Entrepreneurship in Recession

The International Library of Entrepreneurship

Series Editor: David B. Audretsch
Director, Institute for Development Strategies
and Ameritech Chair of Economic Development
Indiana University, USA

Wherever possible, the articles in these volumes have been reproduced as originally published using facsimile reproduction, inclusive of footnotes and pagination to facilitate ease of reference.

For a list of all Edward Elgar published titles visit our website at www.e-elgar.com

Entrepreneurship in Recession

Edited by

Simon C. Parker

MBA '80 Professor of Entrepreneurship
Richard Ivey School of Business, University of Western Ontario, Canada

THE INTERNATIONAL LIBRARY OF ENTREPRENEURSHIP

An Elgar Research Collection
Cheltenham, UK • Northampton, MA, USA

Published by
Edward Elgar Publishing Limited
The Lypiatts
15 Lansdown Road
Cheltenham
Glos GL50 2JA
UK

Edward Elgar Publishing, Inc.
William Pratt House
9 Dewey Court
Northampton
Massachusetts 01060
USA

A catalogue record for this book is available from the British Library

Library of Congress Control Number: 2011922869

ISBN 978 1 84980 045 7

Printed and bound by MPG Books Group, UK

Contents

Acknowledgements

The editor and publishers wish to thank the authors and the following publishers who have kindly given permission for the use of copyright material.

American Economic Association for articles: Simon Kuznets (1940), 'Schumpeter's Business Cycles', *American Economic Review*, **30** (2, Part 1), June, 257–71; Ben Bernanke and Mark Gertler (1989), 'Agency Costs, Net Worth, and Business Fluctuations', *American Economic Review*, **79** (1), March, 14–31; Ricardo J. Caballero and Mohamad L. Hammour (1994), 'The Cleansing Effect of Recessions', *American Economic Review*, **84** (5), December, 1350–68; Patrick Francois and Huw Lloyd-Ellis (2003), 'Animal Spirits Through Creative Destruction', *American Economic Review*, **93** (3), June, 530–50; Gadi Barlevy (2007), 'On the Cyclicality of Research and Development', *American Economic Review*, **97** (4), September, 1131–64.

Blackwell Publishing Ltd (Wiley-Blackwell) for articles: Peter Johnson (1981), 'Unemployment and Self-Employment: A Survey', *Industrial Relations Journal,* **12** (5), 5–15; D.J. Storey and A.M. Jones (1987), 'New Firm Formation – A Labour Market Approach to Industrial Entry', *Scottish Journal of Political Economy*, **34** (1), February, 37–51; Marc Cowling and Peter Mitchell (1997), 'The Evolution of U.K. Self-Employment: A Study of Government Policy and the Role of the Macroeconomy', *Manchester School*, **LXV** (4), September, 427–42; J. Kim DeDee and Douglas W. Vorhies (1998), 'Retrenchment Activities of Small Firms during Economic Downturn: An Empirical Investigation', *Journal of Small Business Management*, **36** (3), July, 46–61; Raquel Carrasco (1999), 'Transitions To and From Self-Employment in Spain: An Empirical Analysis', *Oxford Bulletin of Economics and Statistics*, **61** (3), 315–41.

Elsevier for articles: Richard Highfield and Robert Smiley (1987), 'New Business Starts and Economic Activity: An Empirical Investigation', *International Journal of Industrial Organization*, **5**, 51–66; John A. Pearce II and Steven C. Michael (1997), 'Marketing Strategies that Make Entrepreneurial Firms Recession-Resistant', *Journal of Business Venturing*, **12**, 301–14; Jeffrey R. Campbell (1998), 'Entry, Exit, Embodied Technology, and Business Cycles', *Review of Economic Dynamics*, **1**, 371–408; Adriano A. Rampini (2004), 'Entrepreneurial Activity, Risk, and the Business Cycle', *Journal of Monetary Economics*, **51**, 555–73; Virginie Pérotin (2006), 'Entry, Exit, and the Business Cycle: Are Cooperatives Different?', *Journal of Comparative Economics*, **34**, 295–316; Maitreesh Ghatak, Massimo Morelli and Tomas Sjöström (2007), 'Entrepreneurial Talent, Occupational Choice, and Trickle Up Policies', *Journal of Economic Theory*, **137**, 27–48; A. Roy Thurik, Martin A. Carree, André van Stel and David B. Audretsch (2008), 'Does Self-Employment Reduce Unemployment?', *Journal of Business Venturing*, **23**, 673–86.

Simon C. Parker for article: Emilio Congregado, Antonio A. Golpe and Simon Parker (2009), 'The Dynamics of Entrepreneurship: Hysteresis, Business Cycles and Government Policy', *IZA Discussion Paper No. 4093*, i, 1–29, reset.

Springer Science and Business Media B.V. for articles: David S. Evans and Linda S. Leighton (1990), 'Small Business Formation by Unemployed and Employed Workers', *Small Business Economics*, **2** (4), 319–30; D.J. Storey (1991), 'The Birth of New Firms – Does Unemployment Matter? A Review of the Evidence', *Small Business Economics,* **3** (3), September, 167–78; Nigel Meager (1992), 'Does Unemployment Lead to Self-Employment?', *Small Business Economics*, **4** (2), June, 87–103; David B. Audretsch and Zoltan J. Acs (1994), 'New-Firm Startups, Technology, and Macroeconomic Fluctuations', *Small Business Economics*, **6** (6), December, 439–49; Robert L. Boyd (2000), 'Race, Labor Market Disadvantage, and Survivalist Entrepreneurship: Black Women in the Urban North During the Great Depression', *Sociological Forum,* **15** (4), 647–70.

Taylor and Francis Ltd (http://www.informaworld.com) for articles: Alfonso Alba-Ramirez (1994), 'Self-Employment in the Midst of Unemployment: The Case of Spain and the United States', *Applied Economics,* **26,** 189–204; Ross Gittell and Jeffrey Sohl (2005), 'Technology Centres During the Economic Downturn: What Have We Learned?', *Entrepreneurship and Regional Development*, **17**, July, 293–312.

University of Chicago Press for articles: Andrei Shleifer (1986), 'Implementation Cycles', *Journal of Political Economy*, **94** (6), December, 1163–90; Henry S. Farber (1999), 'Alternative and Part-Time Employment Arrangements as a Response to Job Loss', *Journal of Labor Economics,* **17** (4, Part 2), October, S142–S169; Paul Gompers and Josh Lerner (2003), 'Short-Term America Revisited? Boom and Bust in the Venture Capital Industry and the Impact on Innovation', *Innovation Policy and the Economy*, **3**, January, 1–27.

Every effort has been made to trace all the copyright holders but if any have been inadvertently overlooked the publishers will be pleased to make the necessary arrangement at the first opportunity.

In addition the publishers wish to thank the Library of Indiana University at Bloomington, USA, for their assistance in obtaining these articles.

Introduction

Simon C. Parker

At the time of writing, the world economy is struggling to emerge from a global recession. A credit crunch has gripped the financial markets and economic growth continues to face downward pressures. In response, numerous governments and multinational institutions have injected liquidity into the world's banking systems and national economies. At the same time, policy-makers have redoubled their efforts to promote entrepreneurship as a source of economic growth. The present volume, *Entrepreneurship in Recession*, therefore seems like a timely addition to the International Library of Entrepreneurship.

One of the principles which underpin the selection of papers for this volume is the belief that it is scarcely possible to understand why economies go into recession, or to comprehend the role that entrepreneurs play in this process, without first standing back and reflecting on the causes of the business cycle. The upsides of business cycles are booms; the downsides are recessions. The history of economic thought has long suggested that the seeds of each are contained in the other. This volume considers aspects of cycles and recessions in which the entrepreneur plays a leading role.

The volume is structured in three parts. The first highlights some key theoretical contributions to the topic of recessions, business cycles and entrepreneurship. Of course, theory is not enough: we also need empirical evidence, in order to test the theories and to reveal otherwise hidden aspects of real-world manifestations of these phenomena. The second part of the volume contains several readings which present evidence about entrepreneurship in recession at the levels of the individual entrepreneur, the firm and the industry. A handful of readings which take international and macro-time-series perspectives are also included. The third part recognizes that recessions entail not only falling output but also rising unemployment. The relationships between unemployment and entrepreneurship have been studied intensively. Accordingly, the final part of this volume presents some selected readings on this issue as well.

Part I of the volume commences with a couple of articles which draw on Schumpeter's pioneering contributions to the analysis of business cycles, innovation and entrepreneurship (e.g. Schumpeter, 1927, 1939). The volume kicks off with Simon Kuznets' (1940; Chapter 1) review of Joseph Schumpeter's classic treatise on business cycles. Kuznets' article is a cogent summary and critique of Schumpeter's argument that 'business cycles are the recurrent fluctuations in the rate at which innovations are introduced into the economy, in the intensity with which entrepreneurs exercise their *sui generis* function of overcoming obstacles to new combinations' (Kuznets, 1940, 259). I have chosen to include a review of Schumpeter's contributions rather than excerpts from the original contributions themselves partly for the sake of concision; partly because Schumpeter's meaning is often 'elusive' (Kuznets, 1940, 258); and partly because Kuznets' own critique is well worth reading in its own right. For example, Kuznets criticizes Schumpeter's claim that business cycles are engendered by an unequal distribution of entrepreneurial ability, which causes cyclical fluctuations in the rate of innovation. As Kuznets points out, Schumpeter fails to explain how unequal entrepreneurial abilities translate into 'bunching' of innovations through time which gives rise to booms and recessions (1940, 262–263). Kuznets argues further that Schumpeter also has trouble explaining the existence of *high frequency* business cycles (as opposed to 'long wave' cycles lasting decades), which continue to attract the most interest in practice. Schumpeter's theory relates instead to periods characterized by major disruptive innovations entailing a temporal pattern of rapid change – followed by long periods of hiatus. In practice, only 'the most momentous innovations such as steam power, electricity, etc.' (1940, 264) follow this kind of pattern, which is more akin to 'long waves' than to conventional notions of the business cycle. Several economists have recently explored the issue of disruptive Schumpeterian innovation, business cycles and growth in more formal settings (for a survey, see Aghion and Howitt, 1998).

In summary, as the authors of Chapter 3 in this volume put it, Schumpeterian cycles 'rely on the arrival of major technological breakthroughs that influence all sectors – a general purpose technology (GPT). While the GPT story may be consistent with "long waves", there is little evidence to support the notion that such economy-wide advances can explain high-frequency business cycles' (Francois and Lloyd-Ellis, 2003, 531). Another problem is that, with the exception of radical GPT advances, most inventions tend to emerge continuously over time.

In a different but related line of reasoning, Schumpeter emphasized the role of imitators who swarm into the market after the 'market-making' actions of entrepreneurial pioneers have revealed themselves, and compete away the pioneering entrepreneur's profits. Famously, Schumpeter argued that such imitators help to establish the new order as a new equilibrium for the economy, before another pioneering entrepreneur disrupts the equilibrium again in another wave of 'creative destruction'. A modern neoclassical articulation of this idea – which can explain the 'bunching' phenomenon that Schumpeter was unable to link convincingly with business cycles – appears in Chapter 2 of the volume. In that article, Andrei Shleifer (1986) suggests that although inventions may arrive in a steady stream over time (as noted above), entrepreneurs optimally choose to innovate *simultaneously* to take advantage of high aggregate demand. The result is 'implementation cycles', in which innovations are 'bunched' in particular periods. The reason is that, anticipating the future erosion of profits by imitators, exceptional entrepreneurs who encounter a new innovative opportunity do best by delaying their innovations until a time when profits are the highest. That is during a boom. The clustering of innovations then generates a boom in labour demand, which in turn generates the high demand for output needed to support the boom. On the other hand, when entrepreneurs expect a boom only in the distant future, they may choose to postpone innovations, consigning the economy to a recession. The duration of a recession depends on entrepreneurs' (self-fulfilling) expectations. An interesting feature of Shleifer's model is that business cycles can be the most profitable – or even the unique – outcome chosen by entrepreneurs. Whereas Schumpeter viewed innovation as essentially autonomous, i.e. independent of demand, Shleifer explicitly linked innovation with expected (and actual) demand.

A different model which builds on Schumpeter's theme of 'creative destruction' appears in the third chapter in this volume, by Patrick Francois and Huw Lloyd-Ellis (2003). Francois and Lloyd-Ellis first criticize Shleifer's theory by pointing out that it assumes drastic but costless imitation, and depends critically on the impossibility of storage. For example, if entrepreneurs could store their output, they would do best producing when costs are low (during recessions) and selling when demand is high (during booms). Obviously, this would undermine the existence of cycles. Francois and Lloyd-Ellis are able to relax the assumption of drastic imitation and non-storage yet are still able to show that entrepreneurs choose to release paradigm-shifting innovations together in good times, á là Shleifer. Entrepreneurs devote effort to developing, but not to implementing, new innovations in recessions because that would reveal valuable proprietary information to rivals, thereby reducing the duration of their reign of supremacy prior to the next wave of creative destruction. As a result, recessions are prolonged. However, 'eventually it becomes profitable to implement the stock of innovations that have accumulated during the downturn, and the cycle begins again' (Francois and Lloyd-Ellis, 2003, 532). For their part, booms come to an end because wage costs rise so much that new entrepreneurial activities become less profitable. As a result, the economy slows, giving entrepreneurs incentives to divert effort away from production to new innovations.[1] Thus Francois and Lloyd-Ellis predict that innovation is counter-cyclical, as the opportunity cost of investing in innovation and thereby enhancing future productivity growth is lower in recessions.

More generally, entrepreneurs can respond to recessions by engaging in a range of activities which contribute to long-run productivity and growth. Innovation is only one such activity, though it is certainly an important one; search and schooling are others (Barlevy, 2007, note 1; Chapter 4). In fact, as Gadi Barlevy points out in Chapter 4, R&D actually appears to be pro-cyclical – not counter-cyclical, as Francois and Lloyd-Ellis supposed. Barlevy goes on to highlight a dynamic externality inherent in innovation which can give rise to R&D pro-cyclicality. Radical innovations financed by R&D not only increase economic activity directly, but also indirectly create opportunities for other innovations as well. This indirect 'spillover' effect expands the set of opportunities for entrepreneurs and stimulates greater economic activity. Consequently, if entrepreneurs focus on short-term profitability and do not internalize this dynamic externality when making their investment decisions, R&D spending peaks during booms and collapses during recessions. The implications of this insight are that inefficiently low levels of innovation conducted during recessionary periods make adverse shocks to the macro economy unnecessarily protracted, and increase the costs of future growth. This may provide a rationale for a public policy of counter-cyclical R&D subsidies.

Chapter 5, by Ricardo Caballero and Mohamad Hammour (1994), turns its attention from the supply side of innovation to the demand side of consumer spending. It does so in the Schumpeterian context of 'creative destruction', posing the intriguing question of what happens to the structure of industries when demand falls during a recession. In particular, Caballero and Hammour ask whether recessions cause the rate of entry by entrepreneurs using the latest technology to decline – or whether they cause the rate of exit by less efficient incumbents to increase. The former case is referred to as an 'insulating' effect, protecting incumbent entrepreneurs: Caballero and Hammour's model predicts that this case arises when adjustment costs are linear. In contrast, if adjustment costs are such that the motive for smoothing the innovation creation process over time becomes more valuable, the latter outcome is predicted to hold. Caballero and Hammour motivate their question by way of example: at the start of the Great Depression, the US automotive industry comprised both small-scale craft producers and more efficient mass-producers. As the Depression got under way, plant shutdowns were concentrated among the least efficient craft producers, *at the same time as* new more efficient plants were created. This and other evidence cited by Caballero and Hammour suggests that job destruction is more cyclically responsive than job creation. Caballero and Hammour refer to the pruning of inefficient or outdated techniques and products by more efficient entrepreneurs during recessions as a process of 'cleansing'. Because of cleansing, recessions may improve an economy's productivity over the medium and long term, though these authors carefully refrain from concluding that this makes recessions 'desirable' events.

Offsetting Caballero and Hammour's cleansing argument is a countervailing effect stressed in Chapter 6 by Ghatak, Morelli and Sjöström (2007) (abbreviated to GMS hereafter). Whereas cleansing implies that bad ventures fail so the average quality of active entrepreneurs improves, GMS point out that wages fall in recessions, with the consequence that individuals with relatively low abilities in entrepreneurship now have incentives to turn entrepreneur.[2] This dilutes the average quality of the entrepreneur pool, which is relevant because when lenders lack information about entrepreneurs' hidden abilities (i.e. under conditions of asymmetric information) lenders have to extend loans priced at the quality of the average venture. That entails a cross-subsidy from the most able to the least able entrepreneurs (de Meza and Webb, 1987). As a result, entry into entrepreneurship during recessions worsens the quality of the entrepreneurial pool, increasing the interest rate for all entrepreneurs. The ablest entrepreneurs respond by reducing their demand for labour, which reduces the average wage even further, exacerbating the initial reduction in wages accompanying the recession. Hence entrepreneurs' hiring decisions affected by asymmetric information in entrepreneurial credit markets make recessionary downturns more severe.

A similar theme is explored in Chapter 7, co-authored by one of the architects of current counter-recessionary policies being implemented by the US Federal Reserve – Ben Bernanke. In a classic article written with Mark Gertler, the importance of entrepreneurs' balance sheets is emphasized (Bernanke and Gertler, 1989). In the authors' own words, the basic idea is this: 'In good times, when profits are high and balance sheets are healthy, it is easier for firms to obtain outside funds. This stimulates investment and propagates the good times. Conversely, poor financial health in bad times reduces investment and reinforces the decline in output … this rationalizes a sort of accelerator effect of income on investment … countercyclical agency costs are crucial to the story' (Bernanke and Gertler, 1989, 27).

A central plank of Bernanke and Gertler's argument is that reductions in entrepreneurial wealth are associated with higher agency costs. Lower wealth implies loans are backed by less collateral, so lenders must charge higher interest rates to entrepreneurs in order to break even. This reduces the profits and consumption possibilities of entrepreneurs. Therefore entrepreneurs have less to lose by under-reporting to banks the returns from their investment projects. Anticipating this, banks have to audit entrepreneurs more intensively (hence incurring agency costs). The stage is now set for analysis of a deflationary shock. Deflation redistributes value from borrowers (entrepreneurs) to creditors (banks), reducing entrepreneurs' wealth and increasing agency costs as noted above. The lower investment by entrepreneurs reduces both aggregate demand and aggregate supply, which further worsens deflationary episodes. Interestingly, agency costs bind only in downturns, imparting an asymmetry to productivity shocks. As a result, recessions are predicted to be deep and short, whereas booms are more moderate and protracted – which seems to accord with the evidence cited in this and other articles in the volume.

A recurrent theme in the articles discussed so far is the role that entrepreneurs play in exaggerating variations in economic conditions, by taking decisions which heighten booms and deepen recessions. The mechanism in the chapters by Shleifer and Francois/Lloyd-Ellis is entrepreneurs choosing to implement more innovations in booms than in recessions; in Barlevy it is entrepreneurs spending more on R&D in booms than recessions owing to knowledge spillovers; and in GMS and Bernanke/Gertler it is cyclical variations in the price and availability of credit (owing to asymmetric information problems) which cause entrepreneurs to hire more labour and produce more output in booms than recessions. The final article in Part I of the volume, by Adriano Rampini (2004; Chapter 8), proposes yet another mechanism based on asymmetric information problems, in a model which can be thought of as 'a business cycle frequency version of Knight's theory of entrepreneurship' (Rampini, 2004, 557). Like GMS and Bernanke/Gertler, Rampini studies the effects of counter-cyclical agency costs; unlike them, Rampini explores the pro-cyclical nature of technology (occupational) choice in environments where the source of counter-cyclical agency costs is risk aversion. That is, attitudes towards risk rather than constraints on outside funding is the factor limiting entrepreneurship in this model.

Rampini points out that when productivity shocks are favourable, agents become wealthier. Under decreasing absolute risk aversion, higher productivity and wealth make people more willing to leave safe paid employment and bear risks in entrepreneurship. Entrepreneurship is risky because agents who become entrepreneurs need to bear part of the project-specific risk for incentive reasons. Greater participation in entrepreneurship increases output because entrepreneurship commands a risk premium. A further effect is that entrepreneurs are more willing to supply high levels of effort when wealth and productivity are high. This reduces moral hazard problems, making lenders more willing to fund risky investment projects. However, when shocks are unfavourable, the opposite process occurs: wealth, investment and entrepreneurship all decline. The net result is that entrepreneurs amplify and propagate productivity shocks over time.

Part II of the volume presents a range of empirical evidence about the nature and determinants of cycles insofar as they relate to entrepreneurship. There are several distinct sets of papers here. The first set links business entry and exit rates to the state of the business cycle. Four papers take a range of different approaches to explore the macroeconomic evidence about the cyclical nature of entrepreneurship. The first, by Richard Highfield and Robert Smiley (1987; Chapter 9), uses econometric time-series methods to analyse the temporal covariance structure between new business incorporations and economic activity in the USA. Contrary to the bulk of theoretical studies reviewed in the first part of this collection, Highfield and Smiley report that growth in the new incorporation rate appears to be associated with higher unemployment and interest rates in the preceding year. It is also associated with lower unemployment and interest rates in the following years. Thus it seems that firms enter to seize opportunities created by sluggish economic activity, stimulating increased economic activity in later periods.

The counter-cyclical nature of these findings seems to contradict the theoretical predictions of pro-cyclical entrepreneurship in Part I of this volume. However, Highfield and Smiley actually study not new business starts (as implied by the title of their article), but *incorporations* of (mainly existing) businesses – which account for only a small minority of start-ups. The next three studies focus on new venture creation specifically, rather than incorporations, and instead obtain unanimous support for pro-cyclical entrepreneurship. In the first of these articles, David Audretsch and Zoltan Acs (1994; Chapter 10) estimate a pooled cross-section–time-series regression using data on 117 US industries for six time periods over 1976–86. Audretsch and

Acs report that new firm start-ups respond positively to macroeconomic growth, a low cost of capital and high unemployment rates. The significant positive relationship between new firm start-up rates and GNP growth rates provides clear evidence of pro-cyclical entrepreneurship.

In the next of these papers, Jeffrey Campbell (1998; Chapter 11) analyses data from individual plants rather than aggregate industries (as in Audretsch and Acs, 1994). Applying similar methods of temporal cross-correlations as those used by Highfield and Smiley (1987), Campbell shows that the manufacturing plant entry rate in the US covaries positively with output and total factor productivity growth, while the exit rate is a leading indicator of all these variables. Thus, entry is pro-cyclical (correlated with current productivity growth) while exit is counter-cyclical (positively correlated with future productivity growth). Campbell relates these findings to some of the earlier theoretical concepts explored in this volume, namely the Schumpeterian notion of creative destruction and Caballero and Hammour's notion of the 'cleansing' effect of recessions. As Campbell puts it, 'a persistent improvement to embodied technology induces obsolete plants to cease production, causing exit to rise. Later, as entering plants embodying the new technology become operational, both output and productivity increase' (1998, 371).

Chapter 12, by Congregado et al. (2009), is a contemporary contribution to the literature on business cycles and entrepreneurship. Using an unobserved components time-series model, Congregado et al. show that in Spain, the employer self-employment rate is pro-cyclical while the own-account self-employment rate is counter-cyclical.[3] To the extent that job creation performance can be associated with 'high quality' entrepreneurship, this suggests that the quality as well as the quantity of entrepreneurship varies positively over the business cycle. According to Congregado et al., employers benefit the most from economies of scale and respond to booms by hiring more workers, drawing low ability own-account workers out of self-employment and into paid-employment. Yet these authors do not detect business cycle effects on entrepreneurship in the USA. An important policy implication of this study is that business cycle fluctuations can have persistent effects on entrepreneurship well into the future, a phenomenon known as *hysteresis*. This accentuates the importance of macro-stabilization policies, especially during recessions, if governments wish to promote high rates of entrepreneurship in their economies in the long run.

While Congregado et al. (2009) break down entrepreneurship into employer and non-employer types, the next article by Virginie Pérotin (2006; Chapter 13) provides a different decomposition. It distinguishes between labour-managed ventures ('worker co-operatives') and 'conventional' enterprises. Pérotin draws on an earlier theoretical analysis by Ben-Ner (1988), which argued that worker co-operatives are created primarily in recessions and exit in recoveries when conventional employment becomes more attractive relative to labour-managed employment. Using a sample of French data, Pérotin finds support for the notion of more pronounced counter-cyclicality in the number of worker co-operatives: higher unemployment rates and lower GDP growth rates are associated with increases in the number of new co-operative firms the following year. However, Pérotin also found that the effect of the business cycle on exit is similar for both types of ventures.

The next two papers, by Ross Gittell and Jeffrey Sohl (2005; Chapter 14) and Paul Gompers and Josh Lerner (2003; Chapter 15) turn their attention to a different aspect of entrepreneurship in recession. They focus on technological entrepreneurship and the role of venture capital (VC). Gittell and Sohl report that many of the USA's leading high-technology centres, including

Silicon Valley, fared poorly during the business downturn of the early 2000s. This experience seems to have refuted predictions that the 'new economy' would be able to foster recession-proof growth. Gittell and Sohl attribute the causes of poor economic performance in these centres during the downturn to several factors, including limited product diversity, high wages, and the low quality of VC-backed projects in the late 1990s just prior to the recession. Gittell and Sohl cite the experience between the late 1990s and the early 2000s as evidence that VC exaggerates rather than moderates regional economic cycles.

For their part, Gompers and Lerner (2003) discuss the cyclical nature of the venture capital industry, and suggest that the inherent structure of VC funds together with information lags in the venture investment process are responsible for the recurrence of accentuated booms and busts in the VC industry. Like Gittell and Sohl, Gompers and Lerner pay particular attention to the *quality* of VC in the late 1990s, prior to the bursting of the dot com bubble in April 2000 and the subsequent dramatic shrinkage of the VC industry. Gompers and Lerner argue that, while *on average* VC can have a powerful impact on innovation, its impact declines sharply during booms such as the one of the late 1990s. Gompers and Lerner go on to criticize policy-makers for boosting VC-based government programmes at times when the private VC market is the most active, duplicating investment in 'hot' sectors which the private sector already funds extensively. While they do not claim that policies of this kind were directly responsible for the declining quality of VC investments at the height of the boom, Gompers and Lerner do contend that they 'had the consequence of throwing gasoline on the fire: i.e., they have exacerbated the cyclical nature of venture funding' (2003, 3). Instead, these authors argue that policy-makers should focus on technologies which are not currently popular among private investors, and should provide 'follow-on capital to firms already funded by venture capitalists during periods when venture inflows are falling' (2003, 25).

Most of the articles so far have highlighted implications for public policy. A different and no less pressing question concerns the strategies which entrepreneurs themselves can adopt, both prior to and during a recession. This question is addressed in the next two articles, which both study small publicly owned US manufacturing firms trading through the 1990–91 recession. The first of these articles, by J. Kim DeDee and Douglas Vorhies (1998), argues that companies should adopt effective retrenchment strategies to maximize performance during recessions. DeDee and Vorhies identify the following business areas as ripe for retrenchment: financial management, marketing, product development and R&D, and production management. These authors claim that restructuring internal departments by product lines and along functional responsibilities enhance performance during recessions. So does improving enterprises' new product development capabilities. Consistent with the theoretical predictions of the studies in Part I of this volume, the best-performing enterprises reduce their R&D expenditures during recession. According to DeDee and Vorhies, other strategies that prove effective include increasing emphasis on manufacturing on a customer-order basis. A focus on high quality products and large orders turn out to be counter-productive, counter-recessionary policies on the other hand. So is an over-emphasis on drastic cost-cutting, especially in advertising and sales-related areas.

This last recommendation receives additional support from John Pearce and Steven Michael (1997; Chapter 17), who focus specifically on marketing strategies. These authors argue that a company's marketing strategies preceding a recession strongly affect the impact of an economic downturn on firms, as well as the odds that these firms recover later. Like DeDee and Vorhies, Pearce and Michael find that cutting back on sales and advertising – commonly advised retrenchment strategies – are associated with worse rather than superior performance. As they put it, 'a simple emphasis on incentives and efficiency alone hurts a firm as recession hits' (Pearce and Michael, 1997, 302). These authors advise entrepreneurs to maintain marketing activities in the core business during recessions, while cautiously expanding with an emphasis on marketing efficiency during upturns. Part of the reason is, they argue, that marketing raises firms' levels of awareness of recessions; enables them to make the necessary internal adjustments; and helps them respond to new opportunities created in the downturn. Pearce and Michael acknowledge that their prescriptions contradict the 'conventional wisdom' that retrenchment works best in bad times. But they point out that recessions are qualitatively different types of 'bad times' than more commonly studied sources of distress for firms, which are usually company-specific rather than economy-wide.

From the relatively mild 1990–91 recession we turn, in the final paper in Part II, to the deep and traumatic experiences of the Great Depression in the 1930s. In Chapter 18, Robert Boyd (2000) shifts the focus from the firm to the individual, and thereby paves the way for the largely individual-level studies discussed in Part III of the volume. Boyd explores the experience of an especially vulnerable socio-demographic group, namely urban black American women, who (Boyd argues) responded to harsh economic conditions by becoming 'survivalist' entrepreneurs. These are defined as 'persons who become self-employed in response to a desperate need to find an independent means of livelihood' (Boyd, 2000, 648). Boyd shows that the Depression drove black American women to start marginal businesses in occupations with low barriers to entry such as boarding and lodging, house keeping, hairdressing and beauty culture. More advantaged white women in contrast avoided these occupations and sought work in the mainstream labour market.

Boyd's results are suggestive but not definitive, since only the outcomes and not the precise mechanisms driving individuals' choices are explored in his study. To shed greater light on these issues, Part III of this volume is devoted to a range of studies which analyse how workers respond to redundancy and the experience of unemployment in terms of starting new ventures and becoming self-employed. As noted earlier, unemployment is a central feature of recessions, and so to fully understand the impact of recessions on individual choices, and the resultant effects on entrepreneurship, it is necessary to discover how individuals cope with it.

The first article in Part III, by Peter Johnson (1981; Chapter 19), surveys some of the early British literature from the 1960s and 1970s on transitions from redundancy to self-employment. Johnson's conclusions are that inflows to self-employment from redundancies are numerically modest. Only 5 per cent or so of redundant British workers start their own ventures. These workers are more likely to have worked as managers than as unskilled manual workers, and are more likely to have worked in small rather than large plants. Chapter 20, by David Storey (1991), provides a slightly more up-to-date review of UK studies from the 1980s, concluding that whereas time-series studies tended to detect a positive relationship between unemployment and self-employment, cross-section studies usually found the opposite. Storey also discusses how public policies, such as employment assistance schemes, taxes and social security benefits, affect entrepreneurship. This theme is taken up more fully in the articles that follow.

In contrast to these two mainly descriptive review studies, Chapter 21 by Storey and A.M. Jones (1987) provides some industry-level econometric evidence from recession-hit English northern locations in the 1970s. The evidence highlights a positive link between job shedding and new firm formation rates. Storey and Jones cite earlier work finding that between one-quarter and one-half of people starting up new businesses in Britain claim to have been unemployed immediately prior to starting up. Storey and Jones distinguish between 'prosperity-pull' and 'recession-push' forces driving the unemployment–self-employment relationship – a theme which has been enthusiastically taken up by subsequent researchers. The prosperity-pull argument is that recessions reduce the value of personal assets, making entry into entrepreneurship by credit-constrained individuals harder. At the same time, expected profits in entrepreneurship are reduced. Offsetting these negative forces are recession-push effects, which emphasize the greater availability of second-hand plant during recessions owing to plant closures and downsizings, making entry into entrepreneurship easier. At the same time, the expected value (and likelihood) of work in paid employment is reduced, making entrepreneurship relatively more attractive. The net effect of these two forces is theoretically ambiguous and empirical evidence is required to determine which prevails overall.

Before turning to some of the empirical studies which attempt this, it is worth first perusing some descriptive evidence compiled by David Evans and Linda Leighton (1990; Chapter 22). These authors use Current Population Survey and National Longitudinal Survey data to study the relationship between unincorporated self-employment and unemployment among white Americans. Their main findings are as follows. First, unemployed people are twice as likely to enter unincorporated self-employment as employees are, despite being prone to higher exit rates and larger drops in their income as a result of making the switch. The self-employment earnings penalty is especially pronounced for people who have been unemployed for a long duration. This suggests that 'necessity' entrepreneurship is at work for a substantial number of white Americans, which complements the findings (discussed earlier in Chapter 18) of Boyd (2000) relating to blacks during the Great Depression. It is also interesting in the light of Johnson's (1981; Chapter 19) article that Evans and Leighton find that American workers who have been laid off are slightly less likely to become self-employed than those who quit their jobs voluntarily. This evidence casts some doubt on the potential of entrepreneurship to quickly replace jobs lost in recessionary conditions.

Chapter 23 by Nigel Meager (1992) argues that researchers have placed too much emphasis on stock measures of entrepreneurship, and too little on disaggregated entry and exit flows. Meager associates recession push forces with inflows into self-employment, and recession pull forces with outflows from self-employment. Meager attributes inconclusive findings in the literature on the direction of this relationship, and the cyclicality of entrepreneurship, to the ill-advised use of stock measures of self-employment. Chapter 24, by Alfonso Alba-Ramirez (1994), heeds Meager's warning, by examining the influence of past unemployment experience on the probability that *employees who switch jobs* choose to leave paid employment altogether and take up self-employment. Alba-Ramirez finds that both in Spain and the USA a longer spell of previous unemployment is associated with a significantly higher probability of transitioning to self-employment. Workers who lose their jobs ('displaced workers') are significantly more likely to make this transition in Spain than non-displaced workers are; but those who transition into self-employment do jobs of lower quality as measured, for example, by the incidence of part-time rather than full-time work, and the absence of social security coverage. Earnings are also lower for Spanish entrants to own-account self-employment compared with workers who remain in paid employment. In the USA in contrast, displaced workers who previously earned high wages are significantly *more* likely to transition into self-employment than to paid employment and to remain there – contrary to some previous evidence from Evans and Leighton (1989) highlighting the prevalence of low-wage entrants to self-employment. This observation could be capturing the influence of the greater skills and wealth of high-wage involuntarily unemployed workers who can make a go of it in self-employment.

Raquel Carrasco (1999; Chapter 25) provides further evidence showing that entrants to self-employment in Spain tend to be of low labour market quality. Unemployed Spanish men are more likely to enter self-employment than employees; yet they are also more likely than employees to leave self-employment and return to unemployment. In addition, higher unemployment rates push disproportionately more poorly educated Spaniards into self-employment. Interestingly from a public policy perspective, unemployment benefits have a strong negative effect on the probability that Spaniards enter self-employment, especially in boom times when the unemployment rate is low.

The theme of public policy – so prominent in times of recession – is taken up even more directly in Chapter 26 by Marc Cowling and Peter Mitchell (1997). These authors study the evolution of self-employment in Britain over 1972–92. This period includes the 1980s, a time of generally high unemployment in Britain, as well as the recession of 1990–91. The two most important government policies introduced during the 1980s in Britain were the Employment Assistance Scheme, set up in 1983 to provide income support to unemployed workers wishing to start a business of their own; and the Small Firms Loan Guarantee Scheme, set up in 1981 to improve access to finance for entrepreneurs lacking collateral. Cowling and Mitchell find small positive effects of these policies on the aggregate British self-employment rate. Echoing some of the results discussed above, they also find that higher rates of 'short-term unemployment' are associated with lower aggregate self-employment rates, whereas the opposite relationship holds for the 'long-term unemployment' rate. The implication of these findings is that the long-term unemployed cannot compete as effectively in the formal labour market as the short-term unemployed, so are disproportionately 'pushed' into self-employment as a last resort. In contrast, the short-term unemployed have more attractive alternative options and so are less likely to choose self-employment. The implication here, as in so many of the previous articles discussed in Part III, is that self-employment is for many workers an undesirable labour market state. When recessions strike, short-term unemployment necessarily rises; but the depth and severity of the recession determine whether these workers ever join the ranks of the long-term unemployed. If they do, Cowling and Mitchell's results suggest that they are eventually more likely to make their way into self-employment.

If workers lose their jobs, possibly (but not necessarily) in recessions, how do they go about regaining them, and what role if any does entrepreneurship play in this process? This question is addressed, in Chapter 27, by Henry Farber (1999). Like Alba-Ramirez, Farber uses US Displaced Worker Supplements data. Farber finds that job-losers are significantly more likely than non-job-losers to be found in temporary and involuntarily part-time jobs. But the tendency of job-losers to occupy these jobs declines over time, as they eventually regain regular full-time employment. In parallel with the earlier British studies reviewed by Peter Johnson (Chapter 19), self-employment does not play a major part in job-losers' re-employment strategies. While highly educated job losers are more likely to turn to independent contractor self-employment relative to similarly educated non-job-losers, job-losers in general are less likely than non-losers to be classified as 'other self-employed' workers.

The final paper in the collection, by Roy Thurik and co-workers (2008; Chapter 28), returns us to the macroeconomic theme with which the volume started. A key public policy question which has run throughout the articles assembled herein, but never very directly addressed, is whether governments can promote entrepreneurship as a counter-recessionary strategy. The small positive effects detected by Cowling and Mitchell in Chapter 26 from unemployment-to-self-employment schemes such as the UK's Employment Assistance Scheme suggest that scope for such policies exists but is limited. Thurik et al.'s article also addresses this question and comes up with a similar verdict, albeit for a different reason. Thurik et al. observe that unemployment might not only stimulate entrepreneurship through the 'recession push' mechanism, but also that entrepreneurship can create jobs, thereby reducing the unemployment rate later on. Thurik et al. utilize a two-equation vector autoregression model to separate out these two mechanisms, and find support for both of them using pooled time-series–cross-section evidence from a set of 23 OECD (Organisation for Economic Co-operation and Development) countries. Interestingly, the unemployment-reducing effect of entrepreneurship turns out to be considerably stronger than the entrepreneurship-promoting effect of unemployment. Thus it might seem that pro-entrepreneurship policies could actually help governments lift their economies out of recessions. In fact, Thurik et al.'s findings offer little encouragement for such thinking. Whereas a rise in unemployment feeds fairly rapidly into higher rates of self-employment, it takes eight years and more for the self-employed to create jobs that are noticeably associated with lower unemployment rates. So entrepreneurship promotion policies appear to have more of a long-term than a short-term counter-cyclical 'quick fix' character.

To conclude, the articles assembled in this volume provide a lively and varied overview of the literature at the interface of entrepreneurship and recession. People adapt to recessionary conditions in various ways. Some displaced workers are forced into marginal entrepreneurship; many entrepreneurs who are already there struggle to keep their ventures afloat and have to adopt suitable strategies to do so; and for other more resourceful entrepreneurs, recessions offer opportunities to exploit low wage costs and launch new waves of innovation which in the aggregate helps to move the economy out of recession. The literature covered in this collection suggests that entrepreneurs play a central role in the creation and propagation of business cycles. They both affect and are affected by them. Of course, this should not lead us to overlook the prominent role entrepreneurs also play in driving structural growth; but that is an issue best left for another volume of readings.

Notes

1. In a different model, Lloyd-Ellis and Bernhardt (2000) show how wages and production can evolve pro-cyclically owing to entrepreneurs switching into paid employment when the average wage is high (so subsequently reducing wages) – and switching back into entrepreneurship when the average wage is low (so subsequently increasing wages). This outcome of long-term cycles in wages and productivity arises if the distribution of entrepreneurial ability is positively skewed – implying that efficient entrepreneurs are scarce.
2. This might explain the common emergence of worker co-operatives and other 'marginal' enterprises in recessions, which dissolve in economic recoveries when conventional employment opportunities become more readily available (see Chapter 13 by Pérotin).
3. This bears out descriptive and only suggestive evidence documented by Alba-Ramirez (1994; Chapter 24).

References

Aghion, P. and P. Howitt (1998). *Endogenous Growth Theory*, Cambridge MA: MIT Press.

Ben-Ner, A. (1988). The life-cycle of worker-owned firms in market economies: a theoretical analysis, *Journal of Economic Behaviour and Organization*, **10**(3), 287–313.

De Meza, D. and D.C. Webb (1987). Too much investment: a problem of asymmetric information, *Quarterly Journal of Economics*, **102**, 281–292.

Evans, D.S. and L.S. Leighton (1989). Some empirical aspects of entrepreneurship, *American Economic Review*, **79**, 519–535.

Lloyd-Ellis, H. and D. Bernhardt (2000). Enterprise, inequality and economic development, *Review of Economic Studies*, **67**, 147–168.

Schumpeter, J.A. (1927). The explanation of the business cycle, *Economica*, **21**, 286–311.

Schumpeter, J.A. (1939). *Business Cycles: A Theoretical, Historical and Statistical Analysis of the Capitalist Process*, New York: McGraw-Hill.

Part I
Recessions, Business Cycles and Entrepreneurship: Theory

[1]

SCHUMPETER'S BUSINESS CYCLES[1]

The scope of this monumental treatise may be indicated by a brief review of its chapters, classified here, with some violence to the unity and
interpenetration of approaches in the book itself, as introductory, theoretical, historical, and statistical. The introductory chapter discusses business situations as they are apprehended by the business-man; distinguishes
groups of external factors that affect economic change; lists the statistical
series that may be used advantageously in continuous observation of the business conjuncture; and ends with the expected conclusion that empirical linking of factors and symptoms, as reflected in time series and other data, is
insufficient for the understanding of economic change, since observation of
actual economic processes cannot distinguish between interwoven causes and
effects. To make causal analyses a theoretical apparatus is indispensable.

This theoretical apparatus is presented in chapters 2 through 4. Chapter 2 deals with equilibrium and the theoretical norm, *i.e.*, with the stationary economy. Chapter 3 presents the entrepreneur, the innovation, and
the banking system—the triple alliance that contributes a strategic impetus
to economic evolution. Chapter 4 comprises the crux of Professor Schumpeter's theory of business cycles, indicating how the behavior of entrepreneurs
provides the primary model for use in the study of business cycles; how this
primary model is complicated by consideration of secondary factors (errors,
propagation through the credit system, etc.), and of the various types of
cycles to which the primary and secondary factors give rise. These three
chapters are to a large extent a summary of Professor Schumpeter's earlier
writings on the nature of a stationary economy and the theory of economic
change. But in chapter 2 comments on imperfect competition take account
of recent developments in the field; and in chapter 4 business-cycle theory
is expanded and extended materially beyond the somewhat bare statement
of it in Professor Schumpeter's earlier writings.

Chapter 5 in Volume I discusses the bearing of the theoretical model
upon the measurement of cycles in time series. Chapters 8 through 13 in
Volume II deal with the behavior of various economic quantities in Great
Britain, the United States, and Germany, for the pre-war period as represented by annual data. The successive chapters discuss the general price
level, physical quantities (total) and employment, prices and quantities
of individual commodities, expenditures and wages, the rate of interest,
the central credit market and the stock exchange. These chapters may be
termed statistical, although this does not mean that they present a detailed statistical analysis of cycles in the various aspects of the economic
system. In these chapters there is more of theoretical and qualitative dis-

---

[1] *Business Cycles: A Theoretical, Historical, and Statistical Analysis of the Capitalist
Process*, by JOSEPH A. SCHUMPETER. Vols. I and II. (New York: McGraw-Hill. 1939.
Pp. xvi, 448; ix, 647. $10.00.)

cussion than of quantitative analysis; and they may be classified as statistical only by comparison with the other parts of the treatise.

Chapters 6 and 7 in Volume I present historical outlines of economic change in the three countries mentioned, for the years from 1787 to 1913—outlines concerned with the dating of two of the three cycle types that are distinguished on the basis of historical evidence, and with the recording of the more outstanding innovations with which the cycles are associated. Chapters 14 and 15 in Volume II contain a detailed discussion of economic changes from 1919 to date. These four chapters may be characterized as historical, although the last two, which deal with recent years, may be alternatively viewed as an application of all three types of approach to the post-war decades. The recent years are discussed much more intensively and comprehensively than pre-war years, the last two chapters accounting for 300 of the 1,000 pages in the two volumes.

This outline of the scope of the treatise suggests that any thorough summary of its contents would exceed the limits of the present review. Such a summary would be exceedingly difficult because of the character of Professor Schumpeter's discussion. Some of the chapters, as already indicated, are themselves summaries of the author's earlier writings, and would need expansion rather than condensation. Other parts, especially those classified above as historical, are running commentaries upon specific situations, with a wealth of allusions, incisive sidelights, references to existing literature, and theoretical suggestions. Such discussion cannot be summarized effectively. In still other parts, the author's meaning is elusive in that the reader is uncertain what limits of confidence Professor Schumpeter assigns to his statements and what in detail is the basis upon which they are made—a comment of particular application to the discussion of the dating of cycles and the presence or absence of cycles in a given series.

One must therefore select for review only a few of the numerous problems treated in the two volumes. The presentation below deals with three topics that seem to the writer to be of wide bearing and to call for critical evaluation: (a) the relation between distribution of entrepreneurial ability and the cyclical character of economic change; (b) the four-phase scheme of the business cycle and its bearing upon statistical analysis; (c) the three types of cycles distinguished. I shall first attempt to present Professor Schumpeter's view on these three topics, and then formulate the questions which, in my view, are raised by his discussion.

To Professor Schumpeter, business cycles are pulsations of the rate of economic evolution. Economic change in general is attributed to three groups of forces: external factors, for example, the demand of governments for new military weapons; the factor of growth, by which the author means the continuous gradual changes in population and in the volume of savings and accumulation, changes that do not require drastic shifts in the combination of productive factors and thus may be attained by the ordinary, run of the mill economic agent addicted to an habitual and adaptive type of activity; and innovations which represent material changes (or as Professor Schumpeter defines them, changes of first order) in the production functions. It is innovations that are of strategic importance in the evolution of capitalist economy, innovations that are usually introduced by new rather than by old firms, by new men rather than by those who already occupy prominent niches in the functioning system.

Business cycles are recurrent fluctuations in the rate at which innovations are introduced into the economy, in the intensity with which entrepreneurs exercise their *sui generis* function of overcoming obstacles to new combinations. The reason for this discontinuity in the rate of innovations and in the intensity of entrepreneurial endeavor, of the bunching of innovations at one time and their comparative scarcity at others, lies in the distribution of entrepreneurial ability. This ability to dare, to initiate, to overcome obstacles to innovations is, like many other abilities, distributed along a curve which suggests that there are few individuals endowed with such ability to any great degree and many who are equipped only to initiate and follow the pioneering efforts of the few. If then we envisage, in a state of equilibrium, the action of the first entrepreneur, one of high ability, we shall see that his action will be followed by a swarm of imitations, increasing in volume as time passes and as the innovation becomes a more and more accepted pattern of action.

This uprush of innovation, accompanied by expanding credit, rising prices, rising interest rates, a relatively constant volume of total output but usually a shift in favor of producers' goods, constitutes the period of rise in the first approximation to the business cycle. It terminates as soon as the disturbance of the equilibrium has proceeded far enough to upset the existing relations of prices, costs and quantities, thus making it impossible to formulate rationally calculated plans for the future. This terminus is reached all the sooner because innovations are usually concentrated at any given time in one or few industrial areas, and the increase in risk and uncertainty is made more effective by the exhaustion of innovation opportunities. At the turn, the rate of innovation slackens and a period of readjustment ensues in which entrepreneurs take stock and the economy recedes to a new equilibrium level, a level which both growth and innovations make higher than that from which the expansion started. During this period of recession credit volumes, prices and interest rates decline but total output is likely to average larger than the preceding prosperity.

This first approximation, the primary model, thus accounts for a two-phase cycle, a departure upward from equilibrium level and a recession to a new equilibrium level. But conditions under which entrepreneurial activity takes place in reality must next be considered: the errors of forecast; the speculative tendencies of individuals; the thousand and one peculiarities of economic institutions that are likely to prolong and exaggerate a movement once initiated. These surface factors, which, in Professor Schumpeter's view, often claim the attention of business-cycle students to the exclusion of the fundamental process of innovation, may and do intensify the rise during the prosperity phase beyond the level to which it would have been carried by the stream of innovations proper; and during recession they reënforce the deflation, carrying it often below the equilibrium level into depression. When this occurs, the economy returns to equilibrium whenever the forces of depression spend themselves, a point determined largely by the peculiarities of the secondary factors that produce the abnormal contraction. But the equilibrium reached by recovery is not necessarily identical with that which would have been attained had the depression not taken place.

The combination of the first and second approximations yields a four-phase cycle of prosperity, recession, depression, and revival. The upper turning point is determined essentially by the primary model, whereas the revival point is determined largely by secondary factors. But whatever the difference in the causation of prosperity and recession as over against depression and revival, the four-phase model of the cycle must constitute the paramount guide in the statistical study of time series. Cyclical units should be defined not from trough to trough or peak to peak but from the beginning of prosperity, the point where the series begins to rise above the normal level to the end of revival, the point where the series again reaches the new normal. Professor Schumpeter dates the terminal points of the cycles that he distinguishes in accordance with this rule, and advocates for time-series analysis a method, originally proposed by Ragnar Frisch, that calls for establishing points of inflection. Under certain conditions these points of inflection are in the neighborhood of equilibrium levels and their establishment will thus serve to ascertain the terminal dates of the cycles, if not the turning points that divide prosperity from recession and depression from revival. Since inflection points suggest equilibrium levels in cyclical movements only if the rate of cyclical rise or decline diminishes as the curve pulls away from the equilibrium line, Professor Schumpeter accepts this condition as consonant with the theoretical significance of normal levels.

Neither the primary, nor the secondary, model implies necessarily one type of cycle only, *i.e.*, a cycle of approximately the same duration and intensity. On the contrary, differences in the magnitude of various innovations suggest that there may be several kinds of cycles differing in duration and in amplitude as the innovations with which they are associated differ in magnitude and the time they require to attain their proper place in the economy. Presumably the same is true of the secondary factors: they may and do differ with reference to the span of time during which they produce their exaggerating effect upon expansion and liquidation. It is thus theoretically plausible to expect cycles of varying duration and intensity, their types and their interrelations to be determined largely by observation.

Professor Schumpeter finds that in order to account for the cycles that can be observed historically and statistically during the last century and a half three types of cycles should be distinguished: long waves of about fifty years in duration (Kondratieffs); intermediate waves of about eight to nine years in duration (Juglars); and short waves of about forty months in duration (Kitchins). Unfortunately nowhere in the two volumes is there a combined chronology stating the terminal dates of the various types of cycles distinguished by Professor Schumpeter for the three countries with which he deals in his historical and statistical sections. But the historical outlines in Volume I are concerned with establishing the Kondratieffs and the Juglars in the three countries before the World War; and in the detailed discussion of the years since 1919 there are a few specific indications of the dates of some Kitchins.[2]

The concurrence of these three types of cycles, each christened by the name of the economist who was chiefly responsible for claiming validity for it, accounts, according to Professor Schumpeter, for the diversity in the duration and amplitude of cycles observed in time series; and it explains why some "depressions," such as those of 1825-30, 1873-78, and 1929-34, were so long and so deep—a result of coincidence in phase of at least two of the three types of cycles. But all three types of cycles are due to the same fundamental set of causes, described by the primary model; in all we should expect four or two phases as the secondary factors are or are not sufficiently

[2] I have attempted to construct a chronology of the Kondratieffs with the following results:

Prosperity	Recession	Depression	Revival
Industrial Revolution Kondratieff, 1787-1842: Cotton Textile, Iron, Steam Power			
1787-1800	1801-1813	1814-1827	1828-1842
Bourgeois Kondratieff, 1842-1897: Railroadization			
1843-1857	1858-1869	1870-1884-5	1886-1897
Neo-Mercantilist Kondratieff, 1897 to date: Electricity, Automobile			
1898-1911	1912-1924-5	1925-6-1939	

The dates of the first and second Kondratieff are established from the discussion for Great Britain; that of the third from the discussion for the United States. The specific dates for the three countries are presumably somewhat different, but the differences are likely to be minor. It should also be noted that Professor Schumpeter considers that the first Kondratieff is not very clearly shown in Germany. This table above was checked by Professor Schumpeter who has kindly suggested a few changes in its original version.

Professor Schumpeter also provides dates for Juglars. They are presented as roughly corresponding to the dates in Thorp's *Business Annals*, with due allowance for the difference in terminology.

effective to produce depressions and revivals. As to the relations among these three types of cycles, two observations are made by Professor Schumpeter. First, the theoretical model requires that "each Kondratieff should contain an integral number of Juglars and each Juglar an integral number of Kitchins" (p. 172). The immediate consequence of this is that the first years in the prosperity phase of each Kondratieff coincide with Juglar and Kitchin prosperities; and the same is true of the immediately preceding revivals. Second, "barring very few cases in which difficulties arise, it is possible to count off, historically as well as statistically, six Juglars to a Kondratieff and three Kitchins to a Juglar—not as an average but in every individual case" (p. 174). This empirical conclusion, however, is not called for by the theoretical scheme; indeed the latter would lead us to expect irregularity in the number of the shorter type cycles comprised within each cyclical unit of longer duration.

This summary, bare and oversimplified as it is, reveals the significance of Professor Schumpeter's theoretical scheme and empirical findings. The close connection in this scheme between business cycles and the general process of evolution of capitalist economy; the direct bearing of the theoretical model of the cycle, with its equilibrium levels and its four phases, upon the statistical analysis of time series; the specificity of the three-cycle scheme, in the duration, interrelation and concurrence of the three cycle-types—all contribute to an impression of a well integrated intellectual structure that elegantly spans the gap between controlled imagination and diversified reality.

But further reflection and even a partial scrutiny of the evidence presented in the two volumes raise a host of crucial questions and disturbing doubts. In selecting some of these for discussion, we may begin with the association claimed to exist between the distribution of entrepreneurial ability and discontinuity in the making of innovations—in other words, their "bunching." What precisely is the necessary connection between scarcity at any given time of high entrepreneurial ability (and the plenitude of imitators) and the bunching of innovations? Given an infinite supply of possible innovations (inventions and other new combinations), why need entrepreneurial genius defer the next pioneering step until his preceding one has been so imitated and expanded that the upsetting of the equilibrium stops even him in his tracks? If imitators are ready to follow as soon as the entrepreneurial genius has proved that the innovation is successful, the disturbance of equilibrium at that time is certainly not sufficient to bar this genius from turning to new feats and thus initiating an uprush in another industry. Why should we not conceive these applications of high entrepreneurial ability, whether represented by one man or several, as flowing in a continuous stream, a stream magnified in a constant proportion by the efforts of the imitators?

A close reading of Professor Schumpeter's text, both in this book and in his earlier treatise on the *Theory of Economic Development,* indicates that he expects high entrepreneurial ability to pause after the innovation and descend to the lower level of its imitators. The theory definitely calls for discontinuity *over time* in the operation of entrepreneurial ability. But such discontinuity cannot be derived from a distribution of entrepreneurial ability *at any given moment of time,* except on one assumption—namely, that the ability called for is so scarce that it may be completely absent during some periods of time while present at others. But this implies cycles in the supply of entrepreneurial ability, whether the supply be conceived in terms of individuals or of phases in the life of various individuals. I am not sure that Professor Schumpeter would view this assumption as valid.

Further reading and reflection suggest two possible alternative explanations of the bunching of innovations. The first is that *by definition* an innovation so disturbs existing economic relations that its introduction on a significant scale (*i.e.,* by the first entrepreneur plus the imitators) will necessarily prevent any other innovation from being successful so long as a process of readjustment has not taken place. This answer means, of course, that an innovation, by definition, is tantamount to a two-phase cycle, *i.e.,* it is defined as the kind of change that produces, upon its introduction, a phase of prosperity and of recession. And correspondingly, an entrepreneur *sui generis* is one who by definition introduces innovations that by definition result in a two-phase cycle. Hence by definition there is a necessary association between two-phase cycles and the *existence* of entrepreneurs. This, however, is such an obvious tautology as to be inacceptable as a significant interpretation or extension of Professor Schumpeter's position.

The second answer, suggested by Professor Schumpeter's references to the concentration of innovations in restricted industrial areas and by the emphasis in his historical discussion of technological changes, is that the discontinuity or bunching in the rate of innovation rests essentially upon discontinuity or bunching in the supply of possible new combinations, particularly of technological inventions. This, in essence, assumes cyclical fluctuations in the rate at which producers of the technical basis for innovations contribute to the stock of possible new combinations from which entrepreneurs can choose. Thus, it may be said that in the last quarter of the eighteenth century in England there were several major inventions (cotton textiles, iron and steel, steam engine); that thereafter it was not until the 30's of the nineteenth century that another big group of inventions, connected with steam railroads, became accessible to the entrepreneur; and that as a result we have a two-phase cycle of prosperity in the last quarter of the eighteenth century and of recession in the next quarter.

Whether or not this be a proper extension of Professor Schumpeter's theory, the argument that technological and other opportunities for economic innovation are not necessarily continuous over time has some plausibility. There may be periods of hiatus with no big potential change on hand to stimulate and motivate the driving power of entrepreneurial genius. But this generalization, viewed as a basis for a primary model of business cycles, is subject to severe qualifications. Discontinuity of opportunity can be assumed only with reference to the most momentous innovations such as steam power, electricity, etc., *i.e.,* innovations that bear upon Kondratieff cycles. We can hardly expect significant fluctuations in the stock of innovation opportunities of the type that are associated with the Juglar or the Kitchin cycles. Furthermore, even with reference to the major innovations that may be associated with fifty-year spans, there is some indication that the long lapse between the appearance of the inventions is itself partly conditioned by the functioning of the economic system. For example, we may say that electricity did not become available sooner because it had to wait until the potentialities of steam power were exhausted by the economic system and until the attention of inventors and engineers was ready to be diverted to the problems of electricity. If this is so, there may be discontinuity in the *appearance* of inventions, but there is no necessary time lag between those major inventions as sources of significant economic innovations. Thus, even for application to a primary model of the Kondratieff cycle the assumption of discontinuity of technical opportunities would have to be closely scrutinized in the light of historical evidence.

The queries raised above should not be interpreted as denying the importance of entrepreneurial genius or the jerky character of economic evolution. They stem from a critical consideration of one point only, the association between distribution of entrepreneurial ability and cyclical fluctuations in the rate of innovation, an association that appears crucial in Professor Schumpeter's business-cycle theory. Nor need it be emphasized that the discussion above applies exclusively to the first approximation, the primary model, and neglects completely the secondary factors. It is the former that Professor Schumpeter stresses as providing the fundamental explanation of business cycles, and it is the former that contains his specific contribution. The term "secondary factors" subsumes the variety of forces treated in many other business-cycle theories, and there is a tendency in Professor Schumpeter's treatise to slight them, considering them at best as influences inferior to the factors cited in the first approximation.

We may pass now to a consideration of the four-phase model of a cycle conceived in terms of departures from an equilibrium line, and the bearing of this model upon statistical analysis of time series. The procedure preferred by Professor Schumpeter involves establishing points of inflection, first in the original series, then in the line that passes through the first series of inflection points and so on, successively decomposing the total series into several cyclical lines. Professor Schumpeter himself recognizes the difficulties involved in the application of this procedure (see page 211, vol. I). There is first the delicate problem of smoothing the series so as to eliminate the effect of erratic fluctuations on the second order differences used to establish inflection points. A more serious difficulty arises because the assumption that the inflection points are in the neighborhood of equilibrium levels implies a specific pattern of cyclical movements; and there is no ground for expecting cyclical fluctuations in actual series to conform to this pattern.

For these reasons Professor Schumpeter does not recommend the method for general application and recognizes it only as a first approximation and a far from infallible guide. He presents applications of this method in his book to just two series: one used for purely illustrative purposes in chapter 5, a monthly series on revenue freight loadings from 1918-1930 (Chart III, page 218) and the other used for analytical purposes in chapter 8 (Chart IX, page 469), an annual series of wholesale prices in the United States from 1790 to 1930. For the rest, statistical analysis is confined to a graphic portrayal of the series, sometimes reduced to successive rates of percentage change, sometimes smoothed by a simple moving average, and in one case with a fitted trend curve and fitted cycles. The preponderant number of series are, however, left in their original form and the statistical analysis for almost all of them is in the form of qualitative statements of quantitative import, based upon observation of the charts.

The difficulties encountered in the matter of inflection points and the paucity of formal statistical analysis in the treatise lead to a doubt whether Professor Schumpeter's concept of equilibrium and of the four-phase model of business cycles are such as to permit of application to statistical analysis. This doubt is strengthened when it is considered that the concept calls for segregating movements of the equilibrium line caused by external factors and growth from movements caused by innovations. Hence the usual lines of secular trend, drawn so as to bisect the area of cyclical fluctuations, are not acceptable from the viewpoint of Professor Schumpeter's theoretical model. This model requires, as I see it, that the line underlying any given cycle should express at any given time only the level that can be maintained by the activity of the inert adaptive character not properly dignified by the term entrepreneurial. To segregate this level from the slant given to the line by the cumulation of innovations is indeed difficult.

By refusing to deal with secular trend lines based upon formal characteristics (irreversibility, smoothness, etc.) Professor Schumpeter sacrifices the possibility of basing the distinction between long-term movements and cyclical variations upon observable criteria. By refusing to accept peaks and troughs as guides in the determination of cycles he scorns the help provided by that statistical characteristic of cycles in time series. One cannot well escape the impression that Professor Schumpeter's theoretical model in its present state cannot be linked directly and clearly with statistically observed realities; that the extreme paucity of statistical analysis in the treatise is an inevitable result of the type of theoretical model adopted; and that the great reliance upon historical outlines and qualitative discussion is a consequence of the difficulty of devising statistical procedures that would correspond to the theoretical model.

The validity of the three-cycle schema, the last topic under discussion, hinges largely on the nature of the historical evidence and qualitative analysis. As already indicated, Professor Schumpeter does not claim for the Kondratieff-Juglar-Kitchin combination any necessary connection with his theoretical model. But he does present it as a schema called for by historical reality, as a classification fully justified by the way it describes successive business cycles since the last quarter of the eighteenth century in the three countries under observation. Yet, in spite of numerous references to this classification in the historical outlines, in spite of the determinate way in which its validity is claimed in the treatise, there remain serious doubts that such validity has been demonstrated or could be demonstrated with the type of materials and analysis employed by Professor Schumpeter.

The cycle is essentially a quantitative concept. All its characteristics such as duration, amplitude, phases, etc., can be conceived only as measurable aspects, and can be properly measured only with the help of quantitative data. Furthermore, the distinction between cycles and irregular movements traceable to external factors can be made at all adequately only if the successive cycles are measured and averages are struck in which the influence of external factors can be reduced, if not eliminated. This does not mean that observation of cycles on the basis of qualitative information is neither possible nor valuable. For whatever quantities reflect cyclical changes, these changes result from discrete acts by individuals or nonpersonal units in the social system. Some of these discrete acts may be recorded singly and separately in historical records; of others a crude count or impression can be derived from contemporary qualitative reports. The study of such qualitative data in conjunction with statistics is indispensable for a close analysis of the latter. And the former without the assistance of the latter can often give a crude idea of the succession of cyclical phases and of very striking differences in amplitude between one cycle and another. But it is difficult to see how qualitative records can yield much beyond a suggestion of dates of peaks and troughs of a single type of cycle; how one could, on the basis of historical records alone, distinguish the dating and phases of several concurrently existing cycle types.

The question raised bears most upon the establishment of the Kondratieff cycles. To establish the existence of cycles of a given type requires first a demonstration that fluctuations of that approximate duration recur, with fair simultaneity, in the movements of various significant aspects of economic life (production and employment in various industries, prices of various groups of goods, interest rates, volumes of trade, flow of credit, etc.); and second, an indication of what external factors or peculiarities of the economic system proper account for such recurrent fluctuations. Unless the former basis is laid, the cycle type distinguished cannot be accepted as affecting economic life at large—it may be specific to a limited part of the country's economic system. Unless the second, theoretical, basis is established there is no link that connects findings relating to empirical observations of a given type of cycles in a given country over a given period of time with the broader realm of already established knowledge.

Neither of these bases has ever been satisfactorily laid for the Kondratieff cycles. Kondratieff's own statistical analysis refers largely to price indexes, interest rates, or volumes of activity in current prices—series necessarily dominated by the price peaks of the Napoleonic wars, of the 1870's (not unconnected with the Civil War in this country), and of the World War. The prevalence of such fifty-year cycles in volumes of production, either total or for important branches of activity, in employment, in physical volume of trade, has not been demonstrated; nor has the presumed existence of these cycles been reconciled with those of a duration from 18 to 25 years established for a number of production series in this and other countries. Nor has a satisfactory theory been advanced as to why these 50-year swings should recur: the explanations tend to emphasize external factors (inventions, wars, etc.) without demonstrating their cyclical character in their tendency to recur as a result of an underlying mechanism or as effects of another group of external factors of proven "cyclicity."

These doubts as to the validity of the Kondratieff cycles are not dispelled by the evidence Professor Schumpeter submits. The part of his discussion that deals with qualitative, historical evidence leaves unanswered two crucial questions. The first refers to the particular aspect of activity that is considered as revealing the Kondratieff cycles and is thus observed to establish the dates. Such observation obviously cannot relate to economic activity at large, for qualitative data on the course of general economic activity necessarily deal with short-term changes and would not serve to differentiate the underlying Kondratieffs from the much more clearly marked shorter cyclical swings. One must, therefore, in order to set the dates of Kondratieffs, choose some activity particularly sensitive to these long swings.

The natural choice would be the economic innovations whose introduction forms the substance of Kondratieff prosperities. But as Professor Schumpeter observes, such innovations usually make their appearance before the Kondratieff that is associated with them. Thus steam railroads began to be constructed before the railroadization Kondratieff (*i.e.,* before 1843); and electricity was well known before the Kondratieff associated with it began in 1898. One then tends to infer that a Kondratieff begins when the underlying major innovation is being introduced on a large scale and at a rapid rate. But does this mean that the prosperity of a Kondratieff is the period at which the introduction of the innovation displays the maximum absolute or percentage rate of increase?[3] One searches in vain for a definite formulation of the criterion by which historical evidence is analyzed to distinguish the Kondratieff cycles from the Juglars and used to establish for the former the terminal dates and also those of the four phases.

The second question raised by the discussion of the Kondratieffs in the light of historical evidence refers to the treatment of "accidental" external factors and of transient secondary influences. As Professor Schumpeter himself recognizes, any given cyclical turn, in any observable type of cycle, can be attributed to one or several specific historical events, *i.e.,* to some transient accidental circumstances in the neighborhood of the turn. And yet it should be possible in the analysis to distinguish between these accidental concomitants and the underlying cyclical swings. As already indicated, this segregation is accomplished in statistical analysis by averaging or similar devices. In the treatment of qualitative, historical evidence the task is more difficult. It might be facilitated by a classification of various types of factors that would distinguish in advance cyclical factors from others; but even then the concurrence in historical reality of accidental and cyclical factors might necessitate what is essentially a quantitative analysis. It is not clear how Professor Schumpeter deals with the problem. In some cases he recognizes an "accidental" disturbance that produces what appears to be a cyclical turn, but does not disregard this turn as conforming with his schema. In other cases he attributes the departure of reality from the hypothesis to accidental historical conditions (notably in explaining why prices continued to decline in the United States after 1842 when there was supposedly a Kondratieff prosperity). The opportunity in such treatment for personal judgment is perhaps inevitable in the use of qualitative data; but the unfortunate consequences for the effort to establish the validity of the Kondratieff cycles and their dates are not diminished thereby.

As to the statistical basis for the recognition of Kondratieff cycles, Professor Schumpeter's approach, for reasons already indicated, can yield little

---

[3] This criterion would not fit experience in the United States, since the percentage rate of growth in the additions to railroad mileage was at its maximum before 1842; and the absolute rate of addition was at its maximum long after 1860.

of value. The failure to follow articulate methods of time series analysis reduces the statistical methods to a mere recording of impressions of charts, impressions with which it is often difficult to agree. To quote but two instances. (1) In Charts XII and XIII (pp. 486 and 487) Professor Schumpeter presents data on pig iron consumption (annual) for the United States, the United Kingdom and Germany for the period roughly from 1857 to 1913; and comments that the lines reflect "all three cycles . . . very well" (p. 485). But I, for one, cannot detect any traces of Kondratieffs in the lines either for Germany or for the United Kingdom; and would record two long cycles in the American series, one from 1857 to 1875 and the other from 1875 to 1895, rather than a single Kondratieff swing. (2) Chart XLII presents a monthly index of industrial production for the United States from 1897 to 1935. Professor Schumpeter then comments that the movement during 1898-1912 shows a rate of increase lower than that from 1922 to 1929; and this is cited to support the existence of a Kondratieff prosperity (1898-1912), as contrasted with a subsequent Kondratieff recession that is assumed to terminate in 1925.[4] But a glance at the chart suggests to me that the line from 1898 to 1912 is appreciably steeper than the line that would characterize the post-war decade; and that any higher rate that might be shown by a line drawn from 1922 to 1929 would be due exclusively to the position of the terminal years in the shorter-term cycles. Whichever of these judgments of the charts is correct, the ease of disagreement, of which there are many other instances, is an eloquent testimony to the insufficiency of the crude statistical procedures followed in the treatise to provide a basis for establishing cycle types of so elusive a character as the Kondratieffs.

The Kitchins are too short and perhaps too mild to be discernible with the available qualitative historical evidence, especially for the years before 1919. Hence the distinction between the Juglars and the Kitchins is based in the treatise largely upon statistical evidence, *i.e.,* again largely upon the impression conveyed by the charts. The series used for the pre-war years are almost exclusively annual, and the comments refer to the existence of the Kitchins rather than to their dates. Only for the years since 1919 do the plenitude of quantitative and detailed data and the emphasis that Professor Schumpeter places upon a thorough discussion of changes during these recent two decades, lead him to date the Kitchins and use them together with the Kondratieffs and Juglars to explain the successive economic conjunctures in the three countries under his observation.

The evidence brought together in the two volumes, and still more other available measures of cyclical behavior, suggest with some plausibility the

---

[4] To be sure, Professor Schumpeter deprecates the significance of this chart as evidence of Kondratieff phases; but the statistical evidence that he submits for Kondratieffs consists essentially of similar items, each of them qualified.

desirability of distinguishing more than one type of cycle, or recognizing in addition to the shortest unit of cyclical swing observable in the economic system others appreciably longer. But whether the distinction should be drawn in the specific form suggested by Professor Schumpeter is still an unanswered question. Annual series provide too crude a guide for establishing cycles as short as the Kitchins. A mere observation of "notches" on the surface of Juglars, or even of prominent short-term oscillations would not suffice: either result could be produced by random variations, and these short-term variations would have to be analyzed to demonstrate that they could not be due to mere chance. Hence only monthly series could be used as statistical evidence of Kitchins. But the series presented in the treatise cover too short a period to provide sufficient basis for the generalization that Kitchins existed in the past.[5] And no direct evidence seems to be presented to confirm the generalization so explicitly made that it is possible to count three Kitchins for every Juglar.

The critical evaluation above of what appear to be important elements in Professor Schumpeter's conclusions, viewed as a systematic and tested exposition of business cycles, yields disturbingly destructive results. The association between the distribution of entrepreneurial ability and the cyclical character of economic activity needs further proof. The theoretical model of the four-phase cycle about the equilibrium level does not yield a serviceable statistical approach. The three-cycle schema and the rather rigid relationship claimed to have been established among the three groups of cycles cannot be considered, on the basis of the evidence submitted, even tolerably valid; nor could such validity be established without a serviceable statistical procedure. The core of the difficulty seems to lie in the failure to forge the necessary links between the primary factors and concepts (entrepreneur, innovation, equilibrium line) and the observable cyclical fluctuations in economic activity.

And yet this evaluation does injustice to the treatise, for it stresses the weaknesses of the discussion and overlooks almost completely its strength. Granted that the book does not present a fully articulated and tested business-cycle theory; that it does not actually demonstrate the intimate connection between economic evolution and business cycles; that no proper link is established between the theoretical model and statistical procedure; that historical evidence is not used in a fashion that limits the area of personal judgment; or that the validity of three types of cycles is not estab-

---

[5] It is also to be noted that for recent years economic conditions in this country dominated those of Europe to an extent much greater than before the war. It is also in this country that the cycle in general business conditions was observed to be shorter than in England or Germany. Hence an analysis, confined to only the recent decades, would run the danger of ignoring the possible absence of Kitchins in England and Germany during the nineteenth century.

lished. Yet it is a cardinal merit of the treatise that it raises all these questions; that it emphasizes the importance of relating the study of business cycles to a study of the underlying long-term movements; that it calls for emphasis on the factors that determine the rate and tempo of entrepreneurial activity; that it demands a statistical procedure based upon a clearly formulated concept of the business cycle; and that it valiantly attempts to use historical evidence. In all these respects the volumes offer favorable contrast with many a book published in recent years on business cycles, whether of the type in which abstract reasoning is unsullied by contact with observable reality or of the opposite category in which mechanical dissection of statistical series is the sum total of the author's achievement.

Furthermore, both the summary and the critical discussion above necessarily fail to show the achievements of the treatise in providing illuminating interpretations of historical developments; incisive comments on the analysis of cyclical fluctuations in various aspects of economic activity; revealing references to an extraordinarily wide variety of publications in directly and indirectly related fields; thought-provoking judgments concerning the general course of capitalist evolution. It is difficult to convey the flavor of the book except by saying that in many of its parts it reads like an intellectual diary, a record of Professor Schumpeter's journey through the realm of business cycles and capitalist evolution, a journal of his encounters there with numerous hypotheses, diverse historical facts, and statistical experiments. And Professor Schumpeter is a widely experienced traveller, whose comments reveal insight combined with a sense of reality; of wide background against which to judge the intellectual constructs of men and the vagaries of a changing social order.

Thus, whatever the shortcomings of the book as an exposition of a systematic and tested theory of business cycles, these shortcomings are relative to a lofty conception of the requirements such theory should meet. It is the cognizance of these requirements that makes the book valuable even to one who may not be interested in the author's comments on the various and sundry historical, statistical and theoretical matters. But these comments are of high suggestive value and should, if given circulation, prove effective stimuli for further theoretical, historical and statistical study of business cycles and economic evolution. It is my sincere hope that Professor Schumpeter's labor embodied in the treatise will be repaid by an extensive utilization of it by students in the field, aware though they may be of the tentative character of his conclusions and of the personal element in some of his comments and evaluations.

Simon Kuznets

University of Pennsylvania

[2]

Implementation Cycles

Andrei Shleifer

Princeton University

The paper describes an artificial economy in which firms in different sectors make inventions at different times but innovate simultaneously to take advantage of high aggregate demand. In turn, high demand results from simultaneous innovation in many sectors. The economy exhibits multiple cyclical equilibria, with entrepreneurs' expectations determining which equilibrium obtains. These equilibria are Pareto ranked, and the most profitable equilibrium need not be the most efficient. While an informed stabilization policy can sometimes raise welfare, if large booms are necessary to cover fixed costs of innovation, stabilization policy can stop all technological progress.

I. Introduction

At least since Keynes (1936), economists have suspected that an autonomous determinant of agents' expectations can lead them to do business in a way that makes these expectations come true. Several recent studies confirmed this suspicion by exhibiting economies with multiple self-fulfilling rational expectations equilibria. Most notably, Azariadis (1981), Cass and Shell (1983), Grandmont (1983), and Farmer and Woodford (1984), among others, investigate such equilibria in overlapping generations models, while Diamond (1982) and Diamond and Fudenberg (1982) study them in a model with search-mediated trade. None of these studies, however, focuses on

I am grateful for the helpful suggestions of Robert Barsky, Olivier Blanchard, Peter Diamond, Stanley Fischer, Franklin Fisher, Ken Judd, Greg Mankiw, Julio Rotemberg, Garth Saloner, Robert Solow, Lawrence Summers, Robert Vishny, Robert Waldmann, and the referees of this *Journal*.

[*Journal of Political Economy*, 1986, vol. 94, no. 6]

1164   JOURNAL OF POLITICAL ECONOMY

Keynes's specific concern about the influence of the state of long-term expectation, or business confidence, on businessmen's plans to undertake or postpone investment projects. A model addressing this concern is presented in this paper.[1] In the model, entrepreneurs hold partly arbitrary but commonly shared expectations about the future path of the economy and independently choose a pattern of investment that fulfills these expectations. Expectations influence the cyclical behavior of macroeconomic variables, the efficiency properties of the economy, and, in some cases, long-run development as well.

Specifically, the theory describes the possibilities for both cyclical and noncyclical implementation of innovations occurring despite the steady arrival of inventions.[2] The model is one of a multisector economy, in which each sector receives ideas about cheaper means for producing its output. Such inventions arrive to each sector at a constant rate. When a firm in a sector invents a low-cost technology, it can start using it at any time after the invention. Although the inventing firm can profit from becoming the lowest-cost producer in its sector, such profits are temporary. Soon after the firm implements its invention ("innovates"), imitators enter and eliminate all profits. For this reason, the firm would like to get its profits when they are the highest, which is during a general boom. Expectations about the date of arrival of this boom determine whether the firm is willing to postpone innovation until the boom comes.

---

[1] Several recent theoretical studies are related to the current discussion. Weitzman (1982) and Solow (1985) discussed multiple Pareto-ranked equilibria in economies with increasing returns; my work sheds doubt on the importance they attribute to the increasing returns assumption. Rotemberg and Saloner (1984, 1985) study oligopolies that intensify exogenously started booms through price wars or inventory buildups. Their work shares with mine the "unsmoothing" character of private agents' response to macroeconomic fluctuations, though they do not model endogenous cycles. Finally, Judd (1985) discusses a completely different mechanism that leads to innovation cycles. In his model, there is an infinite supply of possible innovations, but when firms introduce too many new products within a short time, they compete for the same consumer resources and reduce profits from each particular product. Furthermore, when imitation leads to price reductions for recently introduced products, consumers substitute toward these products, making entry by yet newer products even less profitable. As a result, after a period of innovation, entrepreneurs wait until the secular growth of the economy renders further innovation profitable. Judd's mechanism is almost the opposite of mine: innovations in his model repel rather than attract other innovations.

[2] Because of the essential role played by innovation in this paper, the theory of business cycles it presents might (incorrectly) be thought to be Schumpeterian. Schumpeter (1939) thought the innovation process to be essentially autonomous and completely independent of market demand. His inventors create markets rather than adapt to enter good markets. In contrast, Schmookler (1962, 1966) believed that innovation occurs in markets in which demand is substantial and profits from innovation can be great. My theory, then, is more Schmooklerian than Schumpeterian. Schmookler, however, insisted that expectations are adaptive and that innovation takes place in the markets in which demand has proven to be high. My work, in contrast, emphasizes foresight as a determinant of the timing of innovation.

If all firms owning inventions share the expectations about the timing and size of the general boom, they can time their innovations to make this boom a reality. When firms in different sectors all anticipate an imminent boom, they put in place the inventions they have saved. By innovating simultaneously, firms give a boost to output and fulfill the expectation of a boom. When, on the other hand, firms expect a boom only in the distant future, they may choose to delay implementation of inventions. When firms in different sectors postpone innovation, the economy stays in a slump. A firm in a given sector affects the fortunes of firms in other sectors by distributing its profits, which are then spent on output of firms in all sectors. In turn, they benefit when profits from other sectors are spent on their own products. By waiting to innovate, all firms contribute to the general prosperity of a boom, which affords them profits that are worth waiting for.

When expectations drive investment, the economy can fluctuate without fluctuations in invention. Any of a number of cycles of different durations can be an equilibrium, depending on agents' anticipations about the length of the slump. The longer is the slump, the bigger is the boom that follows it. One possible equilibrium outcome is the immediate implementation of inventions, in which case output grows without a cycle. When the economy does fluctuate, it falls behind its productive potential as firms postpone innovation but catches up in a boom. Productivity grows in spurts. An economy with these features is described in Sections II–III.

The possibility of a cyclical equilibrium sheds doubt on a frequently articulated view that a market economy smooths exogenous shocks. Inventions here can be interpreted as shocks hitting the economy, which are essentially identical each period. But these shocks can be "saved." If they are, the stock of technological knowledge grows steadily but is embodied into technology periodically. The economy follows a cyclical path when a much smoother path is available.

When expectations are autonomous, the economy can end up in any of its several perfect-foresight stationary cyclical equilibria. These equilibria are Pareto ranked, so the economy can settle into a very bad equilibrium. But expectations need not be truly autonomous; they may reflect agents' preferences over equilibria. For example, some equilibria may generate higher profits for all firms whose actions affect the equilibrium path. If the myriad of firms in the economy could coordinate on production plans supporting this equilibrium, it is arguably the natural outcome to expect. The question then arises whether the most profitable equilibrium is the one preferred by consumers. Section V shows that if innovation does not require fixed costs, the acyclical equilibrium is both the most profitable and the most efficient. In contrast, Section VI supplies an example in which, with contemporaneously incurred fixed costs, the most profitable equilibrium is cyclical, but the most efficient one is acyclical. The example raises the possibility of a disagreement between workers and firm owners over the preferred path of the economy.

In the model discussed in Sections II–VI, long-term development of the economy is independent of which equilibrium obtains. In the long run, all good ideas are put to use, with or without business cycles. Since cycles are inefficient, a countercyclical fiscal policy that could steer the economy to the steady growth equilibrium would be desirable. An example of such a policy, presented in Section VII, is a progressive tax system (or a tax surcharge during booms) that reduces the profitability of innovation during booms and thus eliminates cycles and raises welfare.

In general, however, long-term development might rely on the cycle, and an ignorant countercyclical policy might be harmful. For example, if each innovator must incur a fixed cost in the period prior to innovation (e.g., he must build a plant), large sales during booms may be necessary to enable the entrepreneur to cover his fixed costs. Innovations introduced during slumps may lose money, and even steady growth equilibria may fail to sustain innovation because of an insufficient level of aggregate demand. In this case, only a cyclical equilibrium is compatible with implementation of inventions. In an alternative equilibrium (called "stone-age"), firms never expect a boom and do not innovate at all.

If the government understands that long-term growth can be sustained only with fluctuations, it will forgo stabilization policy. An attempt to eliminate the cycle with aggregate demand management at best will be wasteful and at worst will steer the economy into the stone-age equilibrium. The success of countercyclical policy should be judged in the light of the possibility that an ignorant policy can entail substantial welfare losses if it blocks technological progress.

While focusing on the role of expectations and on coordination, I depart significantly from a down-to-earth theory of investment. Capital in the model is a stock of knowledge embodied into a technology that uses no durable assets. Investment constitutes taking available ideas that are not being used and adding them to the stock of utilized knowledge. The cycles are implementation cycles rather than cycles in physical investment. Knowledge, however, is a very imperfect proxy for a physical asset since it does not offer the same opportunities for physical smoothing of consumption. Section VIII discusses the consequences of introducing capital into the model and considers additional assumptions that must be made to preserve the results. It also discusses additional extensions and presents conclusions.

II. Setup of the Model

A. *The Consumer*

The household side of the economy consists of one representative consumer, who lives for an infinite number of discrete periods. The consumer's preferences are defined each period over a list of N goods, which is constant over time. The lifetime utility function is given by

$$\sum_{t=1}^{\infty} \rho^{t-1} \frac{\left(\prod_{j=1}^{N} x_{tj}^{\lambda} \right)^{1-\gamma}}{1-\gamma}, \tag{1}$$

where $\lambda = 1/N$ and x_{tj} is consumption of good j in period t.

I use Cobb-Douglas preferences within a period to abstract from substitution between different goods.[3] In a model addressing macroeconomic questions, equilibrium in each sector should be determined by aggregate demand and not by prices in other sectors, a property guaranteed by Cobb-Douglas preferences. The infinitely lived consumer formulation assures that the results are not driven by the restricted market participation property of overlapping generations models. All the results I present also hold in a finite-horizon economy.

Assume that in period t each good j is sold at the price p_{tj} on a separate market and that the consumer's income is y_t. If the interest rate paid at time t is denoted by r_{t-1}, the consumer's budget constraint is

$$\sum_{t=1}^{\infty} \frac{y_t - \sum_{j=1}^{N} p_{tj} x_{tj}}{D_{t-1}} = 0, \tag{2}$$

where $D_t = (1 + r_1) \ldots (1 + r_t)$ and $D_0 = 1$.

The assumption of one lifetime budget constraint for the representative consumer relies on perfect capital markets. In particular, it means that an entrepreneur can borrow against the profits (known with certainty) that will be earned from his yet unmade invention. We can think of inventors selling the claims to profits from future inventions in a competitive stock market so that all these claims are traded from the start. The model thus allows for consumers with heterogeneous wealth levels (specifically, inventors and noninventors) and for capital market transactions between them. Once these transactions

---

[3] Cycles of the type I discuss will be easier to sustain, the less substitutability there is between different goods.

are completed, we can think in terms of a representative consumer with a lifetime budget constraint.

Maximization of (1) subject to (2) yields consumption expenditures c_t in period t such that

$$c_t^\gamma = \left(\sum_{i=1}^{N} p_{ti} x_{ti} \right)^\gamma = \rho^{t-1} D_{t-1} \cdot (\Pi \, p_{jt}^\lambda)^{\gamma-1} \cdot \frac{1}{\alpha}, \qquad (3)$$

where α is the Lagrange multiplier on (2). In addition, we get constant expenditure shares for various goods:

$$x_{ti} p_{ti} = \lambda c_t. \qquad (4)$$

Assume that physical storage is impossible. Competitive interest rates adjust to make $y_t = c_t$ so that the consumer wants neither to borrow nor to save. Equilibrium interest rates are given by

$$1 + r_t = \frac{1}{\rho} \cdot \left(\frac{y_{t+1}}{y_t} \right)^\gamma \cdot \frac{\left(\prod_{j=1}^{N} p_{jt+1}^\lambda \right)^{1-\gamma}}{\left(\prod_{j=1}^{N} p_{jt}^\lambda \right)^{1-\gamma}}. \qquad (5)$$

Finally,

$$y_t = \Pi_t + L, \qquad (6)$$

where Π_t are aggregate profits in period t, L is the inelastic labor supply, and wage at each t is taken to be one without loss of generality. Throughout, I measure prices and interest rates in wage units.

B. Market Structure and Innovations

Prior to period 1, output of each good j can be produced by firms with constant returns to scale technologies in which output is equal to the labor input. Every period, firms play a Bertrand price game, without capacity limitations. The Bertrand assumption is equivalent to assuming competition whenever no innovation takes place while letting the innovator be a dominant firm in its market. In period 1, then, equilibrium prices all equal unity.

Each period, one firm in each of n sectors generates an invention. These inventions are made in a very strict order. In the first period, firms in sectors $1, \ldots, n$ get ideas; in the second period, firms in sectors $n + 1, \ldots, 2n$ invent, and so on. In period $T^* = N/n$, firms in the last n sectors invent, and in period $T^* + 1$, the next round of inventions begins with sectors $1, \ldots, n$. This order is permanent for all rounds of invention.

An invention in each sector is a technology that produces one unit of output with $1/\mu$ the labor it took to produce this output with the best technology known up to then. The rate of technological progress μ exceeds one and is the same for all goods and for all times. Thus ideas from the first round permit a unit of output to be produced with $1/\mu$ units of labor, those from the second round with $1/\mu^2$ units, and so forth.[4]

In any period from the date it gets the invention, the firm can enter the market and implement it. Assume that the firm can postpone innovation without the danger that another firm implements it first (until, of course, the next idea arrives to the sector). When it innovates, the firm enters a Bertrand market, in which it becomes the lowest-cost producer. Equilibrium price equals the marginal cost of inefficient firms, but the innovator captures the whole market. He does not want to lower the price since demand is unit elastic, and he cannot raise it without losing all his sales. In the period after innovation, imitators enter and compete away all profits, with the price falling to the marginal cost of the efficient technology, or $1/\mu$ times the old price.

C. The Decision to Innovate

Consider what happens to a firm that innovates when aggregate demand is y_t and the marginal cost of an inefficient producer in its sector is w_{ti}. It gets revenue λy_t for output $\lambda y_t/w_{ti}$, obtained at a unit cost w_{ti}/μ and a total cost $\lambda y_t/\mu$. Its profits are

$$\pi_t = \lambda y_t - \left(\frac{\lambda y_t}{w_{ti}}\right) \cdot \left(\frac{w_{ti}}{\mu}\right) = \frac{\lambda(\mu - 1)y_t}{\mu}. \tag{7}$$

Independence of profits of the unit cost level of inefficient firms is a special feature of the Cobb-Douglas and constant unit cost assumptions; it does not buy any important results. Each firm innovating in period t will make π_t. I use the notation $m \equiv \lambda(\mu - 1)/\mu$, so that $\pi_t = my_t$.

Importantly, I assume that a firm owning an invention chooses its date of innovation (and hence the only date on which it makes profits) to maximize the present value of profits. It may be argued that, in a representative consumer economy, the firm should do what that consumer wants, and hence, if profit maximization leads to an inefficiency, it is an inappropriate objective for the firm. To deal with this

---

[4] Because prices are rapidly falling, it is important to keep in mind that restrictions on the speed of innovation are necessary to keep lifetime utility finite. These restrictions will be discussed later in the paper.

objection, the economy I describe can be replicated as in Hart (1982) so that owners of firms do not consume their firms' output. Suppose that there are two representative consumers on two identical islands, each laboring on his own island and consuming the fruit of his own labor but owning firms and saving on the other island. Suppose that the two islands are in the same equilibrium so that interest rates, incomes, and profits are the same on both. Then any firm that the representative consumer owns cannot affect the prices he faces by altering its date of innovation. In that case, the owner's objective is profit maximization since the firm's choices enter their problem only through the budget constraint and capital markets are perfect. After replication, all the issues I study remain. Having one representative consumer and a profit-maximizing firm is a simplifying but perfectly legitimate abstraction.

III. Construction of a Periodic Equilibrium

The principal decision of the firm holding an invention is to determine when to innovate. In this section, I show that firms in different sectors, receiving ideas at different times, may all choose to innovate in the period of high profits and high aggregate demand, that is, when other firms innovate. This synchronization of innovations gives rise to a multiplicity of perfect-foresight equilibria. One of them is always the steady growth acyclical equilibrium, in which inventions are implemented immediately. From the set of equilibria with fluctuating output, I focus on constant period cycles.

In a perfect-foresight equilibrium, firms form expectations about the path of interest rates and of aggregate demand, and these expectations are fulfilled by the chosen timing of innovations. Firms are assumed to be small so that each firm ignores its own impact on the behavior of aggregate variables. Similarly, when a firm makes its decisions, it cares only about aggregate data, and not about what is happening in any sector other than its own.[5]

Suppose we look for cycles of period $T \leq T^*$, in which inventions accumulated in periods $1, \ldots, T$ are implemented together in period T, called a T-boom. Innovations are imitated in period $T + 1$, which is also the first period of the next cycle. (I speak in terms of periods $1, \ldots, T$, but this should be interpreted as modulo T.)

---

[5] I could alternatively assume a continuum of infinitesimal sectors. The essential assumption is that firms take the behavior of aggregate variables as given and ignore their own impact on those variables. It is therefore misleading to interpret this model as a game between sectors.

The conditions for the existence of a perfect-foresight cyclical equilibrium of period T are twofold. First, it must be the case that if firms inventing in periods $1, \ldots, T - 1$ expect the boom to take place in period T, they choose to innovate in period T rather than in the period in which they get their ideas or any period prior to T. Second, if firms with inventions expect a boom in period T, they must prefer not to wait past period T to innovate; in particular, they should not want to wait until the next boom. I take up these two conditions in order.

To find conditions for postponement, fix T and consider first the periods of no innovation. Prior to the boom, there are no profits earned in the economy, and hence in periods $1, \ldots, T - 1$ income is L. Since prices do not change either, interest rates are given by $1 + r_1 = \ldots = 1 + r_{T-2} = 1/\rho$. Next consider a T-boom. Since a firm will never sit on a new idea until the next idea comes to its sector and makes the first one obsolete, T must satisfy

$$T < T^* = \frac{N}{n}. \tag{8}$$

Since profits are the same in each innovating sector, we have

$$\Pi_T = nTmy_T, \tag{9}$$

which combined with (6) yields

$$\pi_T = \frac{mL}{1 - nTm} = my_T. \tag{10}$$

Note that the condition $T < 1/nm$ is implied by (8). We also apply (5) to get

$$1 + r_{T-1} = \left(\frac{1}{\rho}\right)(1 - nTm)^{-\gamma} \tag{11}$$

since prices do not change from period $T - 1$ to period T.

If a firm getting its idea in period 1 is willing to wait until period T to implement it, so will firms getting their ideas in periods $2, \ldots, T - 1$ since the interest rate is positive throughout and income stays constant at L. For the same reason, if a firm that gets the idea in period 1 wants to postpone implementing it beyond period 1, it will not want to implement it until time T.

We can now calculate the condition under which the firm that gets its idea in period 1 is willing to delay innovation until period T. That condition is $\pi_T/D_{T-1} > \pi_1$ or

$$\rho^{T-1}(1 - nTm)^{\gamma-1} > 1. \tag{12}$$

Expression (12) can be interpreted as follows. Profits in this model are proportional to output, while the discount factor is proportional to output raised to the power γ. The more concave is the consumer's utility, the higher must be the interest rate to keep him from wanting to borrow in the period prior to the boom. Discounted profits are thus proportional to output raised to the power $1 - \gamma$. Also, $(1 - nTm)$ is the share of wages in income, and hence discounted profits are proportional to $(1 - nTm)^{\gamma - 1}$ since the wage bill is constant. The more firms innovate, the higher is the share of profits and hence the higher is income, and the more profitable it is to innovate at that time. This effect, however, is mitigated by declining marginal utility of income and by discounting. In particular, with logarithmic utility, there can be no delay since the discount rate is proportional to profits. I therefore assume throughout that $0 \leqslant \gamma < 1$.[6] But as long as $\gamma < 1$ and (12) is satisfied, interest rates do not rise by enough prior to the boom to offset firms' preference for getting their profits during that boom.

When (12) holds, if all firms but one inventing in periods $1, \ldots, T$ are willing to wait until period T to innovate, that last firm is also willing to wait until period T. We now need to find under what conditions, when all but one of the firms innovate in period T, the last one does not want to wait beyond that. For even when a firm waits until the boom, it may want to wait one more period because of price declines in period $T + 1$ and the resulting possibility of negative interest rates (in wage units) at time T.

Two influences can keep the firm from postponing innovation beyond a boom. First, even despite price declines, discounting may be sufficient to render postponement unprofitable. Second, by the time a firm might want to innovate in the future, the next invention may have arrived in its sector, thus preventing it from profiting from its own idea. I first provide the condition under which a firm does not want to wait beyond a boom even without a danger that its invention will be surpassed, and then I deal with that danger.

Observe first that if the firm does not want to wait until $2T$ to innovate, it will not want to wait until any period before $2T$ either. For if it did, it would also want to postpone innovation from then until $2T$, by (12). Observe also that the firm unwilling to wait until $2T$ would not choose to wait beyond $2T$ since delaying innovation from $2T$ to $2T + t \leqslant 3T$ is just like delaying innovation from T to $T + t \leqslant 2T$ (or even worse if the next idea may be coming into the sector). All we need to find, then, is the condition under which the firm prefers entering at time T to entering at $2T$.

---

[6] In contrast, Grandmont (1983) requires high γ's to generate a cycle in an overlapping generations model.

To get this, apply (5) to obtain

$$1 + r_T = \frac{1}{\rho} \cdot \frac{(1 - nTm)^\gamma}{\mu^{nT\lambda(1-\gamma)}}. \tag{13}$$

The power of μ appears in (13) since imitators drive the price of the goods whose production was innovated last period to $1/\mu$ of their period T levels (and profits to zero). After imitation, the pattern of interest rates in periods $T + 1, \ldots, 2T - 1$ repeats that in periods $1, \ldots, T - 1$, and profits in period $2T$ are again given by (7). To prevent delay until $2T$, then, we need

$$\rho\mu^{n\lambda(1-\gamma)} < 1. \tag{14}$$

Condition (14) excludes the possibility that firms want to postpone their innovation indefinitely; it is also equivalent to the transversality condition for the consumer's problem, guaranteeing that lifetime utility (1) is finite in equilibrium.

The inverse of the left-hand side of (14) raised to the power T is the discount factor between periods T and $2T$. That inverse also equals the interest rate that would prevail in a steady growth equilibrium. Inequality (14) says that, looking from period T, period $2T$ profits (which in wage units are the same) should be discounted. The problem is that prices fall after period T, and hence the period T interest rate may be negative. Nevertheless, by assuming (14) we insist that, on average, the future be discounted at a positive rate, which happens only if technological progress is not too fast.[7]

When (14) holds, no firm wants to postpone innovation beyond a boom even when the next innovation in its sector does not arrive until after the next boom. When (14) fails, a firm wishes to postpone innovation until the boom just prior to the arrival of the next idea into its sector. In this case, only the cycle of length $T^* = N/n$ can be sustained as a periodic perfect-foresight equilibrium, and this cycle always exists when (14) is false. (Proof: Equation [12] reduces to $\rho^{[N/n]-1}\mu^{1-\gamma} > 1$, which is true whenever $\rho\mu^{n/N[1-\gamma]} > 1$.) Because failure of (14) leads to the conclusion of infinite lifetime utility, the usefulness of this case is unclear, and I ignore it from now on.

The main arguments of this section can be summarized in the following proposition.

---

[7] An alternative interpretation of (14) can be made if we take as numeraire the price of a good whose production is innovated in period T. Then by period $2T$, the real price of each good whose production has not been innovated at time T rises by a factor of μ, as do the real wage, aggregate income, and profits. Condition (14) says that the real discount rate between periods T and $2T$ actually exceeds μ. As before, it amounts to saying that the force of time preference dominates the rate of increase of real income and profits.

PROPOSITION 1. Suppose that the pace of innovation is slow enough that (14) holds. Then for every T satisfying (8) and (12), there exists a perfect-foresight cyclical equilibrium in which all accumulated inventions are implemented simultaneously every T periods.

This result has a simple economic interpretation. If firms can receive profits in only one period, they would like to do so at the time of high aggregate demand. The latter obtains when profits are high, and profits are high when many firms innovate. The rise in interest rates in the period prior to the boom is not sufficient to offset this preference for synchronization.

The paths of utility and of the interest rate in wage units over a T-cycle are shown in figure 1. Over time, the magnitude of the cycle stays constant thanks to Cobb-Douglas preferences, which imply that profits in each boom are the same and each round of cost reductions has the same effect on interest rates. A detrended output series exhibits a cyclical pattern with both booms and recessions.

IV. The Multiplicity of Equilibria

Proposition 1 suggests that, for a given set of parameter values, there may be several periodicities T for which there exists a cycle. In particular, it is obvious that $T = 1$ always works, so the 1-cycle—a steady growth equilibrium in which ideas are implemented as soon as they are received—always exists.

To study the multiplicity of perfect-foresight equilibria of a constant period, define the left-hand side of (12) as the function

$$f(T) \equiv \rho^{T-1}(1 - nmT)^{\gamma - 1}.$$

Remember that $mLf(T)$ is the present value that a firm inventing in period 1 attaches to its invention in a T-cycle. We are interested in T's between one and N/n, for which $f(T) > 1$ when parameters satisfy (14). To describe this set, it is useful to start with two calculations. The proofs of these and subsequent claims are collected in Appendix A.

LEMMA 1. The function $f(T)$ attains a minimum at a positive T_M under (14). Furthermore, $f(T)$ is decreasing for $T < T_M$ and increasing for $T > T_M$.

LEMMA 2. Under (14), $f(N/n) < f(1)$.

The lemmas imply that $f(T)$ attains its minimum somewhere to the right of $T = 1$. It may decrease all the way to N/n or reach a minimum before N/n and rise afterward, but not all the way to $f(1)$. In fact, from the restrictions imposed so far, we cannot ascertain either the sign of $f'(N/n)$ or whether $f(N/n)$ is greater or less than unity. The possibilities for the set of T's that keep $f(T)$ above one are then as follows. It can include all T's between one and N/n, only low T's, or both low

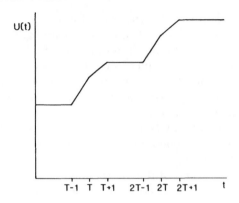

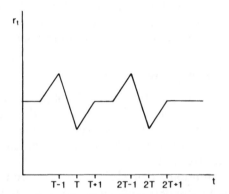

FIG. 1.—Paths of utility and interest over the cycle

T's and high *T*'s, with a break in the middle. The three possibilities are shown in figure 2. They demonstrate the general multiplicity of equilibria in this model.

Multiple equilibria arise naturally when expectations govern the timing of investment. In a 1-cycle, agents always expect a constant but mild boom and promptly innovate to make it come true. In a longer-period cycle, agents expect a low level of aggregate demand for a time and correctly anticipate the moment of a big boom. Compared with short cycles, long cycles have longer (and deeper, after detrending) slumps but also wider spread booms.[8] In addition, there can be equilibria with variable periods of the cycle. As long as firms do not want to wait until the next cycle's boom, the period of the cycle today

_____

[8] In contrast, Diamond and Fudenberg (1982) exhibit a business cycle that at every stage provides agents with a lower utility flow than does the good stationary equilibrium.

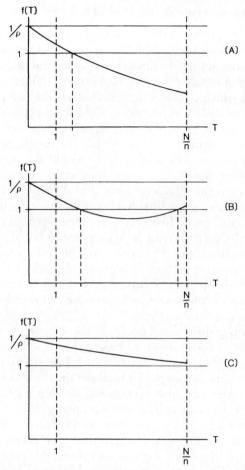

Fɪɢ. 2.—Multiplicity of cyclical equilibria. *A*, only short cycles are feasible; *B*, short and long cycles are feasible; *C*, all cycles are feasible.

does not affect the period of the cycle in the future. Expectations can support any one of these equilibria, as long as beliefs are common to all the market participants.

It is worth noting that, when (12) and (14) hold with a strict inequality, none of these equilibria is sensitive to small perturbations of the aggregate demand process. For example, suppose that a firm in some sector makes a mistake and innovates in a slump. If the impact of this mistake on aggregate demand in the boom is negligible, (12) will continue to hold and other firms will stay with their planned timing of innovation. Equilibria are thus invariant to small exogenous fluctuations of demand.

V. Coordination, Profitability, and Efficiency

When several T-cycles qualify as equilibria, it becomes an issue which one of them should occur. An almost persuasive view argues that expectations are completely autonomous in this model, and therefore any discussion of equilibrium selection is unwarranted. Alternatively, one might ask which equilibrium firms will prefer and then maintain that the most profitable equilibrium is the most plausible one.

To do this, consider a firm in period 1, contemplating its own profits in various equilibria. If its profits are the highest in the T^*-cycle, all firms receiving ideas up until T^* would also prefer a boom at T^* to any earlier boom. Moreover, they know they cannot have a bigger boom than the T^*-boom even after T^* since a new round of inventions precludes delay by some firms. In this case, the T^*-cycle is the most profitable for all firms receiving ideas up until T^*, and in this sense it is focal. (Note that not *all* firms prefer a boom at T^*; if $T^* = 3$, firms getting inventions in period 4 might well prefer the 2-cycle.) Alternatively, if firms getting inventions in period 1 prefer a boom right then to a boom in any future period, it is plausible to expect them to be able to coordinate on immediate innovation. In this case, steady growth is a focal outcome.[9]

In my example, discounted profits in the T-cycle for a firm getting an invention in period 1 are given by $mLf(T)$. By lemmas 1 and 2, this quantity is the highest in the 1-cycle, which I therefore consider to be a plausible outcome. Though this weakens the case for my model as a predictor of cycles, the next section will present a generalization in which the T^*-cycle may well be the most profitable.

The next obvious question is one of the consumer's preference between equilibria. Though it is intuitively appealing that the consumer should prefer the 1-cycle to all others, this proposition is not trivial to show. True, in the 1-cycle, the consumer gets price reductions the soonest, and the production set of the economy expands at the fastest technologically feasible rate. As a result, if we compare a T-cycle with the 1-cycle, in all periods other than T-booms, the consumer is clearly better off in the 1-cycle. In T-booms, however, high profits may compensate for higher prices. Take, for example, period T^* in the T^*-cycle. In that period, innovation occurs in all sectors and, hence (by a standard result in tax theory), there is no static distortion since the markup is the same on all goods. In period T^* in the 1-cycle, we have the same production set and a distortion since only n out of N prices exceed the marginal cost. Hence period T^* welfare is higher in

---

[9] In this model, as well as in the extension with fixed costs from Sec. VI, cycles of period T, with $1 < T < T^*$, cannot be the most profitable for all firms receiving inventions between times 1 and T.

the T^*-cycle. In fact, for extremely high rates of innovation (i.e., rates of innovation that require unreasonably small discount rates ρ for [14] to hold), the consumer prefers the T^*-cycle. For example, let $T^* = 2$, $\gamma = 0$, so that (12) and (14) reduce to $\rho\mu > 1$ and $\rho\mu^{1/2} < 1$. We calculate that $U(1) - U(2) = (1 + \rho\mu^{1/2})[2\mu/(\mu + 1)] - (1 + \rho\mu)$. By setting $\rho = 1/4$ and $\mu = 9$, we satisfy (12) and (14), while $U(1) - U(2) = -.05 < 0$. Nonetheless, the following proposition holds.

PROPOSITION 2. Assume (14) and that $\mu \leq T$. Then the consumer's lifetime utility is higher in the 1-cycle equilibrium than it is in the T-cycle equilibrium.

The restriction $\mu \leq T$ is economically meaningless; however, it is weaker than the restriction $\mu < 2$. If we think of a period as a year, a "reasonable" value for the size of innovation in an average sector cannot be nearly that high.

The consumer thus prefers immediate innovation and will end up with it if firms can coordinate the timing of innovation to settle on the most profitable equilibrium. On the other hand, if expectations are truly autonomous and lead to a cyclical outcome, the consumer's welfare falls short even of its second-best potential attained through immediate innovation. Of course, no equilibrium in this model is efficient.

To pinpoint the sources of inefficiency in the model, consider its deviations from the Walrasian paradigm. First, firms do not act as price takers, and, in particular, firms recognize the effect of their innovation today on tomorrow's price. Second, the innovator's output improves the productive opportunities of imitators since the latter cannot imitate until innovation has taken place. This externality can be described with missing markets and turns out not to matter as long as imitators earn zero profits.[10] Absence of price taking is thus the culprit of inefficiency. In fact, it can be shown that if firms act as price takers in a similar model generalized to allow for decreasing returns (so that there are profits in equilibrium), we could not obtain a delay of innovation even with production externalities introduced by imitation.

[10] Because of constant returns, imitators always earn zero profits (since they always play the Bertrand game against at least the innovator). Hence they cannot afford to pay anything for the right to imitate. Even if we open personalized markets for imitation rights (following Arrow [1970]) but let the innovator set the price, he could sell nothing at any positive price; nor will he give away his idea at zero price. As a result, personalized markets will clear at a small positive price, at which both supply and demand equal zero in all periods. Put another way, in making his decisions the innovator can ignore these markets, and therefore their absence is irrelevant.

VI.   The Case of Fixed Costs

Suppose that innovation requires a one-time expenditure of F units of labor at the time the innovation is implemented. Imitation, as before, comes free in the period after innovation. This change raises the relative desirability of innovation during a large boom and allows for the most profitable equilibrium to be cyclical.

Adaptation of the earlier analysis yields

$$\pi_T = \frac{mL - F}{1 - nTm} = my_T - F, \tag{10'}$$

for which we need to assume that

$$mL - F \geq 0. \tag{15}$$

The condition for preference for delay from period 1 to period T then is

$$\rho^{T-1}(1 - nTm)^{\gamma-1}\left(\frac{L}{L - nTF}\right)^{\gamma} > 1. \tag{12'}$$

Fixed costs improve the possibilities for existence of T-cycles because, with fixed costs, aggregate demand is lower in a T-boom, and therefore r_{T-1} is lower. In fact, the ratio of profits in period T to what they would have been if a firm innovated in period 1 is the same with or without fixed costs. The essential difference fixed costs make is that they lower the interest rate in period $T - 1$ and thus raise *discounted* T-boom profits. (Note that, as long as $mL - F \geq 0$, $F < \lambda L$ and $nTF < nT\lambda L < L$.) The condition that a firm not wish to wait until the next boom remains (14), so we sum up with the following proposition.

PROPOSITION 3. Whenever there exists a T-cycle in a model without fixed costs, there also exists a T-cycle if fixed costs are low enough ([15] holds). Furthermore, with fixed costs, a T-cycle exists for some parameter values that do not admit a T-cycle without fixed costs (e.g., logarithmic preferences).

Proposition 3 shows that the multiplicity of equilibria is at least as big a problem now as it was without fixed costs. Moreover, since the relative profitability of long-period equilibria rises with F, a firm obtaining an invention in period 1 may now prefer the T^*-cycle, even when (14) holds.

LEMMA 3. If F is just below mL, the T^*-cycle is the most profitable, provided that

$$\rho^{(N/n)-1} \cdot \left[\mu - \left(\frac{n}{N}\right)(\mu - 1)\right] > 1. \tag{16}$$

It should be noted that condition (16) implies the existence of a T^*-cycle. For parameter values satisfying (14) and (16) simultaneously, firms may very well end up in a T^*-cycle. At the same time, if F is just below mL, the consumer prefers the 1-cycle. The reason is that profits are virtually equal to zero, and hence "high" profits at T^* cannot offset the lower path of prices of the 1-cycle. In this special case, the consumer's preference for immediate innovation is clear-cut. Fixed costs thus introduce the possibility that firms will "choose" an equilibrium that the consumer dislikes. If expectations accommodate this selection, we end up with a perfect-foresight equilibrium whose efficiency may be substantially lower than that of a less profitable equilibrium.

VII. Public Stabilization Policy and Long-Run Growth

In an economy that develops in a T-cycle, fiscal policy can eliminate fluctuations. Such a policy can raise welfare when steady growth is the socially preferred and feasible equilibrium. Consider first the economy without fixed costs, discussed in Sections II–III. Let the government step in in the first period after a boom and introduce a progressive income tax schedule $\tau(y_t)$, to be applied to all income. The proceeds of the tax are thrown into the sea.

In this economy, income and profits in period t are reduced by a factor of $[1 - \tau(y_t)]$, and interest rates are again given by (5), where the income is after-tax. The firm should now maximize its owner's discounted after-tax profits. Under these modifications, it does not pay a firm to postpone innovation until period T if τ satisfies

$$\rho^{T-1}\left\{\frac{1 - \tau\left(\dfrac{L}{1 - nTm}\right)}{(1 - nTm)[1 - \tau(L)]}\right\}^{1-\gamma} \leq 1. \qquad (17)$$

Set $\tau(L) = \tau(L/(1 - nm)) = 0$ and, for each $T > 1$, let $\tau(L/(1 - nTm))$ be the tax rate satisfying (17) with equality. In this case, profits are lower in the boom, so even though the interest rate prior to the boom is also lower, since $\gamma < 1$, discounted profits from investing in the boom fall. The economy is thus stabilized on the 1-cycle; the government collects no taxes but stands ready to implement its policy. A progressive tax (or tax surcharge) here resembles an automatic stabilizer (Baily 1978). Furthermore, at the time of the announcement, the policy has an infinite multiplier, as income jumps from L to $L/(1 - nm)$ without any government expenditure. Finally, the policy raises both welfare and profits and hence should receive universal support.[11]

Even if the government sets its tax variables suboptimally but still stabilizes the economy on steady growth, the amount of harm such a policy can do is limited. If the government sets $\tau(L/(1 - nm)) > 0$, it collects revenues, buys goods, and throws them into the sea. Still, such a policy can only waste what is collected; it cannot arrest technological progress.

This, however, is not the case in a more general model. What makes the cases studied in Sections II–VI special is that long-run development of the economy is independent of the particular cyclical path that it follows. Eventually, all good ideas are put to use, with or without business cycles. While fiscal policy stabilizes growth, it has no consequences for development.

An alternative possibility is that the cycle is essential for development. This would be the case if, for example, firms could not cover their fixed costs when they expect other firms to innovate as soon as they invent. Thus aggregate demand during steady growth is too low to sustain it as an equilibrium. Only in a boom of a cyclical equilibrium might aggregate demand be high enough to enable firms to cover fixed costs. In addition, there will exist a stone-age equilibrium in which, because firms do not expect other firms to innovate, innovation is unprofitable and never takes place. Cyclical synchronization of innovations is thus essential for implementation of inventions. Appendix B presents an example of such an economy.

If cyclical growth is essential for innovation, stabilization policy can do more harm than good. The reason is that if taxes render innovation unprofitable even during booms, there may be no times when the firm can earn a profit from implementing its invention. As a result, the economy will settle in the stone-age equilibrium. Too aggressive a fiscal policy, while getting rid of the cycle, can actually endanger technological progress.

VIII. Conclusion

The examples discussed in this paper have attempted to illustrate the impact of entrepreneurs' expectations about the future path of macroeconomic variables on their decisions to undertake or postpone investment projects. An economy in which aggregate demand spillovers favor simultaneous implementation of projects in different sectors was shown to exhibit cyclical equilibria, with duration of slumps

---

[11] One potential disadvantage of this policy is that it is not subgame perfect. When it comes to a boom, the government would prefer not to tax and waste the income.

governed largely by expectations. In some examples, business cycles were either the most profitable or even unique outcomes. Furthermore, although countercyclical policy stabilizes the economy in some cases, an aggressive intervention can interfere with long-run development.[12]

The model I discussed can be amplified to study the nature of cyclical equilibria in a somewhat more realistic context. For example, if inventions come in different sizes (e.g., different μ's relative to the same F), firms with big ideas need not wait for the boom, even when firms with small ideas do. Alternatively, a very large unanticipated innovation (or some other shock) can have a large enough impact on aggregate demand so as to trigger a boom prior to its otherwise anticipated time.[13] Finally, if inventions arrive into some sectors more often than they do into others, economywide equilibrium can consist of overlapping cycles of different periodicities, as emphasized by Schumpeter (1939).

Some extensions of the model are suggestive of ways of getting to a unique equilibrium. For example, suppose some periods (such as the Christmas season) are characterized by an especially high marginal utility of consumption and therefore by low interest rates preceding them. The present value of profits earned from innovating in such periods might be especially high, resulting in their selection as booms. Although in the model without fixed costs cyclical equilibria with seasonal booms might be focal, they are not unique. With fixed costs, however, such equilibria can be made unique.

In evaluating the usefulness of this model, it might be fruitful to recall four conditions that seem to be responsible for cyclical equilibria. First, there must be a constantly replenished supply of pure profit opportunities. Second, these opportunities cannot be exploited forever without pure profits' being eliminated by entry. Third, profits in different sectors of the economy must spill over into higher demand in other sectors. Fourth, this spillover must be significant at the moment profits are received: intertemporal smoothing of consumption should not make the moment of receipt of income irrelevant for demand. As this discussion suggests, I do not regard innovation to be the critical part of the story: it is simply an extremely convenient way to model temporary pure profit opportunities. Furthermore, I consider the first three conditions to be quite appropriate for a market economy.

---

[12] This paper has not considered micro interventions, such as patent policy. For example, a policy granting each innovator a permanent patent ensures immediate implementation of inventions. Such a policy, however, is socially very costly.

[13] Farrell and Saloner (1984) studied a different mechanism for such a domino effect; some results similar to theirs hold in my model.

Absence of capital, however, is a critical assumption that cannot be eliminated without substituting an alternative. For suppose we add capital to the model. Then in a period of a slump, when the consumers realize that they will be better off in the future, they will attempt to dissave and to consume now, thereby reducing the future capital stock and smoothing out consumption between periods. In this case, there will be no general boom, and implementation cycles will be impossible in equilibrium. As I specified the model, physical dissaving is not feasible because there is no capital.[14] When all the adjustment to fluctuations in income occurs through interest rates, the incentives for firms not to wait for the boom are insufficient to eliminate cycles.

With capital, we need additional assumptions to accommodate implementation cycles. First, borrowing constraints can restrict opportunities for consumption smoothing. The results of this paper can be developed in an overlapping generations model of capital with the conclusion that, if entrepreneurs cannot borrow against future profits, cyclical equilibria are feasible. An alternative formulation, which is perhaps a fruitful subject for future research, is to consider a model with durable irreversible investment as in Arrow (1968). The effect of durable capital should be to limit the amount of physical dissaving that the economy can do. As a result, durable capital might accommodate implementation cycles, though I have not verified this possibility. Finally, the economy may be subject to uninsurable and unanticipated shocks, in which case the mechanism discussed in this paper will work to accentuate cycles, though it will not cause them.

Appendix A

Proof of Lemma 1

Setting $f'(T) = 0$, we obtain $T_M = (1/nm) + [(1 - \gamma)/\ln \rho]$. Taking logs of both sides of (14), we get that $\ln \rho + n\lambda(1 - \gamma)\ln \mu < 0$, so

$$\frac{1}{\ln \rho} > - \frac{1}{n\lambda(1 - \gamma)\ln \mu}.$$

Therefore,

$$T_M = \frac{1}{nm} + \frac{1 - \gamma}{\ln \rho} > \frac{1}{nm} - \frac{1 - \gamma}{n\lambda(1 - \gamma)\ln \mu}$$

$$= \frac{1}{n\lambda} \left(\frac{\mu}{\mu - 1} - \frac{1}{\ln \mu} \right) > 0,$$

---

[14] With fixed costs standing in for capital, as in Sec. VII, physical dissaving again is not feasible.

where the last inequality follows since $\ln \mu > (\mu - 1)/\mu$ for $\mu > 1$. The sign of the derivative of $f(T)$ is the sign of $(1 - nTm)\ln \rho + nm(1 - \gamma)$, which is negative for $T < T_M$ and positive for $T > T_M$.

Proof of Lemma 2

First, it can be verified that

$$\mu\left(1 - \frac{n}{N}\right) + \frac{n}{N} < \mu^{1 - (n/N)} \quad \text{when } \mu > 1 \text{ and } 0 < \frac{n}{N} < 1. \qquad (A1)$$

Now the claim of the lemma amounts to asserting that

$$X \equiv \left[\mu - \left(\frac{n}{N}\right)(\mu - 1)\right]^{1 - \gamma} \cdot \rho^{(N/n) - 1} < 1.$$

But (14) implies that $\rho < \mu^{-n/N(1 - \gamma)}$, so

$$X < \left[\mu - \left(\frac{n}{N}\right)(\mu - 1)\right]^{1 - \gamma} \cdot [\mu^{-(1 - \gamma)n/N}]^{(N - n)/n}$$

$$= \left\{\left[\mu - \left(\frac{n}{N}\right)(\mu - 1)\right] \cdot \mu^{-(N - n)/N}\right\}^{1 - \gamma}.$$

The last expression is smaller than one provided that $\mu - (n/N)(\mu - 1) < \mu^{1 - (n/N)}$, which is just (A1).

Proof of Lemma 3

Applying (10'), we can compute that

$$\pi_{T^*} = \rho^{(N/n) - 1} \cdot \mu^{1 - \gamma} \cdot \left(\frac{L}{L - NF}\right)^{\gamma} \cdot (mL - F)$$

and

$$\pi_1 = \frac{mL - F}{1 - nm}.$$

Therefore,

$$\frac{\pi_{T^*}}{\pi_1} = \mu^{1 - \gamma} \cdot \left(\frac{L}{L - NF}\right)^{\gamma} \cdot (1 - nm) \cdot \rho^{(N/n) - 1}$$

$$\approx \mu(1 - nm)\rho^{(N/n) - 1}$$

when $F \approx mL$. But $\mu(1 - nm) = \mu - (n/N)(\mu - 1)$, so when (16) holds, $\pi_{T^*}/\pi_1 > 1$, as claimed.

Proof of Proposition 2

Notation

Denote $\alpha = n/N$ so that $T^* = 1/\alpha$. Let $L(T)$ be the equilibrium *lifetime* utility of the agent in a T-cycle equilibrium for $T = 1, \ldots, T^*$. I will prove later that to compare $L(1)$ with $L(T)$ it is enough to look at the first T periods. Accordingly, denote by $U(T)$ the total utility attained over the first T periods in a T-cycle equilibrium and by $U(1)$ the total utility attained over the first T periods in a 1-cycle equilibrium. Denote by $v(T)$ utility in a T-boom. Also, for each of the first T periods of the 1-cycle equilibrium define $f_t = \Pi_{j=1}^{N} x_{tj}^{\lambda}$, where x_{tj} is equilibrium consumption of good j in period t in the 1-cycle, and define g_t as the corresponding quantity for a T-cycle. Thus

$$U(1) = \sum_{i=1}^{T} \rho^{i-1}(f_t^{1-\gamma})$$

and

$$U(T) = \sum_{i=1}^{T} \rho^{i-1}(g_t^{1-\gamma}).$$

The proof is long and tedious, so I outline the steps first. Step 1 proves that, when welfare in a 1-cycle equilibrium is compared with that in the T-cycle equilibrium, it is enough to look at the first T periods of the individual's life. Steps 2 and 3 restrict the parameter space to the cases that are most favorable to T-cycle welfare: step 2 shows that it is sufficient to look at $\gamma = 0$, and step 3 shows that, for $\gamma = 0$, it suffices to look at the highest permissible ρ, which by (14) is $\rho = \mu^{-n/N}$. Step 4 shows that $v(t)$ is never greater than μ^{α}, the value it attains when $T = T^*$. Step 5 shows that $U(1) > U(T)$ as long as $\mu < T$ and completes the proof.

Step 1

$L(1) > L(T)$ iff $U(1) > U(T)$. For both the 1-cycle equilibrium and the T-cycle equilibrium, the history of periods $T + 1, \ldots, 2T$ is the same as the history of periods $1, \ldots, T$, except nT prices are $1/\mu$ of their old levels. This makes the utility in period $T + x$ (where $x = 1, \ldots, T$) equal to $\rho^T \cdot \mu^{nT\lambda(1-\gamma)}$ times the utility in period x. Extending this argument to future periods, we get

$$L(1) = \frac{U(1)}{1 - \rho^T \mu^{nT\lambda(1-\gamma)}}$$

and

$$L(T) = \frac{U(T)}{1 - \rho^T \mu^{nT\lambda(1-\gamma)}}.$$

Inequality (14) ensures that these expressions are finite, and thus the assertion is proved.

Step 2

Other things equal, if $U(1) > U(T)$ for $\gamma = 0$, then $U(1) > U(T)$ for $\gamma > 0$. Observe that $\partial U(1)/\partial f_t = (f_t)^{-\gamma} \cdot \rho^{t-1}$ and $\partial U(T)/\partial g_t = (g_t)^{-\gamma} \cdot \rho^{t-1}$. In the 1-cycle, income (in wage units) stays constant over time, but prices are falling. Thus

$$f_i > f_j \quad \text{for } i > j. \tag{A2}$$

Also, before period T, the individual enjoys both higher income and lower prices in the 1-cycle than he does in the T-cycle. Thus

$$g_i < f_i \quad \text{for } i < T. \tag{A3}$$

If $g_T < f_T$ also, as may be the case if $T < T^*$, we are done with proving that $U(1) > U(T)$. The question is what happens when

$$g_T > f_T, \tag{A4}$$

so we assume from now on that this is the case. Our maintained hypothesis is that

$$\sum_{i=1}^{T} \rho^{i-1} f_i > \sum_{i=1}^{T} \rho^{i-1} g_i.$$

Now suppose that $\gamma > 0$ and apply the mean value theorem to find that

$$U(T) - U(1) = \sum_{i=1}^{T} \rho^{i-1} h_i^{-\gamma}(g_i - f_i),$$

where

$$f_T < h_T < g_T \qquad \qquad (A5)$$

and

$$g_i < h_i < f_i \quad \text{for } i < T. \qquad \qquad (A6)$$

Now combine (A5), (A2), and (A6) to show that $h_T > f_T > f_i > h_i$ for $i < T$. The last inequality implies that, for any $i < T$, we have

$$h_i^{-\gamma} > h_T^{-\gamma}. \qquad \qquad (A7)$$

Using (A7) and (A3), we then obtain that

$$\sum_{i=1}^{T} \rho^{i-1} h_i^{-\gamma}(g_i - f_i) < \sum_{i=1}^{T} \rho^{i-1} h_T^{-\gamma}(g_i - f_i)$$

$$= h_T^{-\gamma}\left(\sum_{i=1}^{T} \rho^{i-1} g_i - \sum_{i=1}^{T} \rho^{i-1} f_i \right) < 0$$

by assumption. This proves the claim.

Step 3

If $\gamma = 0$ and $U(1) > U(T)$ for some ρ_1, then $U(1) > U(T)$ for all $\rho < \rho_1$. We are taking step 2 into account and also assuming that

$$\sum_{t=1}^{T-1} \rho_1^{t-1}(f_t - g_t) > \rho_1^{T-1}(g_T - f_T).$$

Multiply both sides by ρ^{T-1}/ρ_1^{T-1} to obtain

$$\sum_{t=1}^{T-1} \frac{\rho^{T-1}}{\rho_1^{T-t}} (f_t - g_t) > \rho^{T-1}(g_T - f_T).$$

But $\rho^{T-1}/\rho_1^{T-t} < \rho^{t-1}$ when $\rho < \rho_1$. Hence

$$\sum_{t=1}^{T-1} \rho^{t-1}(f_t - g_t) > \sum_{t=1}^{T-1} \frac{\rho^{T-1}}{\rho_1^{T-t}} (f_t - g_t) > \rho^{T-1}(f_T - g_T).$$

Q.E.D.

Since (14) imposes an upper bound on ρ in terms of μ and since we are taking $\gamma = 0$, we assume from now on that $\rho = \mu^{-\alpha}$.

Step 4

Utility in a T-boom, $v(T)$, is bounded above by μ^α. A calculation reveals that

$$v(T) = \frac{1}{1 - T\alpha[(\mu - 1)/\mu]} \, \rho^{T-1}$$

$$= \rho^{T-1} \frac{\mu}{(T^* - T)\alpha(\mu - 1) + 1}$$

$$= \frac{\mu(T^* - T)\alpha}{(T^* - T)\alpha(\mu - 1) + 1} \, \mu^\alpha.$$

The last equality follows since $\rho = \mu^\alpha$. By the mean value theorem,

$$\mu^{(T^* - T)\alpha} = 1 + (\mu - 1)(T^* - T)\alpha \cdot y^{-T\alpha}$$

for some $1 < y < \mu$. Then $y^{-T\alpha} < 1$, and so

$$\mu^{(T^* - T)\alpha} < 1 + (\mu - 1)(T^* - T)\alpha.$$

Using the last expression for $v(T)$ implies that $v(T) < \mu^\alpha$.

Step 5

$U(1) > U(T)$ for $\mu < T$. When $\rho = \mu^{-\alpha}$ and $\gamma = 0$, we can compute that

$$U(1) = \frac{1}{1 - \alpha[(\mu - 1)/\mu]} \cdot T.$$

Applying the mean value theorem to $f(x) \equiv 1/x$ for x between one and $1 - \alpha[(\mu - 1)/\mu]$, we obtain

$$U(1) = T\left\{1 - \alpha\,\frac{\mu - 1}{\mu}\left[\frac{-1}{(1 - Y)^2}\right]\right\}$$

for some $0 < Y < \alpha[(\mu - 1)/\mu]$. But then $U(1) > T\{1 + \alpha[(\mu - 1)/\mu]\}$.
   When $\rho = \mu^{-\alpha}$, $\gamma = 0$, and $v(T) < \mu^\alpha$, we have

$$U(T) \leq 1 + \mu^{-\alpha} + \ldots + \mu^{(-T+1)\alpha} + \mu^\alpha < (T - 1) + \mu^\alpha.$$

The last inequality follows since each of the $T - 2$ middle terms is less than one. Applying the mean value theorem for $f(x) = x^\alpha$ for x between one and μ, we obtain $(T - 1) + \mu^\alpha = (T - 1) + 1 + (\mu - 1)\alpha Z^{\alpha - 1}$ for some $1 < Z < \mu$. But since $Z^{\alpha - 1} < 1$, we have $U(T) < T + \alpha(\mu - 1)$.
   Putting the bounds on $U(1)$ and $U(T)$ together, we get

$$U(1) - U(T) > T + T\alpha\,\frac{\mu - 1}{\mu} - T - \alpha(\mu - 1) = \alpha(\mu - 1)\left(\frac{T}{\mu} - 1\right) > 0$$

by assumption. This completes the proof.

Appendix B

This Appendix describes an economy that grows either in cycles or with no innovation at all. Suppose that an innovating firm must incur a fixed cost in the period prior to innovation. If the innovation reduces the unit cost from that of the currently *used* technology by a factor of μ, then this fixed cost is F.

If, however, a round of innovation has been skipped and the innovation improves the currently used technology by a factor of μ^2, then the fixed cost is $2F$ (similarly $3F$ for μ^3, etc.). This technology captures the notion that more dramatic innovations are costlier to implement. In other respects, the economy is the same as that of Section II of the text.

Calculation of equilibria generally follows Section III, except now y_t exceeds c_t by the amount of fixed-cost investment needed for period $t + 1$ innovation. If an innovation requires a fixed cost aF, the cost to the firm is $aF(1 + r_t)$ since aF must be saved in period t and savings earn interest. Thus fixed costs are a limited form of capital. With savings in the model, interest rate expressions must be modified to allow for divergence of income from consumption.

Consider an economy in which $T^* = 2$ and $\gamma = 0$. Thus half of all sectors receive an invention each period. I will present an example in which (1) equilibria in which each sector implements every nth round of invention as soon as it arrives, while skipping the first $n - 1$ rounds, do not exist (in particular, for $n = 1$, steady growth equilibrium does not exist); (2) the 2-cycle exists; (3) the stone-age equilibrium, in which entrepreneurs expect no innovation to take place—and none does—also exists.

Requirement 1 amounts to the condition that an innovating firm's profits be negative in an equilibrium in which every k periods $N/2$ sectors reduce costs by a factor of μ^k, followed next period by the same reduction in the other $N/2$ sectors. For $k = 1$, this is the steady growth equilibrium. The condition that ensures that 1 is satisfied is

$$\frac{\mu^k - 1}{\mu^k} \cdot \frac{1}{N} \left\{ \frac{L - (N/2)Fk}{1 - [(\mu^k - 1)/2\mu^k]} \right\} - \frac{Fk}{\rho\mu^{k/2}} < 0, \quad \text{for } k = 1, 2 \ldots . \quad \text{(B1)}$$

To satisfy requirement 2, we calculate the 2-cycle. The interest rate before the boom is $1 + r_1 = 1/\rho$, and the interest rate before the slump is $1 + r_2 = 1/\rho\mu$ since all prices fall after the boom. Profits are given by

$$\pi_1 = m(L - NF) - F(1 + r_2) = \frac{1}{N} \frac{\mu - 1}{\mu} (L - NF) - F(1 + r_2) \quad \text{(B2)}$$

and

$$\pi_2 = m\mu L - F(1 + r_1) = \frac{1}{N} (\mu - 1)L - F(1 + r_1) \quad \text{(B3)}$$

in the slump and boom, respectively. We are seeking parameters for which

$$\frac{\pi_2}{1 + r_1} > 0 > \pi_1 \quad \text{(B4)}$$

or

$$\rho \left[\frac{1}{N}(\mu - 1)L \right] - F > 0 > \frac{1}{N} \left(\frac{\mu - 1}{\mu} \right) (L - NF) - \frac{F}{\rho\mu}. \quad \text{(B5)}$$

The last condition for the 2-cycle is (14) from Section III, which here reduces to

$$\rho\mu^{1/2} < 1. \quad \text{(B6)}$$

Finally, for the stone-age equilibrium to exist (requirement 3), it must be unprofitable for a firm to innovate alone in a period, or

$$\frac{\mu - 1}{\mu} \frac{1}{N} L - \frac{F}{\rho} < 0. \quad \text{(B7)}$$

Let $L = 100$, $\mu = 2$, $\rho = .7$, and $NF = 60$. For these parameter values, conditions (B1) and (B5)–(B7) can be shown to hold. In this case, equilibria with innovation but without synchronization do not exist, and bunching is necessary for technological progress.

Macroeconomic stabilization policy of the type described in Section VII will not work in this economy. To establish this, let τ_1 and τ_2 be the income tax rates for busts and booms, respectively, and observe that, as before, taxation reduces consumption and income. Because the consumer's utility is linear in income, after-tax interest rates will not be affected by the imposition of taxes. However, a firm pays for its plant at pretax interest rates, which increase as a result of imposition of the tax. These interest rates are given by

$$1 + R_1 = \frac{1}{\rho(1 - \tau_2)} \tag{B8}$$

and

$$1 + R_2 = \frac{1}{\rho\mu(1 - \tau_1)}. \tag{B9}$$

In this example, taxation strictly raises the cost of capital. As a result, if innovation was not profitable in a slump before taxes were introduced, it will not be profitable with taxes. Nor will taxes make innovation in a steady growth equilibrium profitable, thereby permitting such equilibrium to reappear. Furthermore, a firm may no longer be able to break even if it innovates in a boom. Profits in a 2-boom are now given by

$$\pi_2 = \left[\frac{1}{N}(\mu - 1)L - F(1 + R_1) \right] \cdot (1 - \tau_2). \tag{B10}$$

For the parameter values from the example and $\tau_2 > .15$, π_2 is negative. This means that a tax rate of 15 percent or higher on a 2-boom's income sends the economy into the stone-age equilibrium, which exists regardless of the level of the tax.

References

Arrow, Kenneth J. "Optimal Capital Policy with Irreversible Investment." In *Value, Capital, and Growth: Papers in Honour of Sir John Hicks*, edited by J. N. Wolfe. Edinburgh: Edinburgh Univ. Press, 1968.
———. "Political and Economic Evaluation of Social Effects and Externalities." In *The Analysis of Public Output*, edited by Julius Margolis. New York: Columbia Univ. Press (for N.B.E.R.), 1970.
Azariadis, Costas. "Self-fulfilling Prophecies." *J. Econ. Theory* 25 (December 1981): 380–96.
Baily, Martin N. "Stabilization Policy and Private Economic Behavior." *Brookings Papers Econ. Activity*, no. 1 (1978), pp. 11–50.
Cass, David, and Shell, Karl. "Do Sunspots Matter?" *J.P.E.* 91 (April 1983): 193–227.
Diamond, Peter A. "Aggregate Demand Management in Search Equilibrium." *J.P.E.* 90 (October 1982): 881–94.
Diamond, Peter A., and Fudenberg, Drew. "An Example of 'Animal Spirits' and Endogenous Business Cycles in Search Equilibrium." Mimeographed. Cambridge: Massachusetts Inst. Tech., 1982.
Farmer, Roger, and Woodford, Michael. "Self-fulfilling Prophecies and the Business Cycle." Working Paper no. 82-12. Philadelphia: Univ. Pennsylvania, Center Analytic Res. Econ. and Soc. Sci., 1984.

Farrell, Joseph, and Saloner, Garth. "Standardization, Compatibility, and Innovation." Working Paper no. 345. Cambridge: Massachusetts Inst. Tech., April 1984.

Grandmont, Jean-Michel. "Endogenous Competitive Business Cycles." Discussion Paper no. 8316. Paris: CEPREMAP, 1983.

Hart, Oliver D. "A Model of Imperfect Competition with Keynesian Features." *Q.J.E.* 97 (February 1982): 109–38.

Judd, Kenneth L. "On the Performance of Patents." *Econometrica* 53 (May 1985): 567–85.

Keynes, John Maynard. *The General Theory of Employment, Interest and Money.* London: Macmillan, 1936.

Rotemberg, Julio J., and Saloner, Garth. "A Supergame-Theoretic Model of Business Cycles and Price Wars during Booms." Working Paper no. 349. Cambridge: Massachusetts Inst. Tech., July 1984.

———. "Strategic Inventories and the Excess Volatility of Production." Mimeographed. Cambridge: Massachusetts Inst. Tech., April 1985.

Schmookler, Jacob. "Invention, Innovation, and Business Cycles." In *Variability of Private Investment in Plant and Equipment,* pt. 2, *Some Elements Shaping Investment Decisions.* Materials submitted to U.S. Congress, Joint Economic Committee, 87th Cong. Washington: Government Printing Office, 1962.

———. *Invention and Economic Growth.* Cambridge, Mass.: Harvard Univ. Press, 1966.

Schumpeter, Joseph A. *Business Cycles: A Theoretical, Historical, and Statistical Analysis of the Capitalist Process.* New York: McGraw-Hill, 1939.

Solow, Robert M. "Monopolistic Competition and the Multiplier." Mimeographed. Cambridge: Massachusetts Inst. Tech., 1985.

Weitzman, Martin L. "Increasing Returns and the Foundations of Unemployment Theory." *Econ. J.* 92 (December 1982): 787–804.

[3]

Animal Spirits Through Creative Destruction

By Patrick Francois and Huw Lloyd-Ellis*

We show how a Schumpeterian process of creative destruction can induce rational, herd behavior by entrepreneurs across diverse sectors as if fueled by "animal spirits." Consequently, a multisector economy, in which productivity improvements are made by independent, profit-seeking entrepreneurs, exhibits regular booms, slowdowns, and downturns as part of the long-run growth process. Our cyclical equilibrium has higher average growth, but lower welfare than the corresponding acyclical one. We show how a negative relationship can emerge between volatility and growth across cycling economies, and assess the extent to which our model matches several features of actual business cycles. (JEL E0, E3, O3, O4)

Are business cycles simply random shocks around a deterministic trend, or are there more fundamental linkages between short-run fluctuations and long-run growth? Macroeconomists have tended to study the sources of fluctuations and the determinants of growth separately, but there are several reasons to question this standard dichotomy. First, postwar cross-country evidence suggests a significant negative partial correlation between volatility and growth, after controlling for standard growth correlates (e.g., Gary Ramey and Valerie A. Ramey, 1995). This

* Francois: CentER, Tilburg University, The Netherlands, and Department of Economics, University of British Columbia, Vancouver, Canada (e-mail: p.francois@kub.nl); Lloyd-Ellis: Department of Economics, Queen's University, Kingston, Ontario, Canada K7L 3N6 (e-mail: lloydell@qed.econ.queensu.ca). We are grateful to Daron Acemoglu, Gadi Barlevy, Paul Beaudry, Francisco Gonzalez, Elhanan Helpman, Michael Krause, Joanne Roberts, Shouyong Shi, Gregor Smith, Gianluca Violante, Alwyn Young, and two anonymous referees for helpful suggestions. We also thank seminar participants at the University of Colorado-Boulder, the University of Illinois-Urbana Champain, Northwestern University, Queen's University, the University of Toronto, the University of British Columbia, the University of Lausanne, the October 2000 Canadian Institute for Advanced Research (CIAR) meetings in Montreal, the 2001 meetings on New Approaches to the Study of Economic Fluctuations (NASEF) in Hydra, and the 2001 Canadian Macroeconomics Study Group (CMSG) meetings in Vancouver. The research of Francois is funded by a fellowship of the Royal Netherlands Academy of Arts and Sciences. Lloyd-Ellis gratefully acknowledges funding from Social Sciences and Humanities Research Council of Canada (SSHRCC) and the CIAR.

correlation is economically significant even among OECD countries. Second, while it is clear that some portion of aggregate volatility is the result of exogenous disturbances, the recurring asymmetry between the responses of the economy during upturns and downturns, is suggestive of an endogenously determined component. Third, there is increasing evidence that the strength of cyclical upturns is related to the depth of preceding downturns. Finally, as argued by Victor Zarnowitz (1998), even for fluctuations that are typically associated with obvious aggregate shocks, the causal links are not always clear.

The view that growth and cycles are intimately linked is often associated with Joseph Schumpeter (1927). He argued that growth occurs through a process of "creative destruction"— competition among entrepreneurs in the search for new ideas that will render their rivals' ideas obsolete. This idea is central to modern theories of endogenous long-run growth starting with Paul S. Segerstrom et al. (1990), Gene Grossman and Elhanan Helpman (1991), and Philippe Aghion and Peter Howitt (1992). However, Schumpeter also argued that this process of entrepreneurial innovation is responsible for the regular short-run fluctuations in economic activity, which he termed the "normal" business cycle. The key to explaining such business cycles, he argued, was to understand why entrepreneurial activity would be clustered over time.

A source of clustering, suggested by Schumpeter himself, has been recently formalized by a

VOL. 93 NO. 3   FRANCOIS AND LLOYD-ELLIS: ANIMAL SPIRITS   531

number of authors (for a survey see Aghion and Howitt, 1998). However, such "Schumpeterian cycles" rely on the arrival of major technological breakthroughs that influence all sectors—a general purpose technology (GPT). While the GPT story may be consistent with "long waves," there is little evidence to support the notion that such economy-wide advances can explain high-frequency business cycles. An alternative theory of why activity in diverse sectors of the economy may be clustered is developed by Andrei Shleifer (1986). He shows that when imitation limits the longevity of monopoly profits, a strategic complementarity arises that could lead entrepreneurs to implement innovations at the same time, even if the innovations themselves arrive uniformly through time. The clustering of implementation results in a boom in labor demand, which in turn generates the high demand for output necessary to support the boom. The temporary nature of the associated monopoly profits induces entrepreneurs to delay implementation until demand is maximized, so that a self-reinforcing cycle arises. Shleifer interprets his theory as a formalization of John Maynard Keynes' (1936) notion of "animal spirits."[1]

There are, however, several important limitations to Shleifer's theory of implementation cycles. Firstly, since innovations arrive exogenously, long-run growth is exogenous, so the theory has no implications for the impact of cycles on growth. Secondly, because of the multiplicity of equilibria that arise in his model, it is not possible to obtain precise predictions even for the effect of growth on cycles. Thirdly, the temporary nature of profits relies on the assumption of drastic, but costless imitation. It is not clear how robust the results would be to a less abrupt erosion of profits. Finally, Shleifer's theory depends critically on the impossibility of storage. If they could, innovators would choose to produce when costs are low (i.e., before the boom), store the output, and then sell it when

demand is high (i.e., in the boom). Such a pattern of production would undermine the existence of cycles.

In this article, we draw on the insights of Schumpeter (creative destruction) and Shleifer (animal spirits), to develop a simple theory of endogenous, cyclical growth. We show how a multisector economy, in which sector-specific, productivity improvements are made by independent, profit-seeking entrepreneurs, can exhibit regular booms, slowdowns, and downturns in economic activity as an inherent part of the long-run growth process. We establish the existence of a unique cyclical growth path along which the growth rate and the length and amplitude of cycles are endogenously determined. Our theory does not rely on the arrival of GPTs nor on drastic imitation, and allows for the possibility of storage. Specifically, we show that the process of creative destruction itself can induce endogenous clustering of implementation *and* innovation.

Creative destruction implies that the dissemination of knowledge caused by implementation eventually leads to improvements that limit a successful entrepreneur's time of incumbency. Anticipating this, entrants will optimally time implementation to ensure that their profits arrive at a time of nondepressed aggregate activity and that they maximize the length of their incumbency. It is these effects which lead to clustering in entrepreneurial implementation and, hence, to an aggregate level boom. If an entrepreneur implements before the boom, he reveals the information underlying his productivity improvement to potential rivals who may use this information in designing their own productivity improvements. By delaying implementation until the boom he delays reaping the rewards but maximizes his expected reign of incumbency. During the delay, entrepreneurs rely on maintaining secrecy regarding the nature of the innovations that they hold.[2]

Our cycle not only features clustering of implementation, but also endogenous clustering of innovation. It is this feature which generates

---

[1] The expression "animal spirits" is often associated with stochastic changes in the expectations of investors that turn out to be self-fulfilling. In the cyclical equilibrium that we study, however, the behavior of entrepreneurs may have the *appearance* of being fueled by animal spirits, but in fact expectations are *deterministic*.

[2] As Wesley M. Cohen et al. (2000) document, firms do indeed view secrecy as the best form of protection—patenting is a less desired means of protecting knowledge.

the endogenous interactions between long-run growth and short-run fluctuations. After the boom, wage costs are so high that it is initially not profitable to undertake new entrepreneurial activities. As the next boom approaches, however, the present value of new innovations grows until at some point it becomes profitable to allocate entrepreneurial effort to innovation. As labor effort is withdrawn from production, per capita output (and measured productivity) gradually decline. Eventually it becomes profitable to implement the stock of innovations that have accumulated during the downturn, and the cycle begins again.

We adopt a broad interpretation of innovation to include any improvement that is the outcome of purposive design in search of profit. Entrepreneurs are the source of refinements to process, organization, and product improvements that increase productivity within narrowly defined sectors. The knowledge created by such entrepreneurial activity is both tacit and sector specific. Unlike R&D, or scientific knowledge, the improvements created may not be formally expressible (as in a blueprint or design) and need not lend themselves to protection by patent. It is our view that such mundane entrepreneurial decisions are the major source of high-frequency productivity improvements, not the patentable R&D improvements of a laboratory, which are often the focus in the growth literature.[3] In modern production activities much of the entrepreneurial function has been allocated to managers and other skilled workers. It may therefore be more useful to think of innovation as requiring a reallocation of labor effort within firms. This interpretation is thus not unlike that of Robert E. Hall (2000) who emphasizes the role of "reorganization" in a recession.

Although our model is rather stylized, it has clear predictions for the interactions of long-run growth and short-run fluctuations. Firstly, the

cycle in our model shows a positive feedback from both the duration and depth of downturns to the magnitude of succeeding upturns. This feature is consistent with the evidence of Paul Beaudry and Gary Koop (1993), M. Hashem Pesaran and Simon M. Potter (1997), and Filippo Altissimo and Giovanni L. Violante (2001). Secondly, the cycles generated by our model exhibit asymmetries in upturns and downturns that have some features in common with the evidence of Kenneth M. Emery and Evan F. Koenig (1992), Daniel E. Sichel (1993), and Nathan S. Balke and Mark A. Wynne (1995). In particular, business cycles typically exhibit rapid growth in output at the beginning of the boom, a gradual slowdown, and then a decline which occurs at a fairly constant rate. Thirdly, consistent with the evidence of Ramey and Ramey (1995) and Kory Kroft and Lloyd-Ellis (2002), variation in the productivity of entrepreneurship induces a negative relationship between long-run growth and output volatility.

Recently, several authors have developed related, non-GPT models of endogenous growth and cycles. Francois and Shouyong Shi (1999) modify the Grossman and Helpman (1991) growth model by allowing exogenous, drastic imitation (as in Shleifer, 1986), by introducing a technological innovation process requiring accumulated inputs through time, and by treating the interest rate as exogenous. That model also inherits Shleifer's (1986) nonrobustness to storage. In Kiminori Matsuyama (1999) the clustering of innovations also results from the short-term nature of monopoly rents, though through a different channel. In his framework, growth arises due to increasing product variety. Thus the upsurge in growth there arises through drastic innovations that represent wholly new (though partially substitutable) products, and is driven by a few leading sectors. This again lends itself more easily to a long-cycle interpretation. Scott Freeman et al. (1999) develop a model of cycles featuring a "time to build" component in innovation. As they emphasize, this technology describes "big" research or infrastructure projects, once again suggesting a long wave application of the cycle.

The present paper proceeds as follows. Section I presents the economy's fundamentals, defines a general equilibrium, and shows that

---

[3] This view was shared by Schumpeter (1942, p. 132): "... The function of entrepreneurs is to reform or revolutionize the pattern of production by exploiting an invention or, more generally, an untried technological possibility ... . This function does not essentially consist in either inventing anything or otherwise creating the conditions which the enterprise exploits. It consists in getting things done."

one equilibrium of the model is an acyclical growth path that is qualitatively identical to that studied by Grossman and Helpman (1991). Section II presents the main results of the paper. We posit a cycle and derive the equilibrium behavior of households, firms, and entrepreneurs that would be consistent with such a cycle. We then derive the sufficient conditions required for a unique cyclical equilibrium to exist, and show that the cyclical equilibrium is stable. Section III examines the implications of our equilibrium growth process for the endogenous relationship between long-run growth and short-run volatility. We also compare the long-run growth and welfare in the acyclical and cyclical equilibria. Section IV considers the implications of our model for some qualitative features of the business cycle and compares these to available evidence. The final section summarizes and considers some potential extensions of the model. Technical details of proofs and derivations are relegated to a not-for-publication Appendix which is available on the *AER* web site at http://www.aeaweb.org/aer/contents/ or from the authors upon request.

I. The Model

A. *Assumptions*

Time is continuous and indexed by t. We consider a closed economy with no government sector. Households have isoelastic preferences

$$(1) \quad U(t) = \int_t^\infty e^{-\rho(s-t)} \frac{c(s)^{1-\sigma}}{1-\sigma} \, ds$$

where ρ denotes the rate of time preference and we assume that $\sigma \in (0, 1)$. Each household maximizes (1) subject to the intertemporal budget constraint

$$(2) \quad \int_t^\infty e^{-[R(\tau)-R(t)]} c(\tau) \, d\tau$$

$$\leq B(t) + \int_t^\infty e^{-[R(\tau)-R(t)]} w(\tau) \, d\tau$$

where $w(t)$ denotes wage income, $B(t)$ denotes the household's stock of assets at time t and $R(t)$ denotes the discount factor from time zero to t.

Final output is produced by competitive firms according to a Cobb-Douglas production function utilizing intermediates, k, indexed by i, over the unit interval:

$$(3) \quad y(t) = \exp\left(\int_0^1 \ln k_i(t) \, di\right).$$

Final output is storable (at an arbitrarily small cost), but cannot be converted back into an input for use in production. We let p_i denote the price of intermediate i.

Output of intermediate i depends upon the state of technology in sector i, $A_i(t)$, and the labor resources devoted to production, l_i, in a linear manner:

$$(4) \quad k_i^s(t) = A_i(t) l_i(t).$$

Labor receives the equilibrium wage $w(t)$. There is no imitation, so the dominant entrepreneur in each sector undertakes all production and earns monopoly profits by limit pricing until displaced by a higher productivity rival. We assume that intermediates are completely used up in production, but can be produced and stored for use at a later date. Incumbent intermediate producers must therefore decide whether to sell now, or store and sell later.

Competitive entrepreneurs in each sector attempt to find ongoing marginal improvements in productivity by diverting labor effort away from production and towards innovation.[4] They finance their activities by selling equity shares to households. The probability of an entrepreneurial success in instant t is $\delta x_i(t)$, where δ is a parameter, and x_i is the labor effort allocated to entrepreneurship in sector i. At any point in time, entrepreneurs decide whether or not to allocate labor effort to innovation, and if they do so, how much. The aggregate labor effort

---

[4] This process can equivalently be thought of as a search for product improvements, process improvements, organizational advances, or anything else which creates a productive advance over the existing state of the art.

allocated to entrepreneurship is given by $X(t) = \int_0^1 x_i(t) \, dt$.

New innovations dominate old ones by a factor e^γ. Entrepreneurs with innovations must choose whether or not to implement their innovation immediately or delay implementation until a later date. Once they implement, the knowledge associated with the innovation becomes publicly available, and can be built upon by rival entrepreneurs. However, prior to implementation, the knowledge is privately held by the entrepreneur. We let the indicator function $Z_i(t)$ take on the value 1 if there exists a successful innovation in sector i which has not yet been implemented, and 0 otherwise. The set of periods in which innovations are implemented in sector i is denoted by Ω_i. We let $V_i^I(t)$ denote the expected present value of profits from implementing an innovation at time t, and $V_i^D(t)$ denote that of delaying implementation from time t until the most profitable time in the future.

Finally, we assume the existence of arbitrageurs who instantaneously trade assets to erode any profit opportunities. There are three potential assets in our economy: claims to the profits of intermediate firms, stored intermediate output, and stored final output. As we shall see, in all of the equilibria discussed below, only claims to the profits of intermediate firms will be traded—intermediate and final output are never stored. However, the potential for stored output to be traded imposes restrictions on the possible equilibria that can emerge.

In summary, our model is formally identical to that developed by Grossman and Helpman (1991), but with an elasticity of intertemporal substitution, $1/\sigma$, that exceeds unity. However, we have expanded the set of possible strategies by divorcing the realization of innovations from the decision to implement them (as in Shleifer, 1986) and by allowing intermediate output to be potentially storable.

B. *Definition of Equilibrium*

Given an initial stock of implemented innovations represented by a cross-sectoral distribution of productivities $\{A_i(0)\}_{i=0}^1$ and an initial distribution of unimplemented innovations,

$\{Z_i(0)\}_{i=0}^1$, an equilibrium for this economy satisfies the following conditions:

- Households allocate consumption over time to maximize (1) subject to (2). The first-order conditions of the household's optimization require that

$$(5) \quad c(t)^\sigma = c(s)^\sigma e^{R(t) - R(s) - \rho(t-s)} \quad \forall \, t, s,$$

and that the transversality condition holds

$$(6) \quad \lim_{s \to \infty} e^{-R(s)} B(s) = 0.$$

- Final goods producers choose intermediates to maximize profits. The derived demand for intermediate i is then

$$(7) \quad k_i^d(t) = \frac{y(t)}{p_i(t)}.$$

- Intermediate producers set prices. It follows that the price of intermediate i is given by

$$(8) \quad p_i(t) = \frac{w(t)}{e^{-\gamma} A_i(t)},$$

and the instantaneous profit earned is

$$(9) \quad \pi_i(t) = (1 - e^{-\gamma}) y(t).$$

Note crucially that firm profits are proportional to aggregate demand.
- Labor market clearing:

$$(10) \quad \int_0^1 l_i(t) \, di + X(t) = 1.$$

Labor market equilibrium also implies

$$(11) \quad w(t)(1 - X(t)) = e^{-\gamma} y(t).$$

- Free entry into arbitrage. For all assets that are held in strictly positive amounts by households, the rate of return between time t and time s must equal $[R(s) - R(t)]/(s - t)$.

- There is free entry into innovation. Entrepreneurs select the sector in which they innovate so as to maximize the expected present value of the innovation. Also

$$(12) \quad \delta \max[V_i^D(t), V_i^I(t)] \le w(t), \ x_i(t) \ge 0$$

with at least one equality.

- In periods where there is implementation, entrepreneurs with innovations must prefer to implement rather than delay until a later date

$$(13) \quad V_i^I(t) \ge V_i^D(t) \qquad \forall \ t \in \Omega_i.$$

- In periods where there is no implementation, either there must be no innovations available to implement, or entrepreneurs with innovations must prefer to delay rather than implement:

$$(14) \quad \text{Either } Z_i(t) = 0,$$

$$\text{or if } Z_i(t) = 1, \ V_i^I(t) \le V_i^D(t)$$

$$\forall \ t \notin \Omega_i.$$

The familiar acyclical growth path analyzed by Grossman and Helpman (1991) satisfies these conditions. The key feature of this equilibrium is that innovation occurs every period and implementation occurs immediately, so that $Z_i(t) = 0 \ \forall \ i, t$. Growth is steady and consumption behavior is described by the familiar differential equation

$$(15) \quad \frac{\dot{c}(t)}{c(t)} = \frac{r(t) - \rho}{\sigma},$$

where $r(t) = \dot{R}(t)$ denotes the instantaneous interest rate. The properties of this equilibrium are already well known, so its derivation is relegated to the unpublished Appendix, but the following will be useful for comparison with the cyclical equilibrium:

PROPOSITION 1: *If*

$$(16) \quad (1 - e^{-\gamma})\gamma(1 - \sigma) < \frac{\rho}{\delta} < e^\gamma - 1,$$

then there exists an acyclical equilibrium with a constant growth rate given by

$$(17) \quad g^a = \frac{[\delta(1 - e^{-\gamma}) - \rho e^{-\gamma}]\gamma}{1 - \gamma(1 - \sigma)e^{-\gamma}}.$$

The first inequality in (16) implies that $r(t) > g^a(t)$ at every moment. Along a balanced growth path, this condition must hold for utility to be bounded. However, this condition also ensures both that no output is stored, and that the implementation of any innovation is never delayed. The return on storage is the growth in the price of the intermediate good in noninnovating sectors, which in turn equals $g^a(t)$. Thus, since $r(t) > g^a(t)$, it never pays to store the intermediate.

II. The Cyclical Equilibrium

There is a second growth path that satisfies the equilibrium conditions above. Along this path, innovations are implemented in clusters rather than in a smooth fashion. In this section we derive the optimal behavior of agents in such a cyclical equilibrium and the evolution of the key variables under market clearing. We derive sufficient conditions for existence and show that market clearing implies a unique positive cycle length and long-run growth rate.

Suppose that the implementation of entrepreneurial innovations occurs at discrete intervals. An implementation period is denoted by T_v where $v \in \{1, 2, \dots, \infty\}$, and we adopt the convention that the vth cycle starts in period T_{v-1} and ends in period T_v. The evolution of final output during a typical cycle between implementation periods is depicted in Figure 1. A boom occurs when accumulated innovations are implemented at T_{v-1}. After that there is an interval during which no entrepreneurial effort is devoted to improvement of existing technologies and consequently where all resources are used in production. During this interval, no new innovations are implemented so that growth

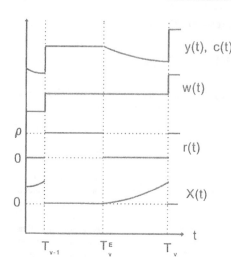

FIGURE 1. THE CYCLICAL GROWTH PATH

boom. Note that a sufficient condition for the boundedness of the consumer's optimization problem is that $\ln(c_0(T_v)/c_0(T_{v-1})) < R(T_v) - R(T_{v-1})$ for all v, or that

$$(19) \qquad \frac{1}{T_v - T_{v-1}} \ln \frac{c_0(T_v)}{c_0(T_{v-1})} < \frac{\rho}{1-\sigma}.$$

In our analysis below, it is convenient to define the discount factor that will be used to discount from some time t during the cycle to the beginning of the next cycle. This discount factor is given by

$$(20)$$

$$\beta(t) = R(T_v) - R(t)$$

$$= R(T_v) - R(T_{v-1}) - \int_{T_{v-1}}^{t} r(s)\, ds.$$

slows to zero. At some time T_v^E innovation commences again, but successful entrepreneurs withhold implementation until time T_v. Entrepreneurial activity occurs throughout the interval $[T_v^E,\ T_v]$ and causes a decline in the economy's production, as resources are diverted away from production towards the search for improvements. At T_v all successful entrepreneurs implement, and the $(v + 1)$th cycle starts with a boom.

Over intervals during which the discount factor does not jump, consumption is allocated as described by (15). However, as we will demonstrate here, along the cyclical growth path, the discount rate jumps at the boom, so that consumption exhibits a discontinuity during implementation periods. We therefore characterize the optimal evolution of consumption from the beginning of one cycle to the beginning of the next by the difference equation

$$(18) \quad \sigma \ln \frac{c_0(T_v)}{c_0(T_{v-1})}$$

$$= R(T_v) - R(T_{v-1}) - \rho(T_v - T_{v-1}).$$

where the 0 subscript is used to denote values of variables the instant after the implementation

A. *Entrepreneurship*

Let $P_i(s)$ denote the probability that, since time T_v, no entrepreneurial success has been made in sector i by time s. It follows that the probability of there being no innovation by time T_{v+1} conditional on there having been none by time t, is given by $P_i(T_{v+1})/P_i(t)$. Hence, the value of an incumbent firm in a sector where no innovation has occurred by time t during the vth cycle can be expressed as

$$(21) \quad V_i^I(t) = \int_t^{T_{v+1}} e^{-\int_t^\tau r(s)\, ds} \pi_i(\tau)\, d\tau$$

$$+ \frac{P_i(T_{v+1})}{P_i(t)} e^{-\beta(t)} V_{0,i}^I(T_{v+1}).$$

The first term here represents the discounted profit stream that accrues to the entrepreneur with certainty during the current cycle, and the second term is the expected discounted value of being an incumbent thereafter.

In the acyclical equilibrium, the role of secrecy is not relevant because innovators would always prefer to implement even if it were possible that, by delaying, they could protect their knowledge. Since simultaneous innovation can only occur with a second-order probability in that equilibrium, it is assumed away. In the cyclical equilibrium considered here, secrecy (i.e., protecting the knowledge embodied in a new innovation by delaying implementation) can be a valuable option. Innovations are withheld until a common implementation time, so that simultaneous implementation is a possibility. However, as the following lemma demonstrates, such duplications do not arise in the cyclical equilibrium:

LEMMA 1: *In a cyclical equilibrium, successful entrepreneurs can credibly signal a success immediately and all innovation in their sector will stop until the next round of implementation.*

Unsuccessful entrepreneurs have no incentive to falsely announce success. As a result, an entrepreneur's signal is credible, and other entrepreneurs will exert their efforts in sectors where they have a better chance of becoming the dominant entrepreneur.[5]

In the cyclical equilibrium, entrepreneurs' conjectures ensure no more entrepreneurship in a sector once a signal of success has been received, until after the next implementation. The expected value of an entrepreneurial success occurring at some time $t \in (T_v^E, T_v)$ but whose implementation is delayed until time T_v is thus:

$$(22) \qquad V_i^D(t) = e^{-\beta(t)} V_{0,i}^I(T_v).$$

Since no implementation occurs during the cycle, the entrepreneur is assured of incumbency until at least T_{v+1}. Incumbency beyond that time depends on the probability that there has not been another successful innovation in that sector up until then. The symmetry of sectors implies that innovative effort is allocated evenly

over all sectors that have not yet experienced an innovation within the cycle. Thus the probability of not being displaced at the next implementation is

$$(23) \qquad P_i(T_v) = \exp\left(-\int_{T_v^E}^{T_v} \delta \tilde{x}_i(\tau)\, d\tau\right)$$

where $\tilde{x}_i(\tau)$ denotes the quantity of labor that would be allocated to entrepreneurship if no innovation had been discovered prior to time τ in sector i. The amount of entrepreneurship varies over the cycle, but at the beginning of each cycle all industries are symmetric with respect to this probability: $P_i(T_v) = P(T_v)\ \forall\ i$.

B. *Within-Cycle Dynamics*

Within a cycle, $t \in [T_{v-1}, T_v]$, the state of technology in use is unchanging. A critical variable is the amount of labor devoted to entrepreneurship, the opportunity cost of which is production. In order to determine this, we first characterize wages paid to labor in production.

LEMMA 2: *The wage for $t \in [T_{v-1}, T_v]$ is pinned down by the level of technology*

$$(24)$$

$$w(t) = e^{-\gamma} \exp\left(\int_0^1 \ln A_i(T_{v-1})\, di\right) = w_v.$$

Competition between firms attempting to hire does not drive the wage up to labor's marginal product because firms earn monopolistic rents. However, it does ensure that labor benefits proportionately from productivity advancements. We denote the improvement in aggregate productivity during implementation period T_v (and, hence, the growth in the wage) by e^{Γ_v}, where

$$(25) \qquad \Gamma_v = \int_0^1 \left[\ln A_i(T_v) - \ln A_i(T_{v-1})\right] di.$$

Since wages are determined by the level of

---

[5] With an arbitrarily small signaling cost, the equilibrium involves strictly dominant strategies. This equilibrium relies on the memoryless nature of the Poisson process governing innovation. However, with memory a similar shutting down of innovation after a success would arise if innovative effort is directly observable. However, the direction of this effort cannot be observed, or incumbents might allocate effort in their own sectors to deter entry.

technology in use, and since this does not change within the cycle, wages are constant within the cycle.

Following an implementation boom, the economy passes through two distinct phases:

The Slowdown.—As a result of the boom, wages rise rapidly and the present value of engaging in innovation falls below the wage, $\delta V^D(t) < w(t)$. During this phase, no labor is allocated to entrepreneurship and no new innovations come on line so final output must be constant

$$(26) \qquad g(t) = \frac{\dot{w}(t)}{w(t)} = 0.$$

With zero growth, the demand side of the economy dictates that the interest rate just equal the discount rate,

$$(27) \qquad r(t) = \sigma g(t) + \rho = \rho.$$

Since the economy is closed, and there is no incentive to store either intermediate or final output when $r(t) \geq 0$, it must be the case that:

$$(28) \qquad c(t) = y(t).$$

During the slowdown, the expected value of entrepreneurship, $\delta V^D(t)$, is necessarily growing at the rate of interest, $r(t) = \rho$, but continues to be dominated by the wage in production. Since the wage is constant during the cycle, $\delta V^D(t)$ must eventually equal $w(t)$. At this point, entrepreneurship commences. The following lemma demonstrates that it does so smoothly:

LEMMA 3: *At time* T_v^E, *when entrepreneurship first commences in a cycle,* $w_v = \delta V^D(t)$ *and* $X(T_v^E) = 0$.

The Downturn.—For positive entrepreneurship to occur under free entry, it must be that $w_v = \delta V^D(t)$. Since the wage is constant throughout the cycle, $\delta V^D(t)$ must also be constant during this phase. Since the time until

implementation for a successful entrepreneur is falling and there is no stream of profits because implementation is delayed, the instantaneous interest rate must be zero.

$$(29) \qquad r(t) = \frac{\dot{V}^D(t)}{V^D(t)} = \frac{\dot{w}(t)}{w(t)} = 0.$$

With a positive discount rate, $\rho > 0$, a zero interest rate implies that consumption must be declining. Since the economy is closed, it follows once again that, because there is no incentive to store output, (28) holds. Hence, per capita output must also decline:

$$(30) \qquad g(t) = \frac{r(t) - \rho}{\sigma} = -\frac{\rho}{\sigma}.$$

This occurs during the downturn because labor flows out of production and into entrepreneurship (knowledge capital is being built). Using (11), (30), and the fact that $X(T_v^E) = 0$, yields the following expression for aggregate entrepreneurship at time t:

$$(31) \qquad X(t) = 1 - e^{-(\rho/\sigma)[t - T_v^E]}.$$

The proportion of sectors that have not yet experienced an entrepreneurial success by time $t \in (T_v^E, T_v)$ is given by

$$(32) \qquad P(t) = \exp\left(-\int_{T_v^E}^{t} \delta x(\tau) \, d\tau\right).$$

Recalling that labor is only devoted to entrepreneurship in sectors which have not innovated since the start of the cycle, the labor allocated to entrepreneurship in each sector is then

$$(33) \qquad x(t) = \frac{X(t)}{P(t)}.$$

Differentiating (32), and substituting in (33), we thus obtain the aggregate rate of entrepreneurial success,

$$(34) \quad \dot{P}(t) = -\delta x(t)P(t) = -\delta X(t).$$

We characterize an equilibrium in which the cycle is never long enough that all sectors innovate, $P(T_v) > 0$. The parameter restrictions that ensure this are discussed in subsection E of this section.

The dynamic movement of variables implied by our hypothesized cycle is sketched in Figure 1. The resulting allocation of labor to entrepreneurship (31) determines the size of the output boom at the end of the cycle. Denote the interval over which there is positive entrepreneurship by $\Delta_v^E = T_v - T_v^E$. Then we have:

PROPOSITION 2: *In an equilibrium where there is positive entrepreneurship only over the interval* $(T_v^E, T_v]$, *the growth in productivity during the succeeding boom is given by*

$$(35) \quad \Gamma_v = \delta \gamma \Delta_v^E - \delta \gamma \left(\frac{1 - e^{-(\rho/\sigma)\Delta_v^E}}{\rho/\sigma} \right).$$

Equation (35) tells us how the size of the productivity boom depends positively on the amount of time the economy is in the entrepreneurship phase, Δ_v^E. The size of the boom is convex in Δ_v^E, reflecting the fact that as the boom approaches, the labor allocated towards innovation is increasing, which also implies that the boom size is increasing in the depth of the downturn.

C. *Market Clearing During the Boom*

For an entrepreneur who is holding an innovation, $V^I(t)$ is the value of implementing immediately. Just prior to the boom, when the probability of displacement is negligible, the value of implementing immediately must equal that of delaying until the boom:

$$(36) \quad \delta V^I(T_v) = \delta V^D(T_v) = w_v.$$

During the boom, since entrepreneurs prefer to implement immediately, it must be the case that $V_0^I(T_v) > V_0^D(T_v)$. Thus the return to innovation at the boom is the value of immediate (rather than delayed) incumbency. It follows

that free entry into entrepreneurship at the boom requires that

$$(37) \quad \delta V_0^I(T_v) \le w_{v+1}.$$

The opportunity cost to financing entrepreneurship is the rate of return on shares in incumbent firms in sectors where no innovation has occurred. Just prior to the boom, this is given by the capital gains in those sectors:

$$(38) \quad \beta(T_v) = \log\left(\frac{V_0^I(T_v)}{V^I(T_v)} \right).$$

Note that since the short-term interest rate is zero over this phase, $\beta(t) = \beta(T_v)$, $\forall\, t \in (T_v^E, T_v)$. Combined with (36) and (37) it follows that asset market clearing at the boom requires

$$(39) \quad \beta(T_v) \le \log\left(\frac{w_{v+1}}{w_v} \right) = \Gamma_v.$$

Provided that $\beta(t) > 0$, households will never choose to store final output from within a cycle to the beginning of the next because it is dominated by the long-run rate of return on claims to future profits. However, unlike final output, the return on stored intermediate output in sectors with no innovations, is strictly positive because of the increase in its price that occurs as a result of the boom. Even though there is a risk that the intermediate becomes obsolete at the boom, if the anticipated price increase is sufficiently large, households may choose to purchase claims to intermediate output rather than claims to firm profits.[6]

If innovative activities are to be financed at time t, households cannot be strictly better off buying claims to stored intermediates. Two types of storage could arise with equal returns.

---

[6] One may suppose that incumbents have an incentive to store intermediate production and threaten to use it to undercut any future innovator in their sector. However, such a threat is not credible. If faced with an innovator holding a productive advantage that will be implemented at time T, an incumbent would sell stockpiled intermediates before time T and obtain a higher price than by delaying and selling it in competition with the new innovator.

In sectors with unimplemented innovations, innovators could implement immediately but delay sales until the boom. The best way to do this is to produce an instant prior to the boom and to sell an instant afterwards. Since the revenue is the same, the difference between producing before and after the boom is that the former involves the current wage and the latter involves the higher future wage. Thus, the return on claims to stored intermediates is $\ln(w_{v+1}/w_v) = \Gamma_v$. In sectors with no innovation, similar trade in such claims leads to an identical return on stored intermediates of $\ln(p_{i,v+1}/p_{i,v}) = \Gamma_v$.

It follows that the long-run rate of return on claims to firm profits an instant prior to the boom must satisfy

$$(40) \qquad \beta(T_v) \geq \Gamma_v.$$

Because there is a risk of obsolescence, this condition implies that at any time prior to the boom the expected rate of return on claims to stored intermediates is strictly less than $\beta(t)$.

Combining (39) and (40), and observing that $\beta(T_v) = \sigma\Gamma_v + \rho\Delta_v^E$, yields the following implication of market clearing during the boom for the long-run growth path:

PROPOSITION 3: *Long-run asset market clearing implies that*

$$(41) \qquad \Gamma_v = \frac{\rho\Delta_v^E}{1 - \sigma}.$$

It follows that asset market clearing yields a unique relationship between the length of the downturn and the size of the subsequent productivity boom.

Figure 2 depicts the two conditions (35) and (41) graphically. As shown by the solid lines, combining the two conditions yields a unique (positive) equilibrium pair (Γ, Δ^E) that is consistent with the within-cycle dynamics and the asset market-clearing condition. Combining them implies that Δ^E must satisfy

$$(42) \qquad \left(1 - \frac{\rho}{\delta\gamma(1-\sigma)}\right)\Delta^E = \frac{1 - e^{-(\rho/\sigma)\Delta^E}}{\rho/\sigma}.$$

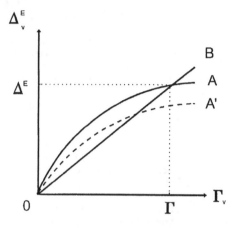

FIGURE 2. EQUILIBRIUM RECESSION LENGTH
AND BOOM SIZE

Note that although we did not impose any stationarity on the cycles, the equilibrium conditions imply stationarity of the size of the boom and the length of the downturn. For a unique positive value of Δ^E that satisfies this condition to exist it is sufficient that $\rho < \delta\gamma(1 - \sigma)$.

D. *Optimal Entrepreneurial Behavior*

It has thus far been assumed that entrepreneurs are willing to follow the innovation and implementation sequence hypothesized in the cycle. The equilibrium conditions that we have considered so far effectively assume that entrepreneurs who plan to innovate will implement at T_v and that they start innovation at T_v^E. However, the willingness of entrepreneurs to delay implementation until the boom and to just start engaging in innovative activities at exactly T_v^E depends crucially on the expected value of monopoly rents resulting from innovation, relative to the current labor costs. This is a forward-looking condition: given Γ and Δ^E, the present value of these rents depend crucially on the length of the subsequent cycle, $T_{v+1} - T_v$.

Since Lemma 3 implies that entrepreneurship starts smoothly at T_v^E, free entry into entrepreneurship requires that

$$(43) \qquad \delta V^D(T_v^E) = \delta e^{-\beta(T_v^E)}V_0^I(T_v) = w_v.$$

Since the increase in the wage across cycles reflects only the improvement in productivity: $w_{v+1} = e^{\Gamma} w_v$, and since from the asset market-clearing conditions, we know that $\beta(T_v^E) = \Gamma$, it immediately follows that the increase in the present value of monopoly profits from the beginning of one cycle to the next must, in equilibrium, reflect only the improvements in aggregate productivity:

$$(44) \qquad V_0^I(T_{v+1}) = e^{\Gamma} V_0^I(T_v).$$

Equation (44) implies that, given some initial implementation period, and stationary values of Γ and Δ^E, the next implementation period is determined. Notice once again that this stationarity is not imposed, but is an implication of the equilibrium conditions. Letting $\Delta_v = T_v - T_{v-1}$, we therefore have the following result:

PROPOSITION 4: *Given the boom size, Γ, and the length of the entrepreneurial innovation phase, Δ^E, there exists a unique cycle length, Δ, such that entrepreneurs are just willing to commence innovation, Δ^E periods prior to the boom.*

In the unpublished Appendix we show that the implied cycle length is given by

$$(45) \qquad \Delta = \Delta^E + \frac{1}{\rho} \ln[1 + \mu\Delta^E],$$

where

$$(46) \qquad \mu = \frac{\left(\dfrac{\rho}{\delta\gamma(1 - \sigma)} - (1 - e^{-\gamma}) \right)}{\left(\dfrac{1 - e^{-\gamma}}{\rho} - \dfrac{e^{-\gamma}}{\delta} \right)} > 0.$$

E. *Existence*

The equilibrium conditions (12), (13), and (14) on entrepreneurial behavior also impose the following requirements on our hypothesized cycle:

- Successful entrepreneurs at time $t = T_{v-1}$ must prefer to implement immediately, rather than delay implementation until later in the cycle or the beginning of the next cycle:

$$(E1) \qquad V_0^I(T_{v-1}) > V_0^D(T_{v-1}).$$

- Entrepreneurs who successfully innovate during the downturn must prefer to wait until the beginning of the next cycle rather than implement earlier:

$$(E2) \quad V^I(t) < V^D(t) \qquad \forall\, t \in (T_v^E, T_v).$$

- No entrepreneur wants to innovate during the slowdown of the cycle. Since in this phase of the cycle $\delta V^D(t) < w(t)$, this condition requires that

$$(E3) \quad \delta V^I(t) < w(t) \qquad \forall\, t \in (T_{v-1}, T_v^E).$$

- The downturn is not long enough that all sectors innovate:

$$(E4) \qquad\qquad P(T) > 0.$$

The following proposition demonstrates that there is a nonempty parameter space such that the triple $(\Delta^E, \Delta, \Gamma) > 0$ solving (35), (41), and (45) also implies that conditions (E1), (E2), (E3), and (E4) are satisfied.

PROPOSITION 5: *If*

$$(47) \quad \max[(1 - e^{-\gamma})\gamma(1 - \sigma), \gamma(1 - \sigma) - \sigma]$$

$$< \frac{\rho}{\delta} < \gamma(1 - \sigma) - \sigma(1 - e^{-(1 - \sigma/\sigma)\gamma})$$

then there exists a unique cyclical equilibrium growth path, $(\Delta^E, \Delta, \Gamma)$.

To understand this proposition it is useful to refer to Figure 3 which illustrates the implied evolution of $V^I(t)$, $V^D(t)$, and $w(t)/\delta$. The inequality $(1 - e^{-\gamma})\gamma(1 - \sigma) < \rho/\delta$ on the left of (47) is sufficient for (E1) to hold. It ensures that, during the cycle, the instantaneous interest rate always exceeds the instantaneous growth rate. As a result, at the beginning of a cycle, implementation is never delayed, because any

Entrepreneurship in Recession

THE AMERICAN ECONOMIC REVIEW

JUNE 2003

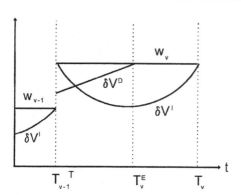

FIGURE 3. EVOLUTION OF VALUE FUNCTIONS AND WAGE

gain in profits from delay is less then the rate at which it is discounted. This is equivalent to the transversality condition that the long-run interest rate exceeds the long-run growth rate.

During the downturn, the left-hand inequality in (47) ensures that $V^I(t)$ approaches $V^D(t)$ from below so that implementation is delayed until the next boom, (E2). To understand this, note that the boom is the only time during the cycle at which the increment in output exceeds the increment in the discount factor. Although, the increment in *productivity*, Γ, exactly equals the increment in the discount factor, β, the reallocation of resources back into production implies that output increases by more than the increment in productivity. Thus, the increase in profits at the boom exceeds the rate at which they are discounted and this will induce delay prior to the boom provided that the probability of being displaced is sufficiently low. Hence the upper bound on $\gamma\delta$ required for this condition to hold.

The right-hand inequality in (47) is necessary and sufficient for condition (E4) to be satisfied, so that not all sectors innovate during the cycle. This is a possibility because through the downturn an increasing amount of innovative effort, $X(t)$, is allocated across fewer and fewer sectors. This condition effectively ensures that the entrepreneurial phase does not proceed for too long, which can be seen from equation (41) to require a low value for $\rho/\delta\gamma$, as implied by the condition.

The right-hand inequality is also sufficient to ensure that the value of immediate implementation, $V^I(t)$, declines monotonically during the slowdown. The weaker necessary and sufficient condition that (47) implies is $\rho/\delta < e^\gamma - 1$. This condition ensures that, over this phase, forgone profit by delaying implementation (proportional to $e^\gamma - 1$) exceeds the benefit from such delay, a higher probability of retaining incumbency (proportional to ρ/δ). Since, at the beginning of the cycle, $\delta V^I(T_{v-1}) = w_v$, condition (E3) follows.

The parameter restrictions imposed by (47) are stronger than those needed for the existence of the acyclical equilibrium in (16). Note, however, that while they are sufficient for existence they are not necessary. In particular, the cyclical equilibrium can exist even if the condition that $\gamma(1 - \sigma) - \sigma < \rho/\delta$, is violated. Table 1 gives some parameter examples that satisfy (47), and yield long-run growth rates in the 2–3 percent range. The increase in consumption at the boom must equal the increase in output, which in turn must exceed the increase in the discount factor. This is only possible here if σ is small enough, and certainly less that unity. Introducing physical capital weakens this restriction since some of the output boom is diverted to investment. We discuss such an extension in Francois and Lloyd-Ellis (2003).

F. Stability

There are two notions of stability that we must consider. The first relates to the stability of the instantaneous equilibrium. In every instant, labor chooses between entrepreneurship and production, entrepreneurs choose between implementing today or delaying until tomorrow, and incumbents must decide whether to sell now or store. It is straightforward to demonstrate stability by considering errors in the decisions of agents and showing that such perturbations result in movement back towards equilibrium in the next instant (in the unpublished Appendix).

A second notion of stability relates to the dynamic convergence of the economy to its long-run growth path. Like the acyclical growth path, the cyclical equilibrium is "jump stable." As our analysis demonstrates, there is a unique triple $(\Gamma, \Delta^E, \Delta)$ that is consistent with equilibrium. Thus the economy necessarily jumps to this long-run path since no other $(\Gamma, \Delta^E, \Delta)$ triple can hold, even in the short run, without violating the equilibrium conditions. Note finally that there is one element of indeterminacy in the cycling equilibrium; the length of the first cycle Δ_0 is indeterminate on the interval $[\Delta^E, \Delta]$ since there is no previous entrepreneurship phase to pin it down.

III. Implications for Growth, Welfare, and Volatility

In this section we compare the long-run growth rates in the cyclical and acyclical economies and examine the impact of changes in the productivity of innovative effort.

A. *Growth and Welfare in Cyclical and Acyclical Economies*

Let the average growth rate in the cycling equilibrium be denoted

$$(48) \qquad g^c = \frac{\Gamma}{\Delta},$$

and recall the acyclical equilibrium growth, g^a, given in (17). Then we have

PROPOSITION 6: *The long-run growth rate in the cyclical equilibrium g^c exceeds that in the acyclical equilibrium, g^a.*

The cyclical equilibrium yields higher average growth because all entrepreneurship occurs in the downturn when growth is negative and the interest rate is low relative to the economy's long-run average. Thus compared with the acyclical economy where the interest rate is constant, the same expected flow of profits for the same expected length of incumbency has higher value in the cycling economy, thereby inducing more entrepreneurship and higher growth.

Although the long-run growth rate is higher in the cyclical equilibrium, the same is not true of welfare. Consider two economies that start with an identical stock of implemented technologies and zero unimplemented innovations.

Suppose one of the economies is in a cyclical equilibrium at the beginning of a cycle and the other is in an acyclical equilibrium. Then:

PROPOSITION 7: *Welfare in the acyclical economy exceeds that in the cyclical one.*

There are three key differences that determine relative welfare in the two economies: (1) the long-run growth rate in the cyclical economy is higher, (2) the initial consumption in the cyclical economy is higher because some labor is allocated to innovation in the acyclical economy, whereas none is during this phase of the cyclical equilibrium, and (3) until the next boom, the short-run growth rate in the cyclical economy is zero or negative, whereas it is positive in the acyclical one. Proposition 7 demonstrates this last factor dominates, so that welfare is lower in the cyclical economy.

B. *Impact of Entrepreneurial Productivity*

Consider the impact of an increase in entrepreneurial productivity δ on the cyclical growth path.

LEMMA 4: *An increase in δ results in shorter cycles, smaller booms, and shorter recessions.*

To understand these results first consider Figure 2. For a given cycle length and downturn length (Δ, Δ^E), an increase in δ causes the size of the boom to be larger because entrepreneurship is now more productive. This is illustrated by the outward shift in OA to OA'. However, now the economy would be to the right of OB, so that the asset market is out of equilibrium, with $\beta < \Gamma$ just prior to the boom, so that there is an incentive to store. Arbitrageurs would be willing to offer incumbents and entrepreneurs incentives to produce more intermediate output than needed to supply current demand. In particular, entrepreneurs with unimplemented innovations would respond by bringing production forward slightly from the boom. But if all entrepreneurs do this, the boom would actually occur earlier and the incentive to store would disappear. Applying this argument recursively, one can see that the length of the downturn (and hence the entire) cycle would fall until it is just

THE AMERICAN ECONOMIC REVIEW

JUNE 2003

TABLE 1—GROWTH AND VOLATILITY

Benchmark parameters				Long-run growth (percent)	Volatility, Σ	Cycle length, Δ
δ	γ	ρ	σ			
2.0	0.120	0.025	0.25	2.67	0.194	3.8
2.4				3.26	0.186	2.6
1.8				2.38	0.200	4.9
	0.115			2.44	0.190	4.4
	0.125			2.91	0.201	3.4
		0.022		2.70	0.189	3.3
		0.028		2.64	0.199	4.4
			0.20	2.68	0.202	2.7
			0.27	2.66	0.191	4.4

short enough to ensure that for the (smaller) size of the boom that results, the incentive to produce early and store has been removed (i.e., $\beta = \Gamma$ just prior to the boom). Thus, as noted in the lemma, the cycle length, recession length, and boom size would all fall.

The economy's volatility is also affected by a change in δ. Since the standard deviation is not well-defined in our context, we measure volatility as the average absolute size of deviations in long output from trend:

$$(49) \quad \Sigma = \frac{1}{\Delta} \int_0^{\Delta - \Delta^E} |\Gamma - g^c t| \, dt$$

$$+ \frac{1}{\Delta} \int_{\Delta - \Delta^E}^{\Delta} \left| \Gamma - \frac{\rho}{\sigma}(t - (\Delta - \Delta^E)) - g^c t \right| dt.$$

The variable δ affects this through numerous channels; Δ, Δ^E, and g^c. Though the affects on phase lengths are unambiguous (see Lemma 4), the relationship between g^c and Σ is not analytically clear. The first three rows of Table 1 shows how growth, volatility, and cycle length vary with changes in δ, within the parameter space given by (47). These numerical examples illustrate what extensive simulations show is a more general result:

The long-run relationship between growth, g^c, and volatility, Σ, across economies with different levels of entrepreneurial productivity is negative.

Thus, the relationship between growth and volatility across cyclical equilibria is, at least superficially, consistent with the empirical results of Ramey and Ramey (1995) and Kroft and Lloyd-Ellis (2002). Note, however, that this relationship does not represent the impact of volatility on growth, nor the impact of growth on volatility. Rather it is an induced relationship due to variation in the productivity of entrepreneurship.

Our emphasis on the consequences of cross-country variation in δ, rather than γ, stems from our view that the former parameter captures country-specific factors, whereas the latter captures (on average) characteristics of a technological possibilities frontier which is common to all countries. Thus, differences in entrepreneurial productivity may reflect variations in the quality of education, institutional arrangements and culture, for example. It is possible, however, that δ also reflects technological possibilities as well. For example, one referee speculates that the combination of a low δ and a high γ may be characteristic of a mature technological stage. If so, then such a stage would be associated with cycles, whereas early stages (high δ, low γ) would involve steadier growth.

IV. Implications for the Business Cycle

In this section we consider the extent to which some essential features of the implied cyclical process are qualitatively consistent with the facts. In our conclusion we also discuss several extensions to the model that we believe will allow it to match the data more closely.

A. *The Downturn is Not a Consequence of Mismeasurement*

The downturn in our cycle results from the allocation of labor to entrepreneurship in anticipation of the upcoming boom. Since this reallocation represents an investment in intangible assets, one may wonder whether the implied downturn is really just a result of mismeasurement which would disappear if we included intangible investment, $I(t)$, in computing aggregate GDP. If we did so, aggregate GDP during the downturn would be

$$(50) \quad GDP = c(t) + I(t) = y(t) + w_v X(t)$$

$$= \pi(t) + w_v[1 - X(t)] + w_v X(t)$$

$$= (1 - e^{-\gamma})y(t) + w_v.$$

Thus, the downturn does not arise from mismeasurement—even though the wage is constant through the cycle—GDP declines because profits decline. This is because imperfect competition in the intermediate sector implies that the total marginal cost of labor leaving production (i.e., its marginal product) exceeds the private marginal cost (i.e., the wage). Although workers are equally well off in the two activities, the reallocation has a negative externality on current profits. A similar implication emerges from the GPT-driven downturn in Helpman and Manuel Trajtenberg (1998).

B. Stock Market Implications

Our model also has predictions for the cyclical behavior of the stock market. Here, the stock market consists of three types of firms: incumbents in sectors where no new innovations have occurred, "terminal" incumbents in sectors where innovations have occurred, and new entrants in those sectors that have not yet implemented but have value. In the slowdown, only the first type of firm exists, but during the downturn all three are present. At any point in time the total value of firms on the stock market is given by

$$(51) \quad \Pi(t) = (1 - P(t))[V^T(t) + V^D(t)]$$

$$+ P(t)V^I(t),$$

where $V^T(t)$ denotes the value of "terminal" firms who are certain to be made obsolete during the next wave of implementation. The value of these firms can be written as

$$(52) \quad V^T(t) = V^I(t) - \frac{P(T_v)}{P(t)} V^D(t).$$

Substituting into (51) yields

$$(53) \quad \Pi(t) = V^I(t) + (1 - P(t))$$

$$\times \left[1 - \frac{P(T_v)}{P(t)} V^D(t) \right].$$

During the slowdown, $P(t) = 1$ so that $\Pi(t) = V^I(t)$. Immediately prior to the boom $P(t) = P(T_v)$, so that again $\Pi(T_v) = V^I(T_v)$. Thus, the evolution of the aggregate value of the stock market during the cycle resembles that of incumbent firms in sectors that have not yet innovated, $V^I(t)$, (see Figure 3) except that during the downturn it is always higher, reflecting the fact that incumbents with uncertain longevity are being replaced by new entrants who will have incumbency for at least one full cycle length.

Thus, the stock market falls during the slowdown, in anticipation of the subsequent recession, and rises during the downturn, in anticipation of the subsequent boom. This cyclical anticipation of future profits implicit in aggregate stock prices accords well with the findings of Hall (2001), who compares the growth rate of cash flows implicit in securities values with the actual five-year forward growth rate of cash flow (see his Figure 9). While, of course, much of the variation in profits reflect unexpected shocks to the economy, Hall's results are consistent with the view that a significant component of cyclical fluctuations is indeed anticipated by equity markets.

C. The Clustering of Implementation

As in the pure real business cycle (RBC) model, productivity improvements in our cycle are clustered over time and are procyclical. Susanto Basu (1996) finds that, once one takes account of variations in capital utilization and labor hoarding over the cycle, the implied movements in total factor productivity (TFP) may be small and not strongly procyclical. However, Robert G. King and Sergio Rebelo (1999) argue that once one endogenizes variations in factor utilization, large fluctuations in output can result from small changes in TFP. Moreover, the implied TFP movements are hardly ever negative, and hence more

Entrepreneurship in Recession

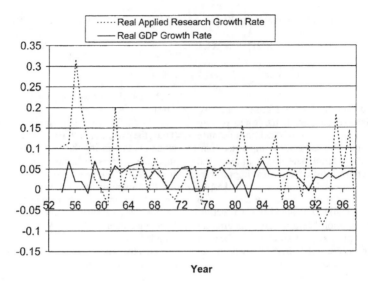

FIGURE 4. APPLIED RESEARCH AND GROWTH IN THE UNITED STATES

Source: National Science Foundation.

consistent with their interpretation as technology improvements.

There is, however, more direct evidence of procyclical clustering of implementation during booms. Paul A. Geroski and Chris F. Walters (1995) investigate high-frequency movements in both the granting of patents in the United States to U.K. firms and the implementation of major innovations in the United Kingdom for the period 1948–1983. They find that the implementation of innovations and patenting activity are procyclical,[7] and that they occur in small (several year) clusters. More generally, Zvi Griliches' (1990) survey on patents also concludes that the basic procyclicality of patenting, first suggested by Jacob Schmookler (1966), has not been overturned.

---

[7] Though Geroski and Walters term their observations "innovations," their data involves the actual implementation of innovations.

D. *The Countercyclicality of Innovative Effort*

One often-used measure of innovative effort is R&D expenditure. Antonio Fatas (2000) documents that growth in real R&D expenditures in the United States is positively correlated with real GDP growth. However, if we consider only privately funded R&D and distinguish between basic research, which is not generally driven by commercial considerations (and is a small proportion of the total), and applied research which is, then this stylized fact is not so clear. There is, in fact, no significant correlation between growth rates in real applied research (NSF data) and real GDP for the United States over the period 1953 to 1999. As may be seen in Figure 4, although the big increases during the 1960's appear to occur during booms, those of 1973–1974, 1981, and 1991 occur during recessions.

On the whole then, the evidence on R&D expenditures is not strongly supportive of either a pro- or countercyclical view. However, innovation is a much broader concept than that measured by R&D investment. Much of the entrepreneurial function in modern production is undertaken by skilled workers and managers within industries.[8] Since much of their innovative effort occurs without separately measured expenditures or occupational reallocation, the usual aggregate data sets are not helpful. Instead, what we require is detailed information about plant-level activities. Although the evidence so far is disparate, a number of studies (discussed below) have used either specialized data sets based on surveys or proxies to obtain related estimates.[9]

A frequently emphasized feature of business cycles is the apparent employment of labor during recessions beyond that which is technologically necessary to meet regular production requirements. Recently, the RBC literature has argued that this behavior reflects "labor hoarding"—like capital, there are significant costs to adjusting labor (e.g., hiring and firing costs) which cause firms to hold on to skilled labor during recessions. However, another interpretation is that this labor is actually doing something productive—coming up with new ideas and approaches that will be useful in the future. In a survey of U.S. manufacturing plants, Jon A. Fay and James L. Medoff (1985) find that during a trough quarter the typical plant paid for about 8 percent more labor hours than technologically necessary. Only half of this was hoarded labor—the remainder was used in other productive activities. Of the respondents that reassigned workers during recessions (more than half of respondents), about one-third allocated them to "reworking output" and another third to "training."

One might suspect that innovative activities are more likely to require skilled, nonproduction workers, so that during downturns the ratio of skilled to unskilled workers should rise. Although this is typically the case in the data, it is

possible that this is motivated by labor hoarding since the costs of adjustment for skilled workers are relatively high. However, such a motivation would not lead to an absolute increase in skilled employment during downturns, which has been documented by Victor Aguirregabiria and Cesar Alonso-Borrego (2001). Using Spanish manufacturing data (a balanced panel of 1,080 nonenergy manufacturers from 1986–1991), they find the employment of white collar workers to be significantly countercyclical.

More direct evidence of what managers are doing during downturns is provided by Stephen Nickell et al. (2001). They investigate whether managerial innovations occur in downturns using two unique data sets. The first, based on the Confederation of British Industries Pay Databank (66 manufacturing firms during the period 1981–1986) includes information on two measures of innovation—the removal of restrictive practices and the introduction of new technology. The second data set includes small- to medium-sized manufacturing firms in engineering, plastics, electronics, and food, drink, and tobacco. This categorizes levels of managerial innovation from 1991–1994 and compares them to lagged performance variables from the period 1988–1991.[10] Both data sets support the view that when demand is slack and profitability low, managers and workers devote more time to innovation.

E. Downturns and Subsequent Productivity Growth

In the cyclical process implied by our model, larger downturns are associated with bigger booms. This is broadly consistent with the aggregate empirical characterizations of Pesaran and Potter (1997) and Altissimo and Violante (2001). More direct evidence is provide by Vincenzo Atella and Beniamino Quintieri (1998). Using Italian data for nine industries from 1967 to 1990, they find strong evidence that down-

---

[8] This interpretation of innovation is not unlike the "reorganization" activity emphasized by Hall (2000). Note that although incumbents in our model would not engage in innovation within their own product line, they may innovate in other product lines.

[9] If we interpret innovative effort even more broadly to include any withdrawal of labor from production to productivity-enhancing activities, it is also suggestive that postsecondary educational investments are countercyclical (Plutarchos Sakellaris and Antonio Spilimbergo, 2000).

[10] The managerial innovation variables included: significant change in structure; organization leaner as result of change; significant changes resulting in more decentralized organization; significant changes in human resources management practices and industrial relations; and the implementation of just-in-time technologies.

548   THE AMERICAN ECONOMIC REVIEW   JUNE 2003

turns tend to be followed by subsequent increases in TFP. The correlation of negative demand movements with subsequent TFP growth was greater than either public capital or R&D expenditures. In a similar study for 2-digit SIC industries in the United States (using the NBER annual productivity database from 1958–1991), Jim Malley and V. Anton Muscatelli (1999) find that demand reductions to manufacturing as a whole are significantly positively correlated with subsequent TFP growth.

V. Concluding Remarks

This paper has established the existence of cycles along a balanced growth path of a completely standard multisectoral Schumpeterian growth model that allows for the possibility of delayed implementation and storage. Specifically, we show that even with multiple sectors, in general equilibrium, with reasonable assumptions on preferences, technology and market competition, no static increasing returns to scale, no stochastic expectations, no threshold effects, and rational forward-looking behavior, there exists a business cycle that is interlinked with the economy's growth process. Moreover, we establish conditions under which a unique cycling equilibrium arises.

The endogenous cycles generated by our model have several features that we believe are crucial to understanding actual business cycles. First and foremost, the cyclical fluctuations are the result of independent actions by decentralized decision makers. They are not the result of economy-wide shocks or economy-wide technological breakthroughs, but emerge as a result of pecuniary demand externalities that induce coordination. This is true of both the boom, which reflects Shleifer's (1986) formalization of "animal spirits" in the joint implementation of innovations, and of the downturn, which reflects the common incentives of entrepreneurs in anticipation of the upcoming boom. Second, as in our cycle, the quantitative analyses of Emery and Koenig (1992), Sichel (1993), and Balke and Wynne (1995) suggest that the average cycle starts with a growth spurt which is then followed by a growth slowdown before the economy enters a period of relatively constant decline during the downturn. Thirdly, as is con-

sistent with the findings of Pesaran and Potter (1997) and Altissimo and Violante (2001) there is a positive feedback from downturns to subsequent cyclical upturns. Finally, the equilibrium relationship between growth and volatility is negative, which is consistent with the cross-country evidence of Ramey and Ramey (1995).

A valuable feature of the model developed here is its parsimony. Apart from a slight generalization of preferences, the model is identical to Grossman and Helpman (1991, Ch. 4). The ultimate value of theoretical endeavors aimed at understanding the interactions between growth and cycles will be in their ability to provide a convincing account of the high-frequency data. While the model fits some features of the "normal" business cycle, we do not claim to have done that yet. However, the model's simplicity allows it to be used as a platform for these more empirically motivated extensions. The central mechanism described here is robust to extensions which shall be explored in future work, and which we briefly describe below:

- Tangible capital assets.—Although we allow for saving through intangible assets and for the possibility of storing output, we assume away physical capital as a vehicle for smoothing aggregate consumption over time. Introducing physical capital that is completely liquid would destroy the cyclical equilibrium because households would try to consume the anticipated benefits of the boom in advance by dis-saving. However, suppose (realistically) that capital exhibits "putty-clay" characteristics, and the capital–labor ratio cannot be adjusted fully except through expansion, then the cyclical equilibrium would still exist. During the downturn, capital would be left idle as complementary labor resources shift out of production. Because of the high opportunity cost (the return on intangible assets), investment in new capital would be delayed until after the initial boom that is associated with implementation and the increased utilization of existing capital.
- Abruptness of the boom.—The growth spurt and the start of the slowdown are unrealistically abrupt. In reality expansions tend to be spread out over time, so that positive growth is more common than zero or negative

growth. The introduction of tangible physical capital will also help here. The innovation boom will lead to a rise in capital's marginal product and trigger a sustained period of investment in which output grows smoothly and continuously as capital is accumulated.

- Aggregate uncertainty.—The length and other characteristics of actual business cycles vary from cycle to cycle and look rather different from the deterministic equilibrium cycle described here. However, introducing a degree of aggregate uncertainty would be possible without changing the basic analysis. For example, the stochastic arrival of GPTs that raises productivity in all sectors, say, would cause the size and length of booms and recessions between GPTs to vary over time.

REFERENCES

Aghion, Philippe and Howitt, Peter. "A Model of Growth through Creative Destruction." *Econometrica*, March 1992, *60*(2), pp. 323–51.

_____. *Endogenous growth theory*. Cambridge, MA: MIT Press, 1998.

Aguirregabiria, Victor and Alonso-Borrego, Cesar. "Occupational Structure, Technological Innovation, and Reorganization of Production." *Labour Economics*, January 2001, *8*(1), pp. 43–73.

Altissimo, Filippo and Violante, Giovanni L. "The Non-linear Dynamics of Output and Unemployment in the U.S." *Journal of Applied Econometrics*, July–August 2001, *16*(4), pp. 461–86.

Atella, Vincenzo and Quintieri, Beniamino. "Productivity Growth and the Effects of Recessions." *Giornale degli Economisti e Annali di Economia*, December 1998, *57*(3–4), pp. 359–86.

Balke, Nathan S. and Wynne, Mark A. "Recession and Recoveries in Real Business Cycle Models." *Economic Inquiry*, October 1995, *33*(4), pp. 640–63.

Basu, Susanto. "Procyclical Productivity: Increasing Returns or Cyclical Utilization?" *Quarterly Journal of Economics*, August 1996, *111*(3), pp. 719–51.

Beaudry, Paul and Koop, Gary. "Do Recessions Permanently Change Output?" *Journal of Monetary Economics*, April 1993, *31*(2), pp. 149–63.

Cohen, Wesley M.; Nelson, Richard R. and Walsh, John P. "Protecting Their Intellectual Assets: Appropriability Conditions and Why U.S. Manufacturing Firms Patent (or Not)." National Bureau of Economic Research (Cambridge, MA) Working Paper No. 7552, February 2000.

Emery, Kenneth M. and Koenig, Evan F. "Forecasting Turning Points: Is a Two-State Characterization of the Business Cycle Appropriate?" *Economics Letters*, August 1992, *39*(4), pp. 431–35.

Fatas, Antonio. "Do Business Cycles Cast Long Shadows? Short-Run Persistence and Economic Growth." *Journal of Economic Growth*, June 2000, *5*(2), pp. 147–62.

Fay, Jon A. and Medoff, James L. "Labor and Output over the Business Cycle: Some Direct Evidence." *American Economic Review*, September 1985, *75*(4), pp. 638–55.

Francois, Patrick and Lloyd-Ellis, Huw. "Co-Movement, Capital and Contracts: Endogenous Business Cycles Through Creative Destruction." Mimeo, Queen's University, 2003.

Francois, Patrick and Shi, Shouyong. "Innovation, Growth, and Welfare-Improving Cycles." *Journal of Economic Theory*, April 1999, *85*(2), pp. 226–57.

Freeman, Scott; Hong, Dong Pyo and Peled, Dan. "Endogenous Cycles and Growth with Indivisible Technological Developments." *Review of Economic Dynamics*, April 1999, *2*(2), pp. 403–32.

Geroski, Paul A. and Walters, Chris F. "Innovative Activity over the Business Cycle." *Economic Journal*, July 1995, *105*(431), pp. 916–28.

Griliches, Zvi. "Patent Statistics as Economic Indicators: A Survey." *Journal of Economic Literature*, December 1990, *28*(4), pp. 1661–707.

Grossman, Gene and Helpman, Elhanan. *Innovation and growth in the global economy*. Cambridge, MA: MIT Press, 1991.

Hall, Robert E. "Reorganization." *Carnegie-Rochester Conference Series on Public Policy*, June 2000, *52*, pp. 1–22.

_____. "Struggling to Understand the Stock Market." *American Economic Review*, May

2001 (*Papers and Proceedings*), *91*(2), pp. 1–11.

Helpman, Elhanan and Trajtenberg, Manuel. "A Time to Sow and a Time To Reap: Growth Based on General Purpose Technologies," in Elhanan Helpman, ed., *General purpose technologies and economic growth*. Cambridge, MA: MIT Press, 1998, pp. 55–83.

Keynes, John Maynard. *The general theory of employment, interest and money*. London: Macmillan, 1936.

King, Robert G. and Rebelo, Sergio. "Resuscitating Real Business Cycles." *Handbook of macroeconomics, volume 1B*. Amsterdam: North-Holland, 1999.

Kroft, Kory and Lloyd-Ellis, Huw. "Further Cross-Country Evidence on the Link between Growth, Volatility and Business Cycles." Mimeo, Queen's University, 2002.

Malley, Jim and Muscatelli, V. Anton. "Business Cycles and Productivity Growth: Are Temporary Downturns Productive or Wasteful?" *Research in Economics*, December 1999, *53*(4), pp. 337–64.

Matsuyama, Kiminori. "Growing Through Cycles." *Econometrica*, March 1999, *67*(2), pp. 335–47.

Nickell, Stephen; Nicolitsas, Daphne and Patterson, Malcolm. "Does Doing Badly Encourage Management Innovation?" *Oxford Bulletin of Economics and Statistics*, February 2001, *63*(1), pp. 5–28.

Pesaran, M. Hashem and Potter, Simon M. "A Floor and Ceiling Model of US Output." *Journal of Economic Dynamics and Control*, May 1997, *21*(4–5), pp. 661–96.

Ramey, Gary and Ramey, Valerie A. "Cross-Country Evidence on the Link Between Volatility and Growth." *American Economic Review*, December 1995, *85*(5), pp. 1138–51.

Sakellaris, Plutarchos and Spilimbergo, Antonio. "Business Cycles and Investment in Human Capital: International Evidence on Higher Education." *Carnegie-Rochester Conference Series on Public Policy*, June 2000, *52*, pp. 221–56.

Schmookler, Jacob. *Invention and economic growth*. Cambridge, MA: Harvard University Press, 1966.

Schumpeter, Joseph. "The Explanation of the Business Cycle." *Economica*, December 1927, (21), pp. 286–311.

_____. *Capitalism, socialism and democracy*. New York: Harper, 1942.

Segerstrom, Paul S.; Anant, T.C.A. and Dinopoulos, Elias. "A Schumpeterian Model of the Product Life Cycle." *American Economic Review*, December 1990, *80*(5), pp. 1077–91.

Shleifer, Andrei. "Implementation Cycles." *Journal of Political Economy*, December 1986, *94*(6), pp. 1163–90.

Sichel, Daniel E. "Business Cycle Asymmetry: A Deeper Look." *Economic Inquiry*, April 1993, *31*(2), pp. 224–36.

Zarnowitz, Victor. "Has the Business Cycle Been Abolished?" *Business Economics*, October 1998, *33*(4), pp. 39–45.

[4]

On the Cyclicality of Research and Development

By Gadi Barlevy*

Economists have recently argued recessions play a useful role in fostering growth. Yet a major source of growth, R&D, is procyclical. This paper argues one reason for procyclical R&D is a dynamic externality inherent in R&D that makes entrepreneurs short-sighted and concentrate their innovation in booms, even when it is optimal to concentrate it in recessions. Additional forces may imply that procyclical R&D is desirable, but equilibrium R&D is likely to be too procyclical, and macroeconomic shocks are likely to have overly persistent effects on output and make growth more costly than in the absence of such shocks.

This paper examines how research and development activity (henceforth R&D) varies over the business cycle. The notion that macroeconomic shocks which induce business cycles might also affect activities that drive long-run growth, including R&D, implies such shocks can have long-lived consequences, far beyond the duration of any particular cyclical episode. This possibility has important implications for various macroeconomic questions, ranging from how to identify macroeconomic shocks (particularly the applicability of long-run identification restrictions) to how to properly account for the social costs of macroeconomic instability.

Several recent papers have argued that recessions should ideally promote various activities that contribute to long-run productivity and thus to growth.[1] This view rests on the notion that the opportunity cost of achieving productivity growth—the forgone output or sales that could have been achieved instead—is lower in recessions, providing incentive to undertake such activities in downturns. If negative macroeconomic shocks encourage growth-enhancing investments, as this view suggests, economic contractions would tend to be shorter and less persistent then they would be otherwise. Cyclical fluctuations might even contribute positively to welfare if they allow the economy to grow at a lower resource cost.

Some growth-enhancing activities—such as schooling—are indeed countercyclical, in accordance with this view. As already noted previously by some economists, however, measured R&D activity seems to be procyclical. This is surprising, since R&D seems like an activity that should similarly be concentrated in recessions: it is labor intensive, and while labor productivity in producing goods appears to decline in recessions, work surveyed in Zvi Griliches (1990) suggests productivity in innovation is acyclical. The purpose of this paper is to provide insight into why R&D might be procyclical despite forces that would make it countercyclical. Is the procyclical pattern in R&D evidence that business cycles impose a larger welfare cost because they affect growth, making shocks inefficiently more persistent and increasing the cost of achieving growth? Or is the simple opportunity cost model inappropriate when it comes to R&D?

* Federal Reserve Bank of Chicago, 230 South La Salle St., Chicago, IL 60604 (e-mail: gbarlevy@frbchi.org). I am grateful to the editor and two anonymous referees who made extremely valuable suggestions for improving the paper. I would also like to thank Jeff Campbell, Marty Eichenbaum, Jonas Fisher, Huw Lloyd-Ellis, Merritt Lyon, Kiminori Matsuyama, Alex Monge, Joanne Roberts, and Fabrizio Zilibotti for their comments, as well as seminar participants at Northwestern University, the Stockholm School of Economics, Queens' University, the London School of Economics, the NBER Summer Workshop, the Canadian Macro Study Group, and the Society of Economic Dynamics.

[1] See, Robert E. Hall (1991), Dale T. Mortensen and Christopher A. Pissarides (1994), and João Gomes, Jeremy Greenwood, and Sergio Rebelo (2001) on how recessions affect search; Russell Cooper and John Haltiwanger (1993), Ricardo J. Caballero and Mohamad L. Hammour (1994), Philippe Aghion and Gilles Saint-Paul (1998), and Eric Canton and Harald Uhlig (1999) on how they affect technical change; and David N. DeJong and Beth F. Ingram (2001), Jarros Dellas and Plutarchos Sakellaris (2003), and Barlevy and Daniel Tsiddon (2006) on how they affect human capital accumulation.

This paper argues that externalities inherent in R&D can induce a procyclical bias in R&D relative to the socially optimal path for R&D. That is, a decentralized market will tend to allocate an inefficiently low fraction of innovation to recessions. By itself, this suggests a role for policy intervention, e.g., countercyclical R&D subsidies. I further argue that this bias is quantitatively significant, and is an important reason why R&D is procyclical despite forces that tend to make it countercyclical. While other forces also account for the procyclicality of R&D, and some of these may even make moderately procyclical R&D desirable, the implication is that macroeconomic shocks serve to distort R&D, making growth more costly than it would be in their absence and inefficiently prolonging the effects of such shocks. Absent countercyclical R&D subsidies, there may be a greater role for stabilization policy than implied by calculations on the cost of macroeconomic volatility that ignore its effects on growth, e.g., Robert E. Lucas, Jr. (1987).

The bias I describe stems from the fact that new ideas often benefit others beyond the innovators who came up with them. In particular, others might be able to improve on a new idea once it has been introduced, incorporate some of its features, or adopt it in full once patents expire. It has been observed since at least Kenneth Arrow (1962) that if innovators cannot appropriate the spillovers from their research, R&D will be inefficiently low. But there is a less appreciated temporal aspect to such spillovers, namely that the benefits that accrue to others typically occur later in time; rival innovators need time to improve upon or imitate an idea, or must wait for a patent to expire before using it. The incentive for an innovator to undertake R&D thus heavily weights the short-term benefits of innovation that accrue principally to her. Whereas a benevolent planner would take into account that research undertaken in a recession yields benefits when economic conditions improve, private agents discount these longer-run benefits and fail to fully exploit downturns to carry out innovation at a lower cost. The more procyclical are profits, the stronger this distortion will be. If profits are sufficiently procyclical, innovation can fall enough in recessions to turn R&D procyclical on the basis of this distortion alone.

This bias is related to work by Andrei Shleifer (1986), which argues that entrepreneurs introduce new technologies *en masse* in booms in order to capture high profits. However, Shleifer examines when firms implement new technologies, not when they undertake R&D. When Patrick Francois and Huw Lloyd-Ellis (2003) endogenize innovation in Shleifer's model, they find it is countercyclical: entrepreneurs engage in R&D in recessions, then wait to implement their ideas in booms. By contrast, I assume firms do not wait to implement new ideas, e.g., because they are impatient. If innovators must implement immediately, the higher profits in booms could potentially conflict with the incentives to engage in intertemporal substitution. The new insight here is to show that because of dynamic externalities, entrepreneurs tend to chase short-term profits at the expense of intertemporal substitution, engaging in too little R&D during recessions.[2]

To illustrate this point, I construct an equilibrium model of R&D that captures the intertemporal substitution view: there is a fixed supply of resources that can be used for either production or innovation, and the relative productivity of the two uses fluctuates over time in a way that leads the opportunity cost of innovation to fall in recessions. The model further incorporates a dynamic spillover whereby successful innovation today benefits future entrepreneurs. I solve for the equilibrium of this model and discuss its tendency to underprovide R&D in recessions. I then calibrate the model to gauge whether the bias is large, and whether the model can accord with the key facts regarding the behavior of R&D over the cycle.

The paper is organized as follows. Section I presents evidence on the procyclicality of R&D. Section II sorts through potential sources of procyclical R&D to focus the subsequent theory. Section III presents the model and illustrates its inherent procyclical bias. Section IV calibrates the model to assess the quantitative significance of the bias. Section V concludes.

---

[2] Another difference with Shleifer's model is that in his model these cycles arise when new ideas are implemented with delay. Since there are no cycles when there is no delay, it is impossible to examine the cyclical behavior of entrepreneurs who must implement immediately in that model. Here, cycles are driven by exogenous shocks.

I. Evidence on the Cyclicality of R&D

Although various authors have previously noted that R&D is procyclical, it is worthwhile reviewing the evidence and confirming that the procyclical pattern of R&D is robust. This section summarizes the evidence and provides additional findings that will guide the subsequent theory.

There are two main data sources on R&D activities in the United States. The first is the National Science Foundation (NSF), which conducts annual surveys on the R&D activities of private and public entities. Among private entities, questionnaires are administered to a subset of firms from the universe of companies surveyed by the Census Bureau. Large companies that are known to be active in R&D are included in this subset with certainty; additional firms are randomly sampled each year from the remaining population of firms. Companies are questioned about their R&D expenditures, defined as activities whose purpose is to do one or more of the following: pursue a planned search for new knowledge, whether or not the research has reference to a specific application; apply existing knowledge to problems involved in the creation of a new product or process, including work required to evaluate possible uses; or apply existing knowledge to problems involved in the improvement of a present product or process. Firms are also asked how these activities are funded, what expenses these R&D expenditures are allocated to, and the number of scientists and engineers employed in R&D.

The other source of data on R&D expenditures is the Standard & Poor's Compustat database of publicly traded companies. As part of their 10-K filing, publicly traded companies must disclose their expenditures on research and development, defined as "planned search or critical investigation aimed at discovery of new knowledge" and "translation of research findings or other knowledge to an existing product or process whether intended for sale or use." While publicly traded firms are a more selected sample than those surveyed by the NSF, the virtue of Compustat is that it allows us to relate R&D expenditures to firm and industry data.

In documenting how R&D activity evolves with macroeconomic conditions, I use data from both datasets and confirm that both yield similar patterns. I then consider evidence on potential explanations for these patterns using firm- and industry-level data from Compustat. Appendix A provides more details on how the data were assembled.

A. *The Cyclicality of Research and Development*

I begin with data from the NSF. Figure 1 plots the growth in real R&D expenditures performed and financed by private industry as reported by the NSF between 1958 and 2003. Expenditures are deflated using the implicit GDP deflator, as the NSF suggests. As evident from Figure 1, the growth rate of R&D covaries positively with real GDP growth. The correlation between the two series is 0.39, and regressing growth in real R&D expenditures on real GDP growth yields a coefficient of 0.69 with a standard error of 0.25. It is also apparent from Figure 1 that growth in real R&D expenditures tends to fall in National Bureau of Economic Research (NBER) recession years, although in the recessions of both the early 1980s and 1990s R&D growth remained steady during the recession and declined only afterward. As mentioned earlier, various papers have already noted that R&D expenditures as reported by the NSF tend to grow more rapidly in booms than in recessions. Griliches (1990) surveys the evidence on patents, and suggests both patents and R&D (the latter based on NSF data) are procyclical. Antonio Fatas (2000) plots essentially the same two series (up through 1997), although his measure of R&D includes publicly funded R&D. Matthew C. Rafferty (2003) reports that aggregate R&D expenditures as reported by the NSF are positively correlated with certain cyclical measures. Klaus Walde and Ulrich Woitek (2004) use NSF data for the United States and Organisation for Economic Co-operation and Development (OECD) data on R&D expenditures for other G7 countries. They conclude that R&D is positively correlated with output and capital investment. Finally, Diego Comin and Mark Gertler (2006) decompose NSF data on R&D by frequency and find that R&D expenditures are procyclical at business cycle frequencies and even more so at medium-run frequencies of between 8 and 50 years.[3]

---

[3] Paul A. Geroski and C. F. Walters (1995) also use aggregate data to argue that innovation is procyclical. However,

1134   THE AMERICAN ECONOMIC REVIEW   *SEPTEMBER 2007*

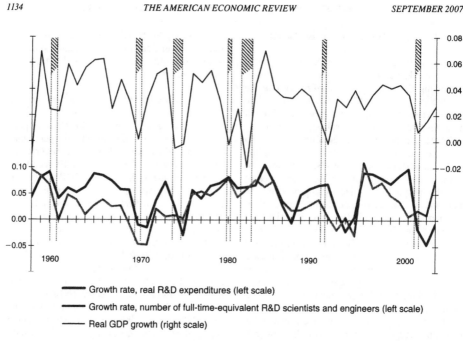

FIGURE 1. MEASURES OF R&D OVER THE BUSINESS CYCLE

Source: NSF.

One potential problem with data on R&D expenditures is that since there is no long series on the price of R&D, deflating by the GDP deflator may lead to spurious fluctuations in R&D that reflect price mismeasurement rather than true changes in R&D activity. Moreover, firms may not be consistent in which activities they consider to be R&D. I therefore turn to the growth rate in the number of full-time equivalent scientists and engineers employed in R&D in industry as reported by the NSF, narrowly defined to include "all persons engaged in scientific or engineering work at a level which requires a knowledge of physical or life sciences or engineering or mathematics" and whose "experience is equivalent to completion

of a 4-year college course with a major in these fields, regardless of whether or not they actually hold a degree in this field." Although scientists and engineers account for only a part of all R&D inputs, the virtue of this measure is that it does not depend on prices and is thus more likely to reflect true R&D activity. This growth rate is also depicted in Figure 1. As evident from the figure, the growth rate in employment of scientists and engineers closely tracks the growth rate in R&D expenditures; the correlation between the two series is 0.61 over the period in which both series are available. However, while employment growth in R&D is procyclical, it is more weakly correlated with GDP growth. The correlation between the two is only 0.10, and regressing the growth in employment of scientists and engineers on the growth in real GDP does not yield a statistically significant coefficient. Still, the fact that employment growth is highly correlated with R&D expenditures suggests changes in R&D expenditures reflect changes in real resources devoted to research

---

their evidence is for the United Kingdom and looks at the output of innovation—patents and successful innovations—rather than R&D expenditures. In the opposite direction, Saint-Paul (1993) tries to isolate the effects of demand shocks on R&D from all other shocks, and fails to find a significant effect of demand shocks on R&D.

VOL. 97 NO. 4   BARLEVY: ON THE CYCLICALITY OF RESEARCH AND DEVELOPMENT   1135

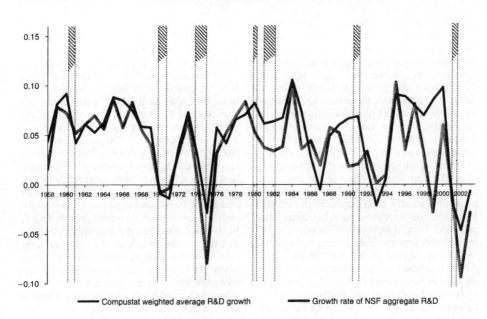

FIGURE 2. R&D GROWTH, NSF VERSUS COMPUSTAT

and development activities rather than spurious mismeasurement.

I next turn to the Compustat data. In contrast to NSF data, Compustat reports only R&D expenditures, not employment. Also, it is not a representative sample; the firms in Compustat are publicly traded and tend to be large (measured either by assets or employees). However, since a disproportionate share of R&D expenditures in the NSF is made by large firms, R&D patterns among these firms may capture quite well the behavior of total R&D expenditures. Figure 2 shows the weighted average growth of R&D expenditures among R&D-performing firms in Compustat. That is, I took all domestically incorporated firms in Compustat each year that reported positive R&D in both that year and the previous year, and then averaged the log growth in their R&D expenditures, weighting by the initial level of R&D expenditures of each firm. To minimize the effect of outliers, I removed observations where the absolute value of the log change in R&D expenditures ranked in the top 5 percent of all observations

in constructing Figure 2, although I included these observations in all of the subsequent work, since omitting them did not affect any of the conclusions. The Compustat series is consistent with the NSF series, both in level and in the way the two evolve over time. Nevertheless, there are a few differences. Average growth of R&D expenditures among Compustat firms fell more sharply in the early 1980s than in the NSF data. In addition, R&D growth in the late 1990s appeared to be more erratic among Compustat firms, although both datasets show a sharp decline in real R&D expenditures around the 2001 recession. Average growth of R&D in Compustat is actually more correlated with real GDP growth than the NSF series; the correlation between the two series for the same period between 1958 and 2003 is 0.49, and regressing average growth in R&D on growth in real GDP yields a higher coefficient of 0.94 with a standard error of 0.25.

Since Compustat reports R&D data by firm, we can use these data to examine whether the procyclical pattern in R&D is also apparent

1136   THE AMERICAN ECONOMIC REVIEW   SEPTEMBER 2007

at the industry level.[4] That is, do firms tend to expand R&D at a faster rate when output in the industry they operate in is rising? Fortunately, Compustat assigns each firm a four-digit standard industry classification (SIC) code. For many firms it also reports the North American Industry Classification System (NAICS) industry code. Even when Compustat fails to assign a NAICS code, in many cases I was able to assign one based on the assigned SIC code using conversion tables provided by the Census Bureau.

Measuring output at the industry level is somewhat more problematic than at the aggregate level; in particular, which is a better indicator of a booming industry, gross output or value added? In the absence of a clear answer, I consider both measures. First, using the NBER Manufacturing and Productivity database compiled by Eric Bartelsman, Randy Becker, and Wayne Gray (2000), I construct real gross output for 459 four-digit SIC industries from 1958 to 1996. This dataset provides highly disaggregated data and covers an extended period. However, it encompasses only manufacturing. While this excludes certain R&D-intensive industries, such as computer programming services and communications, R&D is heavily concentrated in manufacturing. According to both the NSF and Compustat, the share of R&D expenditures in manufacturing has consistently ranged between 70 and 80 percent of total R&D expenditures since 1990, and over 90 percent earlier. NSF data suggest manufacturing accounts for a similar share of employment of scientists and engineers. To incorporate data outside of manufacturing, I also used data from the Bureau of Economic Analysis (BEA) on real gross output and real value added by industry. The BEA provides these estimates at the three-digit industry level rather than at the four-digit level (and using the NAICS classification as opposed to SIC). These data also cover a shorter period than the NBER database: gross output data are available for 1988–2004, and value added is available at the three-digit level for 1978–2004, and at the two-digit level for 1947–2004.

Armed with this data, I assigned each firm in Compustat its respective industry output

measure whenever available. I then regressed the growth of real R&D expenditures of each firm on its industry's output growth along with firm fixed effects.[5] This regression should capture the extent to which firms deviate from their long-run growth rate of R&D as industry conditions vary. The results are reported in the first row of Table 1. As evident from the table, the coefficient on industry output is positive and highly significant for all three measures. To isolate the reaction of firms to industry-specific (as opposed to aggregate) output growth, I introduced year effects to absorb both cyclical effects and changes in patent policy or R&D subsidies that affect all industries. As can be seen in the table, the coefficients on output growth decline for all three measures, but they remain positive and statistically significant. Hence, even after controlling for aggregate conditions, industries where production is increasing tend to undertake more R&D, not less. Firms do not appear to substitute toward R&D when industry output is low, or divert resources from R&D when industry output is high.

B. *Further Investigating R&D Procyclicality*

Since Compustat contains additional firm-level information, we can use it to further scrutinize the procyclical pattern in R&D activity documented above. For example, is the procyclical pattern in R&D picking up some other firm-level variation that is correlated with industry or aggregate output? Does the procyclicality of R&D vary systematically across industries, and if so what type of industries have more procyclical R&D?

I begin with variables for which aggregate R&D may be proxying. One commonly invoked explanation for the procyclicality of R&D is that firm earnings fall in recessions, making it difficult to finance innovation. According to this view, the positive coefficient on industry output

---

[4] While the NSF does break down total R&D expenditures by SIC industry codes, many of these series contain missing values or are deliberately withheld for privacy reasons.

[5] Matthew C. Rafferty and Mark Funk (2004) also regress R&D growth among Compustat firms against the growth in gross output using fixed effects, although they used only gross output from the NBER Manufacturing and Productivity database. But their regression includes additional explanatory variables, among them the firm's own sales, which make it difficult to interpret the coefficient on growth in industry output as a pure measure of cyclical sensitivity.

TABLE 1—CORRELATION OF R&D WITH INDUSTRY OUTPUT MEASURES
Dependent variable: Growth in real R&D

	4-digit SIC code manufacturing only gross output 1959–1996	3-digit NAICS code all industries gross output 1988–2004	3-digit NAICS code all industries value added 1978–2004
Output growth	0.2102	0.9229	0.4140
(no time fixed effects)	0.0262	0.0468	0.0303
Output growth	0.1354	0.3631	0.1861
(with time fixed effects)	0.0292	0.0649	0.0365
Firm fixed effects	Yes	Yes	Yes
N	29,618	43,557	62,715
# of firms	3,454	6,160	7,719
# of industries	130	51	54

Notes: Value added data are available from 1950 on for 2-digit NAICS codes. For industries where the 3-digit code accounted for virtually all of the value added in the respective 2-digit industry, I used the 2-digit output and tracked data back to 1950. Observations prior to 1978 account for less than 2 percent of my observations.

is really standing in for omitted measures of firm balance sheet positions that vary over the cycle, and including these should greatly reduce the implied procyclicality of R&D. Since Compustat includes financial information on firms, we can test this prediction. Table 2 repeats the regressions from Table 1, but adds various balance sheet variables. Specifically, I add the current year cash flow (before R&D expenses) and the residual cash flow in the previous year after R&D expenses, as well as current and lagged values of firm assets, firm liabilities, plant, property, and equipment, short-term debt (debt due within one year), and long-term debt. All variables are deflated by the implicit GDP deflator. Not only is growth industry output still significant, but the coefficient is also essentially unchanged. The increase in R&D expenditures in periods of rising industry output is evidently not a reflection of unaccounted changes in firm balance sheet positions, since firms increase the rate of growth of their R&D regardless of their cash positions. Adding second- and third-order terms of all of the balance sheet variables above left the coefficient on output growth similarly unchanged.

The fact that including balance sheet information does not change the coefficient on industry output might seem surprising at first. However, this result should be interpreted with caution. In particular, it does not mean credit constraints are unimportant for R&D. In fact, although not reported in the table, the coefficient on lagged cash flow is significant in two of the specifications reported in Table 2, suggesting that

similarly sized firms (as measured by assets) with more cash do tend to have higher R&D growth. Rather, the results in Table 2 imply that the tendency of firms to accelerate their R&D when industry output rises does not reflect how relatively cash-rich or cash-poor they are. This result is consistent with Charles P. Himmelberg and Bruce C. Petersen (1994) who argue R&D is sensitive to cash flow, but that this relationship is also hard to detect because firms tend to smooth R&D in response to temporary cash flow shocks by, among other things, curtailing their investment in physical capital. In other words, cash-rich firms undertake more R&D activity than cash-poor firms, but regardless of the scale of their R&D activity, both tend to minimize the disruptive effect of temporary fluctuations in cash flows on their R&D.

I next turn to evidence on R&D cyclicality by industry. Since this paper argues firms undertake more R&D in booms to capture the higher present discounted value of the profits they expect to earn if successful, it seems natural to ask whether firms in industries where the present discounted value of profits rises more in booms tend to have more procyclical R&D. For reasons that will become clear once I present the model, we should also expect industries where the present discounted value of profits is only modestly procyclical to have *counter*cyclical R&D.

To test this prediction, I partitioned firms into two-digit SIC codes. For two-digit codes in which relatively few firms reported R&D (i.e., agriculture, retail trade, and wholesale trade), I

TABLE 2—PARTIAL CORRELATION OF R&D WITH INDUSTRY OUTPUT MEASURES
AFTER CONTROLLING FOR BALANCE SHEET VARIABLES[a]
Dependent variable: Growth in real R&D

	4-digit SIC code manufacturing only gross output 1959–1996	3-digit NAICS code all industries gross output 1988–2004	3-digit NAICS code all industries value added 1978–2004[b]
Output growth	0.2057	0.9116	0.4115
(no time fixed effects)	0.0270	0.0475	0.0307
Output growth	0.1331	0.3538	0.1875
(with time fixed effects)	0.0301	0.0657	0.0370
Firm fixed effects	Yes	Yes	Yes
N	28,389	42,598	61,336
# of firms	3,429	6,124	7,674
# of industries	129	51	55

[a] Balance sheet variables included in all regressions (but not reported in the table) are current year cash flow (before R&D expenditures), lagged cash flow (after R&D expenditures), and current and lagged assets, liabilities, plant property and equipment, short-term debt and long-erm debt, all deflated by the implicit GDP deflator.

[b] Value added data are available from 1950 on for 2-digit NAICS codes. For industries where the 3-digit code accounted for virtually all of the value added in the respective 2-digit industry, I used the 2-digit output and tracked data back to 1950. Observations prior to 1978 account for less than 2 percent of my observations.

aggregated firms into their respective one-digit industries. Conversely, for industries within two-digit codes that are particularly R&D intensive, (i.e., pharmaceuticals, communication equipment, computers, and computer programming), I divided the original two-digit code into multiple industries. This left me with 44 industries. I first needed a measure of the procyclicality of present discounted profits for these industries. I used the stock market values of publicly traded firms in each industry as a stand-in for present discounted profits, since these should in theory reflect the discounted value of future dividends of these firms. Thus, I took all domestically incorporated firms in each industry where available, and regressed the growth rate in the real stock prices of firms on the growth of real GDP and a constant. Let $\hat{\beta}_{stock}$ denote the coefficient on real GDP growth from this regression, which represents how stock market values in a given industry covary with the business cycle. Next, for each industry, I took all domestically incorporated R&D-performing firms and regressed the growth rate in real R&D expenditures of each firm on the growth rate of real GDP and a constant. Let $\hat{\beta}_{R\&D}$ denote the coefficient on real GDP growth in this regression. Figure 3 plots $\hat{\beta}_{stock}$ and $\hat{\beta}_{R\&D}$ across industries, where the size of each point corresponds to the inverse of the standard error in estimating $\hat{\beta}_{R\&D}$. The

reason for weighting is that some sectors have few firms that report any R&D (e.g., transportation, utilities, insurance, and finance), and $\hat{\beta}_{R\&D}$ is poorly estimated in those sectors. As evident from the figure, industries with more procyclical stock values tend to have more procyclical R&D growth. For example, computer programming and semiconductors, whose stock market values are far more procyclical than all remaining industries, also have highly procyclical R&D, while primary metals, petroleum, mining, and agriculture, whose stock market values are the least procyclical, display weakly countercyclical R&D growth (although in all three cases $\hat{\beta}_{R\&D}$ is statistically indistinguishable from zero).[6]

Regressing $\hat{\beta}_{R\&D}$ on $\hat{\beta}_{stock}$ using the same set of weights yields the following relationship:

$$\hat{\beta}_{R\&D} = -1.58 + 0.39 \times \hat{\beta}_{stock}.$$
$$\quad\;\;(0.30)\;\;(0.04)$$

[6] As an aside, neither stock market values nor R&D are particularly procyclical for pharmaceuticals. This is probably because innovation is an exceptionally drawn out process due to regulation, insulating the industry from cyclical fluctuations. Although pharmaceuticals account for a significant share of total R&D, they do not contribute much to the cyclical patterns in R&D this paper focuses on. One should therefore avoid drawing inference from that sector for the phenomena studied here.

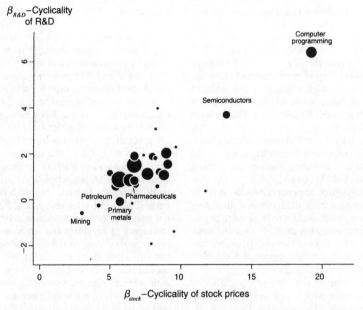

FIGURE 3. CYCLICALITY OF STOCK PRICES (β_{stock}) AND R&D ($\beta_{R\&D}$) ACROSS INDUSTRIES
(Observations weighted by the standard error of the estimate of R&D cyclicality in each industry)

Since $\hat{\beta}_{stock}$ is estimated, in principle we should adjust the standard errors to reflect estimation error. However, since the samples used to estimate $\hat{\beta}_{stock}$ were typically large, this variable is fairly tightly estimated, especially for those industries that have many observations on R&D and as such receive the most weight in the regression above. Moreover, since the regression is meant to be suggestive rather than a true structural relationship, it seems improper to impose additional structure in order to make these corrections. The constant in this regression is negative, suggesting that industries where stock market values are only modestly procyclical will tend to exhibit countercyclical R&D. While this finding is consistent with the model I present below, one has to be careful in interpreting this finding. In particular, this intercept is extrapolated, since I estimate $\hat{\beta}_{stock}$ to be positive and highly significant in all 44 industry categories. Moreover, while I estimate negative values of $\hat{\beta}_{R\&D}$ in several industries, in none of the cases is this negative value statistically significant at the 10 percent level. Thus, evidence

that industries in which stock market values are only moderately procyclical tend to have countercyclical R&D is at best indirect.

II. Previous Explanations for the Procyclicality of R&D

Before attempting to model the procyclical bias in R&D described in the introduction, I first review some of the theories advanced in the literature for the procyclicality of R&D. The purpose of this section is to help focus the subsequent theoretical model by determining what elements are and are not important for studying the *cyclical* behavior of R&D.

As already noted in the previous section, one common explanation for the procyclicality of R&D involves credit market frictions. This hypothesis is explicitly developed in Aghion et al. (2005). In their model, the opportunity cost of R&D is lower in recessions. But downturns also reduce the amount of internal funds available for firms to finance ongoing R&D projects. Aghion et al. show that if firms had unlimited access to credit, they would concentrate growth-enhancing activities in recessions. But if firms anticipate they will be borrowing-constrained, they would instead focus their R&D efforts in booms for fear that they will not be able to bring projects initiated in recessions to fruition. While this explanation is intuitive, the evidence described in the previous section suggests it is unlikely to account for the procyclical pattern in R&D we observe, at least insofar as credit constraints are reflected in firm balance sheets. This conclusion is lent further credence by the observation that the lion's share of the cyclical fluctuations in R&D comes from large, publicly traded firms, which are generally less likely to suffer from financing difficulties. I therefore chose not to incorporate credit constraints in modelling the evolution of R&D over the business cycle. This does not imply, however, that credit constraints are not important for understanding R&D more generally.

Another explanation for the procyclicality of R&D is that recessions do not create opportunities for intertemporal substitution. There are two different versions of this argument. According to one view, the specialized labor employed in R&D is not readily substitutable for production workers at high frequencies. While there is some truth that scientists and engineers may not be easily shifted to production, NSF data suggest that on average 40 percent of wage payments in R&D are allocated to support staff, who are more easily reallocated into production. Moreover, an important input into R&D is managerial attention, which certainly could be alternatively devoted to production issues. A separate argument for why recessions might not encourage intertemporal substitution is that R&D relies on produced goods as an input. If more goods can be produced during booms, there will be more resources available to use for R&D. Aghion and Saint-Paul (1998) explore this possibility formally, and show that innovation will be procyclical if productivity-improving activities use final goods rather than factor inputs.[7] But they then reject this view, arguing that data on how demand shocks affect long-run

productivity are inconsistent with this assumption. More directly, as Griliches (1984) observes, the primary input into R&D is labor, not produced goods. Hence, although some R&D certainly involves produced goods, I will assume in my model that R&D uses only labor inputs that could alternatively be used for production.

A more compelling explanation for the procyclicality of R&D is that labor supply itself varies over the cycle. Specifically, if labor resources are procyclical, it may not be desirable to divert already scarce labor resources in recessions from production to R&D or to draw resources from R&D in booms when labor resources are more plentiful. Indeed, this is how Antonio Fatas (2000) generates procyclical R&D. While it is true that, as Austan Goolsbee (1998) argues, the supply of scientists and engineers is inelastic in the short run, an inflow of labor resources can still allow those capable of doing R&D to concentrate on these activities and provide them with relevant support services. I abstract from this possibility in my initial analysis, although I will allow for cyclical variation in labor supply later when I look at the quantitative aspects of the model.

III. A Model of R&D and Analysis of a Special Case

To study the evolution of R&D over the business cycle, I adapt a standard real business cycle model to include an innovation sector as modeled by Grossman and Helpman (1991). Production in the model economy involves two factors of production: capital and labor. These can be used to produce a single final good via a two-step process. This final good in turn can be used for three purposes: consumption, production of new capital, and as an indirect input into the production of final goods (a feature sometimes referred to as roundabout production). Labor resources, in addition to being used for production, can be used to carry out R&D in order to augment labor productivity in producing this final good. Thus, production and R&D compete for labor resources. This section lays out the model, and then focuses on a special case of the model that can be solved analytically to illustrate its key features. In the next section, I calibrate the general version of the model in order to analyze its quantitative properties.

---

[7] Following Luis A. Rivera-Batiz and Paul M. Romer (1991), this is known as the lab-equipment model. Comin and Gertler (2006) also assume R&D uses final goods, and note that this assumption helps to generate procyclical R&D.

I assume households in the economy can be represented by a single agent with constant-relative risk-aversion utility over the amount of the final good C_t consumed at date t:

$$(1) \qquad U(C_t) = \frac{C_t^{1-\gamma} - 1}{1 - \gamma}.$$

Utility is discounted at rate ρ. The representative agent is endowed with a constant labor endowment L per unit time and an initial capital stock at date t_0 normalized to one. Since the agent is assumed to derive no utility from leisure, the entire labor endowment will be supplied at every date. As alluded to in the previous section, however, variable labor supply can be an important source of procyclical R&D. Although it will be more convenient to abstract from variation in labor supply for now, I will introduce such variation in the next section.

Turning to technology, consider first the production of capital goods. I assume a linear technology whereby one unit of the final good can be converted into q units of capital. Assuming capital depreciates at rate δ, the instantaneous rate of change in the capital stock is

$$(2) \qquad \dot{K}_t = qI_t - \delta K_t,$$

where I_t denotes the amount of final goods allocated to the production of capital.

Next, consider the production of the final good. I assume it is constructed in two stages. First, labor is converted into a continuum of intermediate goods indexed by $j \in [0,1]$. Second, the intermediate goods are combined with capital to produce the final good.

Let us begin with the second stage. It will be convenient to proceed as if all intermediate goods must first be assembled into a composite good, whose quantity I is denoted by X_t, according to a Cobb-Douglas technology. That is, x_{jt} of each good j together yield

$$(3) \qquad X_t = \exp\left[\int_0^1 \ln x_{jt}\, dj\right].$$

The production of the final good is itself Cobb-Douglas in the composite good and capital, i.e.,

X_t units of composite good and K_t units of capital yield Y_t units of the final good, where

$$(4) \qquad Y_t = z_t K_t^\alpha X_t^{1-\alpha}.$$

The coefficient z_t reflects productivity in the final goods sector. To capture the fact that labor productivity in the goods sector varies over the business cycle, I let z_t follow a Markov switching process between two states, $Z_1 \geq Z_0$, with a constant hazard rate μ. This is the only source of fluctuations in the model. I treat these fluctuations as exogenous, although one could potentially endogenize them.[8]

I next turn to the production of intermediate goods. For reasons that will become clear below, I assume the production of each intermediate good entails both a fixed cost and a variable cost. The fixed cost is assumed to be denominated in final goods, i.e., F_t units of final good have to be sacrificed per instant if a given intermediate good is to be produced. As the subscript suggests, this amount is time varying, in a way described in more detail below. Once this fixed cost is incurred, labor can be converted into intermediate goods according to a good-specific linear technology. Let L_{jt} denote the amount of labor employed in the production of good j. The amount x_{jt} of intermediate good j produced at date t is given by

$$(5) \qquad x_{jt} = \lambda_{jt} L_{jt}.$$

The coefficient λ_{jt} is assumed to have the following structure:

$$(6) \qquad \lambda_{jt} = \lambda^{m_{jt}}$$

for some $\lambda > 1$, where m_{jt} is an integer that denotes the generation of technology used for producing good j at date t. Good j starts out at some generation m_{jt_0} at the initial date t_0, but agents can advance to higher-generation technologies by engaging in R&D. That is, starting with generation m_j, devoting R_j units of labor to

---

[8] For example, Jess Benhabib and Roger E. A. Farmer (1994) describe an economy with spillovers in which the scale of production, and thus the productivity of individual producers, fluctuate endogenously over time. Fluctuations in z_t could also reflect changes in utilization rates in response to some other shock.

1142   THE AMERICAN ECONOMIC REVIEW   SEPTEMBER 2007

R&D on good j gives rise to a hazard ϕR_j of discovering generation $m_j + 1$ in the next instant, which given $\lambda > 1$ will be more productive than its predecessor. In line with the evidence on the acyclicality of productivity in the innovation sector in Griliches (1990), I assume ϕ does not vary with time.

The discovery of a new technology, in addition to increasing the productivity in good j by a factor of λ, leads to two additional outcomes. First, it allows innovators to begin working on the next generation technology. R&D is therefore incremental, in the sense that the mth generation has to be created before the $(m + 1)^{th}$ technology can be. Each new discovery immediately becomes public knowledge, allowing rivals to incorporate it as they work on subsequent generations. This feature introduces a dynamic externality, since whenever a researcher discovers a new generation, she allows others to build on and profit from her work.

Second, I assume each new discovery spawns inferior imitations. That is, new ideas can be copied, albeit imperfectly, in the sense that knock-off versions are more costly to operate. Although the imitation technology will never actually be used, it plays an important role in the analysis. In particular, the technology available to rivals affects the profits the leading producer can earn in a decentralized market. Without imitations, rivals could use older generation technologies, which have higher variable costs but the *same* fixed cost as the leading producer. In the model, this feature generates counterfactual implications about the markup producers charge. I therefore assume discoveries spawn imitations which have a *lower* fixed cost than the leading version (but a higher variable cost), resulting in more empirically plausible markups. This assumption can be defended on the grounds that imitators do not incur the fixed costs of patent protection that a leading-edge producer would. To simplify the analysis, I assume the imitation technology involves zero fixed cost and has a marginal cost that is λ times the marginal cost of the leading technology, although this exact specification is not essential.

Let $M_t = \int_0^1 m_{jt}\, dj$ denote the average generation across intermediate goods, and let $R_t = \int_0^1 R_{jt}\, dj$ denote total employment in R&D aggregated over all intermediate goods. One can show that in any equilibrium (and along

the optimal path), each sector will use the same amount of labor $L_{jt} = L - R_t$. Substituting in this expression, we have

$$(7) \quad Y_t = z_t K_t^\alpha X_t^{1-\alpha} = z_t [\lambda^{M_t}(L - R_t)]^{1-\alpha} K_t^\alpha.$$

Output grows as labor productivity improves and more capital is accumulated. To avoid the situation where the economy outgrows the fixed cost, I scale this fixed cost in proportion to the rate at which output increases, namely λ^{M_t}. Specifically,

$$(8) \qquad\qquad F_t = \lambda^{M_t} F$$

for some constant $F > 0$. The notion that fixed costs grow over time is plausible; for example, the cost of overhead labor should naturally rise with overall labor productivity.[9]

This describes the economic environment. In the remainder of this section, I focus on a special case of this model which is analytically tractable. In particular, I restrict $\gamma = 0$ so that the agent is risk-neutral, and set $q = \delta = 0$ so that the value of capital is always fixed at one (i.e., capital can be viewed as a fixed factor, such as land). Finally, in the absence of capital accumulation, (8) must be modified to $F_t = \lambda^{(1-\alpha)M_t} F$, the rate at which output grows. To insure the fixed cost does not exceed the total amount of output that could ever be produced (i.e., when all labor resources are allocated to production), I also restrict $F < Z_0 L^{1-\alpha}$. None of the other parameters is assigned a value.

Consider first what a benevolent social planner would do in this economy. She would maximize the well-being of the representative household, choosing how much labor to allocate to R&D and each intermediate good (and if capital were accumulable, how much capital to produce) as well as which technology to use to produce each

---

[9] This begs the question why I did not model the fixed cost directly in terms of labor. The reason is that the value of labor in a decentralized market would change one for one with z_t. As a result, the fixed cost F_t will vary greatly over the cycle. But, in practice, real wages tend to be somewhat rigid over the cycle, even though they do grow over longer time horizons. Fixed costs should therefore not vary much over the cycle, a feature I wanted the model to adhere to. Assuming the fixed cost is denominated in final goods captures rigidity in the salaries of overhead labor without unnecessarily complicating the model.

intermediate good. Clearly, the planner would always use the leading-edge technology for any good. It is also easy to show that she should allocate the same amount of labor, $L - R_i$, to each intermediate good. The planner's problem thus reduces to choosing a path for R&D:

$$(9) \quad V_i(M_{t_0}) = \max_{R_t} E\left[\int_{t_0}^{\infty} \lambda^{(1-\alpha)M_t}\left[z_t(L - R_t)^{1-\alpha} - F\right] \right.$$

$$\left. \times e^{-\rho(t-t_0)} dt \,|\, z_{t_0} = Z_i \right]$$

subject to the constraint that

$$\dot{M}_t = \phi R_t,$$

i.e., the change in the average generation of technology corresponds to the fraction of successful entrepreneurs who discover the next generation in their respective line. For this problem to be well defined, we need to ensure the planner cannot achieve infinite utility. This requires that the economy cannot grow faster than the discount rate ρ. Since the maximal growth rate occurs when all labor resources are used in R&D, this condition can be written as

$$(10) \quad \rho > (1 - \alpha)\phi L \ln \lambda.$$

We can rewrite the planner's problem recursively as follows:

$$(11)$$

$$\rho V_i(M)$$

$$= \max_{R \in [0,L]} \left\{ \begin{array}{l} \lambda^{(1-\alpha)M}[Z_i(L - R)^{1-\alpha} - F] \\ + \mu(V_{1-i}(M) - V_i(M)) + \dfrac{\partial V_i}{\partial M}\phi R \end{array} \right\}.$$

I now establish the following result (for proofs of all results, see the Appendix):[10]

PROPOSITION 1: *In any interior path, optimal innovation is countercyclical along the optimal path, i.e., $R_0 > R_1$.*

[10] All propositions relate to interior solutions where R&D is always positive. An earlier version of this paper dealt with corner cases. One can typically guarantee an interior solution by assuming L is sufficiently large.

This claim formalizes the intertemporal substitution view: since the returns to production are low when z_t is low, it is preferable to shift resources toward R&D in these periods. There are, however, two aspects of this special case that make countercyclical R&D particularly desirable. First, labor L is assumed to be constant over time. If, instead, labor were more plentiful when z is high, it might not be necessary to divert resources from R&D to take advantage of temporarily high productivity in the goods sector. Second, the assumption of risk-neutrality, which I impose for analytical convenience, contributes to making countercyclical R&D more desirable. In particular, a drawback of shifting resources from production to innovation during recessions is that it makes output more volatile; the decline in the amount of labor used in production compounds the already low productivity. To the extent this makes consumption more volatile, risk-neutrality may overstate the desirability of countercyclical R&D. In the next section I explicitly take into account these two considerations.

I now show that in the same environment for which Proposition 1 dictates a countercyclical path for R&D, equilibrium R&D in a decentralized market can be procyclical. I first need to specify how the decentralized economy is organized, and then solve for its equilibrium.

I assume both intermediate and final goods are produced by profit-maximizing firms. The technology for producing final goods is freely available, so profits in this sector will equal zero in equilibrium. By contrast, intermediate goods producers are assumed to enjoy some market power: the entrepreneur who discovers the mth generation for producing good j earns a patent that grants him exclusive rights to use this technology; without this patent, no innovation would ever take place. In what follows, I focus on equilibria where R_{jt} is the same across all goods j, and where in addition the common value of R&D in all sectors, R_t, can be expressed as a function of aggregate productivity z_t at date t alone. This restriction is natural, given these features are true for the optimal path. Formally, I restrict attention to symmetric Markov perfect equilibria. Let R_i denote the level of R&D common to all sectors when productivity $z_t = Z_i$ for $i \in \{0, 1\}$.

I normalize the wage per unit labor to one. Let p_{jt} denote the equilibrium price of intermediate good j. Given the Cobb-Douglas aggregator X, the demand of final goods producers for each intermediate good j will be unit elastic. Thus, each intermediate-goods producer would want to charge as high a price as possible: his revenue will be constant regardless of the price he charges, but at higher prices he can produce fewer goods and lower his costs. If, however, he were to charge too high of a price, his rivals could underprice him and steal his business. Here, the relevant threat involves the knock-off version of his own technology, which has no fixed cost but a marginal cost that is λ times as large. Hence, a producer would engage in limit pricing by setting his price equal to the marginal cost of this rival technology, i.e., $p_{jt} = \lambda^{-(m_\mu - 1)}$. Note that at this price, the producer would be charging a markup λ over his own marginal cost.

Let $e_{jt} = p_{jt} x_{jt}$ denote total expenditures by final goods producers on intermediate good j. Given the Cobb-Douglas specification for X, final goods producers will equalize expenditures across all intermediate goods, so $e_{jt} = e_t$ for all j. Each intermediate goods producer thus earns e_t in revenue, and given my normalization of the wage to one, incurs variable costs equal to the number of workers he employs. The latter expression is equal to $\lambda^{-m_\mu} x_{jt}$, or, alternatively, $\lambda^{-m_\mu} e_t / p_{jt}$. Using the expression for p_{jt} derived above, profits are given by

$$(12) \qquad \pi_{jt} = \left(1 - \frac{1}{\lambda}\right) e_t - P_t F_t,$$

where P_t denotes the price of the final good. Profits are thus the same for all goods j, i.e., $\pi_{jt} = \pi_t$ for all j. Equation (12) helps to explain the reason for some of my earlier assumptions. It states that profits net of fixed costs are equal to total sales e_t times one minus the inverse markup. This equation holds more generally for any constant marginal cost technology,

$$(13) \qquad \pi_t = \left(1 - \frac{1}{\lambda_t}\right) et - FC_t,$$

where λ_t represents a potentially time-varying markup and FC_t represents the fixed cost at date t. In analyzing the cyclical behavior of profits, Valerie E. Ramey (1991) divides both sides of equation (13) by sales e_t to arrive at an expression for the ratio of profits to sales. Since

empirically profits are more procyclical than sales, she finds this ratio is highly procyclical. But as evident from (13), in the absence of fixed costs this ratio inherits the cyclical properties of the markup λ_t. Empirically, markups are moderately countercyclical. We would thus need to allow for fixed costs of production to have any hope of according with the data. We also need to ensure that the markup λ_t is not so countercyclical as to offset the role of the fixed cost. This explains why I needed to allow for an imitation technology with lower fixed costs. If the next most efficient producer had the same fixed cost as the leading producer, the resulting markup would be sufficiently countercyclical to make π_t / e_t acyclical. Getting the model to match the cyclical behavior of profits is important, since in the model it is profits that ultimately drive R&D.

I next solve for the equilibrium values of e_t and P_t. Since there is no capital accumulation, in equilibrium the representative household spends all of its income on final goods. Thus, household expenditures on final goods $P_t(Y_t - F_t)$ equal household income, i.e., the sum of aggregate profits $\Pi_t = \int_0^1 \pi_t \, dj$ and factor payments

$$(14) \qquad P_t(Y_t - F_t) = \Pi_t + r_t K + L,$$

where r_t denotes the rental rate of capital at date t. Given the Cobb-Douglas technology for final goods, expenditures on intermediate goods e_t should account for a fraction $1 - \alpha$ of the total cost of final goods production. Since the market for final goods is perfectly competitive, the latter equals the market value of final goods produced, i.e., $e_t = (1 - \alpha) P_t Y_t$. Similarly, expenditures on capital goods $r_t K$ equal $\alpha P_t Y_t$. Substituting into (14) and rearranging yields

$$(15) \qquad \pi_t = (\lambda - 1)(L - R_t) - P_t F_t.$$

As for the price of final goods P_t, competition in the market for final goods implies P_t equals the minimum cost to produce a single unit of the good, i.e.,

$$P_t = \min_{x_{jt}, K_t} \left\{ \int_0^1 p_{jt} x_{jt} \, dj + r_t K_t \right\}$$

$$\text{s.t. } z_t K_t^\alpha \left(\exp\left[\int_0^1 \ln x_{jt} \, dj \right] \right)^{1-\alpha} = 1.$$

Using the fact that $p_{jt} = \lambda^{-(m_p - 1)}$, $r_t K_t = \alpha P_t Y_t$, and $K_t = 1$ for all t, one can show that

$$(16) \qquad P_t = \frac{\lambda(L - R_t)^\alpha}{(1 - \alpha)z_t \lambda^{(1-\alpha)M_t}}.$$

Hence, profits can be expressed as

$$(17) \quad \pi_t = (\lambda - 1)(L - R_t) - \frac{\lambda(L - R_t)^\alpha F}{(1 - \alpha)z_t}.$$

Finally, let v_j denote the value of a successful innovation of intermediate good j. Entrepreneurs who succeed in innovation earn profits (17) as long as their technology is the most advanced. Since profits π_{jt} are the same for all j, and R_{jt} is assumed to be the same for all j, v_j will be the same for all j as well. Let v denote the common value of a successful innovation in all sectors, and let v_i denote this value if productivity at date t_0 is equal to Z_i. Let $\mathbb{I}_{jt}$ be an indicator that equals one if the leading-edge producer of good j at date t_0 is still the leading-edge producer at date t, and zero otherwise. Since the representative agent owns all claims in equilibrium, v_i must leave him indifferent to buying an additional claim. This indifference condition implies

(18)

$$v_i = E\left[\int_{t_0}^{\infty} \mathbb{I}_{jt} \cdot \frac{U'(C_t)/P_t}{U'(C_{t_0})/P_{t_0}} \pi_t e^{-\rho(t-t_0)} dt \,\big|\, z_{t_0} = Z_i\right]$$

$$= E\left[\int_{t_0}^{\infty} \mathbb{I}_{jt} \cdot \frac{P_{t_0}}{P_t} \pi_t e^{-\rho(t-t_0)} dt \,\big|\, z_{t_0} = Z_i\right],$$

where the expectation above is taken over all possible paths for z_t and $\mathbb{I}_{jt}$. A firm trying to become the leading producer will choose R to maximize the expected value from a successful innovation net of R&D costs, $\phi Rv - R$. It follows that in equilibrium $\phi v_i \le 1$ for $i \in \{0, 1\}$, with strict equality if $R_i > 0$.

Substituting in for π_t and P_t in (18) yields

$$(19) \quad v_i = E\left[\int_{t_0}^{\infty} \mathbb{I}_{jt} \cdot \frac{(L - R_{t_0})}{(Z_t)} \frac{\lambda^{(1-\alpha)M_t}}{\lambda^{(1-\alpha)M_{t_0}}}\right.$$

$$\times \left[(\lambda - 1)z_t(L - R_t)^{1-\alpha} - F\right]$$

$$\left.\times\, e^{-\rho(t-t_0)} \, dt \,\big|\, z_{t_0} = Z_i\right].$$

As in (10), we once again need to assume that growth is not too rapid:

$$(20) \qquad \ln \lambda < (1 - \alpha)^{-1}.$$

I now establish the following result.

PROPOSITION 2: *Given (20), there exist two values F^* and $\bar{F}$ such that if $F > F^*$ and $F < \bar{F}$, then there exists a pair $R_0 < R_1$ where $\phi v_0(R_0, R_1) = 1$. By contrast, when $F = 0$, any solution for the system $\phi v_0(R_i, R_{1-i}) = 1$ must satisfy $R_0 > R_1$.*

Proposition 2 suggests that if fixed costs are large, so that profits are highly volatile, there can be an equilibrium with procyclical R&D. At the same time, fixed costs cannot be too large, or else profits will be so low that entrepreneurs have no incentive to try to achieve them. Conversely, if fixed costs are small, so that profits are only as volatile as sales, equilibrium R&D will be countercyclical. Intuitively, if profits are only modestly procyclical, the value of innovation in booms will rise, but by less than the cost of R&D. Procyclical R&D requires that profits be more procyclical than the cost of R&D to ensure that innovation is more profitable in booms. Recall that earlier I found that industries with only moderately procyclical stock prices indeed appear to have countercyclical R&D.

Why is it that, with moderately sized fixed costs, the decentralized market fails to reproduce a countercyclical path for R&D as the planner prefers? The reason is that in a decentralized market, entrepreneurs care too much about the short-term benefits from their R&D, correctly expecting that the benefits from their research in the more distant future are more likely to accrue to others. Formally, consider the ratio of the real value of a successful innovation in a boom to its value in a recession. This ratio is given by

(21)

$$
\frac{v_1/P_1}{v_0/P_0} = \left\{ E\left[\int_{t_0}^{\infty} \mathbb{I}_t \cdot \lambda^{(1-\alpha)M_t} \right.\right.
$$

$$
\times \left[z_t(L - R_t)^{1-\alpha} - \frac{F}{\lambda - 1} \right]
$$

$$
\left.\left. \times e^{-\rho(t-t_0)} dt \Big| z_{t_0} = Z_i \right] \right\}
$$

$$
\left\{ E\left[\int_{t_0}^{\infty} \mathbb{I}_t \cdot \lambda^{(1-\alpha)M_t} \right.\right.
$$

$$
\times \left[z_t(L - R_t)^{1-\alpha} - \frac{F}{\lambda - 1} \right]
$$

$$
\left.\left. \times e^{-\rho(t-t_0)} dt \Big| z_{t_0} = Z_i \right] \right\}.
$$

The analogous expression for the benevolent planner is the ratio of the marginal value improving the technology, $\partial V / \partial M$, in a boom relative to a recession. This expression is given by

(22)

$$
\frac{\partial V_1/\partial M}{\partial V_0/\partial M} = \left\{ E\left[\int_{t_0}^{\infty} \lambda^{(1-\alpha)M_t} \right.\right.
$$

$$
\times \left[z_t(L - R_t)^{1-\alpha} - F \right]
$$

$$
\left.\left. \times e^{-\rho(t-t_0)} dt \Big| z_{t_0} = Z_1 \right] \right\}
$$

$$
\left\{ E\left[\int_{t_0}^{\infty} \lambda^{(1-\alpha)M_t} \right.\right.
$$

$$
\times \left[z_t(L - R_t)^{1-\alpha} - F \right]
$$

$$
\left.\left. \times e^{-\rho(t-t_0)} dt \Big| z_{t_0} = Z_0 \right] \right\}.
$$

Comparing the two expressions reveals two differences. First, in the decentralized market, the fixed cost is scaled by a factor of $(\lambda - 1)^{-1}$. This is because entrepreneurs care not about the output they produce but about the profits they earn. While they earn only a proportion of the output they produce, they bear all of the cost of the output they use to cover their fixed cost. Entrepreneurs therefore weight the output they produce and the output they use up differently, unlike the planner. This distortion is not relevant for our purposes, and can be nullified by setting $\lambda = 2$ so the markup is 100 percent. Second, and more importantly, the entrepreneur multiplies the flow value at each date by $\mathbb{I}_t$, an indicator of whether he will still be the leading producer at date t. Since the probability that $\mathbb{I}_t = 1$ decreases with t, the integrals in (21) assign more weight to values closer to date $t = t_0$ than the integrals in (22), i.e., private agents care less about the long-run benefits of innovation than the planner. The ratio of the respective values of innovation will thus be distorted in the direction of the ratio of profits in booms to profits in recessions, since these are the expressions that receive the largest weight under (22). The bigger the ratio of profits in booms to their value in recessions, the more entrepreneurs value innovations in booms than in recessions, and the more biased R&D will be toward booms.

Although the special case of the model above is analytically convenient for demonstrating the bias, it is far too stylized to help us gauge if the bias can play a significant role in making equilibrium R&D procyclical. To address this question, I shall now return to the general model and analyze its quantitative implications.

IV. Quantitative Analysis

A key feature of the general model absent from the special case above is capital accumulation. In this section I discuss some of the issues that arise when capital can be accumulated. I then proceed to solve the model numerically for specifically calibrated parameter values. The section concludes with several robustness exercises, notably allowing for variable labor supply.

A. *Analysis of the General Model*

In analyzing the general model, it will prove helpful to restrict γ to one. This is the value I use in the subsequent calibration, and the case of log utility turns out to be analytically convenient. The planner's problem in this case reduces to

$$V_i(K_{t_0}, M_{t_0}) = \max_{R, I_t} E\left[\int_{t_0}^{\infty} \ln\left(z_t K_t^{\alpha}\right)\left[\lambda^{M_t}(L - R_t)\right]^{1-\alpha}\right.$$

$$\left. - \lambda^{M_t}F - I_t\right)e^{-\rho(t-t_0)}\, dt\big|z_{t_0} = Z_i\right]$$

s.t. 1. $\dot{M}_t = \phi R_t$

2. $\dot{K}_t = qI_t - \delta K_t.$

Let $k = \lambda^{-M}K$ and $\iota = \lambda^{-M}I$. Using the law of motion for M, one can show that $V_i(K_{t_0}, M_{t_0}) = v_i(k_{t_0}) + M_{t_0}((\ln \lambda)/\rho)$, where $v_i(k)$ satisfies

(23)

$$\rho v_i(k) =$$

$$\max_{\iota, R}\left\{\ln\left(Z_i k^{\alpha}(L - R)^{1-\alpha} - F - \iota\right)\right.$$

$$+ \frac{\phi R \ln \lambda}{\rho}$$

$$+ \frac{\partial v_i}{\partial k}(q\iota - (\delta + \phi R \ln \lambda)k) + \mu\left(v_{1-i}(k)\right.$$

$$\left. - v_i(k))\right\}.$$

The planner now has *two* relevant control variables, investment and R&D. The first-order conditions for the maximization problem with respect to each are given by

$$\frac{1}{Z_i k^{\alpha}(L - R)^{1-\alpha} - F - \iota} = q\frac{\partial v_i}{\partial k}$$

$$\frac{(1 - \alpha)Z_i k^{\alpha}(L - R)^{-\alpha}}{Z_i k^{\alpha}(L - R)^{1-\alpha} - F - \iota} = \left(\frac{1}{\rho} - k\frac{\partial v_i}{\partial k}\right)\phi \ln \lambda.$$

Substituting the first equation into the second yields the following formula for R_i, the value of R&D when productivity is equal to z_i:

(24)

$$R_i = L - \left[\left(\frac{1}{\rho(\partial v_i/\partial k)} - k\right)\frac{\phi \ln \lambda}{q(1 - \alpha)Z_i k^{\alpha}}\right]^{-1/\alpha}.$$

Rather than two numbers R_0 and R_1, an optimal plan now corresponds to two functions $R_0(k)$ and $R_1(k)$. This raises a question of what it means for R&D to be procyclical, since changes in z_t affect not only how much R&D is desirable at a given k but also k itself. I shall refer to a policy as procyclical if $R_1(k) > R_0(k)$ for any k in the limiting set the economy settles down to in the long run, i.e., for any value of k that occurs infinitely often with probability one. Similarly, a policy is said to be countercyclical if $R_1(k) < R_0(k)$ for all such k.

Next, consider the decentralized equilibrium of the economy. The production side of the economy is essentially the same as in the special case analyzed earlier, except that the price of final goods P now explicitly depends on the level of capital. In particular, (16) generalizes to

(25)

$$P = \frac{\lambda^{1-M}(L - R)^{\alpha}}{z(1 - \alpha)k^{\alpha}}.$$

The main difficulty in solving for an equilibrium is that once we move away from the assumption of risk-neutrality, evaluating the value of a successful innovation v in (18) necessitates an expression for consumption C_t. Without accumulable capital, consumption is equal to net output $Y_t - F_t$. When capital is accumulable, we instead need to explicitly solve the household's problem to derive C_t, i.e., we must determine how a household should optimally divide its wealth between consumption, capital, and claims to the profits of intermediate good producers.

Since the household must own all of the claims on profits in equilibrium, it will be convenient to proceed as if there were a mutual fund company that pooled all entrepreneurs into a single portfolio on behalf of the household. Arbitrage requires the value of this portfolio to be the same as the cost of buying up all firms, which is just $\int_0^1 v\, dj = v$. To insure the fund continues to own all incumbents, it must pay the research expenses of any potential innovator in exchange for the rights to the patent if the innovator is successful, i.e., the fund deducts an operating expense R out of dividends. Thus, as far as the household is concerned, it can allocate its wealth either to physical capital or to an asset whose price is v and which yields a dividend of $\Pi = \pi - R$ per unit time, where π is given by (15).

Let w denote the household's nominal wealth and σ denote the fraction of its wealth that it allocates to capital. Given the linear technology for producing capital goods, the price of a unit of capital, P_K, is equal to qP. If aggregate productivity remains constant, the nominal return per unit of capital is $r + \dot{P}_K$, and the number of units of capital it holds is $\sigma w/P_K$. Similarly, the nominal return per share of the mutual fund it owns is $\Pi + \dot{v}$, and the number of shares it owns in the mutual fund is $(1 - \sigma)w/v$. In equilibrium, however, $\dot{v} = 0$. In addition to the returns to its assets, the household also earns labor income and spends some of its resources on consumption. Hence, the evolution of nominal wealth w while z_t is constant is given by

$$(26) \quad \dot{w} = \left[\left(\frac{r}{P_K} + \frac{\dot{P}_K}{P_K}\right)\sigma + \frac{\Pi}{v}(1 - \sigma)\right]w$$

$$+ L - \lambda^M Pc,$$

where $c = \lambda^{-M}C$. If productivity z_t did change, the nominal value of the physical capital the household owns would jump together with P_K. The nominal value of wealth held in the mutual fund would not change, however, since the value of the mutual fund is $v = \phi^{-1}$ independently of aggregate productivity. Hence, the wealth of the household will jump from w to w^* where

$$(27) \quad w^* = \left[\frac{P'_K}{P_K}\sigma + (1 - \sigma)\right]w$$

and P'_K is the price of capital under the new level of productivity. Let W denote the aggregate wealth of the economy. In equilibrium, of course, $w = W$. However, since individual households act as price takers, they treat the path of W as given and assume it determines the values of the prices it faces. Let $R_i(W)$ denote the equilibrium employment in R&D when $z_t = Z_i$ and aggregate wealth is W_i. We can then express k in terms of W, since $W = P_K K + v = q\lambda^M Pk + \phi^{-1}$. Using the expression for P in (25), we have

$$k_i(W) = \left[\frac{(W - \phi^{-1})Z_i(1 - \alpha)}{q\lambda(L - R_i(W))^\alpha}\right]^{\frac{1}{1-\alpha}}.$$

We can similarly express the nominal quantities r, P, and Π as functions of W. This implies

we can express the household problem recursively in terms of two state variables, w and W:

$$(28) \quad \rho V_i(w, W)$$
$$= \max_{\sigma, c}\left\{\ln c + \frac{\phi R \ln \lambda}{\rho} + \frac{\partial Vi}{\partial w}\dot{w}\right.$$
$$+ \frac{\partial V_i}{\partial W}\dot{W} + \mu\left(V_{1-i}(w^*, W^*)\right.$$
$$\left. - V_i(w, W))\right\},$$

subject to (26) and (27), the free entry condition $\phi v = 1$, and the laws of motion for W, i.e., if z_t remains constant over the next instant, then

$$(29)$$
$$\dot{W} = \left(r + \dot{P}_K\right)\lambda^M k + \Pi + L - \lambda^M Pc(W, W),$$

while if z_t changes over the next instant, W will jump to W^*, where

$$W^* = q\lambda^M P_{1-i}k_i(W) + \phi^{-1}.$$

The first-order conditions for the household problem with respect to σ and c are given by

$$(30) \quad \left(\frac{r}{P_K} + \frac{\dot{P}_K}{P_K}\right) - \phi\Pi$$
$$= \mu\frac{\partial V_{1-i}(w^*, W^*)/\partial w^*}{\partial V_i(w, W)/\partial w}\left[1 - \frac{P_{1-i}}{P_i}\right];$$

$$(31) \quad \frac{1}{Pc(w, W)} = \frac{\partial V_i}{\partial w}.$$

An equilibrium is a set of functions $w_i^*(w)$, $V_i(w, W)$, and $R_i(W)$ which satisfy the system of equations (27), (28), and (30).

B. *Calibration and Results*

The equations that define an equilibrium must be solved numerically, requiring me to assign particular values to the various parameters of the model. Since the model is essentially a standard real business cycle model with endogenous growth, many of the parameters I use have already been discussed in the real business cycle literature. The values I use are as follows:

TABLE 3

γ	1.00	α	0.33	λ	1.20
ρ	0.05	Z_0	0.94	ϕ	0.10
q	1.00	Z_1	1.06	F	3.60
δ	0.08	μ	0.20	L	30.80

The first two parameters correspond to utility terms. As already anticipated, I assume log utility by setting the coefficient of relative risk aversion γ to one. Normalizing a unit of time in the model to correspond to a year, I set the discount rate ρ to 5 percent. The next several parameters relate to production. First, I set $q = 1$ so consumption and investment goods trade one for one, a common assumption in real business cycle models. I set the depreciation rate of capital δ to 8 percent per year. The share of capital in the production of final goods α is set to one-third. To match the 6 percent unconditional standard deviation of detrended productivity growth we observe in the data, I set Z_0 to 0.94 and Z_1 to 1.06. I set the transition rate μ so that a complete cycle is ten years, slightly longer than the eight-year frequency often used to identify business cycle fluctuations. For λ, I follow Julio Rotemberg and Michael Woodford (1999) in calibrating the markup to 20 percent. The productivity term ϕ turns out to be a scaling parameter; I normalize it to 0.10.

The remaining two parameters, F and L, are chosen to match the growth rate of GDP per capita and the average GDP share of R&D. Empirically, the average growth rate of GDP per capita is 2 percent per year. The GDP share for total R&D (both private and public) has been roughly stable at about 2.5 percent for much of the post–World War II period. However, the relevant share for my purposes is private R&D, which has trended during this period from 1 percent prior, to just over 2 percent. To err on the side of caution, I forced the model to match the higher R&D share of 2 percent. This implies to a lower value for F and hence *less* procyclical R&D. If, instead, I had calibrated F to match a smaller R&D share, I would have needed a higher value of F to drive down profits and make R&D sufficiently less attractive that fewer resources

would be devoted to it. It is not obvious whether the appropriate output measure in the model is gross output or output net of fixed costs. However, at $F = 3.6$, R&D accounts for 2.0 percent of gross output and 2.2 percent of net output, so the distinction is relatively minor. Interestingly, for these parameter values, the model generates reasonable time variation in R&D, even though it was not designed to: the standard deviation of log R&D share in the model is 0.139 and 0.136 for gross and net output, respectively, compared to 0.137 for the log share of total R&D in NSF data from 1953 to 2002.

As a fraction of output, the parameters in Table 3 imply a fixed cost equal to 8.1 percent of gross output (and 8.8 percent of net output). By comparison, Ramey (1991) and Susanto Basu (1996) suggest nonproduction workers as a proxy for overhead labor. Nonproduction workers account for 20 percent of the labor force during the postwar period. Since labor accounts for two-thirds of output, this suggests an overhead cost of 13 percent of output. If anything, my estimate is overly conservative.

To solve the model, I use a collocation method in which I approximate the respective value functions with n^{th} order polynomials, where I choose the coefficients of the polynomial by requiring that the asset equations hold exactly at $n + 1$ points. Thus, to solve the planner's problem, I approximate $v_i(k)$ using a polynomial in k. To solve for the decentralized equilibrium, I approximate $R_i(W)$ and $w_i^*(w)$ using polynomials in W and w, respectively, and the function $V_i(w, W)$ with the polynomial $\sum_{k=0}^{n}\sum_{\ell=0}^{n-k}a_{k\ell}w^kW^\ell$. The coefficients of each respective polynomial are chosen so that either the equilibrium conditions or the planner's first-order conditions hold exactly at particular values of k, w, and W, respectively.[11] The results reported here are based on $n = 4$, although I confirmed that higher-order polynomials yielded nearly identical results.

---

[11] Following the recommendation of Kenneth L. Judd (1998), these points correspond to the roots of the Chebyshev polynomials, adapted to the limiting interval for the relevant variable. For $V_i(w, W)$, I use the triangular array $\{w_iW_j\}_{1 \le i \le j \le n+1}$, where w_i and W_j represent the roots of Chebyshev polynomials adapted to the limiting interval for equilibrium wealth. Note that I need to approximate $V(w, W)$ both on and off the equilibrium path (in which $w = W$) to approximate both $\partial V_i/\partial w$ and $\partial V_i/\partial W$.

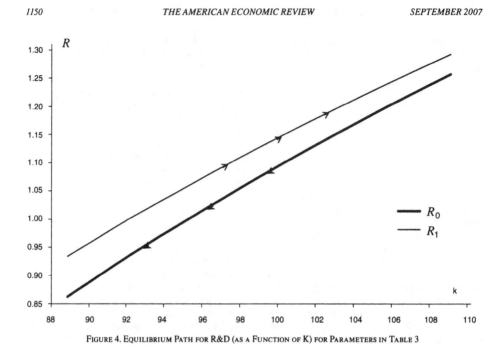

FIGURE 4. EQUILIBRIUM PATH FOR R&D (AS A FUNCTION OF K) FOR PARAMETERS IN TABLE 3

The purpose of solving for equilibrium is to determine whether, at the calibrated parameter values, the model can deliver procyclical R&D, and what role the bias plays in accounting for this pattern. It is important to note, however, that at this stage I have abstracted from a variable labor supply, which itself should contribute to procyclical R&D.

Figure 4 plots the functions $R_i(k)$ along the equilibrium path over the limiting set for k. For the values in Table 3, equilibrium R&D is procyclical. The extent of this procyclicality is modest: R&D in a boom is about 3–8 percent higher for a given value of k than in a recession. Moreover, since an increase in z_t stimulates capital accumulation, which raises k and provides even further incentive to undertake R&D, the actual path for R&D will appear to be even more procyclical. By contrast, solving the planner's problem reveals that the optimal path for R&D is countercyclical, i.e., $R_0(k) > R_1(k)$ for all limiting values of k. This suggests the procyclical bias in R&D must be large at empirically plausible parameter values, enough to turn R&D procyclical all by itself in an environment where it should be countercyclical.

One caveat in comparing the equilibrium and optimal paths for R&D is that the two differ not only in their implied cyclicality of R&D but also in the average level of R&D. At the assigned values, optimal R&D is much higher than equilibrium R&D. One might therefore ask if the planner would still prefer a countercyclical path if she were restricted to the same average level of R&D as prevails in equilibrium. This question can be addressed using a perturbation argument. Suppose aggregate productivity fluctuates between $Z_0 = 1 - \varepsilon$ and $Z_1 = 1 + \varepsilon$ for a small value ε. Let R denote nonstochastic steady-state equilibrium R&D when $Z_0 = Z_1 = 1$. For ε small, the planner's constrained optimum can be approximated by $R_0 = (1 - \zeta) R$ and $R_1 = (1 + \zeta)$ for some ζ. For $\varepsilon = 0.01$, I find that the household's value function is decreasing in ζ in the neighborhood of $\zeta = 0$. Thus, for small shocks, the optimal policy that is constrained to keep average R&D unchanged would opt to concentrate R&D in recessions. I confirm that this remains true for $\varepsilon = 0.06$, i.e., starting from a constant path for R&D, a small countercyclical perturbation from a constant R&D path raises welfare, while a small procyclical perturbation lowers it. The model unambiguously views procyclical equilibrium R&D as inefficient.

C. Robustness

The calibration exercise above reveals that the procyclical bias in R&D can be strong enough to account for the procyclicality of R&D all by itself. It also suggests that optimal policy should reverse the timing of R&D. The remainder of this section explores the robustness of these two results. To preview the remainder of the section, I first argue that small changes in certain parameters can significantly weaken the magnitude of the bias, enough that equilibrium R&D will no longer be procyclical. This suggests the bias toward procyclical R&D might not be able to account for the procyclicality of R&D by itself. I then argue that variable labor supply, which I have emphasized throughout as a potentially important consideration, can restore the procyclicality of R&D in these cases. Interestingly, plausible degrees of variable labor supply cannot, on their own, generate procyclical R&D, suggesting both elements are important. Finally, I argue that once we allow for variable labor supply, it may no longer be optimal to turn R&D countercyclical, although it will still be desirable to shift some R&D from booms to recessions.

I begin by examining the effects of changing some of the parameters in Table 3. One parameter of interest is the fixed cost F. Recall that the magnitude of the fixed cost determines how much profits vary with z_t. If I set F to zero (while adjusting L to keep average growth at 2 percent), equilibrium R&D turns countercyclical, just as predicted by Proposition 2 for the special case of the model analyzed earlier. So how large must the fixed cost be for equilibrium R&D to be procyclical? The answer turns out to be 3.3, which corresponds to 7.9 percent of gross output and 8.6 percent of net output at the implied parameter values. It would therefore not take a much smaller fixed cost than the one I originally calibrated to turn R&D countercyclical. That said, fixed costs are probably higher than my estimate, not lower. Aside from the observation that the share of nonproduction workers all by itself is roughly 13 percent, profit rates in the United States are quite small, while smaller values of F would imply large profit rates (as well

as counterfactually large R&D shares, since becoming a leading-edge producer turns more lucrative).

Another parameter of interest is the markup λ, especially given the difficulty in estimating marginal cost properly. Since markups determine profits, it is not surprising that this parameter has important implications for the magnitude of the procyclical bias in R&D. Again, as I varied λ, I adjusted L and F to match a 2 percent average growth rate and a 2 percent share of R&D in gross output. Since a higher markup by itself implies higher profits, we need a higher fixed cost (measured as a fraction of output) to lower profits back down and keep the equilibrium share of R&D at 2 percent. But since a higher fixed cost is associated with more volatile profits, a higher markup λ should lead to more procyclical R&D, while a lower markup should lead to less procyclical R&D. I find that λ must be at least 1.15 for R&D to remain procyclical; for values of λ below this cutoff, there will be some values of k that prevail in the long-run for which $R_0(k) > R_1(k)$. When $\lambda = 1.10$, equilibrium R&D will be strictly higher in recessions for all limiting values of k. Thus, slightly smaller markups (in an absolute sense) dramatically lower the magnitude of the bias inherent to R&D.

Yet another important parameter is μ, which governs the persistence of fluctuations. If profits revert to their long-run average very quickly, firms will expect roughly similar profit streams regardless of whether they undertake R&D in recessions or in booms. This suggests that the bias will lessen as z_t becomes less persistent, i.e., at higher values of μ. In fact, μ does not need to be much higher for the procyclicality evident in Figure 4 to break down. If $\mu \geq 0.23$, which implies cycles that last on average about nine years rather than ten, there will be levels of k in the limit set for which $R_0(k) > R_1(k)$. A similar issue arises if we allow for asymmetric transition rates. Suppose the transition rate for z_t is given by μ_0 in recessions and μ_1 in booms. As an example, suppose we set $\mu_0 = 0.5$ and $\mu_1 = 0.125$, so that the average cycle still lasts ten years on average, but recessions last only two years while booms last eight years. To leave the unconditional standard deviation of productivity unchanged, I also recalibrate $Z_0 = 0.88$ and $Z_1 = 1.03$. Equilibrium R&D in this case turns out to be countercyclical. More generally, the bias appears to become weaker whenever at least one of the states is not very persistent. This pattern is consistent with the findings in Comin and Gertler (2006) that R&D is more procyclical at medium-term frequencies than at high frequencies; shocks that cause profits to remain below average for extended periods are more likely to depress R&D than high-frequency shocks.

In sum, the finding that the procyclical bias can account for procyclical R&D appears somewhat fragile: a slightly lower fixed cost, a slightly lower markup, or a slightly less persistent process all lead to countercyclical equilibrium R&D. This does not deny the main point of the quantitative exercise, however, which is that the procyclical bias in R&D can be significant. Specifically, making profits more volatile by introducing fixed costs leads to large shifts in R&D activity toward booms. What the robustness analysis instead suggests is that there are probably additional forces that contribute to the procyclical pattern in R&D, which I have not accounted for. As noted earlier, one important consideration I have ignored up to now is that labor supply varies over the cycle. I now modify the model to incorporate this possibility.

Rather than introduce leisure as a separate argument in the utility function and allowing households to choose their labor supply, I follow Fatas (2000) in assuming labor varies exogenously over the cycle. Although this ignores certain welfare issues, this approach should still serve us well in gauging whether the model is able to account for cyclical patterns in R&D. In particular, if I did introduce a preference for leisure, I would have had to calibrate preferences so that the implied endogenous variation in hours would accord with the same volatility in hours I already match with exogenous variation. As long as variation in hours does not affect other aspects of the model such as the marginal utility of consumption, the implied equilibrium paths should be the same whether labor varies endogenously or exogenously. Empirically, the standard deviation of detrended hours is on the order of 6 percent, roughly the same as for total factor productivity. I therefore assume that when $z_t = Z_0$ then $L_t = 0.94 \cdot L$ and when $z_t = 1$ then $L_t = 1.06 \cdot L$, where L is the same as in Table 1.

Before examining whether this modification can salvage the ability of the model to generate procyclical R&D for slight perturbations of the

parameters in Table 3, I first ask whether variable labor can generate procyclical R&D on its own. In particular, suppose I weaken the procyclical bias in R&D by setting the fixed cost F to zero. Could fluctuations in labor supply generate a procyclical pattern in R&D? The answer is no: when I set $F = 0$ and recalibrate L to match a steady-state growth rate of 2 percent, equilibrium R&D turns out to be countercyclical. Variable labor supply is compatible with procyclical R&D when $F = 0$ only when the standard deviation of labor is at least 11 percent, almost twice as much as labor productivity. Thus, when I minimize the extent of the procyclical bias in R&D in the model, it needs extraordinarily volatile labor supply to overcome the incentive to concentrate innovation activity in recessions. Although previous papers with variable labor have been able to generate procyclical equilibrium R&D without introducing fixed costs to make profits more volatile, e.g., Fatas (2000) and Comin and Gertler (2006), they also abstract from changes in the opportunity cost of R&D over the cycle. The findings here suggest that if this feature were incorporated, these models would have a difficult time generating procyclical R&D in equilibrium without further modifications.

Although variable labor supply cannot generate procyclical R&D in the absence of fixed costs, it can contribute to making equilibrium R&D procyclical when fixed costs lead to moderately volatile profits that are not quite enough to make equilibrium R&D procyclical. To gauge the ability of variable labor supply to amplify the procyclicality of R&D, I re-solve the model for the benchmark parameters in Table 3 allowing fluctuations in labor supply of 6 percent. Figure 5 compares the implied equilibrium path for R&D with the path in Figure 4 where labor is constant over time. With variable labor supply, the long-run range for k is wider, and for each k the variation in R&D dwarfs the variability when labor is assumed fixed. More precisely, whereas the standard deviation of the log share of R&D when labor is fixed over time is 0.139, with variable labor supply this standard deviation almost triples to 0.414. The empirical counterpart between 1953 and 2002, as noted earlier, is 0.137. This suggests that once we allow for variable labor supply, the model predicts overly volatile R&D. Recall, however, that fairly modest changes to some of the parameters can turn

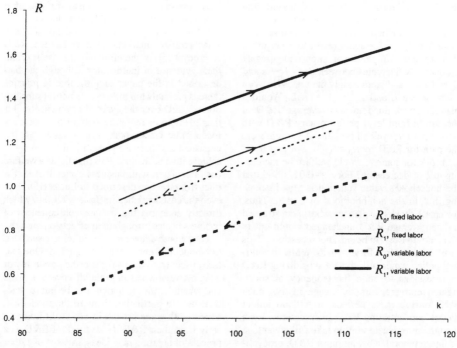

FIGURE 5. EQUILIBRIUM R&D FOR PARAMETERS IN TABLE 3, FIXED AND VARIABLE LABOR

R&D countercyclical in the absence of labor supply shocks. For example, suppose we set $\mu_0 = 0.5$ and $\mu_1 = 0.125$, and in addition we lower the markup λ to 1.15. In the absence of variable labor supply, equilibrium R&D would be moderately countercyclical. However, with variable labor supply, equilibrium R&D is procyclical. The implied standard deviation of the log share of R&D is 0.193, much closer to its empirical counterpart. Allowing for slightly countercyclical markups can presumably bring the volatility of R&D even lower so as to accord with what we observe in the data. Quantitatively, then, both the procyclical bias and variable labor supply play important roles in accounting for the procyclicality of R&D, since the only way for the model not to generate overly volatile R&D is if neither factor generates procyclical R&D by itself.

Finally, I turn to the question of the nature of optimal policy. When I assumed constant labor supply over time, I found that the optimal path for R&D was countercyclical. That is,

it is desirable not just to reallocate some R&D from booms to recessions on the margin to offset the tendency of private agents to undertake too much R&D in booms. Policymakers should actually reverse the timing of R&D, as intertemporal substitution arguments dictate. However, when labor supply varies over time, it is no longer obvious that reversing R&D is still optimal. Intertemporal substitution argues that we should allocate more resources to production in booms when the return to this activity is relatively high, and we should allocate more resources to R&D in recessions when the return to this activity is relatively high. When labor resources are fixed, this necessitates shifting labor resources between the two activities. But if labor resources are more abundant in booms, it might not be necessary to draw down resources from innovation to allocate more resources to production and take advantage of its temporarily high return. Similarly, if labor resources are more scarce in recessions, it might be too costly

1154   THE AMERICAN ECONOMIC REVIEW   SEPTEMBER 2007

to take away resources from this activity and devote it to innovation. To gauge whether optimal policy remains countercyclical with variable labor supply, I once again resort to a perturbation argument. In particular, suppose aggregate productivity fluctuates between $Z_0 = 1 - \varepsilon$ and $Z_1 = 1 + \varepsilon$, and labor supply fluctuates between $L_0 = 1 - \varepsilon L$ and $L_1 = (1 + \varepsilon)L$. Would a planner constrained to keep average R&D at the equilibrium level prefer to vary R&D with or against the cycle? Formally, if we represent the path for R&D by $R_0 = (1 - \zeta)R$ and $R_1 = (1 + \zeta)R$ for some ζ, would welfare be increasing in ζ or decreasing? For $\varepsilon = 0.01$, I find that the household's value function is now increasing in ζ in the neighborhood of $\zeta = 0$. Thus, for small shocks, a planner who is constrained to keep average R&D unchanged would opt to concentrate R&D in booms, not recessions. This result remains true for $\varepsilon = 0.06$. While the optimal policy would still dictate subsidizing R&D in recessions to undo the tendency of short-sighted entrepreneurs to engage in too much R&D during these periods, it will no longer dictate concentrating R&D in recessions. Even though entrepreneurs fail to take full advantage of intertemporal substitution in R&D, procyclical R&D may not be inherently inefficient. Still, macroeconomic shocks lead to an unnecessarily high cost of achieving growth by allocating too much R&D to boom periods when its cost is highest.

V. Conclusion

This paper examines why R&D activity might be procyclical despite the notion that recessions are the ideal time to undertake such activities. The main result of the paper is that because of dynamic externalities, there is a tendency in decentralized markets toward engaging in too much R&D in booms. Quantitatively, it appears that this bias could generate procyclical equilibrium R&D in an environment where the optimal path for R&D is countercyclical. Moreover, this bias implies that society would be better off reallocating some of its R&D from booms to recessions, precisely because it allows the economy to grow at a lower resource cost. However, this conclusion does not necessarily imply that R&D should be countercyclical. In particular, certain considerations absent from the basic model of

intertemporal substitution, such as variable labor supply, can make it desirable to undertake more R&D in booms, just not to the full extent it is in a decentralized market. The mere fact that R&D is procyclical is therefore not in itself *prima facie* evidence of inefficiency, although the bias described in the paper suggests that in practice there is probably too little intertemporal substitution of R&D over the cycle. Procyclical R&D is thus likely to increase the welfare costs of macroeconomic shocks, both because shocks are too persistent and because growth is more costly to achieve than necessary. This highlights a welfare cost associated with business cycles that is distinct from the one described in Lucas (1987), or even the cost described in Barlevy (2004), which directly concerns the welfare consequences of business cycles through their effects on growth.

I close with a few remarks on some issues that the model presented here has ignored. One feature absent from the analysis is the possibility of a lag between when an initial discovery is made and when the idea it spawns can be put to practical use. In particular, firms in the model can expect with some probability to profit immediately from their R&D. If we think of R&D as a process of creating new ideas, this seems rather far-fetched. One could instead interpret R&D in the model as consisting mostly of actions involving the development of ideas as opposed to the creation of ideas; good ideas are always available, but entrepreneurs need to hire labor resources to make them practical. The increase in R&D during recessions should then be seen as an acceleration in the development of existing projects. This interpretation is reasonable, given that on average roughly 70 percent of R&D expenditures are at the development stage, according to NSF estimates. However, the notion that ideas are always readily available and are not the result of deliberate effort is unsatisfactory. If research activity declines in recessions, there shouldn't be as many ideas around for entrepreneurs to develop in booms. It would be preferable to model research and development as separate stages, both of which require resources that could alternatively be used in production, and study their behavior over the cycle. Comin and Gertler (2006) make some progress in this direction. It seems reasonable to conjecture that research and development will remain biased toward booms in such a model. Intuitively, as

VOL. 97 NO. 4   BARLEVY: ON THE CYCLICALITY OF RESEARCH AND DEVELOPMENT   1155

long as shocks are persistent, positive shocks today will increase the probability of higher profits T periods from now. The incentive to increase R&D in response to a favorable macro shock will be mitigated given discounting and the weaker correlation across long horizons, but it should not disappear altogether. Another force that might mitigate these incentives is if research were cumulative, so that the chance of a successful discovery would be lower if the firm did not undertake much research prior to the favorable shock (in contrast to the way it is modelled here). In industries where research builds heavily on past work and where diffusion lags are long, such as pharmaceuticals, the incentive to concentrate research in booms may be negligible. However, in industries where diffusion lags between discovery and implementation are considerably shorter, such as software and computer equipment, there may still be a marked procyclical bias in the timing of research activities.

Another feature missing from the model is the possibility of strategically delaying using an idea that has already been developed. In particular, firms might choose to engage in R&D during recessions, when the opportunity cost of innovation is relatively low, but then wait to implement their ideas when profits are high. Shleifer (1986) and Francois and Lloyd Ellis (2003) advocate this view. There is reason to believe, however, that the possibility of strategic delay is not too important in practice. First, if entrepreneurs are sufficiently impatient, they may not want to wait to implement new technologies. Second, empirical evidence suggests firms are not very reluctant to release the results of their research. For example, Griliches (1990) reports that firms tend to take out patents—and thus publicize their new ideas—very soon after undertaking R&D efforts and long before they actually put their new ideas to use. In addition, strategic delay over the cycle would imply a mismatch between R&D activity and patenting over the business cycle, since R&D activity should peak in recessions while patents should peak in booms. However, Griliches reports that R&D and patents are highly synchronized over the business cycle. These findings suggest strategic delay is not widespread in practice. Nevertheless, given the emphasis in Shleifer (1986) on booms as periods of mass implementation, it is certainly worth incorporating this feature in future work.

APPENDIX A: DATA CONSTRUCTION

NSF Data

Data on real R&D expenditures performed and financed by industry are taken from National Patterns of Research Development Resources, 2003, Appendix B, Table B-10, column 23. Data on full-time equivalent employment from 1957 to 1999 were taken from Tables H-19 and B-25 in the NSF Industrial Research & Development Information System, which reports the number of employees for January of each year. I assign each January's observation to the previous year. Beyond 1999, I took data from various NSF reports. Data for January 2000 was taken from Table 1 in the NSF report "U.S. Industrial R&D Expenditures and R&D-to-Sales Ratio Reach Historical Highs in 2000." Data for January 2001 were taken from Table 1 in the NSF report "Largest Single-Year Decline in U.S. Industrial R&D Expenditures Reported for 2002." Data for January 2002 and January 2003 were taken from Table 3 in the NSF report "Increase in US Industrial R&D Expenditures Reported for 2003 Makes Up For Earlier Decline." All reports are available from the NSF Web site, www.nsf.gov.

Compustat

All Compustat variables were taken from the North American Industrial dataset. The particular data used correspond to the following original series in Compustat:

- R&D expenditures: item46
- Cash flow (after R&D expenditures): item14 + item18
- Cash flow (before R&D expenditures): item14 + item18 + item 46

- Assets: item6
- Liabilities: item181
- Short term debt (due within one year): item44
- Long term debt (due beyond one year): item 9
- Net value of capital stock: item8
- Market value of equity at year end: item24 × item25 + item10

All series are deflated by the implicit GDP deflator to arrive at real values. To match the timing, I assigned the stock price to the year after it was reported. To compute average growth in R&D, I took all firms that reported positive amounts of R&D at some point. From these, I excluded firms that were incorporated outside the United States, as indicated by a Compustat variable FINC that is different from zero. In addition, I eliminated all duplicate entries of the same firm (often identified by the presence of PRE-FASB in their title). Although few firms have duplicate records, some of these are large companies (e.g., Ford Motor Company, General Motors, General Electric) and leaving in duplicate records would have affected weighted averages. In computing the cyclicality of stock prices, my selection criterion was analogous: I took all firms for which a closing price, numbers of shares outstanding, and the value of preferred stock were available, and then eliminated firms incorporated outside the United States and duplicate entries.

Industry Output

Industry output is constructed from three sources. First, I obtained a series for real gross output for various four-digit SIC codes in manufacturing from the NBER manufacturing industry database compiled by Bartelsman, Becker, and Gray. For each four-digit industry, I calculated nominal gross output as the sum of value added and material costs. To arrive at real gross output, I divided this measure by the shipments deflator provided by Bartelsman et al. for each industry.

Second, I obtained measures of real gross output by three-digit NAICS codes across all industries from the BEA, which compiles this series from 1987 to 2004. Note that some industries are available at a more disaggregate level than three digits (for example, motor vehicles are distinguished from other transportation equipment, and legal services and computer system design are distinguished from miscellaneous professional and technical services), while some are available only at a more aggregated level (for example, real output is not reported for separate three-digit industries for wholesale trade or retail trade). I paired each Compustat firm to the gross output reported for its respective NAICS code by the BEA.

Third, the BEA reports real value added for the same NAICS industry categories from 1947 to 2004.

APPENDIX B: PROOFS OF PROPOSITIONS

PROOF OF PROPOSITION 1:
For given values of $\{R_i\}_{i=0,1}$, the system given by (11) reduces to ordinary linear differential equations in $V(Z_i, M)$. Standard theorems ensure this system has a unique solution. Hence, starting with values for R_i, we can use the method of undetermined coefficients to find the unique value functions $V(Z_i, M)$ associated with a given pair (R_0, R_1). I conjecture that the value function $V(\cdot, \cdot)$ takes the form

$$V(Z_i, M) = v_i \lambda^{M(1-\alpha)}.$$

Differentiating this function with respect to M yields

$$\frac{\partial V}{\partial M} = (1-\alpha) v_i \lambda^{M(1-\alpha)} \ln\lambda.$$

Substituting this into (11) yields a system of independent linear equations in the coefficients v_i:

$$\rho v_i = Z_i(L-R_i)^{1-\alpha} - F + \mu\left(v_{1-i}-v_i\right) + (1 - \alpha) v_i \phi R_i \ln \lambda.$$

Since the right-hand sice of (11) is strictly concave in R_i, the first-order condition is both necessary and sufficient to characterize the optimal R_i. The first-order condition is given by

(B1) $$- (1 - \alpha)Z_i\lambda^{M(1-\alpha)}(L-R_i)^{-\alpha} + \frac{\partial V}{\partial M}\phi \le 0,$$

with equality if $R_i > 0$. Substituting the expression for $V(\cdot,\cdot)$, we obtain

(B2) $$R_i = \begin{cases} L - \left(\dfrac{Z_i}{v_i\phi\ln\lambda}\right)^{1/\alpha} & \text{if } v_i > \left(\dfrac{Z_i}{\phi L^\alpha\ln\lambda}\right), \\ 0 & \text{otherwise.} \end{cases}$$

If we substitute this expression into the asset equation (11), we obtain a pair of equations with v_{1-i} as a function of v_i that hold at the optimal R_i:

$$v_{1-i} = g_{1-i}(v_i) = \begin{cases} \dfrac{\rho + \mu - (1 - \alpha)\phi L \ln \lambda}{\mu}v_i - \dfrac{\alpha}{\mu} Z_i^{1/\alpha}(v_i\phi \ln \lambda)^{1-(1/\alpha)} + \dfrac{F}{\mu} & \text{if } v_i > \dfrac{Z_i}{\phi L^\alpha \ln \lambda}, \\ \dfrac{\rho + \mu}{\mu} v_i - \dfrac{Z_i L^{1-\alpha}}{\mu} + \dfrac{F}{\mu} & \text{otherwise.} \end{cases}$$

The optimal program thus corresponds to any pair (v_0^*, v_1^*) which solves the equations

$$v_1^* = g_1(v_0^*) \qquad v_0^* = g_0(v_1^*),$$

where each $g_{1-i}(\cdot)$ is continuous and differentiable, since the left- and right-hand derivatives at $v_i = Z_i/(\phi L^\alpha \ln \lambda)$ are both equal to $(\rho + \mu)/\mu$. Since $\rho > (1 - \alpha)\phi L\ln \lambda$, it follows that $\partial g_{1-i}(v_i)/\partial v_i > 1$ for all v_i. To prove the system of equations has a unique solution, note that since $\partial g_{1-i}/\partial v_i > 1 > 0$ for all v_i, the function $g_{1-i}(\cdot)$ must be invertible. An equilibrium therefore involves a value v_0^* such that $g_1(v_0^*) - g_0^{-1}(v_0^*) = 0$. Differentiating this condition with respect to v_0^* yields

$$\frac{d}{dx}[g_1(x) - g_0^{-1}(x)] = \frac{dg_1}{dx} - \left(\frac{dg_0}{dx}\right)^{-1} > 0.$$

This monotonicity insures there is at most one value of v_0^*. To establish existence, note that since I have assumed $F \le Z_i L^{1-\alpha}$, $g_1(0) < 0$ and $g_0^{-1}(0) > 0$. Hence, $g_1(0) - g_0^{-1}(0) < 0$, and is finite. The fact that $\lim_{x\to\infty} dg_1/dx > 1 > \lim_{x\to\infty}(dg_0/dx)^{-1}$ implies $(\partial/\partial x)[g_1(x) - g_0^{-1}(x)]$ is strictly bounded away from 0, and so $g_1(x) - g_0^{-1}(x) \to \infty$ as $x \to \infty$. The existence of v_0^* and v_1^* follows from continuity.

Next, suppose that the optimal path dictates $R_i > 0$ for both i. I need to show $R_0 > R_1$. I begin by showing that $v_1^* > v_0^*$. Since $R_i > 0$, the asset equations imply

$$v_{1-i}^* = \frac{\rho + \mu - (1 - \alpha)\phi L \ln \lambda}{\mu}v_i^* - \frac{\alpha}{\mu} Z_i^{1/\alpha}(v_i^*\phi\ln\lambda)^{1-(1/\alpha)} + \frac{F}{\mu}$$

$$\equiv av_i^* - bZ_i^{1/\alpha}(v_i^*)^{1-(1/\alpha)} + \frac{F}{\mu}.$$

94

Consider the fixed point $\hat{v}_i$ which solves $\hat{v}_i = g_{1-i}(\hat{v}_i)$, i.e.,

$$\hat{v}_i = a\hat{v}_i - bZ_i^{1/\alpha}(\hat{v}_i)^{1-(1/\alpha)} + \frac{F}{\mu}.$$

It is easy to show $\hat{v}_i$ exists, is unique, and must be positive. Implicit differentiation implies

$$\frac{d\hat{v}_i}{dZ_i} = \frac{\frac{b}{\alpha}\left(\frac{\hat{v}_i}{Z_i}\right)^{1-(1/\alpha)}}{(\alpha-1) + \frac{1-\alpha}{\alpha}b\left(\frac{Z_i}{\hat{v}_i}\right)^{1/\alpha}} > 0$$

so that $Z_0 < Z_1 \Rightarrow \hat{v}_0 < \hat{v}_1$. Since $dg_i^{-1}/dx < 1$, we know that for any $x < \hat{v}_1$, it must be true that $x - g_0^{-1}(x) < 0$. Since

$$g_1(\hat{v}_0) - g_0^{-1}(\hat{v}_0) = \hat{v}_0 - g_0^{-1}(\hat{v}_0)$$

and since $\hat{v}_0 < \hat{v}_1$, then $g_1(\hat{v}_0) - g_0^{-1}(\hat{v}_0) < 0$. Since $g_1(v_0^*) - g_0^{-1}(v_0^*) = 0$ and $g_1(x) - g_0^{-1}(x)$ is increasing in x, it follows that $v_0^* > \hat{v}_0$. Moreover, since $dg_i^{-1}/dx > 1$, the fact that $g_1(\hat{v}_0) = \hat{v}_0$ implies $g_1(x) > x$ for any $x > \hat{v}_0$, including v_0^*. This implies $g_1(v_0^*) > v_0^*$. But since $v_1^* = g_1(v_0^*)$, it follows that $v_1^* > v_0^*$.

Next, I use the fact that $v_1^* > v_0^*$ to argue $v_1/Z_1 < v_0/Z_0$, which is sufficient to establish $R_1 < R_0$. Combining the equations $v_{1-i}^* = g_{1-i}(v_i^*)$ for both values yields the equation

$$av_0^* - bZ_0^{1/\alpha}(v_0^*)^{1-(1/\alpha)} - v_1^* = av_1^* - bZ_1^{1/\alpha}(v_1^*)^{1-(1/\alpha)} - v_0^*,$$

which can be rearranged to yield

$$\frac{v_0^*}{v_1^*} = \frac{(a+1) - b\left(\frac{Z_i}{v_1^*}\right)^{1/\alpha}}{(a+1) - b\left(\frac{Z_0}{v_0^*}\right)^{1/\alpha}}$$

so that

$$v_1^* > v_0^* \Leftrightarrow \frac{v_1^*}{v_0^*} < \frac{Z_i}{Z_0}.$$

Given the expression for R_i in (B2), this implies $R_0 > R_1$.

PROOF OF PROPOSITION 2:

I first derive expressions for the value of a successful innovation v_i at each level of productivity Z_i. For any z_t-measurable function $X(\cdot)$, the integral

$$W_i(M_{t_0}) = E\left[\int_{t_0}^{\infty} \theta_t \cdot \lambda^{(1-\alpha)M_t} X(z_t) e^{-\rho(t-t_0)} dt \,\middle|\, z_{t0} = Z_i\right]$$

for any z_t-measurable $R(\cdot)$ given $M_t = \phi R$ can be characterized by the recursive system of equations

$$\rho + \mu = W_i(M) = \lambda^{(1-\alpha)M}X(Z_i) + \mu W_{1-i}(M) + \left[\frac{\partial W_i}{\partial M} - W_i(M)\right]\phi R_i.$$

Define $R_i = R(Z_i)$. Using the method of undetermined coefficients, we can verify that $W_i(M) = w_i\lambda^{(1-\alpha)M}$, where

$$w_i = \frac{\omega(R_{1-i})X(Z_i) + \mu X(Z_{1-i})}{\omega(R_i)\omega(R_{1-i}) - \mu^2},$$

where we define

$$\omega(x) = \rho + \mu + (1 - (1 - \alpha)\ln\lambda)\phi x.$$

Using the expression for profits π, and setting $y_i = L - R_i$, the value of a successful innovation v_i can be written as

(B3) $$v_i = \frac{(\lambda - 1)\left[\omega(L - y_{1-i})y_i + \mu\dfrac{Z_{1-i}}{Z_i}y_{1-i}^{1-\alpha}y_i^{\alpha}\right] - [\omega(L - y_{1-i}) + \mu]\dfrac{\lambda y_i^{\alpha}F}{(1-\alpha)Z_i}}{\omega(L - y_i)\omega(L - y_{1-i}) - \mu^2}.$$

In an interior equilibrium, $v_0 = v_1 = \phi^{-1}$. We can easily rule out the case where $y_i = 0$ in equilibrium, since this implies the marginal product of labor is infinite and hence must yield higher utility than using it in R&D. For $y_i \neq 0$, we can rewrite v_0 and v_1 in terms of y_1 and $\xi = y_0/y_1$ as

(B4) $$v_0 = \frac{(\lambda - 1)\left[\omega(L - y_1)\xi + \mu\dfrac{Z_{1-i}}{Z_i}\xi^{\alpha}\right]y_1 - [\omega(L - y_1) + \mu]\dfrac{\lambda\xi^{\alpha}Fy_1^{\alpha}}{(1-\alpha)Z_0}}{\omega(L - y_1)\omega(L - \xi y_1) - \mu^2};$$

(B5) $$v_1 = \frac{(\lambda - 1)\left[\omega(L - \xi y_1) + \mu\dfrac{Z_0}{Z_1}\xi^{1-\alpha}\right]y_1 - [\omega(L - \xi y_1) + \mu]\dfrac{\lambda Fy_1^{\alpha}}{(1-\alpha)Z_1}}{\omega(L - y_1)\omega(L - \xi y_1) - \mu^2}.$$

A necessary condition for equilibrium is that $v_0 - v_1 = 0$, which can be rearranged to yield the condition

(B6) $$\frac{\lambda Fy_1^{\alpha-1}}{Z_1(\lambda - 1)(1 - \alpha)}(A_0 - A_1(y_1)\xi - A_2(y_1)\xi^{\alpha}) - 1 + \xi + h(\xi) = 0,$$

where

$$A_0 = \frac{\omega(L) + \mu}{\omega(L)};$$

$$A_1(y_1) = \frac{(1 - (1 - \alpha)\ln\lambda)\phi y_1}{\omega(L)};$$

$$A_2(y_1) = \frac{\omega(L - y_1) + \mu}{\omega(L)}\frac{Z_1}{Z_0};$$

and

$$h(\xi) = \frac{\mu}{\omega(L)}\left[\frac{Z_1}{Z_0}\xi^\alpha - \frac{Z_0}{Z_1}\xi^{1-\alpha}\right].$$

For convenience, let us define

$$Q(\xi,y_1) \equiv \frac{\lambda F y_1^{\alpha-1}}{Z_1(\lambda-1)(1-\alpha)}(A_0 - A_1(y_1)\xi - A_2(y_1)\xi^\alpha) - 1 + \xi + h(\xi)$$

so that we can now rewrite (B6) more compactly as $Q(\xi,y_1) = 0$.

RESULT 1:
I first wish to show that there exist values F^* and $\overline{F}$ such that if $F > F^*$ and $F < \overline{F}$, there exists an F^* such that for all $F \in (F^*,\overline{F})$, there exist pairs (y_0, y_1) where $y_0 > y_1$ and $Q(y_0/y_1, y_1) = 0$. I then use this solution to derive values $R_1 > R_0$ which further satisfy the equilibrium conditions $v_0(R_0, R_1) = v_1(R_0, R_1) = \phi^{-1}$.
I begin with the following lemma.

LEMMA 1: *Suppose* $\ln \lambda < (1-\alpha)^{-1}$. *For any* $F > 0$, *there exists a unique* $\hat{y}_F > 0$ *such that* $v_0(\hat{y}_F, \hat{y}_F) = v_1(\hat{y}_F, \hat{y}_F)$. *Moreover, there exists an* $F^* > 0$ *such that* $v_1(\hat{y}_F, \hat{y}_F) < \phi^{-1}$ *for* $F < F^*$ *and* $v_1(\hat{y}_F, \hat{y}_F) > \phi^{-1}$ *for* $F > F^*$.

PROOF:
Consider the equation $v_0(y, y) = v_1(y, y)$. Substituting in and rearranging yields

(B7) $\quad \mu(Z_1 + Z_0)\dfrac{y^{1-\alpha}}{F} + \dfrac{\lambda}{(\lambda-1)(1-\alpha)}(1 - (1-\alpha)\ln\lambda)\phi y = \dfrac{\lambda(\omega(L)+\mu)}{(\lambda-1)(1-\alpha)}.$

Since $\ln \lambda < (1-\alpha)^{-1}$, the left-hand side of this equation is monotonically increasing in y and ranges from 0 to ∞ as y ranges from 0 to ∞. Since the right-hand side in (B7) is a strictly positive constant, there exists a unique value $\hat{y}_F$ for which the equation is satisfied. Moreover, this $\hat{y}_F$ is monotonically increasing in F. Taking limits, $\hat{y}_F \to 0$ as $F \to 0$, while $\hat{y}_F \to L + (\rho + 2\mu)/[(1 - (1-\alpha)\ln\lambda)\phi]$ as $F \to \infty$, i.e., the value at which $\omega(L - \hat{y}_F) = -\mu$.
At $y_0 = y_1 = y$, the value of a successful innovation is given by

$$v_i(y,y) = (\lambda-1)\frac{\left(\omega(L-y) + \mu\dfrac{Z_{1-i}}{Z_i}\right)y - \dfrac{(\omega(L-y)+\mu)\lambda F y^\alpha}{(\lambda-1)(1-\alpha)Z_i}}{\omega^2(L-y) - \mu^2}.$$

Setting $y = \hat{y}_F$ and using (B7), this expression reduces to

$$v_i(\hat{y}_F, \hat{y}_F) = (\lambda-1)\frac{\left(\omega(L-\hat{y}_F) + \mu\dfrac{Z_{1-i}}{Z_i}\right)\hat{y}_F - \dfrac{\mu(Z_1+Z_0)\hat{y}_F}{Z_i}}{\omega^2(L-\hat{y}_F) - \mu^2}$$

$$= \frac{(\lambda-1)\hat{y}_F}{\omega(L-\hat{y}_F) + \mu}.$$

Hence, $v_1(\hat{y}_F, \hat{y}_F)$ is monotonically increasing in $\hat{y}_F$, which in turn is monotonically increasing in F. As noted above, $\hat{y}_F \in [0, L + \frac{\rho + 2\mu}{(1 - (1 - \alpha)\ln\lambda)\phi})$, which implies v_i ranges between 0 and ∞. The existence of F^* follows from continuity.

Returning to the original proof, for any value of F, define the set

$$\Omega_F = \left\{ (y_0, y_1) \mid y_1 > 0, \ Q\left(\frac{y_o}{y_1}, y_1\right) = 0 \right\}.$$

My strategy will be to show that for $F > F^*$ as defined in the lemma, there exists an element $(y_0, y_1) \in \Omega_F$ such that $(y_0 > y_1)$ and where $v_0(y_0, y_1) = v_1(y_0, y_1) = \phi^{-1}$.

For any value of $\xi \geq 1$, consider the values of y_1 for which $(\xi y_1, y_1) \in \Omega_F$. For $\xi_1 = 1$, we know from the lemma that there exists a unique such value, namely $y_1 = \hat{y}_F$. I now argue that for any $\xi > 1$, there exists a unique value $\hat{y}_\xi$ such that $(\xi \hat{y}_\xi, \hat{y}_\xi) \in \Omega_F$.

I begin by rearranging $Q(\xi, y_1)$ to get

$$Q(\xi, y_1)$$

$$= \frac{\lambda F}{Z_1(1 - \alpha)(\lambda - 1)} \left(\left[\frac{Z_1}{Z_0}\xi^\alpha - \xi \right] \frac{(1 - (1 - \alpha)\ln\lambda)\phi}{\omega(L)} y_1^\alpha + \frac{\omega(L) + \mu}{\omega(L)} \left[1 - \frac{Z_1}{Z_0}\xi^\alpha \right] y_1^{\alpha - 1} \right) - H(\xi),$$

where $H(\xi) = h(\xi) - 1 + \xi$ does not depend on y_1. For $\xi \geq 1$, the coefficient on y_1^α is positive, while the coefficient on $y_1^{\alpha - 1}$ is negative. Hence, for a fixed ξ, $Q(\xi, y_1)$ is monotonically increasing in y_1, so there can be at most one value of y_1 for which $Q(\xi, y_1) = 0$. If we take the limit as $y_1 \to 0$, the limit tends to $-\infty$ since $y_1^{\alpha - 1}$ rows arbitrarily large and its coefficient is negative. If we instead take the limit as, $y_1 \to \infty$, the limit tends to ∞ since y^α grows arbitrarily and its coefficient is positive. The existence of $\hat{y}_\xi$ follows from continuity. Continuity also implies that the path $(\xi \hat{y}_\xi, \hat{y}_\xi)$ for $\xi \geq 1$ forms a continuous path in (y_0, y_1) space.

As $\xi \to \infty$, the path $(\xi \hat{y}_\xi, \hat{y}_\xi)$ must limit to $(y_0, 0)$ for some y_0. This is illustrated graphically in Figure B1, where the heavy line depicts a segment of the set Ω_F. A fixed ξ corresponds to a ray in (y_0, y_1) space, and increasing ξ implies rotating this ray clockwise toward the y_0 axis. Using the expressions for $v_0(y_0, y_1)$ and $v_1(y_0, y_1)$, taking the limit as $y_1 \to 0$, implies

$$v_1 = 0;$$

$$v_0 = \frac{(\lambda - 1)\omega(L)y_0 - \frac{\omega(L) + \mu\lambda F}{(1 - \alpha)Z_0}y_o^\alpha}{\omega(L - y_0)\omega(L) - \mu^2}.$$

There can therefore be only two limiting values of y_0 at which $v_0(y_0, 0) = v_1(y_0, 0)$, namely $y_0 = 0$ and

$$y_0 = \tilde{y}_0 \equiv \left[\frac{(\omega(L) + \mu)\lambda F}{\omega(L)(\lambda - 1)(1 - \alpha)Z_0} \right]^{\frac{1}{1 - \alpha}}.$$

Thus, as ξ grows arbitrarily large, the path $(\xi \hat{y}_\xi, \hat{y}_\xi)$ must tend to either $(0, 0)$ or $(\tilde{y}_0, 0)$. Suppose the limit were $(0, 0)$. In this case, we can construct a function $\hat{x}_\xi$ where $\hat{x}_\xi > \hat{y}_\xi$ and $(\xi \hat{x}_\xi, \hat{x}_\xi) \to (\hat{x}_0, 0)$ as $\xi \to \infty$, where $\hat{x}_0 \in (0, \tilde{y}_0)$. Since $Q(\xi y_1, y_1) > 0$ whenever $y_1 > \hat{y}_\xi$ for $\xi > 1$, it follows that $Q(\xi \hat{x}_\xi, \hat{x}_\xi) > 0$. But then by continuity, $Q(y_0, 0) \geq 0$, which one can directly show is not true. It follows that $\lim_{\xi \to \infty}(\xi \hat{y}_\xi, \hat{y}_\xi) = (\tilde{y}_0, 0)$.

Finally, I need to show that there exists a $\xi > 1$ for which $v_0(\xi\hat{y}_\xi, \hat{y}_\xi) = v_1(\xi\hat{y}_\xi, \hat{y}_\xi) = \phi^{-1}$. By definition, $v_0(\xi\hat{y}_\xi, \hat{y}_\xi) = v_1(\xi\hat{y}_\xi, \hat{y}_\xi) =$ for all ξ. The issue is whether this joint value is equal to ϕ^{-1}. To determine this, note that at $\xi = 1$, $\hat{y}_\xi = \hat{y}_F$. If $F > F^*$, then $v_0(\hat{y}_F, \hat{y}_F) > \phi^{-1}$. Next, I just argued that $\lim_{\xi\to\infty}(\xi\hat{y}_\xi, \hat{y}_\xi) = (\tilde{y}_0, 0)$, at which point $v_0(\xi\hat{y}_\xi, \hat{y}_\xi) = v_1(\xi\hat{y}_\xi, \hat{y}_\xi) = 0$. If $v_0(\xi\hat{y}_\xi, \hat{y}_\xi) < \infty$ for all $\xi \geq 1$, then by continuity there must exist a value of $\xi > 1$ such that $v_0(\hat{y}_F, \hat{y}_F) = \phi^{-1}$ as long as $F > F^*$. However, $v_0(\xi\hat{y}_\xi, \hat{y}_\xi)$ may not be bounded for all $\xi \geq 1$, since the denominator can vanish. It is then possible that as we trace out ξ, the value of $v_0(\xi\hat{y}_\xi, \hat{y}_\xi)$ jumps from $+\infty$ to $-\infty$ and $v_0(\xi\hat{y}_\xi, \hat{y}_\xi)$ might vary from a value greater than ϕ^{-1} to 0 without ever equalling ϕ^{-1}.

However, we can rule out this possibility as long as we can guarantee that $\omega(L - \tilde{y}_0)\,\omega(L) - \mu^2 > 0$, i.e., the present discounted values of profits are well defined at the point $(\tilde{y}_0, 0)$. Plugging in the value above of $\tilde{y}_0$, we can rearrange this as a statement about the parameter F:

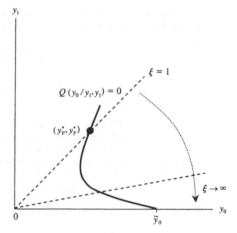

FIGURE B1. THE SET $\Omega_F = \{(y_0, y_1) | Q(y_0/y_1, y_1) = 0\}$

$$F < (1 - \alpha)Z_0 \frac{\lambda - 1}{\lambda}\left[\frac{\omega(L)}{\omega(L) + \mu}\right]^\alpha \left[\frac{\omega(L) - \mu}{\phi(1 - (1 - \alpha)\ln\lambda)}\right]^{1-\alpha} \equiv \bar{F}.$$

As long as $F < \bar{F}$, then by continuity there exists a $\hat{\xi}$ such that $\omega(L - \xi\hat{y}_\xi)\,\omega(L - \hat{y}_\xi) - \mu^2 \geq 0$ for all $\xi > \hat{\xi}$. Thus, even if $v_0(\xi\hat{y}_\xi, \hat{y}_\xi)$ were not always finite, the last point at which the denominator changes signs must be from being negative to being positive, and from that point on $v_0(\xi\hat{y}_\xi, \hat{y}_\xi)$ must transition from $+\infty$ down to 0, and at some point it must equal ϕ^{-1} as claimed.

RESULT 2:

I next show that if $F = 0$, then any solution to the system of equations $v_0(y_0, y_1) = v_1(y_0, y_1) = \phi^{-1}$ must have $y_0 < y_1$ and hence $R_0 > R_1$. Note that when $F = 0$, this equation reduces to

(B8) $$1 - \xi = h(\xi).$$

It will suffice to show that any solution ξ^* which solves (B8) lies in the unit interval $(0, 1)$, since this implies $y_0 < y_1$, and hence that $R_0 > R_1$.

I begin by establishing there exists a $\xi^* \in (0, 1)$ which solves (B8). If $\xi = 0$, we have

$$1 - \xi = 1 > 0 = h(\xi)$$

while if $\xi = 1$, we have

$$1 - \xi = 0 < \frac{\mu}{\omega(L)}\left[\frac{Z_1}{Z_0} - \frac{Z_0}{Z_1}\right] = h(\xi),$$

where we use the fact that $\omega(L) > 0$ given that $\rho > (1 - \alpha)\phi L \ln\lambda$. The existence of ξ^* follows from continuity.

To prove there is no solution $\xi^* > 0$, differentiate $h(\cdot)$ to obtain

$$h'(\xi) = \frac{\mu}{\omega(L)}\left[\alpha\frac{Z_1}{Z_0}\xi^{\alpha-1} - (1-\alpha)\frac{Z_0}{Z_1}\xi^{-\alpha}\right].$$

For $\xi \geq 1$, we have

$$\alpha\frac{Z_1}{Z_0}\xi^{\alpha-1} - (1-\alpha)\frac{Z_0}{Z_1}\xi^{-\alpha} > -(1-\alpha)\frac{Z_0}{Z_1}\xi^{-\alpha} > -1.$$

Since at $\xi = 1$, $h(\xi) > 1 - \xi$, a necessary condition for there to exist a $\xi^* > 1$ such that $1 - \xi^* = h(\xi^*)$ is that there exists a $\xi > 1$ such that $h'(\xi) < -1$. So there can be no $\xi > 1$ for which $1 - \xi = h(\xi)$. Hence, $R_0 > R_1$ in any interior equilibrium.

REFERENCES

Aghion, Philippe, George-Marios Angeletos, Abhijit Banerjee, and Kalina Manova. 2005. "Volatility and Growth: Credit Constraints and Productivity-Enhancing Investment." National Bureau of Economic Research Working Paper 11349.

Aghion, Philippe, and Gilles Saint-Paul. 1998. "Virtues of Bad Times: Interaction between Productivity Growth and Economic Fluctuations." *Macroeconomic Dynamics*, 2(3): 322–44.

Arrow, Kenneth. 1962. "Economic Welfare and the Allocation of Resources for Invention." In *The Rate and Direction of Inventive Activity: Economic and Social Factors*, ed. Richard Nelson, 609–26. Princeton: Princeton University Press.

Barlevy, Gadi. 2004. "The Cost of Business Cycles under Endogenous Growth." *American Economic Review*, 94(4): 964–90.

Barlevy, Gadi, and Daniel Tsiddon. 2006. "Earnings Inequality and the Business Cycle." *European Economic Review*, 50(1): 55–89.

Bartelsman, Eric, Randy Becker, and Wayne Gray. 2000. *NBER-CES Manufacturing Industry Database, June 2000*. http://www.nber.org/nberces/nbprod96.htm.

Basu, Susanto. 1996. "Procyclical Productivity: Increasing Returns or Cyclical Utilization?" *Quarterly Journal of Economics*, 111(3): 719–51.

Benhabib, Jess, and Roger E. A. Farmer. 1994. "Indeterminacy and Increasing Returns." *Journal of Economic Theory*, 63(1): 19–41.

Caballero, Ricardo J., and Mohamad L. Hammour. 1994. "The Cleansing Effect of Recessions." *American Economic Review*, 84(5): 1350–68.

Canton, Eric, and Harald Uhlig. 1999. "Growth and the Cycle: Creative Destruction versus Entrenchment." *Journal of Economics*, 69(3): 239–66.

Comin, Diego, and Mark Gertler. 2006. "Medium-Term Business Cycles." *American Economic Review*, 96(3): 523–51.

Cooper, Russell, and John Haltiwanger. 1993. "The Aggregate Implications of Machine Replacement: Theory and Evidence." *American Economic Review*, 83(3): 360–82.

DeJong, David N., and Beth F. Ingram. 2001. "The Cyclical Behavior of Skill Acquisition." *Review of Economic Dynamics*, 4(3): 536–61.

Dellas, Harris, and Plutarchos Sakellaris. 2003. "On the Cyclicality of Schooling: Theory and Evidence." *Oxford Economic Papers*, 55(1): 148–72.

Fatas, Antonio. 2000. "Do Business Cycles Cast Long Shadows? Short-Run Persistence and Economic Growth." *Journal of Economic Growth*, 5(2): 147–62.

Francois, Patrick, and Huw Lloyd-Ellis. 2003. "Animal Spirits through Creative Destruction." *American Economic Review*, 93(3): 530–50.

Geroski, Paul A., and C. F. Walters. 1995. "Innovative Activity over the Business Cycle." *Economic Journal*, 105(431): 916–28.

Gomes, João, Jeremy Greenwood, and Sergio Rebelo. 2001. "Equilibrium Unemployment." *Journal of Monetary Economics*, 48(1): 109–52.

Goolsbee, Austan. 1998. "Does Government R&D Policy Mainly Benefit Scientists and Engineers?" *American Economic Review*, 88(2): 298–302.

Griliches, Zvi. 1984. "Comment on R&D and Innovation: Some Empirical Findings." In *R&D Patents and Productivity*, ed. Zvi Griliches, 148–49. Chicago: University of Chicago Press.

Griliches, Zvi. 1990. "Patent Statistics as Economic Indicators: A Survey." *Journal of Economic Literature*, 28(4): 1661–1707.

Grossman, Gene M., and Elhanan Helpman. 1991. "Quality Ladders in the Theory of Growth." *Review of Economic Studies*, 58(1): 43–61.

Hall, Robert E. 1991. "Labor Demand, Labor Supply, and Employment Volatility." In *NBER Macroeconomics Annual 1991*, ed. Olivier J. Blanchard and Stanley Fischer, 17–47. Cambridge, MA: MIT Press.

Himmelberg, Charles P., and Bruce C. Petersen. 1994. "R&D and Internal Finance: A Panel Study of Small Firms in High-Tech Industries." *Review of Economics and Statistics*, 76(1): 38–51.

Judd, Kenneth L. 1998. *Numerical Methods in Economics.* Cambridge, MA: MIT Press.

Lucas, Robert E., Jr. 1987. *Models of Business Cycles (Yrjo Jahnsson Lectures Series).* London: Blackwell Publishing.

Mortensen, Dale T., and Christopher A. Pissarides. 1994. "Job Creation and Job Destruction in the Theory of Unemployment." *Review of Economic Studies*, 61(3): 397–415.

Rafferty, Matthew C. 2003. "Do Business Cycles Influence Long-Run Growth? The Effect of Aggregate Demand on Firm-Financed R&D Expenditures." *Eastern Economic Journal*, 29(4): 607–18.

Rafferty, Matthew C., and Mark Funk. 2004. "Demand Shocks and Firm-Financed R&D Expenditures." *Applied Economics*, 36(14): 1529–36.

Ramey, Valerie A. 1991. "Markups and Business Cycles: Comment." In *NBER Macroeconomics Annual Volume 6*, ed. Olivier J. Blanchard and Stanley Fisher, 134–90. Cambridge, MA: MIT Press.

Rivera–Batiz, Luis A., and Paul M. Romer. 1991. "Economic Integration and Endogenous Growth." *Quarterly Journal of Economics*, 106(2): 531–55.

Rotemberg, Julio, and Michael Woodford. 1999. "The Cyclical Behavior of Prices and Costs." In *Handbook of Macroeconomics Volume 15*, ed. John Taylor and Michael Woodford, 1051–1135. Amsterdam: Elsevier Science, North-Holland.

Saint-Paul, Gilles. 1993. "Productivity Growth and the Structure of the Business Cycle." *European Economic Review*, 37(4): 861–83.

Shleifer, Andrei. 1986. "Implementation Cycles." *Journal of Political Economy*, 94(6): 1163–90.

Taylor, John B., and Michael Woodford. 1999. *Handbook of Macroeconomics Volume 1b.* Amsterdam: Elsevier Science, North-Holland.

Walde, Klaus, and Ulrich Woitek. 2004. "R&D Expenditure in G7 Countries and the Implications for Endogenous Fluctuations and Growth." *Economics Letters*, 82(1): 91–97.

[5]

The Cleansing Effect of Recessions

By Ricardo J. Caballero and Mohamad L. Hammour*

We investigate industry response to cyclical variations in demand. Production units that embody the newest process and product innovations are continuously being created, and outdated units are being destroyed. Although outdated units are the most likely to turn unprofitable and be scrapped in a recession, they can be "insulated" from the fall in demand by a reduction in creation. The structure of adjustment costs plays a determinant role in the responsiveness of those two margins. The calibrated model matches the relative volatilities of the observed manufacturing job creation and destruction series, and their asymmetries over the cycle. (JEL E00, L00, J00)

This paper investigates the response of industries to cyclical variations in demand in the framework of a vintage model of "creative destruction."[1] Our premise is that the continuous process of creation and destruction of production units that results from product and process innovation is essential for understanding not only growth, but also business cycles.[2] This idea goes back at least to Joseph A. Schumpeter (1939, 1942), although we do not go so far as to adopt his view that the process of creative destruction is itself a major *source* of economic fluctuations (as in Andrei Shleifer [1986]). Our emphasis here is on variations in demand as a source of economic fluctuations, and on the way a continuously renovating productive structure responds to them.

A stark example of this effect of demand on industry structure has been recently documented by Timothy F. Bresnahan and Daniel M. G. Raff (1991, 1992) in their study of the effect of the Great Depression

*Caballero: Department of Economics, Massachusetts Institute of Technology, Cambridge, MA 02139; Hammour: Department of Economics, Columbia University, School of International Affairs, New York, NY 10042. We thank John Haltiwanger for helpful comments and for providing us with job-flow data. We also thank Olivier Blanchard, Peter Diamond, Julio Rotemberg, three anonymous referees, and workshop participants at Boston College, Boston University, the University of Chicago, Columbia University, the University of Maryland, UQUAM, the NBER Summer Institute 1991 and the NBER EFRR 1992 meeting in Palo Alto for useful comments. Caballero thanks the National Science Foundation and the Alfred P. Sloan Foundation for financial support.

[1] In independent work, Dale Mortensen and Christopher Pissarides (1991, 1992) study issues similar to the ones considered in this paper in the context of a search model of unemployment.

[2] For an analysis of creative destruction in Leif Johansen's (1959) vintage model of embodied technical progress, see Robert M. Solow (1960), Edmund S. Phelps (1963), Eytan Sheshinski (1967), and references therein. For two recent models of growth through creative destruction, see Gene R. Grossman and Elhanan Helpman (1991) and Philippe Aghion and Peter Howitt (1992).

For recent analyses of the empirical significance of creative destruction for growth, see Eric J. Bartelsman and Phoebus J. Dhrymes (1991), Martin N. Baily et al. (1992), and Charles R. Hulten (1992). Using price-based estimates of embodied technical change, Hulten (1992) argues that as much as 20 percent of the change in total factor productivity can be directly associated with capital embodiment. Bartelsman and Dhrymes (1991) and Baily et al. (1992) use plant-level data to decompose improvements in aggregate productivity into a component due to resource allocation from relatively inefficient to relatively efficient plants, and another due to improvements in technology purely at the plant level. Both studies find that a major part of technical progress arises from factor reallocation, a fact consistent with the view of an economy subject to ongoing creative destruction. Compounded over the period 1972–1987 for a sample of 22 industries, the results in Baily et al. (1992) indicate that aggregate growth is made up of 6.7 percent due to reallocation and 3.5 percent due to plant-level technical progress (results for "all industries except 3573" in their table 1, p. 207).

on the American motor vehicles industry. Using Census panel data, they find that the large contraction in automotive production was the occasion for a permanent structural change in the industry. At the beginning of the Depression, the diffusion of mass-production techniques in manufacturing had only been partial, and a substantial segment of the industry was still based on skilled craftsmanship. Plant shutdown, which accounted for a third of the decline in industry employment during the Depression, was concentrated in smaller, less productive craft-production plants, while plants that had adopted the mass-production system had a competitive advantage that made them more likely to survive. The result was a true shakeout or "cleansing" of the productive structure, as most plant shutdowns were permanent. Interestingly, creation was still taking place alongside this massive destruction process, with a sizable number of new plants entering even in the depths of the Depression.[3]

In general, industries undergoing continuous creative destruction can accommodate variations in demand in two ways: they can vary either the rate at which production units that embody new techniques are created or the rate at which outdated units are destroyed. The central question becomes: along which of these two margins will business cycles be accommodated?

Since a representative-firm economy is unsuited to answer this question, we address it in the context of a simple theoretical model of creative destruction with heterogeneous technologies.[4] Production units embody the most advanced techniques available at the time of their creation. Creation costs slow down the process of technology adoption and lead to the coexistence of production units of different vintages. This decouples the two margins and permits a meaningful analysis of the issue at hand.

The interaction of two margins can challenge one's intuition. We isolate two effects. Old production units, having an inferior technology, can more easily turn unprofitable and be scrapped in a recession than new ones. However, units in place may not experience the full fall in demand if it is accommodated by a reduction in the creation rate. We investigate the extent to which this "insulating" effect of creation will operate and reduce the responsiveness of destruction to demand. The structure of adjustment costs turns out to play a determinant role in the extent to which insulation will take place. When adjustment costs are linear, we show that insulation is complete, and the industry responds *exclusively* on its creation margin. As the motive for smoothing the creation process over time becomes more important, insulation becomes more limited, and the destruction margin becomes more responsive.

What is the empirical evidence on the cyclical responsiveness of creation and destruction? We next turn to the U.S. evidence on gross job creation and destruction collected by Olivier J. Blanchard and Peter A. Diamond (1990) and Steven Davis and John Haltiwanger (1990, 1992). As emphasized by Blanchard and Diamond, the simultaneous high observed rates of job creation and destruction in narrowly defined sectors lend plausibility to the view of an economy subject to ongoing creative destruction. This view is further confirmed by the strong persistence of job destruction at the plant level documented by Davis and Haltiwanger (1990). We analyze Davis and Haltiwanger's (1990, 1992) data on manufacturing job flows in light of our model. The evidence is that job destruction is much more cyclically responsive than job creation. Thus, the insulating effect of creation seems very imperfect. According to our model, this is due to the structure of creation costs that gives a motive for smoothing the creation process. Interestingly, the data exhibit features that provide a natural experiment to test this explanation. Noting that business cycles are highly asymmetric, with recessions shorter but much sharper than expansions, our model would predict that those asymmetries would be smoothed out in the

---

[3]In the 1929–1931 period, industry 1408 saw 13 new plant entries and 60 exits. During 1931–1933, those numbers were 9 and 45.

[4]A steady-state variant of this model has been used by Boyan Jovanovic and Saul Lach (1989) to study technology diffusion.

creation process. The evidence confirms this prediction: creation is roughly symmetric around its mean, while destruction is highly asymmetric.

The view that emerges from interpreting the greater cyclicality of job destruction along creative-destruction lines is one of recessions as times of "cleansing," when outdated or relatively unprofitable techniques and products are pruned out of the productive system—an idea that was popular among pre-Keynesian "liquidationist" theorists like Hayek or Schumpeter (see J. Bradford De Long, 1990), but *need not* be taken to imply, as those authors did, that recessions are "desirable" events.

In Section I, we lay out our basic vintage model of creative destruction and characterize its steady state. Section II introduces demand fluctuations into the model, and asks which of the creation or destruction margins will respond to them. Section III interprets the data on manufacturing job flows in terms of our model and ends with a calibration exercise in which the model's theoretical response to the observed path of manufacturing activity is calculated and compared to the actual response.

I. A Vintage Model of Creative Destruction

In this section, we present the basic features of the model of creative destruction that is used throughout the paper. The first subsection describes the basic statistics of the model; Subsection B turns to market equilibrium conditions; and Subsection C characterizes the model's steady state.

A. *Production Units: Distribution and Flows*

We model an industry experiencing exogenous technical progress. New production units that capture the most advanced techniques are continuously being created, and outdated ones are being destroyed. Because the creation process is costly, production units with different productivities coexist.

More specifically, labor and capital combine in fixed proportions to form *production units*. A production unit created at time t_0 embodies the leading technology at t_0, and produces the same constant flow $A(t_0)$ of

output throughout its lifetime. Technical progress makes the productivity $A(t)$ of the leading technology at time t grow at an exogenous rate $\gamma > 0$.

Although we interpret the creation process as one of technology adoption, it could also be interpreted as one of product innovation. In this case, there is a continuum of perfectly substitutable products that yield different utilities. A production unit created at t_0 will be producing a unit flow of the most advanced product in existence at t_0, which yields utility $A(t_0)$.

Since production units that were created at different times (and thus have different productivities) may coexist, we must keep track of their age distribution. Let

$$f(a,t) \qquad 0 \le a \le \bar{a}(t)$$

denote the cross-section density of production units aged a at time t, where $\bar{a}(t)$ is the age of the oldest unit *in operation* at time t.[5] The boundary $f(0,t)$ is given by the rate at which new units are created, and the age $\bar{a}(t)$ at which units become obsolete is determined by the destruction process. Our assumptions will be such that $f(a,t)$ and $\bar{a}(t)$ are continuous functions.

The density $f(a,t)$ can be aggregated to obtain the total number (or "mass") of production units at any time t:

$$N(t) = \int_0^{\bar{a}(t)} f(a,t)\, da.$$

Because of fixed proportions, $N(t)$ is a measure of both the industry's employment and its capital stock in operation. Industry output is given by

$$(1) \qquad Q(t) = \int_0^{\bar{a}(t)} A(t-a) f(a,t)\, da.$$

We now turn to the flows that determine the evolution of the density $f(a,t)$. Production units are subject to an exogenous de-

---

[5] Of course the use of the word "density" is an abuse of terminology.

VOL. 84 NO. 5   CABALLERO AND HAMMOUR: CLEANSING EFFECT OF RECESSIONS   1353

preciation (or failure) rate $\delta > 0$ and to the endogenous process of creative destruction. Since, as we describe below, the latter turns out to affect $f(a,t)$ only at its boundaries, we know that at any time t the number of units that have survived for a years is given by

$$(2) \quad f(a,t) = f(0, t-a)e^{-\delta a}$$

$$0 < a \leq \bar{a}(t).$$

Measures of production unit flows can be obtained by differentiating $N(t)$ over time, taking (2) into account:[6]

$$\dot{N}(t) = f(0,t)$$

$$-\left\{ f(\bar{a}(t),t)\left[1-\dot{\bar{a}}(t)\right] + \delta N(t) \right\}.$$

The first term $f(0,t)$ measures the rate of creation of production units, and the second measures the rate of destruction. When normalized by $N(t)$, they are denoted by $CC(t)$ and $DD(t)$, respectively. The rate of destruction has three components: $f(\bar{a}(t),t)$ units will be destroyed because they have reached the obsolescence age $\bar{a}$; $-f(\bar{a}(t),t)\dot{\bar{a}}(t)$ are destroyed because $\bar{a}$ changes over time; and $\delta N(t)$ units depreciate. With some abuse of terminology, we call the sum of the first two components "endogenous destruction." Our assumptions are such that endogenous creation and destruction are always positive, that is, $f(0,t) > 0$ and $\dot{\bar{a}}(t) < 1$, for all t.

Finally, it will be useful to have an expression for the change in output as a function of the above flows:[7]

$$(1') \quad \dot{Q}(t) = A(t)f(0,t)$$

$$-\left\{ A(t-\bar{a}(t))f(\bar{a}(t),t) \right.$$

$$\left. \times \left[1-\dot{\bar{a}}(t)\right] + \delta Q(t) \right\}.$$

B. Market Equilibrium

We now turn to supply and demand conditions in this model, and to the economics of creative destruction. We model a perfectly competitive industry in partial equilibrium. Because our main argument does not depend on the presence or absence of uncertainty, we assume perfect foresight.

Supply is determined by free entry and perfect competition. There is a cost c of creating a new production unit:[8]

$$c = c(f(0,t)) \qquad c(\cdot) > 0, c'(\cdot) \geq 0.$$

Here, c is allowed to depend on the creation rate $f(0,t)$ to capture the possibility that, for the industry as a whole, fast creation may be costly, and adjustment may not take place instantaneously. This can be due to different reasons. It can arise from a concave production function in the sector producing the industry's capital stock, or from standard convex capital installation and labor training costs.[9] Industry-wide convexity could also have been derived from a nondegenerate distribution of linear individual adjustment costs across potential entrants (see e.g., Peter Diamond, 1993).

As long as creation is taking place, free entry equates a unit's creation cost to the present discounted value of profits over its lifetime. More formally, set the operating cost of a production unit—including wages —to 1 by choosing it as a numeraire, and let $P(t)$ denote the price of a unit of output. The profits generated at time t by a produc-

---

[6] The derivation involves the partial differential equation $f_t + f_a + \delta f = 0$, $0 < a < \bar{a}(t)$, which follows directly from (2) and corresponds to the basic McKendrick-von Foerster equation in population dynamics (see R. M. Nisbet and W. S. C. Gurney, 1982).

[7] Differentiate (1) using

$$\partial A(t-a)/\partial t = -\partial A(t-a)/\partial a.$$

[8] An alternative specification is $c = c(f(0,t)/N(t))$. Normalizing the creation rate by $N(t)$ may be more appealing because it makes the model scale-free. But it complicates things by introducing an additional benefit of creating a production unit, equal to the reduction in future creation costs due to the increase in $N(t)$. We choose the simpler specification to avoid this added complexity.

[9] In this case, because we did not choose the scale-free specification mentioned in footnote 8, we would need to assume a fixed number (normalized to 1) of symmetric, perfectly competitive firms to derive a marginal adjustment cost of the form $c = c(f(0,t))$.

tion unit of age a are

$$\pi(a,t) = P(t)A(t-a) - 1.$$

Now let $T(t)$ measure the maximum lifetime of a unit created at t, which by perfect foresight satisfies

(3) $\bar{a}[t + T(t)] = T(t)$.

At any time t, the free-entry condition is

(4) $c(f(0,t))$

$$= \int_t^{t+T(t)} \pi(s-t,t)e^{-(r+\delta)(s-t)}\,ds$$

where $r > 0$ is the exogenously given instantaneous interest rate.

To see what determines exit note that, assuming $P(t)$ is continuous, whenever a unit is being destroyed it must be the case that the profits it generates have reached zero. Since such a unit must be the oldest in operation at that time, $\bar{a}(t)$ must satisfy

(5) $P(t)A(t-\bar{a}(t)) = 1$.

This condition relates the price $P(t)$ to $\bar{a}(t)$. From this it is simple to see that the continuity of $\bar{a}(t)$ implies the continuity of $P(t)$, and that $P(t)$ must be decreasing if there is endogenous destruction $(\dot{\bar{a}}(t) < 1)$.[10] Since we restrict our attention to cases in which the latter is always taking place, it follows that $P(t)$ is always decreasing and that production units will be destroyed the *first* time their profits hit zero.

The demand side of the model is quite simple. We assume a unit-elastic demand function, and take total spending $\bar{D}(t)$ on the industry's output to be an exogenous and continuous function of time:

(6) $P(t)Q(t) = \bar{D}(t)$.

An equilibrium in this industry is a path $\{f(0,t),\bar{a}(t),T(t),P(t),Q(t)\}_{t \geq 0}$ that satisfies equations (1)–(6), summarized below, for all $t \geq 0$, given an initial density $f(a,0)$, $a > 0$, of production units:

(1) $Q(t) = \int_0^{\bar{a}(t)} A(t-a)f(a,t)\,da$

(2) $f(a,t) = f(0,t-a)e^{-\delta a}$

$$0 < a \leq \bar{a}(t)$$

(3) $\bar{a}(t + T(t)) = T(t)$

(4) $c(f(0,t))$

$$= \int_t^{t+T(t)}[P(s)A(t)-1]e^{-(r+\delta)(s-t)}\,ds$$

(5) $P(t)A(t-\bar{a}(t)) = 1$

(6) $P(t)Q(t) = \bar{D}(t)$.

Since the paths of $T(t)$, $P(t)$, and $Q(t)$ are immediately determined from the path $\{f(0,t),\bar{a}(t)\}$ by equations (1)–(3) and (5), we will focus on the latter path as a sufficient description of equilibrium.

Note that, instead of using the free-entry and free-exit conditions, equations (4) and (5) could alternatively have been derived as the first-order conditions for maximization of a number of perfectly competitive firms that hold the production units in this industry. This highlights the efficiency of the resulting equilibrium outcome, and its compatibility with different institutional arrangements. It can also be used to establish the existence and uniqueness of equilibrium.[11]

C. *Steady State*

Before we turn to the response of our industry to demand fluctuations, it is instructive to characterize its steady-state (or balanced-growth) equilibrium, assuming that demand is a constant $\bar{D}^*$ over time.

---

[10] To see this, differentiate (5):

$$\dot{P}(t) = -\gamma[1 - \dot{\bar{a}}(t)]P(t).$$

[11] See Hugo Hopenhayn (1990) for a general discussion of existence and uniqueness of a dynamic industry equilibrium in the presence of heterogeneity and creation costs.

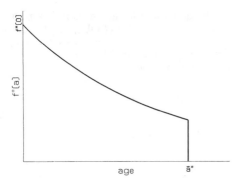

FIGURE 1. STEADY-STATE CROSS-SECTIONAL DENSITY

In steady state, the lifetime of production units is constant: $T(t) = \bar{a}(t) = \bar{a}^*$, for all t; their age distribution is time-invariant: $f(a,t) = f^*(a)$, for all t; and by (5) the price $P(t)$ must be decreasing at constant rate γ. Equation (2) implies that the distribution of production units in steady state is the truncated exponential distribution illustrated in Figure 1:

$$f^*(a) = f^*(0)e^{-\delta a} \qquad 0 < a \le \bar{a}^*.$$

The creation rate and destruction age $(f^*(0), \bar{a}^*)$ are jointly determined from free-entry and market-equilibrium conditions (4) and (6) in steady state. Using (1) and (5), we get

$$(7) \qquad c(f^*(0)) = \frac{e^{\gamma \bar{a}^*} - e^{-(r+\delta)\bar{a}^*}}{\gamma + r + \delta}$$
$$- \frac{1 - e^{-(r+\delta)\bar{a}^*}}{r + \delta}.$$

$$(8) \qquad f(0) = \frac{(\gamma + \delta)\bar{D}^*}{e^{\gamma \bar{a}^*} - e^{-\delta \bar{a}^*}}.$$

For future use, creation normalized by N, which is equal to $f^*(0)(1 - e^{-\delta \bar{a}^*})/\delta$, is given in steady state by

$$(9) \qquad CC^* = \frac{\delta}{1 - e^{-\delta \bar{a}^*}}.$$

The special case when the creation cost is a constant c, independent of the creation rate, will be examined closely in what follows. In this case system (7)–(8) is recursive. We can first solve (7) for the steady-state efficient lifetime $\bar{a}^*$ that balances the benefits and costs of updating technology, independently of demand and the rate of creation.[12] Then we can obtain $f^*(0)$ from (8), given $\bar{a}^*$ and the level of demand $\bar{D}^*$.

II. Business Cycles

We now turn to the response of the creative-destruction process modeled above to cyclical fluctuations in demand. From a pure accounting point of view, our industry has two margins along which it can accommodate a fall in demand $\bar{D}(t)$. As can be seen from (1'), it can either reduce the rate of creation $f(0,t)$ or increase the rate of endogenous destruction $f(\bar{a}(t), t)[1 - \dot{\bar{a}}(t)]$, which amounts to reducing the age $\bar{a}(t)$ at which units are destroyed [since $f(\bar{a}(t), t)$ is given at t]. The issue is which of these two margins, $f(0,t)$ or $\bar{a}(t)$, will respond to demand fluctuations, and to what extent?

The problem's difficulty comes from the interaction between two margins. For a given creation rate, a fall in demand will cause the most outdated units to turn unprofitable and be scrapped. But if the recession is partly accommodated by a fall in the creation rate, units in place may not suffer its full impact. We argue that the extent to which creation will thus "insulate" existing units from variations in demand depends on the costs of fast creation in the industry, that is, on $c'(f(0,t))$. The insulating effect of creation will be more complete, the smaller is $c'(f(0,t))$. In the extreme case where $c'(f(0,t)) = 0$ and adjustment takes place instantaneously, creation will

---

[12] The effect of different parameters on $\bar{a}^*$ is quite intuitive in this case: $\bar{a}^*$ decreases with γ, since faster technical progress raises the opportunity cost of delaying renovation; it increases with c so as to give more time to recoup higher creation costs; and it increases with r and δ, because they lead to heavier discounting of future profits and make it more difficult to recover creation costs in a short time.

$$(10) \quad f(0,t) = \frac{\dot{\overline{D}}(t) + \delta \overline{D}(t) + P(t) A(t - \overline{a}(t)) f(\overline{a}(t),t) [1 - \dot{\overline{a}}(t)] - \dot{P}(t) Q(t)}{P(t) A(t)}$$

fully accommodate demand fluctuations, and destruction will not respond. We start by examining this special case to clarify the insulation mechanism in our model, and then look at what happens more generally when insulation is incomplete.

A. *The "Insulation" Effect: An Extreme Case*

The insulating effect of creation can be best understood in the extreme case where the cost of creation c is a constant, independent of the rate $f(0,t)$ at which it is taking place. In this case adjustment is instantaneous, and as long as the nonnegativity constraint on $f(0,t)$ is not binding, the insulation effect is complete. Demand fluctuations are accommodated *exclusively* on the creation margin, and destruction does not respond.[13] To see why, note that there is a very simple way to solve equilibrium conditions (1)–(6) when $c(f(0,t))$ is constant. As we saw in the analysis of the steady state, the system of equations is recursive in this case. We can first solve for $\overline{a}(t)$, using the free-entry condition (4) together with (3) and (5). Given that these equations do not depend on the path of $\overline{D}(t)$ and $f(0,t)$, they can be solved independently. But since this is exactly what we did in the analysis of steady state when c was constant, the solution is the same constant lifetime $\overline{a}^*$ we obtained there, and accordingly a price $P(t)$ falling at constant rate γ.

Given this, we can then solve for the creation rate $f(0,t)$ to satisfy market equilibrium condition (6), using (1) and (2). In other words, the creation rate adjusts continuously to accommodate demand and,

from (1′), is given by equation (10), above, which we assume yields a nonnegative $f(0,t)$.[14] In the resulting equilibrium, demand fluctuations are fully accommodated by adjustments at the creation margin $f(0,t)$, while $\overline{a}(t)$ remains constant at the destruction margin. The creation process neutralizes the effect of demand fluctuations on the price $P(t)$, thus fully "insulating" existing units from changes in demand. $P(t)$ falls at a constant rate γ that reflects the rate of technical progress, providing the right signal for production units to operate for the constant lifetime $\overline{a}^*$.

Note that the above analysis does not imply that the destruction rate will be constant in equilibrium, but only that it does not respond to demand through variations in the age $\overline{a}(t)$ at which units are destroyed. Variations in the destruction rate reflect an "echo" effect of the history of demand on the number $f(\overline{a}^*,t)$ of units that reach the age of obsolescence $\overline{a}^*$.

It is clear from the above proof that, in the case of constant creation cost, the full-insulation result is robust to any modification of the model that preserves the independence of (3)–(5) from $\{\overline{D}(t)\}$ and $\{f(0,t)\}$. In particular, it does not hinge on certainty, on perfect competition, or on the degree of industry-wide returns to scale. Perfect foresight is not necessary because, as long as it is known that the nonnegativity constraint on $f(0,t)$ will never be binding, implementing equilibrium behavior does not

---

[13]The insulation effect is *not* due to asymmetric adjustment costs on the creation and destruction margins. Insulation would still be complete if we were to add linear destruction costs, since doing so is equivalent to adding the present value of those costs to the cost of creation.

[14]By replacing equation (6) in (10) and noticing that $f(\overline{a}(t),t) \geq 0$ for all t, one may show that a *sufficient* condition for positive entry in the full insulation case is:

$$\dot{\overline{D}}(t) / \overline{D}(t) > -(\delta + \gamma).$$

Since creation cannot be negative, a fall in demand larger than $\delta + \gamma$ may break insulation, for any further fall in demand beyond the point of zero creation must be accommodated on the destruction side.

require expectations of future demand. Fully accommodating demand on the creation side only requires knowledge of *current* conditions. Perfect competition is not necessary either, since a monopolist's first-order conditions would only add a markup to equations (4) and (5) and preserve the recursive structure of system (1)–(6).[15]

Robustness with respect to industry-wide returns to scale is also straightforward but will be discussed in some detail for future reference. Assume the simple case where short-run increasing or decreasing returns are due to an industry-wide externality. More specifically, suppose that the output at t of a production unit of age a is $q(t)^\beta A(t-a)$, where $q(t) \equiv Q(t)/A(t)$ is aggregate output detrended by the leading technology and is taken as given by firms. In this case, it is simple to see that equilibrium conditions (1)–(6) remain unchanged if we substitute $\tilde{Q}(t) \equiv Q(t)/q(t)^\beta$ and $\tilde{P}(t) \equiv P(t)q(t)^\beta$ for $Q(t)$ and $P(t)$, respectively. We can then apply the same argument as before on the transformed system to prove that $\bar{a}(t)$ is constant in equilibrium.

B. *Creation and Destruction over the Cycle*

The full-insulation effect in the previous section was primarily due to the special case of constant creation costs. In reality, the industry may not be able to create all the necessary production units instantaneously in response to a rise in demand. In this section we show that if $c'(f(0,t))$ is positive, insulation will only be partial, and destruction will also respond to demand fluctuations.

Once we allow c to depend on $f(0,t)$, system (1)–(6) loses its analytic tractability and must be solved numerically. The solution method we devised is described in the Appendix: we turn (1)–(6) into a system of time-varying delay differential equations in $(f(0,t), \bar{a}(t))$ (see H. Gorecki et al., 1989), develop a "multiple-shooting" method for

finding an equilibrium solution for given *arbitrary* values for the path $T(t)$, and then use an iterative procedure to converge to the right expectations for this path. For all numerical solutions we use the simple linear functional form

$$(11) \quad c(f(0,t)) = c_0 + c_1 f(0,t)$$

$$c_0, c_1 > 0.$$

To show the way both creation and destruction respond to demand, we generated a sinusoidal demand $\bar{D}(t) = 1 + 0.07\sin(t)$ and solved for the resulting periodic equilibrium.[16] Figure 2 depicts the response of the normalized creation and destruction rates (CC and DD) to the change in demand, $\bar{D}(t)$. It is clear that the insulation effect is imperfect, and a fall in demand is accommodated partly by a fall in the creation rate and partly by a rise in the destruction rate.

With increasing creation costs, the industry will smooth the creation process, since it is costly to accommodate demand fluctuations fully with variations in $f(0,t)$. Reducing the rate of technology adoption to a near standstill in a recession may require firms to catch up at prohibitively expensive rates in the ensuing expansion. Thus creation will not fully insulate existing units, and part of the contraction will have to take place at the destruction margin.[17] From a purely formal point of view, destruction responds to demand because equations (3)–(5) are no longer independent of the path of $f(0,t)$ and demand.

III. Application to Job-Flow Data

In this section we explore the broad consistency of our model with U.S. data on

---

[15]In this case, the elasticity of demand would have to be greater than 1 for the monopolist's problem to be well defined.

[16]We set $r = 0.065$, $\delta = 0.15$, $\gamma = 0.028$, $c_0 = 0.3$, and $c_1 = 1.0$. The cost parameters are entirely arbitrary at this stage. Later we calibrate them using U.S. manufacturing data on job flows.

[17]Had we introduced uncertainty in our model, a very similar effect would have emerged from a "time to build" feature of the creation process. In this case, unexpected changes in demand cannot be accommodated instantaneously on the creation margin and will therefore lead to a response on the destruction margin.

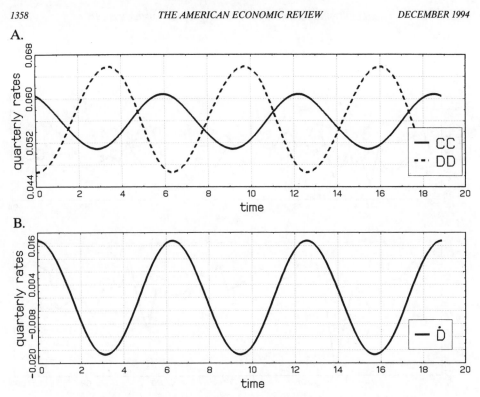

FIGURE 2. A) CREATION AND DESTRUCTION ($c_0 = 0.3$, $c_1 = 1.0$); B) CHANGE IN DEMAND (SYMMETRIC)

gross job flows. Although this is not meant to be a thorough investigation of labor markets, we find the match of nontrivial aspects of the job flow data a success for such a stylized model.

A. *A Look at the Data*

Production units in our model combine labor and capital in fixed proportions to produce output. One could therefore think of each unit as creating a job in the industry and use job-flow data to measure production unit flows.

Data on job creation and destruction that correspond roughly to our theoretical CC and DD series have been constructed by Davis and Haltiwanger (1990, 1992) and by Blanchard and Diamond (1990) using different sources. We focus on the data of Davis and Haltiwanger, who draw on the Longitudinal Research Database to con-

struct quarterly series for U.S. manufacturing plants for the period 1972:2–1986:4.[18,19]

Since our model analyzes the response of job flows to demand fluctuations, we examine the corresponding relationship in the data. We use output $Q(t)$ to pin down demand empirically and take the growth rate

[18] Blanchard and Diamond's (1990) series are monthly and cover both manufacturing (for the period 1972–1981) and the economy as a whole (1968–1986). They are based on employment-flow data, from the Bureau of Labor Statistics for the manufacturing series and from the Current Population Survey for the economy-wide series.

[19] Because we lack within-plant measures of gross flows, there is an issue of whether the Davis-Haltiwanger series give us a useful measure of total gross job flows. One indication that they do is that they have major features in common with the Blanchard-Diamond series which are collected from workers rather than plants.

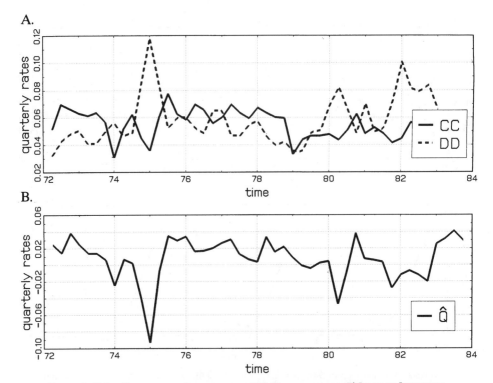

FIGURE 3. A) JOB CREATION AND DESTRUCTION IN U.S. MANUFACTURING; B) INDEX OF INDUSTRIAL
PRODUCTION (RATE OF GROWTH)

of the index of industrial production as a measure of output growth.[20] Figure 3 depicts job creation, job destruction, and output growth for the manufacturing sector. The relation between these series is analyzed in Table 1 using two-digit SIC data.

Regressions are run by constraining all coefficients to be equal across sectors, except for a constant.[21]

The first block ($\hat{Q}$) in Table 1 presents results from the regression of sectoral rates of job creation and job destruction on leads and lags of the corresponding rates of growth of the indexes of industrial production. The first result that arises is that the rate of job destruction is more responsive to changes in sectoral activity than is the rate of job creation (the sums of coefficients are -0.384 and 0.218, respectively). This can be seen directly from Figure 3 and is one of

---

[20] In our basic model $Q(t)$ is a smoothed [by the movements in $P(t)$] version of exogenous demand $\bar{D}(t)$. The degree of smoothing depends on the elasticity of demand, which, for simplicity, we assume to be 1 in the model. Interestingly, $Q(t)$ can be as volatile as $\bar{D}(t)$ [and $P(t)$ completely rigid] in the external-economies version of the model briefly discussed in Section II-A. Similarly, in our basic partial-equilibrium analysis we have assumed a constant consumption wage. However, allowing for a procyclical consumption wage, as would probably be the case in general equilibrium if shocks are correlated across industries, would dampen the effect of demand shocks but would not alter the basic qualitative features of our analysis.

[21] We also ran the regressions using aggregate manufacturing instead of sectoral industrial production on the right-hand side. The results were virtually unchanged.

TABLE 1—JOB CREATION AND DESTRUCTION RESPONSE TO OUTPUT GROWTH

Regressor	Timing	Creation		Destruction	
		Coefficient	Standard deviation	Coefficient	Standard deviation
$\hat{Q}$	2 leads	0.029	0.006	0.030	0.010
	1 lead	0.065	0.007	−0.068	0.010
	contemporaneous	0.108	0.007	−0.185	0.010
	1 lag	0.013	0.007	−0.103	0.010
	2 lags	0.003	0.006	−0.058	0.010
	Sum:	0.218	0.013	−0.384	0.017
$\hat{Q}^+$	2 leads	0.052	0.012	0.012	0.016
	1 lead	0.102	0.012	0.002	0.016
	contemporaneous	0.131	0.012	−0.065	0.016
	1 lag	0.059	0.012	−0.025	0.016
	2 lags	0.055	0.012	−0.008	0.016
	Sum:	0.399	0.026	−0.066	0.023
$\hat{Q}^-$	2 leads	0.002	0.010	0.006	0.014
	1 lead	0.022	0.011	−0.149	0.014
	contemporaneous	0.093	0.012	−0.293	0.015
	1 lag	−0.012	0.012	−0.139	0.015
	2 lags	−0.021	0.012	−0.059	0.015
	Sum:	0.084	0.020	−0.634	0.024

Notes: The table shows the response of job creation and job destruction to changes in the growth rate of the index of industrial production for each sector ($\hat{Q}$), and to the latter split into values above and below its mean ($\hat{Q}^+$ and $\hat{Q}^-$, respectively). The data are quarterly observations for the two-digit SIC manufacturing industries, for the period 1972:2–1986:4. The coefficients are constrained to be equal across all sectors, except for a constant (not shown).

the key findings of Davis and Haltiwanger (1990, 1992) and Blanchard and Diamond (1990). In terms of our model, the insulating effect of job creation seems far from complete. As can be seen in the simulated example in Figure 2, our model can easily match the fact that destruction is more responsive than creation.[22]

[22] Davis and Haltiwanger (1992) show that the large variance of job destruction relative to that of job creation is mostly the result of the behavior of old, large, multi-unit establishments. Young, small, single-unit establishments exhibit the opposite pattern; that is, job creation is more volatile than job destruction. Our model is silent with respect to the size and multi-unit dimensions, given that its perfectly competitive linear setting makes no predictions about the division of production into firms and plants. However, it can easily rationalize the age-dependence of the relative volatility of job creation and destruction, since presumably older plants have a relatively large fraction of the outdated production units that our model predicts exhibit cyclical destruction, while young plants have mostly new production units.

This kind of behavior can be generated in our model by costly speed of adjustment $c'(f(0,t)) > 0$. In fact, as our calibration exercise below shows, only a small elasticity of creation costs (around 0.2) is needed to explain the facts. In any case, the data exhibit features that provide a natural experiment to test this mechanism. Observed business cycles are highly asymmetric, with recessions shorter but much sharper than expansions. In this context, our model predicts that those asymmetries would be smoothed out in the creation process.

The evidence is summarized in the second and third blocks in Table 1, which split the regressors between periods in which the rates of growth of sectoral output are above their mean ($\hat{Q}^+$) and periods in which they are below it ($\hat{Q}^-$). Looking first at job creation, we find that it is more responsive to expansions in sectoral activity than to contractions (the sum of coefficients for $\hat{Q}^+$ and $\hat{Q}^-$ are 0.399 and 0.084, respectively). Going back to Figure 3, this corresponds to

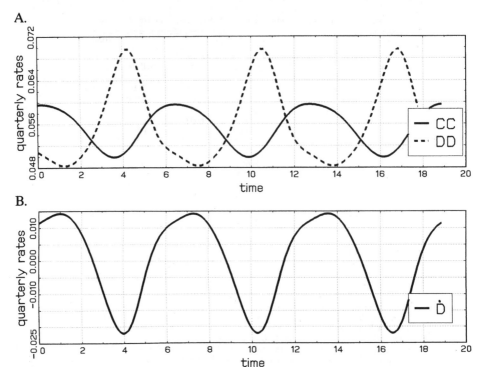

FIGURE 4. A) CREATION AND DESTRUCTION ($c_0 = 0.3$, $c_1 = 1.0$); B) CHANGE IN DEMAND (ASYMMETRIC)

the fact that job creation is roughly symmetric around its mean, while output growth is highly asymmetric, with recessions that are shorter-lived but much sharper than expansions. It is not surprising, then, that our regression yields an asymmetric response of job creation to expansions and recessions.

If we turn to job destruction, we find quite the opposite effect, with a sum of coefficients that is substantially larger in absolute value for recessions than it is for expansions (-0.634 vs. -0.066). Asymmetries in output are thus not only preserved in the response of job destruction (which would hold if the sum of coefficients were symmetric), but are actually amplified.

The fact that asymmetries in demand are smoothed out in the response of job creation and amplified in the response of destruction matches our model's predictions well. To show this, we simulated a periodic

equilibrium with the *asymmetric* process for demand $\bar{D}$ depicted in Figure 4.[23] It is clear that the creation process is roughly symmetric, while destruction is highly asymmetric. Firms use predictions of future demand in trying to smooth job creation; thus, the asymmetries in demand are smoothed out by the averaging of demand over the unit's lifetime. On the other hand, destruction depends only on current conditions; thus asymmetries are reflected directly on it. Moreover, if creation declines only mildly in response to a sharp contraction, the equilibrium price falls more sharply, which induces

[23]This process was generated with the equation $\bar{D}(t) = 0.05[\cos(t) + \sin(t)] - 0.016 \sin(2t) - 0.003 \cos(3t)$. The initial level is set to $\bar{D}(0) = 1$, and model parameters are set to $r = 0.065$, $\delta = 0.15$, $\gamma = 0.028$, $c_0 = 0.3$, and $c_1 = 1.0$.

additional destruction. This is the reason why destruction not only preserves, but *amplifies* the asymmetries in demand; it must "make up" for the symmetry in creation.

B. Calibration Exercise

We now present the results of an exercise based on aggregate manufacturing series that provides a synthesis for the previous discussion. We calibrate the model and use it to generate the equilibrium job creation and destruction series that are consistent in theory with the observed path of employment. In other words, we use the model to split observed net changes in employment into their gross creation and destruction components. We then repeat the exercise using the observed path of output and compute the creation and destruction series that are consistent in theory with the path of demand implied by observed output movements. In both cases, the model-generated series are compared with actual observations.

Solving for an equilibrium requires an initial age distribution of jobs, and expectations of what demand would be after the end of the sample period. We handle this problem by solving for a *periodic* equilibrium, with a period equal to the sample period. The model's response was simulated for the period 1972:2–1983:4 using the method described in the Appendix.[24]

The parameter values we used to calibrate the model are summarized in Table 2. We chose a yearly interest rate $r = 6.5$ percent and a depreciation/failure rate $\delta = 15$ percent. To choose the rate of technical progress γ, we approximated trend values by averages over the sample. Since there was very little growth in manufacturing em-

TABLE 2—CALIBRATED PARAMETERS

Variable	Symbol	Value
Interest rate	r	0.065
Depreciation rate	δ	0.150
Rate of technical progress	γ	0.028
Adjustment cost parameters	c_0	0.403
	c_1	0.500

ployment over the sample period (and one can easily show the direct link between demand and employment growth), we attributed all of the average growth rate of output to technical progress and set $\gamma = 2.8$ percent.

While our results are not very sensitive to the above parameters, they strongly depend on the parameters c_0 and c_1 of the adjustment-cost function (11). These parameters were chosen as follows. First $\bar{a}^*$ was calibrated based on equation (9), which relates the steady-state lifetime of jobs to job turnover CC*. Using the average value of CC over the sample for CC*, we find that $\bar{a}^* = 7.42$ years. This, together with the parameter values above, allows us to calculate from (7) the present discounted value of profits a production unit can generate in steady-state. By the free-entry condition, this must be equal to the steady-state creation cost, and it is found to be $c^* = 0.525$ (equivalent to a half year's operating costs for the production unit). This leaves us with only one free adjustment-cost parameter, since c_0 and c_1 are related in steady state to c^* by (11):

$$c^* = c_0 + c_1 f^*(0)$$

where $f^*(0)$ is given by equation (8). We searched for the value of c_1 that minimizes the weighted sum of squared residuals of the creation and destruction series and found a value of 0.5.[25] This corresponds to a relatively small elasticity for the creation

---

[24]Although the Davis and Haltiwanger (1990, 1992) job-flow series extend to 1986:4, we chose a shorter period for three reasons. (i) Numerical problems get worse as the simulation period gets longer. (ii) Because we are solving for a periodic equilibrium, we need demand to be roughly at the same level at the beginning and at the end of the period. (iii) Our model has little to say about the behavior of job destruction in 1985–1986, which exhibits two sharp peaks that are not associated with much action on the demand side.

[25]We used the inverse of the covariance matrix of creation and destruction as a weighting matrix. Our grid evaluated the model at values of c_1 0.1 units apart. We calibrated c_1 using the employment-driven simulations, which gave us higher values of c_1 than the demand-driven simulations. The qualitative conclusions are unaffected by our choice, however.

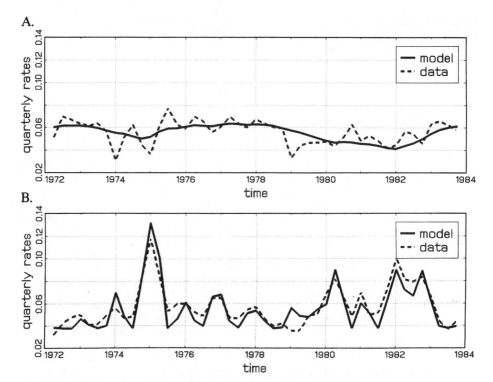

FIGURE 5. A) EMPLOYMENT-DRIVEN JOB CREATION ($c_0 = 0.403$, $c_1 = 0.500$); B) EMPLOYMENT-DRIVEN
JOB DESTRUCTION ($c_0 = 0.403$, $c_1 = 0.500$)

cost function, which reflects the fact that, although the insulation mechanism breaks down easily, creation has enough volatility in the data so costs of fast creation cannot be too large.

An issue we faced in the output-driven simulation concerned the observed procyclicality of average labor productivity, which our basic model is not designed to explain. To capture this, we introduced an output externality along the lines discussed in Section II-B and set the externality parameter β equal to 0.18 (as estimated by Caballero and Richard K. Lyons [1992]). Note, however, that our particular interpretation of procyclical productivity is not crucial here, since all it does is dampen the output fluctuations used to drive the simulation by a factor of β. The employment-driven simulation is unaffected.

The results of the employment-driven and output-driven simulations are given and compared to the data in Figures 5 and 6.[26] Job creation appears too smooth compared to the data, which is at least partly due to the absence of uncertainty in our model. In general, however, the model can clearly account for the relative volatility of job creation and destruction, and for the greater symmetry of the former compared to the latter.

[26]Note that the output-driven simulation cannot be expected to capture seasonal movements in observed job flows (which are not seasonally adjusted) because the driving process, industrial production, is seasonally adjusted.

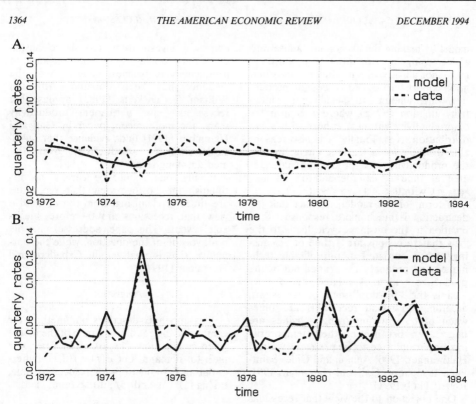

FIGURE 6. A) OUTPUT-DRIVEN JOB CREATION ($c_0 = 0.403$, $c_1 = 0.500$); B) OUTPUT-DRIVEN JOB DESTRUCTION ($c_0 = 0.403$, $c_1 = 0.500$)

IV. Concluding Remarks

This paper has examined industry response to demand fluctuations in a vintage model of creative destruction, where the response can take place along two possible margins. We have argued that responses to demand fluctuations on the creation margin have an "insulating" effect on existing production units, reducing the sensitivity of the destruction side. The extent to which this happens depends on the structure of creation costs. Empirically, the model seems to provide a good basis for interpreting the data of Davis and Haltiwanger (1990, 1992) on gross job flows.

The central features in our analysis are heterogeneity across production units and their turnover. Although they arise quite naturally in the context of creative destruction, these features can also appear in other

environments. Hopenhayn and Richard Rogerson (1991) and Caballero (1992) provide examples of models in which two margins arise because of idiosyncratic productivity or demand shocks.[27]

Several extensions can be introduced without modifying the basic results of the paper. For example, there is evidence that new plants tend to have larger failure rates, which can be easily accommodated in our

---

[27]A meaningful treatment of two margins of adjustment requires heterogeneous production units. In our paper, this arises because of embodied technical progress ($\gamma > 0$) coupled with creation costs. In the absence of technical progress ($\gamma = 0$) all production units would be identical, and the two margins would not generally be active simultaneously, unless we introduce another source of heterogeneity, such as idiosyncratic shocks.

model by making the exogenous failure rate a decreasing function $\delta(a)$ of a. Furthermore, not all surviving production units in a given cohort turn out to be equally productive, which amounts to specifying a productivity function $A(t, z)$, where z is an index of productivity within a cohort with some distribution $g(z)$. Finally, it is also reasonable to allow for a learning curve; that is, the productivity of a production unit created at time t_0 can depend on its age, $A(t_0, a)$, with $0 < A_a(\cdot, \cdot) < \gamma A(\cdot, \cdot)$.

In terms of our model, the fact that job destruction is much more responsive than creation to the business cycle leads to the view that recessions are a time of "cleansing," when outdated or unprofitable techniques and products are pruned out of the productive system. A related, but distinct idea is the "pit-stop" view of recessions, according to which recessions are times when productivity-improving activities are undertaken because of their temporarily low opportunity costs (see e.g., Davis and Haltiwanger, 1990; Aghion and Gilles Saint-Paul, 1991; Jordi Galí and Hammour, 1991; Robert Hall, 1991).

One objection to the view that recessions are times of cleansing is that it implies countercyclical productivity, while average labor productivity is in fact procyclical. However, one can show that this effect on productivity is likely to be small and may be dwarfed by other factors (labor hoarding, externalities, etc.) that make measured productivity procyclical.[28,29] An appropriate

empirical investigation into the cleansing effect must look at the *dynamic* response of productivity to business cycles. There, the evidence has been debated. Although William T. Dickens (1982) argues that recessions leave permanent productivity scars, the more recent paper by Galí and Hammour (1991) finds evidence that recessions improve productivity over the medium–long term.

Finally, one should be careful to distinguish the positive view that recessions are times of cleansing, from the normative view that recessions are therefore "desirable" events. This paper addresses only the positive side of the question, while the normative side is analyzed in Caballero and Hammour (1994).

APPENDIX

This appendix describes our method for computing the equilibrium path of the model given by equations (1)–(6), given a periodic path for demand. Let $\phi(t) \equiv f(0, t)$. Differentiating (4) and (6) with respect to time, taking (1), (2), and (5) into account, yields

$$(A1) \quad \dot{\bar{a}}(t) = 1 + \frac{\dot{\bar{D}}(t) + \delta \bar{D}(t) - e^{\gamma \bar{a}(t)}\phi(t)}{\gamma \bar{D}(t) + \phi(t - \bar{a}(t))e^{-\delta \bar{a}(t)}}$$

$$(A2) \quad \dot{\phi}(t) = \frac{1}{c_1}\bigg((r + \delta + \gamma)[c_0 + c_1\phi(t)]$$
$$- (e^{\gamma \bar{a}(t)} - 1) + \gamma \frac{1 - e^{-(r+\delta)T(t)}}{r + \delta}\bigg)$$

---

[28]Starting from steady state and using calibrated values for model parameters ($\delta = 0.15$, $\gamma = 0.028$, $\bar{a}^* = 7.4$ years), the effect of destroying 10 percent of the jobs in an industry at the low-productivity margin is a 1.1-percent improvement in average labor productivity. It will be even smaller relative to trend if accompanied by a fall in the creation rate.

[29]This idea finds strong support in Bresnahan and Raff's (1991) study of the motor-vehicles industry during the Great Depression. Although average labor productivity fell during the Depression, they found that "output per worker in the industry did not decline nearly so much as output per worker at a typical continuing plant from 1929 to 1933. Because the exiting plants were low in labor productivity and because their numbers were large in the aggregate, they account for this large composition effect" (p. 330).

This phenomenon is documented for a broader set

of industries in the Baily et al. (1992) study mentioned in footnote 2, which decomposes productivity growth into a part that takes place at the plant level and a part due to resource reallocation across plants. For the three periods 1972–1977, 1977–1982, and 1982–1987, the plant-level components were 2.80 percent, −6.08 percent, and 7.16 percent, while the reallocation components were 1.83 percent, 2.90 percent, and 1.82 percent (results for "all industries except 3573," in Baily et al.'s table 1 [p. 207]). Thus, the cyclical contraction in *aggregate* productivity that took place in the middle of the period was smaller than the contraction that took place at the typical plant. This difference was due to the positive reallocation component of productivity growth, which was in fact larger than in the first and last periods.

where $\{T(t)\}$ is related to $\{\bar{a}(t)\}$ through equation (3):

(A3) $\bar{a}(t + T(t)) = T(t)$.

The differential system (A1)–(A3) has several interesting but complex features. First, equation (A1) for $\ddot{a}(t)$ includes the second variable $\phi(t - \bar{a}(t))$ delayed. Second, this delay is not only flexible, but depends on $\bar{a}(t)$. Third, equation (A2) for $\dot{\phi}(t)$ includes $T(t)$, which by (A3) is a flexible lead that depends on the function $\bar{a}(\cdot)$.

In order to solve this system, we limit ourselves to the case of a periodic driving force $\bar{D}(t)$, with period R. Our algorithm calculates at each iteration i a one-period path $X_i \equiv \{\phi_i(t), \bar{a}_i(t)\}_{0 \leq t < R}$ of creation and destruction, *given* a history of past creation $H_i \equiv \{\phi_i(t)\}_{t < 0}$ and expected lifetimes $E_i \equiv \{T_i(t)\}_{0 \leq t}$. With the given history and expectations, system (A1)–(A2) can be solved forward for any initial values for $(\phi(0), \bar{a}(0))$. Using a multiple-shooting procedure, X_i is chosen to be a "periodic" solution for (A1)–(A2), in the sense that

$$(\phi_i(0), \bar{a}_i(0)) = (\phi_i(R), \bar{a}_i(R)).$$

The algorithm proceeds as follows:

Initialization.—Set $i = 1$ and the initial history H_1 and expectations E_1 to arbitrary values (e.g., their steady-state values for an average level of demand $\bar{D}^*$).

Iteration i.—Generate the one-period solution X_i, given H_i and E_i. If $i > 1$ and $|X_i - X_{i-1}|$ is less than some small ε, the procedure has converged. Use X_i as the equilibrium solution and terminate the algorithm. Otherwise, calculate H_{i+1} and E_{i+1} for the next iteration by extending the "periodic" function X_i to the whole real time interval. H_{i+1} is set equal to the resulting periodic history of $\phi(t)$, and E_{i+1} is obtained from the periodic expectation of $\bar{a}(t)$ using equation (A3). Once this is done, increment i and repeat the iteration.

We ran the two theoretical simulations in Figures 2 and 4 using this method. The employment- and output-driven simulations in Figures 5 and 6 were run with the same method, except that equation (A1) was modified so that we can take output and employment as given, rather than demand.

For the employment-driven simulation, equation (A1) was modified as follows. Since the path of $N(t)$ is taken as given, we rewrite (A1) in terms of employment. Recalling the expression

$$\dot{N}(t) = f(0, t) - \{f(\bar{a}(t), t)[1 - \dot{\bar{a}}(t)] + \delta N(t)\}$$

derived in Section I-A, we get

(A1') $\ddot{a}(t) = 1 + \dfrac{\dot{\bar{N}}(t) + \delta \bar{N}(t) - \phi(t)}{\phi(t - \bar{a}(t)) e^{-\delta \bar{a}(t)}}$.

We replace (A1) by (A1') and use the solution method described above.

As for the output-driven simulation, recall that we introduced an externality β along the lines described in Section II-A. In this case equilibrium conditions (1)–(6) only hold if we substitute $\hat{Q}(t) \equiv Q(t)/q(t)^\beta$ and $\hat{P}(t) \equiv P(t)q(t)^\beta$ for $Q(t)$ and $P(t)$, respectively, where $q(t) \equiv Q(t)/A(t)$. In other words, by (5), we need to dampen observed output fluctuations $\hat{Q}(t)$ (where a "hat" designates a growth rate) by a factor of β and use

$$\hat{\tilde{Q}}(t) = \hat{Q}(t) - \beta[\hat{Q}(t) - \gamma].$$

With this in mind, we rewrite (A1) in terms of "dampened" output. The latter is related to demand through equations (5) and (6):

$$\bar{D}(t) = \tilde{Q}(t) e^{-\gamma[t - \bar{a}(t)]}$$

where units were chosen so that $A(0) = 1$. Replacing for $\bar{D}(t)$ and $\dot{\bar{D}}(t)$ in (A1) and rearranging, we get

(A1'') $\ddot{a}(t) = 1 + \dfrac{\left[\dot{\tilde{Q}}(t) + \delta \tilde{Q}(t)\right] e^{-\gamma t} - \phi(t)}{\phi(t - \bar{a}(t))}$

$$\times e^{(\gamma + \delta)\bar{a}(t)}.$$

We replace (A1) by (A1'') and solve.

Note that to run these simulations in continuous time, we need a continuous path for $N(t)$ and $Q(t)$, whereas the observed path is discrete. To handle this problem, we regress the growth rates of these two series on as many $\sin(i\omega t)$ and $\cos(i\omega t)$ terms, $i = 1, 2, \ldots$, as we have degrees of freedom, where $\omega \equiv 2\pi/R$. We use the resulting continuous and periodic representation to run the simulations.

REFERENCES

Aghion, Philippe and Howitt, Peter. "A Model of Growth Through Creative Destruction." *Econometrica*, March 1992, *60*(2), pp. 323–51.

Aghion, Philippe and Saint-Paul, Gilles. "On the Virtue of Bad Times." Mimeo, European Bank for Reconstruction and Development, June 1991.

Baily, Martin Neil; Hulten, Charles and Campbell, David. "Productivity Dynamics in Manufacturing Plants." *Brookings Papers on Economic Activity*, Microeconomics 1992, pp. 187–249.

Bartelsman, Eric J. and Dhrymes, Phoebus J. "Productivity Dynamics: U.S. Manufacturing Plants, 1972–1986." Columbia University Department of Economics Discussion Paper No. 584, September 1991.

Blanchard, Olivier J. and Diamond, Peter. "The Cyclical Behavior of the Gross Flows of U.S. Workers." *Brookings Papers on Economic Activity*, 1990, (2), pp. 85–155.

Bresnahan, Timothy F. and Raff, Daniel M. G. "Intra-Industry Heterogeneity and the Great Depression: The American Motor Vehicles Industry, 1929–1935." *Journal of Economic History*, June 1991, *51*(2), pp. 317–31.

_____. "Technological Heterogeneity, Adjustment Costs, and the Dynamics of Plant-Shut-Down Behavior: The American Motor Vehicle Industry in the Time of the Great Depression." Mimeo, Stanford University, 1992.

Caballero, Ricardo J. "A Fallacy of Composition." *American Economic Review*, December 1992, *82*(5), pp. 1279–92.

Caballero, Ricardo J. and Hammour, Mohamad L. "On the Timing and Efficiency of Creative Destruction." National Bureau of Economic Research (Cambridge, MA) Working Paper No. 4768, June 1994.

Caballero, Ricardo J. and Lyons, Richard K. "External Effects in U.S. Procyclical Productivity." *Journal of Monetary Economics*, January 1992, *29*(1), pp. 209–25.

Davis, Steven J. and Haltiwanger, John. "Gross Job Creation and Destruction: Microeconomic Evidence and Macroeconomic Implications," in Olivier J. Blanchard and Stanley Fischer, eds., *NBER macroeconomics annual*. Cambridge, MA: MIT Press, 1990, pp. 123–68.

_____. "Gross Job Creation, Gross Job Destruction, and Employment Reallocation." *Quarterly Journal of Economics*, August 1992, *107*(3), pp. 818–63.

De Long, J. Bradford. 'Liquidation' Cycles: Old-Fashioned Real Business Cycle Theory and the Great Depression." National Bureau of Economic Research (Cambridge, MA) Working Paper No. 3546, October 1990.

Diamond, Peter. "On Time: Lectures on Models of Equilibrium." Mimeo, Massachusetts Institute of Technology, 1993.

Dickens, William T. "The Productivity Crisis: Secular or Cyclical?" *Economics Letters*, 1982, *9*(1), pp. 37–42.

Galí, Jordi and Hammour, Mohamad L. "Long-Run Effects of Business Cycles." Mimeo, Columbia University Graduate School of Business, April 1991.

Gorecki, H.; Fuksa, S.; Grabowski, P. and Korytowski, A. *Analysis and synthesis of time delay systems.* New York: Wiley, 1989.

Grossman, Gene M. and Helpman, Elhanan. *Innovation and growth in the global economy.* Cambridge, MA: MIT Press, 1991.

Hall, Robert E. "Labor Demand, Labor Supply, and Employment Volatility," in Olivier J. Blanchard and Stanley Fischer, eds., *NBER macroeconomics annual*. Cambridge, MA: MIT Press, 1991, pp. 17–47.

Hopenhayn, Hugo A. "Industry Equilibrium Dynamics: A General Competitive Theory." Mimeo, Stanford University, 1990.

Hopenhayn, Hugo and Rogerson, Richard. "Job Turnover and Policy Evaluation: A General Equilibrium Analysis." Mimeo, Stanford University, 1991.

Hulten, Charles R. "Growth Accounting When Technical Change Is Embodied in Capital." *American Economic Review*, September 1992, *82*(4), pp. 964–80.

Johansen, Leif. "Substitution versus Fixed Production Coefficients in the Theory of Economic Growth: A Synthesis." *Econometrica*, April 1959, *27*(2), pp. 157–76.

Jovanovic, Boyan and Lach, Saul. "Entry, Exit, and Diffusion with Learning by Doing." *American Economic Review*, September 1989, *79*(4), pp. 690–99.

Mortensen, Dale and Pissarides, Christopher. "Job Creation and Job Destruction in the Theory of Unemployment." Mimeo, Northwestern University, 1991.

_____. "The Cyclical Behavior of Job Creation and Job Destruction." Mimeo, Northwestern University, 1992.

Nisbet, R. M. and Gurney, W. S. C. *Modeling fluctuating populations*. New York: Wiley, 1982.

Phelps, Edmund S. "Substitution, Fixed Proportions, Growth and Distribution." *International Economic Review*, September 1963, *4*(3), pp. 265–88.

Schumpeter, Joseph A. *Business cycles: A theoretical, historical, and statistical analysis of the capitalist process*. New York: McGraw-Hill, 1939.

_____. *Capitalism, socialism, and democracy*. New York: Harper, 1942.

Sheshinski, Eytan. "Balanced Growth and Stability in the Johansen Vintage Model." *Review of Economic Studies*, April 1967, *34*(2), pp. 239–48.

Shleifer, Andrei. "Implementation Cycles." *Journal of Political Economy*, December 1986, *94*(6), pp. 1163–90.

Solow, Robert M. "Investment and Technological Progress," in K. J. Arrow, S. Karlin, and P. Suppes, eds., *Mathematical methods in social sciences*. Stanford, CA: Stanford University Press, pp. 89–104.

[6]

Available online at www.sciencedirect.com

ScienceDirect

Journal of Economic Theory 137 (2007) 27–48

JOURNAL OF
Economic
Theory

www.elsevier.com/locate/jet

ELSEVIER

Entrepreneurial talent, occupational choice, and trickle up policies

Maitreesh Ghatak[a,*], Massimo Morelli[b], Tomas Sjöström[c]

[a] *London School of Economics, London, UK*
[b] *Ohio State University, Ohio, USA*
[c] *Rutgers University, NJ, USA*

Received 1 August 2001; final version received 23 February 2006
Available online 19 April 2006

Abstract

We study market inefficiencies and policy remedies when agents choose their occupations, and entrepreneurial talent is subject to private information. Untalented entrepreneurs depress the returns to entrepreneurship because of adverse selection. The severity of this problem depends on the outside option of entrepreneurs, which is working for wages. This links credit, product and labor markets. A rise in wages reduces the adverse selection problem. These multimarket interactions amplify productivity shocks and may generate multiple equilibria. If it is impossible to screen entrepreneurs then all agents unanimously support a tax on entrepreneurs that drives out the less talented ones. However, if screening is possible, e.g., if wealthy entrepreneurs can provide collateral for their loans, then wealthy entrepreneurs do not support surplus enhancing taxes.
© 2006 Elsevier Inc. All rights reserved.

JEL classification: D82; E44; J24; O16

Keywords: Occupational choice; Adverse selection; Entrepreneurial talent

1. Introduction

When an occupation is subject to adverse selection, talented individuals receive less than the full marginal social return of their talents. This typically creates inefficiencies. For example, if consumers cannot distinguish high-quality from low-quality goods, then the competitive equilibrium price will reflect the average quality [2]. As a consequence, producers of high-quality

---

* Corresponding author. Tel.: +44 207 852 3568; fax: +44 207 955 6951.
  E-mail addresses: m.ghatak@lse.ac.uk (M. Ghatak), morelli.10@osu.edu (M. Morelli), tsjostrom@fas-econ.rutgers.edu (T. Sjöström).

doi:10.1016/j.jet.2006.02.007

goods may produce too little or leave the market. Alternatively, suppose setting up a new business requires credit. If the probability that a loan is repaid depends on the unobserved talent of the entrepreneur, then the equilibrium interest rate will reflect the average talent in the market [21]. Therefore, untalented entrepreneurs impose a negative externality on talented entrepreneurs. This negative externality reduces the incentives of talented entrepreneurs to borrow and invest.

These consequences of adverse selection are well known. However, they have been derived in partial equilibrium models. In partial equilibrium, the entrepreneur's outside option is exogenously given. But suppose the outside option of the entrepreneur is to work for wages. The wage depends on investment and output decisions made by other entrepreneurs, which are influenced by the adverse selection problem. In this case it may be misleading to treat the outside option as exogenous when analyzing the adverse selection problem.

In this paper, we develop a general equilibrium model of occupational choice, where the entrepreneur's outside option is endogenized. The returns to different occupations depend on the quality of the pool of entrepreneurs, i.e., the extent of the adverse selection problem. But the severity of the adverse selection problem depends on the outside option of the entrepreneurs, which in turn depends on the returns to different occupations. Thus, there is a two-way interaction between allocation of talent and the returns to different occupations. This two-way interaction can make the adverse selection problem more severe. Policies such as subsidies to entrepreneurs may have unintended consequences. Unlike the Akerlof model, multiple equilibria can exist even if firms and banks are not price takers. On the other hand, our model yields a richer set of policy remedies. In particular, the adverse selection problem may be remedied by policies that influence the outside option, for example by raising the minimum wage.

In our model agents can choose between supplying labor as workers and becoming entrepreneurs. Entrepreneurs borrow capital from banks and sell their output in the product market. Entrepreneurial talent is private information, so adverse selection may occur in the credit or the product market (but not in the labor market). No screening instruments are available in the basic model. The product price or the interest rate depend on the *average* talent level in the pool of active entrepreneurs. This in turn depends on the wage in the labor market, which is the outside option of entrepreneurs. The wage is endogenously determined in general equilibrium. In equilibrium, the least talented entrepreneurs will typically be indifferent between remaining entrepreneurs and becoming workers. Because they are less talented than the average of the pool of active entrepreneurs, they impose a negative externality on other entrepreneurs. After a wage increase, the least talented entrepreneurs switch occupations, so the average quality of the pool goes up. This *pool quality effect* causes the price to go up or the interest rate to go down. Thus, a wage increase can be good not only for workers, but also for entrepreneurs, since it implies better terms for them in the product or credit markets.

The pool quality effect can potentially lead to a *positive* relationship between wages and aggregate labor demand. When the wage goes up, the improved terms in the product or the credit market may induce the remaining entrepreneurs to hire *more* labor. The more elastic is labor demand, the stronger is the pool quality effect on labor demand.

The model has significant policy implications. Policies that benefit workers, such as a minimum wage increase, drive the least talented entrepreneurs out of business. These entrepreneurs and their workers will transfer to firms run by more talented entrepreneurs. The talented entrepreneurs obtain better terms in the product and credit markets due to the pool quality effect, which justifies their expansion even at a higher wage. The benefits initially given to workers *trickle up* to the remaining entrepreneurs. This can potentially make *all* agents better off. Indeed, if there is no screening,

M. Ghatak et al. / Journal of Economic Theory 137 (2007) 27–48   29

then there will be *unanimous* support for such trickle up policies, because all entrepreneurs will benefit from the quality of the pool effect. [1]

Policies that increase the demand for labor (for example, by improving the productivity of labor) will typically lead to higher wages, which in turn will tend to raise the average quality of the entrepreneurs. Again, this improves the returns to entrepreneurship via improved terms in product and credit markets. Due to the interaction between multiple markets there is a *multiplier* effect that creates further incentives to expand production and employment. Policies that encourage firms to expand employment can finance themselves, since higher labor demand leads to higher wages, which raises overall surplus through the pool quality effect.

We extend the basic model to allow borrowers to have different (observable) levels of wealth that can be used as a screening instrument. With a "separating" contract, wealthy talented entrepreneurs are protected from the negative externalities caused by untalented entrepreneurs. Accordingly, they will not benefit from a tax on entrepreneurs, even if it raises total social surplus. Therefore, in the presence of screening instruments, surplus enhancing policies no longer have unanimous support. Even though it cannot induce a pool quality effect on separating contracts, a wage increase can have a non-standard effect on labor demand even in the screening model, by a new type of *extensive margin effect*. When the wage increases, it becomes easier to separate talented entrepreneurs from untalented entrepreneurs, and so the collateral required for a separating contract decreases. More agents therefore obtain separating contracts which have low interest rates, and this increases labor demand. Thus, the basic model and the model with screening uncover, two separate effects that may lead to an upward sloping labor demand curve, with important implications for policies such as a minimum wage, or a tax on entrepreneurs.

Multiple equilibria can exist in our model. If there is no screening, then the equilibria are Pareto-ranked. This situation is similar to Murphy et al. [18]. Everyone prefers the wages to be high, including the entrepreneurs. As a result there is a clear incentive to coordinate on the surplus maximizing equilibrium. But when screening is possible, the multiple equilibria are typically *not* Pareto-ranked. Rich talented entrepreneurs prefer wages to be low, but those who are talented and poor prefer high wages, because this relaxes their credit constraints.

In models of occupational choice with *exogenously* determined credit constraints it is never optimal to tax entrepreneurs [4,11,12,5,17,19]. De Meza and Webb [9] pointed out that credit constraints might be relaxed if the borrower's outside option becomes more attractive, but they also treated this outside option as exogenous. None of these articles considered the *two-way* interaction between the labor and credit markets which is the focus of our analysis. In the literature, on poverty traps due to credit constraints, lowering the cost of credit (e.g., through credit subsidies) encourages entrepreneurship and investment [3]. But this argument ignores the potentially important *selection* effect highlighted in our model. If entrepreneurial talent is private information, credit subsidies will encourage less talented agents to become entrepreneurs, so the average quality of the pool falls. This exacerbates the adverse selection problem. Naturally, banks will respond by raising interest rates or imposing higher collateral requirements. As we will show, this can cancel out the intended beneficial effects of the policy.

The literature on the "cleansing" effect argues that in a recession, the quality of the pool of entrepreneurs improves due to failures of bad projects (see [8]). Our model leads us to question

---

[1] Historically, the architects of the "Scandinavian model" argued in favor of high minimum wages. These economists were aware that less productive firms would be driven out of business, but they hoped that the unemployed workers would eventually be hired by more productive firms, which would stimulate growth [1]. In our model it is the quality of the pool effect which induces high-quality firms to absorb the unemployed workers.

this view. In a recession the outside options are depressed. Therefore, less talented agents try to become entrepreneurs, which *worsens* the quality of the pool. In response to this, banks adopt tougher lending policies, which depresses the demand for labor. More generally, our analysis suggests that interventions in the labor market can change the outside option for entrepreneurs, and hence affect the severity of credit constraints.

Mankiw [14] discusses the possibility of multiple equilibria in a credit market with adverse selection. The intuition is that when interest rates rise, borrowing becomes less attractive, and high-quality (low risk) borrowers are the first to drop out. This lowers the quality of the pool of borrowers, so banks require a higher interest rate in order to break even. However, if the banks are not price takers (i.e., if they can choose which contracts to offer), then only the equilibrium with the lowest interest rate survives.[2] In our model, multiple equilibria occur for a different reason. When borrowing becomes less attractive, low-quality (high risk) entrepreneurs are the first to drop out and become workers, which *raises* the quality of the pool of borrowers. In itself, this cannot generate multiple equilibria. Instead, multiple equilibria occur because the outside option to borrowing is endogenously determined through occupational choice, and the returns in the credit and labor markets are linked due to technological/demand complementarities. This can generate multiple equilibria even if the banks are not price takers.

The paper is organized as follows. In Section 2 we present a model of adverse selection and occupational choice between complementary activities that encompasses our leading examples of product market and credit market adverse selection. In Section 3 we prove the existence of equilibria. Section 4 identifies economic policies that raise social surplus. Section 5 contains an example of multiple equilibria. In Sections 2–5 we assume no screening instruments are available, and focus on the pool quality effect. In Section 6 we extend the basic model for the case of adverse selection in the credit market, by allowing banks to screen borrowers using collateral. In Section 7 we make some concluding observations.

2. The model

2.1. Environment

We consider a one-period competitive economy with a continuum of agents. The population size is normalized to 1. Each agent is endowed with 1 unit of labor which he supplies inelastically. Thus, the total labor endowment of the economy is 1. All agents have access to a self-employment technology that yields them an autarchy income normalized to zero. Agents can supply their labor as workers or entrepreneurs. Firms produce a good x. In addition, there is a numeraire commodity m. The quality of x varies. Specifically, the x good comes in two varieties: satisfactory and unsatisfactory. To simplify, we suppose only satisfactory x goods give utility to consumers. Unsatisfactory x goods are useless. If a consumer consumes $\hat{x}$ units of the satisfactory version of the x good, and m units of the numeraire, then his utility is $U = \hat{x} + m$. The unsatisfactory x good does not add to his utility and so does not show up in the utility function.

Each firm consists of one entrepreneur and l ordinary workers who produce the x good (adding physical capital would make no substantive difference). The amount of ordinary labor l is chosen by the entrepreneur. Potential entrepreneurs do not have any liquid wealth and need to borrow to pay wages. The wage rate is denoted by w and the (gross) interest rate by r. The production function

---

[2] Mas-Colell et al. [15] make a similar point about Akerlof's [2] model.

M. Ghatak et al. / Journal of Economic Theory 137 (2007) 27–48   31

is $f(l)$, which is strictly increasing, strictly concave, and twice continuously differentiable. Banks are competitive and face a constant (gross) opportunity cost of 1 per unit of capital.

Agents are heterogeneous in terms of their talent as entrepreneurs. Let $\theta \in \{\theta_L, \theta_H\}$ denote the quality of an agent's entrepreneurial input, where $\theta_H > \theta_L$. If $\theta = \theta_H$ then the agent is a *high type*, and if $\theta = \theta_L$ then the agent is a *low type*. The high types make up a fraction q of the population, the rest are low types. The true θ is the agent's private information. An entrepreneur of type θ is *successful* with probability θ and *unsuccessful* with probability $1 - \theta$. If the entrepreneur is successful, then the x good he produces has satisfactory quality. If he is unsuccessful, then the output is unsatisfactory. Thus, an entrepreneur of type θ will produce a satisfactory product with probability θ, and an unsatisfactory product with probability $1 - \theta$.

If an agent of type θ works as an entrepreneur then he suffers a disutility $c_e(\theta)$. The disutility of being a worker is denoted $c_w(\theta)$. These disutilities are incurred simply by working in a particular occupation (there is no effort choice, and each agent supplies one unit of labor). Define $b(\theta) \equiv c_w(\theta) - c_e(\theta)$. For some results, the following assumption is required.

Assumption 1.

$$b(\theta_H) > b(\theta_L).$$

Assumption 1 is a single-crossing property with regard to occupational choice. It implies that entrepreneurship is more desirable (or less costly) for high types than for low types. For example, the disutility from entrepreneurial activity may be decreasing in the type of an agent. Alternatively, extra income may be generated by higher-quality entrepreneurs. However, if there is adverse selection in the credit market, then the extra income cannot be appropriated by lenders: it is a *private* benefit. (If the private benefit also depends on l, then our results will be strengthened if l and θ are complements.)

Depending on who bears the cost of the quality uncertainty concerning the x good, we consider two versions of the adverse selection problem that fit our framework. The key issue is whether or not the consumers can observe the quality of the x good before purchasing it.

Case I: *Product market adverse selection*. In this case, the quality of the x good cannot be observed by consumers before purchase. Therefore, all firms sell the x good at the same price p. The consumers suffer from the quality uncertainty, which depresses p. Specifically, let μ denote the fraction of the total supply of the x good which is satisfactory. Since all firms will sell the same quantity, μ equals the average θ among the active entrepreneurs. Given the linear utility function, the equilibrium price of x must be $p(\mu) = \mu$. [3] Since all entrepreneurs can sell their output at the market price, they will all repay their loans. Therefore, the interest rate does not depend on μ. Competition among banks ensure that the interest rate is fixed at $r = 1$.

Case II: *Credit market adverse selection*. In this case, the quality of the x good can be observed by consumers before purchase. Now p denotes the price of *satisfactory* x goods. By the linearity of the utility function, $p = 1$. Successful entrepreneurs produce satisfactory x goods, and they will sell their output at the price $p = 1$. Unsuccessful entrepreneurs produce unsatisfactory x goods, and they will not be able to sell their output at any positive price. Due to limited liability, entrepreneurs repay their loans only when they are successful (and so can sell their output). Since banks cannot observe the quality of the entrepreneur when making a loan, and there are

---

[3] With a more general utility function, the price of x would also depend on the quantity consumed. This would complicate the model without adding much to the key insights.

no screening instruments, the banks suffer from the quality uncertainty. To ensure that banks break even on average this raises the interest rate. The interest rate is determined by the ex ante probability that the loan is repaid, which is μ, the average θ among the active entrepreneurs. The zero profit condition for the competitive banks yields the interest rate $r(\mu) = 1/\mu$.

2.2. Labor demand

Consider the profit function

$$\pi(p, r, w) \equiv \max_{l \geqslant 0} \{pf(l) - wrl\}.$$

By the envelope theorem,

$$\pi_p(p, r, w) = f(l), \quad \pi_r(p, r, w) = -wl, \quad \pi_w(p, r, w) = -rl.$$

Let μ denote the average quality of all active entrepreneurs (i.e., the average level of θ). As explained in the previous section, p or r can depend on μ. Therefore, we write $p(\mu)$ and $r(\mu)$, where $p'(\mu) \geqslant 0$ and $r'(\mu) \leqslant 0$. This allows us to treat both cases in one framework. In case I, $p'(\mu) > 0 = r'(\mu)$, and in case II, $p'(\mu) = 0 > r'(\mu)$. Notice that

$$\frac{d}{d\mu}\pi(p(\mu), r(\mu), w) = \pi_p p' + \pi_r r' = f(l)p' - wlr' > 0. \tag{1}$$

That is, all firms benefit from an increase in the *average* quality of the entrepreneurs.

The expected payoff of an entrepreneur of type θ is denoted by $v(\pi(p, r, w), \theta)$. In case I, he sells the good at $p = p(\mu)$ with $p' > 0$. The interest rate is $r \equiv 1$, so in case I we have

$$v(\pi(p(\mu), 1, w), \theta) = \pi(p(\mu), 1, w) - c_e(\theta). \tag{2}$$

In case II, if he is successful then he sells at the price $p \equiv 1$ (and repays the loan). The interest rate is $r = r(\mu)$ with $r' < 0$. The entrepreneur succeeds with probability θ, so in case II we have

$$v(\pi(1, r(\mu), w), \theta) = \theta\pi(1, r(\mu), w) - c_e(\theta). \tag{3}$$

In both cases I and II, each entrepreneur will set l to maximize $pf(l) - wrl$.[4] Let $l = h(wr/p)$ denote the solution to this problem. The first-order condition for an interior solution is

$$pf'(l) = wr. \tag{4}$$

Since p or r depends on the *average* quality of active entrepreneurs, all entrepreneurs choose the same l. Thus, the firm's demand for labor can be expressed as a function of w and μ,

$$\tilde{l}(w, \mu) \equiv h\left(\frac{wr(\mu)}{p(\mu)}\right), \tag{5}$$

where $h = (f')^{-1}$ if the solution is interior. From our assumptions regarding the production function, $\tilde{l}(w, \mu)$ is differentiable. Since $f(l)$ is concave, $h(.)$ is decreasing. In other words, labor demand, $\tilde{l}$, is decreasing in the *real wage*, defined as $wr(\mu)/p(\mu)$. The real wage is clearly increasing in w. Also, by assumption, $p' > 0$ or $r' < 0$, and so $wr(\mu)/p(\mu)$ is strictly decreasing

---

[4] In case II, if the entrepreneur fails then he defaults on his loan and earns zero. He will choose l to maximize his profit conditional on success, which is $pf(l) - wrl$.

M. Ghatak et al. / Journal of Economic Theory 137 (2007) 27–48   33

in μ. Therefore, labor demand is decreasing in the nominal wage rate, w and increasing in average quality of active entrepreneurs, μ.

2.3. Occupational choice

The alternative to being an entrepreneur is being a worker. The average quality of entrepreneurs affects p or r, and hence the occupational choice decision of agents of type θ depends on μ. An agent of type θ is indifferent between being an entrepreneur and a worker if

$$v(\pi(p(\mu), r(\mu), w), \theta) = w - c_w(\theta). \tag{6}$$

We call this the occupational choice condition.

In case I, (6) takes the form

$$p(\mu) f(\tilde{l}(w, \mu)) - w\tilde{l}(w, \mu) + b(\theta) = w. \tag{7}$$

In case II, (6) takes the form

$$\theta \left(f(\tilde{l}(w, \mu)) - \frac{w}{\mu} \tilde{l}(w, \mu) \right) + b(\theta) = w. \tag{8}$$

Condition (6) implicitly defines $\mu \in [\theta_L, \theta_H]$ as a function of θ and w. Given θ and w, let $\mu^\theta(w)$ denote the μ that satisfies (6). Clearly, (6) cannot be satisfied if w is too high (everyone then strictly prefers being a worker). Moreover, to avoid trivial cases we assume that even low type agents want to become entrepreneurs at zero wage:

$$v(\pi(p(\mu), r(\mu), 0), \theta_L) > -c_w(\theta_L) \quad \forall \mu \geqslant \theta_L. \tag{9}$$

Given this, (6) cannot be satisfied if w is too low (every agent strictly prefers being a entrepreneur). For w such that (6) cannot be satisfied for any μ, $\mu^\theta(w)$ is not defined.

Given our assumptions on $f(.)$, $\mu^\theta(w)$ is a differentiable function of w. Abusing notation slightly, let $\mu^H(w)$ and $\mu^L(w)$ denote $\mu^\theta(w)$ for $\theta = \theta_H$ and $\theta = \theta_L$, respectively. Notice that $\mu^\theta(w)$ is the average quality of the pool of entrepreneurs such that an agent of type θ is indifferent between being entrepreneur and worker when the wage is w.

For a given θ, by totally differentiating (6) with respect to w, we find that $\mu^\theta(w)$ is *increasing* in w:

$$\frac{d\mu^\theta(w)}{dw} = \frac{1 - v_\pi \pi_w}{v_\pi \left(\pi_p p' + \pi_r r' \right)} > 0.$$

The intuition is that the higher is w, the less attractive it is to be an entrepreneur. To restore indifference, entrepreneurship must be made more attractive. Since (1) holds, this is done by increasing the average quality of the entrepreneurs.

The following result shows how the occupational choice decision of an agent is affected when the wage rate changes.

Lemma 1. *Suppose agents of type θ are indifferent between becoming entrepreneurs or workers. If following an increase in w agents of type θ at least weakly prefer entrepreneurship, the real wage wr/p must fall in case II, and also in case I if $b(\theta) > 0$.*

Proof. In case I, an agent of type θ weakly prefers being an entrepreneur to being a worker if

$$\frac{p(\mu)}{w} f(l) - l + \frac{b(\theta)}{w} \geqslant 1. \tag{10}$$

Starting with equality in (10), so long as $b(\theta) > 0$, an increase in w must be accompanied by a fall in the real wage for (10) to continue to hold.

In case II the analogous condition is

$$\theta \left(f(l) - \frac{w}{\mu} l \right) + b(\theta) \geqslant w. \tag{11}$$

Starting with equality in (11), regardless of the sign of $b(\theta)$, an increase in w must be accompanied by a fall in the real wage for (11) to continue to hold. $\square$

The above (partial equilibrium) result tells us what should be the compensating changes in $p(\mu)$ or $r(\mu)$ when w changes, in order for the marginal entrepreneur not to switch occupations. We next ask what will happen to labor demand if changes in the wage rate are accompanied by compensating changes in $p(\mu)$ or $r(\mu)$ so as to keep the marginal entrepreneur indifferent. Recall that if the average quality is $\mu = \mu^\theta(w)$ and the wage is w, then a type θ agent is indifferent between being entrepreneur and worker. The labor demand of firms, when μ adjusts to satisfy the occupational choice condition of type θ, is

$$\tilde{l}(w, \mu^\theta(w)) = h \left(\frac{w r(\mu^\theta(w))}{p(\mu^\theta(w))} \right). \tag{12}$$

Notice that this differs from the standard labor demand function (5) which considers only the direct effect of w, holding μ constant. We may refer to (12) as a *quasi labor demand function.* Since h is a decreasing function, Lemma 1 and (12) imply the following.

Proposition 1. $\tilde{l}(w, \mu^\theta(w))$ *is increasing in w in case II, and also in case I if $b(\theta) > 0$.*

Thus, if μ adjusts to keep type θ indifferent between being entrepreneur and worker, then the standard (partial equilibrium) negative intensive-margin effect of an increase in w on labor demand is dominated by a positive *pool quality* effect caused by an increase in μ. The improvement in the quality of the pool raises prices or lowers interest rate ($p'(\mu) > 0$ in case I, and $r'(\mu) < 0$ in case II).

3. Market equilibrium

From now on, Assumption 1 is made in order to simplify the analysis. The following relationships implicitly define w', $\overline{w}$ and $\underline{w}$:

$$\theta_{\mathrm{H}} = \mu^{\mathrm{L}}(w'), \tag{13}$$

$$\theta_{\mathrm{H}} = \mu^{\mathrm{H}}(\overline{w}), \tag{14}$$

$$q\theta_{\mathrm{H}} + (1 - q)\theta_{\mathrm{L}} = \mu^{\mathrm{L}}(\underline{w}). \tag{15}$$

M. Ghatak et al. / Journal of Economic Theory 137 (2007) 27–48   35

Let $\lambda \in [0, 1]$ denote the fraction of low type agents who become entrepreneurs in equilibrium. The average quality of the active entrepreneurs is

$$\mu = \frac{q\theta_H + (1-q)\lambda\theta_L}{q + (1-q)\lambda}. \tag{16}$$

If $\lambda = 0$ then there are no low type entrepreneurs so the quality of the pool is at its maximum, $\mu = \theta_H$. If $\mu = \theta_H$ and $w = w'$ then the low type agents are indifferent between being entrepreneurs and workers. If $w > w'$, then the low type agents strictly prefer to be workers. If $w = \overline{w}$ and $\mu = \theta_H$, then the high type agents are indifferent between being entrepreneurs and workers. If $w > \overline{w}$, then even high type agents prefer to be workers (since μ cannot exceed θ_H), which cannot be part of an equilibrium. Notice that Assumption 1 implies $w' < \overline{w}$.

If $w < w'$, then we must have $\lambda > 0$ (otherwise $\mu = \theta_H$, but then the low type agents would strictly prefer to be entrepreneurs, by the definition of w'). If $0 < \lambda < 1$ then the low type agents must be indifferent between being entrepreneurs and workers. Assumption 1 implies that in this case the high type agents *strictly* prefer to be entrepreneurs. If $w < \underline{w}$, then all agents strictly prefer to be entrepreneurs, even though the quality of the pool is at its minimum, $\mu = q\theta_H + (1-q)\theta_L$ (if $w = \underline{w}$ then the low type agents are indifferent). If $w > \underline{w}$ then we must have $\lambda < 1$ (otherwise $\mu = q\theta_H + (1-q)\theta_L$, but then the low type agents would strictly prefer to work for wages, by definition of $\underline{w}$).

If a wage w such that $\underline{w} \leqslant w < w'$ is part of an equilibrium, then the low type agents must be indifferent between the two occupations. Accordingly, the fraction λ must be such that $\mu = \mu^L(w)$. That is,

$$\frac{q\theta_H + (1-q)\lambda\theta_L}{q + (1-q)\lambda} = \mu^L(w).$$

This allows us to solve for the unique λ which corresponds to a given wage w such that $\underline{w} \leqslant w < w'$:

$$\lambda = \frac{q}{1-q} \frac{\theta_H - \mu^L(w)}{\mu^L(w) - \theta_L}. \tag{17}$$

The total number of active entrepreneurs is

$$q + (1-q)\lambda = q\frac{\theta_H - \theta_L}{\mu^L(w) - \theta_L}. \tag{18}$$

It will simplify the exposition to define the demand and supply of labor to include entrepreneurial labor. That is, each firm demands one unit of entrepreneurial labor, and l units of ordinary labor. Given that the population size is normalized to one, each person supplies one unit of labor inelastically, and the autarchy option of each agent is 0, aggregate labor supply is $L^s(w) = 1$ for all $w > 0$.

For $w = \overline{w}$, the high types are indifferent between the two occupations, and the aggregate labor demand consists of the segment

$$L^d(\overline{w}) = \left[0, q\left(h\left(\frac{\overline{w}r(\theta_H)}{p(\theta_H)}\right) + 1\right)\right]. \tag{19}$$

For w such that $w' \leqslant w \leqslant \overline{w}$, all high types are entrepreneurs, but no low types, and so aggregate labor demand is

$$L^{\mathrm{d}}(w) = q \left(h \left(\frac{wr(\theta_{\mathrm{H}})}{p(\theta_{\mathrm{H}})} \right) + 1 \right). \tag{20}$$

For w such that $\underline{w} \leqslant w < w'$, low types are indifferent between the two occupations, and Eq. (18) implies that aggregate labor demand is

$$L^{\mathrm{d}}(w) = q \frac{\theta_{\mathrm{H}} - \theta_{\mathrm{L}}}{\mu^{\mathrm{L}}(w) - \theta_{\mathrm{L}}} \left(h \left(\frac{wr(\mu^{\mathrm{L}}(w))}{p(\mu^{\mathrm{L}}(w))} \right) + 1 \right). \tag{21}$$

Finally, for $w < \underline{w}$, all agents are entrepreneurs, and

$$L^{\mathrm{d}}(w) = h \left(\frac{wr(\theta_{\mathrm{H}})}{p(\theta_{\mathrm{H}})} \right) + 1. \tag{22}$$

We are now ready to state:

Proposition 2. *An equilibrium exists.*

Proof. The labor supply curve is a vertical line $L^{\mathrm{s}}(w) = 1$ for all $w > 0$. The labor demand is continuous, because $h\,(.)$ and $\mu^{\theta}(.)$ are continuous. Since $0 \in L^{\mathrm{d}}(\overline{w})$ and $L^{\mathrm{d}}(\underline{w}) \geqslant 1$, there exists an equilibrium wage w^*, where $\underline{w} \leqslant w^* \leqslant \overline{w}$. $\quad\square$

Considering the expressions for $L^{\mathrm{d}}(w)$, there are three channels through which changes in the wage rate affects total labor demand. The first is the standard *intensive margin effect*: higher wages reduce labor demand per firm. The second is the standard *extensive margin effect*: higher wages reduce the total number of firms (λ falls) and so labor demand falls via this channel as well. The third effect, which we emphasize in this paper, is the *pool quality effect*: higher wages lead to an increase in the average quality of entrepreneurs, which raises prices and/or reduces the interest rate, which in turn raises labor demand.

For $w' \leqslant w \leqslant \overline{w}$, the aggregate labor demand curve is downward sloping due to the first effect. The two other effects do not operate because there are no low type entrepreneurs.

If $\underline{w} \leqslant w < w'$ then all three effects are in operation, and L^{d} may slope up or down. Totally differentiating L^{d} with respect to w we get

$$\frac{dL^{\mathrm{d}}(w)}{dw} = q \frac{\theta_{\mathrm{H}} - \theta_{\mathrm{L}}}{\mu^{\mathrm{L}}(w) - \theta_{\mathrm{L}}} \left[\frac{dh(\phi(w))}{dw} - \frac{(\tilde{l} + 1)}{\mu^{\mathrm{L}}(w) - \theta_{\mathrm{L}}} \frac{d\mu^{\mathrm{L}}(w)}{dw} \right], \tag{23}$$

where $\phi(w) \equiv wr(\mu^{\mathrm{L}}(w))/p(\mu^{\mathrm{L}}(w))$. The two terms within parenthesis have opposite signs. Proposition 1 implies that the combination of the intensive margin and the pool quality effects is positive in net terms. The first term captures this. However, the extensive margin effect is negative, and the second term captures this (recall that $d\mu^{\mathrm{L}}(w)/dw > 0$).

Let ε denote (the absolute value of) the standard elasticity of labor demand. It captures the direct effect of w on labor demand, but not the indirect effect via the occupational choice condition. Using the first-order condition,

$$\varepsilon \equiv -\frac{w}{\tilde{l}} \frac{\partial \tilde{l}}{\partial w} = -\frac{f'(l)}{lf''(l)}. \tag{24}$$

M. Ghatak et al. / Journal of Economic Theory 137 (2007) 27–48
37

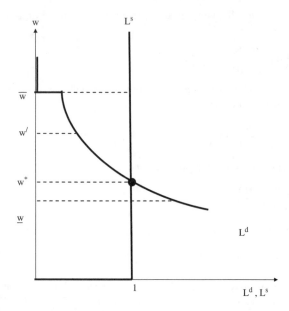

Fig. 1. Unique equilibrium.

Simplifying Eq. (23) we find the following expression whose sign is the same as $dL^d(w)/dw$ for $w < w'$:

$$\left[\frac{b(\theta_L)}{w(1+l)}\frac{\mu^L(w)-\theta_L}{\mu^L(w)}\frac{l}{(1+l)}\right]\varepsilon - 1$$

in case I and

$$\left[\frac{\tilde{l}}{\left(1+\tilde{l}\right)}\frac{\mu^L(w)-\theta_L}{\mu^L(w)+\theta_L\tilde{l}}\right]\varepsilon - 1$$

in case II.

By the occupational choice condition, $b(\theta_L) < w(1+l)$. The rest of the terms within the parentheses in both the expressions lie between 0 and 1. Thus, if $\varepsilon < 1$ then the aggregate labor demand is downward sloping even when $\underline{w} \leqslant w < w'$, in spite of the pool quality effect. Then there is a unique market equilibrium wage w^*. Fig. 1 illustrates such a case. Intuitively, the combination of the intensive margin effect and the pool quality effect is weak if ε is small (e.g., if the production function is Leontief). In this case, the extensive margin effect dominates and labor demand has the usual negative slope. But if $\varepsilon > 1$, the combination of the intensive margin effect and the pool quality effect is strong and it is possible for labor demand to have an upward sloping part. This raises the possibility of multiple equilibria, which is discussed in Section 5.

If the equilibrium wage is less than w', any shock (e.g., relating to technology, transactions costs) will not only have a direct effect on the labor market, but also an indirect effect via occupational choice and changes in the quality of the pool. For example, a technological shock that shifts the labor demand curve to the right will have the direct effect of raising wages in the labor market.

38   *M. Ghatak et al. / Journal of Economic Theory 137 (2007) 27–48*

If low quality entrepreneurs are active, the wage increase will cause some of them to switch occupations. This will improve the quality of the pool of entrepreneurs, thereby raising prices or lowering the interest rate, which will further boost labor demand and so on. Accordingly, such shocks will have a multiplier effect, and their short-run and long-run effects will be different.

4. Surplus enhancing economic policies

The basic distortion in this model is the negative externality untalented entrepreneurs impose on other entrepreneurs. In case I, the existence of low type entrepreneurs reduces the price high type entrepreneurs receive for their output. In case II, the existence of low type entrepreneurs, who frequently fail, raises the interest rates for high type entrepreneurs. We therefore consider policies that reduce λ, the fraction of low type agents who become entrepreneurs, and thereby raise social surplus. In particular, we focus on *trickle up* policies which directly benefit workers but indirectly end up helping entrepreneurs. They do so by inducing the least talented entrepreneurs to switch occupations, thereby improving the quality of the pool of entrepreneurs, which alleviates the adverse selection problem.

To focus on the interesting case, suppose that the market equilibrium is such that $0 < \lambda < 1$.[5] The total social surplus is the sum of the payoff of all agents. It can be expressed as

$$S = qv(\pi(p(\mu), r(\mu), w), \theta_H) + (1 - q)\lambda v(\pi(p(\mu), r(\mu), w), \theta_L)$$
$$+ (1 - q)(1 - \lambda)\{w - c_w(\theta_L)\}, \tag{25}$$

where μ is given by (16). The first two terms in (25) capture the payoff to the high and low type entrepreneurs, respectively, and the third term captures the payoff to the workers (who are all low types).

The expression (25) involves w, which is simply a transfer from entrepreneurs to workers. Alternatively, the social surplus can be expressed as the total value of output, minus the total disutility of labor. The total number of firms is $q + \lambda(1 - q)$. Each firm has l workers and one entrepreneur. Labor market clearing implies $(q + \lambda(1 - q))(l + 1) = 1$ so the number of workers in each firm is

$$l = \frac{1}{q + \lambda(1 - q)} - 1. \tag{26}$$

The total social surplus can therefore be written as

$$S = \{q\theta_H + \lambda(1 - q)\theta_L\}f(l) - qc_e(\theta_H) - (1 - q)\lambda c_e(\theta_L)$$
$$- (q + (1 - q)\lambda)lc_w(\theta_L). \tag{27}$$

This expression does not involve w.

Using (26) we can write S as a function of λ:

$$S(\lambda) = \{q\theta_H + \lambda(1 - q)\theta_L\}f\left(\frac{1}{q + \lambda(1 - q)} - 1\right)$$
$$- qc_e(\theta_H) - (1 - q)\{\lambda c_e(\theta_L) + (1 - \lambda)c_w(\theta_L)\}. \tag{28}$$

---

[5] If $\lambda = 0$ or 1, then small changes in economic policy will not change the social surplus, as λ will not change. In any case the case $\lambda = 0$ is uninteresting, because there are no low type entrepreneurs and as a result, no adverse selection problem. If $\lambda = 1$, then every agent is a self-employed entrepreneur who hires no workers. This case can be ruled out by making an Inada assumption, namely, $f'(0) = \infty$.

M. Ghatak et al. / Journal of Economic Theory 137 (2007) 27–48

The socially optimal λ_0 maximizes $S(\lambda)$. Notice that

$$S'(\lambda) = (1-q)\left\{\theta_L f(l) - \mu(\lambda)(1+l)f'(l) + b(\theta_L)\right\}, \tag{29}$$

where l is given by (26), and

$$\mu(\lambda) \equiv \frac{q\theta_H + \lambda(1-q)\theta_L}{q + \lambda(1-q)}.$$

At an interior optimum, $S'(\lambda_0) = 0$, so

$$\theta_L f(l_0) + b(\theta_L) = \mu(\lambda_0)(1+l_0)f'(l_0), \tag{30}$$

where

$$l_0 = \frac{1}{q + \lambda_0(1-q)} - 1.$$

The function S incorporates general equilibrium effects and may not be globally concave in λ. However, our argument does not rely on concavity.

The left-hand side of (30) is the marginal social benefit of a low type entrepreneur, who produces output worth $\theta_L f(l_0)$, and enjoys a private benefit $b(\theta_L)$. The right-hand side is the social cost. Since the low type entrepreneur hires l_0 workers, if he switches occupation then $1 + l_0$ agents are free to work in other firms, where they will be expected to contribute $\mu(\lambda_0)(1+l_0)f'(l_0)$ to social surplus.

If we evaluate (29) at the competitive equilibrium, we find that

$$S'(\lambda) = (1-q)\left\{\theta_L f(l) - lw + b(\theta_L) - w\right\} < 0, \tag{31}$$

where we have used (4), and the inequality is due to the occupational choice condition ((7) in case I and (8) in case II). Therefore, reducing the number of low-quality entrepreneurs will (locally) raise total social surplus. This is natural, since the low-quality entrepreneurs impose a negative externality on other entrepreneurs.

Consider, therefore, imposing a tax t on all entrepreneurs (which does not depend on how much labor they hire). The tax revenue is redistributed as a lump-sum subsidy to all agents to balance the budget. In case I, the occupational choice condition (7) becomes

$$p(\mu)f(\tilde{l}(w,\mu)) - w\tilde{l}(w,\mu) + b(\theta) - t = w. \tag{32}$$

(The lump-sum subsidy is given to *all* agents so it does not appear in the occupational choice condition.) In case II, the entrepreneur is only able to pay the tax if he succeeds, so the occupational choice condition (8) becomes

$$\theta\left(f(\tilde{l}(w,\mu)) - \frac{w}{\mu}\tilde{l}(w,\mu) - t\right) + b(\theta) = w. \tag{33}$$

Given θ, t and w, let $\mu^\theta(w,t)$ denote the μ that satisfies (32) in case I, and (33) in case II. It can be verified that

$$\frac{\partial\mu^L(w,t)}{\partial w} > 0, \quad \frac{\partial\mu^L(w,t)}{\partial t} > 0. \tag{34}$$

Starting at a competitive equilibrium where $\lambda = \lambda^* \in (0,1)$, imposing a tax $t > 0$ will make it less desirable to be an entrepreneur, so the equilibrium value of λ must fall. (Suppose λ does not fall. Then the demand for labor does not fall, so the equilibrium wage does not fall either. But then it follows from (34) that the quality of the pool, $\mu^L(w, t)$, must strictly improve to keep the low types indifferent between the two occupations. But then λ must fall, a contradiction.)

What is the effect of a tax $t > 0$ on social surplus? We restrict attention to a situation where low types are indifferent between being entrepreneurs and workers before and after the tax. Consider the function:

$$\sigma(\lambda, \mu, w) \equiv qv(\pi(p(\mu), r(\mu), w), \theta_H) + (1 - q)\lambda v(\pi(p(\mu), r(\mu), w), \theta_L)$$
$$+ (1 - q)(1 - \lambda)\{w - c_w(\theta_L)\}. \tag{35}$$

If prices take their market equilibrium values $(p(\mu^*), r(\mu^*), w^*)$, computed when $t = 0$, then $\sigma(\lambda, \mu^*, w^*)$ is independent of λ by the low type's occupational choice condition (6). This corresponds to an artificial exercise: if some low type entrepreneurs switch occupation and prices do not change, then there is no effect on the social surplus as expressed in (25), since the low types are indifferent between the two occupations (each individual who chooses an occupation does not think that his choice will affect prices). But in fact, if λ falls due to a tax (but is still interior), then the equilibrium prices must change. From the balanced budget assumption, the taxes and subsidies cancel out when social surplus is computed. Wage payments are a transfer from entrepreneurs to workers, so they too cancel out. But the increase in $p(\mu)$ or fall in $r(\mu)$ will make the remaining entrepreneurs better off. Thus, when λ falls due to a tax $t > 0$, the true social surplus $S(\lambda)$, where the price changes are accounted for, will exceed the "pseudo surplus" $\sigma(\lambda, \mu^*, w^*)$. Conversely, if instead we were to subsidize entrepreneurs ($t < 0$), then λ would increase and the true social surplus $S(\lambda)$ would be smaller than $\sigma(\lambda, \mu^*, w^*)$. But $\sigma(\lambda, \mu^*, w^*)$ does not depend on λ. This shows that if $0 < \lambda^* < 1$ then $S(\lambda)$ must be maximized at $\lambda_0 < \lambda^*$. That is, there are *too many* low-quality entrepreneurs in the competitive equilibrium. (At a corner solution, it is possible that $\lambda_0 = \lambda^*$.)

Proposition 3. *Suppose* $\lambda = \lambda^*$ *in market equilibrium (without taxes or subsidies) and let* λ_0 *denote the socially optimal* λ. *Then* $\lambda_0 \leqslant \lambda^*$, *with strict inequality if* $0 < \lambda^* < 1$.

Moreover, all agents *unanimously* favor a tax on entrepreneurs.

Proposition 4. *If in market equilibrium* $0 < \lambda^* < 1$, *then all agents strictly gain from the introduction of a small tax on entrepreneurs.*

Proof. Since $0 < \lambda^* < 1$, a low type agent is indifferent between the two occupations. If the tax is small enough that this indifference is maintained, then the changes in the welfare of a low type entrepreneur is the same as the changes in the welfare of a worker. In case I, the difference between the expected payoff of a high type and a low type entrepreneur is a constant, $c_e(\theta_L) - c_e(\theta_H)$. Therefore, the effect on the welfare of a high type entrepreneur is the same as the effect on the welfare of a low type entrepreneur. In case II, the type θ entrepreneur's expected payoff is

$$v(\pi(1, r(\mu), w), \theta) = \theta(\pi(1, r(\mu), w) - t) - c_e(\theta).$$

Therefore,

$$\theta_L(v(\pi(1, r(\mu), w), \theta_H) + c_e(\theta_H)) = \theta_H(v(\pi(1, r(\mu), w), \theta_L) + c_e(\theta_L)).$$

Thus, the change in $v(\pi(1, r(\mu), w), \theta_H)$ has the same sign as the change in $v(\pi(1, r(\mu), w), \theta_L)$. So in both cases, either all agents experience an increase in welfare, or they all experience a

M. Ghatak et al. / Journal of Economic Theory 137 (2007) 27–48   41

reduction in welfare. But, since λ falls and $S'(\lambda) < 0$ at the market equilibrium, the total surplus goes up. Therefore, all agents strictly gain. □

Proposition 4 shows that there will be unanimous agreement for a trickle up proposal to redistribute income from entrepreneurs to workers. The unanimity will persist until λ has been reduced to λ_0. At that point, if $\lambda_0 > 0$ then taxing entrepreneurs even further will reduce the social surplus and make all agents worse off. If $\lambda_0 = 0$, then further tax increases will simply transfer surplus from entrepreneurs to workers in a zero-sum fashion.

If an agent is randomly chosen as social planner and can tax entrepreneurs as long as nobody voices any opposition, then he would choose a tax rate such that the corresponding market equilibrium is efficient. There is unanimous support for this, because all agents are hurt by the adverse selection problem. However, there will be no unanimity on economic policy if there is wealth heterogeneity among the entrepreneurs, as shown in Section 6.

5. Multiple equilibria

We illustrate the possibility of multiple equilibria with an example. Consider case II, with the production function $f(l) = (1 + l)^{\alpha}$, where $0 < \alpha < 1$. (This is a Cobb–Douglas production function where the entrepreneur himself provides productive labor.) In this case, $p \equiv 1$ and $r(\mu) = 1/\mu$. Assume $0 < b(\theta_L) \leqslant b(\theta_H)$. The demand for labor (not counting the entrepreneur's own labor) is

$$h(wr) = \left(\frac{\alpha}{wr}\right)^{\frac{1}{1-\alpha}} - 1$$

if $wr \leqslant \alpha$, and

$$h(wr) = 0$$

if $wr > \alpha$. The profit function is

$$\pi(1, r, w) = \frac{\alpha^{\frac{\alpha}{1-\alpha}} - \alpha^{\frac{1}{1-\alpha}}}{(wr)^{\frac{\alpha}{1-\alpha}}} + wr \qquad (36)$$

for $wr \leqslant \alpha$, and $\pi(1, r, w) = f(0) = 1$ otherwise.
We assume

$$\alpha\theta_H q < b(\theta_L) < \alpha\theta_H q^{1-\alpha}. \qquad (37)$$

Also, to simplify calculations we set $\theta_L = 0$.
The inequality (37) implies that if $\mu = q\theta_H$ and $w = b(\theta_L)$, then

$$wr(\mu) = \frac{b(\theta_L)}{q\theta_H} > \alpha, \qquad (38)$$

so $h(wr(\mu)) = 0$. That is, no entrepreneur will hire any workers. Moreover, since the low types always fail, they are indifferent between the two occupations when the wage is $b(\theta_L)$. Low type entrepreneurs never repay their loans, and hence they do not care about the interest rate $r(\mu)$. Accordingly, $\underline{w} = w' = b(\theta_L)$. Therefore, there is an equilibrium where $w = b(\theta_L)$, and all agents become entrepreneurs, so $\mu = q\theta_H$. At this low pool quality, the interest rate is so high that

42 *M. Ghatak et al. / Journal of Economic Theory 137 (2007) 27–48*

no entrepreneur hires any workers. (Since the demand for labor includes entrepreneurial labor by convention, $L^D(b(\theta_L)) = 1$.)

If $w > b(\theta_L)$, then no low type agent becomes entrepreneur, and $wr(\mu) = w/\mu = w/\theta_H$. As long as $w/\theta_H \leqslant \alpha$, a high type entrepreneur will hire

$$h\left(wr(\mu)\right) \equiv \left(\frac{\alpha}{wr(\mu)}\right)^{\frac{1}{1-\alpha}} - 1$$

workers. A high type agent prefers to be entrepreneur as long as

$$\theta_H \pi(1, r(\mu), w) + b(\theta_H) \geqslant w. \tag{39}$$

The aggregate demand for labor (including entrepreneurial labor) would then be

$$L^D(w) = q\left(h\left(\frac{w}{\theta_H}\right) + 1\right) = q\left(\frac{\alpha\theta_H}{w}\right)^{\frac{1}{1-\alpha}}.$$

Labor market clearing requires $L^D(w) = 1$, which is true if

$$w = \alpha\theta_H q^{1-\alpha} > b(\theta_L). \tag{40}$$

The inequality is due to (37). Also, $w/\theta_H = \alpha q^{1-\alpha} < \alpha$. Substituting $w = \alpha\theta_H q^{1-\alpha}$ and $r = 1/\theta_H$ into the expression (36), we can verify that (39) holds for any $b(\theta_H) > 0$. Thus, there is an equilibrium where only the high types are entrepreneurs, and the wage is given by (40). The interest rate is low enough such that the high types find it worthwhile to hire all the low types as workers.

In this example, there is both a low wage equilibrium where $w = b(\theta_L)$, and a high wage equilibrium where $w = \alpha\theta_H q^{1-\alpha} > b(\theta_L)$.[6] How can we evaluate the multiple equilibria in terms of welfare? It turns out that in general, not just in this example, the high wage equilibrium Pareto dominates the low wage equilibrium.

Consider Fig. 2, which depicts a general case of multiple equilibria. For w such that $w' < w < \overline{w}$, as we move along the labor demand schedule $L^D(w)$, a wage increase is matched by a fall in λ, hence an increase in μ (so p rises in case I, r falls in case II). For $w \leqslant w'$ and $w \geqslant \overline{w}$, λ is constant (1 or 0). Thus, there must be fewer entrepreneurs at the high wage equilibrium w_1^* than at the low wage equilibrium w_0^*. But the total labor supply (including entrepreneurial labor) is constant at 1. Therefore, firm-level labor demand must be higher at the high wage equilibrium. Indeed, this increase in firm-level demand is what causes the labor demand to slope up.[7] This implies the real wage wr/p must be strictly lower in the high wage equilibrium, even though the nominal wage w is higher.[8] Moreover, the price p is at least as high in the high wage equilibrium as in the low wage equilibrium. This implies that entrepreneurs are strictly better off in the high wage equilibrium. Formally, in case I the payoff of an entrepreneur is $\max_l p\left(f(l) - \frac{w}{p}l\right) + b(\theta)$, and since w/p is lower and p is higher they must be better off in the high wage equilibrium. Similarly,

---

[6] These two equilibria are reminiscent of the "cottage production" equilibrium and "modern industrialization" equilibrium in Murphy et al. [18]. However, in their model the multiple equilibria were due to positive pecuniary externalities, whereas in our model they are due to negative information externalities.

[7] The argument is strengthened if labor supply is upward sloping since then high type entrepreneurs have to absorb a higher number of workers who are supplying more labor individually compared to the low wage equilibrium.

[8] In the example, $wr < \alpha$ in the high wage equilibrium, while $wr > \alpha$ in the low wage equilibrium.

M. Ghatak et al. / Journal of Economic Theory 137 (2007) 27–48   43

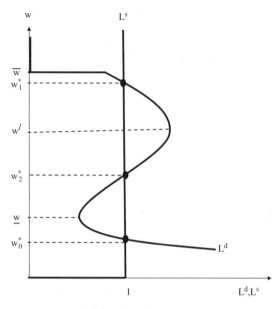

Fig. 2. Multiple equilibria.

in case II the payoff is $\max_l \theta (f(l) - wrl) + b(\theta)$ and so because wr is lower they are better off. Workers obviously are better off in the high wage equilibrium, because they care about the nominal wage only. (Even if they consume the good the firms produce, the price per unit of quality is constant.) Therefore, the high wage equilibrium Pareto dominates the low wage equilibrium. (Some low types switch occupation as the wage increases, but by revealed preference, they are even better off than if they had remained entrepreneurs.) To summarize:

Proposition 5. *If multiple equilibria exist, then they are Pareto-ranked.*

It is well known that multiple Pareto-ranked equilibria can exist in the standard Akerlof model, but this relies on a very strong assumption of price-taking behavior. If this assumption is dropped then only the "best" equilibrium survives [14,15]. In our framework, even if those who purchase the product in case I, and banks in case II, can offer any contract they want (so that they are not price takers), the coordination problem will not disappear since our mechanism works through multimarket interactions. An individual competitive bank, say, will correctly anticipate that lowering the interest rate will not boost aggregate labor demand enough to bring the economy out of a low wage equilibrium. It will only lead to losses for the bank. Only if all banks simultaneously lower interest rates can aggregate labor demand increase, wages go up, and the pool improve.

6. Screening

In the presence of adverse selection, a natural contractual response is to attempt to screen the individuals. Specifically, we will now assume publicly observed wealth can be used as collateral in the credit market adverse selection problem, i.e., case II (as in [7,6]). Wealthy high type entrepreneurs will not suffer from the existence of low type entrepreneurs if they can obtain loans at low interest by providing sufficient collateral.

In the previous sections the positive link between wages and aggregate labor demand was driven by the pool quality effect, for which individual labor demand $h(wr/p)$ had to be elastic. With screening, the aggregate demand for labor may slope upwards even when individual labor demand is completely inelastic. Therefore, we simplify the analysis in this section by assuming that the production technology is Leontief. In each firm it takes n workers to produce R units of output.

Workers who do not work for a firm can produce a subsistence income $\underline{w} > 0$ which sets a lower bound for the equilibrium wage rate. Assume $R > n\underline{w}$. Each agent has some initial wealth denoted by a. The cumulative distribution function for initial wealth is continuous, and is denoted by G. All wealth is observable but not liquid. Entrepreneurs need to borrow wn to pay wages. To simplify the exposition, assume $0 < \theta_L < \theta_H = 1$, and θ_L is low enough such that low types would never become entrepreneurs if types were publicly observed. There is a private non-pecuniary benefit associated with entrepreneurship, $b(\theta_H) = b(\theta_L) = M > 0$, which is not appropriable by banks. (Assumption 1 is not needed when screening is possible.)

Banks compete by offering credit contracts of the form (c, r), where c is the collateral, and r is the gross interest rate on the loan. A borrower of type θ repays the loan with probability θ. If he does not repay, the bank seizes the collateral and liquidates it. The collateral is worth c to the borrower but, if liquidated, it is only worth ϕc to the bank, where $0 < \phi < 1$. A partial equilibrium in the credit market consists of a set of contracts such that no contract makes losses, and no additional contracts can be introduced that will earn strictly positive profits, assuming the original contracts are left unmodified.

In order to focus on the interesting cases, we assume:

Assumption 2.

$$\theta_L \left(R - n\underline{w} \right) + M > \underline{w} > \theta_L R - n\underline{w} + M.$$

This assumption implies that when the wage is the lowest possible ($w = \underline{w}$), a low type would still not want to become entrepreneur if he had to pay the whole wage cost $n\underline{w}$ (which would be the case with self-financing). However, if he pays the wages only if successful (which would be the case with bank-financing), he would want to be an entrepreneur. Since $\theta_H = 1$, the first inequality also implies that high types strictly prefer to be entrepreneurs when $w = \underline{w}$.

Since wealth is observed, agents with different wealth levels can be offered different contracts. The contract offered to an agent of wealth level a is denoted $(c(a), r(a))$. There are two possibilities: if both high and low types of wealth class a accept the credit contract and become entrepreneurs, then the contract is *pooling*. If only high types accept it, then the contract is *separating*. Agents who do not become entrepreneurs are workers, earning the wage w (there is no disutility of labor).

A low type agent who accepts the contract (c, r) gets a payoff

$$\theta_L \left(R - rwn \right) + M - (1 - \theta_L)c.$$

If instead he supplies ordinary labor he receives w. Thus the contract (c, r) is separating if and only if $c \geqslant c^*(r, w)$, where

$$c^*(r, w) \equiv \max \left\{ 0, \frac{\theta_L(R - rwn) + M - w}{1 - \theta_L} \right\}.$$

M. Ghatak et al. / Journal of Economic Theory 137 (2007) 27–48   45

If $c^*(r, w) > 0$ then clearly $c^*(r, w)$ is strictly decreasing in the wage rate as well as the interest rate. If $c = c^*(r, w) > 0$ then low types are indifferent between becoming entrepreneurs and working for wages. We assume that they work for wages in this case. Competition among banks implies $r = 1$. Thus, all separating contracts will be of the form $(c^*(1, w), 1)$. They will, of course, only be offered to agents who have sufficient wealth, $a \geqslant c^*(1, w)$, to meet the collateral requirement. Assumption 2 implies $c^*(1, w) < wn$ for all $w \geqslant \underline{w}$.

The payoff of a high type who accepts the separating contract is $v^s(w) \equiv R - nw + M$. For a high type to accept the contract, his participation constraint must be satisfied, i.e., $v^s(w) \geqslant w$. The upper bound on the equilibrium wage rate is $\overline{w}$ such that $v^s(\overline{w}) = \overline{w}$. That is,

$$\overline{w} = \frac{R + M}{1 + n}.$$

For simplicity, assume $R \geqslant \overline{w}n$, so a high type entrepreneur with a separating contract makes non-negative monetary profits for all $w \in [\underline{w}, \overline{w}]$. Assumption 2 implies $R - n\underline{w} + M > \underline{w}$, i.e., $\overline{w} > \underline{w}$.

Next, consider a *pooling contract* $(c(a), r(a))$, with $c(a) < c^*(1, w)$. This contract attracts both high and low type borrowers with wealth a. The pooling contract yields zero expected profit to the bank if

$$\left[q + (1 - q)\theta_L\right]r(a)nw + (1 - q)(1 - \theta_L)\phi c(a) = nw. \tag{41}$$

As $c^*(1, w) < wn$, and $\phi c(a) \leqslant c(a) < c^*(1, w)$, it directly follows from (41) that $r(a) > 1$. Thus, the payoff of high type borrowers is lower with a pooling than with a separating contract (they cross-subsidize low type borrowers). From (41), $r(a)$ varies inversely with $c(a)$, so the payoff for a high type entrepreneur with a pooling contract is increasing in $c(a)$. Therefore, competition among banks for high type borrowers leads to $c(a) = a$. Accordingly, $r(a)$ is decreasing in a.

The payoff of a high type borrower under a pooling contract (with $c(a) = a$) is $v^P(a, w) = R - r(a)nw + M$, where $r(a)$ is given by (41). It is clear upon inspecting (41) that $r(a)$ is increasing in w, so $v^P(a, w)$ is decreasing in w (the greater the size of the loan, the greater the cross-subsidization of low types). As $r(a)$ is decreasing in a, $v^P(a, w)$ is increasing in a. Therefore, there is a wealth cutoff-level $\hat{a}(w)$ such that $v^P(a, w) \geqslant w$ if and only if $a \geqslant \hat{a}(w)$. Thus, $\hat{a}(w)$ is the lowest wealth level consistent with a pooling contract. Specifically, $\hat{a}(w) = 0$ if $v^P(0, w) \geqslant w$, and otherwise, $\hat{a}(w) > 0$ is determined by the equation $v^P(\hat{a}(w), w) = w$.

To summarize:

Proposition 6. *When screening is possible through collateral requirements*:

(i) *If $c^*(1, w) \leqslant \hat{a}(w)$ then agents with wealth $a \geqslant c^*(1, w)$ are offered a separating contract, while agents with wealth $a < c^*(1, w)$ get no credit.*

(ii) *If $c^*(1, w) > \hat{a}(w)$ then agents with wealth $a \geqslant c^*(1, w)$ are offered a separating contract, while agents with wealth a such that $\hat{a}(w) \leqslant a < c^*(1, w)$ are offered a pooling contract, and agents with wealth $a < \hat{a}(w)$ get no credit.*

When wealth can be used as a screening instrument, pooling contracts and separating contracts can *coexist* in equilibrium. Agents with wealth less than $c^*(1, w)$ either become workers or get a pooling contract where they put all their wealth as collateral. Within a wealth class that receives pooling contracts, a bank cannot hope to attract only high types by reducing the interest and raising the collateral requirement, because the borrowers already put *all* their wealth down as collateral

46   M. Ghatak et al. / Journal of Economic Theory 137 (2007) 27–48

($c(a) = a$). Notice that the assumption that guarantees existence of equilibrium is that wealth is publicly observable. With unobserved wealth, there would be values of q (sufficiently high) such that pooling contracts would be inconsistent with equilibrium (as in [20]).

By our convention, the supply of labor is 1 at any $w \in [\underline{w}, \overline{w}]$. Since the technology has fixed coefficients, each firm demands $n + 1$ units of labor at any $w \in [\underline{w}, \overline{w}]$, including entrepreneurial labor. The marginal agent, who is just on the threshold of being credit constrained, has wealth $a = \min\{\hat{a}(w), c^*(1, w)\}$.

We know that $c^*(1, w)$ is decreasing in w and $\hat{a}(w)$ is increasing in w. If $\hat{a}(w) > c^*(1, w)$, then the marginal agent receives a separating contract. In this case, an increase in w relaxes credit constraints, because separation becomes easier and separating contracts are given to *more* agents. If $\hat{a}(w) < c^*(1, w)$, then the marginal entrepreneur receives a pooling contract. In this case, an increase in w tightens credit constraints, because pooling contracts become less profitable and are given to *fewer* agents. Thus, the demand for labor $L^D(w)$ slopes *up* if $\hat{a}(w) > c^*(1, w)$, and *down* if $\hat{a}(w) < c^*(1, w)$. Notice that when labor demand is increasing in w it is due to an extensive margin effect *working through the equilibrium level of collateral*. This effect was naturally absent in the model without any screening instrument. As in the model without screening, it is easy to see that the upward sloping regions of $L^d(w)$ can generate multiple equilibria. (Examples are readily constructed, but we omit the details.)

Turning now to policy implications, unlike in Section 4, it is not possible to obtain consensus on the policy to eliminate the distortions. Consider imposing a tax t on entrepreneurs, which he only pays if he succeeds (the tax revenue is redistributed via a lump-sum transfer to all agents). In effect, this reduces his revenue from R to $R - t$. The contract $(c, 1)$ is separating if and only if

$$c \geqslant \max\left\{0, \frac{\theta_L (R - t - wn) + M - w}{1 - \theta_L}\right\}.$$

The right-hand side of the inequality is decreasing in t. The tax makes it easier to screen the borrowers, so the banks respond by lowering the collateral requirements. Therefore, for any given w, *more* borrowers can obtain a separating contract if a positive tax is imposed on entrepreneurs. If there are no pooling contracts in equilibrium, then the demand for labor will increase. On the other hand, $\hat{a}(w)$ will also increase, so if pooling contracts are offered in equilibrium, fewer agents can obtain a pooling contract. Thus, the effects of a tax increase depend on whether the marginal entrepreneur gets a separating or a pooling contract. But unlike in Section 4, there can never be unanimous support for a tax increase. Wealthy high type agents, who can afford a separating contract, always strictly prefer lower taxes on entrepreneurs.

Consider finally a credit subsidy $\sigma > 0$ paid up front to any entrepreneur who invests. In effect, this reduces the necessary loan size from wn to $wn - \sigma$. Therefore, the contract $(c, 1)$ is separating if and only if

$$c \geqslant \max\left\{0, \frac{\theta_L (R - (wn - \sigma)) + M - w}{1 - \theta_L}\right\}.$$

The right-hand side of the inequality is increasing in σ. Since the subsidy makes entrepreneurship more attractive, the banks must use tougher lending policies in order to screen the borrowers. Thus, they increase the collateral requirements, so *fewer* borrowers can obtain a separating contract. If there are no pooling contracts in equilibrium, then the credit subsidy makes it harder to invest and reduces the demand for labor. On the other hand, if the credit subsidy is big enough, then pooling contracts will become profitable. In this case, the credit subsidy will increase the number of agents who get a pooling contract, hence it will increase the demand for labor. Again, the effects of the policy depend on whether the marginal entrepreneur gets a separating or a pooling contract.

In the screening model, multiple equilibria are generated by an extensive margin effect, and they cannot be Pareto-ranked. Unskilled agents are better off under a high wage equilibrium. But high types who have sufficient wealth for a screening contract strictly prefer the low wage equilibrium. For them, the interest rate is always 1, but the real cost of labor is higher in the high wage equilibrium. (In Section 5, the real cost of labor wr/p was actually lower at the high wage equilibrium, due to the pool quality effect.)

7. Conclusion

We have studied a channel through which the equilibrium consequences of adverse selection depend on outside options which in turn depend on the endogenous inefficiencies caused by adverse selection. This channel is occupational choice. Its importance depends on the degree of interlinkage between the markets among which agents are choosing, and on the degree of complementarity between various occupations. In the presence of such complementarities, small productivity shocks can have large effects.

If it is impossible to screen the agents, there will be unanimous support for a redistribution of income from entrepreneurs to workers. Such policies improve the quality of the entrepreneurial pool, so the benefits initially enjoyed by workers trickle up to benefit entrepreneurs. With screening, however, some talented entrepreneurs may be immune to the adverse selection problem, so benefits do not "trickle up" to them. Thus, screening instruments are potentially harmful, since they partition the agents into classes with conflicting interests, and surplus enhancing policies no longer get unanimous support. If liquidity constraints prevent poor agents from lobbying for their favorite policies, as in Esteban and Ray [10], then surplus enhancing taxes on entrepreneurs may not materialize. Endogenous policy choice in this kind of environment seems like an interesting topic for future research.

The logic of our model can be applied to a variety of different contexts. The following elements need to be present: the returns to two occupations, say A and B, are positively related (e.g., a rise in the price of the good made by those in occupation A raises demand for inputs produced in B); there is occupational choice, and one occupation (say A) is subject to adverse selection. If the returns to occupation B are low then the adverse selection in occupation A is severe, which depresses the returns to occupation A. This reduces demand for the output generated in occupation B, justifying the low returns in it. Consider the following example. Suppose certain "motivated" agents derive a non-pecuniary payoff from working in the public sector (A). When wages in the private sector (B) are high, only motivated agents work in the public sector, so the quality of the public sector activities will be high. If this increases the productivity of labor in the private sector, the demand for labor in the private sector will be high. This in turn will support high private sector wages. [9]

Acknowledgments

We thank the Institute for Advanced Study for providing an excellent research environment. Morelli is grateful for financial support from the National Science Foundation under Grant SES-0213312. Comments and suggestions by the Associate Editor, two anonymous referees, Madhav

---

[9] See Machiavello [13] for a model along these lines.

48 *M. Ghatak et al. / Journal of Economic Theory 137 (2007) 27–48*

Aney, Rocco Machiavello, Giacomo Rodano, Colin Rowat, and helpful feedback from several seminar audiences are gratefully acknowledged. Special thanks are due to one referee whose suggestions led to significant improvements. The usual disclaimer applies.

References

[1] J. Agell, K.E. Lommerud, Egalitarianism and growth, Scand. J. Econ. 95 (1993) 559–579.

[2] G. Akerlof, The market for 'lemons': quality uncertainty and the market mechanism, Quart. J. Econ. 84 (1970) 488–500.

[3] A.V. Banerjee, Contracting constraints, credit markets, and economic development, in: M. Dewatripont, L. Hansen, S. Turnovsky (Eds.), Advances in Economics and Econometrics: Theory and Applications, Eighth World Congress of the Econometric Society, vol. III, Cambridge University Press, Cambridge, 2003.

[4] A.V. Banerjee, A. Newman, Occupational choice and the process of development, J. Polit. Economy 101 (1993) 274–298.

[5] D. Bernhardt, H. Lloyd-Ellis, Enterprise, inequality and economic development, Rev. Econ. Stud. 67 (2000) 147–168.

[6] D. Besanko, A. Thakor, Collateral and rationing: sorting equilibria in monopolistic and competitive credit markets, Int. Econ. Rev. 28 (1987) 671–689.

[7] H. Bester, Screening vs. rationing in credit markets with imperfect information, Amer. Econ. Rev. 75 (1985) 850–855.

[8] R.J. Caballero, M.L. Hammour, The cleansing effect of recessions, Amer. Econ. Rev. 84 (1994) 1350–1368.

[9] D. DeMeza, D. Webb, Does credit rationing imply insufficient lending?, J. Public Econ. 78 (2000) 215–234.

[10] J. Esteban, D. Ray, Wealth constraints, lobbying and the efficiency of public allocation, Europ. Econ. Rev. 44 (2000) 694–705.

[11] O. Galor, J. Zeira, Income distribution and macroeconomics, Rev. Econ. Stud. 60 (1993) 35–52.

[12] M. Ghatak, M. Morelli, T. Sjostrom, Occupational choice and dynamic incentives, Rev. Econ. Stud. 68 (2001) 781–810.

[13] R. Macchiavello, Occupational, choice public service motivation and development, Mimeo, London School of Economics, 2004.

[14] G. Mankiw, The allocation of credit and financial collapse, Quart. J. Econ. 101 (1986) 455–470.

[15] A. Mas-Colell, M. Whinston, J. Green, Microeconomic Theory, Oxford University Press, Oxford, 1995.

[17] D. Mookherjee, D. Ray, Persistent inequality, Rev. Econ. Stud. 70 (2003) 369–393.

[18] K. Murphy, A. Shleifer, R. Vishny, Industrialization and the big push, J. Polit. Econ. 97 (1989) 1003–1026.

[19] T. Piketty, The dynamics of wealth distribution and the interest rate with credit rationing, Rev. Econ. Stud. 64 (1997) 173–189.

[20] M. Rothschild, J. Stiglitz, Equilibrium in competitive insurance markets: an essay in the economics of imperfect information, Quart. J. Econ. 90 (1976) 630–649.

[21] J. Stiglitz, A. Weiss, Credit rationing in markets with imperfect information, Amer. Econ. Rev. 71 (1981) 393–410.

[7]

Agency Costs, Net Worth, and Business Fluctuations

By BEN BERNANKE AND MARK GERTLER*

This paper develops a simple neoclassical model of the business cycle in which the condition of borrowers' balance sheets is a source of output dynamics. The mechanism is that higher borrower net worth reduces the agency costs of financing real capital investments. Business upturns improve net worth, lower agency costs, and increase investment, which amplifies the upturn; vice versa, for downturns. Shocks that affect net worth (as in a debt-deflation) can initiate fluctuations.

Many students of the business cycle have suggested that the condition of firm and household balance sheets (equivalently, the state of borrower "solvency" or "credit-worthiness") is an important determinant of macroeconomic activity. For example, Frederic Mishkin (1978) and Ben Bernanke (1983) argued that the weakness of borrowers' balance sheets contributed to the severity of the Great Depression, while Otto Eckstein and Allen Sinai (1986) put firm balance sheet variables at the center of their analysis of cyclical dynamics. Numerous studies have connected balance sheet conditions with household and firm spending decisions.

In this paper we present a formal analysis of the role of borrowers' balance sheets in the business cycle. Our vehicle is a modified "real business cycle" model, in which a characteristic of the investment technology is an asymmetry of information between the entrepreneurs who organize and manage physical investment and the savers from whom they borrow. Specifically, we assume a "costly state verification" problem, as in Robert Townsend (1979, 1988). This informational asymmetry makes the Modigliani-Miller theorem inapplicable, opening up the possibility of an interesting interaction between real and "financial" (i.e., balance sheet) factors.

Several aspects of balance sheets are potentially of interest to macroeconomists: The particular balance sheet variable upon which we focus is borrower net worth.[1] Net worth is important, we believe, for the following reason: Whenever there is an asymmetry of information between borrowers and lenders, optimal financial arrangements will typically entail deadweight losses (agency costs), relative to the first-best perfect-information equilibrium; these costs manifest themselves as a higher cost of "external," as compared to "internal," funds. For the particular model used here, and for most standard principal-agent models, it is true that the greater the level of net worth of the potential borrower, the less will be the expected agency costs implied by the optimal financial contract.[2] Thus periods of financial "distress" (when borrower net worth is low) are also times of relatively high agency costs in investment.

At the macroeconomic level, the proposition that borrower net worth and the agency costs of investment are inversely correlated has at least two significant implications.

*Princeton University, Princeton, NJ 08544 and University of Wisconsin, Madison, WI 53706, respectively. Numerous colleagues and several referees provided useful advice. Barry Nalebuff was especially helpful.

---

[1] More specifically, the focus is on "collateralizable" net worth, as opposed to, for example, human capital. For simplicity of modeling, we do not distinguish in this paper among assets that are more or less easy to sell or borrow against. The issues raised by varying balance sheet liquidity are deserving of further research.

[2] This proposition is quite general. For example, in his analysis of the perhaps more familiar Bengt Holmstrom, 1979, principal-agent setup, in which agents' unobserved actions affect project returns, David Sappington, 1983, demonstrated a similar inverse relationship between the agent's wealth and the agency costs of the principal-agent relationship. See Bernanke and Mark Gertler, 1987, for another example and for references. For a model in which this result need not hold, see Joseph Stiglitz and Andrew Weiss, 1987.

First, since borrower net worth is likely to be procyclical (borrowers are more solvent during good times), there will be a decline in agency costs in booms and a rise in recessions. We will show that this is sufficient to introduce investment fluctuations and cyclical persistence into an environment which is rigged to exhibit neither of these features when agency costs are not present; a kind of accelerator effect emerges. Second, shocks to borrower net worth which occur independently of aggregate output will be an initiating source of real fluctuations. A possible example of this is the "debt-deflation," first analyzed by Irving Fisher (1933): During a debt-deflation, because of an unanticipated fall in the price level (or, alternatively, a fall in the relative price of borrowers' collateral, for example, farmland), there is a decline in borrower net worth. This has the effect of making those individuals in the economy with the most direct access to investment projects suddenly un-creditworthy (i.e., the agency costs associated with lending to them are high). The resulting fall in investment has negative effects on both aggregate demand and aggregate supply. We perform a preliminary analysis of the macro effects of a shock to borrower net worth using the model developed below.

We have tried to conduct our analysis solely from first principles. In particular, we derive the form of all financial arrangements endogenously, and we do not rule out randomizing strategies and lotteries. The model is thus necessarily simple, and our analysis should be viewed as an attempt to obtain qualitative insights, rather than to provide an empirically realistic description of real-financial interactions. Other papers in this area which proceed in a general manner similar to ours include those of Roger Farmer (1984), Bruce Greenwald and Joseph Stiglitz (1986), and Stephen Williamson (1987).

The plan of this paper is as follows: Section I lays out the assumptions of the model. Section II analyzes the benchmark-perfect information case. The equilibrium in this case is rigged to involve no business cycle dynamics (investment is constant and output fluctuations are serially independent). Section III introduces asymmetric information

and agency costs. Section III, Parts A, B consider optimal lending contracts and the entrepreneurial investment decision for this case. Implications for macroeconomic equilibrium dynamics are investigated in Section III, Parts C, D; we show that, in contrast to the perfect-information case, the economy with agency costs exhibits persistent fluctuations in investment and output, and that redistributions between borrowers and lenders (as in a debt-deflation) have real aggregate effects. Section IV concludes. Additional results on the nature of the optimal contract under "costly state verification" are presented in the Appendix.

I. The Model

Our starting point is a generic "real business cycle model," that is, a stochastic neoclassical growth model. This framework allows us to illustrate starkly the role of financial factors, since in the standard version of the real business cycle model (for example, Edward Prescott, 1986), the assumption of perfect markets implies that financial structure is irrelevant. Specifically, we study an overlapping generations (OG) model, in the general form used by Peter Diamond (1965). The OG approach has the advantage of providing a tractable framework for dynamic general equilibrium analysis, into which heterogeneity among borrowers and lenders is easily incorporated. The OG setup also allows us to abstract (for the present paper) from long-term financial relationships.[3] The "generations" in our model should be thought of as representing the entry and exit of firms from credit markets, rather than as literal generations; a "period" in our model should therefore be interpreted as the length of a typical financial contract (for example, a bank loan).

As in Diamond (1965) we will assume that each generation of individuals lives for two periods; and that individuals are able to earn labor income only in the first period of life,

---

[3] For equilibrium analyses of the implications of long-term relationships in agency settings, see Edward Green, 1987, and Gertler 1988.

so that they must save to finance second-period consumption. In Diamond's paper it is assumed that saving can be done either by investing in physical capital or by purchasing government bonds: For an expositional reason that will be explained, we make consumption-good inventories, rather than government bonds, the alternative mode of savings to capital investment. Our model also differs from Diamond's original (which was non-stochastic) in that, in the spirit of the real business cycle literature, we allow for shocks to the aggregate production function.

The modifications to Diamond's model just described are minor and have no particularly surprising implications. The significant distinction between our model and Diamond's is that we replace his simple capital production technology (in which output is transformed into capital one-for-one) with a technology that involves asymmetric information. Specifically, we assume that only the entrepreneurs who direct physical investment can costlessly observe the returns to their individual projects; outside lenders must jointly incur a fixed cost to observe those returns. This "costly state verification" model was first analyzed by Townsend (1979, 1988);[4] he showed that the optimal financial arrangements in this setting will involve (most likely randomized) auditing strategies by lenders, which introduce dissipative agency costs into the process. A main goal of this paper is to draw a connection between the condition of borrower balance sheets and these agency costs, and to demonstrate how this connection may play a role in the business cycle.

The detailed assumptions of the model are now stated.

Time. Time is infinite in the forward direction and is divided into discrete periods indexed by t.

Agents. There are overlapping generations of two-period lived agents (and an initial "old" generation in period zero). It will be convenient to assume that there are a countable infinity of agents in each generation. (An implication of this assumption is that

we will generally have to deal in per capita, rather than aggregate, quantities.)

There are two classes of agents. An exogenous fraction η of individuals in each generation are called "entrepreneurs." The rest of the population will be called "lenders." Entrepreneurs and lenders differ in endowments and preferences; much more importantly, they differ in that only entrepreneurs have direct access to the investment technology (see below).

The class of entrepreneurs is itself not homogeneous: We will assume that individual entrepreneurs are indexed by a parameter ω, which in the population of entrepreneurs is uniformly distributed on $[0, 1]$. Low-ω entrepreneurs will have a lower cost of investment, and thus may be thought of as more "efficient." (Again, see below.)

Goods. There are two goods, a capital good and an output good. Output produced in a given period t may be consumed by agents during t, or it may be invested in the production of the capital good (which becomes available for use in $t+1$). We also allow output to be stored directly as an inventory. The gross rate of return on storage is r, $r \geq 1$; that is, a unit of output stored in t yields r units in $t+1$.

Capital cannot be consumed but can be used in the production of output. Capital is assumed to depreciate fully in one period (this is expositional reasons only).

Production Technologies. There are separate production technologies for output and for capital. The output good is produced by a constant returns technology using capital and labor. We will assume below that labor supplies are fixed;[5] we may therefore write the production function in per capita[6] terms. For any period t, the production function for per capita output y_t is assumed to be

$$(1) \qquad y_t = \tilde{\theta}_t f(k_t),$$

---

[4] See also Douglas Gale and Martin Hellwig, 1985.

[5] We focus here on explaining investment fluctuations rather than employment fluctuations. Extensions of the results to the case with variable employment is straightforward in principle.

[6] Throughout "per capita" means "per member of a given generation."

where k_t is the amount of capital per head, and $\tilde{\theta}_t$ is a random aggregate productivity shock. We assume that some production can take place without capital, that is, $f(0) > 0$. We take the random variable $\tilde{\theta}$ to be i.i.d. over time, to be distributed continuously over a finite positive support, and to have a mean equal to θ.

Output in period t can be transformed into period-$(t+1)$ capital (without the use of labor) by means of an investment technology. This investment technology comes in discrete, nondivisible units, called "projects." Each entrepreneur is endowed with one of these projects (and we assume that it is too costly to trade or transfer a project away from the original owner). A project belonging to an entrepreneur of type ω takes as input $x(\omega)$ units of the output good y, where $x(.)$ is increasing in ω. With less than $x(\omega)$ units of y, nothing is produced, and the marginal product of increments of y to a project that already has its requisite quantity of input is zero.

Any project that is undertaken in t produces a quantity of capital, which is available for use in $t+1$. The amount of capital produced by a given project is a discrete random variable with possible outcomes κ_i, $i = 1, 2, \ldots, n$, with $\kappa_j \geq \kappa_k$ for $j > k$. (In the main text we will focus on the case $n = 2$.) The probability of outcome κ_i is π_i, and the expected outcome is κ. Note that project outcomes do not depend on the entrepreneur's type ω, although the quantity of inputs does (high-ω entrepreneurs require higher inputs); this is a simple way of motivating an upward-sloping supply curve of capital goods. The distribution of outcomes is identical *ex ante* across projects and is not affected by any action or effort of the individual entrepreneur.

To introduce issues of asymmetric information into the model, we assume that the realized outcome of any particular investment project is costlessly observable only by the entrepreneur who operates (was endowed with) that project. Other agents in the economy can learn the realized returns of a given project only by employing an auditing technology. This technology absorbs γ units of the capital good when operated, but reveals

the outcome of the audited project to everyone in the economy and without error.[7] An entrepreneur who underreports the return to his project and is not audited can enjoy extra consumption equal to the marginal product of his extra capital. We assume that it is not possible, without auditing, to infer the outcome of a particular entrepreneur's project, for example, it is not possible for others to observe the entrepreneur's second-period holdings of capital or his realized consumption. We will assume that random auditing is feasible; that is, lenders can pre-commit to auditing with some probability (which may depend on the announced outcome). Finally, it makes things a bit simpler to assume that project outcomes are realized, announcements are made, and auditing takes place before the current value of $\tilde{\theta}$ is known; thus, incentive constraints relevant to decisions in t need depend only on expected values of functions of $\tilde{\theta}_{t+1}$.

Investment projects undertaken in a given period have mutually independent outcomes, so that there is no aggregate (per capita) uncertainty about the quantity of capital produced, that is, expected and actual capital per head are the same. Let i_t be the number of investment projects undertaken in t per capita, and let h_t be the fraction of projects initiated in t that are audited. (Both i_t and h_t will be endogenous in general equilibrium.) For any period t, then, next-period capital stock per head, k_{t+1}, is given by

$$(2) \qquad k_{t+1} = (\kappa - h_t \gamma) i_t.$$

We also assume

$$(3) \qquad \theta f'(0)\kappa > rx(0) + \gamma,$$

$$(4) \qquad \theta f'(\kappa \eta) < rx(1).$$

---

[7]Alternatively, we could have assumed that auditing results are private information to the auditor. Then a role would arise for zero-profit intermediaries between lenders and entrepreneurs. These intermediaries would internalize all auditing costs and, by holding perfectly diversified portfolios, could eliminate the need to be monitored by depositors (see Douglas Diamond, 1984, and Stephen Williamson, 1987).

(3) and (4) will be sufficient to guarantee that it is always profitable for some but not all entrepreneurs to operate.

Endowments. Every individual has a fixed-labor endowment, which must be used during the first period of life. The labor endowment of an entrepreneur is L^e, the endowment of a lender is L. As a normalization, we assume that the economywide per capita labor endowment, $\eta L^e + (1-\eta)L$, is equal to one; this way we avoid carrying around the distinction between per capita and per labor-input variables.

Preferences. Individual preferences are defined over lifetime consumption (there is no disutility of labor). We assume that entrepreneurs care about only expected consumption when old, that is, they are risk-neutral and do not consume when young. Lenders consume in both periods; lenders born in t have identical utility functions of the form

$$(5) \qquad U(z_t^y) + \beta E_t(z_{t+1}^o),$$

where z_t^y and z_{t+1}^o are the consumption of the representative period-t lender when young and old, respectively, $U(.)$ is of the usual concave form, and β is a discount factor.

The key restriction imposed by our specification of preferences is that both borrowers and lenders in t are risk-neutral with respect to period-$(t+1)$ consumption; as in Sappington (1983), the assumption of risk-neutrality permits us to concentrate on the role of the agent's wealth in mitigating agency costs, rather than on issues of risk-sharing. The assumptions that entrepreneurs and lenders have different utility functions and, in particular, that entrepreneurs do not consume when young are inessential.

We will focus on the behavior of this model economy in a competitive market environment. In such an environment, our agents' labor supply and consumption/saving behavior are easy to describe. Labor is supplied inelastically, so that, if the market wage per unit of labor endowment is w_t, entrepreneurs have per capita incomes of $w_t L^e$ and lenders have per capita incomes of $w_t L$. (By our normalization assumption,

overall per capita income of the young generation is w_t.) Entrepreneurs do not consume when young, so average entrepreneurial saving, S_t^e, is given simply by

$$(6) \qquad S_t^e = w_t L^e.$$

Entrepreneurial saving will be an important variable in the subsequent analysis.

Lenders do consume in the first period, so that their saving depends on the interest rate as well as the wage. We will make assumptions to guarantee that saving always exceeds capital formation ((see (9) below), so there is always storage of inventories in equilibrium. Thus the marginal rate of return is fixed at r, the rate of return to storage. Maximization of (5) implies that there is an optimal consumption for lenders when young, denoted $z_y^*(r)$. Average savings by lenders, S_t, is thus

$$(7) \qquad S_t = w_t L - z_y^*(r).$$

The main import of (6) and (7) is the establishment of a direct link between wages (marginal productivities) and saving. This link, not empirically unreasonable in itself, is supposed to proxy for the more general idea that savings (and wealth) are greater when the economy is doing well.

We turn now to characterizing the rest of the competitive equilibrium for our model economy.

II. Equilibrium with Perfect Information

As a benchmark, we first consider the competitive equilibrium of our model when auditing is free ($\gamma = 0$), so that information is perfect. We begin by solving for equilibrium in period t, given the inherited capital stock per head, k_t; we then turn to the (trivial) dynamics.

Let $\hat{q}_{t+1}$ be the expected (as of t) relative price of capital in $t+1$; then $\hat{q}_{t+1}\kappa$ is the expected gross return from each investment project. The opportunity cost of investing for a type-ω entrepreneur is $rx(\omega)$. Assuming that entrepreneurs invest when they can earn nonnegative profits, the efficiency level $\bar{\omega}$ of the entrepreneur who is just indifferent

VOL. 79 NO. 1 BERNANKE AND GERTLER: BUSINESS FLUCTUATIONS 19

between investing and storing satisfies

$$(8) \qquad \hat{q}_{t+1}\kappa - rx(\bar{\omega}) = 0.$$

The projects of entrepreneurs with efficiency levels ω of $\bar{\omega}$ or better (i.e., $\omega \le \bar{\omega}$) produce an expected surplus, relative to storage. (Note that $\bar{\omega}$ is a function of $\hat{q}_{t+1}$.)

We assume, as noted in the previous section, that economywide savings always exceed the amount required by profitable projects

$$(9) \qquad \eta S^e + (1-\eta)S > \int_0^{\bar{\omega}} x(\omega)\, d\omega,$$

for any $\bar{\omega}$, for any realization of θ, and for any inherited level of k_t. (For this to be plausible, the entrepreneurial sector needs to be a relatively small part of the economy.) Thus some saving always funds inventory accumulation in equilibrium and the marginal rate of return is always r.

The interesting issue is the joint determination, in period t, of $\hat{q}_{t+1}$ and the next-period capital stock per head, k_{t+1}. Let i_t be the number of projects undertaken (per capita) in t. Then we have

$$(10) \qquad i_t = \bar{\omega}\eta,$$

$$(11) \qquad k_{t+1} = \kappa i_t.$$

(10) follows from the observation that any entrepreneur of efficiency level $\bar{\omega}$ or better (which, since ω is uniform, is a fraction $\bar{\omega}$ of all entrepreneurs) will find it profitable to invest when the cost of funds is r. Thus (10) states that investment per capita equals the fraction of entrepreneurs who invest times the fraction of the population who are entrepreneurs. (11) says that the per capita future capital stock will be the average productivity of an investment project (which, by the law of large numbers, is non-stochastic) times the per capita number of projects.

Combining (8), (10), and (11) yields a "capital supply curve" for the perfect information case (call it the SS curve):

$$(12) \qquad \hat{q}_{t+1} = rx(k_{t+1}/\kappa\eta)/\kappa \quad [\text{SS}]$$

The SS curve is upward-sloping (see Figure

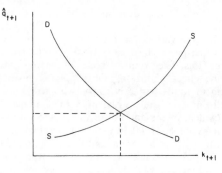

1). A higher expected value of $\hat{q}_{t+1}$ raises the number of entrepreneurs who can profitably invest, so that a larger share of savings is devoted to capital formation instead of to consumption good inventories.

The "capital demand curve" for the perfect information case, DD, is just the condition that the expected price of capital equals its expected marginal product

$$(13) \qquad \hat{q}_{t+1} = \theta f'(k_{t+1}) \quad [\text{DD}],$$

where, recall, θ is the mean of $\tilde{\theta}_{t+1}$ and f' denotes the derivative. The DD curve is downward-sloping (see Figure 1); the marginal product of capital is higher when the capital stock (per head) is smaller. In each period t, $\hat{q}_{t+1}$ and k_{t+1} are determined as the solution of (12) and (13), that is, as the intersection of the capital supply and demand curves in Figure 1.[8]

The dynamics in the perfect information case are extremely simple: Since (12) and (13) are independent of period-t state variables, $\hat{q}$ and k are constant over time. Investment is fixed and the quantity of production of the output good fluctuates in proportion to the (serially uncorrelated) productivity shock. The amount of consumption is positively serially correlated, since in high-productivity periods there is both more consumption and more inventory accumulation.

[8] The solution exists and is unique. Existence is guaranteed by (3) and (4), uniqueness by the fact that DD always slopes downward and SS always slopes upward.

We have thus developed a benchmark case in which investment is constant. This was the motivation for introducing inventories which pay a fixed-gross yield: The presence of this fixed-return mode of saving has the effect of making the supply of investment funds perfectly elastic with respect to the interest rate, while investment demand (which, in the absence of information problems, depends only on the expected marginal productivity of capital and the marginal cost of producing new capital) is fixed over time. In contrast, when information asymmetries are present, investment demand will vary and be history-dependent.

III. Equilibrium with Asymmetric Information

A. *The Optimal Financial Contract*

We now re-introduce imperfect information ($\gamma > 0$) and begin the process of deriving the dynamic macroeconomic equilibrium for this case. This is done in stages: We begin by considering the situation of an entrepreneur who with certainty intends to undertake his project,[9] but for whom the required project input exceeds his personal savings ($x(\omega) > S^e$). In this case, the entrepreneur must borrow in order to invest. Our task is to determine the optimal arrangements under which this borrowing can take place.

The entrepreneur is assumed to be borrowing from a lender (or consortium of lenders) who have an opportunity cost of funds r. At this point our analysis is partial equilibrium, in that we assume that the entrepreneur's own savings (S^e), the expected relative price in the next period of the produced capital good ($\hat{q}$), and the safe rate of return (r) are taken as exogenous.

The optimal contract is found by application of the revelation principle. Formally, the entrepreneur's problem is to maximize his expected next-period consumption, subject to the constraints that (i) the lender(s) receive an expected rate of return of no less

than r, (ii) the entrepreneur has no incentive to lie about realized project outcomes, and (iii) the state-contingent consumptions and auditing probabilities[10] are feasible. The control variables are outcome-dependent auditing probabilities and the entrepreneur's realized consumption levels, which may be contingent both on the project outcome and on whether an audit has occurred.

The Appendix formally states the problem and gives a number of results for the n-state case. For the main text, we choose to specialize to the case $n = 2$. This is for the sake of concreteness; for $n = 2$, it is possible to write out the optimal contract explicitly, while for a larger number of states we have only been able to obtain indirect characterizations. It is worth stressing, however, that the n-state optimal contract does have the "net worth property," that expected agency costs are decreasing in the amount of entrepreneurial savings contributed to the project. Therefore, we can safely claim that allowing for an arbitrary number of possible project outcomes in our macroeconomic analysis would not affect the qualitative nature of our results.

With $n = 2$, there are two possible project outcomes: In state 1 (which occurs with probability π_1), the project produces κ_1 units of the capital good; in state 2 (probability π_2) it produces κ_2 units. State 1 is the "bad" state ($\kappa_1 < \kappa_2$). For an entrepreneur of type ω, the amount borrowed is $x(\omega) - S^e$, and the lenders' required expected return is $r(x(\omega) - S^e)$.

The Appendix shows that, under the optimal contract no auditing occurs when the best possible state (here, state 2) is an-

---

[9] We ignore for the moment his option of putting his savings into consumption-good inventories.

[10] We are allowing general random auditing strategies, which (as Townsend, 1979, first pointed out) may be significantly more efficient than nonrandom strategies. An implication of permitting random auditing is that the optimal contract will not be in the form of a debt contract, as it is when auditing is nonrandom (Dilip Mookherjee and Ivan Png, 1987; Townsend, 1988). Importantly, our macro results are essentially the same whether stochastic auditing is permitted or not. Thus, we do not have to rely on financial contracts taking a particular debt or equity form. For our purposes, the important distinction is between internal and external finance, not between debt and equity per se.

nounced. Thus, for $n = 2$, lenders audit only when the entrepreneur declares the bad state (state 1). Let p be the probability of an audit in the bad state, let c_i be the entrepreneur's consumption payoff when he announces state i ($i = 1, 2$) and is not audited, and let c^a be his consumption payoff when he announces the bad state and is audited.[11] Then the optimal contract is found by choosing the vector $\{p, c_1, c_2, c^a\}$ to solve[12]

$$(14) \quad \max \pi_1\left(pc^a + (1-p)c_1\right) + \pi_2 c_2$$

subject to

$$(15) \quad \pi_1\left[\hat{q}\kappa_1 - p(c^a + \hat{q}\gamma) - (1-p)c_1\right]$$
$$+ \pi_2\left[\hat{q}\kappa_2 - c_2\right] \geq r(x - S^e),$$

$$(16) \quad c_2 \geq (1-p)\left(\hat{q}(\kappa_2 - \kappa_1) + c_1\right),$$

$$(17) \quad c_1 \geq 0,$$

$$(18) \quad c^a \geq 0,$$

$$(19) \quad 0 \leq p \leq 1,$$

where $\hat{q}$ is the expected (next-period) relative price of capital.

Constraint (15) (which specializes the appendix inequality (A2)) requires that lenders receive an expected return of r; this constraint can be shown always to bind. Constraint (16) (which corresponds to the appendix inequality (A3)) is the truth-telling constraint on the entrepreneur; it requires that the contract be structured so that the entrepreneur has no incentive to misreport the good state as the bad state. (16) binds if $p > 0$. Constraints (17) and (18) require that the entrepreneur's consumption in the bad state be nonnegative.[13] These "limited liabil-

ity" constraints restrict the entrepreneur's ability to pay lenders if the project's outcome is bad; as we shall see, the presence of these constraints is the basic reason that the entrepreneur's net worth is important. (19) is a feasibility constraint on p.

The optimal contract for $n = 2$ (the solution to (14)–(19)) is relatively simple. There are two regimes: In the first regime, the entrepreneur's net worth is sufficiently large that he is able to pay lenders their required return even in the worst state.[14] That is,

$$(20) \quad \hat{q}\kappa_1 \geq r(x(\omega) - S^e).$$

There is no agency problem in this case, since the entrepreneur can always pay off. Optimal auditing probabilities are always zero, and the lender's payoff is independent of the project's outcome. This might be called the "full-collateralization" case, since the entrepreneur's contribution is so large relative to the input requirement that the lenders face no idiosyncratic risk.[15] The entrepreneur's expected consumption in the full-collateralization case, $\hat{c}_{fc}$, is the expected project output less the required return to lenders:

$$(21) \quad \hat{c}_{fc} = \hat{q}\kappa - r(x(\omega) - S^e),$$

where, recall, $\kappa = \pi_1\kappa_1 + \pi_2\kappa_2$ is the mean project output.

If entrepreneurial savings S^e are insufficient, so that (20) fails, we are in the "incomplete collateralization" case, and there will be positive agency costs. In this case the incentive constraint (16) and the "limited liability" constraints (17) and (18) are binding,[16] as well as the outside return constraint

---

[11]More precisely, c^a is the payoff if the entrepreneur is audited and found to be telling the truth. The optimal payoff if the entrepreneur is audited and found to be lying is easily shown to be zero.

[12]The dependence of the control variables and of x on ω is suppressed in (14)–(19).

[13]A separate restriction for c_2 is unnecessary, since (16) and (19) imply $c_2 \geq 0$.

[14]Recall that we are assuming that project outcomes are realized and announcements made before θ_{t+1} (and thus q_{t+1} is known). Thus, this ability to repay needs to hold only for the expected value of q, not for the realized value. The alternative assumption complicates the analysis slightly, because incentive constraints would depend on the realized value of q_{t+1}; but qualitative results are unchanged.

[15]If $\kappa_1 = 0$, then "full collateralization" requires $S^e \geq x(\omega)$.

[16](17) and (18) bind because it is optimal to concentrate the entrepreneur's payoff in the good state, thereby minimizing his incentive to misreport.

(15) (which always binds). The optimal auditing probability p, conditional on the entrepreneur's announcement of state 1, is now given by

$$(22) \qquad p = \frac{r(x(\omega) - S^e) - \hat{q}\kappa_1}{\pi_2\hat{q}(\kappa_2 - \kappa_1) - \pi_1\hat{q}\gamma}.$$

The equation (22) is obtained from (15) through (18), which all hold with equality in this case.

The optimal auditing probability p is just sufficient to guarantee that the entrepreneur will report honestly when the good state occurs. Under the assumption that $\pi_2(\kappa_2 - \kappa_1) - \pi_1\gamma > 0$, which we will maintain, p is always positive when there is incomplete collateralization ((20) fails). (It can also be shown that, whenever expected entrepreneurial consumption is positive, $p < 1$.) The optimal auditing probability, and thus expected agency costs (which we identify with expected auditing costs, equal to $\pi_1 p\hat{q}\gamma$), is decreasing in the entrepreneur's contribution to the project, S^e. The intuition for the inverse relation of S^e and expected auditing costs is as follows: When S^e is low, lenders require a large total return, which reduces the entrepreneur's consumption in the good state. (The entrepreneur's consumption in the bad state is always optimally zero.) With a low c_2, the entrepreneur has less at risk if he falsely claims the bad outcome when the good state has occurred; thus he must be audited more frequently.

Expected entrepreneurial consumption when there is incomplete collateralization, $\hat{c}_{ic}$, is given by

$$(23) \qquad \hat{c}_{ic} = \alpha\{ \hat{q}\kappa - r(x(\omega) - S^e) - \pi_1\hat{q}\gamma \},$$

where $\alpha \equiv [\pi_2\hat{q}(\kappa_2 - \kappa_1)]/[\pi_2\hat{q}(\kappa_2 - \kappa_1) - \pi_1\hat{q}\gamma] > 1$. Note that $\partial\hat{c}_{ic}/\partial S^e = \alpha r > r$; when collateralization is incomplete, the return to "inside" funds exceeds the return to "outside" funds. This is because additional inside funds not only replace outside funds but also reduce expected agency costs. Hence the average "cost of capital" in this model depends upon the mixture of internal and external finance.

B. *The Entrepreneurial Investment Decision*

The derivation of the optimal financial contract assumed that the entrepreneur is committed both to undertaking his investment and to contributing all of his personal savings to the project. As the next step toward constructing a market equilibrium, we now consider the effects of relaxing these provisional assumptions.

In the perfect information case, we distinguished two types of entrepreneurs, those that could profitably invest and those that could not. In the imperfect information case, it turns out, we must allow for three types of entrepreneurs. For any given period t, let $\underline{\omega}$ and $\bar{\omega}$ be the levels of entrepreneurial ability that satisfy

$$(24) \qquad \hat{q}\kappa - rx(\underline{\omega}) - \hat{q}\pi_1\gamma = 0,$$

$$(25) \qquad \hat{q}\kappa - rx(\bar{\omega}) = 0.$$

Entrepreneurs with efficiency levels less than $\underline{\omega}$ have projects whose expected net return[17] is positive, *even if announcements that the bad state has occurred precipitate auditing with probability one* ($p = 1$). Call entrepreneurs with $\omega \leq \underline{\omega}$ "good" entrepreneurs. Entrepreneurs with efficiency levels $\omega \leq \bar{\omega}$, on the other hand, are guaranteed to have positive expected net returns only if there is no auditing ($p = 0$), that is, when there are no dissipative agency costs; designate entrepreneurs in this range but who are not "good" (i.e., $\underline{\omega} < \omega \leq \bar{\omega}$) as "fair" entrepreneurs.[18] Finally, "poor" entrepreneurs ($\omega > \bar{\omega}$) have projects that have negative expected net returns even if agency costs are zero.

Note again that, as in Section II, both $\underline{\omega}$ and $\bar{\omega}$ are (increasing) functions of the expected relative price of capital, $\hat{q}$. Thus, our

---

[17]Defined as the expected value of output, less the opportunity cost of inputs and expected auditing costs.

[18]$\bar{\omega}$ is defined exactly as in the perfect information case; compare (8). Thus, for a given $\hat{q}$, both "good" and "fair" entrepreneurs would be "profitable" under perfect information. (Note, though, that the value of $\hat{q}$ in equilibrium is likely to differ in the two cases.)

classification of entrepreneurs is conditional on the value of $\hat{q}$.

Also, for any given ω, let us define the "full-collateralization" level of entrepreneurial saving, $S^*(\omega)$, to be the quantity that exactly satisfies (20). That is,

$$(26) \qquad S^*(\omega) = x(\omega) - (\hat{q}/r)\kappa_1.$$

An entrepreneur of type ω who contributes savings in amount greater than or equal to $S^*(\omega)$ to his project will be able to borrow and invest with zero probability of auditing (and thus with no expected agency costs). $S^*(\omega)$ is a (decreasing) function of $\hat{q}$.

We are now in a position to represent the opportunity sets of different types of entrepreneurs graphically (see Figure 2). For each class of entrepreneurs (good, fair, or poor), the solid line graphs expected entrepreneurial consumption (conditional on undertaking the project) as a function of the amount of savings contributed by the entrepreneur.[19] The dotted line, which in each graph is a ray from the origin with slope r, is the opportunity cost of saving, as determined by the alternative storage technology.

The optimal choices of each class of entrepreneur are easy to discover using Figure 2. Consider first the poor, or inefficient, entrepreneurs. For this group, the total return to storage exceeds the return to investment for any level of savings. Thus, poor entrepreneurs will put their savings into inventory (equivalently, become lenders) and will not undertake their projects.

Good entrepreneurs are in the opposite situation. As long as the quantity of savings that the entrepreneur contributes to his project is less than the full-collateralization level $S^*(\omega)$, the marginal (and average) return to investing in the project is greater than the return to holding inventories. Thus the good entrepreneur will put all of his savings into

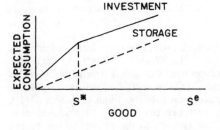

GOOD

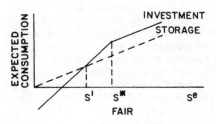

FAIR

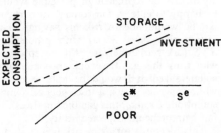

POOR

FIGURE 2

his own project,[20] up to the point where his contribution equals $S^*(\omega)$; beyond this point, he is indifferent between investing in his own project and either storing inventories or lending to others. If the good entreprenur's total savings are less than $S^*(\omega)$, his project will be audited with positive probability, so that agency costs are present. If $S^e \geq S^*(\omega)$, the project can be undertaken with zero-agency costs.

The fair entrepreneur's case is a bit more complicated. First, note that his opportunity set has three regions: If $S^e < S'(\omega)$ (where

[19] This line is defined by (23) for $S^e \leq S^*(\omega)$ and by (21) for $S^e > S^*(\omega)$, for a representative ω in each range. Figure 2 ignores the nonnegativity constraint on entrepreneurial consumption. This is harmless, since, as we shall see, entrepreneurs will not want to invest in the range where nonnegativity binds.

[20] Recall that we are assuming risk-neutrality, so that diversification is not an issue.

S' is defined, as in the diagram, as the level of savings at which the total returns to storage and investment are equal), the entrepreneur will store or lend rather than invest. If $S'(\omega) \leq S^e < S^*(\omega)$, then the entrepreneur will invest (contributing all his funds to the project), and will face a positive auditing probability. Finally, if $S^e \geq S^*(\omega)$, the entrepreneur will invest and will contribute enough to the project to ensure full collateralization. (He will be indifferent about the disposition of his savings in excess of $S^*(\omega)$.) Thus the fair entrepreneur's decision about whether to invest or store, as well as the auditing probability if he does invest, may depend on his level of savings.

We say "*may* depend" because of an interesting wrinkle that arises in this case. The upper envelope of the dashed and solid lines, which defines the fair entrepreneur's opportunity set, is *convex* between zero and $S^*(\omega)$. This means that the (risk-neutral) intermediate-quality entrepreneur in principle would be happy to enter a fair lottery. In particular, he would like to risk his savings in a lottery that pays $S^*(\omega)$ with probability $S^e/S^*(\omega)$, zero otherwise. An entrepreneur who wins this gamble would become fully collateralized and would be able to invest without agency costs; a loser gets zero consumption. *Ex ante*, this gamble improves the fair entrepreneur's expected utility.[21]

This incentive for extra risk-taking seems to arise generically in models in which agency costs are decreasing in the wealth of the agent (so that there may be increasing returns to wealth over a range).[22] It is a legitimate objection to our approach that lotteries of this sort are not seen in reality.[23] Presum-

ably risk-aversion, which we exclude, is the major explanation. Any other factor which introduces concavity into the relationship between returns and wealth (for example, if agency cost savings diminish as wealth rises; see Bernanke-Mark Gertler, 1987) would also reduce the incentive for this sort of gambling.

For present purposes, in the spirit of maintaining internal consistency, we will assume that this "savings lottery" among the fair entrepreneurs (or equivalently, between the fair entrepreneurs and, say, lenders) does take place. (Our basic macro results are essentially the same whether we allow the lottery or rule it out arbitrarily.) Under this lottery, a fraction $g(\omega) = S^e/S^*(\omega)$ of entrepreneurs of type ω win their gamble and become fully collateralized investors; the rest get zero consumption and do not invest.

The outcomes of the good and fair entrepreneurs show two contrasting ways in which the quantity of borrower wealth affects investment efficiency. All investors with $\omega \leq \bar{\omega}$ would invest in a world without information problems,[24] since the net returns to their projects when there are no agency costs are positive. With asymmetric information, all "good" entrepreneurs still invest, but they do so with positive expected agency costs. These agency costs decrease in the level of entrepreneurial savings, S^e. Only a fraction of "fair" entrepreneurs invest;[25] those that do experience no agency costs. This occurs because, as a class, the fair entrepreneurs become essentially self-financing. (On net, the fair entrepreneurs are able to borrow from lenders only the difference between full collateralization and the input cost of their projects.) Thus, investment by the intermediate class of entrepreneurs is restricted essentially to the amount of "internal equity" they can generate. The result that entrepreneurs known to be more efficient can borrow externally (albeit with a higher cost

---

[21] This can be shown formally by modifying the problem (14)–(19) to allow the entrepreneur to enter any fair savings lottery. Only intermediate-quality entrepreneurs will actively desire to enter such a lottery, because of the shape of their payoff functions; good and poor entrepreneurs will be indifferent.

[22] See Bernanke–Gertler, 1987, for another example. Although he does not consider them, lotteries would also seem to ameliorate the principal-agent problem studied by Sappington.

[23] It does seem, though, that people who need a "stake," say to open a business, may exhibit risk-loving behavior.

[24] Poor entrepreneurs, with $\omega > \bar{\omega}$, do not invest in either case.

[25] If lotteries were ruled out, it would still be the case that only a fraction of fair entrepreneurs invest; agency costs would preclude the relatively less efficient ones from undertaking projects.

of funds externally than internally), but that more marginal projects must be largely self-financing, is at least suggestive of real-world arrangements.

C. Within-Period Equilibrium

We show now how the expected price and the quantity of new capital are determined within a period, given the inherited capital stock, and assuming $\gamma > 0$.

In any period t, the inherited per capita capital stock k_t is predetermined. With labor supplied inelastically, output is determined by the production function and the random productivity shock θ (compare (1)). The wage and therefore lender and entrepreneurial saving in t are determined.

We would like to know the supply and demand curves for capital. Consider the determination of capital supply, for a given expected relative price of capital, $\hat{q}$.[26] For $\omega \leq \underline{\omega}$, define $p(\omega)$ to be the probability that an entrepreneur of type ω is audited (in the bad state). The function $p(\omega)$ is defined by

$$(27) \quad p(\omega) = \max\left(\frac{rx(\omega) - \hat{q}\kappa_1 - rS^e}{\hat{q}(\pi_2(\kappa_2 - \kappa_1) - \pi_1\gamma)}, 0\right)$$

for $\omega \leq \underline{\omega}$ (compare (22)). $p(\omega)$ is decreasing in $\hat{q}$ and in S^e; $p(\omega) = 0$ for $S^e \geq S^*(\omega)$.

Fair entrepreneurs (with types between $\underline{\omega}$ and $\bar{\omega}$), because of the "collateralization lottery," do not face the agency cost of auditing when they invest; but only the fraction of fair entrepreneurs who win the lottery are able to invest. Let $g(\omega)$, defined for $\underline{\omega} < \omega \leq \bar{\omega}$, be the fraction of fair entrepreneurs of type ω who can invest (and $1 - g(\omega)$ be the fraction who are excluded). Using the fact that $g(\omega) = S^e/S^*(\omega)$, and substituting from (26), we have

$$(28) \quad g(\omega) = \min\left(\frac{rS^e}{rx(\omega) - \hat{q}\kappa_1}, 1\right)$$

for $\underline{\omega} < \omega \leq \bar{\omega}$. The quantity $g(\omega)$ increases

in $\hat{q}$ and S^e, and for $S^e \geq S^*(\omega)$, we have $g(\omega) = 1$.

Again, entrepreneurs of type $\omega > \bar{\omega}$ do not invest.

Total capital formation (per head) in this case is given by

$$(29) \quad k_{t+1} = \left[\kappa\underline{\omega} - \pi_1\gamma\int_0^{\underline{\omega}} p(\omega)\, d\omega\right]\eta$$
$$+ \left[\kappa\int_{\underline{\omega}}^{\bar{\omega}} g(\omega)\, d\omega\right]\eta,$$

where the expression in the first set of brackets reflects capital formation (net of auditing costs) by good entrepreneurs, and the second expression in brackets is capital formation by fair entrepreneurs. (29) can be rewritten as

$$(30) \quad k_{t+1} = \left\{\kappa\bar{\omega} - \left[\int_0^{\underline{\omega}} \pi_1\gamma p(\omega)\, d\omega\right.\right.$$
$$\left.\left. + \int_{\underline{\omega}}^{\bar{\omega}} \kappa(1 - g(\omega)\, d\omega\right]\right\}\eta \quad [SS].$$

(30) is the capital supply curve for the $\gamma > 0$ case. It is depicted in Figure 3 as the $S'S'$ curve, along with the perfect information capital supply curve (SS) (derived in Section II) for reference. Several points can be made about the $S'S'$ curve.

First, $S'S'$ lies to the left of SS, that is, capital supply is always less in the imperfect information case. ((From (9) and (10), $k_{t+1} = \kappa\bar{\omega}\eta$ when $\gamma = 0$; from (30), $k_{t+1} \leq \kappa\bar{\omega}\eta$ when $\gamma > 0$.) This is because imperfect collateralization when $\gamma > 0$ increases the agency costs for those projects undertaken and (perhaps more significantly) leads to a decline in the number of projects that can be profitably initiated.

Second, the $S'S'$ curve is upward-sloping in $(\hat{q}_{t+1}, k_{t+1})$ space. This can be verified by differentiating the expression for k_{t+1} in (30) with respect to $\hat{q}_{t+1}$, using (27), (28), and the definitions of $\underline{\omega}$ and $\bar{\omega}$ ((24) and (25)). (Note that the dependence of the cutoff efficiency levels $\underline{\omega}$ and $\bar{\omega}$ on $\hat{q}_{t+1}$ must be explicitly taken into account.) Since as $\hat{q}$ gets large enough the system approaches "full collateralization" ($p(\omega)$ and $1 - g(\omega)$ approach zero), the $S'S'$ and SS curves coincide at high values of $\hat{q}$.

---

[26]$\hat{q}$ means $\hat{q}_{t+1}$. We continue to drop the time subscript where there is no ambiguity.

Entrepreneurship in Recession

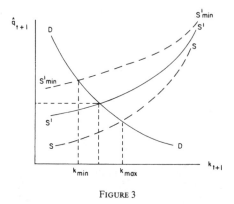

FIGURE 3

Third, unlike that of the SS curve, the position of the $S'S'$ curve depends on a period-t state variable, namely, entrepreneurial savings S^e (which enters into the expressions for $p(\omega)$ and $1 - g(\omega)$). High values of S^e (which move the system closer to full collateralization) push the $S'S'$ curve down toward the SS curve; lower values of S^e move the $S'S'$ curve up and away from the SS curve. $S'S'$ reaches its farthest point from SS when S^e is at its minimum value.[27] The dashed line marked $S'S'_{(min)}$ in Figure 3 describes this boundary.

The determination of the demand for capital is much simpler: Capital demand in the $\gamma > 0$ case is given by the identical DD curve as in the $\gamma = 0$ case (equation (13)). The intersection of $S'S'$ and DD (see Figure 3) determines capital formation in period t. Output which is saved in t but is not invested is stored, to be consumed in the subsequent period. This fully determines the within-period equilibrium.[28]

Two useful comparative statics results follow directly. First, consider the effect of a

---

[27]Given L^e, the minimum possible value of S^e occurs when wages are minimum, which in turn occurs when capital per head is zero and θ is at its minimum possible value. Assumptions made above suffice to guarantee that this minimal wage is positive.

[28]Condition (3) guarantees that the $S'S'_{(min)}$ curve intersects the vertical axis below the DD curve, so that investment is positive no matter how severe the agency problem. For an analysis of investment collapse induced by agency problems, see Bernanke-Gertler, 1987.

rise in current income, emanating from an increase in either the inherited capital stock k_t or the value of the productivity shock θ_t. In either case young entrepreneurs (as well as young lenders) will accumulate more savings. Higher entrepreneurial saving (S^e) lowers agency costs and therefore shifts the $S'S'$ curve down to the right, raising k_{t+1} and lowering $\hat{q}_{t+1}$. This effect is not present in the perfect information case. We see, therefore that the presence of agency costs induces a channel of dependence of investment on income as long as the incentive constraint binds for some entrepreneurs.

Second, imagine a redistribution of (labor) endowment from entrepreneurs to lenders, that is, raise L and lower L^e so that $\eta L^e + (1 - \eta)L$ is still equal to one. The motivation for this exercise is to model an aspect of "debt-deflation," a situation in which a combination of unindexed debt contracts and unexpected deflation redistributes wealth from the debtor class to the creditor class.[29] A fall in L^e lowers S^e, shifting the $S'S'$ up to the left; $\hat{q}_{t+1}$ rises and k_{t+1} falls. Thus a redistribution from borrowers to lenders depresses capital spending. The intuition is that lower entrepreneurial wealth raises the agency costs associated with capital finance, reducing the net return to investment.[30]

D. Dynamics

We are now equipped to consider aggregate dynamics for the $\gamma > 0$ case.

As we have already seen, the (benchmark) perfect information ($\gamma = 0$) case has no interesting dynamics; the capital stock is fixed

---

[29]The original discussion of debt-deflation is Fisher, 1933. See Bernanke, 1987, and James Hamilton, 1987, for some evidence that debt-deflation was an important feature of the Great Depression. Why debt contracts are in practice typically unindexed is a deep puzzle which we will not discuss here.

[30]If we had assumed diminishing rather than constant returns to the storage technology, the debt-deflation (by driving a larger share of savings into storage, the alternative asset) would also cause the safe rate of return to fall; this is the "flight to quality" phenomenon. Note though that, since $\hat{q}$ rises, debt-deflation cannot explain a stock market crash without introducing additional factors (such as aggregate demand externalities).

and production varies only with the productivity shock $\tilde{\theta}$. The $\gamma > 0$ case is different because of the dependence of the capital supply curve on entrepreneurial savings S^e. The $S'S'$ curve is shifted by variations in either the current capital stock k_t or the productivity shock $\tilde{\theta}_t$, either of which affects the value of the entrepreneurs' labor endowments and thus their savings. Thus future capital depends on both current capital and productivity, leading to a nontrivial dynamics.

Consider how a productivity shock is propagated over time when $\gamma > 0$. In the informationally constrained region, a (temporary) rise in $\tilde{\theta}$ stimulates investment by increasing entrepreneurial net worth (since incomes increase). The $S'S'$ curve shifts rightward. The expansion persists because the rise in the future capital stock makes investment in the subsequent period higher than it would otherwise be. Through the same mechanism, negative productivity shocks may induce a persistent investment downturn. This is our attempt to capture in a formal model the following sort of intuition: In good times, when profits are high and balance sheets are healthy, it is easier for firms to obtain outside funds. This stimulates investment and propagates the good times. Conversely, poor financial health in bad times reduces investment and reinforces the decline in output. Note again that this rationalizes a sort of accelerator effect of income on investment; note also that countercyclical agency costs are crucial to the story.

The dynamic effects of productivity disturbances may be asymmetric in this setup. (Sharp investment downturns are more likely than sharp upturns.) For example, suppose the initial level of capital equals the value the economy attains under perfect information; denote this value as k_{max}. Next, for the case $k_t = k_{max}$, let θ^* be the minimum value of $\tilde{\theta}$ which generates a level of S^e large enough to make all "good" and "fair" entrepreneurs fully collateralized.[31] Diagram-

matically, θ^* is the minimum realization of $\tilde{\theta}$ which makes the capital supply curve ($S'S'$) exactly overlap the perfect information supply curve (SS), given $k_t = k_{max}$. In this case, a realization of $\tilde{\theta}$ above θ^* has no effect on investment. The $S'S'$ does not move outward since all the efficient entrepreneurs are already fully collateralized. In contrast, a realization of $\tilde{\theta}$ below θ^*, by pushing some entrepreneurs below full collateralization and moving the $S'S'$ curve left, induces an investment downturn.

An explicit characterization of the stochastic steady state of this model cannot be obtained without some additional assumptions (for example, about functional forms). We may note several points, however: First, as long as some part of the support of $\tilde{\theta}$ is below θ^*, then even if the economy begins at k_{max}, there is some probability that it will be in the informationally constrained region in the next period. Second, if the economy begins at the minimum possible equilibrium capital stock k_{min} (at the intersection of the DD and $S'S'_{min}$ curves), and assuming that $\tilde{\theta}$ is a nondegenerate and continuously distributed random variable, the capital stock will almost certainly rise over time. Third, independent of initial conditions, the equilibrium capital stock in each period (it is easy to show) will lie in the interval $[k_{min}, k_{max}]$. We conclude that for most plausible parameterizations the system will be in the interior of the informationally constrained region with some positive probability in any given period, even asymptotically.

A distributional shock, as described in Section III, Part C, will also initiate interesting dynamics. In particular, a redistribution from borrowers to lenders that does not affect total income will lower investment not only in the current period, but for a number of subsequent periods as well. Thus balance sheet considerations may initiate, as well as propagate, cyclical fluctuations.

IV. Conclusion

We have constructed a simple neoclassical model of intrinsic business cycle dynamics in which borrowers' balance sheet positions play an important role. The critical insight

[31] Given (6), (25), (26), and (13), θ^* is defined by $\theta^* = [x(\bar{\omega}) - (\hat{q}(k_{max})/r)\kappa_1]/[f(k_{max}) - f'(k_{max})k_{max}]$.

is that the agency costs of undertaking physical investments are inversely related to the entrepreneur's/borrower's net worth. As a result, accelerator effects on investment emerge: Strengthened borrower balance sheets resulting from good times expand investment demand, which in turn tends to amplify the upturn; weakened balance sheets in bad times do just the opposite. The aggregate effects of productivity shocks may be asymmetric (since the agency problem may only bind on the "down" side). Further, redistributions or other shocks that affect borrowers' balance sheets (as may occur in a debt-deflation) will have aggregate real effects.

We have investigated extensions of this approach in related work. Our 1987 paper studies the macroeconomic implications of agency costs in a richer model of the investment process. In that model, projects differ *ex ante* (not just *ex post*, as in the costly state verification model), borrowers are able to obtain private information about project quality by incurring an evaluation cost, and borrowers must decide whether to proceed with projects that they have evaluated. The analysis of that model shows that the concept of "agency costs" relevant to macroeconomic fluctuations is much broader than the monitoring costs of the present paper: "Agency costs" should include any deviation from first-best outcomes associated with the necessity of external finance (whether it be through debt or other instruments). This result is important for interpreting the model empirically. Our companion paper also verifies the robustness of this basic approach to variations in assumptions about endowments and the information structure, and to permitting coalitions among entrepreneurs.

We have not discussed policy implications in the present paper. While, as in most OG models, the competitive solution of our model economy is not guaranteed to be Pareto optimal, it is efficient in a limited, intra-generational sense.[32] Issues of effi-

ciency and policy are taken up at greater length in our 1987 paper. In particular, that paper discusses whether a policy of "debtor bailouts" (redistributions from lenders to borrowers) may be desirable when borrower net worth is low. Also addressed there is the issue of whether agency costs typically lead to "under"- or "over" - investment on average.

Finally, it is important to find out whether the qualitative results of this paper go through when borrowers and lenders are able to make contacts that last many periods. This has been done by Gertler (1988). In an *n*-period setting, he shows that the concept of "borrower net worth" should be augmented to include not just current endowments (as in the present paper), but also the "most secure" portion of expected future profits; thus, agency costs depend not only on current wealth but also on expected future conditions. He demonstrates that this can induce additional interesting cyclical dynamics into the aggregate economy.

APPENDIX: OPTIMAL CONTRACTING WITH STOCHASTIC AUDITING

This appendix studies the optimal financial contract between risk-neutral[33] entrepreneurs and lenders when there is private information about project outcomes but lenders have access to a costly auditing technology, as described in the text. We allow explicitly for a randomized auditing strategy by the lenders. As in the main text, we are assuming that borrowing and investment occurs in a given period t, and that project realization, auditing, and "settling up" by entrepreneurs and lenders occurs in $t+1$. Settling up is done via transfers of the produced capital good, and takes place before the period-$(t+1)$ value of capital, in terms of the consumption good, is known. Time subscripts are omitted below for legibility.

There are n possible outcomes of the investment project. In state i, κ_i units of the capital good are produced. Assume $0 \le \kappa_1 < \kappa_2 < \cdots < \kappa_n$ and denote the probability of the ith outcome by π_i, $\pi_i > 0$. After

---

to manipulate the relative price of capital in order to relax incentive constraints.

[33] The assumption of risk-neutrality differentiates our analysis from that of Townsend, 1988, and Mookherjee and Png, 1987, who consider the risk-averse case. Interestingly, the risk-neutral case seems to avoid some apparent anomalies that can arise in the optimal contract with risk aversion.

[32] Our dynamic equilibrium replicates the solution to a planning problem in which there are restrictions on intergenerational trades and the planner is not allowed

privately observing the true state j, the entrepreneur announces a state, say k, to the lenders. The lenders can verify the true state only by incurring an auditing cost of γ units of capital. We assume that lies of the form $k < j$ are feasible; in this case, the entrepreneur can "hide" the extra capital $\kappa_j - \kappa_k$. The expected value of this hidden capital is $\hat{q}(\kappa_j - \kappa_k)$ units of consumption, where $\hat{q}$ is the expected relative price of capital. Lies of the form $k > j$ are assumed infeasible, that is, the entrepreneur cannot show the lenders produced capital that does not exist.

We look for the optimal incentive-compatible contract. Let c_i be the entrepreneur's contractual consumption when he announces outcome i and is not audited, and let c_i^a be his consumption when he announces i, is audited, and is found to be telling the truth. (It is straightforward to show that the entrepreneur's optimal consumption when he is audited and found to be lying is zero (see Mookherjee and Png, 1987); we impose this from the beginning.) We allow a general stochastic auditing strategy: The lenders can commit in advance to auditing an announcement of outcome i with probability p_i. The total input cost of the project is x (here we hold the entrepreneur's "efficiency," ω, fixed). The entrepreneur's contribution is his savings S^e, and the interest rate is r, so that the lenders' total required return is $r(x - S^e)$. The entrepreneur's (borrower's) formal problem is

$$(A1) \quad \max_{\{c_i^a, c_i, p_i\}} \sum_{i=1}^{n} \pi_i \left(p_i c_i^a + (1 - p_i) c_i \right)$$

subject to

$$(A2) \quad \sum_{i=1}^{n} \pi_i \left[\hat{q}\kappa_i - \left(p_i c_i^a + (1 - p_i) c_i \right) - \hat{q} p_i \gamma \right]$$

$$\geq r(x - S^e) \qquad (\lambda_1)$$

$$(A3) \quad p_i c_i^a + (1 - p_i) c_i \geq (1 - p_j)\left(c_j + \hat{q}(\kappa_i - \kappa_j) \right)$$

$$i = 2, \dots, n \quad j < i \quad (\lambda_{2ij})$$

$$(A4) \quad c_i \geq 0 \qquad i = 1, 2, \dots, n \qquad (\lambda_{3i})$$

$$(A5) \quad c_i^a \geq 0 \qquad i = 1, 2, \dots, n \qquad (\lambda_{4i})$$

$$(A6) \quad p_i \geq 0 \qquad i = 1, 2, \dots, n \qquad (\lambda_{5i})$$

$$(A7) \quad 1 \geq p_i \qquad i = 1, 2, \dots, n \qquad (\lambda_{6i})$$

where the multipliers associated with each set of constraints are in the right margin in parentheses, and $\hat{q}$ is the expected value of q_{t+1}. The entrepreneur's objective, (A1), is to maximize expected consumption, subject to the constraint that lenders receive their required return (A2), the truth-telling constraint (A3), nonnegativity constraints on c_i and c_i^a, (A4) and (A5), and the restriction that auditing probabilities be between zero

and one, (A6) and (A7). The first-order conditions for c_1^a, c_i^a $(i = 2, \dots, n)$, c_1, c_i $(i = 2, \dots, n-1)$, c_n, p_1, p_i $(i = 2, \dots, n-1)$, and p_n are, respectively,

$$(A8) \quad \pi_1 p_1 (1 - \lambda_1) + \lambda_{41} = 0$$

$$(A9) \quad \pi_i p_i (1 - \lambda_1) + p_i \sum_{j=1}^{i-1} \lambda_{2ij} + \lambda_{4i} = 0$$

$$i = 2, \dots, n$$

$$(A10) \quad \pi_1 (1 - p_1)(1 - \lambda_1)$$

$$- (1 - p_1) \sum_{k=2}^{n} \lambda_{2k1} + \lambda_{31} = 0$$

$$(A11) \quad \pi_i (1 - p_i)(1 - \lambda_1) + (1 - p_i) \sum_{j=1}^{i-1} \lambda_{2ij}$$

$$- (1 - p_i) \sum_{k=i+1}^{n} \lambda_{2ki} + \lambda_{3i} = 0$$

$$i = 2, \dots, n-1$$

$$(A12) \quad \pi_n (1 - p_n)(1 - \lambda_1)$$

$$+ (1 - p_n) \sum_{j=1}^{n-1} \lambda_{2nj} + \lambda_{3n} = 0$$

$$(A13) \quad \pi_1 (c_1^a - c_1)(1 - \lambda_1) - \lambda_1 \pi_1 \hat{q}\gamma$$

$$+ \sum_{k=2}^{n} \left(c_1 + \hat{q}(\kappa_k - \kappa_1) \right) \lambda_{2k1} + \lambda_{51} - \lambda_{61} = 0$$

$$(A14) \quad \pi_i (c_i^a - c_i)(1 - \lambda_1) - \lambda_1 \pi_i \hat{q}\gamma$$

$$+ (c_i^a - c_i) \sum_{j=1}^{i-1} \lambda_{2ij}$$

$$+ \sum_{k=i+1}^{n} \left(c_i + \hat{q}(\kappa_k - \kappa_i) \right) \lambda_{2ki} + \lambda_{5i} - \lambda_{6i} = 0$$

$$i = 2, \dots, n-1,$$

$$(A15) \quad \pi_n (c_n^a - c_n)(1 - \lambda_1)$$

$$- \lambda_1 \pi_n \hat{q}\gamma + (c_n^a - c_n) \sum_{j=1}^{n-1} \lambda_{2nj} + \lambda_{5n} - \lambda_{6n} = 0.$$

From (A8) or (A9), it is immediate that $\lambda_1 \geq 1$, so that the lenders' return constraint (A2) always binds. Adding the difference between the LHS and RHS of

(A2) to the objective (A1) reveals that the problem is unchanged if we replace (A1) with

(A1)′ $$\min_{\{c_i^a, c_i, p_i\}} \sum_{i=1}^{n} \pi_i \hat{q} p_i \gamma.$$

Thus we have

Result 1. The optimal contract minimizes expected auditing costs, subject to the constraints (A2)–(A7).

Result 1 and the fact that (A2) binds imply that expected auditing costs under the optimal contract are nondecreasing in the return required by lenders (the RHS of (A2)). For fixed r, this required return is decreasing in S^e, the collateral of the entrepreneurs. Thus we have

Result 2. Expected auditing costs under the optimal contract are nonincreasing in the quantity of the entrepreneur's collateral S^e (and they are strictly decreasing in S^e when expected auditing costs are positive at the initial point).

We have noted that $\lambda_1 \geq 1$. There are two interesting subcases, $\lambda_1 = 1$ and $\lambda_1 > 1$. If $\lambda_1 = 1$, then we are in the case of no auditing; that is, $p_i = 0$, all i. (Proof: If $\lambda_1 = 1$, then from (A9) we have $p_i \lambda_{2ij} = 0$ ($i = 2, \ldots, n$; $j < i$). (A12) and the fact that $p_n \lambda_{2nj} = 0$ implies $\lambda_{2nj} = 0$, $j < n$. Using (A11) and working recursively backward from $i = n - 1$, we conclude $\lambda_{2ij} = 0$ ($i = 2, \ldots, n$; $j < i$.) From (A13)–(A15), this implies $\lambda_{5i} > 0$, all i; that is, $p_i = 0$.) On the other hand, if $p_i > 0$ for any i, then $\lambda_1 > 1$. (Proof: If some $p_i > 0$, then $\lambda_{5i} = 0$. Suppose that $\lambda_1 = 1$. From (A13)–(A15), $\lambda_{5i} = 0$ implies that some λ_{2ij} or λ_{2ki} must be positive. But, as shown just above, this implies $\lambda_1 > 1$, a contradiction.)

Consider first the no-auditing case ($\lambda_1 = 1$). With no auditing there is no deadweight loss; the "first best" is attained. The next result characterizes when this is possible.

Result 3. The optimal contract involves no auditing if and only if the lender's required return is less than the value of the worst possible outcome of the project; that is, $p_i = 0$, all i, iff $r(x - S^e) \leq \hat{q} \kappa_1$.

PROOF:

Suppose $p_i = 0$, all i. From (A3), this implies $c_i \geq \hat{q}(\kappa_i - \kappa_1)$, $i = 2, \ldots, n$. Substituting this into (A2) yields $r(x - S^e) \leq \hat{q} \kappa_1$, which proves sufficiency. Now suppose $r(x - S^e) \leq \hat{q} \kappa_1$. Then the contract $\{c_i = \hat{q} \kappa_i - r(x - S^e)$, $p_i = 0$, c_i^a irrelevant$\}$ satisfies the constraints and involves no auditing. Since auditing costs are minimized, this contract is optimal, by Result 1.

When $r(x - S^e) > \hat{q} \kappa_1$, we are in the case $\lambda_1 > 1$, and the optimal contract involves some positive probability of auditing. We give a few results for this case ($\lambda_1 > 1$ is maintained).

Result 4. In any state in which there is a positive probability of auditing, the entrepreneur receives positive consumption only if he is audited; that is, $p_i > 0 \to c_i = 0$.

PROOF:

Our proof is for $i = 2, \ldots, n - 1$; similar arguments apply for $i = 1$ and $i = n$. Assume $1 > p_i > 0$. (If $p_i = 1$,

the value of c_i is irrelevant.) Comparing (A11) and (A9), note that the first two terms of (A11) are proportional to $-\lambda_{4i}$. If $\lambda_{4i} > 0$, then (A11) implies $\lambda_{3i} > 0$ and we are done. Suppose that $\lambda_{4i} = 0$. Then, in (A14), the first and third terms, which are proportional to λ_{4i}, disappear. Since $\lambda_{5i} = 0$, for (A14) to hold there must be some $k > i$ such that $\lambda_{2ki} > 0$. (A11) then again implies $\lambda_{3i} > 0$, so that $c_i = 0$.

Result 5. The entrepreneur receives no consumption in the worst state; $c_1^a = c_1 = 0$.

PROOF:

$\lambda_{41} > 0$ (if $p_1 > 0$) and $\lambda_{31} > 0$ (if $p_1 < 1$) follow immediately from (A8) and (A10).

Result 6. Let $\hat{c}_i = p_i c_i^a + (1 - p_i) c_i$ be the entrepreneur's expected consumption in state i. Then $\hat{c}_i$ is nondecreasing in i, that is, the entrepreneur does better in better states.

PROOF:

For some $\hat{c}_i$, we wish to show that $\hat{c}_k \geq \hat{c}_i$, any $k > i$. $\hat{c}_1 = 0$, so let $i > 1$. If $\lambda_{3i} > 0$ and $\lambda_{4i} > 0$, then $\hat{c}_i = 0$ and the result is immediate. Suppose instead then that either $\lambda_{3i} = 0$ or $\lambda_{4i} = 0$. Then from (A11) or (A9), there exists some $j < i$ such that $\lambda_{2ij} > 0$. This implies $\hat{c}_i = (1 - p_j)(c_j + \hat{q}(\kappa_i - \kappa_j))$. For any $k > i$, we know from (A3) that $c_k \geq (1 - p_j)(c_j + \hat{q}(\kappa_k - \kappa_j)) > (1 - p_j)(c_j + \hat{q}(\kappa_i - \kappa_j)) = \hat{c}_i$. Thus expected consumption is actually strictly increasing in the range where it is positive.

Result 7. There is never any auditing in the highest state; $p_n = 0$.

PROOF:

Suppose $p_n > 0$. Then $\lambda_{5n} = 0$ and, from Result 4, $c_n = 0$. Now if $c_n^a = 0$ also, (A15) can hold only if $\lambda_{5n} > 0$, and we have a contradiction. Suppose instead that $c_n^a > 0$. Then $\lambda_{4n} = 0$. Comparing (A15) with (A9), we see that the first and third terms of (A15), which are proportional to λ_{4n}, must be zero. But then once again (A15) can hold only if $\lambda_{5n} > 0$, a contradiction.

Result 8. The probability of auditing is nonincreasing in the announced state (p_i is nonincreasing in i).

PROOF:

For any p_i, $i = 2, \ldots, n - 1$, we wish to show that $p_{i-1} \geq p_i$. If $p_i = 0$, this is trivial, so take $p_i > 0$. By Result 4, $c_i = 0$. Now there are two possibilities to consider, $c_i^a = 0$ and $c_i^a > 0$.

Suppose $c_i^a = 0$. Then for (A14) to hold, there must be some $k > i$ such that $\lambda_{2ki} > 0$. Thus $\hat{c}_k = (1 - p_i)(\hat{q}(\kappa_k - \kappa_i))$, where $\hat{c}_k$ is defined as in Result 6. We know that $\hat{c}_k \geq (1 - p_{i-1})(c_{i-1} + \hat{q}(\kappa_k - \kappa_{i-1}))$. Since $c_{i-1} + \hat{q}(\kappa_k - \kappa_{i-1}) > \hat{q}(\kappa_k - \kappa_i)$, it must be that $p_{i-1} \geq p_i$.

If $c_i^a > 0$, then $\lambda_{4i} = 0$, and the first and third terms of (A14), which together are proportional to λ_{4i}, equal zero. For (A14) to hold, there must again be some $k > i$ such that $\lambda_{2ki} > 0$, and the argument is the same as before.

REFERENCES

Bernanke, Ben and Gertler, Mark, "Financial Fragility and Economic Performance," NBER Working Paper No. 2318, July 1987.

_____, "Nonmonetary Effects of the Financial Crisis in the Propagation of the Great Depression," *American Economic Review*, June 1983, *73*, 257–76.

Diamond, Douglas, "Financial Intermediation and Delegated Monitoring," *Review of Economic Studies*, July 1984, *51*, 393–414.

Diamond, Peter, "Government Debt in a Neoclassical Growth Model," *American Economic Review*, December 1965, *55*, 1126–50.

Eckstein, Otto and Sinai, Allen, "The Mechanisms of the Business Cycle in The Postwar Era," in Robert Gordon, ed., *The American Business Cycle: Continuity and Change*, University of Chicago Press for NBER, 1986.

Farmer, Roger, "A New Theory of Aggregate Supply," *American Economic Review*, December 1984, *74*, 920–30.

Fisher, Irving, "The Debt-Deflation Theory of Great Depressions," *Econometrica*, October 1933, *1*, 337–57.

Gale, Douglas and Hellwig, Martin, "Incentive-Compatible Debt Contracts I: The One-Period Problem," *Review of Economic Studies*, October 1985, *52*, 647–64.

Gertler, Mark, "Financial Capacity, Reliquification, and Production in an Economy with Long-Term Relationships," unpublished manuscript, June 1988.

Green, Edward, "Lending and the Smoothing of Uninsurable Income," unpublished manuscript, 1987.

Greenwald, Bruce and Stiglitz, Joseph, "Information, Finance Constraints, and Business Fluctuations," unpublished manuscript, June 1986.

Hamilton, James D., "Monetary Factors in the Great Depression," *Journal of Monetary Economics*, March 1987, *19*, 145–69.

Holmstrom, Bengt, "Moral Hazard and Observability," *Bell Journal of Economics*, Spring 1979, *10*, 74–91.

Mishkin, Frederic, "The Household Balance Sheet and the Great Depression," *Journal of Economic History*, December 1978, *38*, 918–37.

Mookherjee, Dilip and Png, Ivan, "Optimal Auditing, Insurance, and Redistribution," unpublished manuscript, revised April 1987.

Prescott, Edward C., "Theory Ahead of Business Cycle Measurement," *Quarterly Review*, Federal Reserve Bank of Minneapolis, Fall 1986, 9–33.

Sappington, David, "Limited Liability Contracts Between Principal and Agent," *Journal of Economic Theory*, February 1983, *29*, 1–21.

Stiglitz, Joseph and Weiss, Andrew, "Macroeconomic Equilibrium and Credit Rationing," unpublished manuscript, July 1987.

Townsend, Robert, "Optimal Contracts and Competitive Markets with Costly State Verification," *Journal of Economic Theory*, October 1979, *21*, 265–93.

_____, "Information Constrained Insurance: The Revelation Principle Extended," *Journal of Monetary Economics*, March/May 1988, *21*, 411–50.

Williamson, Stephen, "Financial Intermediation, Business Failures, and Real Business Cycles," *Journal of Political Economy*, December 1987, *95*, 1196–1216.

[8]

ELSEVIER

Available online at www.sciencedirect.com

SCIENCE @ DIRECT°

Journal of Monetary Economics 51 (2004) 555–573

Journal of
MONETARY
ECONOMICS

www.elsevier.com/locate/econbase

Entrepreneurial activity, risk, and the business cycle [☆]

Adriano A. Rampini*

Department of Finance, Kellogg School of Management, Northwestern University, 2001 Sheridan Road, Evanston, IL 60208, USA

Received 13 August 2001; received in revised form 10 January 2003; accepted 17 June 2003

Abstract

This paper analyzes a model in which the risk associated with entrepreneurial activity implies that the amount of such activity is procyclical and results in amplification and intertemporal propagation of productivity shocks. In the model risk averse agents choose between a riskless project and a risky project with higher expected output ('the entrepreneurial activity'). Agents who become entrepreneurs need to bear part of the project-specific risk for incentive reasons. More agents become entrepreneurs when productivity is high, because agents are more willing to bear risk and need to bear less risk for incentive reasons. Furthermore, cross-sectional heterogeneity can be countercyclical.
© 2003 Elsevier B.V. All rights reserved.

JEL classification: D82; E32; E44; G39

Keywords: Agency costs; Entrepreneurship; Risk aversion; Amplification; Propagation

---

[☆] I thank Andrea Eisfeldt, Thomas Sargent, and José Scheinkman, as well as Andrew Abel, Malcolm Baker, Marco Bassetto, Alberto Bisin, Denis Gromb, Lars Hansen, Narayana Kocherlakota, Arvind Krishnamurthy, Deborah Lucas, Alexander Monge, Mitchell Petersen, Lars Stole, Robert Townsend, Richard Rogerson (the associate editor), an anonymous referee, seminar participants at the University of Chicago, the University of Pennsylvania (Wharton), the University of Colorado at Boulder, the 1999 SED Annual Meeting, the 1999 Workshop in Economic Theory (Venice), the 1999 SITE Summer Workshop, the 2000 World Congress of the Econometric Society, the 2001 NBER Summer Institute, the 2001 SAET Biennial Conference, and the 2002 AFA Annual Meeting for helpful comments. I gratefully acknowledge financial support from the University of Chicago and the Alfred P. Sloan Foundation.
*Tel.: 847-467-1841; fax: 847-491-5719.
E-mail address: rampini@northwestern.edu (A.A. Rampini).

0304-3932/$ - see front matter © 2003 Elsevier B.V. All rights reserved.
doi:10.1016/j.jmoneco.2003.06.003

556   *A.A. Rampini / Journal of Monetary Economics 51 (2004) 555–573*

1. Introduction

This paper analyzes a model of entrepreneurial activity and argues that entrepreneurial activity is procyclical due to the risk associated with it. Thus, a model with endogenous entrepreneurial activity may result in greater amplification and intertemporal propagation of aggregate shocks. We argue that the risk aversion of entrepreneurs, who cannot fully diversify the idiosyncratic risk of their projects for incentive reasons, is an additional mechanism making economic activity more volatile. Considering entrepreneurial risk aversion is important since the economic activity of small firms is particularly affected by downturns[1] and ownership of such firms is highly concentrated, typically in the hands of just one principal owner.[2]

We study an economy where risk averse agents face a choice between a riskfree project and a risky project which is more productive but requires an unobservable effort ('the entrepreneurial activity'). Thus, for incentive reasons, agents who take the risky project, i.e. entrepreneurs, need to bear part of the project-specific risk. Since agents are more willing to bear risk when productivity is high and, in fact, need to bear less risk for incentive reasons, entrepreneurial activity is procyclical even under the optimal contract. In other words, countercyclical agency costs imply that the more productive risky technology dominates the riskless one when productivity is sufficiently high. Thus, countercyclical agency costs result in agents' technology choices being procyclical and hence amplify technology shocks.

Aggregate output can be quite sensitive to changes in the amount of entrepreneurial activity. The reason is that at a point where an agent is indifferent between the riskless and the risky project, the expected output of the risky project exceeds the output of the riskless project because agents have to be compensated for risk. Thus, changes in entrepreneurial activity can have a first-order effect on output.

Furthermore, intertemporal smoothing through storage can make technology adoption correlated across time even if productivity shocks are independent. High storage has a similar effect to high productivity. The higher the amount carried over from the previous period, the better off agents are this period, which makes them more willing to bear project-specific risk and hence a larger fraction of them become entrepreneurs ceteris paribus. In addition, high productivity today implies both increased entrepreneurial activity today and increased storage for tomorrow, which in turn implies increased entrepreneurial activity tomorrow. Thus, the model implies intertemporal propagation, although this effect is relatively small quantitatively.

Under the optimal contract entrepreneurs need to bear a larger part of the project-specific risk when productivity is low. This may be interpreted, as we will argue, as entrepreneurs being more leveraged in bad times. The fact that agents need to hold more project-specific risk in a downturn also implies that the cross-sectional

---

[1] See Bernanke et al. (1996) who review the empirical evidence on the effect of economic downturns on the access to credit and the economic activity of 'high agency cost' borrowers, specifically small firms.

[2] Data from the *1993 National Survey of Small Business Finances* suggests that the ownership share of the principal owner of businesses with less than 500 employees is 81%. For evidence on the effect of entrepreneurial risk on portfolio choice see Heaton and Lucas (2000).

A.A. Rampini / Journal of Monetary Economics 51 (2004) 555–573   557

variation of consumption can be countercyclical; there may be more inequality in bad times. This is of particular interest since countercyclical cross-sectional variation has recently gotten attention in the asset pricing literature as one way to reconcile asset pricing models with empirical evidence on asset returns.[3]

The model also has implications for differences across countries. We expect more productive economies to be better able to share project-specific risk and hence to have more entrepreneurial activity. In addition, this model predicts that an economy with a less developed financial market, e.g., an economy where agents have to bear all the project-specific risk, may have more volatile as well as lower output. Thus, financial development can be negatively related to output variability because entrepreneurial activity can be more volatile when the financial system is less developed.[4]

The model is in a similar spirit to Kihlstrom and Laffont (1979) who study an entrepreneurial model with roots in the work of Knight. In their model, more risk averse individuals become workers while the less risk averse become entrepreneurs. In our model, wealth effects imply that risk aversion varies over the business cycle, and as agents become less risk averse, more of them become entrepreneurs. Thus, we provide a business cycle frequency version of Knight's theory of entrepreneurship.

Banerjee and Newman (1991) analyze a model where agents face an occupational choice similar to the one in our paper in a study of the distribution of wealth. However, their results are quite different from ours since in their model it is the poorer agents who choose the risky project.

The interaction between financial contracting and aggregate economic activity through countercyclical agency costs has received considerable attention recently.[5] Following Bernanke and Gertler (1989), this literature studies the effects of countercyclical agency costs in models with costly state verification of risk neutral entrepreneurs with limited liability à la Townsend (1979) and Gale and Hellwig (1985).[6]

We think that our model complements the existing literature on the effects of countercyclical agency costs by pointing out the procyclical nature of technology choice in environments where agency costs are countercyclical due to risk aversion. In our model it is the risk associated with the entrepreneurial activity rather than

---

[3] See Mankiw (1986) and Constantinides and Duffie (1996) and, for empirical evidence, Heaton and Lucas (1996) and Storesletten et al. (1999).

[4] See, e.g., Greenwood and Jovanovic (1990) and Acemoglu and Zilibotti (1997), for models of the interaction between financial development and growth. See, e.g., King and Levine (1993) and Rajan and Zingales (1998) for empirical evidence.

[5] See Scheinkman and Weiss (1985) for an early model. Holmström and Weiss (1985) study a model in which the use of investment as a screening device amplifies technology shocks. Williamson (1987) studies a model with delegated monitoring in which the amount of 'credit rationing' fluctuates over the business cycle and propagates technology shocks.

[6] See Bernanke et al. (1999) for a synthesis of the literature. Fuerst (1995), Carlstrom and Fuerst (1997), and Fisher (1999) study the quantitative implications of this class of models. See also Greenwald and Stiglitz (1993) for a related model. Kiyotaki and Moore (1997) study the effect of the need to collateralize loans on aggregates and Holmström and Tirole (1996, 1997, 1998) the effect of the demand for liquidity.

558 *A.A. Rampini / Journal of Monetary Economics 51 (2004) 555–573*

constraints on outside funding (due to the limited resources of the insider, i.e., the entrepreneur) that limits the amount of entrepreneurial activity.

The paper proceeds as follows. In Section 2 we describe the model and characterize the solution. In Section 3 we solve an example explicitly, compute certain moments of the example economy, and simulate the economy. We also discuss the cyclical properties of cross-sectional heterogeneity, or inequality, and provide a comparison of the properties of the economy under different regimes of financial intermediation. We conclude in Section 4.

2. Model

In this section we describe the model and characterize the solution of the optimal contracting problem for this economy. We study the optimal contracting problem because we are interested in the dynamics of an economy in which agents only hold the part of project-specific risk which is necessary for incentive reasons. In other words, we think of financial intermediaries offering contracts, e.g., defaultable debt contracts, to entrepreneurs that expose them to the minimal amount of project-specific risk required for them to supply effort towards the success of the project.

2.1. Environment

There is a continuum of agents with unit mass. Time is discrete. Let each agent's utility function $\mathscr{U}$ from a consumption process c and an effort process e be given by

$$\mathscr{U}(c, e) = \mathrm{E}\left[\sum_{t=0}^{\infty} \beta^t u(c_t - e_t)\right]$$

and assume that the momentary utility function u is strictly increasing and strictly concave and satisfies the following assumption:

Assumption 1 (DARA). *The momentary utility function u exhibits decreasing absolute risk aversion, i.e., satisfies $\partial/\partial x(-u''(x)/u'(x)) < 0$.*

Notice that we assume a specific form of non-separability of utility in consumption and effort. Effectively, effort is in terms of the consumption good. Effort can thus be interpreted as an unobservable investment that is required to operate the risky technology. While this assumption about preferences is sufficient to obtain procyclical entrepreneurial activity, it is not necessary.[7] However, the specific form of the non-separability chosen simplifies the analysis considerably.

---

[7] Notice however that in particular the standard assumption of separability of preferences in consumption and effort would not in general deliver this result.

A.A. Rampini / Journal of Monetary Economics 51 (2004) 555–573   559

Each period, the agents can choose one of the following two technologies or projects: A riskless technology that returns $\omega + y$ with certainty[8] and costs $e_0 = 0$ effort and a risky technology that returns $\omega + Y$ with probability p and ω with probability $1 - p$ given effort $e_1 > 0$ and ω with certainty given the low effort level $e_0 = 0$. The aggregate productivity or technology shock, denoted by ω, shifts the output of both technologies by a constant. The reason for this assumption is explained below. We assume that the returns of the risky technology are independent across agents conditional on the aggregate technology shock. Clearly, only the case where $pY - e_1 > y$ is of interest so we take that as given.

Effort is unobservable and hence agents have to be induced to work which, given our assumptions, is optimal if an agent takes the risky project. Thus, agents need to bear project-specific or idiosyncratic risk if they take the risky project. Importantly, we rule out intertemporal incentive provision by assuming that agents' identity cannot be tracked intertemporally.[9] That is, we do not allow compensation of an agent at time t to depend on the outcome of his project at $t - 1$. Thus, we restrict incentive provision to be intratemporal. We make this assumption for tractability reasons only. The main results are preserved even with intertemporal incentive provision, although the effects are somewhat mitigated.

The technology shock ω follows a Markov process. The technology shock is observed at the beginning of each period. As stated above it shifts the output of both technologies by a constant. Given this assumption ω affects only expected returns without affecting variances. Hence, a higher ω is unambiguously preferable. In addition, the additive structure allows us to reduce the dimensionality of the problem from two to one state variable when we restrict attention to the case of technology shocks that are independent over time.

Finally, we also allow storage of the output: For simplicity, we assume that storage s is chosen from the interval $s \in S = [0, \bar{s}]$ with $\bar{s} < +\infty$. We assume that storage is observable by the planner or financial intermediary. Thus, we can without loss of generality assume that the planner or financial intermediary decides on storage. This completes the description of the economic environment.

2.2. Optimal contracting problem

The problem of designing the optimal contract is the following: At the beginning of each period the planner, which we interpret as a financial intermediary, observes the technology shock for that period. The planner then chooses the fraction of the population to be assigned to each technology, the consumption allocation as a

---

[8] The following alternative interpretation of the riskless technology is possible: The technology is risky as well but there is no moral hazard. The output is $\omega + \hat{y}$ with probability p and ω with probability $1 - p$ where $\hat{y}$ satisfies $y = p\hat{y}$. Obviously, full insurance is optimal when agents choose this technology. This alternative interpretation could be adopted throughout the paper, but for clarity we will always refer to the first technology as riskless and the second as risky.

[9] The benefits of multiperiod contracts have been recognized (see Townsend, 1982; Rogerson, 1985; Green, 1987). For models with multiperiod contracts and aggregate fluctuations see Gertler (1992) and Phelan (1994).

560 *A.A. Rampini / Journal of Monetary Economics 51 (2004) 555–573*

function of the technology assignment and output realization and the level of storage for the next period. Let us introduce the technology choice variable α which is the fraction of agents that choose or are assigned to the risky technology and restrict it to $\alpha \in [0, 1]$. That is, agents participate in a lottery that assigns them either to a risky project or to a riskless project with probabilities α and $1 - \alpha$.[10] Finally, output is realized and agents get their consumption allocation. We are now ready to state the Bellman equation for this economy:

$$v(\omega + s, \omega) = \max_{\alpha \in [0,1], c, c_0, c_1 \in \Re, s' \in S} \{\alpha E[u(\tilde{c} - e_1)|e_1] + (1 - \alpha)u(c)$$
$$+ \beta E[v(\omega' + s', \omega')|\omega]\}$$

subject to

$$\alpha E[\tilde{c}|e_1] + (1 - \alpha)c + s' \leqslant \omega + s + \alpha p Y + (1 - \alpha)y$$

and

$$E[u(\tilde{c} - e_1)|e_1] \geqslant u(c_0 - e_0).$$

The notation is as follows: The value function v is a function of two state variables: $\omega + s$, the sum of the technology shock ω and the storage level s, and ω, the technology shock.[11] For agents assigned to the riskless technology the consumption c is just a constant. For agents assigned to the risky technology the consumption is either c_0 or c_1 depending on whether the output of a given agent is low, i.e., ω, or high, i.e., $\omega + Y$, respectively. We write $\tilde{c}$ for the random variable with realizations c_0 and c_1. Note that the momentary expected utility of agents assigned to the risky technology is conditional on the high effort level being induced, which by assumption is optimal. The resource constraint is required to hold in expectation only since there is no within period uncertainty at the level of the population.

For simplicity, we study the case where the technology shock ω follows a Markov chain on the state space $\omega \in \Omega = \{\omega_1, ..., \omega_M\}$ where $\omega_{m+1} > \omega_m$, $\forall m \in \{1, ..., M - 1\}$. Furthermore, we assume that the technology shocks are independent across time, i.e., $\Pi(\omega_{m'}|\omega_m) = \Pi(\omega_{m'}|\omega_{m''})$, $\forall m, m', m''$, or $\Pi_{m,\cdot} = \pi$, $\forall m \in \{1, ..., M\}$, where $\Pi_{m,\cdot}$ denotes the mth row of the transition matrix Π. Thus, any autocorrelation of output or the amount of entrepreneurial activity that we obtain arises endogenously.

With the assumption of independence we can drop the second state variable and the Bellman equation can be written as

$$v(\omega + s) = \max_{s' \in S} \{\Phi^c(\omega + s - s') + \beta E[v(\omega' + s')]\},$$

---

[10] One can interpret the lottery as all agents applying for funding of their risky projects, but only a fraction α of the funding proposals being accepted. Notice that Bernanke and Gertler (1989) introduce a similar lottery in their model.

[11] Equivalently we could choose ω and s as the state variables. We do not do so since the appropriate state variable when technology shocks are independent is $\omega + s$.

A.A. Rampini / Journal of Monetary Economics 51 (2004) 555–573   561

where Φ^c is the expected utility generated in the current period given a value of the state variable net of storage x and is defined as follows:

$$\Phi^c(x) \equiv \max_{\alpha \in [0,1], c, c_0, c_1 \in \Re} \{\alpha(pu(c_1 - e_1) + (1 - p)u(c_0 - e_1)) + (1 - \alpha)u(c)\}$$

subject to

$$\alpha(pc_1 + (1 - p)c_0) + (1 - \alpha)c \leqslant x + \alpha p Y + (1 - \alpha)y$$

and

$$pu(c_1 - e_1) + (1 - p)u(c_0 - e_1) \geqslant u(c_0 - e_0).$$

Thus we can solve the problem in two steps: First, we can analyze the one-period technology adoption and contract design problem, which is the problem that defines Φ^c. Then, taking Φ^c as given we can solve the dynamic problem. We study the one-period technology adoption decision in the next subsection before we return to the dynamic problem.

2.3. The one-period technology adoption decision

In order to understand the technology adoption decision it turns out to be convenient to study the momentary expected utility for a given aggregate technological choice, i.e., $\alpha = 1$ or $\alpha = 0$. For this purpose we introduce the following notation: Let x denote the value of the state variable net of storage for the next period, i.e., net of s'. Define $\Phi(x)$ as the expected momentary utility from choosing the risky technology as a function of x, i.e.,

$$\Phi(x) \equiv \max_{c_0, c_1 \in \Re} \{pu(c_1 - e_1) + (1 - p)u(c_0 - e_1)\}$$

subject to

$$pc_1 + (1 - p)c_0 \leqslant x + p Y$$

and

$$pu(c_1 - e_1) + (1 - p)u(c_0 - e_1) \geqslant u(c_0 - e_0).$$

Strict concavity of Φ is a desirable property for the analysis below. By assumption the utility function u is strictly concave. The only concern in showing that Φ is strictly concave is, then, the convexity of the set of incentive compatible allocations. Proving convexity of that set is equivalent to proving that the certainty equivalent of a Bernoulli lottery is concave in the prizes.[12] One can show that concavity of the

---

[12] To see this equivalence, let $x = c_1 - e_1$, $y = c_0 - e_1$ and $w = c_0 - e_0$. Note that $w - y = e_1 - e_0$ and $x > y$. If the triple (x, y, w) is incentive compatible then $pu(x) + (1 - p)u(y) \geqslant u(w)$. Since $u(\cdot)$ is strictly increasing we can apply the inverse function $u^{-1}(\cdot)$ to this inequality to get $z \equiv u^{-1}(pu(x) + (1 - p)u(y)) \geqslant w$. The right-hand side of the inequality is linear. Thus, it is necessary and sufficient that the certainty equivalent of the lottery with prizes (x, y), which we denote by z above, is concave in the prizes. Note finally that if (x, y, w) and (x', y', w') satisfy $x > y$, $x' > y'$, $w - y = e_1 - e_0$ and $w' - y' = e_1 - e_0$, then for $\lambda \in (0, 1)$ we have $x_\lambda > y_\lambda$ and more importantly $w_\lambda - y_\lambda = e_1 - e_0$ where $x_\lambda \equiv \lambda x + (1 - \lambda)x'$ and analogously for y_λ and w_λ. Hence, if the first two allocations are admissible so is any convex combination.

certainty equivalent obtains for utility functions with constant absolute risk aversion and constant relative risk aversion. We restrict attention to the case of concave certainty equivalents for the rest of this paper:

Assumption 2. *The utility function u satisfies the property that the certainty equivalent of a Bernoulli lottery is concave in the prizes.*

By the theorem of the maximum[13] Φ is continuous and, thus, we have the following lemma:

Lemma 1. *Suppose Assumptions 1 and 2 hold. Then Φ is continuous and strictly concave.*

The assumption of decreasing absolute risk aversion, i.e., Assumption 1, implies that if there is a reversal of the technology choice across the state space at all, then the risky technology is preferable for high values of x and the riskless technology for low values of x. Furthermore, there is at most one reversal of the technology choice. This is stated formally in the next lemma:

Lemma 2. *Suppose Assumption 1 holds. If $E[u(x^{\circ}+\tilde{Z})] \geqslant u(x^{\circ}+\bar{Z})$, then $E[u(x+\tilde{Z})] \geqslant u(x+\bar{Z})$, $\forall x \geqslant x^{\circ}$.*

This lemma is a direct implication of the definition of decreasing absolute risk aversion. The intuition is that the 'wealthier' the agent, i.e., the higher x, the less risk averse the agent. Thus, if an agent with a specific wealth level prefers a lottery over a fixed payment, so will all agents with a wealth level higher than that. To apply the lemma here, define $\tilde{Z}$ to be a random variable taking on values $Y - e_1$ and $-e_1$ with probabilities p and $1 - p$ and let $\bar{Z} = y$. This means that there is a threshold level of wealth such that all agents with a wealth level higher than that will become entrepreneurs. In other words, if an agent lived in autarky, he would become an entrepreneur only if his wealth level exceeded this threshold. Thus, if there were no insurance at all, entrepreneurial activity in this environment would be procyclical. The key question then is whether entrepreneurial activity remains procyclical, once optimal insurance through contracts offered by a financial intermediary is taken into account. The main result is that this is indeed the case: Entrepreneurial activity is procyclical even if agents have access to financial intermediaries.

More generally, we can ask what type of risk we should expect to be 'insurable'. Clearly, we do not expect aggregate risk to be insurable. Idiosyncratic risk, in contrast, should be insurable at least to the extent compatible with incentives. We show, however, that the 'insurability' of idiosyncratic risk varies with aggregates and, in fact, covaries positively with productivity in our model. Agency costs are hence countercyclical in the sense that more utility is lost due to the moral hazard problem when productivity is low.

---

[13] See, e.g., Stokey et al. (1989).

A.A. Rampini / Journal of Monetary Economics 51 (2004) 555–573   563

The main result is summarized in the next proposition, which states that a result similar to Lemma 2 holds if optimal insurance is taken into account:

Proposition 1. *Suppose Assumptions* 1 *and* 2 *hold. If* $\Phi(x^*) \geqslant u(x^* + y)$, *then* $\Phi(x) \geqslant u(x + y)$, $\forall x \geqslant x^*$.

The proof is in the appendix. Proposition 1 implies that even under the optimal contract, an agent chooses to become an entrepreneur only if his wealth exceeds a certain threshold x^*. The intuition is as follows: Suppose an agent at wealth level x^* prefers the entrepreneurial activity to the riskless activity given a contract offered by the financial intermediary. If an agent with a wealth level higher than that had access to the same contract (shifted by the difference in wealth), he would choose the entrepreneurial activity as well because he is less risk averse. But in fact one can do better than that and provide the richer agent with additional insurance (see the corollary to Proposition 1 below).

By choosing whether or not to become an entrepreneur optimally as in Proposition 1, an agent can hence attain an expected utility of $\max\{u(x + y), \Phi(x)\}$. It turns out, however, that the set of expected utilities defined by $\{U : U \leqslant \max\{u(x + y), \Phi(x)\}\}$ is not convex. The non-convexity is around the wealth level x^* where the agent switches from the riskless project to the risky project. The agent's expected utility can thus be increased by convexifying the technology adoption decision in this range. Specifically, the agents sign up with an intermediary. The intermediary assigns a fraction α of the agents to the risky project, the rest to the riskless project. Who gets assigned to which project is determined by a lottery. The agents assigned to the risky project get a contract which is a good deal, i.e., there is cross-subsidization from the agents who run riskless projects to the agents who run risky projects. The intuition is that, loosely speaking, running a risky project and being rich are complements and hence it is optimal to give agents who are entrepreneurs a good deal.

Convexifying the technology adoption results in the expected utility frontier $\Phi^c(x) = co(\{U : U \leqslant \max\{u(x + y), \Phi(x)\}\})$ where *co* stands for taking the convex hull. In practice we get Φ^c directly when solving the constrained optimization problem that defines Φ^c numerically. Obviously, the function Φ^c is by construction continuous and (weakly) concave. Notice that the implications for technology adoption carry over to the case where convexification is taken into account, i.e., entrepreneurial activity is procyclical even in this case. The only difference is that instead of a specific cut off level for wealth at which entrepreneurial activity starts, there is a range of wealth levels in which the fraction of agents who become entrepreneurs increases linearly from 0 to 1 (see the numerical illustration in the next section). We can interpret access to financial intermediaries which can enforce binding contracts that allow for ex post cross-subsidization as an economy being more financially developed. Thus, the model implies that financial development can reduce the volatility of output, a prediction that is empirically testable in a cross section of countries.

The model presented here has interesting implications for the variability of consumption across agents as a function of wealth. The variability of the consumption allocation associated with Φ is decreasing in x. In other words, if c_1 and c_0 solve the maximization problem defining Φ then $\Delta c \equiv c_1 - c_0$ is decreasing in x. This is summarized in the following corollary to Proposition 1.

Corollary 1. *The variability of the consumption allocation associated with Φ is decreasing in x, i.e., $\Delta c \equiv c_1 - c_0$ is decreasing in x.*

The proof is in the appendix. Thus, under the optimal contract entrepreneurs bear less risk when productivity is high or, in other words, incentives need to be steeper in bad times. In terms of claims traded in financial markets this means that insiders have to hold more of the equity in their projects when productivity is low. In good times, entrepreneurs are able to sell more equity to outsiders and hold more bonds, whereas in bad times they have to bear more risk, i.e., they obtain less outside financing of the risky part of their endeavor. We can alternatively interpret this as entrepreneurs being less leveraged when productivity is high, where we take 'less leverage' to mean holding a less risky stake, i.e., less project-specific risk born by the insider. Under this interpretation leverage is countercyclical which reflects the countercyclical nature of agency costs.

2.4. Computation

Given Φ^c from the previous subsection, we can now go back to the dynamic problem. Since Φ^c is a continuous and weakly concave function and taking Φ^c as given, standard arguments[14] imply the following lemma:

Lemma 3. *There exists a unique fixed point v of the operator*

$$(Tf)(\omega + s) = \max_{s' \in S} \{\Phi^c(\omega + s - s') + \beta \mathrm{E}[f(\omega' + s')]\}$$

and v is continuous, strictly increasing and weakly concave.

Given concavity of Φ^c and v, the storage policy is (at least weakly) increasing in the value of today's state variable $\omega + s$, which the numerical illustrations corroborate.

The computation is in two steps: First, the function Φ^c is computed by solving the static optimization problem that defines that function numerically. Second, the dynamic programming problem is solved using the solution for Φ^c from step 1 as the return function. To compute the value function we follow Ljungqvist and Sargent (2000) and discretize the state space, more specifically the storage decision, by letting $s \in S = \{s_1, ..., s_N\}$ where $s_1 = 0$, $s_N = \bar{s}$ and $s_{n+1} = s_n + \bar{s}/(N-1)$, $\forall n \in \{1, ..., N-1\}$. Given aggregate productivity ω_m and storage level s_n we can then write the dynamic

---

[14] See, e.g., Stokey et al. (1989).

program as

$$(Tv)(\omega_m, s_n) = \max_{s' \in S} \left\{ \Phi^c(\omega_m + s_n - s') + \beta \sum_{m'=1}^{M} \Pi_{mm'} v(\omega_{m'}, s') \right\}.$$

Define the $N \times N$-matrix R_m by letting $R_m(n, n') \equiv \Phi^c(\omega_m + s_n - s_{n'})$ and the $N \times 1$-vector v_m by letting $v_m(n) \equiv v(\omega_m, s_n)$. Then

$$Tv_m = \max \left\{ R_m + \beta \sum_{m'=1}^{M} \Pi_{mm'} \imath v_{m'}^{\top} \right\}$$

or

$$Tv = \max\{R + \beta(\Pi \otimes \imath)v^{\top}\},$$

where $\imath$ is an $N \times 1$-vector of ones, $R \equiv \begin{pmatrix} R_1 \\ \vdots \\ R_M \end{pmatrix}$ and $v \equiv (v_1, ..., v_M)$. The Bellman equation can then be solved by iterating to convergence on the last expression.

2.5. Accommodating growth

Economic growth due to exogenous technological change can be easily accommodated in this model. To account for growth we can think of the size of both technologies and the productivity shocks as growing at a continuous growth rate of g, i.e., $Y_t = \exp(gt)Y$, $y_t = \exp(gt)y$, $e_{1t} = \exp(gt)e_1$, $e_{0t} = \exp(gt)e_0$, and $\omega_{mt} = \exp(gt)\omega_m$, $m = 1, ..., M$. If we further assume that the return on storage equals $\exp(g)$ and each agent's momentary utility function exhibits constant relative risk aversion, i.e., $u(c) = c^{1-\sigma}/(1 - \sigma)$, $\sigma > 0$, then we can map the problem of the growing economy into the stationary problem solved above by letting $\tilde{c}_t = \exp(-gt)c_t$, $\tilde{s}_t = \exp(-gt)s_t$ and $\tilde{\beta} = \beta \exp(g(1 - \sigma))$. Obviously, we can also reverse this mapping to simulate a growing economy once the solution for the stationary economy has been computed.

3. A quantitative example

In this section we compute an example economy to illustrate our model of information constrained contracting as a propagation mechanism. In addition, we characterize the cyclical properties of cross-sectional heterogeneity and compare economies which differ in the degree of financial development.

3.1. Parameterization

The parameters of the example economy are chosen to demonstrate the main effects of entrepreneurial risk on economic activity rather than being calibrated to match specific moments of an economy. However, to tie our hands the productivity

Table 1
Parameterization and results for the example economy

Parameterization					
Preferences	β	σ			
	0.99	2			
Technology	p	y	Y	e_0	e_1
	0.5	0.27	1.1	0	0.19
Technology shocks	M	π			
	5	$[0.0625, 0.25, 0.375, 0.25, 0.0625]$			
	Ω				
	0.5105, 0.5215, 0.5325, 0.5435, 0.5545				
Storage	N	$\bar{s}$			
	25	0.066			
Results					
Productivity	$E[\mathscr{Y}_{risky}]$	$\sigma(\mathscr{Y}_{risky})$			
	1.0825	0.011			
Output	$E[\mathscr{Y}]$	$\sigma(\mathscr{Y})$	$\sigma(\mathscr{Y} - e^*)$		
	1.0437	0.0462	0.0342		
Autocorrelation	$\rho(\mathscr{Y}_t, \mathscr{Y}_{t-1})$	$\rho(\mathscr{Y}_t - e_t^*, \mathscr{Y}_{t-1} - e_{t-1}^*)$			
	0.0500	0.0470			

shock process is chosen to match the empirical standard deviation of total factor productivity of about 1% (see, e.g., King and Rebelo, 1999) and the preference parameters are standard. The parameterization of the example economy, as well as the results, are summarized in Table 1. The rate of time preference β is 0.99 and hence a period corresponds to one quarter. Preferences exhibit constant relative risk aversion, i.e., $u(c) = c^{1-\sigma}/(1 - \sigma)$ with a coefficient of relative risk aversion $\sigma = 2$. We next discuss the parameters of the production technology which are chosen such that the expected output of the risky technology net of effort cost implied by the model is about 11% higher than that of the riskless one. Recall that the output of the riskless technology is $\omega + y$. We set $y = 0.27$. The output of the risky technology is $\omega + Y$ with probability p and ω otherwise, where $Y = 1.1$ and $p = 0.5$. The high effort is $e_1 = 0.19$ (and recall that $e_0 = 0$). The technology shocks are described by a Markov chain with $M = 5$, i.e., 5 states, which are equally spaced around a mean of 0.5325 with $\Delta_\omega \equiv \omega_m - \omega_{m-1} = 0.011$, $\forall m \in \{2, ..., 5\}$. Technology shocks are independent over time with distribution $\pi = [0.0625, 0.25, 0.375, 0.25, 0.0625]$, i.e., a symmetric, binomial distribution, and thus the standard deviation of technology shocks is $\sigma(\omega) = \Delta_\omega = 0.011$. It is important to notice that while we refer to ω as the 'technology shock' throughout the paper which simplifies the exposition, this is not equivalent to 'productivity' in the sense of total factor productivity. An appropriate way to define and measure productivity and the variability of productivity in our model is by looking at the expected output of the risky technology and its standard deviation since the technologies are linear in the model. Denote the output of the risky technology by $\mathscr{Y}_{risky}$. The expected output is $E[\mathscr{Y}_{risky}] = E[\omega] + pY = 1.0825$ and, because of the additive structure, the standard deviation is $\sigma(\mathscr{Y}_{risky}) = 0.011$. Thus, productivity has a standard deviation of about 1% as desired.

A.A. Rampini / Journal of Monetary Economics 51 (2004) 555–573   567

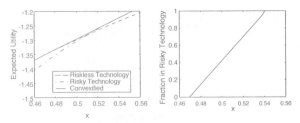

Fig. 1. Expected one period utility for riskless technology, risky technology, and convexified and fraction of agents taking risky technology.

Finally, the storage technology is specified by $N = 25$ and $\bar{s} = 0.066$. This upper bound on storage is not binding in equilibrium.

3.2. Results

To illustrate the technology choice problem we graph the expected one period utility for each technology choice as a function of x, the technology shock net of storage in the left panel of Fig. 1. That is we graph the functions $u(x + y)$ and $\Phi(x)$ as a function of x. The riskless technology dominates the risky technology only for low values of x. The solid line shows the expected utility once convexification is taken into account. For very low x only the riskless project is optimally chosen. For x in a middle range a convex combination of the two projects is assigned with the weight α on the risky project increasing in x (see the right panel of Fig. 1). Finally, for x sufficiently high all the agents are assigned to the risky project.

Following Ljungqvist and Sargent (2000) we compute the value function and the optimal policy, i.e., the optimal technology adoption policy and the optimal storage policy. An optimal policy is a pair of mappings (α^*, s^*) where $\alpha^* : \Omega \times S \mapsto [0, 1]$ and $s^* : \Omega \times S \mapsto S$. For the example under consideration the optimal policy implies that all agents take the risky technology when productivity is high, but entrepreneurial activity drops when productivity is low. For the lowest productivity level and given zero storage, entrepreneurial activity drops from an average level of 86% to 57%.

With the characterization of the optimal policy in hand we are ready to calculate the moments of the example economy and simulate the economy using the Markov matrix Π^* induced by the optimal policy (α^*, s^*) and the associated invariant distribution p^*.

By construction, the technology shock has a mean $E[\omega] = 0.5325$ and a standard deviation $\sigma(\omega) = 0.011$. The conditional expectation of the output of a given technology has the same standard deviation as the technology shock. We argued that an appropriate measure of productivity is the conditional expectation of the output of the risky technology normalized by the unconditional expectation of the output of that technology which we display for a simulation of the example economy in Fig. 2. The unconditional expectation of output $\mathcal{Y}$ of the economy is $E[\mathcal{Y}] = 1.0437$ with a standard deviation of $\sigma(\mathcal{Y}) = 0.0462$. The endogeneity of technology choice amplifies

568 A.A. Rampini / Journal of Monetary Economics 51 (2004) 555–573

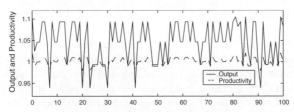

Fig. 2. Simulation of output and productivity for the example economy.

productivity shocks. In fact, the standard deviation of output (in percentage terms) is about 4 times the standard deviation of productivity. Fig. 2 provides a simulation of the example which illustrates this amplification. Since we study a model in which preferences are not separable in consumption and effort, one might argue that output should be corrected for effort cost. The standard deviation of output net of effort cost is $\sigma(\mathcal{Y} - e^*) = 0.0342$ where e^* denotes the optimal effort, a random variable that equals e_1 for the fraction of the population assigned to the risky technology and e_0 for the rest of the population. This reflects amplification of about 3.5 times the standard deviation of productivity even after adjusting for effort cost. Finally, the correlation between output in period t and $t - 1$ is $\rho(\mathcal{Y}_t, \mathcal{Y}_{t-1}) = 0.0500$, i.e., output is autocorrelated despite independent technology shocks, although this effect is small in this specification. This effect is likely to remain relatively small in general, since it is a version of the 'capital accumulation' mechanism which is well known to be a quantitatively unimportant source of persistence. The reason for the positive autocorrelation is that high productivity at time $t - 1$ increases not only entrepreneurial activity and hence output at time $t - 1$ but storage from time $t - 1$ to time t is higher as well, which means that agents are better off at time t and, thus, there is more entrepreneurial activity and higher output at time t, too. Similarly, when we correct for effort, the autocorrelation of output net of effort cost is $\rho(\mathcal{Y}_t - e_t^*, \mathcal{Y}_{t-1} - e_{t-1}^*) = 0.0470$. However, any cost in adjusting the fraction of agents who become entrepreneurs would add additional persistence. If this cost is furthermore asymmetric, i.e., if it is easier to reduce the amount of entrepreneurial activity than to increase it, due to, e.g., search frictions, than such propagation is likely to be asymmetric as well with short downturns and long recoveries. This would be interesting to explore, but is beyond the scope of this paper.

It is worth noting that output contracts considerably when productivity is low and agents move out of the risky technology. At the lowest level of productivity, productivity is 2% below average while output is about 10% below average, since entrepreneurial activity drops to 57% from an average of 86%. The reason is that at a point where an agent is indifferent between the riskless project and the risky project, the expected output of the risky project exceeds the output of the riskless project, since the agent has to be compensated for the utility loss due to risk. Thus, when entrepreneurs switch to the riskless project this has a first-order effect on average output.

A.A. Rampini / Journal of Monetary Economics 51 (2004) 555–573   569

3.3. Cross-sectional heterogeneity

The optimal contract has interesting implications for the cyclicality of inequality in our economy. Inequality in terms of expected utility before agents are assigned to a technology is completely absent. The variance of output across agents is increasing in the fraction of the population assigned to the risky project and hence procyclical. However, this is not the case for the cross-sectional variance of consumption. In general, the cross-sectional variance of consumption is non-monotone in x, the state variable net of storage, since if all agents take the riskless project the cross-sectional variation is zero whereas Corollary 1 implies that when all agents take the risky project the cross-sectional variation is decreasing in x. In the example studied in this section the cross-sectional variance of consumption is countercyclical. The correlation between the cross-sectional variance of consumption and output is about -0.46.

The cross-sectional variance net of effort cost is non-monotone in general as well and turns out to be procyclical in our example which seems interesting by itself. In terms of the implications for empirical work this means that it is hence important not only to adjust 'income' (output) for partial insurance to get 'consumption' but also to decide whether and how to account for 'effort'. Ultimately, the measure of ex post inequality that should be sought is one that accounts for both partial insurance and effort cost.

Thus, the model of entrepreneurial activity presented here provides not just an additional amplification mechanism, but also an explanation for counter cyclical cross-sectional heterogeneity which has recently gotten attention in the asset pricing literature.

3.4. Different regimes of financial intermediation

It is interesting to compare the economy above to an equivalent economy with a less developed financial market, e.g., an economy where financial intermediaries cannot enforce ex post cross-subsidization and hence lotteries are absent. In such an economy, entrepreneurial activity is either 0% or 100%, and hence can be quite volatile. Proceeding as before,[15] the standard deviation of output in this financially less developed economy is 0.1001, which is about 2 times the standard deviation of output in the economy with lotteries. Thus, output volatility is higher in the economy with a less developed financial system. This is because when productivity is very low, entrepreneurial activity stops and output contracts by as much as 25%. At the same productivity, output in the economy with a developed financial system is only 10% below average. Thus, the output dynamics of the two economies with different

---

[15] Notice that the return function in this case is not (weakly) concave, but this does not seem to be a problem computationally in the example studied here.

570 *A.A. Rampini / Journal of Monetary Economics 51 (2004) 555–573*

financial intermediation regimes differ considerably and financial development is negatively related to output variability.[16]

4. Conclusions

In a model where agents can choose to enter an entrepreneurial activity which is risky and where project-specific risk cannot be perfectly diversified away for incentive reasons, we obtain amplification and intertemporal propagation of productivity shocks, although the intertemporal propagation is small quantitatively. Countercyclical agency costs resulting from decreasing absolute risk aversion are responsible for amplification and intertemporal propagation in our model. Absent asymmetric information or risk aversion the technology choice would be independent of the aggregate state and there would be neither amplification nor intertemporal propagation. If, however, agents were forced to bear all project-specific risk in our economy, entrepreneurial activity would be procyclical. What we show in this paper is that entrepreneurial activity remains procyclical even if agents can share as much of the entrepreneurial risk as is compatible with incentives. When productivity is high, agents are not only willing to bear more idiosyncratic risk but in fact are also able to share a larger fraction of that risk with outsiders in our model. Thus, in a sense insiders are more able to sell equity in their projects when productivity is high. The extent to which project-specific risk is insurable hence covaries positively with aggregates and makes entrepreneurial activity relatively more attractive in a boom and relatively less attractive in a downturn. We think that our model complements the existing literature on the effects of countercyclical agency costs (e.g., Bernanke and Gertler, 1989) by extending the theory of entrepreneurship based on risk aversion to a business cycle context and arguing that the risk associated with entrepreneurial activity is an additional force rendering entrepreneurial activity procyclical. We explore the implications of the model for the cyclicality of heterogeneity and show that we can obtain countercyclical cross-sectional variation. The focus of the paper is on the business cycle implications of the model for a single economy, but the model also has cross-sectional implications. In particular, the model predicts that economies with higher productivity are better able to share specific risk and hence have more entrepreneurial activity. Furthermore, financial development can decrease the variability of output as well as inequality.

Appendix

Proof of Proposition 1. Let (c_1^*, c_0^*) be the optimal consumption allocation associated with x^*. Take $x > x^*$. Define $\Delta \equiv x - x^* > 0$. Consider $\hat{c}_1 = c_1^* + \Delta$ and $\hat{c}_0 = c_0^* + \Delta$ which is clearly feasible at x. Incentive compatibility of (c_1^*, c_0^*) at x^* together with

---

[16] If there were no financial intermediation at all and agents had to bear all project-specific risk in this economy, then there would be no entrepreneurial activity and hence no amplification or propagation. Thus, output variability is non-monotone in financial development in general.

A.A. Rampini / Journal of Monetary Economics 51 (2004) 555–573   571

Lemma 2 implies:

$$pu(c_1^* + \Delta - e_1) + (1-p)u(c_0^* + \Delta - e_1) \geqslant u(c_0^* + \Delta - e_0),$$

i.e., $(\hat{c}_1, \hat{c}_0)$ is incentive compatible at x. But then $\Phi(x^*) \geqslant u(x^* + y)$ implies again by Lemma 2 that

$$pu(c_1^* + \Delta - e_1) + (1-p)u(c_0^* + \Delta - e_1) \geqslant u(x^* + \Delta + y),$$

and hence, since $\Phi(x)$ (weakly) exceeds the left-hand side, the conclusion obtains. $\square$

Proof of Corollary 1. Let (c_1^*, c_0^*) and $(\hat{c}_1, \hat{c}_0)$ be as in the proof of the proposition and let (c_1, c_0) be the optimal consumption allocation associated with x. Suppose $c_1 - c_0 > c_1^* - c_0^*$. Then $c_0 < \hat{c}_0$ since by Lemma A.1 the resource constraint must be binding at a solution and hence $(c_1, c_0) \geqslant (\hat{c}_1, \hat{c}_0)$ and $(c_1, c_0) \neq (\hat{c}_1, \hat{c}_0)$ is not feasible. But by Lemma A.2 the incentive compatibility constraint is binding at a solution which implies that the value of the objective evaluated at (c_1, c_0) is lower than the value at $(\hat{c}_1, \hat{c}_0)$ since the right-hand side of the incentive compatibility constraint decreased. A contradiction. $\square$

Lemma A.1. *At a solution to the maximization problem defining Φ the resource constraint is binding.*

Proof. Suppose not. Then it is feasible to increase c_1 which is also incentive compatible and increases the value of the objective. A contradiction. $\square$

Lemma A.2. *At a solution to the maximization problem defining Φ the incentive compatibility constraint is binding.*

Proof. Suppose not. Consider the following feasible variation: $\hat{c}_1 = c_1^* - \varepsilon/p$ and $\hat{c}_0 = c_0^* + \varepsilon/(1-p)$ where the pair (c_1^*, c_0^*) denotes the original solution. Then (c_1^*, c_0^*) is riskier than $(\hat{c}_1, \hat{c}_0)$ in the sense of Rothschild and Stiglitz (1970) since $\int_0^y F^*(c)\,\mathrm{d}c \geqslant \int_0^y \hat{F}(c)\,\mathrm{d}c$, $\forall y$, where $F^*(\cdot)$ and $\hat{F}(\cdot)$ are the cumulative distribution functions induced by the random variables c^* and $\hat{c}$, respectively. Hence, the variation is an improvement. For ε sufficiently small the variation is also incentive compatible which contradicts optimality of (c_1^*, c_0^*). $\square$

References

Acemoglu, D., Zilibotti, F., 1997. Was Prometheus unbound by chance? Risk, diversification, and growth. Journal of Political Economy 105, 709–751.

Banerjee, A., Newman, A., 1991. Risk-bearing and the theory of income distribution. Review of Economic Studies 58, 211–235.

Bernanke, B., Gertler, M., 1989. Agency costs, net worth, and business fluctuations. American Economic Review 79 (1), 14–31.

Bernanke, B., Gertler, M., Gilchrist, S., 1996. The financial accelerator and the flight to quality. Review of Economics and Statistics 78, 1–15.

Bernanke, B., Gertler, M., Gilchrist, S., 1999. The financial accelerator in a quantitative business cycle framework. In: Taylor, J., Woodford, M. (Eds.), Handbook of Macroeconomics, Vol. 1C. North-Holland, Amsterdam, pp. 1341–1393.

Carlstrom, C., Fuerst, T., 1997. Agency costs, net worth, and business fluctuations: a computable general equilibrium analysis. American Economic Review 87, 893–910.

Constantinides, G., Duffie, D., 1996. Asset pricing with heterogeneous consumers. Journal of Political Economy 104, 219–240.

Fisher, J., 1999. Credit market imperfections and the heterogeneous response of firms to monetary shocks. Journal of Money, Credit, and Banking 31, 187–211.

Fuerst, T., 1995. Monetary and financial interactions in the business cycle. Journal of Money, Credit, and Banking 27, 1321–1338.

Gale, D., Hellwig, M., 1985. Incentive-compatible debt contracts: the one-period problem. Review of Economic Studies 52, 647–663.

Gertler, M., 1992. Financial capacity and output fluctuations in an economy with multi-period financial relationships. Review of Economic Studies 59, 455–472.

Green, E., 1987. Lending and the smoothing of uninsurable income. In: Prescott, E., Wallace, N. (Eds.), Contractual Arrangements for Intertemporal Trade. University of Minnesota Press, Minneapolis, pp. 3–25.

Greenwald, B., Stiglitz, J., 1993. Financial market imperfections and business cycles. Quarterly Journal of Economics 108, 77–114.

Greenwood, J., Jovanovic, B., 1990. Financial development, growth, and the distribution of income. Journal of Political Economy 98, 1076–1107.

Heaton, J., Lucas, D., 1996. Evaluating the effects of incomplete markets on risk sharing and asset pricing. Journal of Political Economy 104, 443–487.

Heaton, J., Lucas, D., 2000. Portfolio choice and asset prices: the importance of entrepreneurial risk. Journal of Finance 55, 1163–1198.

Holmström, B., Tirole, J., 1996. Modeling aggregate liquidity. American Economic Review 86 (2), 187–191.

Holmström, B., Tirole, J., 1997. Financial intermediation, loanable funds, and the real sector. Quarterly Journal of Economics 112, 663–691.

Holmström, B., Tirole, J., 1998. Private and public supply of liquidity. Journal of Political Economy 106, 1–40.

Holmström, B., Weiss, L., 1985. Managerial incentives, investment, and aggregate implications: scale effects. Review of Economic Studies 52, 403–425.

Kihlstrom, R., Laffont, J.-J., 1979. A general equilibrium entrepreneurial theory of firm formation based on risk aversion. Journal of Political Economy 87, 719–748.

King, R., Levine, R., 1993. Finance and growth: Schumpeter might be right. Quarterly Journal of Economics 108, 713–737.

King, R., Rebelo, S., 1999. Resuscitating real business cycles. In: Taylor, J., Woodford, M. (Eds.), Handbook of Macroeconomics, Vol. 1B. North-Holland, Amsterdam, pp. 927–1007.

Kiyotaki, N., Moore, J., 1997. Credit cycles. Journal of Political Economy 105, 211–248.

Ljungqvist, L., Sargent, T., 2000. Recursive Macroeconomic Theory. MIT Press, Cambridge.

Mankiw, N.G., 1986. The equity premium and the concentration of aggregate shocks. Journal of Financial Economics 17, 211–219.

Phelan, C., 1994. Incentives and aggregate shocks. Review of Economic Studies 61, 681–700.

Rajan, R., Zingales, L., 1998. Financial dependence and growth. American Economic Review 88, 559–586.

Rogerson, W., 1985. Repeated moral hazard. Econometrica 53, 69–76.

Rothschild, M., Stiglitz, J., 1970. Increasing risk I: a definition. Journal of Economic Theory 2, 225–243.

Scheinkman, J., Weiss, L., 1985. Borrowing constraints and aggregate economic activity. Econometrica 54, 23–45.

A.A. Rampini / Journal of Monetary Economics 51 (2004) 555–573   573

Stokey, N., Lucas, R., Prescott, E., 1989. Recursive Methods in Economic Dynamics. Harvard University Press, Cambridge.

Storesletten, K., Telmer, C., Yaron, A., 1999. Asset pricing with idiosyncratic risk and overlapping generations. Mimeo, Carnegie Mellon University.

Townsend, R., 1979. Optimal contracts and competitive markets with costly state verification. Journal of Economic Theory 21, 265–293.

Townsend, R., 1982. Optimal multiperiod contracts and the gain from enduring relationships under private information. Journal of Political Economy 60, 1166–1186.

Williamson, S., 1987. Financial intermediation, business failures, and real business cycles. Journal of Political Economy 95, 1196–1216.

Part II
Recessions, Business Cycles
and Entrepreneurship: Evidence

[9]

International Journal of Industrial Organization 5 (1987) 51–66. North-Holland

NEW BUSINESS STARTS AND ECONOMIC ACTIVITY

An Empirical Investigation

Richard HIGHFIELD and Robert SMILEY*

Cornell University, Ithaca, NY 14853–4201, USA

Final version received November 1986

This paper identifies two types of factors that influence the rate of creation of new firms; macroeconomic and microeconomic. The macroeconomic climate that appears to be most conducive to the formation of small businesses is what might loosely be called sluggish. Lower rates of growth of GNP, lower inflation rates, and greater growth in the unemployment rate were followed by increases in the rate of new incorporations. The cross-sectional or micro-economic factors which lead to higher rates of entry into different industries include higher growth rates in sales, higher research and development intensity, and higher profit rates. We do not find any of the traditional barriers to entry to be related to the rate of new firm creation.

1. Introduction

What factors influence the rate of the new business starts? This question has been studied in some detail for other economies such as Sweden [Hause and DuRietz (1984)], and for sectors of the U.S. economy such as food [MacDonald (1986)], but never for the U.S. economy as a whole and never for a long period of time. This study presents the analysis of factors influencing the rate of new business starts in a large number of industries, and over a long period of time for the U.S. economy. A number of difficult methodological issues are confronted, and several improvements in empirical estimation techniques are presented.

The importance of understanding the determinants of new business activity should be obvious. An understanding of the dynamics of entry requires an understanding of the determinants of new firm creation as well as entry by existing firms [Caves and Porter (1977)]. Although there are some disputes about the exact numbers, recent empirical work indicates that new small

*Financial assistance for Robert Smiley was provided by the United States Small Business Administration under contract SBA-9241-OA-85. Robert Frank, Paul Geroski, Robert Hutchens, Bruce Phillips, and especially Robert Masson provided helpful comments on an earlier draft. We would like to thank Margaret Forster for excellent research assistance. The conclusions are the authors' and do not reflect official positions of the Small Business Administration.

business starts account for a large proportion of new job creation [Birch (1981)]. Furthermore, small business accounts for a disproportionately large amount of technical innovation [Scherer (1980, pp. 407–438)]. Finally, if economic policy makers should want to influence the rate of new business starts, they must first understand the interrelationships between policy variables and this rate.

In section 2 we present an analysis of the aggregate rate of new business starts (the new incorporations series) for the period 1947–1984. Section 3 presents an analysis of the determinants of new business starts across four-digit industries over the time period 1976–1981. A short conclusion section follows.

2. Time series analysis of new firm startups

One of the potentially confounding problems in cross-sectional industry studies of economic phenomena like entry is the existence of economy-wide factors that can affect behavior in all industries. The preferred method of examining such effects would be analysis of a pooled cross-section–time-series data set covering a sufficient number of data periods to allow modelling and testing of both the macro and industry-specific factors determining entry. In the present case our industry data are available for three two-year periods only, making inference regarding macro effects a practical impossibility. As an alternative we will present a basic analysis of economy-wide effects in this section using aggregate macro data, and will turn to the examination of industry-specific effects in the following section.

Our economy-wide entry variable to be explained is the quarterly growth rate (seasonally adjusted at annual rates) of the number of new U.S. incorporations over the period 1948 to 1984.[1] We use the growth rate in preference to the levels for two reasons. The first is that the number of new incorporations displays a strong upward trend that is quite similar to that of most real activity measures, and it is the deviations from this trend that are of interest. The second reason is a statistical one. The growth rate is approximately stationary[2] over the period studied and our techniques rely on the assumption of stationarity.

For potential explanatory variables we have gathered corresponding time series data on several macro variables which might reasonably be related to

---

[1]This data series is compiled monthly by Dun and Bradstreet from State government data. We compute the growth rate from as follows: $[\ln(INC_t) - \ln(INC_{t-1})] * 400$, where INC_t is the quarterly total.

[2]The concept of weak stationarity (or covariance stationarity) is all that is required here. A time series is weakly stationary if it has constant mean, constant variance and if the covariance between any two points in the series depends only on the amount of time separating them. These properties allow consistent estimation of the time series mean, variance, autocorrelations and cross-correlations with other stationary time series.

the rate of entry of new firms. These are the growth rate of real GNP, the growth rate of real expenditures on new plant and equipment,[3] the change in the unemployment rate, the inflation rate[4] and the real interest rate.[5] Again, all of these series are approximately stationary.

What type of business climate leads to a greater increase in the rate of formation of new firms? At least two different macroeconomic scenarios can be constructed that could lead to increases in new business activity. In a 'naive forecasting' scenario, individuals look at present rates of change and levels of important macroeconomic variables and forecast that these trends will continue. Further, individuals would prefer to start new business when the economy is robust. In this case, high rates of growth of new incorporations would accompany (or would lag by several quarters, since the process of incorporation requires some time) high rates of real GNP growth, low real interest rates, high inflation rates, high new plant and equipment expenditure growth and decreases in the unemployment rate.

An alternative scenario, with very different results, might be called an 'opportunistic' scenario. In this case entrepreneurs begin new business ventures when they sense an opportunity or vacuum in current economic activity. For example, a decrease in expenditures on new plant and equipment might present an opportunity or niche into which a new firm, with a newly constructed plant, might move. Similarly an increasing unemployment rate might indicate a lower cost of attracting qualified workers to a new venture, or even a lower opportunity cost of an entrepreneur's own salary foregone. In this scenario we would also expect low growth rates of real GNP, low rates of inflation, and high real interest rates to lead to increases in the rate of formation of new firms. 'Opportunity' and 'necessity' often have similar symptoms.

In our search for causal determinants of entry at the economy-wide level we will propose no structural model. Rather we will employ methods of statistical time series analysis and engage in a simple forecasting experiment. The concept is that models that incorporate data on causal factors should be able to forecast the growth of entry more accurately than models that do not. This is Granger's (1969) notion of causality, and it is based on the simple (albeit restrictive)[6] rule that the future cannot cause the past. It has been implemented extensively in macroeconomic studies on the role of money[7] and by Ashley, Granger and Schmalensee (1980) to examine the relationship between advertising and consumption.

As a first step in our analysis we have tabulated the sample cross-

[3]From the Bureau of Economic Analysis quarterly P&E survey.
[4]The rate of change in the implicit GNP deflator.
[5]Calculated as the quarterly average 90-day Treasury Bill rate less inflation.
[6]For a comprehensive discussion of causality in econometrics and economic theory, see Zellner (1978).
[7]See, for example, Sims (1972, 1977), Pierce (1977) and Feige and Pearce (1976).

correlations between our new incorporation growth time series and our
macro data series. The cross-correlation between two stationary data series is

$$\rho_{XY} = \text{cov}(Y_{t+k}, X_t)/[\text{var}(X_t)\,\text{var}(Y_t)]^{\frac{1}{2}}, \tag{1}$$

i.e., $\rho_{XY}(k)$ is the correlation between Y and X, k periods earlier in time. In
general $\rho_{YX}(k) \neq \rho_{YX}(-k)$. If X 'causes' Y but Y does not cause X we expect
to find $\rho_{YX}(k) = 0$ for $k \leq -1$ (Y uncorrelated with future X's) but we also
expect to find $\rho_{YX}(k) \neq \emptyset$ for some $k \geq 0$ (Y correlated with past X's).

Sample estimates of (1) were calculated according to Box and Jenkins
(1976) and are tabulated in table 1 for data for the period 1948:3 through
1977:4. The remaining data were held back for a forecasting test discussed
below. The picture painted is an interesting one. The growth rate of new
incorporations is negatively correlated with measures of real activity in the
prior year (real GNP and new plant expenditure growth) and positively

Table 1

Sample cross correlations of *DLINC* with various macro variables; period 1948:3 to 1977:4.[a]

	k	$SE(\hat{\rho}(k))$	Real GNP growth $\hat{\rho}(k)$	Real P&E exp. growth $\hat{\rho}(k)$	Unemp. rate changes $\hat{\rho}(k)$	Real int. rate $\hat{\rho}(k)$	Inflation $\hat{\rho}(k)$
Macro	−12	0.10	0.04	−0.05	−0.08	−0.08	0.05
variables	−11	0.10	0.04	−0.14	−0.01	−0.06	0.05
lagging	−10	0.10	−0.09	−0.24[b]	0.15	0.00	0.03
incorpora-	−9	0.10	−0.22[b]	−0.19	0.27[b]	0.16	−0.08
tion	−8	0.10	−0.30[b]	−0.09	0.23[b]	0.16	−0.09
growth	−7	0.10	−0.20	−0.03	0.18	0.10	−0.01
	−6	0.09	−0.18	0.09	0.07	0.04	0.05
	−5	0.09	−0.02	0.22[b]	0.01	0.07	0.04
	−4	0.09	−0.05	0.29[b]	−0.07	−0.09	0.15
	−3	0.09	0.13	0.31[b]	−0.21[b]	−0.13	0.16
	−2	0.09	0.23[b]	0.34[b]	−0.44[b]	−0.07	0.09
	−1	0.09	0.34[b]	0.11	−0.43[b]	−0.08	0.07
	0	0.09	0.25[b]	−0.13	−0.16	0.11	−0.14
Macro	1	0.09	0.00	−0.31[b]	0.25[b]	0.19[b]	−0.22[b]
variables	2	0.09	−0.31[b]	0.40[b]	0.45[b]	0.02	−0.09
leading	3	0.09	−0.32[b]	−0.44[b]	0.47[b]	0.09	−0.10
incorpora-	4	0.09	−0.30[b]	−0.10	0.21[b]	−0.02	0.04
tion	5	0.09	−0.07	0.01	−0.06	−0.11	0.15
growth	6	0.09	0.03	0.03	−0.06	−0.14	0.20[b]
	7	0.10	0.04	0.11	−0.07	−0.14	0.22[b]
	8	0.10	−0.03	0.04	−0.04	−0.16	0.23[b]
	9	0.10	−0.03	0.03	−0.01	−0.12	0.19
	10	0.10	−0.10	0.11	−0.07	0.01	0.07
	11	0.10	0.04	0.20	−0.08	−0.02	0.03
	12	0.10	0.06	0.11	−0.06	−0.04	0.05

[a]The large sample standard error of $\hat{\rho}(k)$ is $1/\sqrt{n-k}$, here $n = 118$.
[b]$\hat{\rho}(k)$ is greater than two standard deviations from zero.

correlated with these measures in the succeeding year.[8] The same picture is apparent in the cross correlations with the change in the unemployment rate and, somewhat weakly, with the real interest rate. Growth in the incorporation rate is positively associated with growing unemployment rates and higher real interest rates in the preceding year and with falling unemployment and lower interest rates in succeeding years. The cross-correlations with the inflation rate also indicate that periods of incorporation growth follow periods of lower inflation. Taken at face value, these results are generally consistent with the 'opportunistic' scenario. Firms may enter to fill the vacuum created by sluggish economic activity, with the result being that activity increases in later periods.[9]

The notion that slowing real activity causes incorporation growth should, however, not be accepted too readily. The fact that incorporation growth is correlated with real variables at both leads and lags suggests that these variables may in fact be jointly determined. This possibility was examined by computing the cross-correlations between the residuals from an ARMA model for each of the macro variables and the variable resulting when the incorporations series is filtered by the same model.[10] This procedure is designed to remove from the incorporation series any systematic movement that might be induced by the macro variable. If the remaining variation is still correlated at leads but uncorrelated at lags of the macro variable then a tentative inference of causality is possible. Only the inflation rate appears to lead (with the same signs as above) but not lag. Knowledge of the inflation rate may help increase the accuracy of forecasts of the incorporation growth rate, but the reverse is not expected to be true.

As was mentioned at the beginning of this section, one test of the notion that the macro variables discussed above play a role in determining incorporation growth is the predictive test. Indeed Ansley (1977) and Ashley,

---

[8]As our incorporation series represents all incorporations, both new firms and some established firms changing ownership structure, we cannot rule out the possibility that some of this relationship is attributable to owners acting to shield assets in bad times.

[9]The sample was also split in half and the analog to table 1 computed on both the earlier and later periods. The results for both periods give essentially the same impression as that given in table 1, with the earlier period results being slightly stronger than those above, and the later period slightly weaker. The real interest rate results are the only exception. The weak result above does not appear in the later period.

[10]This is called 'prewhitening' the series by Box and Jenkins (1976). Suppose $\phi(B)X_t = \theta(B)e_t$ represents a standard ARMA (p,q) for a model covariance stationary series X_t (one of our macro variables), where $\phi(B) = 1 - \phi_1 B - \cdots - \phi_p B_p^q$, $\theta(B) = 1 - \theta_1 B - \cdots - \theta_q B_q^q$, B is the backshift (or lag) operator such that $BX_t = X_{t-1}$ and e_t represents a zero mean, constant variance noise process. The prewhitened incorporation growth series a_t is calculated as $a_t = \theta^{-1}(B)\phi(B)$(incorporation growth)$_t$. Thus systematic variation in incorporation growth directly induced by systematic variation in X_t is removed. What remains includes systematic variation induced by even random variation in X_t. Of course, if the only channel by which X_t affects or 'causes' incorporation growth is through its systematic (forecastable) variation then we are throwing the baby out with the bath.

Granger and Schmalensee (1980) have argued quite convincingly that cross-correlation analysis is better viewed as a tool for identifying forecasting models (in the sense that a time series analyst identifies the best forecasting model from within a class of possible models) and that post-sample forecasting tests are more appropriate for investigating causality. Here some simple models for forecasting incorporation growth have been devised. The first, which can be considered a benchmark, is a univariate ARMA model for incorporation growth. Such a model will set a level of predictive accuracy that can be expected from forecasting this variable on the basis of its own past alone. Of course, since an ARMA model is a purely statistical model, the form of the model chosen may depend indirectly on all factors determining incorporation growth.[11] To the extent that the factors we have chosen to focus on here are particularly important in determining entry, we would expect to improve upon the performance of the ARMA model.

The evidence from a simple forecasting competition is presented in table 2. One-step-ahead out-of-sample forecasts of the growth rate of incorporations were made for the 28 quarters 1978:1 through 1984:4 using several simple forecasting models.[12] The results of the ARMA forecasts are given on line 1 of the table. The competing models attempted are a univariate transfer function model involving the inflation rate as an exogenous explanatory variable (an idea supported by the cross-correlation analysis above), three

Table 2

Summary of forecasting results; one-step-ahead out-of-sample forecasts of incorporation growth for the period 1978:1 through 1984:4.

Forecasting model	Mean absolute forecast error	Root mean squared forecast error
1. Univariate ARMA model	12.05	14.78
2. Transfer function model input variable: inflation rate	11.85	14.64
3. Bivariate ARMA model incorporation growth and real GNP growth	11.37	14.67
4. Bivariate ARMA model incorporation growth and unemployment rate changes	11.03	14.48
5. Bivariate ARMA model incorporation growth and growth in new plant and equipment expenditures	12.41	16.17
6. Vector autoregression involving incorporation growth, inflation, real GNP growth, unemployment rate changes and growth in new plant and equipment expenditures	11.29	14.93

[11]This fact often goes unrecognized as an explanation of the fact that ARMA forecasts are often competitive with or even superior to forecasts from complex econometric models.
[12]I.e., each model was estimated using data from the period 1948:3 to 1977:4. Future incorporation growth was then predicted, the model updated to include data for 1978:1, another prediction was made, the model updated again, and so on.

separate bivariate ARMA models relating incorporation growth to real GNP growth, the change in the unemployment rate and new plant and equipment expenditure growth, and a vector autoregression involving all five variables. Only the transfer function model involving the inflation rate reflects a strict causal ordering. All of the other models assume joint causation (i.e., they include no exogeneity restrictions).[13] No model relating the real interest rate and incorporation growth was suggested by our analysis.

As seen, none of the models achieves dramatic improvements over the univariate model for incorporation growth. The best model, the bivariate ARMA model with unemployment rate changes, achieves about a 9% reduction in mean absolute forecast error, but a somewhat smaller reduction in root mean squared error, indicating the presence of some large forecasting errors. The second best model, the bivariate ARMA model with real GNP growth, achieves a 6.4% reduction in mean absolute forecast error, and also reduces the root mean squared error by a smaller amount. The coefficients in both models imply the same relationship as indicated by the cross-correlation results. Increases in the unemployment rate and decreases in real GNP growth lead increases in incorporation growth. While a tentative causal relationship appeared in the cross-correlation analysis of the inflation rate, the forecasting improvement achieved by the transfer function model is quite slight.

Although the evidence is by no means overwhelming, the business climate apparently most hospitable to new firm incorporation has not been a robust one: sluggish economic growth seems more likely to spur creation of new firms. The magnitude of the forecasting improvements indicates, however, that most of the variation in growth in incorporations remains unexplained and that none of the macro variables appears to be strongly causal in the sense of Granger. Policy implications are not strong in this setting. Certainly few would suggest the bizarre policy of slowing the economy down in order to create a better climate for new business. What is apparent, however, is an indication that higher incorporation growth goes hand in hand with an economy changing from the worse to the better. This might suggest that further incentives for new business formation could speed recoveries, but we have made no attempt to examine causality in this direction.

3. Entry determinants at the micro level – Cross-sectional relationships

The factors affecting the rate of entry by new firms into different industries are discussed in this section. The section is organized as follows: a model of

[13]In identifying and estimating the transfer function models and bivariate ARMA models we have followed the suggestions of Box and Jenkins (1976) and Tiao and Box (1981), respectively. To estimate the vector autoregression, which involves eight lags of each of the five variables, we employ the Bayesian techniques of Litterman (1984) and Highfield (1984).

the entry process is presented first, followed by a discussion of the measurement of the variables. The empirical results are presented last.

3.1. A model of entry

The rate of entry E_{it} by new firms into industry i in time period t is modeled as a function of the predicted future profit rate Π_{it} and the entry forestalling profit rate Π_{it}^N,

$$E_{it} = f(\Pi_{it} - \Pi_{it}^N) + \mu, \tag{2}$$

where

$f(0) = 0$ by the definition of entry forestalling,
$\Pi_{it} = \Pi(\Pi_{it}^{PAST}, GROWTH, RDEXP)$,
$\Pi_{it}^N = \Pi^N ADS, EXCAPEXP, MESMKT, CAPREQ, RISK, CONC, RDEXP)$,
μ = all entry orthogonal to excess profits.
Π_{it}^{PAST}:   past profit rates in industry i,
GROWTH: past sales growth,
RDEXP: research and development expenditures as a percentage of sales,
ADS: advertising expenditures as a percentage of sales,
MESMKT: the ratio of the plant size necessary to achieve minimum efficient scale, to the size of the market,
CAPREQ: the investment necessary to build a plant of minimum efficient scale,
CAPEXP: new capital expenditures as a percentage of net plant,
EXCAPEXP: CAPEXP—GROWTH,
RISK: a measure of the risk of entry,
CONC: the four firm concentration ratio.

3.2. Discussion

Π_{it}: Predicted post-entry profits are a positive function (Π) of past profits, growth in sales and research and development expenditures. We will test different functional forms for the relationship between past and predicted future profit rates in the paper, but we would expect the overall relationship to be positive. We would expect future profits to be greater and entry more frequent in industries that are growing more rapidly (GROWTH).

A high rate of technical progress in an industry will also indicate a dynamic and evolving situation, and thus might attract new entrants seeking to discover and develop new products and processes. A high ratio of expenditure on research and development to sales (*RDEXP*) would indicate a technologically dynamic industry and signal new entrants.

Π_{it}^N: The entry forestalling profit rate is the highest long run profit rate that will not attract entry. Barriers to entry would positively affect the entry forestalling profit rate, and negatively affect the rate of entry, ceteris paribus.[14] The traditional barriers are the ratio of advertising expenditures to sales (*ADS*), the proportion of industry sales required to operate a plant of minimum efficient scale (*MESMKT*), and the amount of capital required to build a plant of minimum efficient scale (*CAPREQ*).

We also attempt to account for the possibility that some incumbent firms may be attempting to preempt the market through capacity expansion [Spence (1977)]. *CAPEXP* measures capital expenditures lagged one year divided by net plant. Preemption attempts should be indicated when expenditures on plant and equipment exceed industry growth (*EXCAPEXP*).

Risk averse potential entrants will be deterred by high investment risk. We measure risk in two ways. *RISK* is the average variance for industry firms in profits (after taxes as percentage of stockholder's equity) over the five years prior to the period in question. The second risk variable, *BAYRISK*, is a measure of the variability in predicted profits derived from a profit forecasting model discussed below. These are reasonable risk measures for individuals whose investment portfolios are *not* well diversified, which would seem an appropriate description of an individual starting up a new business.[15]

Concentration (*CONC*) and research intensity (*RDEXP*) could, in theory, attract or deter entry. Orr (1974) feels that '... when entering highly concentrated industries, the potential entrant must also consider the possibility that established firms may collude to thwart his entry.' Baron's (1973) model predicts that *lower* concentration may deter entry since a symmetric post entry equilibrium would imply smaller size and a higher likelihood that the entrant will be forced to operate below minimum efficient scale.[16] The possibility that high R&D expenditures might be correlated with frequent entry is discussed above. But new entrants into research intensive industries must also raise more risky financial capital, and the difficulty and cost of assembling the necessary human capital may also deter entry.

3.3. Measures of the variables

The U.S. Small Business Administration has been compiling entry statistics by four-digit industries only since 1976. The data, which originate from Dun

[14]See Bain (1956) and Demsetz (1982) for different points of view regarding barriers to entry.
[15]If an individual is perfectly well diversified, we would want to use the industry beta.
[16]See Masson and Shaanan (1986, pp. 4–5) for a thorough discussion of concentration and entry.

and Bradstreet, are available in two-year increments – 1976–77, 1978–79 and 1980–81.[17] Our entry measures are taken for these three time periods.

The entry rate ($Entry_{it}$) is simply the number of new firms formed in industry i within the time period t, divided by the number of firms in existence in the industry at the beginning of the period. This variable is then transformed as follows:

$$\text{Relative entry rate}_{it} = Entry_{it} - \overline{Entry}_t, \tag{3}$$

where $\overline{Entry}_t$ is the average entry rate across all industries i for period t. This transformation should control for any economy-wide factors (in the separate time periods) affecting entry rates. Problems of econometric estimation are also avoided since (unlike $Entry_{it}$), the Relative entry rate is unbounded.

The independent variables $PROFIT_{it}$, ADS_{it}, $RDEXP_{it}$, $CAPEXP_{it}$ and $RISK_{it}$ are taken from the Compustat tape. In the case of the first four variables, the observations are lagged one year (i.e., for the 1980–1981 period, ADS_{it} is observed in 1979). $PROFIT_{it}$ is after tax income less extraordinary items and discontinued operations, summed for each firm in industry i, and then divided by the sum of equity capital for industry i firms. $RDEXP_{it}$ and ADS_{it} are the sums of research and development expenditures and advertising expenditures as a proportion of sales. $CAPEXP_{it}$ is the sum of capital expenditures divided by the sum of net plant for firms in the ith industry.

In addition to using a simple lagged profits variable to predict future profits (and thus to signal entry), we have developed a somewhat more sophisticated measure of expected profitability.[18] We have formulated a simple forecasting model for profits which has been applied to each industry.

$$PROFIT_{it} = C + \alpha_1 PROFIT_{it-1} + \alpha_2 PROFIT_{it-2} + e_t. \tag{4}$$

The model is a Bayesian implementation of an autoregressive model in which profits in any period are related in a linear way to profits in the two preceding periods: where e_t is a zero mean, normally distributed error term. Forecasts from this model were generated iteratively[19] beginning in 1974, using annual data, and the forecasts for the years 1976, 1978 and 1980 (called $BAYPROF_{it}$)[20] were used as independent variables.

[17]The problems of classifying multiproduct firms into four-digit industries are well known. Aside from modifying national concentration ratios as discussed below, we have made no modifications to the official SIC classification scheme since we were (ultimately) constrained by Dun and Bradstreet's use of existing codes.
[18]Expectations regarding future profitability are also affected by $GROWTH$ and $RDEXP$, in addition to past profit rates.
[19]By 'iterative' we mean that no future data were used in the generation of the profit forecasts. They are true forecasts, not fitted values from the model.
[20]Our profit series for each industry begins in 1971, leaving very few observations with which to estimate the model. A Bayesian method of estimation was employed to overcome this

$BAYRISK_{it}$ is the variance of the predictive distribution of profits (where $BAYPROF_{it}$ is the mean). Due to its autoregressive nature, the model (3) will account for any time trend in profits. $BAYRISK_{it}$ will then be a risk measure taken after accounting for any underlying time trend.

The sources for the remaining variables are the various censuses.[21] $GROWTH_{it}$ is the annual growth rate in sales or value of shipments from 1972–1977. $MESMKT$ is the ratio of the average sales per establishment for establishments in the median size class, to sales for the industry for the year 1977. $CAPREQ$ is $MESMKT$ multiplied by total assets for the industry, for the year 1977. $CONC_{it}$ is the four firm concentration ratio. We have modified $CONC_{it}$ according to Schwartzman and Bodoff (1971) by first identifying the industries for which a national concentration ratio is not appropriate, since markets are regional or local. For these seven industries, we then added Schwartzman and Bodoff's estimates of the difference between average regional (or local) and national rates to our 1977 national rates. The resulting $CONC_{it}$ should adequately reflect national, regional and local concentration, where appropriate.

3.4. Estimation techniques and results

The basic results reported in this section are regressions in which we have pooled observations from the three time periods in our sample. As the independent variable is cross-sectional in nature, there is the possibility that omitted macroeconomic factors can bias the results. To the extent that these economy-wide factors affect entry in a similar way in all industries, we can control for these macro effects by subtracting the mean entry rate $Entry_t$ from the observed, industry specific, entry rate $Entry_{it}$.

The results for the data set that includes measures for all independent variables are presented in table 3. Data are available for one or more time periods for forty industries (four-digit), nearly all of which are manufacturing.[22]

The hypothesis tests are consistent with the finding that high industry growth strongly attracts entry by new firms. This finding is similar to the results of Hause and DuRietz (1984) for Swedish manufacturing industries. Although the F test indicates that the regression equation is clearly significant, the significance of the remaining coefficients is quite limited.

---

problem. Given the data through 1973 we assume a normal prior distribution on profits in 1974. The mean of this distribution being zero and its standard deviation being 0.5 (i.e., a profit or loss rate of 50% of equity capital is one standard deviation from the mean). Using this very spread out distribution as our starting point we infer a prior distribution for the parameters of eq. (3).

[21]Source: U.S. Bureau of the Census (1972, 1977).
[22]See table A.1 in the appendix for the industries included.

Table 3

115 observations; dependent variable: relative entry rate$_{it}$.

Independent variable	Coefficient	Standard error	T statistic
Constant	−0.035987	0.016084	−2.237475
BAYPROF	−0.244044	0.564525	−0.432300
ADS	−0.184650	0.175784	−1.050439
EXCAPEXP	0.029984	0.038803	0.772736
RDEXP	0.374736	0.24009	1.560756
RISK	−0.013461	0.008561	−1.572244
GROWTH	0.360785	0.072860	4.951744*
CONC	−0.000262	0.000187	−1.398997
MESMKT	0.311990	0.225176	1.385541
CAPREQ	0.000042	0.000081	0.519121

$$\bar{R}^2 = 0.322, \ F(10, 105) = 7.0241$$

*Statistically significant at 1%.

There is marginal support for the hypothesis that industries characterized by high R&D expenditures to sales ratios also experience higher rates of entry. Rather than acting as a barrier to entry, research intensity in an industry seems to attract entry by new firms. *RISK*, which measures the variance of past profits, also has the hypothesized sign and is marginally significant ($P = 11.9\%$, two tailed test). High profit rates in the periods prior to the time period of observation do not appear to signal new entry. None of the other coefficients on the deterrents or barriers to entry are statistically significant.[23]

Alternative methods for estimating expected future profits and investment risk were described above. When the equation in table 3 was estimated using $PROFIT_{it}$ (lagged profits) and $BAYRISK_{it}$ (the predicted variance in profits), neither coefficient was significantly different from zero, and the only major result affected was that *RDEXP* was no longer even marginally significant.

The sample size can be substantially enlarged by eliminating independent variables with missing values. In table 4, the variables *ADS, CONC* and *CAPREQ* have been dropped and 20 industries (61 observations) have been added, mostly in natural resource extraction and services. The findings are much stronger than those in table 3: entry occurs much more frequently in research intensive, rapidly growing industries.

There is also a substantial difference in the explanatory power of the profit variable. The Bayesian profit forecast, *BAYPROF*, is positively and significantly related to the subsequent rate of entry by new firms. The profit forecast using simple lagged profits ($PROFIT_{it}$) and the alternative risk measure

---

[23]These observations are consistent with most of the findings of MacDonald (1986) for food industries.

Table 4

176 observations; dependent variable: relative entry rate$_{it}$.

Independent variable	Coefficient	Standard error	T statistic
Constant	−0.029400	0.007565	−3.886144
BAYPROF	0.257411	0.056791	4.532634[a]
EXCAPEXP	0.003874	0.007649	0.506519
RDEXP	0.219136	0.096291	2.275763[b]
GROWTH	0.295167	0.044189	6.679606[a]
MESMKT	−0.067678	0.112233	−0.603017
RISK	−0.001167	0.006799	−0.171614

$$R^2 = 0.316, \ F(7, 169) = 14.5$$

[a]Statistically significant at 1%.
[b]Statistically significant at 5%.

were substituted for *BAYPROF* and *RISK* in regressions not reported here. Neither was significantly different from zero at the 10% level. So with this more extensive industry coverage, the Bayesian autoregressive forecasting technique dominates a simple lagged profit forecast.[24] Entrepreneurs do use previously available profit information in deciding whether to risk their capital, but they use it in a sophisticated fashion.

4. Summary and conclusions

This paper contributes to the industrial organization literature on entry through enabling us to better understand what economic conditions are more hospitable to the creation of new firms, and through application of new methods to better understand these complex relationships. We have identified two types of factors that influence the rate of creation of new firms: macroeconomic and microeconomic factors. Although the evidence is somewhat weak, the macroeconomic climate that appears to be most conducive to the formation of small businesses is what might loosely be called sluggish. Lower rates of growth of GNP, lower inflation rates, and greater growth in the unemployment rate were followed by increases in the rate of new incorporations. These new incorporations in turn tend to lead periods of more robust economic activity. The cross-sectional or microeconomic factors which affect rates of entry into different industries include higher growth rates in sales, higher research and development intensity, and higher profit

[24]The regression in table 4 was also run with the smaller data set used in table 3. I.e., the table 3 regression was run with *ADS*, *CONC* and *CAPREQ* eliminated. The results for the remaining variables are quite similar to those reported in table 3 indicating that the significance of *BAYPROF* in table 4 is due to the expanded data set, not the elimination of the three variables.

rates. We do not find any of the traditional barriers to entry to be related to the rate of new firm creation.

Putting the time series and cross-sectional results together, we have a consistent and interesting picture of entry through the creation of new firms. Individuals decide to form new firms when economic conditions are relatively poor – but they decide to enter industries which are dynamic and robust, as measured by technical progressivity and profitability.

We have utilized some time series techniques which appear to be new to the industrial organization literature. After observing the patterns of leads and lags of new incorporation activity as they are correlated with leads and lags of important macroeconomic variables, we investigate whether knowledge of these macroeconomic variables will allow us to improve on forecasts of the new incorporations growth rate. In the cross-sectional study, we conclude that the lack of relationship in other studies [e.g., McDonald (1986), Orr (1974)] between the profit rate and subsequent new business creation is the result of lack of sophistication in modeling entrepreneurs' expectations about future profit rates.[25] The Bayesian autoregressive model we used to forecast future profit rates seems to indicate quite clearly that present profit rates do influence future entry.

[25]But see Masson and Shaanan (1986).

Appendix

Table A.1

Industries used in analysis.

SIC code	Industry description
Industries used in table 3	
2041	Flour and other grain mill products
2046	Wet corn milling
2065	Confectionary products
2082	Malt beverages
2086	Bottled and canned soft drinks
2121	Cigars
2711	Newspapers
2761	Manifold business forms
2834	Pharmaceutical preparations
2841	Soap and other detergents
2844	Toilet preparations
2911	Petroleum refining
3079	Miscellaneous plastic products
3221	Glass containers
3241	Cement, hydraulic
3443	Fabricated plate work, boiler shops
3444	Sheet metal work
3452	Bolts, nuts, rivets, and washers

Table A.1 (continued)

SIC code	Industry description
3494	Valves and pipe fittings
3531	Construction machinery
3533	Oilfield machinery
3622	Industrial controls
3651	Radio and TV receiving sets
3662	Radio and TV communication equipment
3674	Semiconductors and related devices
3693	X-ray apparatus and tubes
3711	Motor vehicle and car bodies
3714	Motor vehicle parts and accessories
3721	Aircraft
3811	Engineering and scientific instruments
3823	Process control instruments
3825	Instruments to measure electricity
3841	Surgical and medical instruments
3842	Surgical appliances and supplies
3861	Photographic equipment and supplies
3914	Silverware and plated ware
3931	Musical instruments
5012	Automobiles and other motor vehicles
5065	Electronic parts and electronic communication equipment
8911	Engineering and architectural services

Additional industries used in table 4

1021	Copper ores
1211	Bituminous coal and lignite
1311	Crude petroleum and natural gas
1381	Drilling oil and gas wells
1382	Oil and gas exploration services
2111	Cigarettes
3442	Metal doors, sash, and trim
3661	Telephone and telegraph apparatus
5093	Scrap and waste materials – wholesale
5211	Lumber and other building materials – retail
5411	Grocery stores – retail
5712	Furniture stores
5812	Eating places – retail
7011	Hotels, rooming houses, camps, and other lodging places
7372	Computer programming and other software services
7374	Data processing and computer facilities management
7391	Research and development laboratories
7392	Consulting services
7393	Protective services
7395	Photofinishing laboratories

References

Ansley, C.F., 1977, Report on the NBER–NSF seminar on time series, Mimeo. (Graduate School of Business, University of Chicago, IL).

Ashley, R., C.W.J. Granger and R. Schmalensee, 1980, Advertising and aggregate consumption: An analysis of causality, Econometrica 48, no. 5, 1149–1167.

Bain, Joe S., 1956, Barriers to new competition (Harvard University Press, Cambridge, MA).

Baron, David, 1973, Limit pricing, potential entry and barriers to entry, American Economic Review, Sept., 666–674.

Birch, David L., 1981, Who creates jobs?, The Public Interest.

Box, G.E.P. and G.M. Jenkins, 1976, Time series analysis – Forecasting and control (Holden-Day, San Francisco, CA).

Caves, Richard and Michael Porter, 1977, From entry barriers to mobility barriers: Conjectural decisions and contrived deterrence to new competition, Quarterly Journal of Economics 91, 241–261.

Demsetz, Harold, 1982, Barriers to entry, American Economic Review, March, 47–57.

Feige, E.L. and D.K. Pearce, 1976, Economically rational expectations: Are innovations in the rate of inflation independent of innovations in measures of monetary and fiscal policy?, Journal of Political Economy 84, June, 449–552.

Granger, C.W.J., 1969, Investigating causal relations by econometric models and cross-spectral methods, Econometrica 37, July, 424–438.

Hause, John C. and Gunnar DuRietz, 1984, Entry, industry growth and the microdynamics of industry supply, Journal of Political Economy 92, no. 4.

Highfield, R.A., 1984, Forecasting with Bayesian state space models, Technical report (H.G.B. Alexander Research Foundation, Graduate School of Business, University of Chicago, IL).

Litterman, Robert B., 1984, Specifying vector autoregressions for macroeconomic forecasting, Research Department Staff Report no. 92 (Federal Reserve Bank of Minneapolis, Minneapolis, MN).

MacDonald, James M., 1986, Entry and exit on the competitive fringe, Southern Economic Journal 52, no. 3.

Masson, Robert T. and Joseph Shaanan, 1986, Optimal pricing and the threat of entry: Canadian evidence, Working paper (Cornell University, Ithaca, NY).

Orr, Dale, 1974, The determinants of entry: A study of the Canadian manufacturing industries, Review of Economics and Statistics, Feb., 58–66.

Pierce, D.A., 1977, Relationships – and the lack thereof – between economic time series, with special reference to money and interest rates, Journal of the American Statistical Association 72, March, 11–21.

Scherer, Frederic M., 1980, Industrial market structure and economic performance, 2nd ed. (Rand McNally, Chicago, IL).

Schwartzman, David and Joan Bodoff, 1971, Concentration in regional and local industries, Southern Economic Journal 37, Jan., 343–348.

Sims, C.A., 1972, Money, income and causality, American Economic Review LXII, Sept., 540–552.

Sims, C.A., 1977, Exogeneity and causal ordering in macroeconomic models, in: C.A. Sims, ed., New methods in business cycle research: Proceedings from a conference (Federal Reserve Bank of Minneapolis, Minneapolis, MN) 23–43.

Spence, A. Michael, 1977, Entry, capacity, investment and oligopolistic pricing, Bell Journal of Economics 8, Autumn, 534–544.

Standard and Poor's, 1984, Annual industrial compustat tape.

Tiao, G.C. and G.E.P. Box, 1981, Modeling multiple time series with applications, Journal of the American Statistical Association 76, 802–816.

U.S. Bureau of the Census, Census of manufacturers – 1972, Census of retail trade – 1972, Census of wholesale trade – 1972, Census of mineral industries – 1972, Census of construction industries – 1972, Census of service industries – 1972 (Washington, DC).

U.S. Bureau of the Census, Census of manufacturers – 1977, Census of retail trade – 1977, Census of wholesale trade – 1977, Census of mineral industries – 1977, Census of construction industries – 1977, Census of service industries – 1977 (Washington, DC).

Zellner, Arnold, 1978, Causality and econometrics, in: K. Brunner and A.H. Meltzer, eds., Three aspects of policy and policymaking, Carnegie–Rochester Conference Series on Public Policy, Vol. 10 (North-Holland, Amsterdam) 9–54.

[10]

New-Firm Startups, Technology, and
Macroeconomic Fluctuations

David B. Audretsch
Zoltan J. Acs

ABSTRACT. New-firm startup activity is examined within a framework pooling a cross-section of 117 industries over six time periods between 1976 and 1986. A model is introduced relating startup activity both to elements of the business cycle, in particular the macroeconomic growth rate, the cost of capital, and the unemployment rate, and to industry-specific characteristics, especially the technological conditions underlying the industry. The pooled cross-section regression results suggest that macroeconomic fluctuations as well as industry-specific elements contribute to startup activity. While new-firm startups respond positively to macroeconomic growth, they are promoted by a low cost of capital and high unemployment rate. A somewhat surprising result is that new-firm startups are not apparently deterred in capital intensive industries and where R&D expenditures play an important role. The empirical results suggest that new firms may be able to overcome their inherent size and experience disadvantages in such markets through exploiting university research and pursuing innovative activity.

I. Introduction

An important finding of Mills and Schumann (1985) was that small firms account for a greater share of economic activity during economic expansions and a reduced share during contractions. Building upon the theories introduced by Stigler (1939) and Marschak and Nelson (1962), they concluded that small enterprises served an important economic function by infusing productive flexibility into an economy which serves to absorb macroeconomic fluctuations.

But where do these small firms come from? This matter was left unexplored by Mills and Schumann. One source is clearly the startup of new firms. Of course, a literature has recently blossomed consistently showing that entry into markets is impeded when confronted with certain characteristics of industry structure.[1] How can this be reconciled with the observation in the second section of this paper that the startup of new firms is a pervasive phenomenon throughout U.S. manufacturing? One answer is that not only have the bulk of entry studies focused on "net" entry, or the change in the number of firms within an industry over a specified period of time, rather than on gross entry, or the startup of new firms, but that, with only a handfull of exceptions, every study examining entry behavior has been restricted to a cross-section comparison across industries for a single time period. And, while Highfield and Smiley (1987) undertook one of the only studies examining new-firm startups over time, their data were aggregated to the macroeconomic level for the U.S., rendering it impossible to identify the industry-specific component influencing startups.

These constraints have made it virtually impossible to decompose the impact that both macroeconomic fluctuations and industry-specific characteristics exert on startup activity. The purpose of this paper is to provide the first study examining the startup of new firms within both a cross-section and time series context. This enables us not only to identify the extent to which startup activity responds to conditions in the labor market, the credit market, and the overall aggregate economy, but also the manner in which the startup of new firms responds to the technological conditions underlying the particular industry. In the second section of this paper the data source and method used to measure new-firm startups is introduced. The manner in which both industry-specific effects and macroeconomic fluctuations are expected to shape startup activity is explained

Final version accepted on September 16, 1993

David B. Audretsch
CEPR and Wissenschaftszentrum Berlin für Sozialforschung
and
Zoltan J. Acs
Merrick School of Business, University of Baltimore

in the third section. Based on the amount of startup activity in 117 four-digit standard industrial classification (SIC) industries observed in six different years, the pooled cross-section regression model is estimated and the empirical results reported in the fourth section.

Finally, in the last section a summary and conclusion are provided. We find that the startup of new firms is substantially shaped by both macroeconomic fluctuations as well as industry-specific characteristics. In particular, macroeconomic expansion serves as a catalyst for startup activity. However, new-firm startups are apparently promoted by a low cost of capital as well as a high unemployment rate. While the startup of new firms is not deterred either in capital intensive or R&D intensive industries, there is considerable evidence suggesting that industries where university research is important and where small firms tend to be innovative serve as a catalyst for new-firm startups. Thus, the results generally indicate that, at least to some extent, new firms fulfill the Schumpeterian (1950) function of "creative destruction" both by redeploying resources which have been unemployed by the incumbent enterprises as well as by introducing new products through innovative activity.

II. Measuring new-firm startups

Studies examining the determinants of entry generally suffer from two well-known limitations. First, while several notable exceptions exist (Dunne, Roberts and Samuelson, 1988 and 1989), the most common measure of entry used in studies attempting to empirically identify the determinants of entry has been the change in the number of firms over a given period, or what has become referred to as "net entry".[2] Measuring the change in the number of firms does not account for enterprises which exited from the industry during the relevant time period. That is, given an amount of gross entry, the measure of net entry will increase as the number of exits from the industry decreases. Thus, it is quite conceivable that an industry could have a negative amount of net entry, if many firms actually entered the industry (i.e., if gross entry was positive), but even more firms exited from the industry. Because the pattern of industry exits varies across industries, the extent

to which net entry deviates from actual gross entry will also vary substantially from industry to industry.

The second limitation is that entry has typically been measured over a single time period. While it has been possible to measure the number of new-firm startups at the aggregate macroeconomic level (Highfield and Smiley, 1987), this has not been systematically done at the disaggregated industry level.[3]

These two limitations have made it virtually impossible to disentangle the macroeconomic influences on new-firms startups from the microeconomic influences. All that can be concluded from the existing literature is that both are probably important.

To overcome the traditional data limitations, we rely upon the U.S. Small Business Administrations's Small Business Data Base (SBDB). The data base is derived from the Dun and Bradstreet (DUNS) market identifier file (DMI), which provides a virtual census on about 4.5 million U.S. business establishments every other year between 1976 and 1986.

The raw data in the Dun and Bradstreet files have come under considerable criticism. Perhaps one of the most significant weaknesses in the DUNS data is missing records for subsidiaries and branches. Because the Dun and Bradstreet files are compiled on the basis of credit rating, branches and subsidiaries of multi-establishment firms that are unlikely to require credit independently from the parent firm are often not recorded. Similarly, there tends to be chronic underrepresentation in industries where there is a propensity for firms not to apply for credit. In addition, Jacobson (1985) found that in several cases firms and establishments are not included in the data base until several years after they have been established, particularly in rapidly expanding industries, such as certain types of services, and in new industries, such as microcomputers and software-related industries. In order to correct for at least some of these deficiencies inherent in the raw DMI files, the Brookings Institution in conjunction with the Small Business Administration and the National Science Foundation restructured, edited, and supplemented the original DUNS records with data from other sources in constructing the SBDB.[4]

Thus, it should be emphasized that the SBDB has been adjusted to clean up the raw data in the original DMI files. Several important studies have compared the SBDB data with analogous measures from the establishment data of the U.S. Census of Manufactures (Boden and Phillips, 1985; Acs and Audretsch, 1990, Chapter Two), and from the establishment and employment records of the BLS data (Brown and Phillips, 1989). Such comparisons have generally concluded that the SBDB data are remarkably consistent with these other major data bases providing observations on establishments and enterprises. The SBDB has already been applied in a number of other studies to address a wide variety of issues related to intra-industry dynamics. While Evans (1987a and 1987b) and Phillips and Kirchhoff (1989) used the SBDB to examine the relationships between firm age, growth, and size, Acs and Audretsch (1989a and 1989b) and Macdonald (1986) analyzed the determinants of entry, and Audretsch (1991) measured new-firm survival.

The annual number of new-firm startups is aggregated to major manufacturing sectors and shown for alternate years between 1976 and 1986 in Table I. The share of the total number of enterprises in the sector accounted for by new-firms startups is listed in the parentheses. There are three major points from Table I which should be emphasized. First, the number of new-firm startups and their share of the total number of enterprises varies considerably across manufacturing sectors.

Second, the amount of startups varies substantially from year to year. That is, in 1976 there were 11,154 new-firm startups in all of U.S. manufacturing; this fell by nearly one-quarter to 8,525 startups in 1980, and by nearly two-thirds to 4,239 in 1982. By 1984 the number of manufacturing startups had more than doubled to 10,055, which was nearly again at the 1976 and 1978 levels. This volatility in the number of new-firm startups is attributable, at least to some extent, to macroeconomic fluctuations. This is reflected by the fluctuations in annual growth rates of real gross national product (GNP) of 4.9 percent in 1976, 5.3 percent in 1978, −0.2 percent in 1980, −2.5 percent in 1982, 6.8 percent in 1984, and 2.8 percent in 1986.[5] The extent of startup activity for manufacturing as a whole corresponds quite

closely to these macroeconomic fluctuations. In addition, there is also a clear tendency for the number of startups within each manufacturing sector to reflect the phase of the business cycle.

The third major point from Table I is that, while no industrial sector is immune from the influences of macroeconomic fluctuations, the impact varies considerably from sector to sector. New-firm startups in certain sectors, such as petroleum, textiles and apparel, and communications are apparently quite susceptible to the phase of the business cycle, at least over this period of time. By contrast, in the computer and food sectors, the number of startups seems to be less vulnerable to macroeconomic fluctuations. Just as the strong intertemporal tendency towards fewer startups in the transportation (other) sector probably reflects a longer-term decline, the pronounced tendency towards an increase in the number of startups in computers seems to suggest long-term sectorial expansion.

III. Industry and macroeconomic effects

As Blanchflower and Oswald (1990), Lucas (1978), Evans and Jovanovic (1989) and Evans and Leighton (1989) argue, each individual or agent in the economy is assumed to confront a decision between working for a wage with an established enterprise or starting his or her own new firms. These studies suggest that, while many factors influence the entrepreneurial choice, certainly not least important is the extent to which the profits from starting a new firm, Π, exceed the wage alternative, w, so that the probability of a new-firm startup, pr(NF), is positively related to $\Pi - w$, or

$$\text{pr(NF)} = f(\Pi - w) \qquad (1)$$

The profitability of the new startup is simply the difference between the total revenue, price (p) times the firm's output (q), and total cost, determined by the unit cost of producing q units of output, c(q), times the number of units produced, so that the probability of an agent starting a new firm can be expressed as

$$\text{pr(NF)} = f(p*q - c(q) - w) \qquad (2)$$

Rewriting equation (2) and assuming that the market price equals the average cost for firms that

442   *David B. Audretsch*

TABLE I
New-firm startups by industrial sector[a]

	1976	1978	1980	1982	1984	1986
Food	474	481	374	209	480	535
	(2.53)	(2.67)	(2.15)	(1.22)	(2.79)	(3.09)
Textiles and apparel	1172	1254	854	491	1026	992
	(4.03)	(4.20)	(2.95)	(1.69)	(3.41)	(3.34)
Lumber and furniture	1325	1375	868	425	1060	1106
	(3.71)	(3.70)	(2.28)	(1.12)	(2.75)	(2.79)
Paper	126	191	101	50	149	152
	(2.97)	(4.24)	(2.20)	(1.11)	(3.19)	(3.15)
Chemicals	322	390	284	164	332	335
	(2.95)	(3.52)	(2.54)	(1.45)	(2.85)	(2.83)
— Industrial	91	99	98	41	85	84
	(3.62)	(3.76)	(3.69)	(1.55)	(3.12)	(3.09)
— Drugs and medicinals	34	54	22	26	48	49
	(2.75)	(4.47)	(1.82)	(2.11)	(3.60)	(3.50)
— Other	123	154	116	65	130	138
	(2.39)	(3.00)	(2.24)	(1.23)	(2.42)	(2.52)
Petroleum	41	42	57	11	43	46
	(3.21)	(3.16)	(4.01)	(0.76)	(3.02)	(3.17)
Rubber	430	469	312	158	382	385
	(4.72)	(4.78)	(2.97)	(1.44)	(3.26)	(3.18)
Stone, clay and glass	545	493	292	133	337	358
	(3.86)	(3.41)	(2.00)	(0.93)	(2.41)	(2.58)
Primary metals	168	179	141	79	195	201
	(2.97)	(3.07)	(2.36)	(1.32)	(3.22)	(3.25)
— Ferrous metals	85	90	61	45	102	110
	(3.21)	(3.28)	(2.24)	(1.67)	(3.70)	(3.80)
— Non-ferrous metals	83	89	80	34	93	91
	(2.76)	(2.89)	(2.47)	(1.04)	(2.82)	(2.76)
Fabricated metal products	962	1042	782	362	913	877
	(3.19)	(3.30)	(2.37)	(1.07)	(2.65)	(2.52)
Machinery	1519	1731	1407	586	1433	1314
	(3.14)	(3.38)	(2.60)	(1.02)	(2.43)	(2.22)
— Office and computers	50	66	62	43	118	100
	(4.73)	(5.27)	(4.14)	(2.21)	(4.58)	(3.64)
— Other machinery, non-electrical	1469	1665	1345	543	1315	1214
	(3.10)	(3.34)	(2.56)	(0.98)	(2.33)	(2.15)
Electrical equipment	635	620	461	274	665	606
	(4.41)	(3.98)	(2.88)	(1.62)	(3.63)	(3.21)
— Radio and TV equipment	79	82	53	21	43	49
	(5.02)	(4.63)	(3.00)	(1.15)	(2.38)	(2.73)
— Communications equipment	128	94	74	48	168	119
	(5.27)	(3.59)	(2.77)	(1.62)	(5.02)	(3.40)

Table I (Continued)

	1976	1978	1980	1982	1984	1986
— Electronic components	193 (4.83)	204 (4.64)	163 (3.40)	110 (2.10)	233 (3.98)	211 (3.46)
— Other	235 (3.67)	240 (3.54)	171 (2.52)	95 (1.39)	221 (3.03)	227 (3.04)
Motor vehicles	147 (4.55)	149 (4.31)	116 (3.11)	57 (1.49)	147 (3.62)	148 (3.33)
Other transport equipment	247 (5.31)	250 (5.23)	142 (3.17)	76 (1.76)	191 (4.30)	127 (2.99)
Aircraft and missiles	26 (2.50)	36 (3.24)	26 (2.09)	13 (0.94)	33 (2.19)	42 (2.68)
Instruments	312 (3.94)	323 (3.72)	226 (2.41)	160 (1.60)	308 (2.79)	353 (3.01)
— Scientific and measuring	130 (4.56)	120 (3.63)	104 (2.76)	66 (1.55)	145 (2.99)	141 (2.72)
— Optical, surgical & photographic	182 (3.59)	203 (3.78)	122 (2.18)	94 (1.63)	163 (2.63)	212 (3.24)
Other manufacturing	2703 (3.62)	2703 (3.48)	2082 (2.67)	1081 (1.35)	2361 (2.81)	2435 (2.82)
Total manufacturng	11154 (3.56)	11728 (3.60)	8525 (2.56)	4329 (1.27)	10055 (2.86)	10012 (2.80)

ᵃ The share (percentage) of the total number of firms accounted for by new-firm startups is indicated in the parentheses.

have attained the minimum efficient scale (MES) level of output, q^*, plus some additional factor, δ,

$$\text{pr(NF)} = f[q(c(c(q^*) + \delta - c(q)) - w] \quad (3)$$

where δ is determined by the market growth rate, g, the extent to which the startup is able to contribute to innovative activity, t, and the ability of the incumbent firms to retaliate against the entrant, r. The growth rate can be decomposed into a component that is induced by the macroeconomic environment, g_e, and a component representing the growth of the specific market net of the business cycle influence, g_m or $g = g_e + g_m$. As Bradburd and Caves (1982) found, industry profits and presumably prices tend to accompany high rates of market growth. Thus, $\partial\Pi/\partial g = (\partial\Pi/\partial\delta)(\partial\delta/\partial g) > 0$ producing a new or different product also enables the entrepreneur to raise the price, $\partial\Pi/\partial t = (\partial\Pi/\partial\delta)(\partial\delta/\partial t) > 0$. However, the extent to which the incumbent firms are able to engage in retalitory conduct when confronted with

a new startup in the industry, r, will serve to dampen the profitability of the new firm, $\partial\Pi/\partial r = (\partial\Pi/\partial\delta)(\partial\delta/\partial r) < 0$.

One of the more striking stylized facts regarding new-firm startups emerging from several studies is their remarkably small scale of output. For example, Audretsch (1991) reports that about 95 percent of new-firm startups in U.S. manufacturing in 1976 had fewer than fifty employees. Similarly, then mean size of new firms established in 1976 was 9.55 employees. Evans and Jovanovic (1989), and Fazzari, Hubbard, an Peterson (1988) found that entrepreneurs typically are confronted with a binding liquidity constraint. Similarly, Stoll (1984) shows that the cost of credit is positively and systematically related to firm size. That is, a lower cost of credit and/or more accessible credit conditions should increase the startup size, so that $q = q(i)$, where i is the market rate of interest and $\partial q/\partial i < 0$.

Finally, the rate of unemployment influences

equation (1) in two ways. First, as has been well documented in the labor literature, the wage rate is negatively related to the unemployment rate. Second, those unemployed workers may substitute their reservation wage or the value of their unemployment benefits for w in equation (1). In either case, an increase in unemployment should serve to reduce the value of w, resulting in an increase in the number of new-firm startups, ceteris parabus.

Thus, the number of new-firm startups in an industry is influenced by certain elements which are specific to the individual market and elements which reflect the macroeconomic environment. The industry-specific factors are the importance of scale economies and capital intensity, the market growth rate, the ability of incumbent firms to engage in retalitory strategies against new entrants, and the degree to which new firms are able to innovate. The macroeconomic influences associated with the business cycle are the aggregate level of economic growth, the cost of capital, and the unemployment rate. It is hypothesized that these industry specific and macroeconomic factors combine to shape the number of new-firm startups in an industry.

IV. Empirical results

To test the hypotheses raised in the previous section, a panel of data was assembled, where the unit of observation is the number of startups in a given industry for a given year over the period 1976–1986, for alternate years. To capture the extent to which new firms are able to innovate a number of various measurements, reflecting different aspects of what has been termed as the "technological regime" are used.[6] First, as Levin (1978) and Mueller and Tilton (1969, p. 5) argue, industries in which research and development (R&D) plays an important role are generally not conductive to new-firm startups, since "The chief component of these barriers generally is the extent of economies of scale in the R&D process. The second major factor contributing to R&D entry barriers is the accumulation of patents and know-how on the part of incumbent firms."[7] Thus, a negative relationship would be expected to emerge between the 1977 company R&D-sales ratio (from the Federal Trade Commission's Line of Business Survey) and new-firm startups.

As explained in the previous section, in those industries where the small firms tend to be particularly innovative, the number of startups should be greater.[8] To measure the innovative activity of small firms, the small-firm innovation rate is used, which is defined as the number of 1982 innovations from enterprises with fewer than 500 employees divided by small-firm employment. The innovation data, which were introduced by Acs and Audretsch (1987, 1988, and 1990) are from the U.S. Small Business Administration's Innovation Data Base.

In addition, several variables from a survey of 650 industrial R&D managers by a Yale University group (Levin et al., 1982; Levin et al., 1987) measuring the underlying technological conditions in 130 industries were used. These measures include the importance of learning ("How important is moving quickly down the learning curve as a means of capturing and protecting the advantages from new or improved products?"), basic science ("How relevant were the basic sciences of biology, chemistry, and physics (average of three) to technological progress in this line of business over the past 10—15 years?"), product changes, and university research. As Link and Rees (1990) note, small new firms have apparently been more successful at exploiting university research than have their more established larger counterparts, suggesting that the number of startups should be greater in industries where university research plays an important role.[9] By contrast, large laboratories are likely to be more crucial in industries dependent upon basic research, thereby deterring the startup of new firms. New firms would also be expected to be disadvantaged both in markets where the product specification changes with considerable frequency and where learning is particularly important. Not only do Spence (1981) and Fudenberg and Tirole (1983) argue that the incumbent firms have a clear cost advantage in industries where learning plays an important role, but Scherer and Ross (1990, p . 373) observe that, "Small scale entry is particularly handicapped when learning economies exist, since small firms have relatively little cumulative production and hence are slow to progress down learning curves in the absence of substantial spillovers."

Industry growth is measured by the annual percentage change in value-of-shipments using data from the U.S. Department of Commerce, Bureau of the Census, Annual Survey of Manufactures. In the previous section it was argued that new-firm startups are more likely to be impeded in industries where the incumbent firms can easily detect the new firms and respond through some type of retalitory behavior. As has been commonly argued in the industrial organization literature (Scherer and Ross, 1990), this is more likely to be the case is highly concentrated industries where just several enterprises dominate the market. The degree to which an industry is concentred is represented by the four-firm concentration ratio, measured by the Census of Manufactures at the Bureau of the Census. The importance of scale economies and capital intensity is measured by the capital-labor ratio and is expected to exert a negative influence on the number of startups.

To measure macroeconomic growth, the annual percentage change in real GNP is used. The cost of capital is measured by the average three-month interest rate paid on U.S. Treasury Bills. Both of these variables, along with the unemployment rate, are taken from the 1989 *Economic Report of the President*. While both the growth rate of real GNP and the unemployment rate are expected to exert a positive influence on new-firm startups, the interest rate should be negatively related to the number of startups. It should be emphasized that while these macroeconomic variables vary over time but not across industries for any given year, most of the industry-specific variables are measured only at one point in time. It is implicitly assumed that variables such as R&D intensity, and the various characteristics of the underlying technology in an industry are invariant over a relatively short time period. Only the measure of industry growth varies both across time and across industries.

Because of the limited number of industries for which the Yale data on industry technology are available, pooled cross-section regressions were estimated for 117 four-digit standard industrial classification (SIC) industries over the six time observations using new-firm startups as the dependent variable. The regression results are reported in Table II. Equation 1 shows that industries where university research plays an important role tend to be conducive to new-firm startups. However, if the industry is especially dependent upon

basic science, there is less startup activity. New firms are apparently not attracted to industries characterized by frequent product changes. Perhaps somewhat surprisingly, as the positive but statistically non-significant coefficient of learning suggests, new firms do not seem to be deterred from entering industries where learning-by-doing is considered to be important. Thus, while learning may be advantageous to the incumbent enterprises, it apparently does not significantly deter the startup of new firms.

The statistically non-significant coefficient of R&D/Sales combined with a positive small-firm innovation rate suggests that a technological environment where the small firms have the innovative advantage is conducive to new startups. However, if the small firms are not particularly innovative, given a level of R&D intensity, then startup activity tends to be deterred.

The coefficient of the industry growth rate clearly can not be considered to be different from zero. Given the repeated finding in the cross-section studies that one of the most significant determinants of entry is market growth, this result is startling. While the negative and statistically significant coefficient of concentration suggests that new-firm startups tend to be inhibited in an environment where retaliation from the incumbent enterprises is more likely to be effective, the positive coefficient of capital intensity implies that startups are not significantly deterred from entering industries exhibiting substantial scale economies. Although this contradicts the prediction of the previous section, it is consistent with the results from a number of cross-section studies, such as Acs and Audretsch (1989a and 1989b; and Highfield and Smiley, 1987). It is also consistent with the finding of Audretsch (1991) that, although new-firm startups may not be deterred in the presence of capital intensity, their ability to survive over time is significantly less.

New-firm startups are clearly influenced by the stage of the business cycle, as evidenced by the positive and statistically significant coefficient of the growth rate of real GNP. During the expansion phase of the business cycle, while real GNP is expanding, startup activity tends to be high. By contrast, during a recession or trough, when real GNP is declining, startup activity becomes dormant. The interest rate also exerts a strong influ-

TABLE II
Pooled cross-section regression results for new-firm startups (t-statistics listed in parentheses)

	1	2	3	4
University research	2.625	2.167	2.965	2.295
	(3.06)	(3.52)	(3.93)	(3.70)
Basic science	−3.331	−3.127	−3.691	−3.300
	(−3.91)	(−4.61)	(−4.92)	(−4.83)
Product changes	−2.885	−3.433	−3.185	−3.590
	(−3.89)	(−4.10)	(−4.46)	(−4.31)
Learning	0.917	1.761	1.205	1.987
	(1.42)	(2.80)	(1.88)	(3.17)
Company R&D/sales	0.982	2.047	—	—
	(1.45)	(1.83)		
Small-firm innovation rate	5.339	1.013	5.672	1.99
	(3.28)	(0.44)	(3.54)	(0.86)
Industry growth	0.150	0.083	0.150	0.084
	(0.90)	(0.81)	(0.90)	(0.80)
Concentration	−0.145	—	−0.149	—
	(−3.73)		(−3.78)	
Capital intensity	0.064	0.130	0.058	0.138
	(2.21)	(3.48)	(2.22)	(3.70)
GNP growth rate	0.052	0.053	0.052	0.054
	(2.04)	(2.09)	(2.00)	(2.11)
Interest rate	−0.310	−0.307	−0.311	−0.308
	(−8.50)	(−8.41)	(−8.47)	(−8.46)
Unemployment	0.152	0.142	0.153	0.141
	(1.95)	(1.83)	(1.95)	(1.82)
R^2	0.418	0.345	0.416	0.342
F	38.051	30.402	41.058	32.606
Sample Size	702	702	702	702

ence on new-firm startups. Startup activity is apparently choked off to a considerable extent by high interest rates and promoted when the cost of capital is relatively low. Finally, as indicated by the positive and statistically significant coefficient of the unemployment rate, unemployment apparently is conducive to new-firm startups.

The positive coefficient of the capital-labor ratio might be attributable to the impact of capital intensity on startup activity being confounded with that of market concentration, due to the high correlation between concentration and capital intensity, However, in equation 2, when the four-firm concentration ratio is omitted from the regression, the coefficient of the capital labor ratio not only remains positive and statistically significant, but actually doubles in magnitude. Similarly, the company R&D/Sales ratio could be suspected as being multicollinear with the measures of the importance of university research, basic science, product changes, and learning. However, when it is omitted from Equation (3), none of these other coefficients are affected to any noticeable extent. Finally, in Equation (4) omitting both the concentration ratio and R&D intensity variables leaves the coefficients of the other variables virtually unchanged, with the exception that the small-firm innovation rate no longer has a significant impact on new-firm startups, although the coefficient does remain positive.

V. Conclusions

An important finding of this paper is that new-firm startups serve as key agents in implementing the "Schumpeterian" (1950) task of "creative destruction". This function is fulfilled in two ways. First, as incumbent enterprises reduce employment and close plants during an economic contraction, the resulting unemployment triggers an increase in the startup of new firms. That is, at least some of the resources released by the incumbent firms, presumably because they were being applied the least efficiently, will be redeployed by new startups. This redeployment of resources occurs despite the finding in this paper that "all boats are lifted by a rising tide," that is, startup activity is generally driven, to a considerable extent, by the business cycle. During periods of macroeconomic expansion, the startup of new firms increases in virtually every industry. By contrast, startup activity becomes sluggish during a recession.

The second manner in which new startups serve as Schumpeterian firms is through innovative activity. A rather startling result is that the startup of new firms is apparently not deterred either in industries which are capital intensive or R&D intensive, or where learning-by-doing plays an important role. There is at least some evidence suggesting that, under the appropriate technological circumstances, new-firm startups can compensate for their inherent size and experience disadvantages through innovative activity. One source for this innovative activity is apparently university research.

At least two important aspects regarding new-firm startups have been left unexplored by this paper. First, what happens to the firms subsequent to their startup, and how is their ability to survive related to macroeconomic fluctuations? Second, what are the normative implications of startup activity; is it desirable or undesirable? That is, would economic welfare be enhanced or undermined by encouraging the startup of new firms? While these are complicated questions, they surely need to be addressed in future research. In any

case, the results of this paper show that not only is startup activity a pervasive phenomenon in U.S. manufacturing, but that it is clearly connected to both the macroeconomic environment as well as the underlying technological conditions in the industry.

Acknowledgements

We wish to thank Jianping Yang for his computational assistance and Dick Nelson and Rick Levin for providing us with some of the data. All errors and omissions remain our responsibility.

Notes

[1] See for example the studies examining net entry listed in Scherer and Ross (1990) and contained in Geroski and Schwalbach (1991).

[2] For examples of this literature, see Orr (1974) and Duetsch (1984).

[3] Yamawaki (1991) examines the determinates of net entry into 135 three-digit Japanese manufacturing industries for five one-year periods between 1980 and 1984. However, he was not able to identify new-firm startups from his measure of net entry.

[4] For further explanation of the development and editing of the SBDB, see U.S. Small Business Administration (1986 and 1987), Harris (1983), and Brown and Phillips (1989).

[5] The annual growth rates of real gross national product are from the U.S. Department of Commerce, Bureau of Economic Analysis.

[6] For detailed explanations of what is meant by the "technological regime", see Winter (1984), Audretsch (1991), and Acs and Audretsch (1990, chapter seven).

[7] In fact, the notion that R&D intensity impedes entry has at least some empirical support. Orr (1974) found that Canadian net entry was adversely affected by R&D intensity, and Baldwin and Gorecki (1987) found that entry via plant creation is negatively related to R&D.

[8] For an overview of the innovative advantages associated with new and small firms, see Nelson (1984) and Scherer (1991).

[9] For evidence of R&D spillovers, see Acs, Audretsch and Feldman (1992 and 1993).

References

Acs, Zoltan J. and David B. Audretsch, 1990, *Innovation and Small Firms*, Cambridge, MA: MIT Press.

Acs, Zoltan J. and David. B. Audretsch, 1989a, 'Small-Firm Entry in U.S. Manufacturing', *Economica* **56**(2), 255–265.

Acs, Zoltan J. and David B. Audretsch, 1989b, 'Births and Firm Size', *Southern Economic Journal* **56**(2), 467–475.

Acs, Zoltan J. and David B. Audretsch, 1988, 'Innovation in Large and Small Firms: An Empirical Analysis', *American Economic Review* 78 (4), 678–690.

Acs, Zoltan J. and David B. Audretsch, 1987, 'Innovation, Market Structure and Firm Size', *Review of Economics and Statistics* 69 (4), 567–575.

Acs, Zoltan J., Maryann P. Feldman and David B. Audretsch, 1992, 'Real Effects of Academic Research', *American Economic Review* 82 (1), 363–367.

Acs, Zoltan J., Maryann P. Feldman and David B. Audretsch, 1994, 'R&D Spillovers and Recipient Firm Size', *Review of Economics and Statistics* 76 (1).

Audretsch, David B., 1991, 'New-Firm Survival and the Technological Regime', *Review of Economics and Statistics* 73 (3), 441–450.

Baldwin, John R. and Paul K. Gorecki, 1982, 'Plant Creation versus Plant Acquisition: The Entry Process in Canadian Manufacturing', *International Journal of Industrial Organization* 5 (1), 27–42.

Blanchflower, D. and B. Meyer, 1994, 'A Longitudinal Analysis of Young Entrepreneurs in Australia and the United States', *Small Business Economics* 6.

Blanchflower, D. and A. Oswald, 1990, 'What Makes an Entrepreneur?', NBER Working Paper 3252, September.

Boden, Richard and Bruce D. Phillips, 1985, 'Uses and Limitations of USEEM/USELM Data', Office of Advocacy, U.S. Small Business Administration, Washington, DC, November.

Bradburd, Ralph and Richard E. Caves, 1982, 'A Closer Look at the Effect of Market Growth on Industries' Profits', *Review of Economics and Statistics* 64 (4), 635–645.

Brown, H. Shelton and Bruce D. Phillips, 1989, 'Comparison Between Small Business Data Base (USEEM) and Bureau of Labor Statistics (BLS) Employment Data: 1978–1986', *Small Business Economics* 1 (4), 273–284.

Duetsch, Larry L., 1984, 'Entry and the Extent of Multiplant Operations', *Journal of Industrial Economics* 32 (2), 477–487.

Dunne, Timothy, Mark J. Roberts and Larry Samuelson, 1988, 'Patterns of Firm Entry and Exit in U.S. Manufacturing Industries', *Rand Journal of Economics* 19 (4), 495–415.

Dunne, Timothy, Mark J. Roberts and Larry Samuelson, 1989, 'The Growth and Failure of U.S. Manufacturing Plants', *Quarterly Journal of Economics* 104 (4), 671–698.

Evans, David S., 1987a, 'Tests of Alternative Theories of Firm Growth', *Journal of Political Economy* 95 (3), 657–674.

Evans, David S., 1987b, 'The Relationship Between Firm Growth, Size, and Age: Estimates for 100 Manufacturing Industries', *Journal of Industrial Economics* 35 (2), 567–581.

Evans, David S. and Boyan Jovanovic, 1989, 'Estimates of a Model of Entrepreneurial Choice under Liquidity Constraints', *Journal of Political Economy* 95 (3), 657–674.

Evans, David S. and Linda S. Leighton, 1989, 'The Determinants of Changes in the U.S. Self-Employment, 1968–1987', *Small Business Economics* 1 (2), 111–120.

Fazzari, S., R. Hubbard and B. Peterson, 1988, 'Financing Constraints and Corporate Investment', *Brookings Papers on Economic Activity*, 141–207.

Fundenberg, Drew and Jean Tirole, 1983, 'Learning-by-Doing and Market Performance', *Bell Journal of Economics* 14 (3), 522–530.

Geroski, Paul and Joachim Schwalbach (eds.), 1991, *Entry and Market Contestability: An International Comparison*, Oxford: Basil Blackwell.

Harris, Candee S., 1983, *U.S. Establishment and Enterprise Microdata (USEEM): A Data Base Description*, Business Microdata Project, The Brookings Institution, June.

Highfield, Richard and Robert Smiley, 1987, 'New Business Starts and Economic Activity: An Empirical Investigation', *International Journal of Industrial Organization* 5 (1), 51–66.

Jacobson, Louis, 1985, *Analysis of the Accuracy of SBA's Small Business Data Base*, Alexandria, VA: Center for Naval Analysis.

Jovanovic, Boyar, 1994, 'Entrepreneurial Choice When People Differ in Their Management and Labor Skills', *Small Business Economics* 6.

Levin, Richard C., 1978, 'Technical Change, Barriers to Entry, and Market Structure', *Economica* 45 (4), 347–361.

Levin, Richard C., John J. Beggs, Alvin K. Klevorick, Richard R. Nelson, Merton J. Peck, Peter C. Reiss, Robert W. Wilson and Sidney G. Winter, 1982, 'Dynamic Competition: A Program of Research on Technological Change and Market Structure. First Year Progress Report to the National Science Foundation', unpublished manuscript, Yale University, April.

Levin, Richard C., Alvin K. Klevorick, Richard R. Nelson and Sidney G. Winter, 1987, 'Appropriating the Returns from Industrial Research and Development', *Brookings Papers on Economic Activity* 3, 783–820.

Link, Albert N. and John Rees, 1990, 'Firm Size, University Based Research and the Returns to R&D', *Small Business Economics* 2 (1), 25–32.

Lucas, Robert E., Jr., 1978, 'On the Size Distribution of Business Firms', *Bell Journal of Economics* 9 (3), 508–523.

Macdonald, James, 1986, 'Entry and Exit on the Competitive Fringe', *Southern Economic Journal* 52 (3), 640–652.

Marschak, T. and Richard R. Nelson, 1962, 'Flexibility, Uncertainty and Economic Theory', *Metroeconomica* 14 (1), 42–60.

Mills, David E. and Laurence Schumann, 1985, 'Industry Structure with Fluctuating Demand', *American Economic Review* 75 (4), 758–767.

Mueller, Dennis, 1976, 'Information, Mobility, and Profit', *Kyklos* 29 (3), 419–448.

Mueller, Dennis C. and J. Tilton, 1969, 'Research and Development Costs as a Barrier to Entry', *Canadian Journal of Economics* 56 (4), 570–579.

Nelson, Richard R., 1984, 'Incentives for Entrepreneurship and Supporting Institutions', *Weltwirtschaftliches Archiv* 120 (4), 646–661.

Orr, Dale, 1974, 'The Determinants of Entry: A Study of the Canadian Manufacturing Industries', *Review of Economics and Statistics* 56 (1), 58–66.

Phillips, Bruce D. and Bruce A. Kirchhoff, 1989, 'Formation, Growth and Survival: Small Firm Dynamics in the U.S. Economy', *Small Business Economics* **1**(1), 65—74.

Scherer, F. M., 1991, 'Changing Perspectives on the Firm Size Problem', in Zoltan J. Acs and David B. Audretsch (eds.), *Innovation and Technological Change: An International Comparison*, Ann Arbor: University of Michigan Press, pp. 24—38.

Scherer, F. M. and David Ross, 1990, *Industrial Market Structure and Economic Performance*, 3rd edition, Boston: Houghton Mifflin.

Schumpeter, Joseph A., 1950, *Capitalism, Socialism and Democracy*, 3rd edition, New York: Harper and Row.

Spence, Michael A., 1981, 'The Learning Curve and Competition', *Bell Journal of Economics* **12**(1), 49—70.

Stigler, George J., 1939, 'Production and Distribution in the Short Run', *Journal of Political Economy* **47**(2), 305—327.

Stoll, Hans R., 1984, 'Small Firm's Access to Public Equity Financing', in Paul M. Horvitz and R. Richardson Petrit (eds.), *Small Business Finance: Problems in the Financing of Small Business*, Greenwich, Conn: JAI Press, pp. 187—238.

U.S. Small Business Administration, 1987, Office of Advocacy, *Linked 1976—1984 USEEM User's Guide*, Washington, DC, July.

U.S. Small Business Administration, 1986, *The Small Business Data Base: A User's Guide*, Washington, DC, July.

Winter, Sidney G., 1984, 'Schumpeterian Competition in Alternative Technological Regimes', *Journal of Economic Behavior and Organization* **5**, 287—320.

Yamawaki, Hideki, 1991, 'The Effects of Business Conditions on Net Entry: Evidence from Japan', in P. Geroski and J. Schwalbach (eds.), *Entry and Market Contestability: An International Comparison*, Oxford: Basil Blackwell, pp. 168—186.

[11]

REVIEW OF ECONOMIC DYNAMICS 1, 371–408 (1998)
ARTICLE NO. RD980009

Entry, Exit, Embodied Technology, and Business Cycles

Jeffrey R. Campbell*

*Department of Economics, University of Rochester, Rochester, New York 14627; and
National Bureau of Economic Research*

Received June 1, 1997

This paper studies the entry and exit of U.S. manufacturing plants over the business cycle and compares the results with those from a vintage capital model augmented to reproduce observed features of the plant life cycle. Looking at the entry and exit of plants provides new evidence supporting the hypothesis that shocks to embodied technological change are a significant source of economic fluctuations. In the U.S. economy, the entry rate covaries positively with output and total factor productivity growth, and the exit rate leads all three of these. A vintage capital model in which all technological progress is embodied in new plants reproduces these patterns. In the model economy, a persistent improvement to embodied technology induces obsolete plants to cease production, causing exit to rise. Later, as entering plants embodying the new technology become operational, both output and productivity increase. *Journal of Economic Literature* Classification Numbers: L16, E22.   © 1998 Academic Press

1. INTRODUCTION

This paper studies the entry and exist of U.S. manufacturing plants over the business cycle and compares the results with those from a vintage capital model augmented with plant level productivity uncertainty. In most vintage capital frameworks, changes in machine retirement and replacement decisions play critical roles in generating business cycles. Except in specific cases, such as that studied by Cooper and Haltiwanger [11], individual machine retirement and replacement is difficult to observe.

* This paper is a substantially revised version of my Ph.D. dissertation written at Northwestern University. Kyle Bagwell, Marty Eichenbaum, Rob Porter, Jonas Fisher, Boyan Jovanovic, and two anonymous referees have made very useful comments on previous versions. I am grateful to the Alfred P. Sloan Foundation for financial support through a doctoral dissertation grant and the Federal Reserve Bank of Chicago for research support. All remaining errors are mine.

However, the entry and exit of individual plants is observable. Using the Longitudinal Research Database, Davis, Haltiwanger, and Schuh [12] produced quarterly employment weighted entry and exit rates for the U.S. manufacturing sector for a period of 16 years. Because much technological change is embodied in plants as well as machines, examining this data is a natural first step toward understanding patterns of machine retirement and replacement over the business cycle.[1] The next section of this paper presents such an examination. The entry and exit rates both exhibit considerable fluctuations over the sample period, and their fluctuations have noticeable relationships with each other and the business cycle. Peaks in the exit rate tend to lead peaks in the entry rate by about five quarters. As might be expected, entry is procyclical and exit is countercyclical. Entry is positively correlated with current productivity growth and exit is positively correlated with future productivity growth.

To determine whether the observed fluctuations in entry and exit could be caused by shocks to the rate of embodied technological progress, the remainder of this paper studies a general equilibrium model of growth, entry, and exit in which all technological progress is embodied in new plants. Using data on economic obsolescence and physical depreciation of capital goods, Boddy and Gort [6] showed that most technological change is embodied in new capital. Olley and Pakes [26] found that the exit of inefficient plants and their replacement with entrants was a major source of productivity growth in the telecommunications industry following telephone deregulation. This work justifies the assumption that all technological progress is embodied in new plants. As in the models of Greenwood, Hercowitz, and Huffman [18] and Greenwood, Hercowitz, and Krusell [19], the sole source of aggregate uncertainty is variation in the level of capital embodied technology. The model augments King, Plosser, and Rebelo's [23] general equilibrium business cycle framework with a selection model of entry and exit resembling Hopenhayn's [21], in which plants face considerable idiosyncratic productivity uncertainty.[2]

The inclusion of idiosyncratic uncertainty significantly influences both microeconomic decisions and macroeconomic outcomes. As in the investment models of Pidyck [27] and Abel and Eberly [1], irreversibility of exit and ongoing productivity uncertainty induce agents to rationally delay plant exit. An extremely unproductive plant is kept in operation in the hope that a favorable idiosyncratic productivity shock will improve its

---

[1] For an example of technological change embodied in plants, see the description of the titanium dioxide industry in Dobson, Shepherd, and Stoner [13].

[2] Caballero and Hammour [7, 8] present a similar model of entry and exit driven by embodied technological change. However, the focus of their work is on the effects of demand and factor price shocks on gross labor market flows.

value. The responses of such plants to technology shocks determine the aggregate exit rate's fluctuations. As embodied technology continually improves, it becomes less likely that an older plant will receive a technology shock favorable enough to justify its long run operation. A positive innovation to embodied technology hastens this obsolescence process and induces marginal plants to exit. The increase in the aggregate exit rate is followed by increases in entry, productivity, and output as new plants embodying the innovation become productive. Thus, the model economy reproduces the cyclical features of the entry and exit data: Exit is countercyclical and leads output and productivity growth, which both accompany entry.

The remainder of the paper proceeds as follows: The next section presents the empirical study of entry and exit. Section 3 presents the model economy, and Section 4 characterizes the competitive equilibrium for a parameterized version of the model and compares the model economy's characteristics to those of the U.S. data. Section 5 offers concluding remarks.

2. ENTRY, EXIT, AND BUSINESS CYCLES

This section documents the cyclical properties of the plant entry and exit rates, showing that the plant entry rate covaries positively with output and total factor productivity growth and that the exit rate is countercyclical and leads all three of these series. These conclusions are based on an examination of the correlations of the entry and exit rates with each other and with current, future, and past output and total factor productivity growth. To correctly interpret the empirical results, it is essential to understand how the data on entry and exit were constructed. Accordingly, this section begins with a description of the data construction procedure.

2.1. *Data Construction*

To produce the Annual Survey of Manufacturers (ASM), the U.S. Bureau of the Census compiles a plant level data set covering the population of large plants and a random sample of small plants in the manufacturing sector.[3] With quarterly employment observations from the ASM panel data set, Davis, Haltiwanger, and Schuh [12] compiled aggregate time series for job creation and destruction, total employment expansion at growing plants, and total employment contraction at shrinking plants. Dividing these measurements by total manufacturing employment yields job creation and destruction rates.

---

[3] Dunne [15] provides details of the linking process for the ASM panel.

374   JEFFREY R. CAMPBELL

Davis, Haltiwanger, and Schuh [12] consider two types of job creation: that which occurs at plants which were previously active and that which occurs at entering plants. Similarly, they divide job destruction into that at plants which remain in production and that at plants which close down. The job creation rate at entering plants—employment at all entering plants divided by total employment—forms an employment weighted entry rate. The job destruction rate at exiting plants, in a like fashion, forms an employment weighted exit rate.

Two features of the data collection process influence its interpretation. First, the definitions of quarters are not standard. Each year, each respondent plant in the ASM panel reports its employment in the previous four quarters, but the year's first quarter begins on November 15 of the *previous* year. Furthermore, the quarters are not all of equal length. Davis, Haltiwanger, and Schuh [12] correct their reported time series to make their quarters of comparable length, but cannot account for the nonstandard quarterly timing. This implies that, when looking for a contemporaneous relationship between either the entry or exit rate and a conveniently measured macroeconomic aggregate, it is important to examine both their contemporaneous correlation and the correlation of the rate with the aggregate lagged one quarter.

The second important feature regards the measurement of entry itself. To account for attrition from the ASM panel, the Census Bureau collects observations of plant start-ups from the Company Organization Survey and the Social Security Administration. It seems likely that these sources would tend to identify plant start-ups after, rather then before, their actual births. In this case, it is best to view the measured entry rate as a linear combination of the current and past true entry rates. The implications of this for empirical work are the same as those of the series' quarterly timing: To find evidence of a contemporaneous relationship between entry and another variable, it is important to look at both the contemporaneous correlation and its correlations with that variable in the past.[4]

2.2. *The Cylicality of Entry and Exit*

To gauge the cyclicality of entry and exit using the quarterly series, Fig. 1 plots them and Table I reports their summary statistics.[5] A standard error, estimated using Newey and West's [25] implementation of a general-

[4] For further details concerning the construction of the entry and exit data, see Davis, Haltiwanger, and Schuh [12].

[5] The original series of Davis, Haltiwanger, and Schuh [12] was seasonally adjusted by removing quarterly means to produce the series used in this paper. The first moments of the adjusted and unadjusted series are identical by construction.

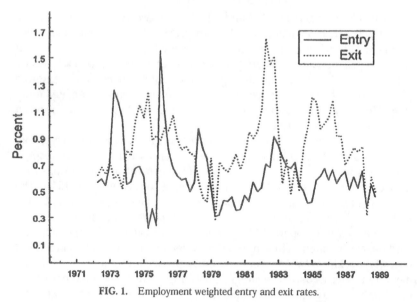

FIG. 1. Employment weighted entry and exit rates.

ized method of moments procedure, appears below each estimated moment in parantheses.[6] The observations begin in the second quarter of 1972 and end in the last quarter of 1988.

The quarterly entry and exit rates reflect the constant restructuring of the U.S. manufacturing sector. Their sample averages, 0.62 and 0.83%, are high. Furthermore, they are quite volatile. Their standard deviations are 0.23 and 0.26%. The cyclical behavior of entry and exit is evident in the data plot. Exit rises during recessions, and entry follows it, increasing during the subsequent recovery. This pattern fits the recession of

[6] Eight sample autocovariances were used to calculate all of the standard errors reported in this paper.

TABLE I
Summary Statistics

Variable	Mean (%)	Std. Dev. (%)
Entry rate	0.62	0.23
	(0.04)	(0.04)
Exit rate	0.83	0.26
	(0.06)	(0.04)

376   JEFFREY R. CAMPBELL

1974–1975 and those occurring from 1980 to 1982. In spite of these cyclical variations, it is clear that not all of the series' fluctuations can be attributed to any particular recession. This is particularly true for entry's rise during 1978 and exit's during the mid 1980s.

Figures 2 and 3 plot the correlations of entry and exit with the past, current, and future per-capita growth rates of nonfarm, nongovernment gross domestic product (GDP). Figure 4 plots the correlations of exit with future and past entry. The figures also present asymptotic 95% confidence intervals for each point on the graph. They were produced with the same procedure used to construct the standard errors in Table I.

Boddy and Gort [5] found that the fraction of investment directed toward new plants increases during booms. The entry rate's dynamic correlations reinforce the conclusion that it is procyclical. Although its contemporaneous correlation with GDP growth is small and insignificant, its correlation with GDP growth one period ago is larger, 0.28, and statistically significant. Although neither of entry's correlations with GDP growth two or three quarters ago are statistically significant, their point estimates are large, 0.25 and 0.26. The exit rate's dynamic correlations also reflect the cyclical pattern found in the data plot. The exit rate is countercyclical and its correlations with future GDP growth are positive,

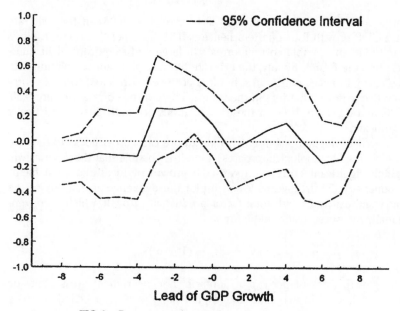

FIG. 2. Dynamic correlations of entry rate with ΔGDP.

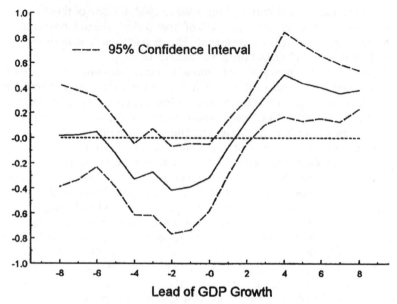

FIG. 3. Dynamic correlations of exit rate with ΔGDP.

large, and statistically significant. The correlation between the exit rate and GDP growth four quarters hence is 0.51. This positive relationship is persistent; the sample correlation is still large and significant eight quarters into the future. Finally, the exit rate has no significant correlation with the current or past entry rates, but it is positively correlated with the entry rate five to seven quarters in the future. These three correlations are 0.30, 0.30, and 0.21. All three of these correlations are individually statistically significant.

If cyclical fluctuations in entry and exit are caused by shocks to the rate of embodied technological progress, then it is possible that these series will exhibit significant correlation with the growth of measured total factor productivity (TFP). Figures 5 and 6 plot the dynamic correlations of the entry and exit rates with total factor productivity growth, which is conventionally measured using the definition

$$z_t \equiv y_t - \alpha n_t - (1 - \alpha)k_t.$$

The growth rates of per-capita nonfarm, nongovernment gross domestic product, hours worked, and the capital stock are y_t, n_t, and k_t. The elasticity of output with respect to labor input, α, is estimated with labor's

378   JEFFREY R. CAMPBELL

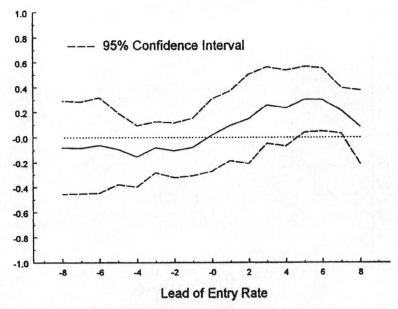

FIG. 4. Dynamic correlations of exit rate with entry rate.

average share of output, as in Solow [29].[7] These correlations are strikingly similar to the analogous correlations with GDP growth. First, the dynamic correlations indicate that entry covaries positively with contemporaneous TFP growth. Although the contemporaneous correlation is small, 0.08, and statistically insignificant, the correlation with TFP growth one quarter ago is larger, 0.20, and statistically significant. Although the correlations two and three quarters in the past are statistically insignificant, their point estimates are large, 0.18 and 0.34. Second, the exit rate covaries positively with future productivity growth. Its correlations with TFP growth three, four, and five quarters hence are 0.38, 0.45, and 0.32. These point estimates are all statistically significant. Whereas exit covaries negatively with contemporaneous GDP growth, it does not covary at all with contemporaneous TFP growth.

[7] To account for the presence of measurement error in hours worked, the variance of TFP growth is estimated using the covariance of two separate measures. The first uses hours data based on the survey of establishment payrolls, and the second uses hours data based on the survey of households. All covariances of TFP with another series are measured using the establishment hours data.

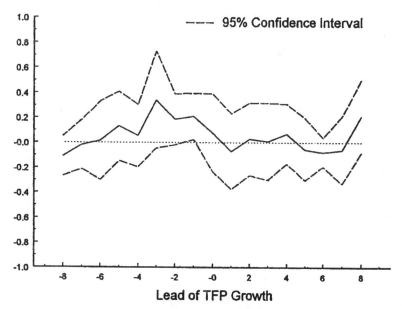

FIG. 5.   Dynamic correlations of entry rate with ΔTFP.

The above empirical results reveal significant relationships of entry and exit with output and productivity growth. The remainder of this paper carries the investigation further by constructing and analyzing a vintage capital model in which fluctuations in entry, exit, output, and productivity reflect shocks to the pace of embodied technological progress.

3. THE MODEL

The model of this paper differs from a standard vintage capital framework by explicitly modeling the idiosyncratic uncertainty experienced by plants. Because the decision to exit is irreversible, this idiosyncratic uncertainty raises the value of the option to operate in the future. These option value considerations significantly impact plants' exit decisions. The remainder of the model is standard. A continuum of plants uses labor to produce a single aggregate good, which can either be consumed or invested in the construction of new plants. Exogenous technological progress continually changes the leading edge technology. As in the vintage capital models of Solow [30] and Cooley, Greenwood, and Yorukoglu [10], the leading edge technology can only be embodied by building new plants. The technology a

380   JEFFREY R. CAMPBELL

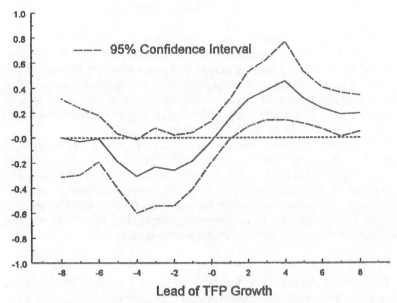

FIG. 6. Dynamic correlations of exit rate with ΔTFP.

plant uses is fixed throughout its lifetime, but different plants implement the same technology with varying degrees of success. After birth, plants are subject to ongoing idiosyncratic productivity shocks. Any plant can be retired to recover a fraction of its capital stock as scrap. This scrap value does not depend on a plant's productivity, so only relatively unproductive plants will exit. Many new plants are constructed using the scrap capital from retired plants, and the reallocation of capital between plants is time consuming. This is captured in the model by assuming that new plants become operational several periods after their construction. Plants which have been constructed but are not yet operational are referred to below as developing plants.

A representative consumer who values leisure and consumption of an aggregate good populates the model economy. There are two types of capital goods she can hold: operational plants and developing plants. During each period, the consumer trades with two types of firms. She sells labor and her portfolio of operational plants to production firms at the beginning of each period. The production firms then produce the aggregate good with these inputs and decide which plants to shut down to recover their scrap. Afterward, the production firms liquidate by selling their operational plants back to consumers. Following the liquidation of the production firms, the consumer trades with investment firms. These firms purchase developing plants from the consumer and advance them one period toward becoming operational. They also purchase the aggregate good from the consumer and use it to construct new plants, which themselves must go through a period of development. At the end of the period, the investment firms also liquidate, selling their portfolios of developing plants back to the consumer. All firms in the model seek to maximize profits. Because their technologies display constant returns to scale, their profits will be zero in a competitive equilibrium.

This market structure, as opposed to one in which consumers rent capital goods to firms every period, naturally prices the economy's capital assets.[8] This is useful for the characterization of exit decisions. The remainder of this section describes the consumer's preferences and the economy's production technology in more detail, presents the decision problems of production firms, investment firms, and the consumer, and summarizes their interaction in a competitive equilibrium.

3.1. *Preferences*

The models specification for preferences is familiar from standard business cycle models. The representative consumer values consumption of an aggregate good and leisure. She has a time endowment of one unit each period, which she must allocate between leisure and labor. The utility function

$$E_0 \sum_{t=0}^{\infty} \beta^t u(c_t, 1 - n_t)$$

represents her preferences over state contingent sequences of consumption, c_t, and leisure, $1 - n_t$. Her subjective discount factor is β, which lies strictly between 0 and 1. Her momentary utility function, $u(c_t, 1 - n_t)$, is

$$u(c_t, 1 - n_t) = \ln(c_t) + \kappa(1 - n_t),$$

where $\kappa > 0$. Hansen [20] justifies this functional form for preferences in a real business cycle model in which labor is indivisible and consumers trade lotteries over employment outcomes.

---

[8]Additional markets in state contingent claims on capital assets and the aggregate good could be added at the expense of considerable extra notation, but spot market prices for physical assets would not change.

382   JEFFREY R. CAMPBELL

3.2. *The Production and Investment Technologies*

The production sector of this economy is populated by a continuum of atomistic plants. Production of this aggregate good requires two inputs: capital and labor. A Cobb–Douglas production function characterizes each plant's technology:

$$y_t = \left(k_t e^{v_t}\right)^{1-\alpha} n_t^{\alpha}.$$

The plant's capital is k_t, its labor input is n_t, and its output of the aggregate good is y_t. The plant's productivity level is v_t. The elasticity of output with respect to labor input, $0 < \alpha < 1$, is common across plants. Plants are of different vintages and have experienced different idiosyncratic shocks, so v_t will vary across plants. Capital is a fixed factor at the plant. It cannot be added to or subtracted from over the plant's lifetime. In contrast, labor is a variable factor. It can be adjusted costlessly.

For each plant a production firm operates, two decisions must be made. First, the firm must determine the plant's labor input. Labor is assumed to come in fixed shift lengths, so that labor input is equivalent to employment. Second, the firm must decide whether or not to retire the plant after production to recover its scrap. When a plant with k_t units of capital is retired, its scrap value is ηk_t units of the aggregate good, where η is a nonnegative constant which is less than 1. If the firm does not retire a plant, then that plant can be sold to the consumer at the end of the period. While the consumer holds the plant between periods, it receives an idiosyncratic shock to its productivity level:

$$v_{t+1} = v_t + \varepsilon_{t+1},$$

$$\varepsilon_{t+1} \sim N(0, \sigma^2).$$

The plant's idiosyncratic productivity level follows a random walk. The random walk's innovation is i.i.d. across time and across plants. It has zero mean, so an average plant's productivity does not rise over its lifetime.

Building a new plant with k_t units of capital requires investing k_t units of the aggregate good. After a new plant is built, it must lie dormant for T^i periods before becoming operational. The case where $T^i = 1$ corresponds to the usual case where capital goods are available for use the period after they are produced. A new plant has access to the leading edge technology when it is built. When the plant finishes its development period, it receives the first draw of its idiosyncratic shock process. This draw reflects its success or failure at implementing the leading edge technology. The initial productivity level, v_{t+T^i}, of a plant begun in period t is a random variable with a normal distribution:

$$v_{t+T^i} \sim N(z_t, \sigma_e^2).$$

TECHNOLOGY AND BUSINESS CYCLES   383

The productivity of a plant with an average implementation of the leading edge technology is z_t. This is an aggregate index of embodied technology. This index is *not* idiosyncratic to the plant. It follows a random walk with a positive drift:

$$z_t = \mu_z + z_{t-1} + u_t,$$

$$u_t \sim N(0, \sigma_z^2).$$

The exogenous technological progress is the model economy's only source of growth and aggregate uncertainty. After a new plant's entry, nothing distinguishes it from an incumbent with an identical productivity level and capital stock. However, the unit root in the plant productivity process implies that the level of the leading edge production technology during its construction, z_t, will have a permanent effect on its productivity. In this sense, the model includes a vintage capital structure.

The assumption that capital is a fixed factor defines a plant to be a stationary collection of capital. In the absence of this assumption, all capital and labor would be employed at the most productive plant every period. In this case, there would be no heterogeneity of operational plants, and reallocation of labor and capital in the model would far exceed that observed in the data. Another implication of the assumption that capital is fixed at the plant level is that old plants cannot implement new technology by updating their capital stock. Productivity studies which determine the impact of productivity growth at existing plants on aggregate productivity growth support this assumption. Using data from three two-digit manufacturing industries—nonelectric machinery, electric machinery, and instruments—Bartlesman and Dhrymes [4] find that growth in average productivity across plants between 1972 and 1986 is actually negative. Aggregate productivity increased in these industries because resources were allocated from plants with low productivity toward those with high productivity. Olley and Pakes [26] find a similar pattern in the telecommunications industry. Additionally, they find that the reallocation of capital through entry and exit drives aggregate productivity growth. Nevertheless, it is clear that embodied technological change can be implemented at existing plants. Gort, Bahk, and Wall [17] find that reductions of the average capital vintage at existing plants significantly increase their productivity. A more general model would resemble Yorukoglu's [32] by allowing new machines embodying the leading edge technology to be used at existing plants, but not as effectively as they are used at new plants.

A final implication of the capital fixity assumption is that the model has no implications for the size distribution of plants. This is because the production possibilities available to one firm operating a plant with a

JEFFREY R. CAMPBELL

particular value of v_t and $k = 1$ are the same as those of another firm operating N plants with that same value of v_t and $k = 1/N$. If the first firm employs n workers at its plant, the second firm can produce exactly the same amount of output by employing n/N workers at each of its plants. If the two firms both decide to retire their plants, they both receive η units of the consumption good in return. Therefore, without loss of generality the capital stock of all plants can be restricted to equal 1. This considerably simplifies the study of the model economy, because plants only differ along one dimension—productivity—instead of two—productivity and size. The application of this model is to the study of aggregate entry and exit rates, which are defined as the fractions of total employment at entering and exiting plants. In the model economy, these statistics are invariant to the size distribution, so this simplification does not require forfeiting empirical relevance.

3.3. *Profit Maximization by Production Firms*

With this specification for the production technology, the profit maximization problem of a production firm can now be described. Given the prices of all plants and the wage rate, a production firm hires labor and trades plants to maximize its profits. The aggregate good is the numeraire in this economy. The wage rate in period t is w_t, the price of a plant with productivity level v_t at the beginning of the period is $q_t^0(v_t)$, and the analogous price at the end of the period is $q_t^1(v_t)$. The firm chooses the number and types of plants to purchase at the beginning of the period, which plants to close at the end of the period, and the plant's employment to maximize current profits. Let $k_t(v_t)$ describe the productivity density of the plants which the firm purchases, $n_t(v_t)$ be the labor allocated to one plant of type v_t, and $s_t(v_t)$ be a function which equals 1 if plants with productivity v_t are retired and equals 0 otherwise.[9] With this notation, a production firm's profit maximization problem is

$$
\max_{k_t(v_t), n_t(v_t), s_t(v_t)} \int_{-\infty}^{\infty} k_t(v_t) e^{v_t(1-\alpha)} n_t(v_t)^{\alpha} \, dv_t + \eta \int_{-\infty}^{\infty} s_t(v_t) k_t(v_t) \, dv_t
$$

$$
+ \int_{-\infty}^{\infty} q_t^1(v_t)(1 - s_t(v_t)) k_t(v_t) \, dv_t - \int_{-\infty}^{\infty} k_t(v_t) q_t^0(v_t) \, dv_t
$$

$$
- w_t \int_{-\infty}^{\infty} k_t(v_t) n_t(v_t) \, dv_t.
$$

[9] Note that $k_t(v_t)$ need not be a *probability* density function.

A production firm's profit equals the output of the aggregate good from production plants plus the scrap obtained from retired plants plus the resale value of plants which are left operational minus the cost of purchasing these plants minus the cost of labor which the firm employs.

The envelope theorem allows this problem to be broken into two steps. First consider the problem of maximizing the firm's output given its capital and labor inputs. This labor allocation problem is

$$\max_{n(v_t)} \int_{-\infty}^{\infty} k_t(v_t) e^{v_t(1-\alpha)} n_t(v_t)^{\alpha} \, dv_t,$$

subject to

$$\int_{-\infty}^{\infty} n_t(v_t) \, dv_t \leq n_t.$$

The firm's total employment is n_t. Solow [30] showed that this problem has a simple analytical solution. Define the firm's *effective capital stock* to be

$$\bar{k}_t = \int_{-\infty}^{\infty} e^{v_t} k_t(v_t) \, dv_t.$$

The effective capital stock is the sum of the number of plants of each type, weighted by their productivity level. The solution to the labor allocation problem is

$$n_t(v_t) = n_t e^{v_t} / \bar{k}_t.$$

A plant's labor input is proportional to its productivity. Substituting this into the firm's production function yields

$$y_t = \bar{k}_t^{1-\alpha} n_t^{\alpha}.$$

The firm's total production is y_t. A Cobb–Douglas production function in labor and *effective* capital represents the aggregate production possibilities.

With the labor allocation problem solved, a firm must still decide which plants to purchase, how much labor to employ, and which plants to retire. In light of this aggregation result, it is clear that the firm's optimal employment will be characterized by the familiar first order condition

$$w_t = \alpha \left(\frac{\bar{k}_t}{n_t} \right)^{1-\alpha}.$$

386   JEFFREY R. CAMPBELL

The firm's plant retirement decision is also easy to characterize. If asset prices equal discounted expected dividend streams, they will be increasing in v_t. A plant's scrap value is invariant to its productivity, so the representative firm will choose to scrap only those plants below a threshold, $\underline{v}_t$. Those plants with productivity levels above the threshold will remain in production. The scrap value of a plant with productivity level $\underline{v}_t$ equals its market value as an operational plant:

$$\eta = q_t^1(\underline{v}_t).$$

This threshold scrap rule is similar to those found in Hopenhayn [21] and Jovanovic [22].

The only remaining decision of a production firm to be characterized is the plant purchase decision. Because there is no bound on the number of plants which a firm can purchase, it must be the case that the optimal purchase, operation, and retirement or sale of plants is an activity which yields zero profits. This zero profit condition is

$$q_t^0(v_t) = (1 - \alpha)\left(\frac{\bar{k}_t}{n_t}\right)^{-\alpha} e^{v_t} + 1\{v_t < \underline{v}_t\}\eta + 1\{v_t \geq \underline{v}_t\}q_t^1(v_t).$$

The indicator function, $1\{\cdot\}$, equals 1 if its argument is true and 0 otherwise. This equation constrains a plant's beginning of period price to equal the dividends it returns plus its value at the end of the period. If the asset is scrapped, this value equals that of the scrap capital. Otherwise, it equals its sale price.

3.4. *Profit Maximization by Investment Firms*

Firms in the investment sector undertake two activities: They advance developing plants toward operation and construct new plants from the aggregate good. The production processes for these activities both display constant returns to scale. To construct a new plant, an investment firm only requires one unit of the aggregate good. To advance a developing plant toward completion, an investment firm need only hold it during one period.

To state the profit maximization problem of an investment firm, let $q_t^{0i}(j)$ and $q_t^{1i}(j)$ be the purchase and sale prices of a developing plant which has advanced j periods in the development process and let $x_t(j)$ denote its purchases of such plants. The profit maximization problem of an investment firm is

$$\max_{x_t(j)} \sum_{j=0}^{T^i-1} \left(q_t^{1i}(j+1) - q_t^{0i}(j)\right)x_t(j).$$

Because the construction of a new plant requires one unit of the aggregate good, $q_t^{0i}(0) = 1$. In order for the investment firm's profits to equal 0, it must be the case that $q_t^{0i}(j) = q_t^{1i}(j + 1)$ for all j between 0 and $T^i - 1$.

3.5. *Utility Maximization by the Consumer*

The consumer begins each period with a portfolio of operational and developing plants. She sells these to the production and investment firms and decides how much labor to supply at the market wage. At the end of the period, she decides how to allocate her income between consumption and savings. Purchases of operational and developing plants are the only means by which the consumer can save. These purchases determine the portfolio of plants with which she begins the following period.

Because the consumer holds all of the economy's capital assets between periods, the first order conditions from her utility maximization problem determine the relationship between asset prices at the end of one period and at the beginning of the next. The first order condition which prices operational plants is

$$q_t^1(v_t) = E\left[\beta \frac{c_t}{c_{t+1}} \int_{-\infty}^{\infty} \frac{1}{\sigma} \phi\left(\frac{v_{t+1} - v_t}{\sigma} \right) q_{t+1}^0(v_{t+1})\, dv_{t+1} \right].$$

Here, the expectations operator is over all sources of aggregate uncertainty. Aggregate uncertainty impacts c_{t+1} and $q_{t+1}^0(v)$ for an arbitrary value of v, but it does not influence the realization of the plant's idiosyncratic productivity level, v_{t+1}. Because operational plants receive their productivity shocks between periods, the consumer's decisions must take account of the uncertain resale value of the operational firms in her portfolio.

Plants which have completed T^i periods of development will receive their first draw of its idiosyncratic productivity process before the next period, so the asset pricing equation for these plants is very similar to that for operational plants:

$$q_t^{1i}(T^i) = E\left[\beta \frac{c_t}{c_{t+1}} \int_{-\infty}^{\infty} \frac{1}{\sigma_e} \phi\left(\frac{v_{t+1} - z_{t+1-T^i}}{\sigma_e} \right) q_{t+1}^0(v_{t+1})\, dv_{t+1} \right].$$

There is no idiosyncratic uncertainty regarding developing plants which will not be operational in the next period, so their asset pricing equations are straightforward:

$$q_t^{1i}(j) = E\left[\beta \frac{c_t}{c_{t+1}} q_t^{0i}(j) \right].$$

388   JEFFREY R. CAMPBELL

Finally, the first order condition regarding the supply of labor is standard:

$$\kappa = w_t/c_t.$$

3.6. *Competitive Equilibrium*

A competitive equilibrium is a state contingent sequence of asset prices, wage rates, asset holdings, consumption, and labor, such that investment and production firms earn zero profits; the asset holdings, consumption, and labor maximize the consumer's welfare given the equilibrium prices and the consumer's budget constraint; and markets for all assets and labor clear at the given prices and quantities. In general no analytical expression exists for the economy's competitive equilibrium, but its approximate computation is feasible. The first and second welfare theorems apply to the model economy, so the problem of computing a competitive equilibrium can be conveniently recast as solving a social planning problem. The state variables for the social planning problem are $K_t(v_t)$, the productivity density of the economy's plants at the beginning of the period; $X_t(j)$, the total number of developing plants which are j periods old; and z_{t-j} for $j = 0, \ldots, T^i - 1$, the current and lagged values of the index of the leading edge technology. The solution to this problem is a set of decision rules expressing the social planner's choice variables, employment, consumption, investment, and a productivity threshold below which plants are retired, as functions of the current state.

Eliminating all sources of nonstationarity is the first step in solving the problem. First note that improvement in the leading edge technology will shift the peak of the function $K_t(v_t)$ to the right as z_t grows. To remove this nonstationarity which is caused by capital augmenting technological progress, it must first be expressed in labor augmenting form. Because the aggregate production function is Cobb–Douglas in capital and labor, this can be easily done. Written this way, the economy satisfies King, Plosser, and Rebelo's [23] restrictions on preferences and technology which guarantee that the economy has a nonstochastic balanced growth path. Scaling all of the social planner's choice variables but hours worked by the level of labor augmenting technology yields a social planning problem for an equivalent economy which is stationary.

To find an approximate solution to this stationary social planning problem, replace its first order necessary conditions with log-linear approximations around its steady state. Because distribution of productivity across plants is a function rather than a scalar, these approximate first order conditions are *functional* equations. Quadrature approximations, the evaluation of which only requires the function's values at a finite number of points, replace the functional equations.[10] This approximation produces a finite dimensional linear dynamical system. Although its dimension is much greater than that of a standard problem, its solutions can be found by applying standard linear algebraic techniques. The approximate system of equations possesses a continuum of solutions. The unique one which also satisfies the social planning problem's transversality condition is an approximate solution to the scaled economy's social planning problem. Scaling the solution by the level of labor augmenting technology yields the desired approximate solution to the original problem. A computational appendix to this paper, available upon request, describes this solution strategy in greater detail.

4. THE MODEL'S BEHAVIOR

This section studies the behavior of a parameterized version of the model economy. As in Kydland and Prescott [24] many of the model's parameter values match features of the steady state growth path with average quantities of the U.S. economy. Two investigations are undertaken using the parameterized model. The first investigation shows that the model can reproduce Bartelsman and Dhrymes' [4] finding that new plants are little more productive than old plants and Bahk and Gort's [2] observation that a plant's productivity grows with age. The endogenous exit of the economy's least productive plants and the resulting selection bias play important roles in reproducing these observations. The second investigation addresses the model's ability to reproduce the empirical relationships documented in Section 2 between entry, exit, and the business cycle.

4.1. *Parameter Values*

The model's parameters which describe the production technology are α, the elasticity of output with respect to employment; μ_z, the average rate of growth in embodied technology; σ_z, the standard deviation of shocks to embodied technological change; σ_e, the standard deviation of new plants' idiosyncratic productivity draws; σ, the standard deviation of incumbent plants' idiosyncratic productivity innovations; and T^i, the development time for new plants. The parameters characterizing preferences are β, the consumer's subjective discount factor, and κ, her marginal utility of leisure. Because the model's labor and product markets are competitive, the elasticity of output with respect to labor input equals labor's share of output. Accordingly, this parameter is set equal to 2/3, labor's average

[10] See Press et al. [28] for an explanation of quadrature approximation of integrals.

390   JEFFREY R. CAMPBELL

share in the U.S. economy. The model's steady state growth rate of output
equals $((1 - \alpha)/\alpha)\mu_z$. Given a value for α, μ_z is chosen to match this
with the average growth rate of the U.S. economy between 1972 and 1988,
0.34% per quarter. Along the steady state growth path, $\beta^{-1}e^{((1-\alpha)/\alpha)\mu_z}$
equals the risk-free gross interest rate. The rate of time preference is set
to equal $1.03^{-1/4}$, so the annual risk-free rate equals 4.4%. The marginal
utility of leisure is set so that the fraction of the consumer's time endowment spent at work, N_0, equals 0.26.

The remaining parameters govern plant level dynamics. As such, they
have no direct analog in the first moments of the U.S. data. In principle,
values for these parameters can be measured directly from microeconomic
data on establishments; but such an exercise is impractical. Although the
parsimonious model of plant level dynamics lends itself to theoretical
tractability, it abstracts from several important features of establishments'
environments. First, the lumpy nature of individual plants' job creation and
destruction decisions suggests that they face employment adjustment costs,
as in Campbell and Fisher [9]. In this model, a plant's employment can be
costlessly adjusted. Second, disturbances to plant's productivity levels have
transitory as well as permanent components. In this model, all shocks
permanently influence productivity. Third, investment in capital equipment
is ongoing over a plant's lifetime.[11]

With these qualifications in mind, the parameters describing the plants'
environment were set using an alternative strategy. First, consider, σ, the
standard deviation of plants' productivity innovations. In the absence of
evidence regarding the magnitude of permanent innovations to plants'
productivity levels, this model's equilibrium was computed using a range of
values for this parameter from 0.01 to 0.06. For the sake of brevity, this
section only reports the results with $\sigma = 0.03$. The cyclical behavior of
entry and exit is robust to the choice of this parameters over the range
considered. Next, the time to deliver, T^i, was set to five quarters. That is, a
plant becomes operational four quarters after the capital goods used in its
construction are produced or freed from their previous use. Waddell et al.
[31] report average construction times for new plants for most manufacturing industries in the early 1960s. A construction time of about one year
was typical for many of these industries.

Two of the model's remaining parameters—the scrap value of old
plants, η, and the standard deviation of entrant's productivity distribution,
σ_e—are set to match exit rates from the model and the U.S. economies. It
is clear that raising the scrap value increases the return to closing an
unproductive plant and thereby induces more exit. How the entrants'

---

[11] See Doms and Dunne [14] for a comprehensive study of U.S. manufacturing plants'
investment behavior.

productivity distribution determines exit rate is less obvious. Two features of the plant level productivity process make σ_e an important determinant of exit. First, embodied technological progress implies that each cohort of new entrants will be more productive than the previous cohort. Second, plants with the same productivity level but different birth dates are identical. With nothing to offset them, these features will imply that older plants exit more frequently than new entrants. In the U.S. economy, new plants are more likely to exit than their older counterparts. The average exit rate for plants less than one year old is 1.64%, compared to 0.83% for all plants. The addition of substantial idiosyncratic uncertainty surrounding a plant's initial draw of v_t can remedy this problem. If σ_e is much larger than σ, then the probability of a new entrant falling below the exit threshold will be higher than that of an incumbent plant with $v_t = z_t$ doing so. Accordingly, η and σ_e were chosen to match the model's steady state overall exit rate and that for young plants with the average exit rates in the U.S. economy. The choice of a large value for σ_e is justified by Bartelsman and Dhrymes' [14] finding that young plants face substantially more productivity uncertainty than their older counterparts.

The final parameter to be determined is the standard deviation of the innovation to embodied technological progress, σ_z. Because no direct observations of z_t are available with which to measure σ_z, this parameter was chosen so that the standard deviation of the exit rate in the model economy equals that in the data, about 0.26%. With this value, the model then tells us the amount of output and productivity variation attributable to embodied technology shocks under the assumption that such shocks cause all fluctuations in the exit rate. When $\sigma = 0.03$ and η and σ_e are

TABLE II
Baseline Parameter Values

Parameter	Value
β	$1.03^{-1/4}$
μ_z	0.66%
α	2/3
σ	3%
σ_e	36%
η	0.835
σ_z	0.59%
T^i	5
N_0	0.26

392   JEFFREY R. CAMPBELL

chosen as described above, $\sigma_z = 0.59\%$. Table II summarizes the set of parameter values used below.[12]

4.2. *Productivity over the Plant Life Cycle*

Along the model's steady state growth path, the ongoing replacement of old unproductive plants with new leading edge plants causes constant aggregate productivity growth. In a standard vintage capital framework, one consequence of this process is that new plants are, on average, more productive than old plants. Available evidence from plant level data sets contradicts this claim. For example, Bahk and Gort [2] observed that the productivity of new plants rises with both age and experience, measured by accumulated output. They interpret these observations as indicative of learning by doing. Bartelsman and Dhrymes [4] found that the average productivity of new plants is not very different from that of incumbent plants.

Although the model economy of this paper embodies a vintage capital structure, it is also capable of reproducing these observations. The two features of the model which drive these results are substantial idiosyncratic uncertainty at the plant level and the endogenous selection of low productivity plants for exit. Surviving plants tended to receive idiosyncratic productivity shocks which caused them to grow, not decline. Therefore, it is possible to find evidence of learning by doing where none exists, if one focuses attention on a balanced panel of surviving plants. For similar reasons, it is inappropriate to compare the average productivity of old plants with their younger (and untested) counterparts to directly measure the importance of vintage capital.

Figure 7 illustrates the effects of selection bias on the steady state distribution of productivity across plants. It graphs the probability density function of $v_t - z_t$, a plant's idiosyncratic productivity level minus the average productivity of the leading edge technology. Along the steady state growth path, this distribution is constant. By construction, the average of

---

[12]An alternative calibration procedure is to choose μ_z and σ_z to match the mean and variance of the growth rate of the real quality adjusted price of producers' durable equipment. This real price is measured as in Greenwood, Hercowitz, and Krusell [19], with Gordon's [16] price index for producers' durable equipment deflated by the implicit GDP deflator for consumption of nondurable goods and services less housing. The resulting values for μ_z and σ_z are 0.72 and 1.1%. Given these values for μ_z and σ_z, the standard deviation of idiosyncratic productivity innovations, σ, can be chosen to match the exit rate's variance in the model with its empirical value. The resulting value of σ is 6.4%. When η and σ_e are then chosen as described above, the resulting values are 0.86 and 32%. The cyclical behavior of the model with these parameters is little different from that reported below. The most substantial difference is that the standard deviation of output growth substantially increases from 0.39 to 0.48%.

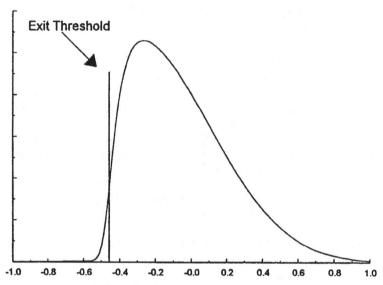

FIG. 7. Steady state distribution of $v_t - z_t$.

$v_t - z_t$ for entering plants is zero. The graph shows that the peak of the productivity distribution is at about -0.2 and that the distribution is skewed to the right because of exit. The exit threshold in the model is -0.46. That is, a plant exits when its productivity is 46% lower than the average implementation of the leading edge technology. The sample selection caused by exit has a significant impact on the average productivity of operational plants relative to the current leading edge, which is -0.05. That is, the average incumbent plant is only about 5% less productive than the average implementation of the leading edge technology. This is in spite of the fact that this leading edge improves at an annual rate of 2.5%.

In addition to impacting aggregate productivity statistics, exit can change observed patterns of plant level productivity dynamics. Consider, for example, the study of learning by doing in plants by Bahk and Gort [2]. Using a panel of plants from the Longitudinal Research Database, these authors measure learning by doing by regressing plant output on inputs and a measure of experience, either accumulated output or age. Although their panel is not balanced, a plant must have survived from its birth until 1986. With this sample, the authors find significant impacts of experience on productivity. A 1% increase in accumulated output, deflated by the average of the plant's last three years' employment to account for cross sectional difference in minimum efficient scale, increases productivity by

394   JEFFREY R. CAMPBELL

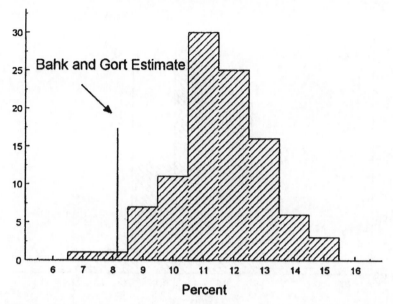

FIG. 8. Histogram of coefficient on accumulated output for simulated productivity
regressions.

7.9%. When experience is measured with age, it increases productivity
1.2% per year.[13]

Figures 8 and 9 plot the histograms of regression coefficients from 100
simulated productivity regressions using data generated from the model's
steady state growth path. For Fig. 8, productivity was regressed against a
constant and the logarithm of accumulated output, deflated by the plants
average employment over the last three years of the sample. For Fig. 9,
productivity was regressed against a constant and plant age. Because the
model generates quarterly data, and Bahk and Gort [2] use annual data,
the simulated coefficients are multiplied by 4 to make them comparable.
Their selection procedure was to use all available data from all plants born
between 1972 and 1983 which survived through 1986. The sample selection
scheme for the simulated regressions approximates this rule. For each
regression, 10 cohorts of 50 plants were simulated. All plants in the first
cohort which survived 13 years were included in the regression sample.
Each succeeding cohort was simulated one less year, and the survivors
were included in the regression sample.

[13] These numbers are taken from Table 1, lines iv and v of Bahk and Gort [2].

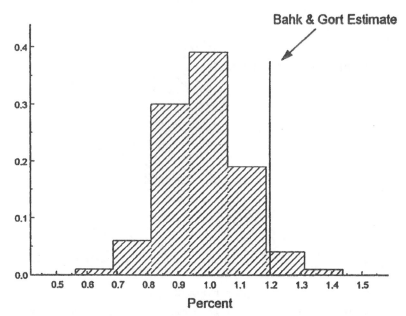

FIG. 9. Histogram of coefficient on plant age for simulated productivity regressions.

Both experiments show that exit can cause average productivity to apparently rise with experience, even if learning by doing does not occur. The coefficient estimates using accumulated output generally exceed Bahk and Gort's [2] estimate. The average regression coefficient is 11.6%, and their standard deviation is 1.5%. Indeed, only 1 coefficient of the 100 is less than 7.9%, the empirical estimate. There also appears to be significant learning by doing when experience is measured with plant age. The average regression coefficient in that case is 1% and their standard deviation is 0.1%. In this case, only two of the simulated coefficients are greater than the empirical value of 1.2%. These simulations fail to match the coefficients estimated by Bahk and Gort [2] exactly, but they produce results of the correct magnitude. Thus, the model economy in which technology is embodied in plants is consistent with the observation that plants' productivity levels tend to rise over time.

4.3. *Responses to Embodied Technology Shocks*

The remainder of this section studies the behavior of the model when the pace of embodied technological change is stochastic. The responses of the model economy to embodied technology shocks reflect the decisions of two kinds of agents: production firms and consumers. First, consider the production firms. Ongoing idiosyncratic uncertainty and exit's irreversibility together impact the exit decisions of firms. This is evident in the steady state exit policy. When an incumbent's productivity is 15% lower than the leading edge, it provides the expected capital services as would the average entrant produced from scrapping the old plant and investing the proceeds. Yet exit does not occur until a plant is 46% less productive than an average entrant. Idiosyncratic uncertainty has driven a considerable wedge between the plant's material scrap value and the exit threshold. Although a plant's productivity may be low today, the option to operate it tomorrow if its fortunes improve is valuable. Accounting for this option value causes a considerable, although rational, delay in exit.

These option value considerations affect the response of the exit threshold to an embodied technology shock. Figure 10 graphs the response of the exit threshold to a 1% improvement in z_t. Because productivity is measured in logarithms, the increase in the exit threshold can be interpreted as a percentage increase. Immediately following an unanticipated 1% increase in z_t, the exit threshold jumps 1.09%. Thereafter, it very slowly declines to its new steady state level 1% higher than before. Although it takes several quarters for the technological improvement to be imple-

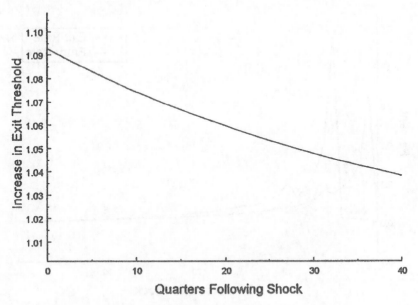

FIG. 10. Response of exit productivity threshold to a 1% increase in z_t.

mented, exit immediately responds to the improvement. The reason is that plants at the bottom of the productivity distribution are only operating because their owners rationally hope that their fortunes will improve. An improvement in z_t lowers the price of capital goods relative to consumption in the long run. This lowers the probability that, if left in place, such a plant's value in operation will ever surpass its scrap value. The option to remain in production becomes less valuable, so these plants exit.

Figure 11 graphs the responses of the entry and exit rates to the embodied technology shock. The responses of the entry and exit rates are expressed in levels, because the rates are already fractions. The jump in the exit threshold causes the following quarter's exit rate to increase by 0.34%. This is a sizeable increase relative to the exit rate's steady state value, 0.83%. The impact of the technology shock on the exit rate is persistent: The exit rate is 0.11% higher three quarters after the shocks. The reinvestment of the scrap capital from exiting plants and an increase in the investment of new capital goods causes the entry rate to rise after five quarters. Five quarters following the improvement, the entry rate jumps 0.48%. The lag is due to the time consuming reallocation of capital. This jump is persistent, being 0.13% above its steady state value eight quarters after the shock.

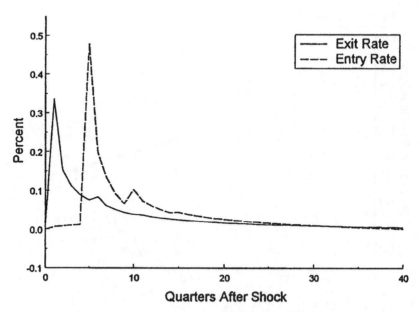

FIG. 11.   Responses of entry and exit rates to a 1% increase in z_t.

398   JEFFREY R. CAMPBELL

The qualitative nature of these responses is robust to the choice of σ, the standard deviation of plants' productivity innovations, but their magnitude declines as σ is increased. With higher values of σ, the quantitative response of the exit threshold to an embodied technology shock is virtually unchanged, but the steady state productivity distribution has more dispersion. The increased dispersion implies that a given percentage increase in the exit threshold affects fewer plants. The calibration of the model with a higher value of σ produces a higher value for the standard deviation of the embodied technology shock because of this reduced response.

The increases of entry and exit following an embodied technology shock cause capital resources to be moved from relatively unproductive plants toward new entrants. This movement affects the economy's production possibilities in two ways. First, the amount of capital which is idle due to reallocation increases. Second, the entrants are more productive than the exiting plants which they replaced. These two effects can be summarized in the behavior of one variable, the economy's effective capital stock. Recall from Section 3.3 that the production possibilities of a single firm can be expressed as a Cobb–Douglas production function of its employment and its effective capital stock. In the model's competitive equilibrium, the production possibilities of the entire production sector are equivalent to those of a single, competitive, representative firm which controls all of the economy's plants. Therefore, a Cobb–Douglas production function in aggregate employment and the aggregate effective capital stock represents the economy's production possibilities:

$$Y_t = N_t^\alpha \overline{K}_t^{1-\alpha},$$

$$\overline{K}_t = \int_{-\infty}^{\infty} K_t(v_t) e^{v_t} \, dv_t.$$

The function $K_t(v_t)$ is as defined in Section 3.6.

This aggregate production function makes clear that the evolution of $\overline{K}_t$ completely summarizes changes in the economy's production possibilities. Furthermore, it also implies that conventionally measured total factor productivity should equal zero if the correct measure of capital input, $\overline{K}_t$, is used in its construction. The actual measure of capital input usually employed in TFP measurement is fixed, reproducible, tangible wealth. This measure is computed as the undepreciated portion of past investment in plant and equipment. Because it does not generally account for quality improvements in capital goods or for idleness due to reallocation, this will be a poor proxy for the economy's effective capital stock. If fixed, reproducible, tangible wealth is employed in standard TFP calculations, then the resulting series will reflect this mismeasurement. Let K_t denote a series for the measured capital stock. Measured TFP is

$$x_t = (1 - \alpha)(\ln \overline{K}_t - \ln K_t).$$

Figure 12 graphs responses of x_t and $\ln \overline{K}_t$ to a 1% increase in z_t. To do so, it computes the response of K_t to the increase by assuming that it is constructed with a perpetual inventory method:

$$K_t = (1 - \delta)K_{t-1} + I_t.$$

The depreciation rate δ is measured as the fraction of the total capital stock lost each period due to exit along the steady state growth path. The investment measure, I_t, is constructed to represent investment in *new* capital goods. It is total investment minus scrap returned from exiting plants.

At the beginning of each period, the effective capital stock available for production is fixed. Therefore, the response of $\overline{K}_t$ to an embodied technology shock is zero in the initial period. As capital goods from exiting plants become idle during reallocation, the effective capital stock declines. Four

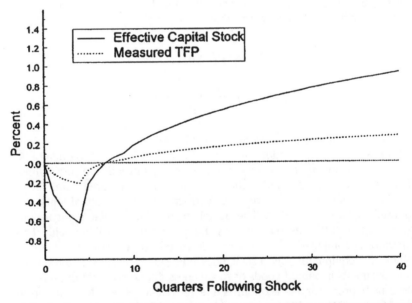

FIG. 12. Responses of effective capital stock and measured TFP to a 1% increase in z_t.

400   JEFFREY R. CAMPBELL

quarters after the shock, it is 0.6% lower. In the fifth period following a shock, it begins to grow as developing plants become operational. In the long run, the shock raises $\overline{K}_t$ by 1.5%. Because the stock of conventionally measured capital is very large relative to the flow of measured investment, it responds very little to the technology shock. This implies that changes in measured TFP largely reflect movements in the stock of effective capital. Because the capital measurement error is multiplied by the elasticity of output with respect to capital, $1/3$, measured TFP moves much less than the effective capital stock.

The responses of the consumer's other choice variables—consumption and employment—are graphed in Fig. 13. Because the technology shock increases the productivity of new plants, it decreases the quality adjusted price of investment goods relative to consumption. As in Barro and King [3] and Greenwood, Hercowitz, and Huffman [18], if the substitution effect of the relative price change outweighs the income effect the consumer will delay gratification by consuming less and working more to increase her investment in physical capital. In the model, the substitution effect dominates, so employment increases 0.45% and consumption falls 0.15% in the period of the shock. Thereafter, consumption steadily rises toward its new steady state value. In contrast, employment immediately falls below its

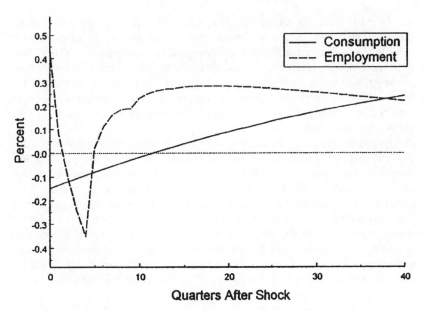

FIG. 13. Responses of consumption and employment to a 1% increase in z_t.

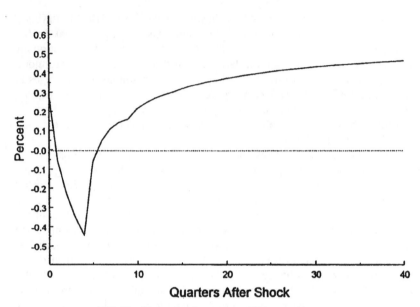

FIG. 14.   Response of output to a 1% increase in z_t.

steady state level. At its trough, four quarters following the technology shock, it is 0.35% below its steady state. This decline in employment reflects the reduced supply of a complementary input, capital. When the first wave of new plants becomes operational, employment immediately increases and overshoots its steady state level. Employment converges to its steady state level very slowly as the economy accumulates effective capital. Ten years after the embodied technology shock, it is still 0.22% above its steady state value.

Aggregate output is just a Cobb–Douglas function of employment and the effective capital stock, so output inherits the expansion–contradiction–expansion pattern which these variables follow after an embodied technology shock. Figure 14 graphs the impulse response of output. The initial boom caused by the increase in labor supply causes output to rise by 0.3%. As its trough, four quarters later, output is 0.45% below its previous steady state value. In the long run, the embodied technology shock raises output by 0.5%. Investment in new capital goods is defined to equal output minus consumption.[14] Consumption's response to the technology shock is very smooth, so investment's response is an amplified version of output's.

---

[14] This is equivalent to the definition given above in the discussion of TFP measurement.

402 JEFFREY R. CAMPBELL

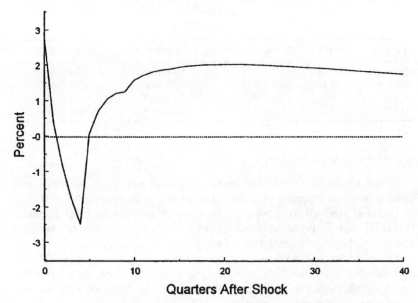

FIG. 15. Response of investment to a 1% increase in z_t.

Figure 15 graphs this response. Like consumption and employment, investment converges to its new steady state level very slowly. Ten years after the shock, it is 1.5% higher than its old steady state. Its long run level is only 0.5% higher.

In summary, two economic decisions profoundly influence the model economy's response to an improvement in embodied technology. These are the consumer's intertemporal substitution of current consumption and leisure for future welfare and the firms' decisions to retire unproductive plants. These responses cause short run fluctuations in output and measured total factor productivity which coincide with increases in plant retirement and replacement. Clearly, this model does not provide a complete theory of the business cycle. The consumer's intertemporal substitution implies that consumption covaries negatively with output and employment in the model, whereas it covaries positively with them in the U.S. economy. Nevertheless, the model provides a framework for understanding how fluctuations in entry and exit and their relationships with the business cycle arise. The analysis now turns to a comparison of the model's observable implications for entry and exit dynamics with those estimated with the U.S. data.

TABLE III
Summary Statistics

Variable	Mean (%)	Std. dev. (%)	U.S. mean (%)	U.S. std. dev. (%)
Entry rate	1.86	0.35	0.62 (0.04)	0.23 (0.04)
Exit rate	0.87	0.26	0.83 (0.06)	0.26 (0.04)
ΔGDP	0.34	0.39	0.34 (0.18)	1.14 (0.14)
ΔTFP	0.22	0.12	0.09 (0.08)	0.84 (0.07)

4.4. *Observable Implications*

In the model economy, the timing of the exit and entry decisions and their impact on output and productivity produce correlations of exit with output and productivity growth which mimic those from the U.S. economy. Table III reports the mean and standard deviation for the output and total factor productivity growth rates and the entry and exit rates from the model economy and analogous statistics from the U.S. economy.[15] All of the statistics from the U.S. economy are measured using data from the same sample period as the entry and exit series. Beside each U.S. statistic is its asymptotic standard error.

By construction, the exit rate's mean and standard deviation are similar in the model and U.S. economies. The mean entry rate in the model economy is much larger than in the U.S. economy, 1.86 versus 0.62%. The intuition for this is simple: In the model employment is increasing in productivity, and only the least productive plants exit. Entrants are more productive than exiting plants on average, and there are more of them. Therefore, entrants' employment must be larger than that of exiting plants. The exact opposite is true in the U.S. economy. Of course, the model abstracts from learning about new technologies through production and therefore may overstate the average size of new entrants. The shocks to the leading edge technology induce significant fluctuations in output growth. The standard deviation of output growth in the model economy is 0.39%, slightly more than one-third of the analogous statistic from the U.S. economy. The standard deviation of total factor productivity growth is 0.12% in the model economy, one-seventh of its value in the U.S. economy.

Figures 16 and 17 plot the dynamic correlations of the entry and exit rates with output growth from the model economy. The entry rate is positively correlated with current and future output growth. The recession

[15] The average exit rate for the model is different from the steady state exit rate because it is calculated as a ratio of levels. Its expected value is $X_0 \exp((\sigma_z^2/2)\sum_{i=0}^{\infty} c_i^2)$, where X_0 is the steady state exit rate and c_i is the ith moving average coefficient of the exit rate's logarithm.

404   JEFFREY R. CAMPBELL

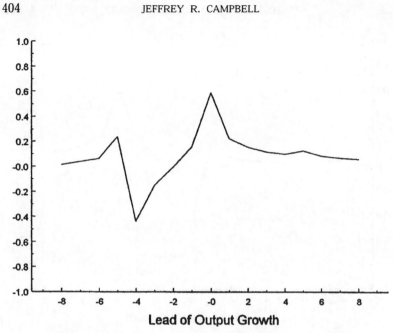

Lead of Output Growth

FIG. 16. Model's dynamic correlations of entry rate with output growth.

immediately following a technology shock generates a large negative
correlation with output growth four quarters earlier. The correlations of
exit with output growth strongly resemble those estimated with the U.S.
data. In particular, exit is strongly positively correlated with future output
growth. It also has a small positive correlation with output growth one
quarter ago. The initial positive labor supply response to a shock generates
this correlation. Figure 18 plots the model's dynamic correlations between
the exit and entry rates. As the impulse response functions suggest, there
is a nearly perfect correlation between the current exit rate and the entry
rate four quarters hence.

Figures 19 and 20 plot the model's dynamic correlations of the entry and
exit rates with measured TFP growth. Unsurprisingly, entry is positively
correlated with current and future TFP growth. As it is with GDP growth,
it is negatively correlated with TFP growth four quarters in the past. The
exit rate has a very strong positive correlation with future TFP growth. The
correlation between exit and TFP growth four quarters hence is 0.75. One
important difference with the U.S. economy is in the contemporaneous
relationship between exit and TFP. The sample correlation is nearly zero
while in the model it is -0.30.

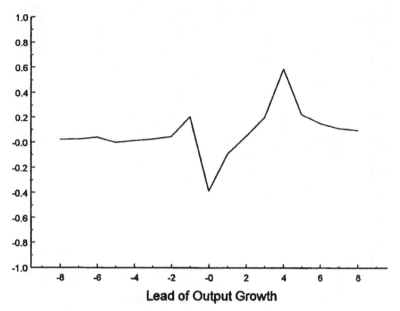

FIG. 17. Model's dynamic correlations of exit rate with output growth.

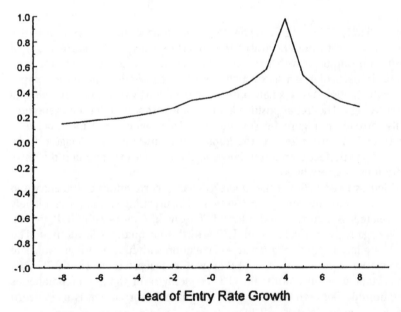

FIG. 18. Model's dynamic correlations of exit rate with entry rate.

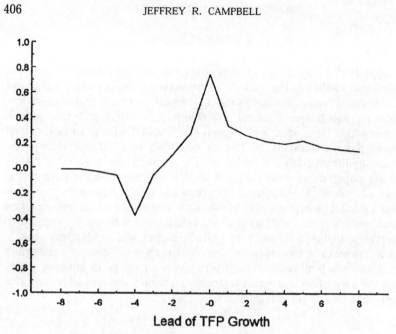

FIG. 19. Model's dynamic correlations of entry rate with TFP growth.

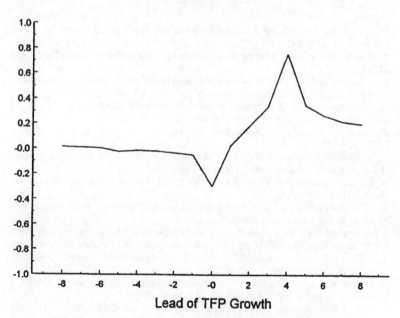

FIG. 20. Model's dynamic correlations of exit rate with TFP growth.

5. CONCLUSION

Models of endogenous capital obsolescence and replacement have been previously applied to the study of business cycles. Cooper and Haltiwanger [11] showed that synchronization of annual machine replacement can generate substantial seasonal movements in output and productivity. Greenwood, Hercowitz, and Krusell [19] showed with a vintage capital model that variation in the rate of embodied technological change can cause significant cyclical fluctuations. The empirical and theoretical results of this paper provide new support for the hypothesis that shocks to the pace of embodied technological progress are a significant source of business cycles. The replacement of old with new machines, as measured by plant entry and exit, exhibits a strong relationship with the business cycle. Increases in the plant exit rate precede output and productivity growth, while increases in the entry rate accompany these. A general equilibrium model in which all technological progress is embodied in entering plants and the pace of such progress is stochastic, mimics the cyclical behavior of entry and exit in the U.S. economy.

REFERENCES

1. A. B. Abel and J. C. Eberly, A unified model of investment under uncertainty, *Amer. Econom. Rev.* **84** (1994), 1369–1384.
2. B.-H. Bahk and M. Gort, Decomposing learning by doing in new plants, *J. Polit. Econ.* **101** (1993), 561–583.
3. R. J. Barro and R. G. King, Time-separable preferences and intertemporal-substitution models of business cycles, *Quart. J. Econom.* **99** (1984), 817–839.
4. E. J. Bartelsman and P. J. Dhrymes, "Productivity Dynamics: U.S. Manufacturing Plants, 1972–1986," working paper, Federal Reserve Board, 1993.
5. R. Boddy and M. Gort, The substitution of capital for capital, *Rev. Econom. Statist.* **53** (1971), 179–188.
6. R. Boddy and M. Gort, Obsolescence, embodiment, and the explanation of productivity change, *Southern Econom. J.* **40** (1974), 553–562.
7. R. J. Caballero and M. L. Hammour, The cleansing effect of recessions, *Amer. Econ. Rev.* **84** (1994), 1279–1292.
8. R. J. Caballero and M. L. Hammour, On the timing and efficiency of creative destruction, *Quart. J. Econom.* **111** (1996), 805–852.
9. J. R. Campbell and J. D. M. Fisher, "Aggregate Employment Fluctuations with Microeconomic Assymetries," working paper 5767, National Bureau of Economic Research, 1996.
10. T. F. Cooley, J. Greenwood, and M. Yorukoglu, The replacement problem, *J. Monetary Econom.* **40** (1997), 457–499.
11. R. Cooper and J. Haltiwanger, The aggregate implications of machine replacement: Theory and evidence, *Amer. Econom. Rev.* **83** (1993), 360–382.
12. S. Davis, J. C. Haltiwanger, and S. Schuh, "Job Creation and Destruction," MIT Press, Cambridge, MA, 1996.

408   JEFFREY R. CAMPBELL

13. D. C. Dobson, W. G. Shepherd, and R. D. Stoner, Strategic capacity preemption: Dupont (1980), *in* "The Antitrust Revolution: The Role of Economics," (J. E. Kwoka, Jr., and L. J. White, Eds.), pp. 157–188, Harper Collins, New York, 1994.

14. M. Doms and T. Dunne, Capital adjustment patterns in manufacturing plants, *Rev. Econom. Dynam.* 1 (1998), 409–429.

15. T. Dunne, "Notes on Corrections Made to PPN's," Data Note Documentation Memorandum 4, Center for Economic Studies, U.S. Bureau of the Census, 1992.

16. Robert J. Gordon, "The Measurement of Durable Goods Prices," Univ. of Chicago Press, Chicago, 1990.

17. M. Gort, B. H. Bahk, and R. A. Wall, Decomposing technical change, *Southern Econom. J.* **60** (1993), 220–234.

18. J. Greenwood, Z. Hercowitz, and G. W. Huffman, Investment, capacity utilization, and the real business cycle, *Amer. Econom. Rev.* **78** (1988), 402–417.

19. J. Greenwood, Z. Hercowitz, and P. Krusell, "The Role of Investment-Specific Technological Change in the Business Cycle," working paper, University of Rochester, 1997.

20. G. D. Hansen, Indivisible labor and the business cycle, *J. Monetary Econom.* **16** (1985), 309–327.

21. H. A. Hopenhayn, Entry, exit and firm dynamics in long run equilibrium, *Econometrica* **101** (1992), 915–938.

22. B. Jovanovic, Selection and the evolution of industry, *Econometrica* **50** (1982), 649–670.

23. R. G. King, C. I. Plosser, and S. T. Rebelo, Production growth, and business cycles I. The basic neoclassical model, *J. Monetary Econom.* **21** (1988), 195–232.

24. F. E. Kydland and E. C. Prescott, Time to build and aggregate fluctuations, *Econometrica* **50** (1982), 1345–1370.

25. W. K. Newey and K. D. West, A simple, positive semidefinite, heteroskedasticity and autocorrelation consistent covariance matrix, *Econometrica* **55** (1987), 195–232.

26. G. S. Olley and A. Pakes, The dynamics of productivity in the telecommunications equipment industry, *Econometrica* **64** (1996), 1263–1297.

27. R. S. Pindyck, Irreversible investment, capacity choice, and the value of the firm, *Amer. Econom. Rev.* **78** (1988), 969–985.

28. W. H. Press, S. A. Teukolsky, W. T. Vetterling, and B. P. Flannery, "Numerical Recipes in C: The Art of Scientific Computing," 2nd ed., Cambridge University Press, Cambridge, U.K., 1992.

29. R. M. Solow, Technical change and the aggregate production function, *Rev. Econom. Statist.* **39** (1957), 312–320.

30. R. M. Solow, Investment and technical progress, *in* "Mathematical Methods in the Social Sciences, 1959," (K. J. Arrow, S. Karlin, and P. Suppes, Eds.), pp. 89–104, Stanford University Press, Stanford, CA, 1960.

31. R. M. Waddell, P. M. Ritz, J. D. Norton, and M. K. Wood, "Capacity Expansion Planning Factors," National Planning Association, Washington, D.C., 1966.

32. M. Yorukoglu, The information technology productivity paradox, *Rev. Econom. Dynam.* **1** (1998), 551–592.

[12]

The dynamics of entrepreneurship: hysteresis, business cycles and government policy

Emilio Congregado, Antonio A. Golpe and Simon Parker

Abstract

This paper estimates an unobserved components model to explore the macro dynamics of entrepreneurship in Spain and the USA. We ask whether entrepreneurship exhibits *hysteresis*, defined as a macro dynamic structure in which cyclical fluctuations have persistent effects on the natural rate of entrepreneurship. We find evidence of hysteresis in Spain, but not the USA, while in both countries business cycle output variations significantly affect future rates of entrepreneurship. The article discusses implications of the findings for the design of entrepreneurship policies.

1. Introduction

As national economies continue to feel the forces of globalization, and large companies proceed with outsourcing and downsizing strategies, efforts to find alternative sources of economic growth are intensifying. For many years, governments around the world have regarded entrepreneurship as a promising candidate in this respect. Growing evidence shows that entrepreneurs create disproportionate numbers of innovations and jobs (Acs and Audretsch, 1990; Audretsch, 2003; Haltiwanger, 2006; Baumol, 2007). Entrepreneurship has also been linked with faster rates of economic growth (Audretsch and Keilbach, 2004, 2007; van Stel, Carree and Thurik, 2005).

Many governments have responded to these forces by devising and implementing portfolios of policies to promote entrepreneurship. These policies include loan guarantee schemes; technology-transfer and innovation programs; employment assistance programs; and subsidized provision of business advice and assistance to small firms (Parker, 2009). Loan guarantee schemes insure banks' loans to entrepreneurs; high rates of business failure mean that these schemes typically run at a loss (Parker, 2009, chapter 16). Innovation policies include direct subsidies to innovators; favorable tax treatment for private sector R&D expenditures; and the provision of seed funds for innovation (Lerner, 1999). Employment assistance programs subsidize welfare recipients to leave the unemployment register by starting new ventures (Bendick and Egan, 1987). Taken together, these interventions often impose sizeable costs on the taxpayer. In the UK at the start of the new millennium, for example, the total cost of small business support amounted to £7.9 billion per annum, or 0.8 per cent of GDP (Storey, 2006).

Given these costs, the lack of robust evidence associating these policies with expanded levels of entrepreneurship is particularly striking. Part of the difficulty of evaluating entrepreneurship policies is that they may have very long-run effects. For example, regional and national data suggest that some entrepreneurship outcomes, especially employment creation and venture growth, can take a decade and more to play out (Fritsch and Mueller, 2008; Carree and Thurik, 2008). These long-run effects are not accurately captured by conventional evaluations, which are usually performed a few years after the policies are implemented, and so capture only short-term impacts (Hart, 2003). An important question therefore concerns the durability of shocks to entrepreneurship, whether these are 'policy' shocks (derived from sudden changes to government policy) or 'economic' shocks (derived from sudden changes to technology, for example).

At the heart of this question is whether entrepreneurship evolves as a trend-stationary or as a non-stationary time-series process. If entrepreneurship is trend-stationary, economic and policy shocks can be regarded as transitory from an aggregate perspective: the rate of entrepreneurship eventually reverts to its underlying, long-run ('natural') rate. Granted, this 'natural rate' might also shift over time; but then one would expect entrepreneurship to be stationary once structural breaks are allowed for. So if the rate of entrepreneurship is trend- (or broken trend-) stationary, entrepreneurship policy shocks will have only temporary effects at the aggregate level. If on the other hand the rate of entrepreneurship is non-stationary, such shocks will have permanent effects.

In a time-series context, hysteresis can be defined and measured in various ways. A popular approach in the empirical literature simply equates hysteresis with the existence of a unit root in a variable (see, Røed 1997, for a survey). An alternative approach proposed by Jaeger and Parkinson (1994) posits a more demanding criterion: hysteresis exists if cyclical changes affect the natural rate of a variable, even as the natural rate follows a unit root process. In which case, temporary shocks have permanent effects while the business cycle does not evolve independently of the natural rate; it then follows that a unit root is a necessary but not a sufficient condition for hysteresis. In this article, we adopt Jaeger and Parkinson's (1994) definition of hysteresis in order to conduct a searching test and to explore whether entrepreneurship exhibits cycles with potentially durable long-run effects.

To test for hysteresis in this way, we follow Jaeger and Parkinson (1994) and decompose entrepreneurship into two unobservable components: a non-stationary 'natural rate' component, and a stationary 'cyclical' component. These components can be estimated by maximum likelihood using the Kalman filter. Although Jaeger and Parkinson's approach has been applied extensively in the literature on unemployment (see Assarson and Janson, 1998; Karamé, 1999; Salemi, 1999; Di Sanzo and Pérez, 2005; Logeay and Tober, 2005), to the best of our knowledge its application to entrepreneurship is novel.

The goal of the present paper is to explore whether aggregate rates of entrepreneurship exhibit persistence or hysteresis. We do so using quarterly time-series data on self-employment rates for Spain and the USA. Different labor market structures and welfare systems mean that conditions for hysteresis might be systematically different in Europe compared with the USA (Di Tella and MacCulloch, 2006; Raurich et al., 2006), so the comparative empirical perspective we take seems to be a natural one. We argue that if entrepreneurship exhibits hysteresis, then entrepreneurship policies might be more powerful than has been thought hitherto, since any increase in entrepreneurship brought about by these policies are incorporated into all future levels of entrepreneurial activity. Furthermore, business cycles would have important effects on the real economy, by impacting on the future trajectory of an economy's natural rate of entrepreneurship.

This article has the following structure. The next section discusses in greater detail theory and evidence about persistence, hysteresis and business cycles in entrepreneurship. The third section describes the data and the estimation methodology. As is common in the literature, entrepreneurship is measured in terms of self-employment rates. Self-employment is an important component of the labor market in many economies. Indeed, in most countries it comprises a larger portion of the workforce than unemployment does (Parker and Robson, 2004). The present inquiry therefore also adds to the labor economics literature on hysteresis, which has focused mainly on unemployment hitherto.[1] The fourth section presents and discusses the results and performs a robustness check on the specification of the model. The final section concludes with a discussion of policy implications and some promising avenues for future research.

2. Persistence, Hysteresis, Business Cycles and Entrepreneurship

Rates of entrepreneurship vary dramatically between countries but exhibit a fairly high degree of temporal stability (Parker and Robson, 2004). Individual-level panel data reveal that the best predictor of someone being self-employed in the next period is whether they are self-employed in the current period (Henley, 2004). This 'state-dependence' property appears to aggregate up to the regional level. For example, Fritsch and Mueller (2007) explain more than one-half of the variance in German regional start-up rates in terms of regional start-up rates from 15 years earlier. The same property also holds at the national level, with several studies being unable to reject the null hypothesis of a unit root in self-employment rates (Parker, 1996; Cowling and Mitchell, 1997; Parker and Robson, 2004; Bruce and Mohsin, 2006).

What might explain these findings? At the individual level, there could be non-pecuniary costs of switching occupation, such as the sudden loss of a pleasant compensating differential, disruption to an accustomed lifestyle, or a stigma from failure (Gromb and Scharfstein, 2002; Landier, 2004). Alternatively, switching costs could be economic in nature involving, for example, lost sector-specific experience, costs of raising start-up capital (if entering entrepreneurship), or re-training costs (if entering paid-employment). Switching costs might also relate to exit barriers caused by incurring sunk costs of capital with limited resale value; prior commitments to customers; or a desire by entrepreneurs to avoid sending an adverse signal of ability by abandoning their ventures (Boot, 1992). In a different vein, Dixit (1989) shows that risk together with sunk costs can give agents an option value of waiting before switching occupation. This reduces the total amount of entry and exit that occurs – as conditions have to become very bad before entrepreneurs close their business and relinquish their sunk costs, or very favorable before they are willing to incur the risk of jeopardizing their assets by entering the market. Risk generates an 'option value' of remaining in the present occupation and deferring a costly switch. Only when average incomes in entrepreneurship reach some upper 'trigger point' will people become entrepreneurs. And they will only leave entrepreneurship in the presence of adjustment costs if incomes drop to some lower trigger point. Between these two trigger points individuals remain in their current occupation (Dixit and Rob, 1994). Dixit and Rob (1994) explicitly refer to this inertia in occupational choice as 'hysteresis'.

At the more aggregated level, theoretical models of multiple entrepreneurship equilibria can explain why ostensibly similar regions and countries exhibit pronounced and enduring differences in entrepreneurship. Thus Landier (2004) studies a model in which serial entrepreneurs possess private information about their abilities which cannot be credibly revealed to banks. High-quality serial entrepreneurship is deterred in economies where the equilibrium cost of capital is high. The cost of capital is high precisely because there is little or no high-quality serial entrepreneurship. But high-quality serial entrepreneurship becomes privately worthwhile in economies where the equilibrium cost of capital is low – which in turn justifies the low cost of capital. Another multiple equilibrium model, by Parker (2005), explains why different geographical areas can possess persistently different rates of entrepreneurship based on self-perpetuating human capital choices within regions which affect payoffs in entrepreneurship and in paid-employment, locking different occupational choice structures into place as stable equilibria.

However, a drawback of these theoretical models is that they are quite stylized. Fundamentally, we lack empirical evidence about whether shocks to entrepreneurship are persistent. As noted in the Introduction, we follow Jaeger and Parkinson (1994) by defining hysteresis as a process in which cyclical shocks affect the 'natural rate' of the variable in question, which evolves as a unit root process. Because the relationship between business cycles and entrepreneurship is also of interest in its own right, the remainder of this section will discuss theoretical perspectives and empirical evidence on entrepreneurship and the business cycle.

In principle, entrepreneurship could evolve either pro- or anti-cyclically, depending on the balance of forces at work in the private sector of the economy. Rampini (2004) proposes a risk-based reason why the number of entrepreneurs is likely to be pro-cyclical. When shocks to the economy are favorable, productivity and wealth in entrepreneurship increase, making agents more willing to bear risk (via decreasing absolute risk aversion) and become entrepreneurs. In addition, anticipating greater returns in favorable states, entrepreneurs also supply higher levels of effort, reducing moral hazard problems and making lenders more willing to fund risky investment projects. When shocks are unfavorable, the opposite process occurs: wealth, investment and entrepreneurship all decline.

A dynamic externality inherent in innovation provides another reason why entrepreneurship and aggregate economic activity might follow similar cycles over time. Radical innovations increase economic activity directly, and frequently indirectly create opportunities for other, subsequent innovations, further increasing opportunities for entrepreneurship and greater economic activity. Because entrepreneurs do not internalize this dynamic externality when making their decisions to innovate and invest, the result is excessive volatility and pro-cyclicality of entrepreneurship, innovation and economic growth (Barlevy, 2007).

These arguments suggest that entrepreneurship is not only pro-cyclical but may also generate and accentuate business cycles. Other theoretical contributions ask whether recessions have a 'cleansing' effect, by removing low-quality enterprises from the market (Caballero and Hammour, 1994). However, because real wages fall in recessions, individuals with relatively low ability have incentives in bad times to enter entrepreneurship and so can *reduce* the average quality of the entrepreneur pool (Ghatak, Morelli and Sjöström, 2007). This might explain the emergence of worker co-operatives and other 'marginal' enterprises in recessions, which dissolve in economic recoveries when conventional employment opportunities become more readily available (Ben-Ner, 1988; Pérotin, 2006). An alternative argument for counter-cyclicality of entrepreneurship relates to monetary policy, since the cost of capital tends to increase in booms and decrease in recessions, inducing exits in the former state and entries in the latter. A problem with this argument though is that aggregate market demand is also higher in booms and lower in recessions, which could dominate changes in the cost of capital in terms of occupational choice. The entrepreneurship literature has referred to these offsetting forces in terms of 'recession push' and 'prosperity pull' effects (Parker, 2009, chapter 4).

The available evidence suggests that venture formation rates and individual transitions into entrepreneurship are higher on average in good economic times and lower on average in bad ones (Audretsch and Acs, 1994; Grant, 1996; Carrasco, 1999). However, this evidence is rather informal in nature. It is based on estimates of the sign of time dummies in individual-level studies of occupational choice rather than being derived from careful analyses of time-series data. It will therefore be interesting to see whether the results obtained in the present paper, derived using a dynamic time-series estimation methodology, bear out these suggestive findings.

Finally, we would argue that previous entrepreneurship research seems to have overlooked an important distinction between different types of entrepreneurs. Entrepreneurs who hire external labor ('employers') belong to a distinct group which could exhibit different cyclical behavior compared with entrepreneurs who work on their own ('own-account entrepreneurs'). Both types of entrepreneur are likely to benefit from higher demand (growth in national income). But employers who run larger ventures and so benefit from economies of scale are likely to gain the most from demand growth (Klepper, 1996). These entrepreneurs can scale up production and expand employment, bidding up wages which draw relatively low-value own-account entrepreneurs out of entrepreneurship and into paid-employment (Lucas, 1978). In which case, one might expect the number of employer entrepreneurs to increase relative to the number of own-account entrepreneurs, making cyclical effects positive for employer entrepreneurs and negative for own-account entrepreneurs. And to the extent that more favorable economic conditions improve opportunities for some own-account entrepreneurs as well, we might expect some own-account entrepreneurs to start hiring labor (Cowling et al., 2004), in which case they switch from own-account to employer status, and reinforce the positive cyclical effects for employers and the negative cyclical effects for the own-account group. Our empirical estimates below will shed light on these conjectures.

3. Data and Methodology

3.1. Data

In common with most previous studies, entrepreneurship in this paper is defined in terms of self-employment, reflecting data availability at the time-series level (Parker, 2009). Our empirical analysis uses quarterly data on non-agricultural self-employment rates, for the USA and Spain. Following previous authors, workers in the agricultural sector are excluded because this sector is structurally different from the rest of the economy. The self-employment rate (S_t) is defined as the share of the workforce that is self-employed in non-agricultural activities. Rates of employer self-employment (E_t) and own-account self-employment (OA_t) are defined as the number of employers and own-account workers respectively, divided by the workforce.

The US self-employment data are seasonally adjusted quarterly observations drawn from the Current Population Survey (CPS, US Bureau of Labor Statistics). The Spanish self-employment data are seasonally adjusted quarterly observations drawn from the Labor Force Survey (EPA, Spanish National Statistics Institute). Owing to data limitations, both samples start in 1987(II) and conclude in 2004(IV). It should be noted at the outset that the self-employed are categorized differently by the American CPS compared with the Spanish EPA – in a way which increases the share of workers classified as self-employed in Spain relative to the USA. In the USA, independent owner-managers and directors of *incorporated* enterprises are classified as employees, while in Spain they are classified as employers. In addition, the Spanish data allow the researcher to distinguish between own-account workers and employers, whereas they cannot be separated in the US case. These differences arise because the Bureau of Labor Statistics (BLS) only partially follows the standards set by the International Labour Organization. In the CPS, individuals are asked: 'Were you employed by government, by a private company, a non-profit organization, or were you self-employed (or working in a family business)?' Persons who respond that they are self-employed are then asked: 'Is this business incorporated?' Persons who respond 'yes' are classified by BLS as wage and salary workers, on the basis that, legally, they are the employees of their own businesses.[2] In the Spanish EPA, workers are asked questions about their main job or business, including 'Were you an employee or self employed?' If self-employed, the respondent was further asked whether they have any employees. Although the Spanish and American self-employment data rest on different definitions, it is still useful to compare results derived from them. The two countries lie at opposite ends of the spectrum in terms of how regulated their labor markets are (Bertola, Boeri and Cazes, 2000), so it will be interesting to see if the structure of entrepreneurship dynamics differs between them.

Finally, real GDP is denoted by Y_t. Data on Spanish real GDP are taken from the Quarterly National Accounts database while data on US GDP are taken from the US Department of Commerce. These data are seasonally adjusted and are expressed in 1995 prices and in billions of chained 2000 US dollars.

3.2. Econometric Methodology

Several macroeconomic studies equate hysteresis in a time series with a unit root process.[3] Others argue that hysteresis arises when changes to the cyclical component of a time-series,

S_t^C, induce permanent changes in the 'natural rate' of the series, S_t^N. This is different to a unit root process. To comprehend the different estimation strategies these approaches call for, decompose the series S_t into the sum of its two (unobservable) components: the non-stationary natural rate component, S_t^N, and the stationary cyclical component, S_t^C:

$$S_t = S_t^N + S_t^C \tag{1}$$

Now define the natural rate component as a random walk plus a term capturing a possible hysteresis effect:

$$S_t^N = S_{t-1}^N + \beta S_{t-1}^C + \varepsilon_t^N \tag{2}$$

where the β coefficient measures, in percentage points, how much the natural rate increases if the economy experiences a cyclical self-employment rate increase of 1 percent. Evidently a unit root in the self-employment rate S_t is a necessary but not sufficient condition for the existence of hysteresis since a unit root could be generated by an accumulation of shocks to the natural rate S_t^N while at the same time $\beta = 0$ (Røed, 1997). In contrast, there is hysteresis if $\beta > 0$.

The specification of the model is completed by writing the cyclical component of the self-employment rate as a stationary second-order autoregressive process:[4]

$$S_t^C = \phi_1 S_{t-1}^C + \phi_2 S_{t-2}^C + \alpha \Delta Y_{t-1} + \varepsilon_t^C \tag{3}$$

augmented with a term, $\alpha \Delta Y_{t-1}$, which relates cyclical self-employment to lagged output growth, where Y_{t-1} is lagged real GDP.[5] This enables the relationship between the business cycle and entrepreneurship to be analyzed. The random shocks ε_t^N and ε_t^C are assumed to be mean-zero draws from the normal distribution with variance-covariance matrix Ω; the state-space form of the model can be written as

$$S_t = \begin{pmatrix} 1 & 1 & 0 \end{pmatrix} \begin{pmatrix} S_t^N \\ S_t^C \\ S_{t-1}^C \end{pmatrix} \tag{4}$$

$$\begin{pmatrix} S_t^N \\ S_t^C \\ S_{t-1}^C \end{pmatrix} = \begin{pmatrix} 1 & \beta & 0 \\ 0 & \phi_1 & \phi_2 \\ 0 & 1 & 0 \end{pmatrix} \begin{pmatrix} S_{t-1}^N \\ S_{t-1}^C \\ S_{t-2}^C \end{pmatrix} + \begin{pmatrix} 0 \\ \alpha \\ 0 \end{pmatrix} \Delta Y_{t-1} + \begin{pmatrix} \varepsilon_t^N \\ \varepsilon_t^C \\ 0 \end{pmatrix} \tag{5}$$

$$\Omega = \begin{pmatrix} \sigma_N^2 & 0 & 0 \\ 0 & \sigma_C^2 & 0 \\ 0 & 0 & 0 \end{pmatrix} \tag{6}$$

To summarize, hysteresis is inferred if the coefficient β is significantly different from zero, whereas pro- or anti-cyclical variation is inferred depending on whether the coefficient α is positive or negative, respectively. The coefficients of the model (4) through (6) are estimated by maximum likelihood using a Kalman filter.

A non-linear version of this model (4) through (6) can also be estimated, to take account of the possibility that entrepreneurship rates respond asymmetrically to the business cycle. For example, positive technology shocks might create valuable opportunities for innovative entrepreneurs which attract entrants into the industry. Yet if negative demand shocks to the broader economy leave innovative sectors unaffected, there may not be a pronounced negative impact on rates of entrepreneurship. More generally, there is a large body of evidence suggesting that macroeconomic time-series exhibit non-linear or asymmetric behavior over various phases of the business cycle.

When we talk about 'positive' or 'negative' shocks, we do so relative to some threshold level of GDP growth, τ (where τ is not necessarily zero). To explore whether asymmetries exist, we estimate a non-linear version of the unobserved components model. Specifically, we replace the state-space equation (5) with the Threshold Auto Regressive (TAR) specification

$$\begin{pmatrix} S_t^N \\ S_t^C \\ S_{t-1}^C \end{pmatrix} = \begin{pmatrix} 1 & \beta & 0 \\ 0 & \phi_1 & \phi_2 \\ 0 & 1 & 0 \end{pmatrix} \begin{pmatrix} S_{t-1}^N \\ S_{t-1}^C \\ S_{t-2}^C \end{pmatrix} + \begin{pmatrix} 0 \\ \alpha^+ \\ 0 \end{pmatrix} I_t^+ \Delta Y_{t-1}^+ + \begin{pmatrix} 0 \\ \alpha^- \\ 0 \end{pmatrix} I_t^- \Delta Y_{t-1}^- + \begin{pmatrix} \varepsilon_t^N \\ \varepsilon_t^C \\ 0 \end{pmatrix} \quad (7)$$

where I_t^+ and I_t^- are the Heaviside indicator functions such that:

$$I_t^+ = \begin{cases} 1 \ if \ \Delta Y_{t-1} \geq \tau \\ 0 \ if \ \Delta Y_{t-1} < \tau \end{cases}$$

$$I_t^- = \begin{cases} 1 \ if \ \Delta Y_{t-1} < \tau \\ 0 \ if \ \Delta Y_{t-1} \geq \tau \end{cases}$$

This model can be estimated via maximum likelihood using the Kalman filter, where α^+ and α^- are among the parameters to be estimated, and τ is obtained by grid search to minimize the residual sum of squares of the autoregressions. In this context a test for asymmetry becomes a test for linearity, i.e. a test for a single regime against the alternative of two regimes. The null hypothesis we are interested in is $H_0 : \alpha^+ = \alpha^-$.

4. Results

This section presents the results in several stages. First, we test what Jaeger and Parkinson (1994) have characterized as a necessary but not sufficient condition for hysteresis, namely the existence of a unit root in the self-employment time-series. Because unit root tests are well-known, our discussion will be deliberately brief. Second, we estimate the linear unobserved components model outlined in the previous section, incorporating a unit root as a maintained hypothesis. This enables hysteresis to be tested directly and the existence of (symmetric) business cycle effects to be examined. The third subsection explores the possibility of asymmetric business cycle effects, by estimating the non-linear TAR unobserved components model. The relaxation of linearity acts as one important robustness check on the results; another is performed in the fourth subsection, where a unit root is no longer imposed on the unobserved components model but instead is tested as a restriction of a free model parameter within a generalized unobserved components model.

4.1. Unit Root Tests

In order to test the hypothesis of non-stationarity, we apply the traditional Augmented Dickey–Fuller (ADF) test and a modified version of the Dickey–Fuller and Phillips–Perron tests proposed by Ng and Perron (2001). This consists of a class of modified tests, $\overline{M}$, with GLS de-trending of the data and use of the modified Akaike information Criteria to select the autoregressive truncation lag. Table 1 reports the results of Ng-Perron tests, $\overline{MZ}_a^{GLS}$ and $\overline{MZ}_t^{GLS}$, originally developed in Stock (1999) with GLS de-trending of the data as proposed by Elliot et al. (1996). In addition, Ng–Perron proposed a similar procedure that corrects the problem associated with the standard Augmented Dickey–Fuller test, $\overline{MSB}^{GLS}$ and $\overline{MPT}^{GLS}$. All test statistics formally examine the unit root null hypothesis against the alternative of stationarity.[6]

Table 1   Unit root tests

Variable	$\overline{MZ}_a^{GLS}$	$\overline{MZ}_t^{GLS}$	$\overline{MSB}^{GLS}$	$\overline{MPT}^{GLS}$	Lag length	ADF	Lag length
Spain							
Self-employment rate	−2.505*	−0.848*	0.339*	8.554*	2	−0.651*	2
Own-account workers rate	0.730*	0.434*	0.594*	27.749*	2	−0.411*	2
Employers rate	0.395*	0.433*	1.096*	72.343*	0	−1.747*	0
US							
Self-employment rate (Non-incorporated)	−2.080*	−0.894*	0.430*	10.650*	0	−1.138*	0
Critical values							
1%	−13.8000	−2.5800	0.17400	1.78000		−3.530	
5%	−8.1000	−1.9800	0.23300	3.17000		−2.905	
10%	−5.7000	−1.6200	0.27500	4.45000		−2.590	

Notes:
Test statistics defined in the text. 'Lag length' refers to the lag length used in the $\overline{M}$ and ADF tests, respectively. The critical values are tabulated in Ng and Perron (2001).
* Rejects null hypothesis at 1% significance level.
** Rejects null hypothesis at 5% significance level.
*** Rejects null hypothesis at 10% significance level.

The results in Table 1 show that the null hypothesis of non-stationarity cannot be rejected for each series, regardless of the test. However, it is well known that structural breaks in time-series can lead to spurious inferences of a unit root. To deal with this possibility, we employ the Zivot and Andrews (1992) minimum *ADF-t(min-t)* procedure. The *min-t* statistics reported in Table 2 show that the null hypothesis of a unit root in the time-series still cannot be rejected for either country. This buttresses our conclusion that a unit root exists in the self-employment rates of both Spain and the USA – and additionally, for each type of self-employment in Spain. As noted above, a unit root is a maintained assumption needed to test for Jaeger and Parkinson's notion of hysteresis. We test this notion of hysteresis now.

Table 2 Unit root tests allowing for structural breaks

Variable	Min-t	Lag length
Spain		
Self-employment rate	−3.882* (1994:4)	2
Own-account workers rate	−3.779* (1991:1)	2
Employers rate	−4.454* (1997:1)	1
US		
Self-employment rate (Non-incorporated)	−4.078* (1997:1)	1
Critical values		
1%	−5.57	
5%	−5.08	
10%	−4.82	

Notes:
Periods corresponding to *min-t* statistics are indicated in parentheses. Critical values for the *min-t* are given by Zivot and Andrews (1992).
Asterisks are as in Table 1.
Min-t statistics are computed using sequential regressions over $1 <$ trend break $< T$ based on the equation $\Delta x_t = \delta_0 + \delta_1 t + \delta_2 DU + \delta_3 DT + \alpha x_{t-1} + \sum_{j=1}^{3} \phi j \Delta x_{t-j} + e_t$, where the dummy variables $DU_t = 1$ and $DT_t = t - TB$ for $t > TB$ and 0 otherwise, and TB denotes the period at which a possible trend break occurs.
Critical values for the *min-t* are given by Zivot and Andrews (1992).

4.2. The Linear Unobserved Component Model

The first two columns of Table 3 present the results of estimating (4) through (6) for aggregate self-employment rates in the USA and Spain, respectively. The parameter β is positive in both countries, but is only statistically significantly different from zero in Spain. This implies that self-employment exhibits hysteresis in Spain. In particular, if the cyclical component of Spanish self-employment increases by 1 percent, the natural rate of Spanish self-employment increases by 0.85 percent. This is a numerically larger effect than Jaeger and Parkinson (1994) detected for Germany, the UK and Canada using unemployment data. Notably, Jaeger and Parkinson did not find evidence of hysteresis for US unemployment, either. It is unclear the extent to which these results reflect greater labor market imperfections and more generous public welfare systems in Europe compared with the USA (Di Tella and MacCulloch, 2006; Raurich et al. 2006).

The effects of hysteresis are illustrated by the plots in Figures 1 and 2. These figures depict, for Spain and the USA, respectively, the self-employment rate and the estimates of the natural rate and the cyclical component. In Spain, where evidence of pronounced hysteresis has been detected, the natural rate component of self-employment follows quite closely the actual self-employment rate. By contrast in the USA the natural rate of self-employment is rather more stable.

Drawing on our earlier conceptual discussion, we explore the Spanish data further by decomposing the aggregate self-employment rate into its two constituent parts, employer (*E*) and own-account (*OA*) self-employment. We do so in order to determine whether hysteresis is being driven by one or both of these elements. We then apply the unobserved components

Table 3   Estimates of the linear unobserved component model

	USA		Spain	
	S	*S*	*E*	*OA*
Natural rate equation				
β	0.430	0.850*	0.560*	1.123*
	(0.335)	(0.286)	(0.214)	(0.228)
Cyclical rate equation				
ϕ_1	0.502	0.367	0.007	0.096
	(0.324)	(0.275)	(0.006)	(0.239)
ϕ_2	−0.130	0.245***	0.002	0.220**
	(0.127)	(0.136)	(0.003)	(0.110)
α	−0.007	−0.013	0.035*	−0.048*
	(0.016)	(0.017)	(0.011)	(0.015)
σ_1	0.000	0.000	0.087*	0.003*
	(0.010)	(0.022)	(0.017)	(0.000)
σ_2	0.103*	0.135*	0.032	0.115*
	(0.010)	(0.012)	(0.034)	(0.015)

Notes:
Standard errors are in parentheses.
Asterisks are as in Table 1.
S, self-employment rate; *E*, employer self-employment; *OA*, own-account self-employment.

model (4) through (6) to each of these two constituent self-employment rates separately. The last two columns of Table 3 report the results. As can be seen, both components of Spanish self-employment exhibit hysteresis separately. Hysteresis seems to be more pronounced for the own-account self-employment rate than for the employer self-employment rate, suggesting that rates of own-account self-employment are especially sensitive to cyclical shocks. Figures 3 and 4 illustrate the findings for each series.

The estimates of α reported in the fourth row of Table 3 suggest that neither the USA nor the Spanish aggregate self-employment series S_t exhibit a significant impact of business cycle variations in output on cyclical self-employment. However, separating out the aggregate self-employment series into its two components of employer and own-account self-employment generates an interesting finding which would otherwise be disguised: α becomes statistically significant, though with opposite signs, for both employers and own-account self-employees. The Spanish employer self-employment rate is pro-cyclical, but the own-account self-employment rate is anti-cyclical. These findings are consistent with our earlier conjectures that the most promising own- account self-employed switch to employer status in good times, while the least promising own-account workers are pulled into paid-employment as the demand for labor expands and employee wages rise.

4.3. Asymmetries

We next check whether our results are robust to the linear specification of the unobserved

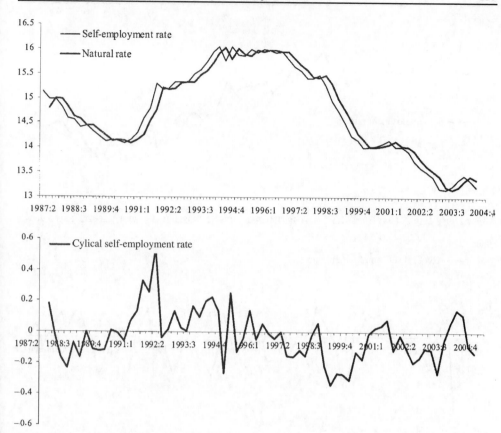

Figure 1   Actual, natural and cylical self-employment rates, Spain

component model. This involves estimating the structure (4), (6) and (7) jointly, to determine whether there is a threshold for income growth which is associated with asymmetric business cycle responses. We wish to check whether the findings in the previous subsection are robust to possible asymmetries, or whether they were merely an artifact of a restrictive technical assumption of linearity.

Table 4 reports the results of estimating the non-linear TAR model. As before, no significant hysteresis is detected in the USA. But in contrast to column 1 of Table 3, where symmetric US business cycle effects were insignificant, column 1 of Table 4 now identifies a significant *asymmetric* US business cycle effect, in which self-employment rates rise in recessions. This is the so-called 'recession push' effect which has been extensively discussed in the entrepreneurship literature (Parker, 2009, chapter 4). The null hypothesis $H_0 : \alpha^* = \alpha^-$ is emphatically rejected: $\chi^2(1) = 10.93$ ($p < 0.01$). This highlights the importance of allowing for asymmetric business cycle effects in the USA.

The evidence for Spain, presented in the remaining columns of Table 4, reveals that hysteresis is still present when the non-linear specification is used, although the β estimates are slightly smaller compared with the corresponding entries in Table 3. Also as in Table 3,

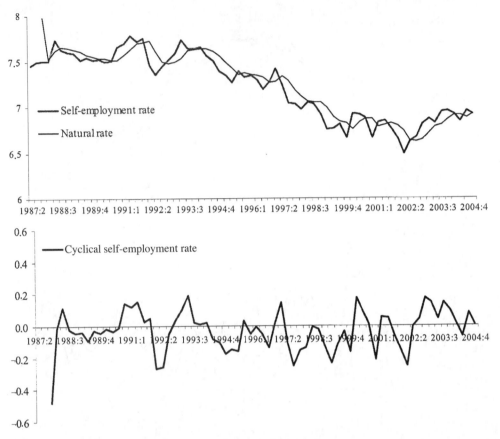

Figure 2   Actual, natural and cyclical self-employment rates, USA

there are no significant business cycle effects for the aggregate self-employment series S_t, although there continue to be positive ones for employers and negative ones for own-account workers. There is little evidence of business cycle asymmetry for either the E or OA series, with $\chi^2(1) = 0.62$ and $\chi^2(1) = 0.38$, respectively. Hence the results for Spain in particular appear to be fairly robust overall.

4.4. Robustness to the Unit Root Restriction

The estimation strategy so far has involved testing for a unit root, and having found one (Section 4.1) imposed it on the structure of the unobserved components model (see e.g. the top left element of the 3×3 matrix in (5)). This assumption can be relaxed in the following 'extended' model, which tests the robustness of the Jaeger and Parkinson (1994) decomposition to the assumed random walk structure of the natural rate, as well as the robustness of the empirical estimates derived above. The space-state form of the linear model is as before, except (5) is now replaced by:

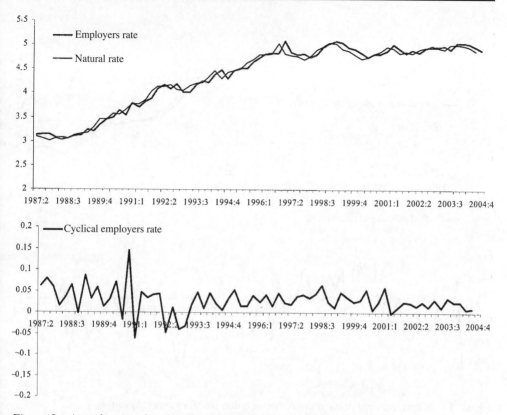

Figure 3   Actual, natural and cyclical employers rates, Spain

$$
\begin{pmatrix} S_t^N \\ S_t^C \\ S_{t-1}^C \end{pmatrix} = \begin{pmatrix} \delta & \beta & 0 \\ 0 & \phi_1 & \phi_2 \\ 0 & 1 & 0 \end{pmatrix} \begin{pmatrix} S_{t-1}^N \\ S_{t-1}^C \\ S_{t-2}^C \end{pmatrix} + \begin{pmatrix} 0 \\ \alpha \\ 0 \end{pmatrix} \Delta Y_{t-1} + \begin{pmatrix} \varepsilon_t^N \\ \varepsilon_t^C \\ 0 \end{pmatrix} \tag{8}
$$

The state space form of the extended non-linear model is analogous and so is suppressed for brevity. Table 5 reports the estimation results for the extended linear model, while Table 6 reports the estimates of the non-linear version of the extended model where separate α^+ and α^- coefficients as well as δ are jointly estimated.

Taking the USA first, the results in column 1 of Table 5 show that the unit root hypothesis can be rejected in the specific context of the unobserved components model ($\delta \neq 1$) – but that pro-cyclicality now becomes statistically significant ($\alpha > 0$). Hysteresis remains insignificant ($\beta \cong 0$). In contrast, the unit root restriction is confirmed in the non-linear specification of the US self-employment rate, with similar results in column 1 of Table 6 to those of column 1 in Table 4.

For Spain, the extended model makes less difference to the results. Estimates of the hysteresis and business cycles parameters β, α and (α^+, α^-) in Tables 5 and 6 are qualitatively similar to those of Tables 3 and 4 where a unit root in the natural rates series was imposed. Indeed, the unit root assumption is not rejected for Spain anywhere in Tables 5 and 6. For

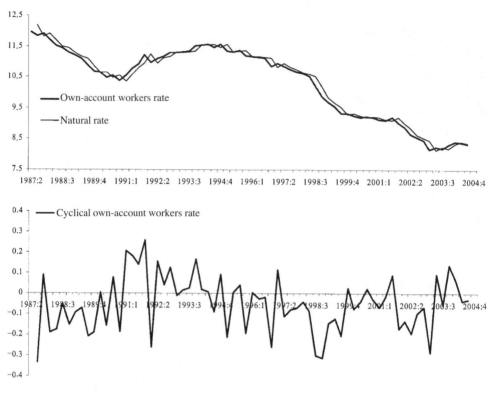

Figure 4   Actual, natural and cyclical own-account workers rates, Spain

Spain, β remains statistically significant while α is again positive and significant for employers and negative and significant for own-account workers. Hence the results for Spain in particular appear to be robust to generalizing the autoregressive structure of the natural rate variable.

5. Conclusions

This paper estimated unobserved components models for the self-employment rate in two developed but otherwise rather different economies: Spain and the United States. Defining hysteresis in terms of the interdependent evolution of a non-stationary natural rate and a stationary cyclical component, thereby distinguishing hysteresis from natural rate shocks, the results provide robust evidence of hysteresis in Spain but not in the USA. This implies that economic and/or policy shocks in Spain have permanent effects on rates of entrepreneurship. In view of the economic importance of entrepreneurship in modern economies, these results suggest that policy-makers need to take particular care when designing pro-entrepreneurship and macroeconomic stabilization policies – especially in Spain. In view of evidence that pro-entrepreneurship policies can have unintended negative as well as positive side-effects on entrepreneurial outcomes (Parker, 2009, chapter 15), the case for public interventions therefore needs to be very compelling, since they can have profound long-run effects. An essential tool

Table 4   Non-linear model estimation results

	USA		Spain	
	S	S	E	OA
Natural rate equation				
β	0.325	0.504***	0.560***	0.919*
	(0.326)	(0.308)	(0.250)	(0.389)
Cyclical rate equation				
ϕ_1	0.441***	0.722*	0.086*	0.308
	(0.326)	(0.258)	(0.012)	(0.354)
ϕ_2	−0.125	0.033	0.032	0.177
	(0.177)	(0.069)	(0.027)	(0.180)
α^+	0.010	−0.008	0.030***	−0.040**
	(0.020)	(0.022)	(0.016)	(0.020)
α^-	0.376*	−0.021	0.047**	−0.058**
	(0.111)	(0.028)	(0.020)	(0.023)
σ_1	0.063**	0.000	0.091*	0.029
	(0.029)	(0.002)	(0.024)	(0.172)
σ_2	0.069**	0.135*	0.021	0.110*
	(0.028)	(0.012)	(0.086)	(0.051)
τ	−0.005	0.012	0.012	0.012

Notes:
The estimates of τ are obtained by grid search methods; no standard error is available for this parameter.
Asterisks are as in Table 1. Abbreviations are as in Table 3.

Table 5   Extended linear model estimation results

	USA		Spain	
	S	S	E	OA
Natural rate equation				
β	0.478	0.840*	0.550***	1.134*
	(0.318)	(0.292)	(0.284)	(0.290)
δ	0.996*	0.999*	1.002*	1.001*
	(0.002)	(0.003)	(0.003)	(0.004)
Cyclical rate equation				
ϕ_1	0.858*	0.372	0.000	0.104
	(0.034)	(0.281)	(0.192)	(0.280)
ϕ_2	−0.930*	0.247***	0.238	0.228
	(0.038)	(0.137)	(0.198)	(0.155)
α	0.053*	−0.008	0.032*	−0.050*
	(0.015)	(0.022)	(0.012)	(0.019)
σ_1	0.093*	0.000	0.091*	0.031
	(0.013)	(0.006)	(0.019)	(0.183)
σ_2	0.000	0.135*	0.019	0.110
	(0.000)	(0.012)	(0.069)	(0.058)

Note: Asterisks are as in Table 1. Abbreviations are as in Table 3.

Table 6   Extended non-linear model estimation results

	USA		Spain	
	S	S	E	OA
Natural rate equation				
δ	0.998*	0.999*	1.002*	1.005*
	(0.246)	(0.003)	(0.003)	(0.004)
Cyclical rate equation				
ϕ_1	0.584**	0.722*	0.001	0.590**
	(0.254)	(0.219)	(0.155)	(0.234)
ϕ_2	−0.156	0.033	0.230	0.035
	(0.179)	(0.083)	(0.187)	(0.080)
α^+	0.019	−0.006	0.031**	−0.040***
	(0.026)	(0.023)	(0.013)	(0.024)
α^-	0.324*	−0.018	0.037***	−0.070*
	(0.123)	(0.031)	(0.021)	(0.026)
σ_1	0.068*	0.000	0.091*	0.097*
	(0.019)	(0.001)	(0.020)	(0.010)
σ_2	0.058*	0.135*	0.021	0.050
	(0.019)	(0.012)	(0.066)	(0.029)
τ	−0.005	0.012	0.012	0.012

Note: Asterisks are as in Table 1. Abbreviations are as in Table 3.

policy-makers need to make informed judgments in this regard is detailed policy evaluations. Our results argue for the use of much longer time horizons in formal evaluation exercises than the few years which are commonly used to gauge entrepreneurship policy impacts.

Our results also shed new light on the important but somewhat neglected issue of business cycle effects on entrepreneurship. Although we found some evidence of pro-cyclicality of entrepreneurship rates in Spain, deeper analysis showed that one should distinguish between own-account and employer components of self-employment. Employers comprise the minority of the self-employed in most countries, including Spain; but they are usually associated with greater economic value-added (Cowling et al., 2004). We found that in Spain employer self-employment rates evolve pro-cyclically whereas own-account self-employment rates evolve counter-cyclically. Therefore the quality as well as the quantity of entrepreneurship in Spain appears to evolve in a pro-cyclical manner. Consequently, effective counter-recessionary economic policies at the macro level become essential for governments wishing to encourage high quality entrepreneurship in order to stimulate employment and innovation. This is of course a highly topical policy issue at the time of writing, when the world economy is in a recession and governments across the globe are looking at entrepreneurship as a creative response to the unfavorable economic conditions.

In contrast to Spain, our results based on US data point to weak or non-existent hysteresis and business cycle effects in entrepreneurship. This might reflect the different nature of institutional and economic conditions in the USA compared with Spain. However, we cannot rule out the possibility that it might simply reflect data limitations, as the aggregate self-employment rate is defined more restrictively by the US statistical authorities. Further research is needed to determine whether it is different national and institutional conditions, or merely different data definitions, which explain the diverse findings. Future work might fruitfully apply the methodology used in this article to a broader range of countries, and should also seek to lengthen the length of the data series that are utilized. A 'micro' look at the causal processes underlying entrepreneurial dynamics would be another natural extension of this paper, complementing our 'macro' analysis of entrepreneurial dynamics. In the context of policy analysis, the impact of particular regulations or macro policies on entrepreneurial entry and longevity could be explored in detail, either within a case study or natural experiment framework. That might help unlock the deep causes of hysteresis and business cycle effects, which were detected in this article, but which deserve much more detailed micro-level analysis to bridge the micro-macro divide.

Notes

* Any opinions expressed here are those of the author(s) and not those of IZA. Research published in this series may include views on policy, but the institute itself takes no institutional policy positions.

    The Institute for the Study of Labor (IZA) in Bonn is a local and virtual international research center and a place of communication between science, politics and business. IZA is an independent nonprofit organization supported by Deutsche Post Foundation. The center is associated with the University of Bonn and offers a stimulating research environment through its international network, workshops and conferences, data service, project support, research visits and doctoral program. IZA engages in (i) original and internationally competitive research in all fields of labor economics, (ii) development of policy concepts, and (iii) dissemination of research results and concepts to the interested public.

    IZA Discussion Papers often represent preliminary work and are circulated to encourage discussion. Citation of such a paper should account for its provisional character. A revised version may be available directly from the author.

1. A different strand of literature explores hysteresis in the realm of international trade and industrial structure: see Franz (1990), Dannenbaum (1998) and Campa (2004).
2. For a detailed explanation of self-employment measurement in the CPS, see Bregger (1996), Manser and Picot (1999), Karoly and Zissmopoulos (2004) or Hypple (2004).
3. See Blanchard and Summers (1986). Layard et al. (1991) popularized the term 'pure' hysteresis for describing the presence of a unit root in time-series.
4. We find that AR(2) processes for the cyclical component fit the data well for all time-series considered. Detailed specification test results are available from the authors on request.
5. Alternative estimates obtained by using unemployment rates instead of real GDP generated similar results and are available on request.
6. Other unit root tests allow for the possibility of non-linear behavior: see Papell et al. (2000), León-Ledesma and McAdams (2004), Camarero and Tamarit (2004) and Camarero et al. (2006, 2008).

References

Acs, Z.J. and Audretsch, D.B. (1990), *Innovation and Small Firms*, MIT Press, Cambridge MA.

Assarson, B. and Janson, P. (1998), 'Unemployment persistence: the case of Sweden', *Applied Economic Letters*, **5** (1), 25–9.

Audretsch, D.B. (2003), 'Entrepreneurship policy and the strategic management of places', in D.M. Hart (ed.), *The Emergence of Entrepreneurship Policy*, Cambridge University Press, Cambridge, 20–38.

Audretsch, D. B. and Acs, Z.J. (1994), 'New firm start-ups, technology and macroeconomics fluctuations', *Small Business Economics*, **6**, 439–49.

Audretsch, D.B. and Keilbach, M. (2004), 'Entrepreneurship capital and economic performance', *Regional Studies*, **38**, 949–59.

Audretsch, D.B. and Keilbach, M. (2007), 'The theory of knowledge spillover entrepreneurship', *Journal of Management Studies*, **44**, 1242–54.

Barlevy, G. (2007), 'On the cyclicality of research and development', *American Economic Review*, **97**, 1131–64.

Baumol, W.J. (2007), 'Small firms: why market-driven innovation can't get along without them', Paper presented at IFN Conference, Stockholm, September.

Ben-Ner, A. (1988), 'The life-cycle of worker-owned firms in market economies: a theoretical analysis', *Journal of Economic Behavior and Organization*, **10**, 287–313.

Bendick, M. and Egan, M.L. (1987), 'Transfer payment diversion for small business development: British and French experience', *Industrial and Labor Relations Review*, **40**, pp. 528–42.

Bertola, G., Boeri, T. and Cazes, S. (2000), 'Employment protection in industrialized countries: The case for new indicators', *International Labor Review*, **139** (1), 57–72.

Blanchard, O.J. and Summers, L.H. (1986), 'Hysteresis and the European unemployment problem', *NBER Macroeconomics Annual*, **1**, 15–78.

Boot, A. (1992), 'Why hang on to losers? Divestitures and takeovers', *Journal of Finance*, **47** (4), 1401–23.

Bregger, J.E. (1996), 'Measuring self-employment in the United States', *Monthly Labor Review*, **119**, 3–9.

Bruce, D. and Mohsin, M. (2006), 'Tax policy and entrepreneurship: new time series evidence', *Small Business Economics*, **26**, 409–25.

Caballero, R.J. and Hammour, M.L. (1994), 'The cleansing effect of recessions', *American Economic Review*, **84**, 1350–68.

Camarero M. and Tamarit, C. (2004), 'Hysteresis vs. natural rate of unemployment: new evidence for OECD countries', *Economics Letters*, **84**, 413–17.

Camarero M., Carrion-I-Silvestre, J.L. and Tamarit, C. (2006), 'Testing for hysteresis in unemployment in OECD countries: new evidence using stationarity panel tests with breaks', *Oxford Bulletin of Economics and Statistics*, **68**, 167–82.

Camarero M., Carrion-I-Silvestre, J.L. and Tamarit, C. (2008), 'Unemployment hysteresis in transition countries: evidence using stationarity panel tests with breaks', *Review of Development Economics*, **12**, 620–35.

Campa, J.M. (2004), 'Exchange rates and trade: how important is hysteresis in trade?', *European Economic Review*, **48**, 527–48.

Carrasco, R. (1999), 'Transitions to and from self-employment in Spain: an empirical analysis', *Oxford Bulletin of Economics and Statistics*, **61**, 315–41.

Carree, M. and Thurik, A.R. (2008), 'The lag structure of the impact of business ownership on economic performance in OECD countries', *Small Business Economics*, **30**, 101–10.

Cowling, M. and Mitchell, P. (1997), 'The evolution of UK self-employment: a study of government policy and the role of the macroeconomy', *Manchester School*, **65**, 427–42.

Cowling, M., Mitchell, P. and Taylor, M. (2004), 'Job creators', *Manchester School*, **72**, 601–17.

Dannenbaum, J. (1998), 'Hysteresis in foreign trade – a new empirical approach', *Jahrbücher für Nationalökonomie und Statistik*, **217**, 589–612.

Di Sanzo, S. and Pérez, A. (2005), 'Unemployment and hysteresis: a nonlinear unobserved components approach', *IVIE Working Papers*, WP-AD 2005-34.

Di Tella, R. and MacCulloch, R. (2006), 'Europe versus America: institutional hysteresis in a simple normative model', *Journal of Public Economics*, **90**, 2161–86.

Dixit, A. (1989), 'Entry and exit decisions under uncertainty', *Journal of Political Economy*, **97**, 620–38.

Dixit, A. and Rob, R. (1994), 'Switching costs and sectoral adjustments in general equilibrium with uninsured risk', *Journal of Economic Theory*, **62**, 48–69.

Elliott, U., Rothenberg, T.J. and Stock, J.H. (1996), 'Efficient tests for an autoregressive unit root', *Econometrica*, **64**, 813–36.

Franz, W. (ed.) (1990), *Hysteresis Effects in Economic Models*, Physica-Verlag, Heidelberg.

Fritsch, M. and Mueller, P. (2007), 'The persistence of regional new business formation-activity over time – assessing the potential of policy promotion programs', *Journal of Evolutionary Economics*, **17**, 299–315.

Fritsch, M. and Mueller, P. (2008), 'The effect of new business formation on regional development over time: the case of Germany', *Small Business Economics*, **30**, 15–29.

Ghatak, M., Morelli, M. and Sjöström, T. (2007), 'Entrepreneurial income, occupational choice, and trickle up policies', *Journal of Economic Theory*, **137**, 27–48.

Grant, D. (1996), 'The political economy of new business formation across the American states, 1970–1985', *Social Science Quarterly*, **77**, 28–42.

Gromb, D. and Scharfstein, D. (2002), 'Entrepreneurship in equilibrium', *NBER Working Paper 9001*, NBER, Cambridge MA.

Haltiwanger, J. (2006), 'Entrepreneurship and job growth', in D.B. Audretsch, R. Strom and Z. Acs (eds.), *Entrepreneurship, Growth and Public Policy*, Cambridge University Press, Cambridge.

Hart, D.M. (ed.) (2003), *The Emergence of Entrepreneurship Policy*, Cambridge University Press, Cambridge.

Henley, A. (2004), 'Self-employment status: the role of state dependence and initial circumstances', *Small Business Economics*, **22**, 67–82.

Hypple, S. (2004) 'Self-employment in the United States: an update', *Monthly Labor Review*, January/February, 24–47.

Jaeger, A. and Parkinson, M. (1994), 'Some evidence on hysteresis in unemployment rates', *European Economic Review*, **38**, 329–42.

Karamé, F. (1999), 'Unemployment persistence: the hysteresis assumption revisited'. Mimeo. EUREQua.

Karoly L.A. and Zissmopoulos, J. (2004), 'Self-employment trends and patterns among older U.S. workers', *Monthly Labor Review*, 24–47.

Klepper, S. (1996), 'Entry, exit, growth and innovation over the product life cycle', *American Economic Review*, **86**, 562–83.

Landier, A. (2004), 'Entrepreneurship and the stigma of failure', Mimeo, Stern School of Business, New York University.

Layard, R., Nickell, S. and Jackman, R. (1991), *Unemployment, Macroeconomic Performance and the Labor Market*, Oxford University Press, Oxford.

León-Ledesma, M. and McAdam, P. (2004) 'Unemployment, hysteresis and transition', *Scottish Journal of Political Economy*, **51**, 1–24.

Lerner, J. (1999), 'The government as venture-capitalist: the long-run impact of the SBIR program', *Journal of Business*, **72**, 285–318.

Logeay, C. and Tober, S. (2005), 'Hysteresis and Nairu in the Euro Area', IMK, Germany, WP 4/2005.

Lucas, R.E. (1978), 'On the size distribution of business firms', *Bell Journal of Economics*, **9**, 508–23.

Manser, M.E. and Picot, G. (1999), 'The role of self-employment in U.S. and Canadian job growth', *Monthly Labor Review*, April, 1999, 10–25.

Ng, S. and Perron, P. (2001), 'Lag length selection and the construction of unit root tests with good size and power', *Econometrica*, **69**, 1529–54.

Papell, D., Murray, C. and Ghiblawi, H. (2000), 'The structure of unemployment', *Review of Economics and Statistics*, **82**, 309–15.

Parker, S.C. (1996), 'A time series model of self-employment under uncertainty', *Economica*, **63**, 459–75.

Parker, S.C. (2005), 'Explaining regional variations in entrepreneurship as multiple occupational equilibria', *Journal of Regional Science*, **45**, 829–50.

Parker, S.C. (2009), *The Economics of Entrepreneurship*, Cambridge University Press, Cambridge.

Parker, S.C. and Robson, M.T. (2004), 'Explaining international variations in self-employment: evidence from a panel of OECD countries', *Southern Economic Journal*, **71**, 287–301.

Pérotin, V. (2006), 'Entry, exit and the business cycle: are cooperatives different?', *Journal of Comparative Economics*, **34**, 295–316.

Rampini, A.A. (2004), 'Entrepreneurial activity, risk and the business cycle', *Journal of Monetary Economics*, **51**, 555–73.

Raurich, X., Sala, H. and Sorolla, V. (2006), 'Unemployment, growth, and fiscal policy: new insights on the hysteresis hypothesis', *Macroeconomic Dynamics*, **10**, 285–316.

Røed, K. (1996), 'Unemployment hysteresis – macro evidence from 16 OECD countries', *Empirical Economics*, **21**, 589–600.

Røed, K. (1997), 'Hysteresis in unemployment', *Journal of Economic Surveys*, **11**, 389–418.

Røed, K. (2002), 'Unemployment hysteresis and the natural rate of vacancies', *Empirical Economics*, **27**, 687–704.

Salemi, M.K. (1999), 'Estimating the natural rate of unemployment and testing the natural rate hypothesis', *Journal of Applied Econometrics*, **14** (1), 1–25.

Stel, A. van, Carree, M. and Thurik, A.R. (2005), 'The effect of entrepreneurial activity on national economic growth', *Small Business Economics*, **24**, 311–21.

Stock, J.H. (1999), 'A class of tests for intregration and cointegration', in R.F. Engle and H. White (eds), *Cointegration, causality and forecasting. A festschrift in honour Clive W.J. Granger*, Oxford University Press, Oxford, 135–67.

Storey, D.J. (2006), 'Evaluating SME policies and programmes: Technical and political dimensions', in M. Casson, B. Yeung, A. Basu and N. Wadeson (eds), *The Oxford Handbook of Entrepreneurship*, Oxford University Press, Oxford, 248–78.

Zivot, E. and Andrews, D.W.K. (1992), 'Further evidence on the great crash, the oil-price shock and the unit root hypothesis', *Journal of Business and Economics Statistics*, **10**, 251–70.

[13]

[13]

Available online at www.sciencedirect.com

SCIENCE ⓓ DIRECT®

ELSEVIER

Journal of Comparative Economics 34 (2006) 295–316

Journal of
COMPARATIVE
ECONOMICS

www.elsevier.com/locate/jce

Entry, exit, and the business cycle:
Are cooperatives different?

Virginie Pérotin

Leeds University Business School, Maurice Keyworth Building, The University of Leeds, Leeds, LS2 9JT, UK

Received 1 September 2004; revised 25 March 2006

Available online 6 May 2006

Pérotin, Virginie—Entry, exit, and the business cycle: Are cooperatives different?

The paper revisits the question of why there are so few labor-managed firms in capitalist economies. Using new data on France, we present a comparative empirical examination of entry and exit among worker cooperatives and conventional firms. We estimate identical equations explaining annual entry and exit flows for the two groups of firms and test for the equality of the coefficients estimated. We find that cooperative creations are more countercyclical, but the effect of the business cycle on exit is the same for both groups of firms. Other factors influencing entry include organizational density and suggest that support structures are important for cooperative entrepreneurship. *Journal of Comparative Economics* **34** (2) (2006) 295–316. Leeds University Business School, Maurice Keyworth Building, The University of Leeds, Leeds, LS2 9JT, UK.
© 2006 Association for Comparative Economic Studies. Published by Elsevier Inc. All rights reserved.

JEL classification: P5; P12; P13

Keywords: Labor-managed firms; Cooperatives; Entry; Exit

1. Introduction

A traditional explanation for the small number of labor-managed firms in capitalist economies is that structural weaknesses cause such firms to disappear, and the theoretical literature has been dominated by models explaining exit, e.g., Vanek (1977) and Ben-Ner (1984). However, the evidence available from Ben-Ner (1988a), Staber (1989) and Pérotin (2004) suggests that

E-mail address: v.perotin@lubs.leeds.ac.uk.

296   *V. Pérotin / Journal of Comparative Economics 34 (2006) 295–316*

labor-managed firms survive rather better than conventional firms (Bonin et al., 1993). Another possibility is that too few labor-managed firms are created, and a small number of studies have looked at entry, including Conte and Jones (1991), Staber (1993), and Russell (1995). This paper takes up the issue again by examining the determinants of both entry and exit among worker cooperatives and conventional firms in France. In particular, we investigate whether differences between the two groups of firms are more marked in relation to entry or to exit. Until now, empirical analyses of entry or exit of labor-managed firms have relied on comparisons of mean creation and hazard rates with conventional firms' or on analyses of worker cooperatives alone. The paper uses new data on aggregate entry and exit flows for both conventional and cooperative firms. The available series are short, but they allow us to conduct multivariate analyses of both entry and exit for both types of firms over the same period.

The French cooperative movement is a particularly well-suited case for looking at these issues. The movement has had a continuous presence since its inception in the mid-19th century and individual worker cooperatives (*sociétés coopératives de production* or SCOPs) often show remarkable longevity. The oldest SCOP currently trading was created in 1882 and 16 of today's SCOPs were created before World War I. This record may be due to the fact that SCOPs, like Italian and Spanish cooperatives, are immune to the main exit processes identified in the theoretical literature, namely, self-extinction by underinvestment and degeneration to the capitalist form, as discussed in Pérotin (1999). Yet SCOPs represent a minute proportion of all French firms, with about 1700 firms employing around 36,000 people out of a total of some 2.5 million firms in France. Problems with firm creation, rather than dissolution, may explain the limited incidence of labor-managed firms even in countries where issues of structural viability have been resolved.

An influential model proposed by Ben-Ner (1988b) suggests that labor-managed firms are created primarily in recessions and exit in recoveries, when membership in an employee-owned firm no longer provides greater benefits than conventional employment. The idea that labor-managed firm creation is countercyclical is supported by empirical evidence on worker cooperative creations in Israel and in the US, as Russell and Hanneman (1992), Russell (1995) and Conte and Jones (1991) report, although not by the evidence for Atlantic Canada provided by Staber (1993). Less empirical evidence is available on cooperative exit, which was found to be related ambiguously to the business cycle by Russell and Hanneman (1992) and unrelated to recessions by Staber (1989). However, ambiguous relationships between entry, exit and business cycle variables have also been observed for conventional firms in several countries, as Reynolds and Storey (1993) discuss. Key issues therefore are to what extent cooperative and conventional entry and exit are counter-cyclical and whether the effect of the cycle is the same for both groups.

Over the last two decades, annual exit rates among SCOPs have been comparable to those of conventional French firms, with an average 10% of cooperatives and 11% of conventional firms exiting annually from 1979 to 2002.[1] Entry rates show less convergence, with an average annual rate of 15% for SCOPs and 12% for conventional firms over the same period. Cooperative flows have also been less stable than conventional ones, especially for entry, which varies between 7 and 35% for SCOPs over the period compared with 10 and 14% for conventional firms. For exit, the corresponding ranges are 5 to 18% for cooperatives and 9 to 15% for conventional firms. Historically, SCOP creations seem to have occurred in waves. Several creation waves coincided with periods of social unrest and political change, i.e., the 1830 and 1848 revolutions, the Paris

---

[1] These are the author's computations based on CG-SCOP (1983–2004) Cordellier (2000), and INSEE (1990, 1999–2005a).

V. Pérotin / Journal of Comparative Economics 34 (2006) 295–316 297

Commune, strikes in 1893–1894 and 1905–1906, the Popular Front government in 1936, and the late 1960s, in addition to the end of each of the two World Wars. However, similar phenomena may affect conventional firms, for which waves of entry follow the end of a large disequilibrium situation, such as the end of World War II in the US, according to Caves (1998).

Immediate connections with the business cycle are difficult to establish from what is known of the historical record. The waves of cooperative creation did not generally happen during recessions in France. High formation phases took place during growth periods in the late 1860s, the mid-1890s and post-World War II, before recessions in 1848, from 1867 to 1870 and from 1968 to 1971, and immediately after recessions in the mid-1890s and from 1905 to 1910.[2] Not much is known about historical patterns of cooperative exit in France beyond the fact that a wave of closures seems to have followed each creation wave. Looking at the recent decades, for which we have data on a continuous period including at least one creation wave in the late 1970s and early 1980s, allows us to examine the respective roles of business cycle and other factors in cooperative entry and to analyze the extent to which any business cycle effects are mirrored in the determinants of cooperative exit.

In order to compare the determinants of entry and exit among cooperatives and conventional firms, we estimate identical equations explaining annual numbers of entering and exiting firms by business cycle and other factors for each group of firms and test for the equality of the coefficients estimated for the two groups. While more than thirty years of recent data are available on SCOP creations and closures, only two decades are available for conventional firms. For both entry and exit, the empirical analysis therefore proceeds in two steps. First, we examine the determinants of cooperative flows on the longer period. Then, we use the shorter series to compare and test for differences in the determinants of cooperative and conventional firm flows.

The theory concerning entry is discussed in the next section. The data and the estimation procedures are presented in section three. Section 4 discusses the results regarding entry. Section 5 covers both the theory and the specification regarding exit; the corresponding results are presented in Section 6. The results are summarized and policy implications are drawn in the concluding section.

2. The theory of firm creation

The standard theory of entry and entrepreneurship suggests that cooperative entry is determined partly by the same set of factors as conventional entry. Additional hypotheses contrast the expected effects of the business cycle on the two types of entry or, in other cases, apply to cooperatives only, with no expected relevance to conventional entry.

Conventional entry, whether by newly-created firms or by existing firms entering new markets, is usually modeled as a function of the difference between the profit expected following entry, which depends on risk, and costs related to entry barriers (Geroski, 1995). In the entrepreneurship literature, this net profit becomes an argument in the utility function of the would-be entrepreneur. When considering whether to create a new firm, i.e., becoming self-employed, or to seek employment with an existing firm, the individual entrepreneur bases the choice on income (Audretsch, 1995). Expected income from creating a firm depends on the risk of bankruptcy and wealth loss to the individual entrepreneur, among other factors. Expected income from wage employment depends on unemployment risk and on the return on alternative investment if the

---

[2] Lévy-Leboyer and Bourguignon (1990) provide extensive information on French growth in the 19th century.

298   *V. Pérotin / Journal of Comparative Economics 34 (2006) 295–316*

entrepreneur has some wealth. The utility optimization framework can also be used to take into account non-pecuniary factors, such as a preference for independence as in Burke et al. (2000) and risk aversion as in Cressy (2000).

Conventional entry is expected to depend positively on incumbent firms' expected profit and on demand growth, which increases expected profit as in, e.g., Dunne et al. (2005). It should depend negatively on the presence of entry barriers and on long-term real interest rates. Entry may also have a positive or negative relationship with unemployment, which increases the pool of potential entrepreneurs by lowering the opportunity cost of entrepreneurship but also lowers their wealth and increases their aversion to risk and credit barriers to entry, as Cressy (2000) discusses. Industry-level barriers to entry are not relevant here because our investigation uses aggregate data.

The determinants of aggregate conventional entry can be summarized in functional form as $Entry = E(\pi, g, u, r)$, where π is the expected profit for incumbent firms, g is demand growth, u is unemployment and r is the long-term real interest rate.

Existing studies often find growth to have a significant impact on entry using industry, regional, or aggregate data (Reynolds and Storey, 1993) but the effect is not always positive, especially at the aggregate level as in, e.g., Highfield and Smiley (1987). Unemployment has been found to have a positive and significant effect on firm creation using French data but the results for other countries are mixed, as Audretsch (1995), Reynolds and Storey (1993), and Hamilton (1985) report.

The hypotheses concerning cooperative entry, to which we now turn, involve different degrees of risk aversion and tastes for non-pecuniary rewards among the relevant potential entrepreneurs, as well as higher overall entry barriers.

For a given membership size, cooperatives may be created for the same reasons as conventional firms. However, as Ben-Ner (1987) points out, an entrepreneur may not want to share the expected profit from a firm creation idea, as would be the case in a cooperative. Choosing the cooperative form implies splitting profit and power with present and future cooperative members and, in the case of SCOPs, also sharing profit with all future employees having more than six months employment with the company.

Many conventional entrepreneurs actually share profit and power with individuals or institutions whose contribution they need. For example, entrepreneurs that need finance or a client base in a particular market or an essential skill they lack enter into partnerships with providers of capital and other inputs. Not having access to the capital market or to cheap bank finance, cooperative founders may need each other for funding and collateral, as suggested by Walras (1865). Other cases may include pre-constituted groups, as in the case of worker buyouts, or individuals with skills appropriate for an industrial setting who value independence, or individuals with non-managerial skills.[3] In most of these cases, cooperative entrepreneurs are likely to have a lower level of wealth and, therefore, be more risk averse than individual entrepreneurs and more vulnerable to unemployment.

Interdependent cooperative founders with limited personal wealth or non-managerial skills fit the model of Conte and Jones (1991). In this model, labor-managed firm entrepreneurs have no access to the capital market, as is common in models of individual entrepreneurship. The prospective cooperative founder chooses among several possibilities, namely, employment in a

---

[3] Dow (2003) discusses Williamson-type arguments regarding specialized human and physical asset ownership and labor-managed firms.

conventional firm, setting up a conventional firm, or creating a cooperative. Risk aversion implies that the cooperative form, in which members split losses as well as profits, becomes more attractive relative to the individual enterprise as the risk of bankruptcy increases. Employment in a conventional firm offers a fixed income and would be preferred to fluctuating cooperative income having the same mean level. However, conventional employment becomes less attractive as the risk of unemployment increases or as conventional firm wages decrease. The predicted effect of business cycle variables on cooperative entry is therefore ambiguous but the implication is that cooperative entry is more likely to be countercyclical than conventional entry.

Additional factors may make cooperative entry more countercyclical than conventional entry. If prospective cooperative entrepreneurs are less wealthy and more vulnerable to unemployment than individual entrepreneurs, recessions are likely to make cooperatives especially attractive to them. In addition, these characteristics imply that cooperative entrepreneurs should prefer cooperative employment when the risk of job cuts increases in conventional firms, because cooperatives offer the possibility of substituting fluctuating wages for alternating periods of employment and unemployment. In contrast, conventional employment requires bearing employment risks without decision power, resulting in potential exposure to moral hazard on the part of investors. Ben-Ner (1988b) notes that recessions offer opportunities for cooperative takeovers to rescue failing conventional firms. However, this type of entry is actually more common among conventional firms than among cooperatives in France, so that this factor may not make cooperative entry comparatively more countercyclical.[4]

Conte and Jones (1991) consider the possibility that individuals with a preference for participation may be more likely to create democratic businesses. People who favor economic democracy belong to a broad spectrum of political currents in France. However, interest in the cooperative form, as opposed to less egalitarian forms of employee ownership, is probably more widespread among individuals supporting the political Left. Left-wing administrations do not necessarily subsidize the cooperative movement but they may set up supportive agencies. In addition, tendering for some government contracts may become more accessible to cooperatives when the Left is in power. More generally, the proportion of potential cooperative entrepreneurs in the population may grow when people feel more confident about human nature and equality and question the status quo, and as a result vote for the Left. It is also like that cooperatives will generally appear more legitimate when politics shift to the Left and information about them is more readily available, so that cooperative-specific barriers to entry are lower. Such barriers include the higher credit and expert advice costs that may result from negative prejudices and lack of information about cooperatives discussed in Conte (1986), Bonin et al. (1993) and Bowles and Gintis (1994).

Legitimacy may also be conferred by the density of existing cooperatives. The organizational ecology literature, e.g., Carroll (1984) and Carroll and Hannan (1989), argues that, as the number of organizations of a given form grows, the form is regarded as more legitimate and this legitimacy in turn results in more organizations of the same kind being created. However, if there is a limit to the number of organizations of a particular kind that a given environment can support,

---

[4] From 1997 to 2001, 84% of entering SCOPs were created from scratch and 7% formed as rescues of failing conventional firms, as reported in CG-SCOP (1983–2004). In contrast, 64% of all firm creations were from scratch and 20% came from rescues of failing firms in the same period, with the balance being mergers and takeovers of sound existing firms, as reported in Rieg (2003). Ben-Ner (1988a) observes that nearly half of SCOP creations result from rescue operations of failing conventional firms or cooperative takeovers of sound conventional firms, also called conversions, but this statistic is due to the fact that the share of rescue takeovers in firm creation peaked in the period covered by his data.

300 *V. Pérotin / Journal of Comparative Economics 34 (2006) 295–316*

increasing competition for resources causes more closures as the size of the movement continues to grow so that it may become more difficult to set up new organizations of that form. Therefore, a quadratic relationship between population size, or density, and the creation of organizations of the same type is likely. This relationship was verified in the case of Israeli cooperatives by Russell and Hanneman (1992, 1995).[5] Density may affect cooperative creations in France through the office of the CG-SCOP that screens and assists new projects. The size of this office is fixed in the short-run but ultimately depends on the size of the movement that supports the CG by its contributions. The CG also advises existing SCOPs and fulfills the normal duties of a trade and lobbying organization. While a larger movement would result in more resources to advise prospective foundings, new and existing SCOPs are in competition for these resources.

In summary, cooperative entry may be determined by the same factors as conventional entry, although the direction of the expected effects is different. In addition, cooperative entry may be affected by the political cycle and organizational density. Hypotheses regarding the determinants of entry of both types of firms can be expressed as $Entry = E(\pi, g, u, r, P, D, D^2)$, where P, D and D^2 represent political cycle and density factors that are expected to affect cooperative but not conventional entry.

3. Specification of firm entry, data, and estimation methods

In order to test the hypotheses from the previous section, we relate data on annual entry flows for each type of firm to a stock market share index, GDP growth, the unemployment rate, real long-term interest rates, a dummy variable indicating the political affiliation of the Prime Minister in office, and organizational density and its square.

Entry flows are the aggregate numbers of newly registered firms every year from 1971 to 2002 for SCOPs and from 1979 to 2002 for all firms in France.[6] For comparison purposes, the population of French firms can be taken to be only conventional firms because the SCOP population represents around 0.05% of the total population of firms and statistics for the total population are rounded to the nearest 1000. We therefore use the terms conventional firms and all firms interchangeably in the remainder of the paper.

For SCOPs, entry flows include all firms recorded as trading as worker cooperatives for the first time in a given year. For both groups of firms, entry figures cover all industries and origins. SCOP entry includes creations from scratch, rescues of failing conventional firms, and conversions of sound conventional companies into SCOPs. Similarly, overall firm entry includes entirely new firms, new subsidiaries of existing ones, and new firms resulting from mergers and takeovers of existing firms.[7] Although our overall hypotheses apply to all forms of entry,

---

[5] Conte and Jones (1991) test for linear density effects at different levels of aggregation, i.e., federal, state, and industry, for US cooperatives and find a positive effect for two of the three levels.

[6] A firm is defined as a trading legal entity with autonomous decision-making, including self-employed individuals as well as companies, producing goods and services in one or more establishments and registered as trading in France. All registrations enter the Sirene database, which is used by the French Statistical Office, INSEE, to compute entry and exit flows. The inclusion of self-employed individuals who do not have employees in the statistics widens the size gap between conventional and cooperative creations. In 1998, the average conventional creation resulted in 2.2 jobs, including 1.1 employees, as reported in Thirion and Demoly (2003) compared with 6.7 jobs in the average new SCOP in that year as computed from CG-SCOP (2003).

[7] Entering subsidiaries include new businesses created by existing firms but not new establishments of existing firms that are not set up as separate firms. INSEE (Counot and Mulic, 2004) indicates that, in 1994 and 1998, 7 to 8% of non-rescue conventional firm creations in industry and services were partly or fully owned by existing businesses. A takeover

V. Pérotin / Journal of Comparative Economics 34 (2006) 295–316 301

the inclusion of entry other than from scratch introduces some heterogeneity, especially among conventional firms. Scale constraints are likely to be greater in takeover operations. New conventional firms created as subsidiaries, as well as a share of the creations resulting from takeovers, are set up by existing businesses, which will be less constrained financially than individual entrepreneurs but may also require higher expected returns to enter.[8]

The variables chosen to test our hypotheses include standard explanatory variables used in studies of aggregate entry; exact definitions and sources can be found in A. Real GDP growth is used to reflect demand growth; this variable is expected to have a positive effect on conventional entry but may have either a positive or a negative effect on SCOP entry. The aggregate unemployment rate may have a positive or negative effect on both types of entry, with a greater expectation that the effect is positive in the case of SCOP entry. Real long-term interest rates are expected to have a negative effect on both types of firm creation. The expected profitability of incumbent firms is usually proxied by a measure of past profitability. We prefer to use a stock market share index because it is more forward looking and should reflect the present value of the future profit streams if capital markets are efficient. This variable is expected to have a positive coefficient in the conventional entry equation, but may have either a positive or negative effect on SCOP entry, depending on whether it reflects profit prospects for cooperatives or risk in conventional employment.[9]

The political cycle variable is a dummy taking the value one when the Prime Minister belongs to the French Socialist Party, reflecting the results of parliamentary elections. The variable's coefficient is expected to be positive for SCOP creations and to have no significant effect on conventional creations. Density is measured by the number of SCOPs trading in October of the previous year and the total number of firms in industry and services at the end of the previous year. For SCOPs, density is expected to have a positive coefficient and density squared should have a negative one. Whether this variable should have any significant effect on conventional entry is unclear.

Following the literature on entry, the explanatory variables have been lagged by one year (except for density which is measured in the previous year) in order to reflect the duration of the process of firm creation, which responds to signals perceived some time before the firm is actually created. The length of the lag used in existing studies varies; Schwalbach (1987) uses averages of the previous five years, whereas Highfield and Smiley (1987) use a one-year lag.

---

results in an entry only if a new company is created in the process. If no new firm is created, e.g., if one of two existing firms takes over the other one without setting up a new company, no entry is registered. Firms that disappear as such after being taken over or merging with other firms are regarded as exiting.

[8] Available data do not allow us to disaggregate entry flows by entry mode. Agarwal and Audretsch (2001) point out that this type of heterogeneity is present in other studies. Another potential source of heterogeneity lies in the fact that the data cannot be disaggregated by industry. However, this deficiency is less problematic, in that disaggregation by industry might not improve greatly our ability to account for entry, although it would increase the sample size. In his review of the empirical literature on entry, Geroski (1995) notes that cross-industry differences in entry do not persist very long, despite stable cross-industry differences in profitability, and that most of the total variation in industry entry over time is within-industry rather than between-industry variation, so that time-varying features of markets that do not necessarily differ across industries are more likely to explain entry.

[9] Alternative estimations were carried out with a measure of profit for existing firms given by the share of profit in value added, which is available for the last two decades from French National Accounts (INSEE, 2005b). The results of these alternative estimations are broadly consistent with the estimates that use the stock market index. We do not report them in detail but comment on certain interesting differences. The full set of results is available upon request from the author.

302   *V. Pérotin / Journal of Comparative Economics 34 (2006) 295–316*

Table 1
Variables means

	1979–2002	1971–2002
SCOP Entry	166.96	138.28
All Entry (1000s)	263.46	n.a.
SCOP Exit	128.79	104.31
All Exit (1000s)	245.96	n.a.
GDP growth	2.15	2.52
Unemployment	9.73	8.22
Left in government	0.63	0.47
Share index	10,121.04	8,928.09
Interest rate	4.80	3.79
Density (SCOPs)	1,259.00	1,068.06
Density (all firms, 1000s)	2,235.29	n.a.

A one-year lag corresponds to anecdotal evidence concerning the time individual entrepreneurs take to set up a firm in France.[10]

The means of these variables are presented in Table 1 for two periods: 1979 to 2002, which is the period for which entry and exit flows are available for both conventional and cooperative firms, and a longer period from 1971 to 2002, for which information on entry and exit flows is available for SCOPs only. SCOP entry averaged 167 and 138 annually for the two periods, respectively. A distinct wave of creations occurred in the late 1970s and early 1980s, followed by a much smaller one in the mid-1990s. Total entry averaged 263,000 over the second period. This later, shorter period was marked by high unemployment at 9.7% on average, high real interest rates averaging 4.8% as high nominal interest rates combined with low inflation, and low growth at 2.2% on average.

Three estimations were performed. One uses SCOP data for the longest period available, i.e., 1971 to 2002, and the other two use SCOP and overall entry data, respectively, for the period in which data for all firms are available, i.e., 1979 to 2002. Since annual entry numbers are count data, taking as a small number of positive discrete values, the entry equations have been estimated by the Poisson Maximum Likelihood (ML) method. Creation levels are assumed to result from a count process so that they are independently Poisson distributed conditional upon the values of the explanatory variables. Hence, in each period, the log of the expected number of creations is a linear function of the independent variables. Formally, annual creation levels y_i are assumed to be observations of independently Poisson distributed discrete variables with parameters λ_i such that:

$$\lambda_i = \exp(x_i' \beta), \qquad (1)$$

where x_i' is the vector of exogenous variables associated with observation i and β is a vector of unknown parameters to be estimated. The parameter λ_i is the expected number of creations so that the elements of β represent semi-elasticities. If y_i has a Poisson distribution, its variance is equal to its mean λ_i so that heteroskedasticity is built into the model because the mean and, therefore, the variance are functions of the regressors.

---

[10] In response to comments, we experimented with different lag lengths. These changes did not alter the results significantly, but yielded less successful estimations.

V. Pérotin / Journal of Comparative Economics 34 (2006) 295–316 303

If the assumption of mean-variance equality is not met, the Poisson ML estimator remains consistent but it may become inefficient. Moreover, with high levels of over-dispersion, the standard errors of the estimated coefficients are inconsistently estimated, as Cameron and Trivedi (1990, 1998) discuss; however, Cox (1983) and Gouriéroux et al. (1984) argue that a little over-dispersion poses no problem. Although the estimator performs well with small samples, dispersion tests suffer from small-sample bias (Cameron and Trivedi, 1998). Given the short length of our series, we use a small-sample test correction proposed by Dean and Lawless (1989) to test for mean-variance equality.[11] Mean-variance equality is rejected for all three equations.[12] Since the Poisson ML estimator remains consistent in this situation, and alternatives such as the Negative Binomial estimators are sensitive to incorrect variance specification and cannot handle under-dispersion, we choose to use the Poisson ML estimator together with robust standard errors that do not require specifying the variance function of y_i, as suggested by Cameron and Trivedi (1998).[13] Another alternative to the Poisson ML estimator is Ordinary Least Squares (OLS) with a semi-log specification because there are no zeros in our dependent variable series. We present OLS estimations with White heteroskedasticity-robust standard errors.

Serial correlation is often absent in count data. We test for this problem in the Poisson ML estimations for up to three lags and with Pearson residuals as proposed by Cameron and Trivedi (1998) and with a Box–Ljung test.[14] The hypothesis of no serial correlation is accepted in all cases.[15] Durbin–Watson statistics for the OLS estimations all fall in the inconclusive zone, suggesting the possibility of positive first-order autocorrelation. However, the pattern of significance of the coefficient estimates is preserved when we correct for autocorrelation, so that only the OLS estimates with heteroskedasticity-robust standard errors are presented.

4. Empirical results on the determinants of firm entry

The equation estimated for SCOPs over the longer period is presented in Table 2. The magnitude of the coefficients estimated by the two methods is quite similar. The signs of the business cycle variables suggest that SCOP entry is countercyclical. A one percentage point increase in unemployment results in a 10% increase or more in cooperative creations. However, the effect of growth is not statistically significant. The stock market share index may have a small negative effect on SCOP creations in that a one-thousand point increase from the mean value of about 8900 results in a 1 to 2% drop in SCOP creations. Thus, our results confirm that perceived risks associated with conventional employment in downturns are a more powerful factor of cooperative creations than are profit prospects, although this coefficient is not significantly different from

---

[11] The test statistic used is T_b from Dean and Lawless (1989). The distribution of this statistic is approximately standard normal, and Dean and Lawless show that the test performs well with sample sizes of 10 or 20.

[12] For the cooperative equation estimated on the longer period, $T_b = 15.25$. The same statistic is 7.90 for the cooperative equation over the shorter period and -78.46 for the overall entry equation.

[13] The robust standard errors come from the equivalent estimator to White's robust variance estimator for the Poisson ML case given in Cameron and Trivedi (1998).

[14] The Box–Ljung statistics is a small sample test (Cameron and Trivedi, 1998). The statistic for this test, T_{BL}, is a function of $\hat{\rho}_k$, the estimated autocorrelation coefficient for lag k, and has a χ^2 asymptotic distribution with m degrees of freedom, where m is the number of lags autocorrelation is tested for. This statistic can be found in Mittelhammer et al. (2000).

[15] We find that $\hat{\rho}_k$ is not significantly different from 0 for $k = 1$ to 3 in all three equations. The statistic T_{BL} is equal to 4.89 for the SCOP equation on the longer period and 2.51 on the shorter period; it is 2.56 for the conventional firm equation.

304   V. Pérotin / Journal of Comparative Economics 34 (2006) 295–316

Table 2
Determinants of SCOP Entry, 1971 to 2002

	Poisson ML			OLS (dependent variable: Log creations)	
Constant	0.30	(1.09)	[0.38]	0.07	[0.09]
GDP growth$_{-1}$	−0.02	(1.35)	[0.43]	-0.46×10^{-2}	[0.10]
Unemployment$_{-1}$	0.10	(4.82)***	[1.70]*	0.14	[1.89]*
Left in government$_{-1}$	0.14	(3.20)***	[1.36]	0.13	[1.13]
Share index$_{-1}$	-0.18×10^{-4}	(3.45)***	[1.76]*	-0.13×10^{-4}	[1.27]
Interest rate$_{-1}$	−0.17	(12.32)***	[6.00]***	−0.16	[5.89]***
Density	0.94×10^{-2}	(14.87)***	[5.60]***	0.93×10^{-2}	[5.40]***
Density^2	-0.43×10^{-5}	(15.40)***	[6.12]***	-0.44×10^{-5}	[4.50]***
	Pseudo R^2 (McFadden) 0.69			Adj. R^2 0.80	
	Pseudo R^2 (dev. based) 0.81			DW 1.07	
	Autocorrelation no				
	Over/under-dispersion yes				

Notes. The asymptotic t-statistics in parentheses have a standard normal distribution. The t-statistics in square brackets are based on standard error estimates that are robust to mean-variance inequality (Poisson estimates) or heteroskedasticity (OLS estimates).
* Statistical significance at the 10% level.
*** Statistical significance at the 1% level.

zero in the OLS estimation. Higher interest rates have the expected negative effect; an increase of one percentage point causes a 16 to 17% decrease in SCOP creations.

The density of cooperatives has the expected quadratic effect; the size of the SCOP population acts as a legitimizing and resource-generating factor until competitive pressures develop. The net impact of density remains positive at the mean; 10% more SCOPs are associated with 2.2% additional new cooperatives. However, this effect becomes negative at a density of 1093 SCOPs, which is below the current density of about 1700. Density effects may actually be more complex. If we include a cubic term, the estimated effect is again positive at current densities possibly because the CG-SCOP expanded once the movement reached a certain scale. However, these results confirm the impact of competition for resources at the creation stage and the importance of support structures. The presence of the Left in government is associated with an increase of 13 to 14% in SCOP creations but this coefficient may not be statistically significant.

The two equations estimated for the shorter period are presented in Table 3. The pattern of significance of the coefficients in the SCOP equation changes slightly compared with the longer-period estimation, although the signs are identical and most of the estimated coefficients have the same order of magnitude.[16] Unemployment affects cooperative creations more significantly over the longer period, while growth may play a more significant role over the last two decades, a period of more stable unemployment.

Cooperative creation is clearly countercyclical in the short period as in the longer one. In the later period, a one percentage point increase in growth is associated with an 8 to 9% decrease in SCOP creations and a one percentage point increase in unemployment could be associated with a 5% increase in SCOP creations. In contrast, a one percentage point increase in growth results in a 3% increase in the number of conventional firms created and a one percentage point

---

[16] Likelihood ratio and Chow tests confirm that the effects change between the 1970s and the later period.

Table 3
Compared determinants of Entry, 1979 to 2002

	SCOPs					All Entry				
	Poisson ML			OLS (dep. variable: Log creations)		Poisson ML			OLS (dep. variable: Log creations)	
Constant	2.84	(6.11)***	[2.82]***	3.19	[3.57]***	−5.39	(0.88)	[1.15]	−4.56	[1.04]
GDP growth$_{-1}$	−0.08	(4.84)***	[1.85]*	−0.09	[2.04]**	0.03	(2.52)**	[2.42]**	0.03	[2.33]**
Unemployment$_{-1}$	0.05	(2.17)**	[0.90]	0.04	[0.84]	−0.02	(1.40)	[2.32]**	−0.02	[2.27]**
Left in government$_{-1}$	0.17	(3.70)***	[1.66]*	0.13	[1.31]	−0.10	(3.26)***	[3.49]***	−0.10	[3.54]***
Share index$_{-1}$	-0.21×10^{-4}	(4.09)***	[2.09]**	-0.18×10^{-4}	[1.84]*	0.28×10^{-5}	(0.75)	[0.85]	0.32×10^{-5}	[0.91]
Interest rate$_{-1}$	−0.15	(8.87)***	[4.64]***	−0.15	[4.57]***	0.02	(1.42)	[2.56]**	0.02	[2.77]**
Density	0.53×10^{-2}	(5.90)***	[2.87]***	0.47×10^{-2}	[2.69]***	0.98×10^{-2}	(1.74)*	[2.27]**	0.90×10^{-2}	[2.25]**
Density^2	-0.24×10^{-5}	(6.01)***	[2.84]***	-0.21×10^{-5}	[2.67]***	-0.21×10^{-5}	(1.70)*	[2.22]**	-0.20×10^{-5}	[2.20]**

SCOPs — Poisson ML:
Pseudo R^2 (McFadden) 0.52
Pseudo R^2 (dev. based) 0.71
Autocorrelation no
Over/under-dispersion yes

SCOPs — OLS:
Adj. R^2 0.53
DW 1.82

All Entry — Poisson ML:
Pseudo R^2 (McFadden) 0.15
Pseudo R^2 (dev. based) 0.65
Autocorrelation no
Over/under-dispersion yes

All Entry — OLS:
Adj. R^2 0.49
DW 1.66

Notes. The asymptotic t-statistics in parentheses (Poisson estimates) or heteroskedasticity (OLS estimates). The t-statistics in square brackets are based on standard error estimates that are robust to mean-variance inequality (Poisson estimates) or heteroskedasticity (OLS estimates).

* Statistical significance at the 10% level.
** Statistical significance at the 5% level.
*** Statistical significance at the 1% level.

306   *V. Pérotin / Journal of Comparative Economics 34 (2006) 295–316*

increase in unemployment could be associated with a 2% decrease in conventional creations, although this coefficient may not be statistically significant (which would confirm the possible ambiguity of the unemployment effect). Interest rates are still negatively related to cooperative entry as expected. However, interest rates have a positive impact on the entry of conventional firms; a one percentage point increase in interest rates is associated with 2% more conventional creations, possibly reflecting the accumulation of assets required before investing in a start-up firm.

In this later period, density again has the expected quadratic effect on cooperative entry; the coefficient becomes negative at around 1100 SCOPs and a 10% increase in the number of existing cooperatives at the mean density is associated with a drop in creations of more than 9%. Interestingly, the same type of overall density effect is observed for the entry of conventional firms, but at the mean density the effect remains positive. Conventional entry grows by 9.2% if density is 10% higher, perhaps reflecting the overall capacity of the economy to sustain new firms, as might be argued by organizational ecology theory (Geroski, 2001).[17] The density effect becomes negative at around 2,330,000 firms, which is slightly below the current density of conventional firms.

Unexpectedly, profit potential measured by the stock market share index has no statistically significant effect on conventional firm creations. However, an increase of 1000 points in this index is associated with a 2% decrease in cooperative creations. The presence of the Left in government may still have the expected positive effect on SCOP creations with a 17% increase but it also has an unexpected negative and significant effect on overall entry, decreasing it by 10%. The impact of a having the Left in government disappears if the share of profit in value added, which averages 39.6% over the period, is substituted for the stock market share index. For both types of creations, this profit variable has strongly significant coefficients with the same signs as those of the share index. A one percentage point increase in the share of profit in value added is associated with a 17% decrease in SCOP creations and with a 7% increase in conventional entry. Over this later period, the Left variable is negatively correlated with the share of profit in value added but positively correlated with the stock market share index and with growth, so that this result suggests that the presence of the Left in government influences entry of the two types primarily through its impact on past capital and labor income shares rather than through legitimation effects or profit prospects as hypothesized.[18]

To summarize these results, SCOP entry is countercyclical, unlike entry as a whole, and it is affected by increased risks associated with conventional employment. The political cycle may influence both types of entry, but in opposite ways, and in a more basic way than was hypothesized. Organizational density has a non-monotonic impact on both cooperative and conventional entry. Likelihood-ratio tests performed on the Poisson estimates and Chow tests performed on the OLS estimates presented in Table 3 confirm that the business cycle variables have significantly

---

[17] Deletion of the density variables leaves the estimated coefficients for the other variables unchanged with the exception of the coefficient for unemployment, which becomes insignificant. This result is consistent with the possibility that density is a scaling variable reflecting the overall capacity of the economy to sustain new firms, which may depend positively on unemployment as a source of potential entrepreneurs and may cancel out the negative effect of unemployment on entry. We find no evidence of a cubic density effect on conventional entry.

[18] The profit variable is the only one that clearly affects conventional entry in that specification; essentially, it summarizes the determinants of entry. In the SCOP equation, this variable picks up all the negative effects on cooperative entry with which it is correlated, including growth, the effect of unemployment on wealth, and interest rates. Although these variables now have a lower effect, the counter-cyclicality of cooperative entry and its relationship with organizational density are confirmed.

V. Pérotin / Journal of Comparative Economics 34 (2006) 295–316 307

different effects on the two types of entry and that the two equations are significantly different overall.[19]

5. The theory and empirical specification of firm exit

Exit is much less well understood than entry. Conventional firms are thought to exit when the present value of future profits no longer exceeds the opportunity cost of operating the firm. Thus, conventional exit may depend on market conditions affecting expected profits, which are typically represented by growth and indicators of current profits. The opportunity cost of keeping the firm in operation includes returns on alternative investments as well as income from wage employment and unemployment. These factors are included with industry characteristics in the few existing empirical analyses of gross exit at the aggregate level, e.g., MacDonald (1986), Audretsch (1991) and Mayer and Chapell (1992). However, this literature yields few clear empirical results, which is not surprising since exit rates are very stable. In addition, aggregate exit data combine several different phenomena because firms exit for different reasons and firms of different ages are vulnerable to different circumstances. Recent studies using establishment and firm-level data, e.g., Agarwal and Audretsch (2001), Disney et al. (2003), and Dunne et al. (2005), highlight the role played by factors such as the conditions under which firms were created, their interaction with the industry life-cycle, and firm age and size. In practice, conventional firm exit includes not only bankruptcies and liquidations but also mergers and takeovers, which may occur in less dramatic situations.[20]

Including recent entry in the regression equation is a way of taking into account the proportion of young firms in the population; these firms have higher exit rates regardless of market conditions, as Boeri and Bellmann (1995) and Disney et al. (2003) report. However, available data do not permit separating out mergers and takeovers. Agarwal and Audretsch (2001) note that this is a common problem in empirical studies of exit. The corresponding heterogeneity principally affects conventional exit because mergers and takeovers are negligible among SCOPs over the sample period. The heterogeneity affecting the SCOP population is mainly related to the fact that SCOPs of different ages and of different origins have different hazard profiles, as Pérotin (2004) demonstrates.[21]

Given our results on SCOP creations, three questions of interest are suggested: first, whether market conditions matter for SCOP survival and, in particular, whether cooperatives exit in re-

---

[19] The likelihood ratio test statistic for a model in which all estimated parameters are different compared to a model in which all parameters are the same in the two equations is T_{LR} is equal to 258.81 (this statistic has a χ^2 distribution with 8 degrees of freedom under the null hypothesis that all parameters are the same). The statistic T_{LR} is equal to 107.66 (with 2 degrees of freedom) when the alternative hypothesis 1 is that all parameters are the same except for those of the business cycle variables. The corresponding F-statistics in Chow tests carried out on the OLS estimations are 4.72 and 5.59.

[20] In our data, a merger or takeover may result in no exit if, for example, one firm becomes owned by another but still exists as a separate firm. However, a merger or takeover may result in one exit if a firm that is taken over ceases to exist as a separate firm and becomes a division of another firm, or even in two exits if two firms merge to form a new, different firm, in which case the data will also register an entry. We had to compute the last four years of conventional exit flows from density and entry. The gain in information from having four extra years should outweigh any distortion that may be introduced into the series from this computation because the conventional entry, exit and density figures tally in most years, with only small discrepancies in both directions.

[21] Unfortunately, the data cannot be disaggregated by industry. Given the stability of inter-industry differences in profitability, this limitation may be less severe than the heterogeneity due to exit modes.

308   *V. Pérotin / Journal of Comparative Economics 34 (2006) 295–316*

coveries, second, whether the political cycle and density have any impact on exit; and finally, whether exit echoes entry in previous years.

Like other types of worker cooperatives in Southern Europe, SCOPs are immune to the self-extinction by under-investment hypothesis found in Vanek (1977). Although the bulk of SCOPs' capital is owned collectively by cooperative members, the French cooperative statute imposes an annual profit plowback and prohibits appropriation of collectively-owned capital by the members, even in case of firm closure (CG-SCOP, 2003). Estrin and Jones (1992, 1998) present empirical evidence confirming the absence of under-investment tendencies among SCOPs. Similarly, the type of degeneration described by Ben-Ner (1988b) does not apply to SCOPs, which have no incentive to hire non-member workers because they share profit with non-members as well as members, as Pérotin (1999) discusses. According to Ben-Ner's model, cooperatives may exit during recoveries because increased and shared profit may be associated with increased uncertainty, which raises the attractiveness of conventional employment with a fixed income. However, in times of rising profit, cooperative members are unlikely to wind down their firm simply to obtain a fixed income elsewhere. Nonetheless, cooperatives lose some of their comparative advantage when jobs are no longer at risk in conventional firms so that those members who can command a higher wage in less egalitarian structures may leave for conventional employment.

Whether SCOPs will exit much in recessions is also unclear. In addition to the X-efficiency advantage that they may have over conventional firms, as suggested by the evidence presented in Doucouliagos (1995) and, particularly for France, in Estrin and Jones (1995), cooperatives may weather recessions by cutting wages and preserving employment, saving on labor turnover costs in the process. To cooperative members, the opportunity cost of keeping the firm in operation is more likely to be unemployment compensation if they are more vulnerable to unemployment than conventional entrepreneurs. Cooperative members may therefore accept lower profit than ordinary investors before closing down. For these reasons, cooperative failure rates may be lower throughout the business cycle and recessions may have an ambiguous effect on exit, because profit prospects are reduced but unemployment increases so that the cost of operating the firm goes down.

The political cycle should affect cooperative closures unambiguously, for reasons that are symmetric to the ones examined for entry. Similarly, density is expected to have a symmetric effect to what was hypothesized for entry. Finally, the level of SCOP births should affect future closures, which is due in part to competition for CG-SCOP resources. A potentially more important effect is related to population dynamics. Creation booms should be reflected in increased numbers of closures in the following years because booms lead to a population with a high proportion of young firms, which have higher failure rates. Among SCOPs, the highest death rates are found in the third year, i.e., at age two, in the period under study, as Pérotin (2004) reports, so that more entry at time $t - 2$ should increase exit at time t.

In the empirical analysis that we present in the next section, exit is allowed to depend on growth, unemployment, a stock market share index, interest rates, the presence of the Left in government, density and its square, and entry lagged by two years. As is customary in the exit literature, variables other than entry are not lagged. As Shapiro and Khemani (1987) remark, the exit lag is thought to be shorter than the entry lag, so that contemporary market conditions should be used; Disney et al. (2003) and Dunne et al. (2005) also use this strategy. Variable definitions are the same as in the entry section, except for the lags. As with entry, alternative equations are estimated in which a profitability variable is substituted for the share index. Any differences are described in the next section.

V. Pérotin / Journal of Comparative Economics 34 (2006) 295–316   309

6. Estimation and empirical results for firm exit

This analysis uses the same techniques and follows the same format as the analysis of entry in Section 4. Equations explaining annual exit are estimated by Poisson ML and by OLS with a semi-log specification and White standard errors. We begin with a SCOP-only estimation over the longest period for which data are available and continue with shorter-period estimations for cooperative and conventional exit. Tests for serial correlation performed on the ML estimations for up to three lags lead us to accept the hypothesis of no autocorrelation in all cases. The OLS estimation for cooperatives over the longer period shows no evidence of first-order autocorrelation, although the estimations on the shorter period may be affected by positive first-order autocorrelation, as the Durbin-Watson statistic falls in the inconclusive region. As with entry, correction for serial correlation preserves the significance pattern of the estimated coefficients in all cases so that only heteroskedasticity robust t-ratios are reported. The SCOP equation for the shorter period does not exhibit any over- or under-dispersion but the longer period estimation and the conventional exit equation do. We report t statistics using robust standard error estimates together with the uncorrected t statistics as we did for the entry equations.[22]

The results are presented in Tables 4 and 5. In all cases, the estimated coefficients are significant less often than in the entry equations, which is consistent with previous empirical work on exit. In addition, the magnitudes of the estimated coefficient are slightly less stable across estimation methods.

Table 4
Determinants of SCOP Exit, 1971 to 2002

	Poisson ML			OLS (dependent variable: Log exit)	
Constant	2.48	$(5.24)^{***}$	$[2.33]^{**}$	1.97	$[2.34]^{**}$
GDP growth	-0.03	(1.56)	$[0.71]$	-0.05	$[1.44]$
Unemployment	0.07	$(3.40)^{***}$	$[1.40]$	0.12	$[2.26]^{**}$
Left in government	-0.63×10^{-2}	(0.13)	$[0.05]$	0.06	$[0.48]$
Share index	0.53×10^{-5}	(0.66)	$[0.17]$	-0.23×10^{-5}	$[0.08]$
Interest rate	0.06	$(2.60)^{***}$	$[1.20]$	0.01	$[0.44]$
Density	0.16×10^{-2}	(1.46)	$[0.72]$	0.25×10^{-2}	$[1.24]$
Density^2	-0.07×10^{-5}	(1.29)	$[0.56]$	-0.11×10^{-5}	$[1.03]$
Entry$_{-2}$	0.26×10^{-2}	$(7.17)^{***}$	$[2.65]^{***}$	0.21×10^{-2}	$[2.21]^{**}$
	Pseudo R^2 (McFadden) 0.71			Adj. R^2 0.84	
	Pseudo R^2 (dev. based) 0.83			DW 2.18	
	Autocorrelation no				
	Over/under-dispersion yes				

Notes. The asymptotic t-statistics in parentheses have a standard normal distribution. The t-statistics in square brackets are based on standard error estimates that are robust to mean-variance inequality (Poisson estimates) or heteroskedasticity (OLS estimates).

** Statistical significance at the 5% level.
*** Statistical significance at the 1% level.

---

[22] The statistic $\hat{\rho}_k$ is not significantly different from 0 for $k = 1$ to 3 in all three equations. The statistic T_{BL} equals 3.41 for the SCOP equation on the longer period and 6.63 on the shorter period; it equals 4.05 for the conventional firm equation. For the SCOP equations, T_b equals 8.42 on the longer period and 1.29 on the shorter period, for which we cannot reject the hypothesis of mean-variance equality. The statistic is -209.99 for the conventional exit equation.

Table 5
Compared determinants of Exit, 1981 to 2002

	SCOPs		All Exit	
	Poisson ML	OLS (dependent variable: Log exit)	Poisson ML	OLS (dependent variable: Log exit)
Constant	6.58 (5.76)*** [2.68]***	6.08 [2.57]***	−13.34 (1.34) [1.54]	−14.44 [1.56]
GDP growth	−0.04 (1.95)* [0.74]	−0.03 [0.43]	−0.33 × 10^{-2} (0.21) [0.17]	−0.36 × 10^{-2} [0.19]
Unemployment	0.06 (3.04)*** [1.43]	0.08 [1.91]*	−0.02 (1.05) [1.13]	−0.02 [1.30]
Left in government	0.03 (0.45) [0.18]	0.01 [0.08]	−0.05 (1.32) [1.17]	−0.06 [1.27]
Share index	0.82 × 10^{-5} (0.98) [0.29]	0.11 × 10^{-4} [0.42]	0.44 × 10^{-5} (0.76) [0.82]	0.36 × 10^{-5} [0.68]
Interest rate	0.16 (4.84)*** [1.86]*	0.15 [1.80]*	0.02 (0.96) [0.86]	0.02 [0.77]
Density	−0.62 × 10^{-2} (2.76)*** [1.26]	−0.55 × 10^{-2} [1.14]	0.02 (1.81)* [2.07]**	0.02 [2.06]*
Density^2	0.26 × 10^{-5} (2.70)*** [1.19]	0.23 × 10^{-5} [1.02]	−0.37 × 10^{-5} (1.82)* [2.08]**	−0.39 × 10^{-5} [2.05]*
Entry_{-2}	0.27 × 10^{-2} (7.33)*** [2.57]**	0.27 × 10^{-2} [2.53]**	0.25 × 10^{-2} (2.15)** [1.42]	0.23 × 10^{-2} [1.33]
	Pseudo R^2 (McFadden) 0.33	Adj. R^2 0.17	Pseudo R^2 (McFadden) 0.19	Adj. R^2 0.28
	Pseudo R^2 (dev. based) 0.49	DW 2.15	Pseudo R^2 (dev. based) 0.56	DW 1.79
	Autocorrelation no		Autocorrelation no	
	Over/under-dispersion no		Over/under-dispersion yes	

Notes. The asymptotic *t*-statistics in parentheses have a standard normal distribution. The *t*-statistics in square brackets are based on standard error estimates that are robust to mean-variance inequality (Poisson estimates) or heteroskedasticity (OLS estimates).

* Statistical significance at the 10% level.
** Statistical significance at the 5% level.
*** Statistical significance at the 1 level%.

V. Pérotin / Journal of Comparative Economics 34 (2006) 295–316   311

From Table 4, the equation estimated for SCOPs over the longer period suggests that at most three factors affect cooperative exit. A one percentage point increase in unemployment is associated with 7 to 12% more cooperative exits and 10% more cooperative births two years earlier, at the mean level of cooperative entry for the period, translate into about 4% more failures (100 more births result in 26% more failures). A one percentage point increase in the long-term interest rate may increase cooperative exit by 1 to 6%, but this coefficient is not always significantly different from zero.

The SCOP equation estimated over the shorter period in Table 5 shows almost identical effects for lagged entry and unemployment as in the longer period, but the interest rate and density variables have different and more strongly significant effects (since no over-dispersion is detected for the SCOP equation, the Poisson standard error estimates are reliable).[23] Neither growth nor unemployment is estimated to have any significant effect on conventional exit. In contrast, a one percentage point increase in unemployment is associated with a 6% increase in cooperative exit and a one percentage point increase in growth corresponds to a 4% decrease in cooperative exit, although this coefficient may not be statistically significant. The value of the stock market share index is not significantly related to either type of exit, but increases in the interest rate result in more cooperative closures, with 16% more closures associated with each percentage point. Overall, our results indicate that cooperatives behave rather like the conventional firm of economic theory, exiting in recessions and when interest rates are high. We find no sign of exit in recoveries on the part of SCOPs.

Neither the stock market share index nor the presence of the Left in government is estimated to have any effect on exit of either type of firm. However, lagged entry has a significant effect on cooperative exit and may also affect conventional exit. The density variables affect both types of exit. The estimated coefficient for lagged entry is about the same in the SCOP equations for both periods, but higher mean entry over the shorter period implies a different elasticity. In the shorter period, a 26 to 27% increase in exit is associated with a 60% increase in annual creations two years earlier rather than the 72% increase found for the longer period. This change is consistent with the finding in Pérotin (2004) that more recent cohorts of SCOPs have been surviving less well in their first two or three years than previous cohorts. For conventional firms, a 25% increase in exit may be associated with a growth in entry at $t - 2$ of less than 40% of the average annual entry in the period, which is also consistent with evidence that SCOPs have higher survival rates than conventional firms at age 2 (Pérotin, 2004).

The coefficients of the density variables have the expected signs for cooperatives, suggesting that a higher density reduces exit by legitimizing cooperatives, up to the level at which competition for resources outweighs legitimacy effects, corresponding to about 1200 SCOPs in our study. For conventional firms, the estimated coefficients have the opposite signs, with the change in sign occurring at a density a little higher than 2,330,000 firms. A possible explanation for this opposite effect is that, for conventional firms, higher density means heightened competition, but at very high levels, buoyant market conditions may keep more firms in operation. The net effects at the sample means are positive for both groups of firms, but the estimated magnitudes may not

---

[23] A likelihood ratio test performed on the Poisson ML estimates suggests structural change between the beginning of the longer period and the shorter, more recent period, although this hypothesis is not supported by a Chow test on the OLS estimates.

be reliable given the uncertainty over the significance of the relevant coefficients, especially for conventional firms, and the possibility that the actual effect of density is more complex.[24]

The estimations presented in Tables 4 and 5 explain exit less effectively than our results in Section 4 explain entry, which is in keeping with the results in the existing empirical literature. However, we find no evidence that SCOPs exit in recoveries. Indeed, a likelihood-ratio test shows the difference between the estimated effects of the two business cycle variables on the two types of exit to be statistically insignificant, even though, taken as a whole, the equations are significantly different. A Chow test performed on the OLS estimates could not reject the hypothesis that the two equations were the same.[25]

7. Conclusion

Some French worker cooperatives have survived for considerably more than a century, and the movement has incorporated, in its statute, provisions that preclude the degeneration and self-extinction that have been conjectured to explain the small numbers of labor-managed firms in market economies. Yet worker cooperatives represent a tiny portion of all French firms, although the movement is sizeable by the standards of industrialized countries. Over the last few decades, entry rates have been rather higher among cooperatives than among French firms in general, while exit rates have been the same or slightly lower. However, the initial population of cooperatives was small and its overall size has stabilized. In this paper, we test the proposition that creation, rather than exit, is where labor-managed firms differ from conventional firms, in particular in their respective responses to the business cycle. We also investigate the influence of the political cycle and organizational density on cooperative creations.

The widespread belief that cooperative creations are more countercyclical than conventional firm entry is confirmed by our analysis. Cooperative creations respond to increases in the risks associated with conventional employment rather than to the prospects of growing profits. More cooperatives are created when unemployment rises and when growth is slower. Cooperative creations also increase when interest rates and profit prospects are lower. In contrast, conventional entry is associated positively with growth and negatively with unemployment, as expected, and it increases with past profitability. Moreover, the difference between the responses of the two groups to the business cycle is statistically significant.

---

[24] A 10% increase in organizational density, which amounts to about 130 firms in that period for SCOPs and 223,500 for firms in general, is associated with an estimated increase in exit of 4% among cooperatives and 77% among conventional firms in these estimations. However, we experimented with a specification including a cubic density term and found it to be relevant for cooperatives, for which increasing density decreases cooperative exits with this specification. Substituting the share of profit in value added for the stock market share index did not improve the clarity or significance of the results. The resulting estimated SCOP equation is very similar to the equation in Table 5 but with less strongly significant coefficients. The conventional equation estimation is much less successful due in part to the extra multicollinearity introduced with the use of the profit variable, which is highly correlated with conventional density variables.

[25] The likelihood ratio statistics for the null hypothesis that all parameters are the same versus the alternative hypotheses that all parameters are different, that the coefficients of the business cycle variables only are different, and that the intercept and coefficients of the other variables are different (with only those of the business variables being the same) are $T_{LR} = 30.93$, 5.01 and 20.06, respectively. The cooperative and conventional exit equations are therefore different but the difference comes from the coefficients of the other variables, those of the business cycle variables being the same for the two groups of firms. The F-statistic for the Chow test of equality of all the coefficients of the exit equation across firm types is 0.67.

V. Pérotin / Journal of Comparative Economics 34 (2006) 295–316   313

The political cycle is found to affect both types of entry in opposite directions, although this result is probably due to the effect of the Left on past capital and labor shares of value added rather than to legitimation effects. Both types of entry respond to density in the way expected for minority and niche organizations. Initially, entry is supported by a higher density; beyond a certain density, entering firms complete with existing firms for resources, but the precise density effects appear to be more complex.

Although our findings on exit are less strong than on entry, they suggest that cooperative exit is not procyclical in France. Cooperative exit responds to the business cycle and to market conditions in the same way a conventional firm is thought to respond, with exit increasing when unemployment and interest rates rise. In contrast to our results for entry, no statistically significant difference is found in the effects of business cycle variables on exit between the two groups of firms. Increased organizational density may lead to greater competition among conventional firms but it limits cooperative exit, although the precise form of the density effect may be complex for exit as well.

Our findings for French cooperatives suggest that, once potential under-investment and degeneration issues are resolved, the main differences between labor-managed and conventional firms are found in entry, rather than exit, behavior. We find no difference in the way the business cycle affects the exit decisions of the two groups, but we do find significant differences in the process of firm creation. Thus, difficulties associated with entrepreneurship may represent a considerable obstacle to the spread of labor-managed firms. Collective entrepreneurship appears to be driven by necessity, i.e., spurred by unemployment and risks associated with conventional employment, in contrast to conventional entry, which is stimulated by growth but limited by rising unemployment. The role of cooperative density confirms the importance of support structures and suggests that enough resources must be invested in cooperative infrastructures in order to counter the effects of competition for resources. These structures would also foster cooperative entrepreneurship in periods of growth.

Clearly, the issue of exit due to structural weaknesses remains relevant for labor-managed firms; exit is especially important in countries that do not have a specific statute for democratic firms to ensure that viable forms are adopted by new entrants. However, several solutions to under-investment and degeneration are known so that some re-focusing of research may be necessary. Our findings need to be confirmed by research covering longer periods and other countries. The issues surrounding cooperative creation are relatively unexplored outside practitioners' circles; however, they may ultimately provide the key to understanding the reasons for the low incidence of labor-management in capitalist economies.

Acknowledgments

The author is grateful to Christian Cordellier, Xiao Yuan Dong, Saul Estrin, Derek Jones, Panu Kalmi, Mark Klinedinst and Tim Mount for comments on earlier versions, as well as to participants in seminars at Universities of Münster, St. Andrews and Leeds, in the Conference on Firms and Markets at Birmingham University, and in the session on Employee Ownership of the Association for Comparative Economic Studies in San Diego. Two anonymous referees made several helpful suggestions. Remaining errors are of course the responsibility of the author.

314 *V. Pérotin / Journal of Comparative Economics 34 (2006) 295–316*

Appendix A
Variable definitions and sources

SCOP Entry	Annual number of SCOPs created (including firms created from scratch, rescue takeovers and conversions of conventional firms). Source: CG-SCOP (1983–2004).
SCOP Exit	Annual number of SCOP closures. Source: CG-SCOP (1983–2004).
ALL Entry	Annual number of entering firms in France (including firms created from scratch—both independently and as subsidiaries of existing firms—and rescue-and non-rescue mergers and takeovers) in 1000s of firms. The numbers are calculated by INSEE using the SIRENE data base, which includes all (compulsory) business registration and deregistration. Sources: INSEE (1990, 1999, 2003), Cordellier (2000), Fabre (2005).
ALL Exit	Annual number of exiting firms in France (including liquidations as well as bankruptcies, mergers and firms taken over by other firms) in 1000s of firms. Sources: as for entry.
Density	For SCOPs, number of existing SCOPs on October 31 of the previous year; for all French firms, number of existing firms (1000s) on 31 December of the previous year. Sources: as for entry and exit.
GDP Growth	Real growth of GDP, 1990 prices. Source: INSEE (1990, 1999–2005a).
Unemployment	Annual rate of unemployment at time of labor force survey, ILO definition. Source: ILO (2005).
Share Index	French stock exchange (SBF) 250-industry share index, 1990 prices. Source: OECD (2003).
Interest Rate	Return on French public and semi-public sector bonds, deflated by the annual rate of price inflation. Source: OECD (2003).
Left in Government	Dummy variable taking the value 1 if the prime minister is a Socialist for more than 6 months of that year. Source: French Prime Minister's Office (Premier Ministre, 2003).

References

Agarwal, Rajshree, Audretsch, David B., 2001. Does entry size matter? The impact of the life cycle and technology on firm survival. Journal of Industrial Economics 49 (1), 21–43.

Audretsch, David B., 1991. New firm survival and the technological regime. Review of Economics and Statistics 73, 441–450.

Audretsch, David B., 1995. Innovation and Industry Evolution. MIT Press, Cambridge, MA.

Ben-Ner, Avner, 1984. On the stability of the cooperative form of organization. Journal of Comparative Economics 8 (3), 247–260.

Ben-Ner, Avner, 1987. Producer cooperatives: Why do they exist in capitalist economies? In: Powell, Walter W. (Ed.), The Nonprofit Sector: A Research Handbook. Yale Univ. Press, New Haven, CT, pp. 434–449.

Ben-Ner, Avner, 1988a. Comparative empirical observations on worker-owned and capitalist firms. International Journal of Industrial Organization 6, 7–31.

Ben-Ner, Avner, 1988b. The life-cycle of worker-owned firms in market economies. A theoretical analysis. Journal of Economic Behavior and Organization 10 (3), 287–313.

Boeri, Tito, Bellmann, Lutz, 1995. Post-entry behavior and the cycle: Evidence from Germany. International Journal of Industrial Organization 13 (4), 483–500.

Bonin, John, Jones, Derek C., Putterman, Louis, 1993. Theoretical and empirical studies of producer cooperatives: Will ever the twain meet? Journal of Economic Literature 31, 1290–1320.

Bowles, Samuel, Gintis, Herbert, 1994. Credit market imperfections the incidence of worker-owned firms. Metroeconomica 45 (3), 209–223.

Burke, Andrew E., FitzRoy, Felix R., Nolan, Michael A., 2000. When less is more: Distinguishing between entrepreneurial choice and performance. Oxford Bulletin of Economics and Statistics 62 (5), 565–587.

Cameron, A. Colin, Trivedi, Pravin K., 1990. Regression-based tests for overdispersion in the Poisson model. Journal of Econometrics 46, 347–364.

Cameron, A. Colin, Trivedi, Pravin K., 1998. Regression Analysis of Count Data. Cambridge Univ. Press, Cambridge, UK.

Carroll, Glenn R., 1984. Organizational ecology. Annual Review of Sociology 10, 71–93.

Carroll, Glenn R., Hannan, Michael T., 1989. Density dependence in the evolution of populations of newspaper organizations. American Sociological Review 54, 524–541.

Caves, Richard E., 1998. Industrial organization and new findings on the turnover and mobility of firms. Journal of Economic Literature 36, 1947–1982.

V. Pérotin / Journal of Comparative Economics 34 (2006) 295–316 315

Confédération Générale des SCOP (CG-SCOP), 1983–2004. Annual statistical abstract. CG-SCOP, Paris.

Confédération Générale des SCOP (CG-SCOP), 2003. Guide juridique des SCOP. SCOP Edit, Paris.

Conte, Michael A., 1986. Entry of worker cooperatives in capitalist economies. Journal of Comparative Economics 10, 41–47.

Conte, Michael A., Jones, Derek C., 1991. On the entry of employee-owned firms: Theory and evidence from US manufacturing Industries, 1870–1960. Working paper No. 91/5. Department of Economics, Hamilton College, Clinton, NY.

Cordellier, Christian, 2000. Créations et cessations d'entreprises: Sous la stabilité, le renouvellement. INSEE Première 740, October.

Counot, Stéphane, Mulic, Sylvie, 2004. Le rôle économique des repreneurs d'entreprise. INSEE Première 975, July.

Cox, D.R., 1983. Some remarks on overdispersion. Biometrika 70 (1), 269–274.

Cressy, Robert, 2000. Credit rationing or entrepreneurial risk aversion? An alternative explanation for the Evans and Jovanovic finding. Economics Letters 66, 235–240.

Dean, C., Lawless, J.F., 1989. Tests for detecting overdispersion in Poisson regression models. Journal of the American Statistical Association 84 (406), 467–472.

Disney, Richard, Haskel, Jonathan, Heden, Ylva, 2003. Entry, exit and establishment survival in UK manufacturing. Journal of Industrial Economics 51 (1), 91–112.

Doucouliagos, Chris, 1995. Worker participation and productivity in labor-managed and participatory capitalist firms: A meta-analysis. Industrial and Labor Relations Review 49 (1), 58–78.

Dow, Gregory K., 2003. Governing the Firm. Workers' Control in Theory and Practice. Cambridge Univ. Press, Cambridge, UK.

Dunne, Timothy, Klimek, Shawn D., Roberts, Mark J., 2005. International Journal of Industrial Organization 23 (5–6), 399–421.

Estrin, Saul, Jones, Derek C., 1992. The viability of employee-owned firms: Evidence from France. Industrial and Labor Relations Review 45 (2), 323–338.

Estrin, Saul, Jones, Derek C., 1995. Workers' participation, employee ownership and productivity: Results from French producer cooperatives. Advances in the Economic Analysis of Participatory and Labor-Managed Firms 5, 3–24.

Estrin, Saul, Jones, Derek C., 1998. The determinants of investment in employee-owned firms: Evidence from France. Economic Analysis 1 (1), 17–28.

Fabre, Virginie, 2005. La hausse des créations d'entreprises se poursuit. INSEE Première 1002, January.

French Government. Prime Minister's Office (Premier Ministre). 2003. Les chefs du gouvernement sous la 5e République. Available at http://www.premier-ministre.gouv.fr/fr/p.cfm?ref=15280.

Geroski, Paul A., 1995. What do we know about entry? International Journal of Industrial Organization 13 (4), 421–442.

Geroski, Paul A., 2001. Exploring the niche overlaps between organizational ecology and industrial economics. Industrial and Corporate Change 10 (2), 507–540.

Gouriéroux, Christian, Monfort, Alain, Trognon, Alain, 1984. Pseudo maximum likelihood methods: Applications to Poisson models. Econometrica 52 (3), 701–720.

Hamilton, Robert T., 1985. Interindustry variation in gross entry rates of 'independent' and 'dependent' businesses. Applied Economics 17, 271–280.

Highfield, Richard, Smiley, Robert, 1987. New business starts and economic activity. An empirical investigation. International Journal of Industrial Organization 5, 51–66.

International Labour Organization (ILO), 2005. Laborsta annual data. ILO Bureau of Statistics, Geneva. Available at http://laborsta.ilo.org.

Institut National de la Statistique et des Etudes Economiques (INSEE), 1990. Annuaire rétrospectif de la France, 1948–1988. Ministère des Finances, Paris.

Institut National de la Statistique et des Etudes Economiques (INSEE), 1999-2005a. Annuaire statistique de la France. Ministère des Finances, Paris.

Institut National de la Statistique et des Etudes Economiques (INSEE), 2005b. Comptes Nationaux. INSEE, Paris. Available at http://www.insee.fr/fr.indicateur/cnat_annu/series.

Lévy-Leboyer, Maurice, Bourguignon, François, 1990. The French Economy in the Nineteenth Century. Cambridge Univ. Press, Cambridge, UK.

MacDonald, James M., 1986. Entry and exit on the competitive fringe. Southern Economic Journal 52, 640–652.

Mayer, Walter J., Chapell, William F., 1992. Determinants of entry and exit: An application of the compounded bivariate Poisson distribution to US industries, 1972–77. Southern Economic Journal, January, 770–778.

Mittelhammer, Ron C., Judge, George G., Miller, Douglas J., 2000. Econometric Foundations. Cambridge Univ. Press, Cambridge, UK.

Organization for Economic Development and Cooperation (OECD), 2003. Main Economic Indicators. ESDS International, University of Manchester.

Pérotin, Virginie, 1999. Why are there so few labor-managed firms? Paper presented at the Conference on Democracy and Development, Columbia University.

Pérotin, Virginie, 2004. Early cooperative survival: The liability of adolescence. Advances in the Economic Analysis of Participatory and Labor-Managed Firms 8, 67–86.

Reynolds, Paul, Storey, David, 1993. Regional characteristics affecting small business formation. A cross-national comparison. ILE Notebook No 18, OECD/GD (93)197. OECD, Paris.

Rieg, Christian, 2003. Légère diminution des créations d'entreprises depuis 2000. INSEE Première 879, January.

Russell, Raymond (Ed.), 1995. Utopia in Zion. The Israeli Experience with Worker Cooperatives. State Univ. of New York Press, Albany, NY.

Russell, Raymond, Hanneman, Robert, 1992. Cooperatives and the business cycle: The Israeli case. Journal of Comparative Economics 16, 701–715.

Russell, Raymond, Hanneman, Robert, 1995. The formation and dissolution of worker cooperatives in Israel, 1924–1992. In: Russell, Raymond (Ed.), Utopia in Zion. The Israeli Experience with Worker Cooperatives. State Univ. of New York Press, Albany, NY, pp. 57–95.

Schwalbach, Joachim, 1987. Entry by diversified firms into German industries. International Journal of Industrial Organization 5, 43–49.

Shapiro, Daniel, Khemani, R.S., 1987. The determinants of entry and exit reconsidered. International Journal of Industrial Organization 5, 15–26.

Staber, Udo, 1989. Age-dependence and historical effects on the failure rates of worker cooperatives: An event-history analysis. Economic and Industrial Democracy 10, 59–80.

Staber, Udo, 1993. Worker cooperatives and the business cycle: Are cooperatives the answer to unemployment? American Journal of Economics and Sociology 52 (2), 129–143.

Thirion, Bernard, Demoly, Elvire, 2003. L'impact sur l'emploi des créations d'entreprises. Insee Première 917. August.

Vanek, Jaroslav, 1977. The Labor-Managed Economy. Cornell Univ. Press, Ithaca, NY.

Walras, Léon, 1865. Les associations populaires de consommation, de production et de crédit. Dentu, Paris.

[14]

ENTREPRENEURSHIP & REGIONAL DEVELOPMENT, 17, JULY (2005), 293–312

Technology centres during the economic downturn: what have we learned?

ROSS GITTELL† and JEFFREY SOHL‡

†Whittemore School of Business and Economics, University of New Hampshire, McConnell Hall, Durham, NH 03824, USA;
e-mail: rgittell@unh.edu
‡Center for Venture Research, Whittemore School of Business and Economics, University of New Hampshire, Durham, NH 03824, USA

This paper documents and assesses the economic performance of metropolitan technology centres in the USA during the business downturn of the early 2000s. We find that many of the USA's leading high-technology centres have performed at or near the national average, but that some of the nation's most prominent technology centres have fared poorly during the downturn, including Silicon Valley. The main factors that accentuated economic decline in technology centres during the recent recession include: a poorly diversified overall economic base; limited diversity within high-technology industries; relatively high (all industry) wages; and high levels of venture capital funding during the end of the 'boom' period of the late 1990s. We find that counter to some of the recent literature on regional development and knowledge-based industry clustering and networking, the rules of regional economic development have not changed dramatically with the so-called 'new economy'. High-technology regions, just as 'traditional' industry regions over the past century, are vulnerable to pronounced economic cycles of growth and decline. The cycles can be particularly pronounced if regional economies are not well diversified and labour costs are not moderated during economic downturns. We also find that venture capital can exaggerate rather than moderate regional economic cycles, such as economic growth years in the USA from the late 1990s to the recession of 2001. The model suggests that free-flowing venture capital dollars may result in an over reliance on these funds, at the expense of a sound business model with sustainable growth and reasonable cash flow. Also, business networks associated with venture capital fund flow might be detrimental at critical economic turning points, often resulting in a rush of dollars in a limited business sector, rather than a diversified set of entrepreneurial ventures.

Keywords: economic growth and decline; technology centres; regional industry clusters; economic diversification; USA economy.

1. Conceptual framework

The recession of the early 2000s in the USA – after a period of strong growth – offers a good opportunity to further knowledge and understanding of regional development and the high-technology sector of the economy. There is strong evidence that high-technology centres and firms contributed significantly to the long period of economic growth in the 1990s in the USA (Progressive Policy Institute 1999). Yet, after a period when the so-called 'new economy' was thought to break long-standing rules about economic cycles and regional and metropolitan area economies,

Entrepreneurship and Regional Development ISSN 0898–5626 print/ISSN 1464–5114 online
© 2005 Taylor & Francis Group Ltd
http://www.tandf.co.uk/journals
DOI: 10.1080/08985620500202582

relatively little is known about the dynamics of high-technology centres during periods of economic decline. This paper attempts to further knowledge and understanding about high-technology centres of the USA economy during such periods.

USA metropolitan areas with a high concentration of employment in the high-technology sector appeared to be the primary beneficiaries of the technology boom and economic growth in the 1990s. During this period, regions with a technology sector concentration tended to grow faster in employment than those lacking high-tech concentration (DeVol and Wong 1999). Drennan (2002), in research completed before the 2001–2003 economic downturn, suggested that specialization in the (broadly defined) information sector contributed substantially to superior USA metropolitan area performance over the last two decades of the twentieth century and would continue to do so in the future.

In the regional development literature the concept of high-technology centres have been studied under different names including clustering, innovation centres and technology centres. The geographic clustering of technology firms has been described as technology districts (Storper 1991), innovation networks (Coombs *et al.* 1996), innovative regional milieu (Malecki and Tootle 1996) and regional innovation systems (Wiig and Wood 1996).

The benefits of high-technology regions in the USA and other nations have also been described. Hassink and Wood (1998) document why geographic clustering of firms in a globally competitive industry (opto-electronics) occurs and is advantageous to a region's economy. They document the positive impact of clustering in terms of fostering research and development (R&D) collaboration and innovation. In a study of Scottish software firms (Collinson 2000) the propensity for technical, financial and commercial components to rapidly align in geographically defined clusters is described and according to Collinson, for Scottish software firms the 'speed of response' facilitated by geographic technology clusters provided a competitive advantage.

Bathelt (2001) identifies the forces behind the economic recovery of one region in the USA, Boston's Route 128 area that occurred in the mid-1990s. The forces identified include the historical resiliency of the region, the existence of multiple sub-sectors and the shared skilled labour pool in the region. The efficacy of these forces was previously supported by the findings of Best (2000). He suggested that the revitalization of Boston's high-tech economy in the mid-1990s was based in large part on geographical concentration of technological capabilities. However, Best suggested that technology concentration *per se* is not sufficient for regional economic advantage, that diversity within high-tech clusters is also necessary to sustain economic advantages. Bee (2003) concurs finding that regional employment growth in technology centres is influenced by technology diversity and industry mix, as characterized by the diversity of high-technology patents that contribute to regional economic growth.

There is a significant body of literature that highlights the importance of knowledge creation and knowledge-based high-technology industry clustering as a source of growth (Romer 1986). This knowledge-based growth, often referred to as the new growth theory, posits the notion that improvements in knowledge provide the basis for increasing returns that propel the process of economic and job growth. This 'new growth', it has been suggested as reviewed above, tends to cluster in geographic regions (Cortright 2002).

Another research stream examines high-tech centres in relation to entrepreneurial activity. In this literature technology centres are, in essence, derived from the development of entrepreneurial networks. It is suggested that public policy should facilitate and promote technology industries and associated networks to enhance regional economic development (Chaston 1996, Shaw 1997, Chell and Baines 2000). Geographically defined inter-firm networks are viewed as both a manifestation of an entrepreneurial centre and as a condition for the development of such centres. This research suggests that entrepreneurial networks contribute to the connectiveness and commonality that help to form a high-tech centre and contribute to economic vitality.

Still another stream of literature on technology centre growth suggests the importance of amenities such as the quality of life and cultural diversity (Florida 2002). These, it is suggested, serve as magnets to attract and retain high-skilled workers and technology entrepreneurs to geographic areas with recreational, cultural and other amenities. There is evidence that these amenities are particularly important in periods of economic growth and tight supply of skilled workers (Collaborative Economics 1999, Morrison Institute 1999, Florida 2002). When labour demand exceeds supply (e.g. in the USA in the late 1990s when many technology centres had unemployment levels below 2%) skilled workers could choose where to work based on where they want to live and technology companies and employment follow.

As the literature review above suggests, geographic areas with concentrations of high-technology activity and their underpinnings are of keen interest to regional economists, economic development professionals, entrepreneurs and suppliers of high-risk capital. High-technology centres are thought of as pathways to economic success. The desire to replicate the culture, capital and economy of Silicon Valley was a goal in the late 1990s that appeared for many areas to be desirable and attainable. The study of technology-based centres during economic downturns offers an opportunity to advance the understanding of this important sector of the economy and consider the sustainability of economic growth based on high-technology concentration.

This inquiry assesses the experience of 25 technology centres in the USA during the economic downturn of the early 2000s and tests empirically the efficacy of the aforementioned factors thought to drive economic growth in technology centres including high-technology industry employment concentration, diversification within technology industries, entrepreneurial activity, business networks, diversity, and quality of life.

This research tries to offer insights into the main contributing contextual and business climate factors of economic resiliency during difficult economic periods. The paper reviews how USA technological centres fared during the economic downturn of 2001 to 2003, considers why some technology centres performed better than others during this period, and tests regional cluster theories.

Why is this important? The literature on regional high-technology development and knowledge-based industry clusters and networking has influenced public policy. A now common view among practitioners is that public policy can and should facilitate and promote technology industries and associated networks to enhance regional economic development (Chaston 1996, Shaw 1997, Chell and Baines 2000). Our inquiry considers the utility of these policies and the associated theory and perspectives reviewed above.

2.   Centres of technological activity

We focus on recent economic experience in USA technology centres. The analysis is empirically based. The objective is to gain insight on regional (in this case USA Metropolitan Statistical Areas, MSAs) high-technology centres during times of economic contraction. An MSA is an official geographical designation used by USA government statistical agencies. It includes central cities and surrounding counties with significant economic connection and residents commuting to work in the central city.

2.1   *USA technology poles*

The Milken Institute in 1999 established a ranking of USA metropolitan areas in high-technology industry output and concentration (DeVol and Wong 1999). The ranking was prompted 'by anecdotes that technology firms are driving booms in fast-growing economies, such as those in Austin, Texas and Seattle, Washington'. Milken researchers studied how the value of high-technology goods produced in USA metropolitan areas through 1998 affected the overall economic growth of those areas. They examined businesses producing electronics, computers, communications equipment, aircraft, movies, medical supplies and related services. The results indicated that strong growth in production of high-technology goods explained 65% of the difference between the areas with the fastest-growing economies and the national average. According to DeVol, 'high-tech industries are determining which areas of the country are succeeding or failing in terms of economic growth...there are still remnants of the old economy, but the new economy is here' (Dworkin 1999: 2).

Of all the 287 metropolitan areas in the nation, the Milken Institute highlighted 25 as 'top ranked' and called them 'tech poles'. The ranking is a composite index for each metropolitan area. The index is calculated by the MSA's percentage of national high-technology real output multiplied by its high-technology real output location quotient. The location quotient is the percentage output of high-technology in each metropolitan area divided by the percentage of output in high-technology in the USA. Table 1 lists the Milken-defined technology poles in rank order with their composite index scores.

The San Jose metropolitan area, which includes much of Silicon Valley, ranked first in the Milken index, far exceeding the second ranked Dallas, Texas, in composite index score.

The Milken Institute published its ranking in the midst of the economic boom of the late 1990s. The metropolitan areas ranking high on the list where proud of their recognition and local economic pundits highlighted the benefits of being technology centres. For example, in Dallas one local business leader was quoted as saying 'Dallas tech pole positioning ends up being a kind of virtuous cycle' (Dworkin 1999).

This paper explores the experience of the tech poles during the early 2000s economic downturn and tries to address whether the prediction by some high-technology pundits of sustained technology cluster-driven economic vitality held in tech poles, and what are the lessons thereof?

First we profile the tech poles and then we describe and then analyse their performance in the early 2000s.

Table 1.   Milken technology poles.

Rank	MSA technology pole	Composite index	Rank	MSA technology pole	Composite index
1	San Jose, CA (SAJ)	23.69	14	Oakland, CA (OAK)	2.21
2	Dallas, TX (DAL)	7.06	15	Philadelphia, PA (PHI)	2.19
3	Los Angeles-Long Beach, CA (LOS)	6.91	16	Rochester, MN (ROC)	1.95
4	Boston, MA (BOS)	6.31	17	San Diego, CA (SAN)	1.93
5	Seattle-Bellevue-Everett, WA (SEA)	5.19	18	Raleigh-Durham-Chapel Hill, NC (RAL)	1.89
6	Washington, DC-MD-VA-WV (WAS)	5.08	19	Denver, CO (DEN)	1.81
7	Albuquerque, NM (ALB)	4.98	20	Newark, NJ (NEA)	1.80
8	Chicago, IL (CHI)	3.75	21	Austin-San Marcos, TX (AUS)	1.78
9	New York, NY (NWY)	3.67	22	San Francisco, CA (SAF)	1.62
10	Atlanta, GA (ATL)	3.46	23	Houston, TX (HOU)	1.62
11	Middlesex-Somerset, NJ (MSH)	3.40	24	Boise City, ID (BOI)	1.43
12	Phoenix-Mesa, AZ (PHO)	2.60	25	New Haven-Stamford, CT (NHB)	1.33
13	Orange County, CA (ORC)	2.59			

Source: DeVol and Wong (1999).

2.2   USA technology pole's economic composition

How similar or dissimilar are the technology poles from the other regions in the USA? The tech poles' industry composition compared to the USA average can be quantified using gini coefficients. Overall metro area composition is the distribution of employment among the main industry sectors (so-called 'supersectors', which are defined as the largest and most comprehensive industry categories used by the new North American Industrial Classification System, NAICS). The supersectors include manufacturing, education and health services, retail trade and construction. The relative mix can be depicted using gini coefficients. The coefficients measure similarity (or dissimilarity) to the USA average industry composition. The formula for gini's is:

$G = \text{SUM} [\text{absolute} (\%Xi - \%Yi)]/2$

SUM = Summation across all sectors in the same area (state, MSA, county)
Absolute = Absolute value
%X = employment ratio on SECTOR i and state 'j'
%Y = employment ratio on SECTOR i and USA or aggregate area.

Gini coefficients range from 0 to 1. A value of 0.20 means that 20% of the employment of a metropolitan area (MSA) would need to shift to a different super-sector in order for that MSA to have employment composition the same as the USA average. A value of 1 is complete dissimilarity and a value of 0 is complete similarity to the USA average. The lower the value the greater the similarity to the USA economy overall.

The tech poles with the most dissimilar industry mixes are Washington, DC, Rochester (Minnesota), San Francisco and San Jose (table 2). Chicago and Seattle have super-sector industry composition most similar to the USA average among the Milken tech poles. DC's ranking is illustrative as it results from more than twice the USA average concentration in professional and technical services and about 30% below the USA concentration in financial activities.

Table 2. Ranking for gini coefficient for NAICS supersectors.

MSA technology pole	Supersector gini coefficient	MSA technology pole	Supersector gini coefficient
Washington, DC-MD-VA-WV	0.21	Phoenix-Mesa, AZ	0.08
Rochester, MN	0.21	Dallas, TX	0.08
San Francisco, CA	0.19	Albuquerque, NM	0.08
San Jose, CA	0.17	New Haven-Bridgeport-Stamford-Danbury-Waterbury, CT	0.08
New York, NY	0.17	Boston, MA-NH	0.08
Middlesex-Somerset-Hunterdon, NJ	0.12	San Diego, CA	0.08
Denver, CO	0.11	Oakland, CA	0.07
Atlanta, GA	0.10	Boise City, ID	0.07
Orange Country, CA	0.10	Raleigh-Durham-Chapel Hill, NC	0.07
Philadelphia, PA-NJ	0.09	Austin-San Marcos, TX	0.06
Los Angeles-Long Beach, CA	0.09	Chicago, IL	0.06
Newark, NJ	0.08	Seattle-Bellevue-Everett, WA	0.06
Houston, TX	0.08		

Source: Bureau of Economic Analysis (2001).

Table 3. Ranking for gini coefficient for high-tech industry.

MSA technology pole	High-tech gini coefficient	MSA technology pole	High-tech gini coefficient
Rochester, MN	0.78	New York, NY	0.28
Boise City, ID	0.70	Boston, MA-NH	0.28
Phoenix-Mesa, AZ	0.60	San Diego, CA	0.26
Austin-San Marcos, TX	0.47	Los Angles-Long Beach, CA	0.26
San Francisco, CA	0.42	Raleigh-Durham-Chapel Hill, NC	0.25
Newark, NJ	0.36	Orange Country, CA	0.24
San Jose, CA	0.36	Albuquerque, NM	0.24
Seattle-Bellevue-Everett, WA	0.35	Oakland, CA	0.22
Middlesex-Somerset-Hunterdon, NJ	0.34	Houston, TX	0.21
Washington, DC-MD-VA-WV	0.33	Philadelphia, PA-NJ	0.20
Dallas, TX	0.33	Chicago, IL	0.19
Atlanta, GA	0.29	New Haven-Bridgeport-Stamford-Danbury-Waterbury, CT	0.17
Denver, CO	0.29		

Source: Bureau of Labor Statistics–Covered Employment Wages (2001).

Gini coefficients can also be calculated within the high-technology sector (using high-technology industries as defined by economy.com, a well-known and respected international economic consulting firm). On this measure Philadelphia, Chicago and New Haven among tech poles have high-tech industry composition most similar to the USA average employment distribution within high-technology while Rochester (Minnesota), Boise (Idaho) and Phoenix (Arizona) have the least similar high-tech compositions to the USA average, due to concentrations of high-technology employment in particular high-tech sub-sectors (table 3). Rochester has 17 times the USA average employment concentration in computer central processing units and periphery equipment manufacturing, Boise and Phoenix have eight and seven times, respectively, the USA concentration in semiconductor and electronic component manufacturing.

The high variation in overall and high-technology industry specific gini coefficients for the 25 tech poles suggests significant diversity in the economic characteristics of the top ranked tech poles. This is confirmed and further illustrated when the high-technology sub-sectors in the individual tech poles with the highest employment concentration relative to the USA average (as measured by location quotients, LQ) are documented (table 4). There is no high-technology sub-sector that more than four of the technology poles have as its leading technology industry in terms of employment concentration relative to the USA average.

Next we consider how overall employment/industry mix and high-technology composition and other factors affected economic performance during the early 2000s downturn.

3. Data and methodology

The tech poles have been impacted by the economic downturn that commenced in the first quarter of 2001. From early 2001 to early 2003, 21 of the 25 technology poles experienced decline in total employment. As with employment composition there were significant differences in tech pole employment performance. Change in total employment in the tech poles ranged from a decline of over 16% in San Jose, the home of 'Silicon Valley', to a 1.5% increase in employment in San Diego.

Milken's leading tech pole, San Jose, had the second greatest employment decline of the 287 MSAs in the USA and San Francisco (another top ranked tech pole) had the third greatest decline. Decline in technical centres was not limited to one geographic region of the USA. Tech poles from all across the USA declined. Interestingly, California and the Northeast were each home to both the best and worst performing technology centres suggesting that neither state nor general regional location had a particularly strong effect on employment performance during the economic downturn from 2001 to 2003.

Overall, the tech poles performed fairly similarly to the USA average during the period 2001–03. Twelve of the poles had employment decline below the USA average of 1.8% during the period, while thirteen experienced more pronounced decline than the USA average over the last two years (table 5).

Yet the tech pole average (not median) employment decline from 2001 to 2003 of 2.8% is considerably higher than the USA average decline. This is because of a pronounced decline in a relatively small number of tech poles. Six tech poles – San Jose, San Francisco, Seattle, Boston, New York City, and Dallas – had sharp employment declines, all with more than double the USA average decline and all ranked among the bottom performing 10% (24 out of 287) of MSAs in the nation.

There was not a similar pronounced increase in any tech pole. The top performing tech pole, San Diego, ranked 48th among the 287 MSAs nationally in growth in total employment with growth of 1.4%. Only 4 of the 25 tech poles experienced employment growth during 2001 to 2003. The fastest-growing MSAs in the USA were not tech poles but centres of retirement and tourism including Fort Meyers (Florida) and Fayetteville (Arkansas), which grew over 6% from March 2001 to March 2003, over four times the rate of growth in San Diego.

The decline in tech-pole employment occurred right after the long period of economic growth in the late 1990s to 2000 (1996–2001) when the tech poles averaged annual employment growth of 2.6%. It also occurred after a period

Table 4. Milken technology poles.

MSA technology pole	Highest LQ subsector	Value of highest LQ	MSA technology pole	Highest LQ subsector	Value of highest LQ
Albuquerque, NM	Wireless Telecom. Carriers	4.09	Newark, NJ	Pharm. & Medicine Mfg	6.40
Atlanta, GA	Software Publishers	2.20	Oakland, CA	Software Publishers	2.00
Ausin-San Marcos, TX	CPU & Periph. Equip. Mfg	4.79	Orange Country, CA	Satellite Telecommunications	4.09
Boise City, ID	Semi & Elec. Comp. Mfg	8.14	Philadelphia, PA-NJ	Pharm. Medicine Mfg	4.04
Boston, MA-NH	Software Publishers	2.71	Phoenix-Mesa, AZ	Semi. & Elec. Comp. Mfg	6.98
Chicago, IL	Sci. Research & Develop. Services	2.12	Raleigh-Durham-Chapel Hill, NC	CPU & Periph. Equip. Mfg	3.36
Dallas, TX	Comm. Equip. Mfg.	3.21	Rochester, MN	CPU & Periph. Equip. Mfg	17.01
Denver, CO	Wired Telecom. Carriers	2.25	San Diego, CA	Sci. Research & Develop. Services	2.84
Houston, TX	Other Telecommunications	7.86	San Francisco, CA	ISP and Web Search Portals	4.44
Los Angles-Long Beach, CA	Satellite Telecommunications	8.47	San Jose, CA	CPU & Periph. Equip. Mfg	3.63
Middlesex-Somerset-Hunterdon, NJ	Other Telecommunications	3.86	Seattle-Bellevue-Everett, WA	Software Publishers	6.07
New Haven-Bridgeport-Stamford-Danbury-Waterbury, CT	Pharm. & Medicine Mfg	2.39	Washington, DC-MD-VA-WV	ISP and Web Search Portals	2.22
New York, NY	Wired Telecom. Carriers	1.93			

Source: DeVol and Wong (1999).

Table 5. Rankings of dependent variables.

Rank	MSA technology pole	Percentage change in total employment (3/01–3/03)	Rank	MSA technology pole	Percentage change in total employment (3/01–3/03)
1	San Diego, CA	1.5	14	Boise City, ID	−2.5
2	Washington, DC-MD-VA-WV	0.9	15	Los Angles-Long Beach, CA	−2.6
3	Albuquerque, NM	0.8	16	Austin-San Marcos, TX	−2.7
4	Rochester, NM	0.3	17	Denver, CO	−2.9
5	Philadelphia, PA-NJ	−0.3	18	Chicago, IL	−3.2
6	Newark, NJ	−0.5	19	Middlesex-Somerset-Hunterdon, NJ	−3.5
7	New Haven-Brideport-Stamford-Danbury-Waterbury, CT	−0.7	20	Dallas, TX	−4.6
8	Houston, TX	−0.8	21	Boston, MA-NH	−5.1
9	Atlanta, GA	−0.8	22	New York, NY	−5.1
10	Phoenix-Mesa, AZ	−0.8	23	Seattle-Bellevue-Everett, WA	−5.5
11	Raleigh-Durham-Chapel Hill, NC	−1.3	24	San Francisco, CA	−11.1
12	Orange Country, CA	−1.6	25	San Jose, CA	−16.5
13	Oakland, CA	−2.3			

Source: Bureau of Labor Statistics–Current Employment Statistics (2001–2003).

when the perspective among tech industry enthusiasts and in many technology centres was of a new dynamic in regional economies. This perceived new dynamic included technology and knowledge-based industry clusters and the end of some traditional economic 'rules' including regional economic cycles. What happened?

The correlation between employment changes during the late 1990s' boom and during the early 2000s decline suggests that what occurred was not a simple boom-bust in tech poles with those centres that had grown the most during the growth period experiencing the sharpest decline during the downturn. The positive (0.13) correlation coefficient between total MSA employment change 1996–2001 and employment change from 2001 to 2003 suggests that the decline in tech poles is not simply explained by boom and bust. There is a more complex relationship.

3.1. How can the downturn in tech centres from March 2001 to March 2003 be explained and why did some tech poles do better than others?

Figure 1 shows the simple correlation between Milken rank and total employment change during the economic downturn from March 2001 to March 2003. The −0.31 correlation suggests that the top ranking among the tech poles tended to suffer more than lesser ranked tech poles. The figure plots the tech poles by Milken rank from twenty-fifth (at the origin) to first (at the vertical top) versus employment change from greatest decrease (at origin) to greatest increase at far right. San Jose (SAJ) and Seattle (SEA) are the most prominent top ranked tech poles with well above the median (for tech pole) employment decline. Washington, DC (WAS) and Albuquerque (ALB) occupy the upper-right hand quadrant and are the two high ranked (above the median of top 25) tech poles that performed best during the economic downturn. The plot depicts that, in general, most of the

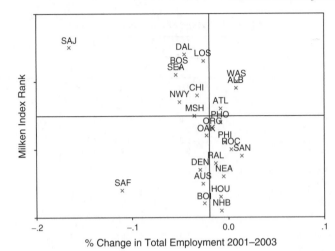

Figure 1. **Milken index rank vs. percentage change in total employment (2001–2003).**

tech poles – regardless of relative rank among the top 25 – performed at or near the
tech pole median (−1.95%) of employment change. Most of the tech poles had total
employment decline just below the USA average (−1.8%) during the last two years.

Further statistical testing of correlation reveals some relationship between
industry composition measures and tech pole employment performance, 2001–
2003, as summarized in table 6. Concentration of employment in high-technology,
professional and technical services, information industries and manufacturing
were all negatively correlated with employment change. The tech poles with
highest concentration of employment in these industries tended to have the most
pronounced employment decline over the last 2 years. In contrast, the tech poles
with the highest employment concentration in retail, other services, and construction
experienced the least employment decline.

The overall gini coefficient (across all industry sectors) of the economy is
negatively correlated with employment change in the early 2000s in the tech centres.
This suggests that less overall diversification in the economy was detrimental to
employment change in the tech centres during the economic downturn. The high-
technology gini coefficient (measured within high-tech) was not significantly correlated with change in employment. This suggests that diversification within high
technology did not help high-technology poles during the downturn. The simple
correlation statistics, however, do not take into account the confluence of factors that
affected tech pole economies during the recent downturn. Econometric analysis can
help control for different factors and isolate the most significant factors affecting tech
poles during the early 2000s' downturn.

4. Econometric modelling and analysis

To help to identify the key factors that contributed to changes in employment from
March 2001 to March 2003 in the tech poles an econometric model was specified.

Table 6. Correlation between industry composition and change in total tech pole employment.

Industry composition	Correlation	Significance	Industry composition	Correlation	Significance
% Employment in High-Tech Industry	−0.68*	0.00	% Employment in Real Estate, Rental, & Housing	−0.09	0.66
% Employment in Professional & Technical Services	−0.55*	0.00	High-tech Gini Coefficient	−0.04	0.83
% Employment in Information	−0.49*	0.02	% Employment in Accommodation & Food Services	0.04	0.86
% Employment in Manufacturing	−0.38**	0.06	% Employment in Administrative & Waste Services	0.10	0.63
% Employment in Management of Companies	−0.33	0.12	% Employment in Transportation & Warehousing	0.17	0.51
Supersector Gini Coefficient	−0.31	0.13	% Employment in Health Care & Social Assistance	0.23	0.27
% Employment in Educational Services	−0.21	0.30	% Employment in Construction	0.30	0.14
% Employment in Arts, Entertainment, & Recreation	−0.20	0.34	% Employment in Other Services	0.31	0.14
% Employment in Finance & Insurance	−0.11	0.60	% Employment in Retail Trade	0.49*	0.01
% Employment in Wholesale Trade	−0.11	0.63			

*, ** denote that the correlation is significant at the 5% and 10% levels, respectively.

304   ROSS GITTELL AND JEFFREY SOHL

The model is used to consider the economic and regional cluster theory described above. The modelling relies on best data available and also proxies for the regional development dynamics under consideration.

4.1 Significance, tests, and results

After testing possible explanatory variables (see more detail below) and model specifications the best model explained 84% of the variance in tech pole employment from March 2001 to March 2003. The model seems to do well explaining the employment decline in the tech poles that experienced the most significant total employment percentage declines, including San Jose (-16.5% actual versus -15.4% predicted) and San Francisco (-11% versus -11.3%). It also does well explaining employment percentage decline in some of the technology centres that had relatively strong economies during the early 2000s such as Albuquerque (0.8% actual versus 1.5% predicted) and Phoenix (-0.8% versus 1%).

There were five significant explanatory variables[1] identified. These include: venture capital per worker, high-technology employment concentration, diversity in high-technology employment, information industry concentration and average (all industry) wages. All these independent variables negatively affected percentage employment decline during the 2001–03 downturn in the tech poles (table 7 shows the model specification). All except for information industry concentration were individually statistically significant at a 5% level of significance (information industry concentration was significant at the 10% level). No other variables considered[1] were significant or added to the model's explanatory power.

The model was corrected for heteroskedasticity using White's estimator (Gujarati 1995). Additionally, the functional form (OLS) and omitted variables were not a problem as the model passed RESET tests, which included the square of the predicted value, the square and cube of the predicted value, and the square, cube, and fourth power of the predicted value.

The best-fit econometric model suggests that metropolitan areas in the so-called new economy are subject to similar regional economic 'rules' as cities and economic regions throughout the twentieth century (Meyer 1963, Gittell 1992, 1999). High employment concentration in cyclical industries and increases in wages in growth

Table 7. Regression results.

Dependent variable: Percentage change in MSA total employment from 3/01 to 2/03.

Variable	Coefficient	Standard error	t-ratio	$P[|T|>t]$
Constant	0.1099390308	0.25403160E − 01	4.328	0.0005
Venture capital per worker	−0.4268356302E − 05	0.12915508E − 05	−3.305	0.0045
Average (all industry) wages	−0.1656595891E − 05	0.55382018E − 06	−2.991	0.0086
High-tech employment	−0.3649647729	0.47032325E − 01	−7.760	0.0000
Diversity in high-tech employment	−0.5658018869E − 01	0.21889597E − 01	−2.585	0.0199
Information industry	−0.5994259756	0.32653785	−1.836	0.0851

(Note: E + nn or E − nn means multiply by 10 to + or −nn power.)
Fit: $R^2 = 0.875801$, Adjusted $R^2 = 0.83699$.

periods (such as the late 1990s in high-technology) leads to pronounced declines during the end of business cycles and economic downturns.

4.2. Model interpretation

In the model, the venture capital per worker coefficient is an estimate of the amount by which the percentage change in total employment increases when venture capital per worker in 1999 increases by $1. Thus, the model estimates that a $1000 increase in venture capital per worker in the late 1990s would result in total employment declining 0.43% between 2001 and 2003. That venture capital investment levels are negatively correlated with percentage change in employment is significant. It suggests that there can be 'too much of a good thing' in terms of money available for start-up and high growth ventures. Tech poles with the highest venture capital money invested per worker in 1999, such as San Jose and San Francisco, tended to experience the greatest percentage declines in employment in the early 2000s. This might reflect that too much capital was chasing too few sound business ventures in 'hot markets' at the end of the exuberant 1990s. This also suggests that place-based networks among venture capitalists and aspiring entrepreneurs might have detrimental aspects, fostering hype, speculation and non-prudent investment especially in the tail end of economic growth periods such as the late 1990s.

In the business networks and regional development literature there is not much attention given to the potential detrimental effects of networking and close group bonds. Just as with inner city youth gangs, close ties and tight networks among businesspersons (such as among venture capitalists and between venture capitalists and aspiring entrepreneurs) can lead to group thinking and irrational behaviour. This behaviour can be motivated by group psychology and individuals and individual firms not wanting to be 'left behind' and thus following the seemingly beneficial behaviour of others without adequate review and consideration of the implications and rationale of their individual actions (Gittell and Thompson 1999).

The experience in the early 2000s in the USA tech poles suggests that it can be hard in places with strong business ties to reverse non-prudent group behaviour. In the case of high-tech centres during the 1990s the ill-informed behaviour was venture investment in non-viable business models. In tech poles such as San Francisco this took the form specifically of investment in dot.coms without substantive products or services to sell and without an adequate plan or prospects to become profitable. Investments were motivated by individuals not wanting to 'miss out' on the perceived opportunities that others were pursuing aggressively and getting rich doing so. Additionally, as reflected in the title *Fast Company* of a prominent new economy business publication, a strong part of the 'group think' of the late 1990s in USA tech centres was the belief that there was great need to act fast to guarantee success in the new economy.

A manifestation of this was the strong flow of venture money into Silicon Valley during the late 1990s. In 1999 venture capital flow in the Valley was over $8000 per worker, compared to the tech pole (top 25 ranked Milken poles) median of $900. The econometric model suggests that the 'rush' of venture capital money had a negative impact during the downturn in Silicon Valley and other tech poles. Firms that got started with venture capital money (and not on sound business models) at the tail end of the economic growth period of the middle to late 1990s had to downsize. Also some older firms may have become over-reliant on the steady flow of venture capital dollars, since the venture capital money was readily available and over two-thirds of venture capital funding is invested in existing portfolio companies (Sohl 2002). With the venture capital money flowing freely at the tail end of the 1990s in some tech poles, the withdrawal from this stream of cash was most painful for those companies that 'subsisted' with venture capital money. In contrast, areas which attracted more modest levels of venture capital investment, such as San Diego (just under $1500 per worker), continued to experience employment growth during the national economic downturn.

An implication of the finding regarding venture capital funding is that while there may be agglomeration economies for the collection and distribution of venture capital dollars in geographic areas, there may be limits to the positive agglomeration effects of venture capital as a local (metropolitan area) market becomes glutted and good money starts chasing not so good deals. Thus, rather than focusing on the development of a sustainable business model with a reasonable cash flow, the rush to take advantage of an active IPO market can drive investors and entrepreneurs to build 'designer' companies fashioned for an exit, rather than building a solid company. Investors may have lacked the foresight to recognize the inherent flaws in the underlying business model and the lack of a clear path to profitability. Implications might include that venture capitalists investing during the mature stage of a growth period might benefit from searching well beyond their natural and normal geographic boundaries.

The cyclical nature of venture capital investing, namely the tendency to invest during or immediately preceding downturns, can be explained in part by Kondratiev waves – defined as long waves in the economic cycle that are an inherent part of the capitalist system (Kondratiev 1984). In the context of the equity financing of technology-based ventures, venture capitalists serve as technology gatekeepers. As gatekeepers, the venture capital industry set the direction of technology through the choice of which technologies to support (Berry 1991). As an influx of money is directed to the chosen technology, this surge is prone to excessive overshoot. Kondratiev wave theory suggests that venture capitalists should curb this speculative nature by building into the screening process the likelihood of overshoot and the consequences of collapse (Berry 1991). Unfortunately, such discipline is not likely if the venture capital industry is strongly effected by 'group think' fostered by close venture capital industry ties and strong bonds/networks with entrepreneurs in particular industry clusters concentrated in regional economies.

Another factor that had a negative effect on employment change in the early 2000s in the tech poles was the average of all industry annual wages (average annual wages per job in 2000). The model also suggests that wage levels in the early 2000s were a negative factor mostly in the tech centres that had tight overall labour markets and high overall average wages, not just in the high-tech industry, such as San Jose ($65 249), San Francisco ($59 397) and New York City ($58 314). High average of all industry wages can contribute to pronounced employment declines, as businesses and employers in all industries not just high-technology seek lower cost areas and fewer workers in periods of recession. In contrast two of the tech poles with the lowest average of all industry average annual wages, Albuquerque ($31 160) and Phoenix ($35 288) had relatively strong employment performance in the early 2000s. The wage coefficient indicates that a $1000 increase in all industry wages accounts for 0.17% of the decrease in total employment between March 2001 and March 2003. Test of the effect of average high-tech industry wages indicated that it was not a significant explanatory variable.

Many public officials and community advocates in technology centres have been most concerned with high-tech wages and in particular whether or not wages in other industries are keeping up with high-tech wages. There is concern that high-tech wages drive up area housing prices and other costs and that wages in other industries including typically low wage service industries should keep pace to ensure what is often called 'liveable wages' across industry sectors. For example, in San Francisco – with the second highest average of all industry wages among the 25 top ranked tech poles – there has been legislation to address the liveable wage issue and require city government and contractors with city government to pay wages well above the minimum. The finding with regards to the effect of wage levels in technology centres during the early 2000s suggests that liveable wage legislation that increases metropolitan area average all industry wages might have unintended consequences. It has the potential to hurt those that it is intended to help. Our findings suggest that policies that raise overall wages in tech poles can contribute to pronounced employment decline during economic downturns.

Employment concentration in high-technology industries, like the other significant explanatory variables in the model, is negatively correlated with the percentage change in total employment in the tech poles in the early 2000s. The model suggests that a tech pole's high-technology employment concentration of 10% of total employment in 2001 (holding everything else constant in the model) could explain 3.6% of decline in total employment from March 2001 to March 2003. With the so-called 'burst of the high-tech bubble', the model indicates that the tech poles with the highest concentrations of high-tech employment would be the most adversely affected. San Jose is the best example, having a high-tech concentration of nearly 23%. The San Jose MSA experienced a 16.5% decline in total employment over the same time period. In contrast, all the other tech poles had high-technology industry concentration below 10% of total employment. San Diego, the tech pole with arguably the strongest economy in the early 2000s, had high-technology industry concentration of 6% in 2001. The high-technology employment concentration finding indicates that tech poles can benefit from diversification outside high-technology. This suggests that the benefits of high-tech industry clusters may not be additive, particularly during economic downturns.

The econometric findings also suggest that diversification within high technology can be beneficial. In the model, the high-tech gini coefficient was significant and negatively related to the percentage change in total employment. The gini coefficient serves as a dissimilarity indicator, the lower the gini the more similar the overall high-tech industry in the MSA is to the USA. Thus the model suggests that the higher the gini (and the less diversity within high-technology) in any tech pole, the more likely that total employment will have declined significantly in that tech pole in the early 2000s.

This finding is different from the simple correlation test above, for which there did not appear to be any effect on employment change from diversity within high-technology industries in tech poles. However, in the regression modelling after controlling for high-technology employment concentration overall and venture capital flow and wages, diversity in high-technology was significant.

High-technology industry ginis result from a region having a high location quotient in a particular technology industry, and not a well diversified base within high-technology. During the most recent recession, concentration of employment in one particular industry within high-tech in an MSA (regardless of the particular industry in high-tech) tended to have negative effect on the MSA economy and contributed to pronounced employment percentage decline. This included San Francisco, with high concentration in internet service providers and web search portals, Austin (Texas), with high concentration in central processing unit and periphery equipment manufacturing and Boise (Idaho) with high concentration in semiconductor manufacturing. The statistical significance of the high-tech gini coefficient suggests that technology clusters that are too concentrated and tech sectors which are too narrow can be detrimental. This supports the finding by Best (2000) regarding the Boston metropolitan area and the benefits of technology industry diversification.

Information industry employment concentration is also significant and negative. The coefficient estimate indicates that an information industry employment concentration of 10% of total area employment in 2001 would explain a 6.0% decline in total employment over the time period. Metropolitan areas with high concentrations in the information industry suffered in the recent recession. As examples Seattle, Dallas, and New York City all had information concentrations around 5% (compared to the 25 top tech pole median of 3.1%) and these MSAs all lost approximately 5% of total employment between March 2001 and March 2003. This finding contrasts with Drennan's (2002) view regarding the enduring benefit of metropolitan area concentration in information industries.

After the five significant variables detailed above were included and various functional forms of the econometric model were tested, no other variable had a statistically significant effect on tech pole total employment change percentage from 2001 to 2003. Neither concentration of employment in other NAICS' super-sectors (such as trade or finance or construction) nor in any particular sub-sector of high-tech and related industries (such as semiconductors, measuring equipment, internet service providers) had any significant effect after controlling for the other variables. Neither did region of the nation (e.g. Northeast or West), relative tax burden, or educational level of the workforce. The latter suggests that a highly educated and skilled workforce can not prevent economic decline. Concentration of adults with higher education does not provide any particular relief during difficult economic times in technology poles.

Business start-up activity also did not have significant affect on economic performance in tech poles during the recent recession. This suggests that entrepreneurship may not be of great benefit to regional economies during periods of general economic weakness. However, the business start-up data is not ideal. The most timely data available on business starts is by state, not by metropolitan area. We used the state measures for the tech poles matching tech poles with state, e.g. San Jose, San Francisco and Los Angeles all with California. The model also does not consider the recession-push theory of entrepreneurship and business start-ups. The recession-push view suggests that many businesses will start up during recession periods and then experience high failure rates, but the new ventures that survive will be a key source of growth and contribute to economic recovery. The time frame for our analysis does not allow for testing of this view, but should be considered in future research.

Entrepreneurship may not be significant in mitigating economic decline in tech poles, but may be one of the major factors in contributing to economic recovery. Recessions can provide a 'push' for entrepreneurial activity, and entrepreneurial ventures can help to foster beneficial economic transition and diversification of regional economies.

The model also indicates that the cost of living did not affect tech pole performance during the economic downturn. This finding, together with the findings related to wages, suggests that it is not overall costs that affect technology economies during periods of economic malaise as much as it is wage costs. This might have policy implications as it indicates that tech poles in which wages respond quickly to labour market conditions, even without changes to overall costs such as housing and energy costs (that are often not very responsive to labour market conditions), may be most resilient to economic decline.

The econometric modelling also indicates that quality of life (as measured by Morgan and Morgan 2003) and diversity (as measured by Florida 2002) do not appear to have affected economic performance during the early 2000s in the tech poles. This suggests that the quality of life and diversity of amenities that may draw workers and entrepreneurs to technology centres, may be a necessary, rather than a sufficient, condition for high-tech growth. In essence, quality of life and diversity may be factors that draw people to a high-tech centre, but might not have a strong enough influence to keep workers and companies there and employed during an economic downturn.

5. Conclusion

There is strong evidence that high-technology centres contributed significantly to the long period of economic growth in the 1990s in the USA. Yet these centres have not been any more resilient during the period of economic decline in the early 2000s than other areas. In fact, some of the more prominent technology centres such as San Jose and Seattle have experienced employment decline significantly more pronounced than the USA average.

In general, less is known about the dynamics of high-technology centres during periods of economic decline than during periods of growth. This is partly an artefact of the emergent literature on regional development (outlined above) produced during the period of extended technology-driven growth in the 1990s. In contrast, this paper attempts to further knowledge and understanding about high-technology centres during the most recent economic downturn.

This analysis suggests that all industry average wages, limited economic diversification, high-technology industry concentration, concentrations within high-technology industry, and venture capital flow at the end of the economic growth period all had a significant negative effect in USA high-tech centres during the most recent recession.

Our findings highlight that high-technology concentration and concentration in the information industry is not always a good thing. This finding is not a surprise to scholars who have studied economic change in the USA and other nation's regions over the last century. In many respects the experience of the early 2000s in high-technology centres in the USA has indicated that high-technology is just another industry and subject to cycles, over-speculation and over-concentration of employment and capital. There are no (or few) 'new rules', much to the chagrin of 'tech gurus' and the new economy pundits who rose to prominence in the late 1990s.

Perhaps the most surprising finding is that 'late' (i.e. at the latter phase of the business cycle) arriving venture capital dollars may add to high-tech centre decline. This suggests that free flowing capital is not always a good thing in tech centres. Rather than an over reliance on a steady stream of venture capital dollars, a good business model with reasonable cash flow, and external capital to fuel growth from this base, is the better strategy. The findings on venture capital flow in the late 1990s and the economic performance of the tech poles in the early 2000s also highlight the potential negative side to strong regional business networks and strong bonds among venture capitalists and between venture capitalists and entrepreneurs in a region. As such, public policy to facilitate the development of technology industry concentrations to enhance regional economic development may need to be broader in scope.

The finding that wage levels negatively affect tech-centre employment indicates that wages, but not necessarily overall costs, are an important factor in economic performance in tech centres. The non-significance of quality of life and diversity suggests that lifestyle amenities might be most relevant during economic growth periods when workers have a choice of where to locate, that quality of life and diversity may be 'selling points' for a tech centre when labour markets are tight, but not an effective glue to hold businesses and workers during down cycles.

The finding on the insignificance of business start-up activity on economic performance in the USA tech poles during early 2000s indicates that entrepreneurial activity is no panacea. Business and economic fundamentals, such as overall economic vitality in the nation, are critical to regional economic success. Business start-up activity in the late 1990s (our proxy for entrepreneurial activity) was not able to counteract the weak economic conditions of 2001–2003 in the USA tech centres, at least in the short-term.

This analysis is meant to provoke and suggest areas for further inquiry. The findings here are limited to what factors may have promoted or dampened economic decline during the early 2000s downturn in USA technology centres. It does not consider the affects of these factors on long-term growth in tech poles or other areas. For example, a set of questions/issues related to long-term growth in the tech poles still need to be considered, such as do the same factors that promote (or dampen) decline during a down phase of an economic cycle in tech poles promote (or dampen) longer-term growth and economic well-being? Another important issue that has been identified here and is a subject for future inquiry is the 'other side' to business networks and close regional ties among leading economic agents. Are there negative consequences for regional development from too strong internal business ties and networks? In the long term, over several stages of the business cycle, are high surges in entrepreneurial activity sustainable on a regional basis? Do the centres with a smaller number of high-growth start-ups during an upswing benefit from less significant decline and exiting of these entrepreneurial ventures? An additional area of enquiry is the international dimensions of our analysis. While USA tech centres were compared, what lessons can be drawn from an analysis of tech centres across nations and over economic cycles?

Significant lessons can be learned from the recent experience of USA tech centres. The technology boom of the late 1990s was not sustained. There are significant challenges ahead for technology centres in the USA and elsewhere. For regions, economic advantage – even with knowledge-based industry concentrations and strong existing business networks – is a dynamic concept, not a static position. The main challenges ahead for technology centres and all regional economies is how to nurture and sustain economic vitality. The experience of the late 1990s in the USA tech centres suggest that continued change, diversification, adjustment and renewal will be necessary in the twenty-first century for regional economies, as it was for regions in the twentieth and nineteenth centuries.

Acknowledgements

The authors would like to thank Laura Hill, Tim Hubbard and Edinaldo Tebaldi for their assistance in the data analysis and manuscript preparation. We would also like to thank the editor and two anonymous referees for their helpful comments that greatly improved this paper.

Note

1. For a full list of significant variables considered, please contact Ross Gittell.

References

Bathelt, H. 2001 Regional competence and economic recovery: divergent growth paths in Boston's high technology economy, *Entrepreneurship & Regional Development*, 13: 287–314.
Bee, E. 2003 Knowledge networks and technical invention in America's metropolitan areas: a paradigm for high-technology economic development, *Economic Development Quarterly*, 17: 115–131.
Berry, B. J. L. 1991 *Long-Wave Rhythms in Economic Development and Political Behavior* (Baltimore, MD: Johns Hopkins University Press).
Best, M. H. 2000 Silicon Valley and the resurgence of Route 128: systems integration and regional innovation, in Dunning, J. H. (ed.), *Regions, Globalization and the Knowledge-Based Economy* (Oxford: Oxford University Press) pp. 459–484.
Bureau of Economic Analysis 2001 Available online at http://www.bea.doc.gov
Bureau of Labour Statistics 2001 Covered employment wages 2001 data. Available online at http://www.bls.gov/cew
Bureau of Labor Statistics 2001–2003 Current employment statistics 2001–2003. Available online at http://www.bls.gov/ces
Chaston, I. 1996 Critical events and process gaps in the Danish Technological Institute SME structured networking model, *International Small Business Journal*, 14: 71–84.
Chell, E. and Baines, S. 2000 Networking, entrepreneurship and microbusiness behaviour, *Entrepreneurship & Regional Development*, 12: 195–215.
Collaborative Economics 1999 *Innovative Regions: The Importance of Place and Networks in the Innovative Economy*, October (Palo Alto, CA: Collaborative Economics).
Collinson, S. 2000 Knowledge networks for innovation in small Scottish software firms, *Entrepreneurship & Regional Development*, 12: 217–244.
Coombs, R., Richard, A., Saviotti, P. P. and Walsh, V. 1996 *Technological Collaboration: Dynamics of Cooperation in Industrial Innovation* (Cheltenham: Edward Elgar Publishing).
Cortright, J. 2002 The economic importance of being different: regional variations in tastes, increasing returns, and the dynamics of development, *Economic Development Quarterly*, 16: 3–16.
DeVol, R. and Wong, P. 1999 *America's High Tech Economy: Growth, Development and Risks for Metropolitan Areas* (Los Angeles, CA: Milken Institute).
Drennan, M. P. 2002 *The Information Economy and American Cities* (Baltimore, MD: Johns Hopkins Press).
Dworkin, A. 1999 Study ranks Dallas 2nd for high-tech, *The Dallas Morning News*, 14 July.
Florida, R. 2002 *The Rise of the Creative Class: And How It's Transforming Work, Leisure, Community and Everyday Life* (New York: Basic Books).

Gittell, R. 1992 Dynamic development cycles and local economic management, *Economic Development Quarterly*, Spring.

Gittell, R. 1999 *Renewing Cities* (Princeton, NJ: Princeton University Press).

Gittell, R. and Thompson, P. 1999 Inner city business development and entrepreneurship: new frontiers for policy and research, in Ferguson, R. and Dickens, T. (eds), *Urban Problems and Community Development* (Washington, DC: Brookings Institute Press).

Gujarati, D. N. 1995 *Basic Econometrics* (Columbus, OH: McGraw-Hill) pp. 379–380.

Hassink, R. and Wood, M. 1998 Geographic 'clustering' in the German opto-electronics industry: its impact on R&D collaboration and innovation, *Entrepreneurship & Regional Development*, 10: 277–296.

Kondratiev, N. D. 1984 *The Long Wave Cycle* (New York: Richardson and Snyder).

Malecki, E. J. and Tootle, D. M. 1996 The role of networks in small firm competitiveness, *International Journal of Technology Management*, 11: 43–57.

Meyer, J. R. 1963 Regional economics: a survey, *American Economic Review*, 53 (1): 19–54.

Morgan, K. O. and Morgan, S. 2003 *State Rankings 2003: A Statistical View of the 50 United States* (Lawrence, KS: Morgan Quitno Press).

Morrison Institute 1999 *The New Economy: A Guide for Arizona. Report produced by the Morrison Institute of Public Policy at the University of Arizona.*

Progressive Policy Institute 1999 *The State New Economy Index.* http://www.neweconomyindex.org/states/.

Romer, P. M. 1986 Increasing returns and long run growth, *Journal of Political Economy*, 94: 1002–1038.

Shaw, E. 1997 The 'real' networks of small firms, in Deakins, D., Jennings, P. and Mason, C. (eds), *Small Firms: Entrepreneurship in the Nineties* (London: Paul Chapman) pp. 7–17.

Sohl, J. 2002 The private equity market in the USA: lessons from volatility, *Venture Capital: An International Journal of Entrepreneurial Finance*, 5 (1): 29–46.

Storper, M. 1991 Technology districts and international trade: the limits to globalization in an age of flexible production. Mimeo from Graduate School of Urban Planning and Lewis Centre for Regional Policy Studies, University of California, LA, September.

Wiig, H. and Wood, M. 1996 What comprises a regional innovation system? An empirical study of innovation in the Norwegian region of More and Romsdal, in Simmie, J. (ed.), *Innovation, Networks and Learning Regions* (London: Jessica Kingsley Publishers) pp. 66–98.

[15]

Short-Term America Revisited? Boom and Bust in the Venture Capital Industry and the Impact on Innovation

Paul Gompers and Josh Lerner, *Harvard University and NBER*

Executive Summary

This chapter seeks to understand the implications of the recent decline in venture activity for innovation. It argues that the situation may not be as grim as it initially appears. While there are many reasons for believing that on average venture capital has a powerful effect on innovation, the effect is far from uniform. During boom periods, the prevalence of overfunding of particular sectors can lead to a sharp decline in the effectiveness of venture funds. While prolonged downturns may eventually lead to good companies going unfunded, many of the dire predictions today seem overstated.

I. Introduction

The past year has seen a dramatic decline in venture capital activity. As figure 1.1 reveals, investment activity has fallen by more than one-half in the past few quarters. Fund-raising by venture capital organizations has similarly undergone a sharp fall, and few observers expect a revival anytime soon.

Already voices have been raised expressing worry about the implications of this decline for technological innovation. If venture capital was really critical for the rapid America's rapid economic growth, as many articles in the business press during the past decade have claimed, its sharp decline must surely be grounds for worry. For instance, *Business Week* recently noted, "most venture capitalists are shelving the expensive change-the-world bets of the past few years. . . The danger is that cutbacks will go too fast and too deep" (Greene 2001).

This chapter seeks to understand the implications of the recent collapse in venture activity for innovation. It argues that the situation may not be as grim as it initially appears. While there are many reasons for

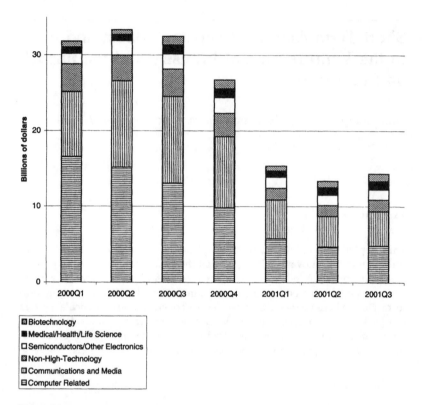

Figure 1.1
U.S. venture capital investments by quarter, 2000–2001. The figure is based on an unpublished Venture Economics database.

believing that *on average* venture capital has a powerful influence on innovation, that influence is far from uniform. In particular, during boom periods, the prevalence of overfunding of particular sectors can lead to a sharp decline in the effectiveness of venture funds. While prolonged downturns may eventually lead to good companies going unfunded, many of the dire predictions seem overstated.

We proceed in three parts. First, we consider the cyclical nature of the venture industry. We explore why shifts in opportunities often do not rapidly translate into increased fund-raising. We also highlight the tendency for the supply of venture capital, when it does finally adjust to shifts in demand, to react in an excessively dramatic manner. We explore how the structure of the venture funds themselves and the information lags in the venture investment process may lead to this overshoot. Similarly, we discuss the determinants of busts, such as we are experiencing today.

We then consider the implications of these shifts for innovation. We review the more general evidence that suggests that venture capitalists have a powerful influence on innovation. We then consider both field-based and statistical evidence that the effects of venture investment on innovation are not uniform. We argue that the effect of these funds on innovation during period of rapid growth, or booms, is attenuated. At the same time, we consider the implications of prolonged troughs, such as the venture industry experienced in the 1970s, and highlight the apparently detrimental consequences of such events.

In the conclusion, we consider some of the implications for public policy. Our analysis suggests that, while the rise of venture capital has been an important contributor to technological innovation and economic prosperity, an effective policy agenda going forward will not simply seek to spur much venture financing. We highlight the fact that many of the steps that policymakers have pursued have had the consequence of throwing gasoline on the fire: i.e., they have exacerbated the cyclical nature of venture funding. Instead, the environment for venture capital investment can be substantially improved by government policies (both federal and state) that encourage private investment and address *gaps* in the private funding process, such as industrial segments that have not historically captured the attention of venture financiers. In short, we argue that policymakers have to view efforts to assist young firms within the context of the changing private sector environment.

II. Cyclicality in the Venture Capital Industry

The recent changes in the venture capital market have been far from the first such cycles. Figures 1.2 and 1.3 depict the changing amount of venture capital funds raised and the returns from these funds. In this section, we will explore what accounts for such extreme variations.

A Simple Framework[1]

To help understand the dynamics of the venture capital industry, it is helpful to employ a simple framework. The two critical elements for understanding shifts in venture capital fund-raising are straightforward: a demand curve and a supply curve. Just as in markets for

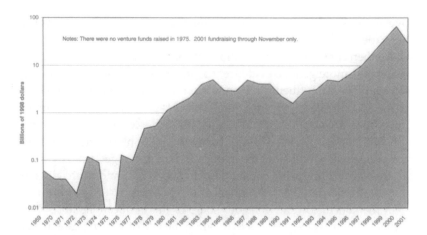

Figure 1.2
Venture capital fund-raising by year, 1969–2001. The figure is based on unpublished
Asset Alternatives and Venture Economics databases.

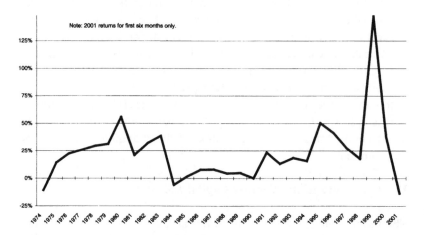

Figure 1.3
Returns to venture capital investments, 1974–2001. The figure is based on an unpublished Venture Economics database.

Short-Term America Revisited?   5

commodities like oil and semiconductors, shifts in supply and demand
shape the amount of capital raised by venture funds. These also drive
the returns that investors earn in these markets.

The supply of venture capital is determined by the willingness of
investors to provide funds to venture firms. That willingness, in turn,
is dependent upon the expected rate of return from these investments
relative to the return they expect to receive from other investments.
Higher expected returns lead to a greater desire of investors to supply
venture capital. As the return that investors expect to earn from their
venture investments increases—that is, as we go up the vertical axis—
the amount supplied by investors grows (we move further to the right
on the horizontal axis).

The number of entrepreneurial firms seeking venture capital determines the demand for capital. Demand is also likely to vary with the
rate of return anticipated by investors. As the minimum rate of return
sought by the investors increases, fewer entrepreneurial firms can meet
that threshold. The demand schedule typically slopes downward:
higher return expectations lead to fewer financeable firms, because
fewer entrepreneurial projects can meet the higher hurdle.

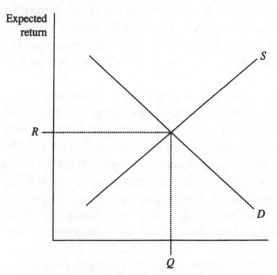

(Willingness of investors to supply capital)/
(number of entrepreneurial firms meeting return requirement)

Figure 1.4
Steady state level of venture capital.

Together, supply and demand should determine the level of venture capital in the economy. This is illustrated in figure 1.4. The level of venture capital should be determined by where the two lines—the supply curve (S) and the demand curve (D)—meet. Put another way, we would expect a quantity Q of venture capital to be raised in the economy, and the funds to earn a return of R on average.

It is natural to think of supply and demand curves as smooth lines. But this is not always the case. Consider, for instance, the venture capital market before the Department of Labor's clarification of the "prudent man" rule of the Employee Retirement Income Security Act in 1979. Before the clarification of ERISA policies, the supply curve may have been distinctly limited: no matter how high the expected rate of return for venture capital was, the supply would be limited to a set amount. The vertical segment of the supply curve resulted because pension funds, a segment of the U.S. financial market that controlled a substantial fraction of the long-term savings, were simply unable to invest in venture funds.

The Impact of Shifts

These supply and demand curves are not fixed. For instance, the shift in ERISA policies led to the supply curve of funds moving outward. Similarly, major technological discoveries, such as the development of genetic engineering, led to an increase in the demand for venture capital.

But the quantity of venture capital raised and the returns it enjoys often do not adjust quickly and smoothly to the changes in supply and demand curves. We can illustrate this by comparing the venture capital market with that for snack foods. Companies like Frito-Lay and Nabisco closely monitor the shifting demand for their products, getting daily updates on the data collected by supermarket scanners. They restock the shelves every few days, adjusting the product offerings in response to changing consumer tastes. They can address any imbalances of supply and demand by offering coupons to consumers or making other special offers.

By way of contrast, in the venture market the quantity of funds provided may not shift rapidly. The adjustment process is often quite slow and uneven, which can lead to substantial and persistent imbalances. When the quantity provided does react, the shift may overshoot the ideal amount, and lead to yet further problems.

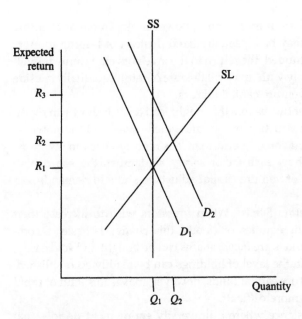

Figure 1.5
Impact on quantity of a demand shock.

This too can be illustrated using our framework, as shown in figure 1.5. It is important to distinguish here between short- and long-run curves. While in the long run the curve may have a smooth upward slope, the short-run curve may be quite different. The long-run supply curve (SL) may have a smooth upward slope, but the supply in the short run may be essentially fixed, if investors cannot or will not adjust their allocations to venture capital funds. Thus, the short-run curve may instead be a vertical line (SS).

This difference is illustrated figure 1.5, which explores the short- and long-run impact of a positive demand shock. The discovery of a new scientific approach, such as genetic engineering, or the diffusion of a new technology, such as the transistor or the Internet, may have a profound effect on the venture capital industry. As large companies struggle to adjust to these new technologies, numerous agile small companies may seek to exploit the opportunity. As a result, for any given level of return demanded by investors, there now may be many more attractive investment candidates.

In the long run, the quantity of venture capital provided will adjust upward from Q_1 to Q_2. Returns will also increase, from R_1 to R_2. In the months or even years after the shock, however, the amount of venture capital available may be essentially fixed. Instead of leading to more companies being funded, the return to the investors may climb dramatically, up to R_3. Only with time will the rate of return gradually subside as the supply of venture capital adjusts.

There are at least two factors that might lead to such short-run rigidities. These are the structure of the funds themselves and the slowness with which information on performance is reported back to investors. We will explore how each factor serves to dampen the speed with which the supply of venture capital adjusts to shifts in demand.

The Nature of Venture Funds   When investors wish to increase their allocation to public equities or bonds, this change is easily accomplished. These markets are *liquid*: shares can be bought and sold easily, and adjustments in the level of holdings can be readily accomplished. The nature of venture capital funds, however, makes this kind of rapid adjustment much more difficult.

Consider an instance where a university endowment decides that venture capital is a particularly attractive investment class and decides to increase its allocation to such investments. From the time at which this new target is agreed upon, it is likely to be several years before the policy is fully implemented. Since venture funds only raise funds every two or three years, if the endowment simply wants to increase its commitment to existing funds, it will need to wait until the next fund-raising cycle occurs for these funds. In many cases, it may be unable to invest as much in the new funds as it wishes.

The reluctance of venture groups to accept their capital stems from the fact that the number of experienced venture capitalists often adjusts more slowly than the swings in capital. Many of the crucial skills for being an effective venture capitalist cannot be taught formally: rather they need to be developed through a process of apprenticeship. Furthermore, the organizational challenges associated with rapidly increasing the size of a venture partnership are often wrenching ones. Thus, groups such as Kleiner Perkins and Greylock have resisted rapidly increasing their size, even if investor demand is so great that they could easily raise many billions of dollars.

If indeed the endowment decides to undertake a strategy of investing in new funds, potential candidates for the university's funds will need to be exhaustively reviewed. Once the funds are chosen, the investments will not be made immediately. Rather, the capital that the university commits will only be drawn down in stages over a number of years.

The same logic works in reverse. If the endowment or pension officers decide to scale back their commitment to private equity, it is likely to take a number of years to do so. An illustration of this stickiness was seen following the stock market correction of 1987. Many investors, noting the extent of equity market volatility and the poor performance of small high-technology stocks, sought to scale back their commitments to venture capital. Despite the correction, flows into venture capital funds continued to rise, not reaching their peak until the last quarter of 1989.[2]

Another contributing factor is the self-liquidating nature of venture funds. When venture funds exit investments, they do not reinvest the funds, but rather return the capital to their investors. These distributions are typically either in the form of stock in firms that have recently gone public or in cash. The pace of distributions varies with the rate at which venture capitalists are liquidating their holdings.

Thus, during *hot* periods with large numbers of initial public offerings and acquisitions—which are likely to be the times when many investors desire to increase their exposure to venture capital—limited partners receive large outflows from venture funds. Even to maintain the same percentage allocation to venture funds during these peak periods, the institutions and individuals must accelerate their rate of investment. Increasing their exposure is consequently quite difficult. Conversely, during *cold* periods, when investors are likely to wish to reduce their allocation to this asset class, they receive few distributions. Thus it is often difficult to achieve a desired exposure to venture capital during periods of rapid change in the market.

The Role of Information Lags   A second factor contributing to the stickiness of the supply of venture capital is the difficulty in discerning what the current state of the venture market is. While mutual and hedge funds holding public securities are "marked to market" on a daily basis, the delay between the inception of a venture investment and the discovery of its quality is long indeed.

The information lags can have profound effects. For instance, when the investment environment becomes more attractive, it can take a number of years to fully realize the fact. While investments in Internet-related securities in the mid-1990s yielded extremely high returns, it took many years for the bulk of institutional investors to realize the size of the opportunity. Similarly, when the investment environment becomes less attractive, as it did during the spring of 2000, investors often continue to plough money into funds. (See, for instance, the discussion in Kreutzer 2001.)

Some of these information problems stem from the firms themselves. The types of firms that attract venture capital are surrounded by substantial uncertainty and information gaps. But these inevitable difficulties are exacerbated by the manner in which the performance of funds is typically reported. The first of these is the conservatism of the valuations. Venture groups tend to be extremely conservative in reporting how much the firms they invest in are worth, at least until the firms are taken public or acquired. While this limits the danger that investors will be misled into thinking that the fund is doing better than it actually is, it also minimizes the information flow about the current state of the market.[3]

This reporting practice, for instance, must lead us to be cautious in evaluating the returns depicted in figure 1.3. Because relatively few firms get taken public during cold markets and many do during hot ones, there are many more dramatic write-ups in firms during the years with active public markets. But the actual value creation process in venture investments is quite different. In many cases, the value of a firm actually increases gradually over time, even as it is being held at cost. Therefore, the low returns during cold periods understate the progress that is being made, just as the high returns during the peak periods overstate the success during those years. Therefore, the signals that venture investors receive are quite limited.

An Illustration   The discussion above ignores many of the complex institutional realities that affect the ebbs and flows of venture capital fund-raising. But even such simple tools can be quite helpful in understanding overall movements in the venture capital activity, as can be illustrated by considering the recent history of the venture capital industry.

As figure 1.2 illustrates, the supply of venture funding began growing rapidly in the mid-1990s. Many practitioners at the time viewed this event glumly, arguing that a boost in venture activity must inevitably lead to a deterioration of returns. Yet the investments during this period enjoyed extraordinary success, as figure 1.3 illustrates. How could these seasoned observers have been so wrong?

The reason is that these years saw a dramatic shift in the opportunities available to venture capital investors. The rapid diffusion of Internet access and the associated development of the World Wide Web ushered in an extraordinary period in the U.S. economy. The ability to transfer visual and text information in a rapid and interactive manner was a powerful tool, one that would transform both retail activities and the internal management of firms.

Such a change led to an increase in the demand for venture capital financing. Thus, for any given level of return that investors demanded, there should have been a considerably greater number of opportunities to fund. Far from declining, the rate of return that venture investments enjoyed actually rose. Much of this rise reflected the fact that the supply of effective and credible venture organizations adjusted only slowly. As a result, those groups who were active in the market during this period enjoyed extraordinary successes.

Why Does the Venture Market Overreact?

Another frequently discussed pathology in the venture market is the other side of the same coin. Once the markets do adjust to the changing demand conditions, they frequently go too far. The supply of venture capital ultimately will rise to meet the increased opportunities, but these shifts often are too large. Too much capital may be raised for the outstanding amount of opportunities. Instead of shifting to the new steady state level, the short-term supply curve may shift to an excessively high level.

The same problem can occur in reverse. A downward shift in demand can trigger a wholesale withdrawal from venture capital financing. Returns rise dramatically as a result. While the supply of venture capital will ultimately adjust, in the interim, promising companies may not be able to attract funding. In this section, we explore two possible explanations for this phenomenon.

Do Public Markets Provide Misleading Information? One possibility is that institutional investors and venture capitalists may overestimate the shifts that have occurred. They may believe that there are tremendous new opportunities, and consequentially shift the supply of venture capital to meet that apparent demand.

This suggestion is captured in figure 1.6. A positive shock to the demand for venture capital occurs, moving the demand curve out from

12   Gompers and Lerner

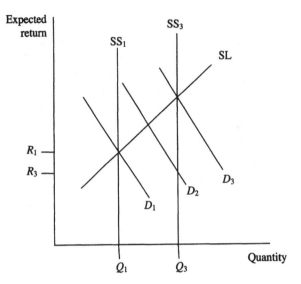

Figure 1.6
Misleading public market signals.

D_1 to D_2. Limited and general partners, however, mistakenly believe that the curve has shifted out to D_3. The short-run supply curve thus shifts from SS_1 to SS_3, leaving excessive investment and disappointing returns in its wake.

Such mistakes may arise because of misleading information from the public markets. Examples abound where venture capitalists have made substantial investments in new sectors, at least partially responding to the impetus provided by the high valuations in that sector. Understanding why public markets overvalue particular sectors is beyond the scope of this piece. Certainly, though, it seems in some cases that investors fail to take into account the effect of competitors: firms appear to be valued as if they were the sole firm active in a sector, and the effects of competitors on revenues and profit margins were not fully anticipated.

Whatever the causes of these misvaluations, historical illustrations are plentiful. One famous example was during the early 1980s, when nineteen disk drive companies received venture capital financing. (For detailed discussions, see Sahlman and Stevenson 1986 and Lerner 1997.) Two-thirds of these investments came in 1982 and 1983, as the valuation of publicly traded computer hardware firms soared. Many disk drive companies also went public during this period. While industry growth was rapid during this period of time (sales increased from $27 million in 1978 to $1.3 billion in 1983), it was questioned at the time whether the scale of investment was rational given any reasonable expectations of industry growth and future economic trends. Indeed, between October 1983 and December 1984, the average public disk drive firm lost 68% of its value. Numerous disk drive manufacturers that had yet to go public were terminated, and venture capitalists became very reluctant to fund computer hardware firms.

Unreasonable swings in the public markets may also lead to over- and underinvestment in venture capital as a whole. Institutions typically try to keep a fixed percentage of their portfolio invested in each asset class. Thus, when public equity values climb, institutions are likely to want to allocate more to venture capital. If the high valuations are subsequently revealed to be without foundations, the level of venture capital will have once again overshot its target.

Do Venture Capitalists Underestimate the Cost of Change? A second explanation for the overshooting is venture capitalists' failure to consider the costly adjustments associated with the growth of their own investment activity. The very act of growing the pool of venture capital under management may cause distractions and introduce organizational tensions. Even if demand has expanded, the number of opportunities that a venture group—or the industry as a whole—can address may at first be limited.

Why might these adjustment costs come about? One possibility is that growth frequently leads to changes in the way in which venture groups invest their capital, which has a deleterious effect on returns. A second possibility is that growth introduces strains in the venture organization itself.

First, consider the types of pressures that rapid growth imposes on the venture investment process. Rather than making more investments, rapidly growing venture organizations frequently attempt to increase their average investment size. In this way, the same number of partners can manage a larger amount of capital without an increase in the number of firms that each needs to scrutinize. This shift to larger investments has frequently entailed making larger capital commitments to firms up front. This has the potential cost of reducing the venture capitalist's ability to control the firm using staged capital commitments.

Similarly, venture firms syndicate less with their peers during these times. By not syndicating, venture groups can put more money to work. As the sole investor, a venture group can allow each of its partners to manage more capital while keeping the number of companies that it is responsible for down to a manageable level. But this syndication can have a number of advantages, such as helping reduce the danger of costly investment mistakes.

Another set of explanations relates to organizational pressures. Limited and general partners may underestimate the consequences of expanding the scale (and the scope) of the fund. An essential characteristic of venture capital organizations has been the speed with which decisions can be made and the parallel incentives that motivate the parties. An expansion of the fund can lead to a fragmentation of the bonds that tie the partnership into a cohesive whole.

One dramatic illustration of these challenges is the experience of Schroder Ventures (Bingham, Ferguson, and Lerner 1996). Schroder's private equity effort began in 1985 with funds focused on British venture capital and buyout investments. Over time, however, they added funds focusing on other markets, such as France and Germany, and particular technologies, such as the life sciences. The venture capitalists—and the institutional investors backing them—realized that there were substantial opportunities in these other markets.

But as the venture organization grew, substantial management challenges emerged. In particular, it became increasingly difficult to monitor the investment activities of each of the groups—a real concern, since the parent organization served as the general partner of each of the funds (and thus was ultimately liable for any losses). Each of the groups saw itself as an autonomous entity, and even in some cases resisted cooperating (and sharing the capital gains) with the others. Although the organization eventually completed a restructuring that allowed it to raise a single fund for all of Europe, the process of change was a slow and painful one.

These tensions are by no means confined to international venture capital organizations. Very similar tensions have appeared in rapidly growing U.S. groups between general partners specializing in life science and in information technology, and between those located in different regions. In some instances, one of these groups has become convinced that another is getting a disproportionate share of rewards in light of their relative investment performance. In other instances, it has become difficult to coordinate and oversee activities.

In some cases, these tensions have led to groups splitting apart. For instance, in August 1999, Institutional Venture Partners and Brentwood Venture Capital—venture funds that had each invested about one billion dollars over several decades—announced their intention to restructure (Barry and Toll 1999). The information technology and life sciences venture capitalists from the two firms indicated that they would join with each other to form two new venture capital firms. Pallidium Venture Capital would exclusively pursue health care transactions, while Redpoint Ventures would focus on Internet and broadband infrastructure investments. Press accounts suggested the decision was largely driven by the dissatisfaction of some of the information technology partners at the firms, who felt that their stellar performance had not been appropriately recognized.

In other cases, a key partner—often dissatisfied with his role or compensation—has departed a venture group, entailing a real disruption to the organization. For instance, Ernest Jacquet left to form Parthenon Ventures shortly after Summit Partners closed on a $1 billion buyout fund ("Summit's Jacquet . . ." 1998). While it is very rare for investors to ask for the return of their contributions from their funds—though, for instance, Foster Capital Management returned $200 million after the several junior partners departed in 1998—these defections can nonetheless affect the workings and continuity of these groups ("Foster Management . . ." 1998).

In short, rapid growth puts severe pressures on venture capital organizations. Even when the problems do not result in an extreme outcome such as the dissolution of the group, the demands on the partners' time in resolving these problems have often been substantial. Thus, during periods of rapid growth, venture capital groups may correctly observe that there are many more opportunities to fund. Rapidly expanding to address these opportunities may be counterproductive, however, and lead to disappointing returns.

III. The Consequences for Innovation

While understanding the causes of cyclicality in the venture industry may be interesting, policymakers are much more likely to be interested in its consequences. In particular, to what extent do these changes affect the innovativeness of the U.S. economy?

In this section, we explore this question. We begin by considering the evidence regarding the overall effect of venture capital on innovation. We then turn to exploring the effect of the boom-and bust pattern on these shifts. We highlight that while the overall relationship between venture capital and innovation is positive, the relationships across the cycles of venture activity may be quite different.

The Basic Rationale

A voluminous theoretical literature has been developed in recent years, as financial economists have sought to understand the mechanisms employed by venture capitalists. These works suggest that these financial intermediaries are particularly well suited for nurturing innovative new firms.

Before considering the mechanisms employed by venture capitalists, it is worth highlighting that a substantial literature has also discussed the financing of young firms. Young firms, particularly those in high-technology industries, are often characterized by considerable uncertainty and informational gaps that make the selection of appropriate investments difficult and permit opportunistic behavior by entrepreneurs after financing is received. This literature has also highlighted the role of financial intermediaries in alleviating moral hazard and information asymmetries.

To briefly review the types of conflicts that can emerge in these settings, Jensen and Meckling (1976) demonstrate that agency conflicts between managers and investors can affect the willingness of both debt and equity holders to provide capital. If the firm raises equity from outside investors, the manager has an incentive to engage in wasteful expenditures (e.g., lavish offices) because he may benefit disproportionately from these but does not bear their entire cost. Similarly, if the firm raises debt, the manager may increase risk to undesirable levels. Because providers of capital recognize these problems, outside investors demand a higher rate of return than would be the case if the funds were internally generated.

Even if the manager is motivated to maximize shareholder value, informational asymmetries may make raising external capital more expensive or even preclude it entirely. For instance, Myers and Majluf (1984) demonstrate that equity offerings of firms may be associated with a "lemons" problem (first identified by Akerlof 1970). If the manager is better informed about the investment opportunities of the firm and acts in the interest of current shareholders, then managers only issue new shares when the company's stock is overvalued. Indeed, numerous studies have documented that stock prices decline upon the announcement of equity issues, largely because of the negative signal that it sends to the market.

These information problems have also been shown to exist in debt markets. Stiglitz and Weiss (1981) show that if banks find it difficult to discriminate among companies, raising interest rates can have perverse selection effects. In particular, the high interest rates discourage all but the highest-risk borrowers, so the quality of the loan pool declines markedly. To address this problem, banks may restrict the amount of lending rather than increasing interest rates.

These problems in the debt and equity markets are a consequence of the information gaps between the entrepreneurs and investors. If the information asymmetries could be eliminated, financing constraints would disappear. Financial economists argue that specialized financial intermediaries, such as venture capital organizations, can address these problems. By intensively scrutinizing firms before providing capital and then monitoring them afterwards, they can alleviate some of the information gaps and reduce capital constraints.

To address these information problems, venture investors employ a variety of mechanisms. First, business plans are intensively scrutinized: of those firms that submit business plans to venture organizations, historically only 1% have been funded. The decision to invest is frequently made conditional on the identification of a syndication partner who agrees that this is an attractive investment. Once the decision to invest is made, venture capitalists frequently disburse funds in stages. Managers of these venture-backed firms are forced to return repeatedly to their financiers for additional capital, in order to ensure that the money is not squandered on unprofitable projects. In addition, venture capitalists intensively monitor managers. These investors demand preferred stock with numerous restrictive covenants and representation on the board of directors. Thus, it is not surprising that venture capital has emerged as the dominant form of equity financing in the U.S. for privately held high-technology businesses.[4]

The Supporting Evidence

It might be thought that it would be not difficult to address the question of the influence of venture capital on innovation. For instance, one could look in regressions across industries and time whether, controlling for R&D spending, venture capital funding has an effect on various measures of innovation. But even a simple model of the relationship between venture capital, R&D, and innovation suggests that this approach is likely to give misleading estimates.

Both venture funding and innovation could be positively related to a third unobserved factor, the arrival of technological opportunities. Thus, there could be more innovation at times that there was more venture capital, not because the venture capital caused the innovation, but rather because the venture capitalists reacted to some fundamental technological shock which was sure to lead to more innovation. To date, only two papers have attempted to address these challenging issues.

The first of these papers, Hellmann and Puri (2000), examines a sample of 170 recently formed firms in Silicon Valley, including both venture-backed and nonventure firms. Using questionnaire responses, they find empirical evidence that venture capital financing is related to product market strategies and outcomes of startups. They find that firms that are pursuing what they term an innovator strategy (a classification based on the content analysis of survey responses) are significantly more likely to obtain venture capital and can obtain it faster. The presence of a venture capitalist is also associated with a significant reduction in the time taken to bring a product to market, especially for innovators. Furthermore, firms are more likely to list obtaining venture capital than other financing events as a significant milestone in the life cycle of the company.

The results suggest significant interrelations between investor type and product market behavior, and a role of venture capital in encouraging innovative companies. Given the small size of the sample and the limited data, they can only modestly address concerns about causality. Unfortunately, the possibility remains that more innovative firms select venture capital for financing, rather than venture capital causing firms to be more innovative.

Kortum and Lerner (2000), by way of contrast, examine patterns that can be discerned on an aggregate industry level, rather than on the firm level. They address concerns about causality in two ways. First, they exploit the major discontinuity in the recent history of the venture capital industry: as discussed above, in the late 1970s, the U.S. Department of Labor clarified the Employee Retirement Income Security Act, a policy shift that freed pensions to invest in venture capital. This shift led to a sharp increase in the funds committed to venture capital. This

Short-Term America Revisited? 19

type of exogenous change should identify the role of venture capital, because it is unlikely to be related to the arrival of entrepreneurial opportunities. They exploit this shift in instrumental variable regressions. Second, they use R&D expenditures to control for the arrival of technological opportunities that are anticipated by economic actors at the time, but that are unobserved by econometricians. In the framework of a simple model, they show that the causality problem disappears if they estimate the effect of venture capital on the patent-R&D ratio, rather than on patenting itself.

Even after addressing these causality concerns, the results suggest that venture funding does have a strong positive effect on innovation. The estimated coefficients vary according to the techniques employed, but on average a dollar of venture capital appears to be three to four times more potent in stimulating patenting than a dollar of traditional corporate R&D. The estimates therefore suggest that venture capital, even though it averaged less than 3% of corporate R&D from 1983 to 1992, is responsible for a much greater share—perhaps 10%—of U.S. industrial innovations in this decade.

The Impact of Market Cycles

The evidence that venture capital has a powerful effect on innovation might lead us to be especially worried about market downturns. A dramatic fall in venture capital financing, it is natural to conclude, would lead to a sharp decline in innovation.

But this reasoning, while initially plausible, is somewhat misleading. For the effect of venture capital on innovation does not appear to be uniform. Rather, during periods when the intensity of investment is greatest, the effect appears to decline. Thus unevenness can be illustrated with both case-study and empirical evidence.

Field-Based Evidence We have already discussed how in many instances the levels of funding during peak periods appear to overshoot the desired levels. Whether caused by the presence of misleading public market signals or the overoptimism on the part of the venture capitalists, funds appear to be deployed much less effectively during the boom period.

In particular, all too often these periods find venture capitalists funding firms that are too similar to one another.[5] The consequences of these excessive investments are frequently the same: highly duplicative research agendas, intense bidding wars for scientific and technical talent culminating with frequent defections from firm to firm, costly litigation alleging intellectual property theft and misappropriation of ideas across firms, and the sudden termination of funding for many of these concerns.

One example was the peak period of biotechnology investing in the early 1990s. While the potential of biotechnology to address human disease was doubtless substantial, the extent and nature of financing seemed to many observers at the time hard to justify. In some cases, dozens of firms pursuing similar approaches to the same disease target were funded. Moreover, the valuations of these firms often were exorbitant: for instance, between May and December 1992, the average valuation of the privately held biotechnology firms financed by venture capitalists was $70 million. These doubts were validated when biotechnology valuations fell precipitously in early 1993: by December 1993, only 42 of 262 *publicly traded* biotechnology firms had a valuation over $70 million.[6]

Most of the biotechnology firms financed during this period ultimately yielded very disappointing returns for their venture financiers and modest gains for society as a whole. In many cases, the firms were liquidated after further financing could not be arranged. In others, the firms shifted their efforts into other, less competitive areas, largely abandoning the initial research efforts. In yet others, the companies remained mired with their peers for years in costly patent litigation.

The boom of 1998–2000 provides many additional illustrations. Funding during these years was concentrated in two areas: Internet and telecommunication investments, which, for instance, accounted for 39% and 17% of all venture disbursements in 1999. Once again, considerable sums were devoted to supporting highly similar firms—e.g., the nine dueling Internet pet food suppliers—or else efforts that seemed fundamentally uneconomical and doomed to failure, such as companies which undertook the extremely capital-intensive process of building a second cable network in residential communities. Meanwhile, many apparently promising areas—e.g., advanced materials, energy technologies, and micromanufacturing—languished unfunded as venture capitalists raced to focus on the most visible and popular investment areas. It is difficult to believe that the impact of a dollar of venture financing was as powerful in spurring innovation during these periods as in others.

Short-Term America Revisited?   21

Statistical Evidence   These suggestive accounts are borne out in a statistical analysis. Using the framework of Kortum and Lerner (2000), we show that the effect of venture capital on innovation was less pronounced during boom periods.

In this analysis, we analyze annual data for twenty manufacturing industries between 1965 and 1992. The dependent variable is U.S. patents issued to U.S. inventors by industry and date of application. Our main explanatory variables are measures of venture funding collected by Venture Economics and industrial R&D expenditures collected by the U.S. National Science Foundation (NSF).

To be sure, these measures are limited in their effectiveness. For instance, companies do not patent all commercially significant discoveries (though in the original paper, we show that the patterns appear to hold when we use other measures of innovation). Similarly, we are required to aggregate venture funding and patents into a twenty-industry scheme that is used by the NSF to measure R&D spending. Finally, our analysis must exclude the greatest boom period of all, the 1998–2000 surge (patent applications can only be observed with a considerable lag).

Table 1.1 presents our estimate of b, the influence of venture capital funding on patent applications, controlling for R&D spending, industry effects, and the year of the observation. Any number greater than one implies that venture capital is more powerful than traditional corporate R&D in spurring innovation. (This is a specification similar to regression 3.2 in that paper, with an added measure for the hottest periods.) We then show the implied coefficient when we estimate the

Table 1.1
Implied effecy of venture capital on innovation, based on the linear patent production function estimated by Kortum and Lerner

Quantity	Coefficient or p-value
Implied potency of venture financing, normal industry-periods	13.57
Implied potency of venture financing, overheated industry-periods	11.53
p-Value, test of difference between normal and overheated industry-periods	0.000

The first row presents implied effect of venture financing on innovation for all manufacturing industries and years between 1965 and 1992 except where the levels of venture inflows are in the top one percent. The second row presents the implied coefficient during the industries and years where inflows are in the top one percent. The final row presents the p-value from a test that the two coefficients are identical.

effect of venture capital on innovation separately for those periods that had the great venture capital investments (defined here as the top one percent of industry-year observations). As the table reports, the effect is some 15% lower during the boom periods, a difference that is strongly statistically significant.

As discussed in Kortum and Lerner (2000), the magnitude of the effect of venture capital on innovation diminishes—but remains positive and significant—when we control for reverse causality: the fact that technological breakthroughs are likely to stimulate venture capital investments. When we repeat the analysis reported here using a number of these complex specifications, the magnitude of the difference between normal and boom periods remains similar, and the percentage difference widens. This statistical result corroborates the field study evidence suggesting that venture capital's effect on innovation is less pronounced during booms.

A Cautionary Note These patterns may lead us to worry less about the short-run fluctuations in venture financing. While their impact on entrepreneurial activity is likely to be dramatic, the effects on innovation should be more modest.

This conclusion, however, must be tempered by the awareness of history: in some cases, surges in venture capital activity have been followed by pronounced and persistent downturns. As alluded to above, just as we can see *overshooting* by investors, so can we see prolonged *undershooting*.

One sobering example is the 1970s. The late 1960s had seen record fund-raising, both by independent venture groups and by Small Business Investment Companies (SBICs), federally subsidized pools of risk capital. Many of the investments by the less established venture groups failed in the subsequent recession, particularly those of the SBICs. (The selection process for these licenses appeared to emphasize political connections rather than investment acumen.) The poor returns generated a powerful reaction, leading both public and private market investors to be unwilling to contribute new capital.

Figure 1.7 depicts one consequence of the period of this reaction. The graph depicts the volume of initial and follow-on offerings in the sector that saw the greatest concentration of venture investments during this period: computer and computer-related firms. The amount of capital raised by these firms fell from $1.2 billion (in today's dollars) in 1968–1969 to just $201 million in the entire period from 1973 to mid-1978,

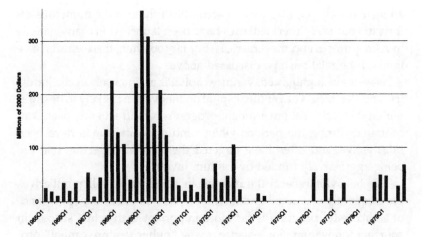

Figure 1.7
Initial public offerings and seasoned equity offerings by computer and computer-related firms, by quarter, 1965–1979. The authors compiled the information from Investment Dealers' Digest, the Securities Data Company database, and other sources.

with absolutely no financing being raised in many quarters. To be sure, many of the firms that raised capital during the boom years and then could not get refinanced had business plans that were poorly conceptualized or were in engaged in doomed battles with entrenched incumbents such as IBM. But many other firms seeking to commercialize many of the personal computing and networking technologies that would prove to have such a revolutionary impact in the 1980s and 1990s also struggled to raise the financing necessary to commercialize their ideas.

At the same time, it is important to note that while venture capital fund-raising and investment has cooled down considerably from the white-hot days of 2000, the level of activity is still extremely high from a historical perspective. In fact, if we ignore the 1999–2000 bubble period in figure 1.2, we find that the venture industry has shown robust growth over the past decade. As a result, the rationale for government intervention to provide funding today seems slim, as we discuss in more detail below.

VI. Conclusions

Government officials and policy advisors are naturally concerned about spurring innovation. Encouraging venture capital financing is an increasingly popular way to accomplish these ends: numerous efforts to spur such intermediaries have been launched in many nations in Asia, Europe, and the Americas. But far too often, these efforts have ignored the relationships discussed above.

As we have highlighted, venture capital is an intensely cyclic industry, and the impact of venture capital on innovation is likely to be differ within the cycle. Yet government programs have frequently been concentrated during the periods when venture capital funds have been most active, and often have targeted the very same sectors that are being aggressively funded by venture investors.

This behavior reflects the manner in which such policy initiatives are frequently evaluated and rewarded. Far too often, the appearance of a successful program is far more important than actual success in spurring innovation. For instance, many "public venture capital" programs, such as the Small Business Innovation Research (SBIR) initiative, prepare glossy brochures full of "success stories" about particular firms. The prospect of such recognition may lead a program manager to decide to fund a firm in a hot industry whose prospects of success may be brighter, even if the sector is already well funded by venture investors (and the impact of additional funding on innovation quite modest). To cite one example, the Advanced Technology Program launched major efforts to fund genomics and Internet tool companies during periods when venture funding was flooding into these sectors (Gompers and Lerner 1999).

By way of contrast, the Central Intelligence Agency's In-Q-Tel fund appears to have done a much better job of seeking to address gaps in traditional venture financing (Business Executives . . . 2001). The SBIR program provides another contrasting example. Decisions as to whether finance firms are made not by centralized bodies, but rather devolved in many agencies to program managers who are seeking to address very specific technical needs (e.g., an Air Force research administrator who is seeking to encourage the development of new composites). As a result, many offbeat technologies that are not of interest to traditional venture investors have been funded through this program.

Public programs, rather than funding hot industries, should address the gaps in the venture financing process. As noted above, venture investments tend to be focused on a few areas of technology that are perceived to have great potential. Increases in venture fund-raising—which are driven by factors such as shifts in capital gains tax rates—

appear more likely to lead to more intense competition for transactions within an existing set of technologies than to greater diversity in the types of companies funded. Policymakers may wish to respond to these industries conditions by (1) focusing on technologies which are not currently popular among venture investors and (2) providing follow-on capital to firms already funded by venture capitalists during periods when venture inflows are falling.

More generally, the greatest assistance to venture capital may be provided by government programs that seek to enhance the demand for these funds, rather than the supply of capital. Examples would include efforts to facilitate the commercialization of early-stage technology, such as the Bayh-Dole Act of 1980 and the Federal Technology Transfer Act of 1986, both of which eased entrepreneurs' ability to access early-stage research. Similarly, efforts to make entrepreneurship more attractive through tax policy (e.g., by lowering tax rates on capital gains relative to those on ordinary income) may have a substantial impact on the amount of venture capital provided and the returns that these investments may yield. These less direct measures may have the greatest success in ensuring that the venture industry will survive the recent upheavals.

In short, while most government programs aimed at spurring venture capital and entrepreneurial innovation likely have achieved a positive social rate of return, the most effective programs and policies seem to be those which lay the foundations for effective private investment. Our analysis suggests that the market for venture capital may be subject to substantial imperfections, and that these imperfections may substantially lower the total social gain achieved by venture finance. Given the extraordinary rate of growth (and now retrenchment) experienced by venture capital over the past decade, the most effective policies are likely those that focus on increasing the efficiency of private markets over the long term, rather than providing a short-term funding boost during the current period of transition.

Notes

We thank Harvard Business School's Division of Research for financial support. This chapter is based in part on Gompers and Lerner (2001). All errors are our own.

1. The supply-and-demand framework for analyzing venture capital discussed here was introduced in Poterba (1989) and refined in Gompers and Lerner (1998b).

2. This claim is based on an analysis of an unpublished Venture Economics database.

3. The problems with the accounting schemes used by venture capital groups are discussed in Cain (1997), Gompers and Lerner (1998a), and Reyes (1990).

4. While evidence regarding the financing of these firms is imprecise, Freear and Wetzel's (1990) survey suggests that venture capital accounts for about two-thirds of the external equity financing raised by privately held technology-intensive businesses from private sector sources.

5. These results are also consistent with theoretical work on *herding* by investment managers. These models suggest that when, for instance, investment managers are assessed on the basis of their performance relative to their peers (rather than against some absolute benchmark), they may end up making investments to similar to each other. For a review of these works, see Devenow and Welch (1996).

6. These figures are based on an analysis of an unpublished Venture Economics database.

References

Akerlof, George A. 1970. "The Market for 'Lemons': Qualitative Uncertainty and the Market Mechanism." *Quarterly Journal of Economics* 84:488–500.

Barry, David G., and David M. Toll. 1999. "Brentwood, IVP Find Health Care, High Tech Don't Mix." *Private Equity Analyst* 9(September):29–32.

Bingham, Kate, Nick Ferguson, and Josh Lerner. 1996. "Schroder Ventures: Launch of the Euro Fund." Case no. 9-297-026. Harvard Business School.

Business Executives for National Security. 2001. *Accelerating the Acquisition and Implementation of New Technologies for Intelligence: The Report of the Independent Panel on the CIA In-Q-Tel Venture.* Washington: Business Executives for National Security.

Cain, Walter M. 1997. "LBO Partnership Valuations Matter: A Presentation to the LBO Partnership Valuation Meeting." Mimeo. General Motors Investment Management Co.

Devenow, Andrea, and Ivo Welch. 1996. "Rational Herding in Financial Economics." *European Economic Review* 40:603–615.

"Foster Management Moves to Dissolve Consolidation Fund." 1998. *Private Equity Analyst* 8(December):6.

Freear, John, and William E. Wetzel. 1990. "Who Bankrolls High-Tech Entrepreneurs?" *Journal of Business Venturing* 5:77–89.

Gompers, Paul, and Josh Lerner. 1998a. "Risk and Reward in Private Equity Investments: The Challenge of Performance Assessment." *Journal of Private Equity* 2(Winter):5–12.

Gompers, Paul, and Josh Lerner, 1998b. "What Drives Venture Capital Fundraising?" *Brookings Papers on Economic Activity: Microeconomics,* 49–192.

Gompers, Paul, and Josh Lerner. 1999. *Capital Market Imperfections in Venture Markets: A Report to the Advanced Technology Program.* Washington: Advanced Technology Program, U.S. Department of Commerce.

Gompers, Paul A., and Josh Lerner. 2001. *The Money of Invention.* Boston: Harvard Business School Press.

Greene, Heather. 2001. "Innovation Drought." *Business Week* (July 9):1Ff. (e. biz supplement).

Hellmann, Thomas, and Manju Puri. 2000. "The Interaction Between Product Market and Financing Strategy: The Role of Venture Capital." *Review of Financial Studies* 13:959–984.

Jensen, Michael C., and William H. Meckling. 1996. "Theory of the Firm: Managerial Behavior, Agency Costs and Ownership Structure." *Journal of Financial Economics* 3:305–360.

Kortum, Samuel, and Josh Lerner. 2000. "Assessing the Contribution of Venture Capital to Innovation." *Rand Journal of Economics* 31:674–692.

Kreutzer, Laura. 2001. "Many LPs Expect to Commit Less to Private Equity." *Private Equity Analyst* 11(January):85–86.

Lerner, Josh. 1997. "An Empirical Exploration of a Technology Race." *Rand Journal of Economics* 28:228–247.

Myers, Stewart C., and Nicholas S. Majluf. 1984. "Corporate Financing and Investment Decisions When Firms Have Information That Investors Do Not Have." *Journal of Financial Economics* 13:187–221.

Poterba, James M. 1989. "Venture Capital and Capital Gains Taxation." In Lawrence Summers, ed., *Tax Policy and the Economy*, volume 3. Cambridge, MA: The MIT Press.

Reyes, Jesse E. 1990. "Industry struggling to forge tools for measuring risk." *Venture Capital Journal* 30(September):23–27.

Sahlman, William A., and Howard Stevenson. 1986. "Capital Market Myopia." *Journal of Business Venturing* 1:7–30.

Stiglitz, Joseph E. and Andrew Weiss. 1981. "Credit Rationing in Markets with Incomplete Information." *American Economic Review* 71:393–409.

"Summit's Jacquet Departing to Form Own LBO Firm." 1998. *Private Equity Analyst* 8(May):3–4.

[16]

Retrenchment Activities of Small Firms during Economic Downturn: An Empirical Investigation

by J. Kim DeDee and Douglas W. Vorhies

Recent advances in the operationalization of retrenchment strategies have aroused interest in the investigation of its relationship to company performance. Limited evidence exists, however, concerning retrenchment's value for procyclical firms as the means to counter declining economic conditions. This study provides a longitudinal analysis of retrenchment activities and financial performance during macroeconomic recession. Results indicate that many common retrenchment activities improve small firm performance during economic downturn.

A basic principle of strategic management theory is the necessity to balance the emphasis between outside and inside operating environments if strategy formulation is to be successful (Pearce 1983). Businesses that managed their strategies properly were better able to prosper and grow. This picture has become less clear because of ever expanding environmental turbulence and the resultant need for firms to retrench to compete, or even to survive (Alevras and Frigeri 1987; Appelbaum, Simpson, and Shapiro 1987; Bailey and Szerdy 1988; Bibeault 1982; Boyle and Desai 1991). Environmental turbulence generates important sets of contextual factors, each with differing impacts on company strategic direction (Hamel and Prahalad 1994) and on the process by which

Dr. DeDee is associate professor of strategic management in the Department of Management and Human Resources at the University of Wisconsin-Oshkosh. His research interests include strategic management practices of small firms and the legal implications of doing business in Eastern Europe.

Dr. Vorhies is assistant professor of marketing in the Department of Marketing at the University of Wisconsin-Oshkosh. His research interests include the development of marketing capabilities and their impact on the competitive behavior of small firms.

strategies are crafted. Defined broadly, such turbulence includes impending reductions and shortages (Cameron, Whetton, and Kim 1987), losses of markets and market share to foreign competitors (Cameron, Sutton and Whetton 1988), industry dynamics and structure, hostility (Covin and Slevin 1989; Hall 1980), or general economic decline (Ewaldz 1990b; McCallum 1991; Touby 1991; Want 1990). Until recently, most research on company retrenchment centered on large complex businesses and had little to do with economic conditions as a reason for environmental decline or with smaller firms' responses to it.

Small firms are now responsible for larger and larger portions of the macroeconomy. Since such options as divesting a strategic business unit, diversifying into a more stable business, or seeking short run financing from a parent company to smooth operating disturbances are not available to small firms, small firms are more likely than large firms to choose retrenchment as a response to recession.

This study deals with small manufacturing firms' uses of retrenchment to react to, or proactively prepare for, possible macroeconomic decline or recession. It is descriptive and empirical: we describe how small firms retrench operations, and we measure the effects of retrenchment on company performance in terms of two performance dimensions—return on common equity and cash flow to sales. Specifically, we studied firms in procyclical industries (those that normally move in the same directions as the macroeconomy) over the duration of the most recent (1989–1992) downward trend in the business cycle to address the following research questions: (1) What retrenchment activities are effective in helping smaller firms deal with economic slowdown? and (2) What actions can management take to mitigate the impact on company performance?

Economic Conditions

The industrial sector remains the bellwether of the U.S. economy, even after a five-decade shift of employment to service businesses. In 1995, manufacturing held only 20 percent of nonfarm employment, down from 41 percent in 1941. Yet, between 1982 and 1990, nearly 2.5 million new jobs were created, helping to drop unemployment to its lowest levels since the early 1970's. Average U.S. productivity increased 4.5 percent annually, a roughly constant share of real GDP. During 1987 and 1988, plant capacity edged upward toward maximum levels. By 1990, U.S. firms, through a clearer understanding of international business dealings and wider uses of technology, were able to counter much foreign encroachment on traditional market strongholds and regain a leadership position as a global exporter. The downward and upward movements that encompass the U.S. economy bar entry to some but provide sustainable competitive advantage to others. While many factors characterize economic slowdown (for example, Gross National Product, Consumer Price Index, unemployment, bond yields, interest rates, disposable personal income), Gross Domestic Product (GDP) is the

Table 1
Real Gross Domestic Product Trends (1988-1992)

Year	Quarter	Percent Change*
1988	2	4.2
	3	2.2
	4	4.0
1989	1	2.3
	2	2.0
	3	1.1
	4	1.2
1990	1	1.8
	2	1.7
	3**	0.2
	4	(4.0)
1991	1	(2.4)
	2	1.4
	3	1.8
	4	0.3
1992	1	2.2

* *New York Times* 6/18/92 C1C2. Percentage change, annual rate, constant dollars, seasonally adjusted
** Start of recession: *Survey of Current Business* (May 1992), published by the National Bureau of Economic Analysis. Key factors of their research: Employment, Sales, Income, Production

indicator of choice among modern economists and management theorists. As a summary measure of production, it excludes net factor income and reflects production attributable to factors located in the United States, making it an excellent research variable for this study.

Real GDP growth ranged from strong to very strong from 1982 through 1989. An examination of Table 1 shows that the GDP slowed and then reversed to negative percentages during 1990. The growth seen in early 1990 was most likely an extension of 1989. The second quarter of 1990, with a drop in *real GDP,* began the most recent economic recession, less severe than a depression, but lasting for at least two consecutive quarters. Negative growth is evident in a minority of quarters (for example, 4/1990 and 1/1991), and very slow growth in a majority of consecutive quarters (for example, 2/1990, 3/1990, 2/1991, 3/1991, and 4/1991). Net growth in 1990 and 1991 was -.3 percent and .8 percent respectively. Thus, the 1990–1991 recession offers an opportunity to study the impact of economic decline on small firms and to see how it influenced the management practices of these firms. While this GDP level approach admittedly fails to encompass the complex range of variables found in the macroeconomy, it does provide a summary point of reference from which other clarifying data might be drawn.

Retrenchment Theories

There is confusion about the meaning of retrenchment and turnaround. The literature summarizes retrenchment as a set of senior management initiatives to reverse declining financial performance and achieve cost and asset reductions, or in some cases revenue generation (Schendel and Patton 1976; Hofer 1980; Bibeault 1982; Heany 1985; O'Neill 1986; Barker and Mone 1994; Pearce and Robbins 1993). For firms facing significant declines in financial performance, restoring profitability and stabilizing operations almost always entails strict cost and/or asset reductions followed by shrinking back to the segments of the

business with the most likely prospects of good margins (Hambrick and Schecter 1983; Hambrick 1985; Finkin 1992; Bailey and Szerdy 1988; Dumaine 1990). At least two categories of research can be derived from these propositions, each of which is necessary but incomplete. In the first, retrenchment is seen as the initial stage of a two-stage turnaround process. Hofer's 1980 field study of 12 financially distressed businesses identified the nature of turnaround situations, types of retrenchment strategies, and guidelines for matching turnaround situations with particular retrenchment approaches. His basic retrenchment strategies of cost cutting, asset reduction, and revenue-generation could be used singly or in concert with each other. Firms using revenue-generating strategies focused primarily on existing product lines and secondly on reintroducing discontinued products and/or short-term manufacturing of new products. Acceptance criteria required all products to be produced quickly and profitably and to utilize excess plant capacity. Furthermore, there was low-to-moderate R & D funding, reduced head counts relative to sales, shorter term price-cutting, and increases in advertising and direct sales programs. Hambrick and Schecter's (1983) study of mature product businesses used multivariate data analysis to identify patterns of cost cutting and asset reductions. They found a significant number of firms that pursued retrenchment strategies of cost and asset reductions and selective product/market pruning, but they did not find any of the revenue generating schemes suggested by Hofer (1980). More recently, Robbins and Pearce's (1992) two-stage paradigm of turnaround identified retrenchment as a distinct process critical to the firm's post-decline performance that may or may not be followed by strategy reorientation.

Cautions apparent from the two-stage turnaround approach suggest the retrenchment phase may be overlapped and possibly obscured by any subsequent recovery stage as the firm implements strategy redirection. Also, while retrenchment is recommended as an integral component of the turnaround process, such recommendations are not specific enough due to a lack of benchmarks on when, what, and how much to retrench in various contexts (Bibeault 1982; Robbins and Pearce 1992).

In the second research category, retrenchment is identified empirically as a stand-alone tactical response to decline in financial performance rather than just a part of the overall turnaround process. Firms in industries where profits rise and fall with the general business cycle (hereafter called procyclical) commonly use retrenchment as a tactical response to poor macroeconomic conditions. Macroeconomic fluctuations such as recessions provide a natural basis to illustrate retrenchment as a stand-alone approach. To date, there are few studies or discussions of a single-phase retrenchment process.

Small Firm Retrenchment during Recession

From the research focusing on negative environmental circumstances as the reason for retrenchment (D'Aveni 1989; Ewaldz 1990a; McCallum 1991; Smart and Vertinsky 1984; Steiner and Solem 1988; Want 1990), Bibeault (1982) defined critical differences among the lowest performers, average performers, and best performers in healthy and sick industries. The firms that either remained profitable or quickly returned to profitability did so only through effective retrenchment strategies. Well-managed companies typically outperformed competitors through disciplined control over the economics of the business, intensive development of appropriate product/market niches, and a leadership style that sustained entrepreneurial drive and commitment among their managers. Slatter (1984, p. 43) endorsed the study of retrenchment in the context of the business cycle:

Retrenchment tends to expose a company's competitive weaknesses, although the source of these weakness-

es is often the result of management decisions or acts of omission during the previous boom phase. Management is usually too busy just meeting demand in a boom period to worry about whether it is losing market share (and hence eroding its relative cost position vis-à-vis competition); decisions to build extra capacity are usually taken at this time with insufficient attention given to the state of market demand when the new capacity comes on stream.

Firms engaged in systematic retrenchment during declining environmental conditions enjoy significant performance benefits over competitors (Hambrick and Schecter 1983; O'Neill 1986; Robbins and Pearce 1992). Smaller firms, however, have been less successful in executing turnarounds, even though their ability to retrench is the crucial factor in their chances of survival (Mills and Schumann 1985). The recession of the early 1990's presents a good opportunity to test these ideas in small firms.

Methods

The intent of this research was to measure two interconnected, yet distinct factors: (1) the retrenchment activities of small firms in light of economic slowdown; and (2) the impact of these retrenchment activities on key financial performance variables in the participating firms. Both objective and subjective data were necessary to profile needs for retrenchment, types of retrenchment policies, and overall company performance prior to and following the turnaround period.

Extraneous Variables

The New York Times, The Survey of Current Business, and related federal government documents were researched to identify significant trends in GDP as a summary measure most likely to impact the retrenchment activities of the firms under study. The time period between 1989–1992 was selected because it reflected the end of the growth period of the 1980's, the recession of 1990–1992,

Table 2
Industries in the Study

Special Industrial Machinery NEC *3559* Component parts and fully assembled limited-use industrial machinery for such industries as chemical refining, distilling, metal smelting, wood drying, plastic forming, and electroplating.

Computer/Communication Equipment *3576:* Lower technology chips, data switches, and network connecting devices for computers and special-use communication hardware.

Computer Peripheral Equipment NEC *3577* Keyboards, graphic displays, magnetic and optical disk and tape drives, optical scanners, plotters, printers, and related input/output devices.

Telephone and Telegraph Apparatus *3661* Communication interface and transmission system components, repeaters, line conditioning devices, switching and multiplexing equipment, and customer premise modems, answering machines, and fax machines.

Radio/TV Broadcast/Communication Equipment *3663* Cellular telephones, fixed and mobile radio systems, transmitters, receivers, fiber optics equipment, satellite communications systems, closed-circuit, cable TV, and studio equipment.

Semi-Conductors/Related Devices *3674* Semi-conductors, integrated circuits, discrete devices, diodes, rectifiers, integrated microcircuits, transistors, solar cells, and light-sensing and emitting devices.

Electronic Components NEC *3679* Receiving antennas, switches, and high and low technology waveguides.

Surgical/Medical Instrument/Apparatus *3841* Manually operated human and veterinary devices (syringes, clamps, hypodermic/suture needles, stethoscopes, laparascopic tools, catheters) and various measuring instruments.

Orthopedic, Prosthetic, Surgical Appliances/Supplies *3842* Materials and equipment for professional and personal healthcare: skeletal and muscular braces, trusses, elastic hosiery, dressings, tapes, and related personal safety items.

Electro-Medical Apparatus *3845* Electrical and battery powered patient-monitoring and diagnostic systems ranging from arc lamps to pacemakers, cardiographs, defibrilators, ultrasonic scanning devices, and magnetic resonance imaging equipment.

and the beginning of macroeconomic recovery in 1992.

The Study

To generate valid conclusions and to control for environmental conditions that could overshadow any performance differences attributable to retrenchment management, it was necessary to limit the sample of firms to those of approximately equal size and to those that faced similar operating and competitive situations. Thus, the sample was limited to companies in ten closely related four-digit Standard Industrial Classification Codes (SIC) with annual revenues between $1 million and $100 million. Table 2 details the SIC codes and shows that the sample represents many machinery, electronics, and computer related firms (SIC 35, 36, 38). There were five reasons for choosing these types of companies. First, they had similar technology levels or product life cycle patterns. Second, their degrees of excess capacity typified those of major U.S. and global industries. Third, despite different geographic locations, they held similar susceptibilities and recovery potential to economic turbulence. Fourth, these industries continue to be prominent in the U.S. economy. Finally, they were some of the first traditional manufacturing industries to face intensifying global competition.

Survey Data

Empirical organizational data for this study were obtained from survey instruments mailed to chief executive officers (CEOs) of 451 manufacturing firms with the pre-selected SIC codes. A comprehensive, non-regionally restricted setting was selected to obtain more generalizable results over non-industry factors such as local regulation, taxation, and wage rates. CEOs were viewed as the most accurate source of gauging each company's management formality and defining changes in company direction. Cover letters addressed each CEO by name and title, and gave an overview of the research with a request for participation. Anonymity was guaranteed to individual respondents to reduce the potential for response bias or unintended error, as proposed by Warwick and Lininger (1975). As further protection against self-report bias, CEOs were asked to complete the questionnaire in the presence of two senior executives who were involved in planning and operationalizing the retrenchment activities undertaken by the business in response to the recent recession. Titles of co-respondents were requested. Following a second mailing, 110 complete and usable questionnaires were received, for a response rate of 24.4 percent.

Operational Definitions

To measure broad organizational responses to economic downturn, the survey instrument was designed to focus on the types of issues management faces during a period of retrenchment. In all, 62 questions were prepared based on the retrenchment literature discussed above. As a result, the survey instrument

asked a series of questions regarding changes to the overall business strategy, product-market strategies, cost cutting and asset allocation, R & D funding and application, production management, advertising, promotion, pricing and distribution, organizational structure, pay/incentives, financial management, and decision-making approaches. To help prevent a possible bias from question order, questions were randomized.

To gauge the degree of emphasis a particular firm gave to the various retrenchment activities, respondents were asked to indicate (1) which activities were emphasized in the year prior to the recession (1989), and (2) which activities were emphasized in response to the recession. This procedure enabled comparisons of firms in terms of their completeness and commitment to the various retrenchment activities. Responses were gauged with Likert-type scale anchors ranging from 1 ("not emphasized at all") through 5 ("given great emphasis") in the overall retrenchment process. (This questionnaire is available from the authors upon request). Likert-type anchors were used for the questionnaire due to their well-known ability to measure attitudes, in this case the attitudes of top management regarding their actions in dealing with retrenchment.

Objective Performance Data

Every firm in this study was publicly traded, allowing access to individual financial data through Standard & Poor's *Compustat Financial Data Base of U.S. Companies.* Several issues guided the selection of financial performance via Compustat as the measure of organizational performance. First, financial performance measures are well known and are among the most commonly used measures of performance in business research (Shrader, Taylor, and Dalton 1984), providing the ultimate measure of firm performance for many researchers and practitioners. Second, there is often a reluctance on the part of managers to report data that they view as sensitive. Therefore, the use of Compustat data eliminated our need to ask respondents to report any sensitive performance information. Third, although organizational performance is best viewed as a multidimensional construct, over the span of several years non-financial measures tend to influence financial performance and are, therefore, largely accounted for in financial performance measures (Venkatraman and Ramanujam 1986). Fourth, the use of objective financial performance measures helps reduce possible methods bias, which can result when subjective performance measures are used in the same study with other subjective measures.

Financial performance was measured for each firm at two separate points in time (fourth quarter 1989 and fourth quarter 1992). This time frame bracketed the range of economic downturn factors mentioned earlier. The first performance measure, return on common equity (net income minus preferred dividend payments divided by common stockholders' equity, reported as a percentage), was selected due to its widespread use as a financial performance indicator. Cash flow to sales (net income plus depreciation divided by sales, reported as a percentage) was selected because it factors out the effects of accounting accruals, which may distort the view of the firm's performance in the short run.

Findings

Characteristics of the Responding Firms

The manufacturing firms responding to the survey were relatively small, as indicated by revenue and assets measured at the end of fourth quarter 1992. The size of the responding firms as measured by mean revenue (calculated from Compustat data) was $8.03 million (std.dev. = $8.13 million), with the largest firm showing revenues of $31.6 million and the smallest showing revenues of $25,000. Size as measured by mean assets (from Compustat) was $25.3 million (std.dev. = $23.8 million), with the largest firm showing assets of $97.3 million and the smallest demonstrating assets of $201,000. As illustrated by these

data, the responding firms from the ten SICs sampled for this study were small and represent a range of firm sizes within the small business category.

Data Analysis

Two series of regression analyses were used to estimate the relationships between the change in the return on common equity (ROCE) and change in cash flow to sales (CFSALES) and the retrenchment variables (X_i). For both dependent variables, the change score was calculated by a subtraction of the Time One results (fourth quarter 1989) from the Time Two results (fourth quarter 1992). Likewise, the change score for the survey-based retrenchment variables (the independent variables) was calculated by subtracting the Time One results from the Time Two results. In addition to the retrenchment variables used in this analysis, size, as measured by the logarithm of Total Assets, was included as a control variable. For analysis of both ROCE and CFSALES, the least squares method was used to estimate the regression coefficients (b_i) in two separate equations of the form:

$$Y_{ROCE} = b_0 + b_1 X_1 + b_2 X_2 + \ldots + b_n X_n + u \text{ (Equation 1)}$$

$$Y_{CFSALES} = b_0 + b_1 X_1 + b_2 X_2 + \ldots + b_n X_n + u \text{ (Equation 2)}$$

where u denotes the random disturbance term. In these equations, the regression coefficient (b_i) represents the change in the dependent variable associated with a one-unit change in the independent variable. Prior to estimating the respective regression equations, all data were standardized (to a mean of zero and a standard deviation of one) to remove any possible effects due to large magnitude differences in units. Following standardization of the data, stepwise regression was used to determine which of the independent variables were significantly related to the respective dependent variables. Results from the stepwise regressions were confirmed by using the forward and backward regression procedures.

Table 3
Regression Estimates of Change in Return on Common Equity Relationship

Variable	Parameter Estimate	Standard Error	t-Value	p-Value	Standardized Estimate
Intercept	0.13	0.05	-2.45	0.02	0.00
Major expenditures on product development R & D	-0.40	0.07	-6.02	0.00	-0.40
Relying on long-term debt as a source of funds	0.14	0.06	2.26	0.03	0.14
Restructuring departments according to product lines	0.30	0.06	5.15	0.00	0.32
Restructuring departments according to functional areas	0.30	0.06	5.20	0.00	0.36
Producing high-quality products	-0.38	0.10	-4.03	0.00	-0.28
Manufacturing on a customer order basis	0.57	0.08	7.29	0.00	0.59
Improving new product development capability	0.43	0.07	5.89	0.00	0.45
Increased productivity from R&D by matching explicit R&D objectives with proposed expenditures	-0.33	0.06	-5.97	0.00	-0.38
Securing large contracts from government and other large customers	-0.21	0.07	-2.86	0.01	-0.19
Reducing sales staff and advertising budgets	-0.20	0.07	-2.87	0.01	-0.19
Involve BOD in decisions on corporate mission, competitive strategies, and organizational structure	-0.20	0.10	-2.08	0.04	-0.22
Involve BOD in decisions on capital allocation and capital structure	-0.42	0.11	-3.94	0.00	-0.45

Regression Equation Characteristics: $R^2 = 0.89$; Adjusted $R^2 = 0.85$; $n = 110$

Evaluation of the final regression equations included tests for violations of the basic assumptions of the regression model. No violations of the regression model assumptions due to deviations in normality, heteroscedasticity, or independence of the error terms was detected. In addition, evidence of influence points and/or outliers were checked and found to be within generally acceptable limits.

Results

Equation 1, which investigated the organizational factors related to overall firm performance, as measured by return on common equity (ROCE), produced a model with an adjusted R^2 = .85; F = 25.03 (see Table 3). It is interesting to note that the mean change in ROCE from the fourth quarter of 1989 to the fourth quarter of 1992 was 9.25 percent (std. dev. = 163.13 percent). This 9 percent increase in average ROCE during the study period demonstrates that the firms studied appear to have developed effective responses to the economic downturn.

The retrenchment variables that were significantly related to ROCE at the .05 level were: (1) major expenditures on research and development (b = -.40); (2) relying on long-term debt for funding (b = .14); (3) restructuring departments by product line (b =.30); (4) restructuring departments along functional responsibilities (b =.30); (5) producing high quality products (b = -.38); (6) manufacturing on a customer-order basis (b =.57); (7) improving new product development capabilities (b = .43); (8) increasing research and development productivity (b = -.33); (9) focusing on large contracts (b =-.21); (10) reducing sales staffs and advertising expenses (b =-.20); (11) involving the Board of Directors in strategic planning (b = -.20): and (12) involving the Board of Directors in capital allocation decisions (b = -.42). The intercept for Equation 1 (ROCE) was significant with a b = .13. Interestingly, size was not significantly related to ROCE.

Equation 2, which investigated the organizational factors related to performance, as measured by cash flow to sales (CFSALES), produced a model with an adjusted R^2 = .86; F = 26.05 (see Table 4). Examination of the mean change in CFSALES demonstrated a decrease of 4 percent (std. dev. = 47 percent). This decrease in the average ratio of cash flow to sales for the firms in this study illustrates the difficulty the firms were having maintaining cash flow levels during this period of economic slowdown.

The retrenchment variables that were significantly related to CFSALES at the .05 level were: (1) narrowing geographic distribution coverage (b = .39); (2) broadening geographic distribution coverage (b = .47); (3) relying on long-term debt for funding (b = .33); (4) decreasing product line breadth (b = -.26); (5) decentralizing managerial responsibility (b = -.30); (6) focusing on better control of firm performance (b = -.21); (7) producing low-cost, low- quality products (b = .77); (8) using value analysis in product development (b = .29); (9) technological leadership (b = .52); (10) capital structure flexibility in terms of raising new funds (b = -.26); (11) attempting to improve bond ratings and common stock performance (b = -.39); and (12) involving the Board of Directors in cost reduction decisions (b = -.80). The intercept term was significant with a (b = -.05). Once again, size was not significant in the analysis.

Table 5, giving the mean differences and associated standard deviations for the retrenchment activities found significantly related to ROCE or CFSALES, completes the picture for the small firms studied. It is important to note that a positive mean difference for an activity shown in Table 5 implies that the retrenchment activity was emphasized in response to the recession, while a negative mean difference implies that the retrenchment activity was de-emphasized in response to the recession. It is also interesting to note that only "major expenditures on product development-oriented R & D" was de-emphasized dur-

Table 4
Regression Estimates of Change in Cash Flow to Sales Relationship

Variable	Parameter Estimate	Standard Error	t-Value	p-Value	Standardized Estimate
Intercept	-0.05	0.06	0.76	0.45	0.00
Narrowing geographic coverage from international to national or from national to regional	0.39	0.08	4.76	0.00	0.37
Broadening geographic coverage from regional to national or from national to international	0.47	0.07	6.32	0.00	0.46
Relying on long-term debt as a source of funds	0.33	0.07	5.04	0.00	0.30
Decreasing product line breadth from full to partial line or from partial line to single line	-0.26	0.09	-2.98	0.01	-0.23
Decentralizing managerial responsibility	-0.30	0.07	-4.14	0.00	-0.25
Achieving better overall control of general firm performance	-0.21	0.08	-2.45	0.02	-0.17
Producing low cost, low quality, discount products	0.77	0.08	10.24	0.00	0.83
Using value analysis for improving present products and developing and using more economical and easily available raw materials	0.29	0.09	3.15	0.00	0.24
Technological leadership	0.52	0.07	7.52	0.00	0.43
Capital structure allowing flexibility to raise additional funds for growth	-0.26	0.06	-4.21	0.00	-0.26
Improving bond ratings and common stock market performance	-0.39	0.07	-5.69	0.00	-0.33
Involving BOD in decisions on cost cutting and asset reduction programs	-0.80	0.07	-10.75	0.00	-0.86

Regression Equation Characteristics: R^2 = 0.89; Adjusted R^2 = 0.86; n = 110

Table 5
Mean Differences and Associated Standard Deviations for Significant Regression Variables

Regression Variable	Mean Difference	Standard Deviation
Narrowing geographic coverage from international to national or from national to regional	.27	.91
Broadening geographic coverage from regional to national or from national to international	.02	1.29
Major expenditures on product development oriented R & D	-.02	1.57
Relying on long-term debt as a source of funds	.12	.96
Restructuring departments according to product lines	.47	1.18
Restructuring departments according to functional areas	.39	.91
Decreasing product line breadth from full line to partial line or partial line to single	.48	1.21
Decentralizing managerial responsibility	.07	.88
Achieving better overall control of general firm performance	.75	1.67
Producing high quality products	.39	.85
Producing low cost, low quality, discount products	.11	.68
Manufacturing on a customer-order basis	.30	.89
Improving new product development capability	.48	1.34
Value analysis for improving products and developing and using more economical and available raw materials	.44	.94
Technological leadership	.14	1.06
Increased productivity from R and D by matching explicit R and D objectives with proposed expenditures	.42	.84
Securing large contracts from government and other large customers	.24	1.02
Reducing sales staffs and advertising budgets	.43	1.67
Capital structure allowing flexibility to raise additional funds for growth	.30	1.02
Improving bond ratings and common stock market performance	.16	1.05
Involving board of directors in decisions on corporate mission, competitive strategies, and organizational structure	.41	.96
Involving board of directors in decisions on capital allocation and capital structure	.34	.98
Involving board of directors in decisions on cost cutting and asset reduction programs	.47	.99

Note: A negative mean implies the firm de-emphasized the activity across the period of interest.

ing the study period. All other activities were emphasized in response to the recession.

Discussion

One major objective of this research was to explore which retrenchment activities contributed most to the performance of small businesses reacting to the pressures of an economic downturn. These retrenchment activities can be grouped into five general areas: financial management, marketing, product development and R & D, production management, and organizational restructuring. Of the financial management factors included in this study, an increase in the emphasis on long-term debt for funding had a positive impact on ROCE. This is most likely due to an increase in financial leverage in these firms during the study period.

In the area of product development, the firms in this study increased their emphasis on improving new product development capabilities during the study period. This increase in product development emphasis was found to be positively related to ROCE. Apparently, during economic downturn, an increase in product development capabilities can be used to boost performance in small firms. However, it appears that "major" expenditures on product development R & D during an economic downturn is not the best approach. Firms in the study decreased these major R & D related expenditures during the study period, which proved to be an appropriate action, as the de-emphasis on these expenditures was positively related to ROCE. It is also interesting to note that increases in R & D productivity were emphasized during the study period, but also had a negative relationship with ROCE. Given these findings it appears that an increase in the emphasis on product development capabilities is appropriate, but careful control over the types of expenditures in related research and development areas is effective. However, care must be taken not to stifle the creative process by over-emphasizing increases in R & D productivity.

In the area of production management, two factors appear to have an impact on performance as measured by ROCE. The first factor deals with an increased emphasis on manufacturing on a customer-order basis. This increase in manufacturing for specific customer orders proved to be strongly related to ROCE and may reflect reducing the expenses of meeting customer requirements by reducing the uncertainty present in marketing a product to a large market (versus a specific customer). Also of interest is that the production of high-quality products was emphasized during this period and was found to be negatively related to ROCE. Apparently, these small firms focused on producing high-quality products, but this focus missed its mark in terms of satisfying customers (who were apparently less interested in quality products during this period), which hurt performance as measured by ROCE.

Several marketing issues appeared to have an impact on ROCE. The first marketing activity that was negatively related to ROCE was an increased emphasis on large contracts secured from large customers and the government. Large orders often require expensive customization to meet special customer requirements. In addition, often large orders are placed only when a discount is offered. This emphasis on large orders appears not to have had the desired benefit to these small firms, as emphasizing large contracts hurt these firms during the economic downturn. This is interesting when contrasted to the positive relationship between manufacturing on a customer-order basis and ROCE. Manufacturing for specific customer orders typically lowers the firm's risk and financial exposure due to large inventories. However, this advantage appears to be partially offset by the discounting necessary to obtain large orders. Perhaps an optimum order size exists to balance these factors. Obviously, this is an area that needs additional exploration and in-depth study. Finally, although cost control is important during periods of economic turmoil, apparently cutting the advertising and sales budget is not a good place to attempt retrenchment. Firms that reduced their marketing efforts by reducing sales staffs and advertising expenditures fared worse than firms that maintained or increased marketing efforts.

Organizational restructuring is also a tactic that firms used to respond to the economic downturn. The small businesses in this study emphasized either functional or product line-based restructuring in their retrenchment activities. For the firms in this study, these restructuring activities appear to have been appropriate responses to the recession, as restructuring by product lines or by functional areas was positively related to ROCE. Another action sometimes employed by firms is to increase the involvement of the Board of Directors (BOD) in the major planning and operating decisions of the firm. It appears that an increase in BOD involvement is not particularly useful, as an increase in BOD involvement in strategic planning activities and capital allocation decisions had a negative impact on ROCE. Thus, it appears that involving the BOD in these issues is counterproductive, perhaps due to the distance between day-to-day operating decision and the BOD's perspective.

The second approach to assessing the impact of the recession on the performance of the small firms in this study focused on the impact on cash flow to sales (CFSALES). Five areas appeared to have an impact on CFSALES: finance, production, marketing, distribution, and organizational restructuring.

Three financial management strategies were emphasized by the firms to meet the challenge of the recession. The first, the improvement of bond ratings and stock performance, proved to be negatively related to CFSALES. By emphasizing stock and bond performance (perhaps through over-emphasis on cost cutting), it appears that these small firms actually hurt their cash flow situation during the study. The second financial management factor, the development of a flexible capital structure to fund growth during this period, hurt performance, as measured by CFSALES. The third, using long-term funding as a source of funds and thereby increasing financial leverage, appears to have been an appropriate action, as it was positively related to CFSALES.

The second area to significantly impact CFSALES was marketing. The two factors with the highest beta coefficients were: (1) an emphasis on producing low-cost, low-quality, discount products ($b = .77$); and (2) an emphasis on using value analysis in ongoing product development ($b = .29$). Apparently, the customers of these small firms were more interested in discount products (those delivering adequate performance at low prices) than on quality products during the recession. This is somewhat to be expected, as customers trim their own budgets. Thus, the firms in this study that emphasized lower-priced, lower-quality products tended to perform better. It is interesting to note that although many firms cut product lines during this period, customers apparently wanted firms to maintain their full lines during this period—decreasing product line breadth during the recession was negatively related to CFSALES ($b = -.26$). Taken together, these factors indicate that the best performing firms maintained product lines but shifted emphasis to lower-price, lower-quality products during the recession.

Analysis of the firm's distribution efforts paints a somewhat conflicting picture. Firms with higher levels of performance, as measured by CFSALES, both broadened geographic coverage and narrowed geographic coverage during the recession. Interestingly, both of these approaches were positively related to CFSALES. However, the mean difference for broadening geographic coverage is very small (.02) with a fairly large standard deviation (1.29), which may indicate that firms were not really broadening geographic coverage. Alternatively, firms may have narrowed coverage in some geographic areas while actually increasing breadth in areas that appeared promising.

In addition to marketing, distribution, and finance, organizational restructuring was also related to CFSALES. Emphasizing the decentralization of management responsibilities was negatively related to CFSALES. Although this finding runs counter to much of the popular management theories about empowerment, during recessions empowerment may be more inefficient and thus hurt cash flow. This finding supports the idea that firms should centralize some decision-making during recession to control costs and reduce the inefficiencies that may be present in a highly decentralized organization. Running somewhat contrary to prior expectations, an emphasis on control over the firm's general performance was negatively related to CFSALES. This finding appears to reflect the need to assert control without stifling all lower management initiative and creativity. Or perhaps this finding reflects an emphasis on the wrong techniques to control performance. This finding definitely needs further exploration and study.

The next two areas of interest, each with one tactic significantly related to CFSALES, were (1) technical leadership, and (2) BOD involvement in cost reduction decisions. Technological leadership was emphasized during the study period and demonstrated a strong positive relationship with CFSALES, thus demonstrating its appropriateness. Also emphasized during the study period but negatively related to CFSALES was involving the Board of Directors in cost reduction decisions. This was strongly and negatively related to CFSALES ($b = -.80$), illustrating a counterproductive action. Thus it appears that involving the Board of Directors in cost cutting may be a poor tactic for small firms during economic downturn.

Summary and Conclusions

This study investigated a set of retrenchment activities that small businesses can use to improve their performance during periods of economic downturn. The good news is that many common retrenchment activities did improve the performance of the small firms studied. For example, organizational restructuring was an effective tactic, as was a focus on lower cost products for customers, combined with careful management of the research and development and product development functions. In essence, it appears that when a recession forces cutbacks among a small manufacturing firm's customers, these companies must be flexible enough to respond to their customers' need for less expensive products. Careful management of costs across the organization and careful management of the research and development and product development areas appear to be vital parts of delivering the cost savings benefits needed by the firms' customers.

Cost cutting is not without its risks, however. This study points out that an over-emphasis on cost cutting (especially in advertising and sales-related areas) is often counterproductive. This finding is especially interesting in that many of the firms studied operate in relatively high-tech industries, where marketing and sales capabilities often are viewed as less important than research and development capabilities. Thus, it appears that managers in these and similar industries can hit a point of diminishing returns in cutting their advertising and sales functions, and if this occurs, performance will be negatively impacted. Furthermore, it appears that an over-emphasis on control by upper management and the BOD can hurt performance during an economic downturn. Most likely, this negative impact stems from attempts by upper management and the BOD to micromanage issues better understood by lower and middle management. Obviously, these conclusions must be viewed as somewhat preliminary in light of the sample employed in this study. However, for managers of small manufacturing firms, these findings present useful insights into common retrenchment activities during periods of economic downturn.

References

Alevras, J., and A. Frigeri (1987). "Picking Up The Pieces After Downsizing," *Training and Development Journal* (September), 29-31.

Appelbaum, S., R. Simpson, and B. Shapiro (1987). "The Tough Test of Downsizing," *Organization Dynamics* 16, 68-79.

Bailey, G., and J. Szerdy (1988). "Is There Life After Downsizing?" *Journal of Business Strategy* 9(1), 8-11.

Barker, V., and M. A. Mone (1994). "Retrenchment: Cause of Turnaround or Consequences of Decline?" *Strategic Management Journal* 15(2), 395-405.

Bibeault, D. G. (1982). *Corporate Turnaround: How Managers Turn Losers Into Winners*. New York: McGraw-Hill.

Boyle, R., and H. Desai (1991). "Turnaround Strategies for Small Firms," *Journal of Small Business Management* 29(3), 33-43.

Cameron, K., R. I. Sutton, and D. A. Whetton (1988). "Issues in Organizational Decline," in *Readings in Organizational Decline*. Ed. K. S. Cameron, R. I. Sutton, and D. A. Whetton. Cambridge, Mass.: Harper and Row.

Cameron, K., D. A. Whetton, and M. U. Kim (1987). "Organizational Dysfunctions of Decline," *Academy of Management Journal* 30(1), 126-138.

Covin, J., and D. Slevin (1989). "Strategic Management of Small Firms in Hostile and Benign Environments," *Strategic Management Journal* 10(1), 75-87.

D'Aveni, R. A. (1989). "The Aftermath of Organizational Decline: A Longitudinal Study of The Strategic and Managerial Characteristics of Declining Firms," *Academy of Management Journal* 32(3), 577-605.

Dumaine, B. (1990). "The New Turnaround Champs," *Fortune* (July), 36-44.

Ewaldz, D. D. (1990a). "Managing in an Economic Downturn," *Across the Board* 27(6), 16-18.

—— (1990b). "Managing in an Economic Downturn," *Small Business Reports* 15(12), 20-25.

Finkin, E. (1992). "Using Cost Management Effectively in the Turnaround Process," *Journal of Business Strategy* 13, 62-64.

Hall, W. K. (1980). "Survival Strategies in a Hostile Environment," *Harvard Business Review* (September-October), 75-85.

Hambrick, D. (1985). "Turnaround Strategies," in *Handbook of Business Strategy*, Ed. W. H. Guth. Boston, Mass.: Warren, Gorham, and Lamont.

Hambrick, D., and S. Schecter (1983). "Turnaround Strategies for Mature Industrial-Product Business Units," *Academy of Management Journal* 26(2), 231-248.

Hamel, G., and C. K. Prahalad (1994). *Competing for the Future*. Boston, Mass.: Harvard Business School Press.

Heany, D. F. (1985). "Business in Profit Trouble," *Journal of Business Strategy* 5(4), 4-12.

Hofer, C. W. (1980). "Turnaround Strategies," *Journal of Business Strategy* 1, 19-31.

McCallum, J. S. (1991). "Perspectives For Managers On Recession," *Business Quarterly* 55(4), 34-39.

Mills, D., and Schumann, L. (1985). "Industry Structure with Fluctuating Demand," *American Economic Review* 75 (September), 758-767.

National Bureau of Economic Analysis, U.S. Department of Commerce (May 1992). *Survey of Current Business*. Washington, D.C.: U.S. Government Printing Office.

New York Times (1992). June 18, C1-C2.

O'Neill, H. M. (1986). "Turnaround and Recovery: What Strategy Do You Need?" *Long Range Planning* 19(1), 80-88.

Pearce, J. A. II (1983). "The Relationship of Internal Versus External Organizations to Financial Measures of Strategic Performance," *Strategic Management Journal* 4(3), 297-306.

Pearce, J. A. II, and D. K. Robbins (1993). "Toward Improved Theory and Research on Business Turnaround," *Journal of Management* 19(3), 613-636.

Robbins, D. K., and J. A. Pearce II (1992). "Turnaround: Recovery and Retrenchment," *Strategic Management Journal* 13(4), 287-309.

Schendel, D. E., and G. R. Patton (1976). "Corporate Stagnation and Turnaround," *Journal of Economics and Business* (16)3, 236-241.

Shrader, Charles B., Lew Taylor, and Dan R. Dalton (1984). "Strategic Planning and Organizational Performance: A Critical Appraisal," *Journal of Management,* 10(2), 149-171.

Slatter, S. (1984). *Corporate Recovery: Successful Turnaround Strategies and Implementation.* Singapore: Penguin.

Smart, C., and I. Vertinsky (1984). "Strategy and The Environment: A Study of Corporate Responses to Crises," *Strategic Management Journal* 5, 199-213.

Steiner, M., and O. Solem (1988). "Factors for Success in Small Manufacturing Firms." *Journal of Small Business Management* (January), 51-55.

Touby, L. A. (1991). "Eight Lessons from the Bad Times for the Good Times: Finding a Business Edge that Works Before, During, and After a Recession," *Working Woman,* 16(12), 40-44.

Venkatraman, N., and Vasudevan Ramanujam (1986). "Measurement of Business Economic Performance: An Examination of Method Convergence," *Journal of Management,* 13(1), 109-122.

Want, J. (1990). "Managing Business Change Cycle," *ABA Banking Journal* 82(4), 78-81.

Warwick, D. P., and C. A. Lininger (1975). *The Sample Survey: Theory and Practice.* New York: McGraw-Hall.

[17]

MARKETING STRATEGIES THAT MAKE ENTREPRENEURIAL FIRMS RECESSION-RESISTANT

JOHN A. PEARCE II
College of Commerce and Finance, Villanova University

STEVEN C. MICHAEL
School of Business Administration, George Mason University

EXECUTIVE SUMMARY

The recession of 1990–1991 adversely affected nearly every industry in the United States, and entrepreneurial manufacturing firms were among those hardest hit by the recession. The failure rate among this group by mid-year 1991 had risen 37% from the previous year. Thus, recessions pose a serious threat to the survival of entrepreneurial firms.

Understanding how the business cycle influences performance and what strategies are effective in such turbulent times has practical value for managers of entrepreneurial firms. In this paper we report a large-scale empirical research study involving subjective and financial information from 118 publicly traded U.S. manufacturing firms. The participating firms are involved in technologically demanding and highly innovative industry segments: Industrial and Computer Equipment; Electrical Equipment and Components; and Measuring, Analysis, and Control Instruments. None of the firms has achieved a market share of more than one half of one percent (< 0.5%). The goal of the study was to determine the components of a marketing strategy that enabled a firm in these industries to withstand the negative financial consequences of a recession.

We find that, in these industries, a company's marketing strategies preceding a recession strongly impact the extent of economic downturn on the firm, and influence its odds of a timely and complete recovery. Our specific prescriptions follow: First, maintain marketing activities in the core business as assurance against recession. Increasing sales and advertising, increasing breadth of production, and increasing geographic coverage improve performance during both the peak and the contraction of the business cycle. Second, during the peak period, cautiously expand with an emphasis on marketing efficiency. Increasing the number of channels of distribution and cutting price have a negative effect unless accompanied by sales-force performance measurement. A simple emphasis on incentives and efficiency alone hurts

Address correspondence to Steven C. Michael, Mail Stop 5F4, George Mason University, School of Business Administration, 136 Enterprise Hall, Fairfax, VA 22030. E-mail: smichae2@sbal.gmu.edu

The authors wish to thank Gerry Hills, two anonymous referees, the editor, and participants at the UIC/AMA Research Symposium in Marketing and Entrepreneurship 1995 for helpful comments and suggestions. Remaining errors are the authors'.

0883-9026/97/$17.00
PII S0883-9026(96)00060-2

a firm as a recession hits. All of these prescriptions run counter to existing views that suggest that recession simply requires cutbacks and retrenchment. Recessions seem to be different from other threats to firm viability, and marketing activities appear to help pull the firm through a macroeconomic downturn.
© *1997 Elsevier Science Inc.*

SCOPE OF THE STUDY

In recessions, typically the "winds of creative destruction" that are the heart of capitalism blow with their mightiest force, creating both opportunities and threats (Schumpeter 1912). As an example, at the rate of business failures increased dramatically during the recession of 1990–1991 (Duncan 1991; Statistical Abstract 1994: Table 846). The entrepreneurial firm is especially affected, with its relatively smaller size, little or no diversification, and considerable resource constraints. What may be its advantage is its greater flexibility. Little research has been done on how to help firms survive recessions, however, and none on entrepreneurial firms' survival, although the issue was identified as an area of research a decade ago by Fahey and Christiansen (1986).

In this paper we consider whether marketing activities can help an entrepreneurial firm survive a recession. We examine marketing strategies employed by entrepreneurial firms in industrial goods businesses before the 1990–1991 recession to examine whether profitability can be associated with expanded marketing activities. We discover an interesting dichotomy: Expanding marketing activities in the core business helps a firm survive, but expansion into new channels and geographies must be done with careful controls in order to prevent overexpansion and decreased profitability during the recession.

The paper is organized as follows. The first section reviews the 1990–1991 recession and its effects on the economy broadly. The second section reviews the business press and previous literature for advice regarding recessions. The third combines literature from economics, marketing strategy, and entrepreneurship to identify propositions regarding the ability to marketing to "recession-proof" a business. Next, the data set is described, and results reported. Recommendations for practice follow.

THE 1990–1991 RECESSION

There have been nine recessions in the United States since World War II, and the most recent one lasted from July 1990 to March 1991. The 1990–1991 recession in the United States followed the country's longest peacetime expansion in history and was different from previous recessions in a number of ways. Compared to other post-WWII recessions, the most unusual features of the 1990–1991 recession were the periods of slow growth both before and after the recession itself.

The recession was short, with a duration of eight months versus the average of 11 months, and mild, with real output (GDP) dropping only 2.2% versus the average 2.8% drop. The recovery was also slower than normal, with real output rising 2.9% in the 18 months following the recession, as compared to the average recovery rate of 9.8% growth in the same time frame (Economic Report of the President 1993: 42). Additionally, declines in employment were smaller than any postwar recession.

The recession of 1990–1991 adversely affected nearly every industry in the United States. Failures and cutbacks in all the weakened industries had a multiplier effect on other industries. Entrepreneurial firms, presumably smaller and more credit-hungry than other firms, were among those hardest hit.

Because of the credit squeeze of the late 1980s, small business was left with few sources of working capital. Coupled with the recession, the result of sharply limited credit was an unprecedented number of small businesses having no choice except to shrink or actually close their doors....The sound loans that were not being made, the new jobs that were not being created, and the untold numbers of new businesses that never got started because of these barriers have left a permanent impact on the economy, never to be recovered (Hogan, 1991: 53).

Entrepreneurial manufacturing firms were among those hardest hit by the recession. Failures among this group by mid-year 1991 had risen 37% over the previous year (Duncan 1991: 8). Thus, recessions pose a serious threat to the survival of entrepreneurial firms.

LITERATURE REVIEW

Despite the practical importance of recessions to entrepreneurial firms, the management and entrepreneurship literature has not explicitly examined how these firms might survive downturns in the business cycle. Existing work is based on personal observation or case study analysis, and most appear to pertain to large corporate organizations. A review of recent articles in the business press suggests the following prescriptions for survival in recessions:

1. *Hold positions in diversified products and markets.* Businesses in cyclically sensitive industries often attempt to recession-proof by diversifying into more recession-resistant sectors. For example, the housing industry suffered in the 1990–1991 recession. Banks were hesitant to lend to commercial land-development companies, but considered the home buyers a less risky investment (Jacob and Neumeier 1991). Some builders recognized this trend and switched markets prior to the recession from commercial building to building new homes. Other builders established effective defenses by expanding into the home-repair and remodeling business or property management, which were sectors of the market traditionally considered less volatile (Altany 1991a, 1991b). Diversification is likely to be a less attractive and less possible option for the smaller firm, however.
2. *Establish niches.* In the clothing industry, specialty stores prospered during the 1990–1991 recession (Mitchell 1992). The Limited, Donna Karana, and Liz Claiborne profited from differentiation strategies promoted by specialty retail shops that appealed to consumers how desired a particular style of clothes. This "style" was not easily substitutable (Jacob and Neumeier 1991). As a second example, companies that marketed commodity chemicals suffered in the last recession, while companies that marketed specialty chemicals generated profits. Specialty chemical companies serve niches that allow them to pass along cost increases to customers, while commodity chemicals have slowing demand and higher costs (Jacob and Neumeier 1991).

    These prescriptions from the business press have limited application, however, for the entrepreneurial firm. Diversification to smooth out cash flows is likely to take away both managerial and financial resources from the entrepreneurial firms' core business. Financing for such acquisitions may not be easily obtained. And establishing a niche and increasing product differentiation is often good advice independent of macroeconomic conditions.

304 J.A. PEARCE AND S.C. MICHAEL

Some existing research in management argues that recession requires a turnaround strategy (Hambrick and Schecter 1983; Hofer 1980; Schendel, Patton, and Riggs 1976). Retrenchment is likewise a documented, and frequently recommended, first step in the turnaround process for a company faced with negative effects (Bibeault 1982; Pearce and Robbins 1993; Sloma 1985). The endorsements of retrenchment are not unanimous (Hardy 1987); there is typically organizational resistance to deep cuts. However, firms that achieve greater reductions are better positioned to achieve turnaround (Goldstein 1988; Slatter 1984). In the business press, McLaughlin observed that companies that enacted moderate cost cuts during recessions not only survived but realized more favorable long-run sales and market-share growth than their competitors who made more severe cuts (McLaughlin 1990). Additional strategies implemented to complement cuts focused on the redirection of resources.

In combination, these findings from prior research suggest that a cost-reduction orientation in favorable economic times best prepares a firm to face the added negative pressures of a recession. Firms that continuously attempt to reduce costs should experience less disruption than competitors that have allowed underutilized, slack resources to accumulate. But this prescription is primarily grounded in an extension of the turnaround model, not specific theorizing regarding recessions. And the empirical work has not generally used large-scale samples for validation.

THEORY

Modern economic theory stresses the role of random events, or shocks, disrupting information transmission in the economic system to create business cycles (Howitt 1991).[1] Within industries, shocks that generate a slowdown in economic activity confuse existing firms as to whether declining prices represent a general weakness in the economy or a breakdown of oligopolistic coordination (Green and Porter 1984). In an oligopoly, firms have quantity constraints that sustain a price above the competitive level. If firms observe price but not quantity, and price is subject to random shocks, then a price decline can occur for two reasons: a recession, or a firm expanding output beyond its appropriate level. Firms that observe price falling assume the collusion has collapsed, so all rush to produce. The expansion in production generates too high a quantity to sustain the oligopolistic price, so price collapses. The testable predictions of this model have been supported by Domowitz, Hubbard, and Petersen (1987). Therefore, information (or the lack of it) creates opportunities in recession.

We believe that information plays a crucial role in helping entrepreneurial firms survive recessions. The firm must engage in constant scanning for information about the macroeconomic environment, as well as industry and competitive conditions, in order to detect opportunities and threats. The generation and dissemination of information about customers, competitors, and market conditions is widely understood to be a marketing function (Kohli and Jaworski 1990; Kotler 1991; Narver and Slater 1990; Slater

---

[1]We do not propose to review the vast and stormy debates regarding the causes of recession. Macroeconomists are divided whether business cycles represent a failure of markets to clear because of market rigidities (the neo-Keynesian perspective) or because of technological shocks and adjustment lags (real business cycle perspective). Both are broadly in agreement that information transmission affects individual and firm decision-making. A historical overview of the issues is found in Howitt (1991). A review of the neo-Keynesian perspective is given in Mankiw (1990), and a review of real business cycle theory is found in Stadler (1994).

and Narver 1994). The firm that performs this task well is described in the marketing strategy literature as having a "market orientation" (Day 1990; Kohli and Jaworski 1990; Kotler 1991; Levitt 1960; Narver and Slater 1990; Slater and Narver 1994), which implies that the firm can recognize and respond to changes in the business environment. Specifically, a firm with an emphasis on marketing as opposed to other business functions is more likely to become aware of the recession, to make necessary internal adjustments, and to identify and pursue external opportunities.

Following the distinction made by Hills and LaForge (1992) in their call for research, we theorize at least two ways in which an emphasis on marketing activities will improve performance in recessions: providing market opportunities, and increasing the returns to various marketing strategies. First, recessions create opportunities. As the Green–Porter model above implies, and as observed by Stigler (1964), the breakdown of oligopolistic coordination creates opportunities for firms, as customers are dissatisfied and willing to move to other suppliers. The firm with an emphasis on marketing activities is likely to become aware of those opportunities more rapidly than a production- or finance-oriented firm, and respond to them with measures designed to capture more market share.

Recessions are also likely to increase the returns to various marketing activities. In order to survive, smaller firms must have some differential advantage that allows them to compete against larger rivals who have economies of scale and scope (Caves and Pugel 1980). One such advantage is flexibility in output volume (Fiegenbaum and Karnani 1991; Mills and Schumann 1984); small firms survive by absorbing more uncertainty. If entrepreneurial firms compete by varying their sales levels, then customers must be identified in expansions through selling efforts and advertising. Through marketing activities, small firms are likely to remain knowledgeable about customer needs, and can adjust production more rapidly than larger competitors. Therefore, small firms are likely to earn a higher return from marketing activities throughout the business cycle.

The existing but incomplete literature suggests that for some companies, in some industries, and in some competitive situations there are advantages to entering a recession having previously implemented strategies--independently or interactively--that emphasized marketing activities. Thus, we hypothesize two possible effects suggested from the theory:

> *P1:* Emphasis on marketing activities relative to competitors will improve performance at the peak of the business cycle for small firms.

> *P2:* Emphasis on marketing activities relative to competitors will improve performance during the contraction of the business cycle for small firms.

The above research suggests a variety of reasons why returns to marketing should be high for entrepreneurial firms. But the theory is coarse-grained; there has been little or no attempt to identify which marketing activities are likely to have higher returns, or to provide help to managers during a recession. Through our analysis below, we attempt to remedy this deficiency.

RESEARCH METHODS

This research was designed to measure two distinct but interconnected factors: activities and financial performance of each participating firm during multiple phases of the business cycle. Objective and subjective data were necessary to profile the strategic activities and performance of each company in the sample frame prior to and during the recessionary period.

Sample

Eleven four-digit industries in three two-digit Standard Industrial Classification Codes (SIC) manufacturing classifications were selected for the study. The sample consisted of all 451 publicly traded manufacturing firms with annual sales revenue between $10 and $100 million in 1990. The two-digit classifications were Industrial and Commercial Machinery and Computer Equipment (35), Electrical and Non-Computer Electrical Equipment and Components (36), and Measuring, Analysis, and Control Instruments (38). All of these firms operate in a single SIC-defined industry, so diversification does not affect results. The participating firms are classified by *Standard & Poor* as involved in technologically demanding and highly innovative industry segments, primarily industrial goods industries. None has achieved a market share of more than one half of one percent ($< 0.5\%$). The small size of the firms place them squarely within the traditional domain of entrepreneurial research. More importantly, firms in these industries have in recent years generated considerably more growth in sales and wealth than the economy on average (Rukeyser 1991: 433; *Statistical Abstract* 1994: Table 869). Thus, these are small firms in wealth-creating industries.

A total of 164 questionnaires were returned, with a response rate of 23.9%. Of these, 114 were included in this analysis since only they were from four-digit SIC codes that demonstrated an impact attributable to the 1990–1991 recession, reflecting either a cyclical or countercyclical classification as judged by Standard and Poor. Previous research has identified industrial goods industries as likely to be most strongly affected by the business cycle. Romer (1991) has shown that price movements in industrial goods markets are interrelated through the business cycle. The effects of recession documented by Domowitz, Hubbard, and Peterson (1987) were most pronounced in industrial goods industries.

Nonresponse bias could exist if there exists a relationship between the model variables (such as performance) and the probability of response. Clearly one reason for nonresponse is unsuccessful performance. Firms with poor performance may have other issues to address besides questionnaires (such as survival) or may be too embarrassed to respond. We undertook an analysis of the nonrespondents to the survey to determine whether their firms differed in a significant way from those firms whose managers supplied our study's marketing data. We compared the financial performance data of respondent and nonrespondent firms from the Industrial and Commercial Machinery and Computer Equipment, Electrical and Non-Computer Electrical Equipment and Components, and Measuring, Analysis, and Control Instruments classifications. The data was obtained from *Standard & Poor's Compustat Financial Data Base on U.S. Companies*. The *t*-test results disclosed no significant differences between respondent and nonrespondent firms on the three performance measures that we investigated: return on equity, return on sales, and return on assets.[2]

[2]A firm may have failed before we created the sample frame, and thus be excluded from our sample and our comparison of respondents to nonrespondents. We believe this risk of bias to be low, however, because our sample frame was created in early 1990, before the full effects of the recession were felt. Also, the study does not include private firms. We see no reason that the effects of recession are different for private versus public firms, but we cannot reject the possibility. We are grateful to a referee for drawing our attention to these sampling issues.

Survey Data

Empirical data for this study were drawn from instruments mailed to the manufacturing firms in the pre-selected SIC codes in late 1990, at the trough of the recession. The sampling frame was created in early 1990, and covered the entire United States. This comprehensive, non-regionally restricted field setting was selected to minimize any influence of non-industry factors such as local regulation and taxation, regional economic conditions, or local wage rates.

Accompanying each questionnaire was a cover letter, individually printed on university stationary and addressed to the company president or chief executive officer. The letter gave a brief overview of the research project and a request for participation. As protection against self-report bias, CEOs were instructed to form a group of three executives to complete the questionnaire. The other participants were to be "two senior executives who were involved in planning and operationalizing activities taken by the business associated with the recent recession." Titles of co-respondents were required but names were optional. Anonymity was guaranteed to all respondents as a step to reduce the potential for response bias or unintended error as proposed by Warwick and Lininger (1975). Additionally, the self-reported measures for each concept were limited to a few clearly defined dimensions, thus facilitating accurate responses.

Changes in the firms' emphasis on marketing and business activities were measured through Likert-type scale inquiries. The respondents were asked to indicate the extent to which 11 different marketing activities were emphasized "in the year prior to the recession." The activities appeared in the questionnaire with the numbers 1 through 5 corresponding to a natural progression from "no emphasis" to "great emphasis." Emphasis scales have been used before in the literature (Dess and Robinson 1984; Hatfield and Pearce 1994). The questions broadly covered the key decision variables in marketing (price, promotion, distribution, and product) used in previous research (Carpenter 1987; Kotler 1991; Robinson 1985). Appendix Table A1 contains the full text of the questions and the mean responses. Appendix Table A2 reports additional descriptive statistics on the firms in the sample.

Objective Data

Questionnaire information was supplemented with quarterly financial information. Return on equity (ROE) performance was measured for each firm quarterly through the business cycle—every three months from Quarter 3 of 1989 through Quarter 1 of 1991. This information was obtained in 1995 from reports made available by the public companies to *Standard & Poor's Compustat Financial Data Base on U.S. Companies*. The time frame was chosen because it covered a complete business cycle. The phases were defined by the movement of GNP in the United States. The peak phase was defined as the third quarter of 1989 through the second quarter of 1990. The contraction phase was demarcated by the third quarter of 1990 through the first quarter of 1991. The performance measure for the peak period, Peak ROE, was computed as the average of quarterly ROE over the four quarters of the peak period. Contraction ROE was computed in a similar way.

ANALYSIS

Factor Analysis

Factor analysis was employed to reduce the data set from a large number of coded items to a small number of representative factors. Specifically, self-reported responses to a list

308 J.A. PEARCE AND S.C. MICHAEL

TABLE 1 Factor Analysis Results

Factor	Item	Loading[1]	Communalities	Eigenvalue
Improve marketing efficiency	Incentive performance reward systems	0.75	0.59	
	Multi-functional task force utilized for R&D/operations coordination	0.69	0.54	
	Use highly skilled, motivated sales staff	0.67	0.55	2.59
Streamline the value chain	Decrease distribution channels	0.84	0.74	
	Restructure/focus departments	0.67	0.66	1.67
Retrench into core business	Reduce sales staff/advertising	0.77	0.66	
	Decrease breadth of production	0.71	0.55	
	Narrow geographic coverage	0.61	0.48	1.53
Expand into new markets	Increase distribution channels	0.74	0.57	
	Broaden geographic coverage	0.69	0.61	
	Price below competition	0.60	0.60	1.06

[1] Highest factor loading reported for each item.
Note: Full text of items included in Appendix Table A1.

of marketing strategy questions employing a 5-point Likert scale (1=not emphasized; 5=given great emphasis) were factor-analyzed utilizing varimax orthogonal rotation. These questions were designed to garner an understanding of pre-recessionary marketing strategies. Factor analysis was utilized because numerous variables were correlated within the coded list and there was a need to explain the variance in the set of coded questions as a function of a much smaller set of underlying variables. Four factors closely related to the original set of items resulted from the analysis, each comprised of at least two items with an eigenvalue that was greater than one (>1.00). A summary of the factor analysis is presented in Table 1.

The first factor, *Improve Marketing Efficiency*, stressed the implementation of sales-force motivation tools and the improvement of new product development through use of a multifunctional task force to address R&D and operational coordination. Factor two, *Streamline the Value Chain*, pertained to pursuing a more efficient marketing effort through decreasing the distribution channels, restructuring departments, and implementing innovative sales and advertising efforts. The third factor. *Retrench into Core Business*, reflected the concentration of efforts with regard to specific products and narrowing geographic coverage. Note that the negative of this factor represents an expansion of marketing efforts in the core business. Factor four, *Expand into New Markets*, reflected efforts to pursue a marketing strategy designed to garner a larger share of the market through increased distribution channels, broader geographic coverage, and price competition.

Summary statistics for all study variables, including factors, are set forth in Table 2. Inter-item reliability analyses (Cronbach's alpha) were applied to all factor measures to assess the level of agreement among the particular measures within each factor. The inter-item reliability measures ranged from 0.47 to 0.57. In summary, it was found that 11 variables reflected the underlying marketing strategies as represented by the four factors. Table 2 also sets forth correlations for study variables. Some degree of correlation was expected among factors given the overlapping of domains. Factor scores for each factor were constructed using only those variables associated with the most significant loading on relevant factors. Specifically, all loading over 0.60 were utilized.

TABLE 2   Descriptive Statistics and Intercorrelations of Study Variables

Variable	N	M	SD	1	2	3	Cronbach Alpha	Eigenvalues
ROE: Peak	104	0.32	59.95					
ROE: Contract	111	−5.92	35.45					
1. Marketing efficiency	98	2.83	0.87				0.57	2.33
2. Streamline	103	1.88	0.72	0.21			0.47	1.60
3. Retrench to core	103	1.48	0.61	0.10	0.29		0.53	1.30
4. New market	102	2.77	0.93	0.20	0.24	−0.01	0.53	1.03

Regression

The dependent variable in this study was performance as measured by return on equity. "ROE is generally the most important indication of management's achievement....Since benefiting shareholders is (management's) goal, ROE is, in an accounting sense, the true bottom-line measure of performance" (Ross, Westerfield, and Jordan 1994). ROE thus appeared to be the best measure of performance of the study.[3] In addition, ROE controlled explicitly for capital structure. Alternatively a simultaneous equations model would have to be employed to separate capital structure effects from product market effects on performance. To clearly understand the impact of the recession on firms, performance was compared across two separate time periods: peak and contraction. The peak phase was defined as the third quarter of 1989 through the second quarter of 1990. The contraction phase was demarcated by the third quarter of 1990 through the first quarter of 1991. Performance in each phase was computed as a simple average.

To understand the relationship between marketing strategies as defined by the four factors and performance given recessionary pressures, simple multiple regression was employed. The independent variables utilized in the partial model to identify the main effects were the four factors. To garner a more complete understanding, however, the addition of interaction terms to the partial model was necessary. Two equations were estimated: one for the peak period and one for the contraction period. Table 3 sets forth regression results on the full model. The table shows statistically significant findings for the peak and contraction phases.

The results in a broad sense support the hypotheses. The single strongest influence on peak performance is negatively associated with retrenchment in the firm's core business, or reducing marketing efforts in the core business. This is shown by the negative coefficient on "Retrench into core business" in Table 3. Therefore, the negative sign emphasizes that marketing efforts in the core business sustain the firm through good times and bad. The second strongest factor--expansion into new markets--has a negative effect unless accompanied by careful controls and incentives, as shown by the positive coefficient on the interaction term of "improving marketing efficiency" and "expansion into new markets." Simply seeking efficiency is not enough, nor is increasing activities into new markets. The two must be combined to improve profitability.

Improving marketing efficiency alone has a negative effect on performance, both during the peak and the contraction phase, as shown by the negative coefficient on "Marketing efficiency" in Table 3. Presumably the emphasis on efficiency and incentives re-

---

[3]Existing research has also established that ROE is typically highly correlated with other performance measures (Schmalensee 1989).

310   J.A. PEARCE AND S.C. MICHAEL

TABLE 3   Results of Regression Analysis for Business Cycle Phases

	ROE	
	Peak (N = 104)	Contraction (N = 111)
Improve marketing efficiency	−90.88**	−42.31*
Streamline the value chain	−48.62	−5.45
Retrench into core business	−159.10**	−78.89**
Expand into new markets	−91.79**	−4.14
Marketing efficiency × streamline	7.55	11.52
Marketing effic. × retren. to core	23.67	12.93
Marketing effic. × new markets	17.91*	4.58
Streamline × retrench to core	5.97	−3.84
Streamline × new markets	8.78	−5.66
Retrench to core × new markets	18.25	8.80
F	2.44**	4.54**
R^2	0.24	0.36
Adjusted R^2	0.14	0.28

*$p < .05$.
**$p < .01$.

duces information flow in the firm. In particular, high emphasis on incentive compensation implies that the sales force bears costs of recession, as commission declines with the general level of macroeconomic activity. This loss may make sales representatives reluctant to share information, and perhaps reduce teamwork and morale as well.

During the contraction phase of the business cycle, the coefficients are reduced but the explanatory power remains high. Again, the single highest returns are to increasing marketing activities in core businesses, as shown by the negative sign on the retrenchment variable. The prior expansion into new markets does not have any effect on performance; neither does streamlining the value chain. An emphasis on efficiency alone before entering a recession has a clear negative effect. Viewing the results across equations for improving marketing efficiency suggests that incentives alone do not improve performance. Instead, increasing efficiency is best employed as part of an expansion strategy.

DISCUSSION

The results offer qualified support for the propositions. First, marketing activities in the core business are clearly the major determinant of profitability in both good times and bad. So Proposition 1 and Proposition 2 are supported. A "market orientation" aids profitability. The return to marketing activities decreases during a contraction, however, as seen by comparing the coefficients from the two regressions. In addition, the pattern of significance in each of the profitability equations is different with respect to the "Expand into new markets" variable. In a contraction, prior expansion yields no payoff. In a peak phase, expansion can hurt profitability, perhaps through overexpansion, unless accompanied by an emphasis on marketing efficiency. In a downturn, that peak phase expansion offers no protection against recession.

The confirmation of Proposition 1 and Proposition 2 suggests that the effectiveness of marketing activities is not moderated by macroeconomic conditions. But more specific conclusions can be drawn. Certain marketing activities, such as expanding the sales force and advertising, are effective throughout the business cycle, while others, such as cautious expansion, have effect primarily in the expansion phase. This research has identified why, when, and in which activities marketing has an effect on performance in recession.

In addition, the research does not support the generic prescription of the turn-around literature that recession requires a simple application of a turnaround strategy. Indeed, a serious emphasis on retrenchment leads to poorer performance in our sample. In short, recession is different. Some existing turnaround literature has argued for a more contingent approach, however. Firms facing performance problems attributable to external causes are advised to use entrepreneurial strategies, ones focused on growth (Robbins and Pearce 1992).[4] This research can be interpreted to define and amplify that prescription, specifically that entrepreneurial strategies are primarily marketing-oriented. Sustained marketing activities can pull a firm through a recession.

It is worth repeating the limitations of the study. First, the sample is composed of firms from technology manufacturing industries. Industry forces may moderate the relationship between marketing strategy and performance during the business cycle discussed here. Second, the firms studied are all publicly traded; recessions may affect private firms differently. Third, other business functions were not explicitly examined.

For researchers, this paper represents at best a first step into understanding how firms, especially entrepreneurial firms, survive the business cycle. Our texts in both entrepreneurship and management stress the importance of understanding the external environment, of which the macroeconomy is a major part. Yet we have little understanding about how firms survive recessions and what advice scholars can give to improve survival. More research is needed, both across the business functions and across the distribution of firm sizes, to determine how macroeconomic activity influences firm strategy, structure, and performance. For example, the availability of financing (perhaps through a deep-pocketed angel) or the degree of diversification might very well affect how small firms survive the business cycle.

For practitioners, a company's marketing strategies preceding a recession strongly impact the extent of economic downturn on the firm. The advice to the entrepreneurial firm is clear. First, maintain marketing activities in the core business as assurance against recession. Second, during the peak period, cautiously expand with an emphasis on marketing efficiency. Both of these propositions are also consistent with the economists' viewpoint of small firms as absorbers of industry and macroeconomic uncertainty, who are vulnerable during downturns. In short, a company's pre-recession condition is important because it sets boundaries on management and marketing actions as well as firm performance during the recession, and increases the firm's ability to survive the winds of creative destruction.

REFERENCES

Altany, D. 1991a. Jump start the recovery: What 30 CEOs are doing to beat recession. *Industry Week*, June 3, 240 (11):39–44.

Altany, D. 1991b. Survival lessons. *Industry Week*, February 4, 240 (3):57–65.

---

[4]That paper and data set did not examine recession explicitly. The cause of performance problems was self-identified as internal or external by the firm. The data did cover the period 1976 to 1985, thus including at least one full business cycle.

Bibeault, D.G. 1982. *Corporate Turnaround: How Managers Turn Losers Into Winners*. New York: McGraw-Hill.

Carpenter, G.S. 1987. Modeling competitive marketing strategies: The impact of marketing mix relationships and industry structure. *Marketing Science* 6 (Spring):208–221.

Caves, R.E., and Pugel, T.W. 1980. Intraindustry differences in conduct and performance: Viable strategies in US manufacturing industries. In *Monograph Series in Finance and Economics, #1980-2*. New York: New York University Graduate School of Business Administration.

Day, G.S. 1990. *Market Driven Strategy: Processes for Creating Value*. New York: Free Press.

Dess, G., and Robinson, R. 1984. Measuring organizational performance in the absence of objective measures: The case of the privately held firm and conglomerate business unit. *Strategic Management Journal* 5:265–273.

Domowitz, I., Hubbard, R.G., and Petersen, B.C. 1987. Oligopoly supergames: Some empirical evidence on prices and margins. *Journal of Industrial Economics* 35:379–398.

Duncan, J. 1991. Business failures soar. *Dun & Bradstreet Reports* 39 (5):8.

Economic Report of the President to the Congress. 1993. Washington, DC: U.S. Government Printing Office.

Fahey, L., and Christensen, H.K. 1986. Evaluating the research on strategy content. *Journal of Management* 12:167–183.

Fiegenbaum, A., and Karnani, A. 1991. Output flexibility: A competitive advantage for small firms. *Strategic Management Journal* 12:101–114.

Goldstein, A.S. 1988. *Corporate Comeback: Managing Turnarounds and Troubled Companies*. New York: John Wiley & Sons.

Green, E., and Porter, R. 1984. Non-cooperative collusion under imperfect price information. *Econometrica* 52:87–100.

Hambrick, D.C., and Schecter, S.M. 1983. Turnaround strategies for mature industrial-product business units. *Academy of Management Journal* 26:231–248.

Hardy, C.H. 1987. Investing in retrenchment: Avoiding the hidden costs. *California Management Review* 29(4):111–125.

Hatfield, L., and Pearce, J.A., II. 1994. Goal achievement and satisfaction of joint venture partners. *Journal of Business Venturing* 9:423–449.

Hills, G.E., and LaForge, R.W. 1992. Marketing and entrepreneurship: The state of the art. In D.L. Sexton and J.D. Kasarda, eds., *The State of the Art of Entrepreneurship*. Boston: PWS-Kent.

Hofer, C.W. 1980. Turnaround strategies. *Journal of Business Strategy* 1(1):19–31.

Hogan, B. 1991. A kinder, gentler recession? *D&B Reports* 39(2):52–53.

Howitt, P. 1991. Macroeconomics: Relations with microeconomics. In J. Eatwell, M. Milgate, and P. Newman, eds., *The New Palgrave: A Dictionary of Economics*. New York: Macmillian.

Jacob, R., and Neumeier, S. 1991. The winners and losers. *Fortune*, January 14:76–80.

Kohli, A.K., and Jaworski, B.J. 1990. Market orientation: The construct, research propositions, and managerial implications. *Journal of Marketing* 54(April):1–18.

Kotler, P. 1991. *Marketing Management*, 7th edition. Englewood Cliffs, NJ: Prentice-Hall.

Levitt, T. 1960. Marketing myopia. *Harvard Business Review* 38 (July–August):45–56.

Mankiw, N.G. 1990. A quick refresher course in macroeconomics. *Journal of Economic Literature* 28:1645–1660.

McLaughlin, M. 1990. How to survive a recession. *New England Business*, July 12, 7:35–37.

Mills, D.E., and Schumann, L. 1985. Industry structure with fluctuating demand. *American Economic Review* 75:758–767.

Mitchell, R. 1992. The Gap: Can the nation's hottest retailer stay on top? *Business Week*, March 9, 3255:58–64.

Narver, J.C., and Slater, S.F. 1990. The effect of a market orientation on business profitability. *Journal of Marketing* 54:20–35.

Robinson, W.T. 1985. Marketing mix reactions to entry. *Marketing Science* 7 (Summer):368–385.

Pearce, J.A., II, and Robbins, D.K. 1993. Toward improved theory and research on business turn-around. *Journal of Management* 19(3):613–636.

Robbins, D.K., and Pearce, J.A., II. 1992. Turnaround: Retrenchment and recovery. *Strategic Management Journal* 13:287–309.

Romer, C. 1991. The cyclical behavior of individual production series, 1889–1984. *Quarterly Journal of Economics* 106:1–31.

Ross, S.A., Westerfield, R.W., and Jordan, B.D. 1995. *Fundamentals of Corporate Finance*. Chicago: Irwin.

Rukeyser, L. 1991. *Louis Rukeyser's Business Almanac*. New York: Simon and Schuster.

Schendel, D.E., Patton, R., and Riggs, J. 1976. Corporate turnaround strategies: A study of profit decline and recovery. *Journal of General Management* 3:3–11.

Schmalensee, R. (1989), Inter-industry studies of structure and performance. In R. Schmalensee and R. D. Willig, eds., *The Handbook of Industrial Organization*, Volume II. New York: Elsevier Science Publishers B.V.

Schumpeter, J.A. 1912. *The Theory of Economic Development*. New York: Oxford University Press.

Slater, S.F., and Narver, J.C. 1994. Does competitive environment moderate the market orientation-performance relationship? *Journal of Marketing* 58:46–55.

Slatter, S.St.P. 1984. *Corporate Recovery: Successful Turnaround Strategies and Their Implementation*. Singapore: Penguin.

Sloma, R.S. 1985. *The Turnaround Manager's Handbook*. New York: Free Press.

Stadler, G.W. 1994. Real business cycles. *Journal of Economic Literature* 32:1750–1783.

Stigler, G. 1964. A theory of oligopoly. *Journal of Political Economy* 72. In K. Leube and T. G. Moore, *The Essence of Stigler*, 1986. Stanford: Hoover Institution.

Statistical Abstract of the United States: 1994. 114th edition. Washington, DC: US Bureau of the Census.

Warwick, D.P., and Lininger, C.A. 1975. *The Sample Survey: Theory and Practice*. New York: McGraw-Hill.

314 J.A. PEARCE AND S.C. MICHAEL

APPENDIX

TABLE A1 Items Used in the Questionnaire

"Indicate the emphasis that your company placed on each of the following activities during the year prior to the recession by making a slash through the appropriate number."	Mean	S.D.
Incentive performance reward systems.	3.18	1.24
Using multidisciplinary task forces for effective R&D, marketing, and operations coordination.	2.31	1.13
Adding highly trained, motivated, and dynamic sales personnel.	2.94	1.18
Decreasing the number of channels of distribution.	1.40	0.86
Restructuring departments according to customers or markets.	2.02	1.10
Reducing sales staff and advertising budgets.	1.81	0.99
Decreasing product line breadth from full line to partial line or partial line to single line.	1.52	0.91
Narrowing geographic coverage from international to national or from national to regional.	1.15	0.56
Increasing the number of channels of distribution.	2.65	1.19
Broadening geographic coverage from regional to national or from national to international.	3.34	1.40
Pricing below competition.	2.26	1.15

Note: Likert scaling phrased as numbered 1 ("not emphasized at all") to 3 ("given average emphasis") to 5 ("given great emphasis").

TABLE A2 Sample Profile

	Mean	Interquartile range
Peak ROE	0.3%	26.1%
Contraction ROE	−5.9%	31.3%
Peak annual sales	$23 million	$29 million
Contraction annual sales	$26 million	$30 million
Peak debt-to-assets ratio	24.1%	29.0%
Contraction debt-to-assets ratio	23.8%	30.2%

Peak is defined as third quarter of 1989 to second quarter of 1990. Contraction is defined as third quarter of 1990 to first quarter of 1991. Interquartile range is defined by subtracting the 75th quartile from the 25th quartile.

[18]

Race, Labor Market Disadvantage, and Survivalist Entrepreneurship: Black Women in the Urban North During the Great Depression[1]

Robert L. Boyd[2]

The resource constraint version of the disadvantage theory of entrepreneurship holds that members of destitute ethnic groups often respond to labor market exclusion by becoming "survivalist entrepreneurs," that is, persons who start marginal businesses in response to a need to become self-employed. Applying this theory, I analyze survivalist entrepreneurship among Black women in the urban North during the Great Depression, when many Black women had to find an independent means of livelihood. I hypothesize that (1) the participation of Black women in entrepreneurial occupations, i.e., occupations that lend themselves to self-employment, was positively associated with the disadvantage of these women in the labor market and (2) Black women would be inclined to participate in those entrepreneurial occupations with low barriers to entry, namely, boarding and lodging house keeping and hairdressing and beauty culture. These occupations, according to a review of historical studies, provided northern Black women with their best opportunities for survivalist entrepreneurship. The analyses of census data support my hypotheses and suggest that the resource constraint version of the disadvantage theory of entrepreneurship is relevant to the economic adjustment strategies of northern Black women during the nation's worst employment crisis.

KEY WORDS: black women; entrepreneurship; Great Depression; northern cities.

[1]Revised version of a paper presented at the annual meeting of the American Sociological Association in Chicago, Illinois, on August 8, 1999.
[2]Department of Sociology, Anthropology, and Social Work, Mississippi State University, P.O. Drawer C, Mississippi State, Mississippi 39762-5503.

INTRODUCTION

The job prospects of disadvantaged groups are always poor, but during times of economic decline and mass unemployment, they are particularly slim. Intergroup competition in the labor market intensifies during such periods and, consequently, those at the bottom of the employment queue—notably, women and ethnic minorities—are often compelled to eke out a living in marginal sectors of the economy. According to the disadvantage theory of entrepreneurship, members of such oppressed groups must sometimes choose between joblessness or self-employment in small-scale entrepreneurial activities (Light, 1979:35). When they choose the latter, they are "survivalist entrepreneurs"—persons who become self-employed in response to a desperate need to find an independent means of livelihood (Light and Rosenstein, 1995:213).

During the Great Depression, Black women in the urban North lost their jobs *en masse*, and their rates of unemployment were remarkably high. These rates were much higher than those of White men and women, and in many northern cities, they were even higher than those of Black men, most notably, in the large industrial centers of the midwest.[3] Applying the disadvantage theory of entrepreneurship, I will show in this article that many Black women in northern cities responded to the widespread unemployment of the Great Depression by becoming survivalist entrepreneurs.

LITERATURE REVIEW

Labor market handicaps may compel oppressed minorities to search for alternatives to wage/salary employment, but these minorities need entrepreneurial resources in order to become independent business owners. Such resources include wealth, human capital, ethnic-group solidarity, and

[3]In point of fact, the percentage of Black women who were unemployed and seeking work in the depression year of 1940 was higher than the comparable percentage of Black men in Detroit (19 vs. 16%), Cleveland (22 vs. 17%), and Chicago (23 vs. 17%), among other midwestern cities (U.S. Bureau of the Census, 1943a:Table 47). These extraordinarily high rates of unemployment resulted from the massive layoffs of Black women in service and manufacturing jobs. Yet, in southern cities the rates were markedly lower—in many cases, less than half the northern rates—for the large agricultural sector of the South absorbed many displaced workers, Black and White (Frazier, 1949:600). Moreover, by some accounts, the unemployment rates of Black women in the North were even higher than those cited above. According to a 1937 census of unemployment cited by Frazier (1949:599–600) the percentages of Blacks and Whites who were unemployed in the North and South were as follows:

	Black women	White women	Black men	White men
North	42.9%	23.2%	38.9%	18.1%
South	26.0%	26.2%	18.0%	16.0%

the cultural values and institutions that promote enterprise. When a group has fewer of these resources than do other groups "as a result of some current or past historical experience," then it is a resource-disadvantaged group (Light and Rosenstein, 1995:153). A modified version of the simple disadvantage theory of entrepreneurship, the "resource constraint version," suggests that the members of such groups tend to respond to joblessness and to limited employment options by becoming petty entrepreneurs rather than by starting small businesses (Light and Rosenstein, 1995:152–153).

Blacks have arguably been the most severely resource-disadvantaged group in American society and thus the sociological literature has attributed their low rate of small business ownership to resource disadvantage, a problem caused by the absence of a tradition of enterprise, the poverty of Black consumers, the social class divisions of Black communities, the lack of informal methods of capital accumulation, and intense oppression by Whites (Butler, 1991:71–77, 143–164; Light, 1972:22–58, 101–126; Waldinger and Aldrich, 1990:62–63). Accordingly, the resource-constraint version of the disadvantage theory holds that the entrepreneurial responses of Blacks to labor market disadvantage will be concentrated in the informal economy, that peripheral sector of cash-based, unregulated, and irregular income-producing activities (Light and Karageorgis, 1994:650, citing Portes and Stepick, 1985). Indeed, the resource-constraint version of disadvantage theory implies that, while Blacks will be underrepresented in small businesses, the need to find sources of nonwage income will cause their overrepresentation in the entrepreneurial pursuits of this peripheral sector (Light, 1979:38–39; Light and Rosenstein, 1995:160–161). Put differently, Black disadvantage in the labor market will be unrelated to Black entrepreneurship in mainstream businesses but positively associated with Black entrepreneurship in marginal enterprises.

I will test this proposition by analyzing the relationship between labor market disadvantage and survivalist entrepreneurship among Black women in the urban North during the Great Depression. I will examine the participation of these women in several "entrepreneurial occupations," that is, occupations that lend themselves to self-employment. These pursuits, I will suggest, provided many Black women with viable alternatives to joblessness and limited opportunity in the Depression-era labor markets of northern cities.

In these labor markets, the "double disadvantage" of racism and sexism (Smith and Tienda, 1988) relegated most Black women to the bottom of the employment queue, and as unemployment became widespread, many of these women were summarily dismissed from their jobs and replaced by Whites. As the economic crisis worsened, thousands of Black women in the urban North, including many who were skilled and educated, were compelled to enter domestic service. Some were so desperate for employment in this low-paying, menial occupation during the Great Depression "that they actually offered their services at the so-called 'slave markets'— street corners where Negro women congregated to await white housewives who came daily to take their pick and bid wages down" (Drake and Cayton, 1945/1962:246).

Faced with such dismal prospects, and with the pressing need to support themselves and their families, it is understandable why Black women in the urban North often searched for sources of nonwage income in the formal and informal sectors of the economy. Surprisingly, however, the entrepreneurial activities of these women during the Great Depression have received little attention in the sociological literature on ethnic enterprise. Indeed, most studies of the occupational pursuits of Black women in northern cities during the early 20th century focus on the employment of these women in domestic service. In part, this is because it was very common for Black women in the urban North to work in the homes of middle- and upper-class Whites as cooks, maids, nurses, and laundresses (Drake and Cayton, 1945/1962:242–252; Marks, 1989:45– 48). But another reason for the relative neglect of survivalist entrepreneur- ship among Black women is that, with some notable exceptions (e.g., Light, 1977), few sociological studies of ethnic enterprise have examined the informal economy of cities in the early twentieth century. And still another reason is that the sociological literature on ethnic enterprise has implied that Blacks in general have failed to mount an entrepreneurial response to labor market disadvantage due to the lack of a cultural inclination toward self-employment (e.g., Frazier, 1949:411; Loewen, 1971:41; Yancy, 1974:118).

Nonetheless, historical studies have shown that, during the early twenti- eth century, Black women were frequently involved in individualistic in- come-producing ventures outside of domestic service. In particular, these studies report, self-employed Black women clustered into several occupa- tions. Many of these women worked in their own homes as dressmakers, seamstresses, or laundresses; many were also proprietors of beauty shops, boarding and lodging houses, eating and drinking places, and retail stores (Levenstein, 1995:116–119; Neckerman, 1993:198). Historical studies fur- ther suggest that two occupations provided Black women with their best opportunities for survivalist entrepreneurship in northern cities during the Great Depression: (1) boarding house and lodging house keeping; and (2) hairdressing and beauty culture.

Boarding and Lodging House Keeping

This was an entrepreneurial pursuit created, on the one hand, by the service provider's need for nonwage income and, on the other, by the consumer's need for temporary, affordable shelter. These respective needs had always been pressing in northern Black communities, and they were at critically high levels during the massive economic and social dislocations of the Great Depression. Under these conditions, an enhanced motivation to become self-employed (a "supply effect") coincided with an expanded consumer market for the service in question (a "demand effect") to foster ethnic enterprise (see Light and Rosenstein, 1995:73–74, 116).

Boarding and lodging house keeping were common among the ethnic groups that migrated to northern cities during the late 19th century. Polish immigrants in Pittsburgh often took in boarders and lodgers during this time (Bodnar *et al.*, 1988:181), and so did Blacks in Philadelphia (Du Bois, 1899/1973:292). In the wake of the Great Migration of 1915–1930, the practice became widespread among Blacks in Detroit, New York, Cleveland, and Milwaukee, among other northern cities (Thomas, 1992:92, citing Kiser, 1969, Kusmer, 1976, and Trotter, 1985). Thousands of Blacks from the South, mostly young, single men, streamed into these cities, looking for places to stay temporarily while they searched for housing and jobs. Many of the migrants were taken in by families that needed boarders and lodgers in order to pay rent. Most of these families belonged to the Black working-class that emerged in the 1920's, when Blacks gained access to the industrial jobs of the North. As these families sought better living conditions, "they were often compelled to occupy homes or apartments that were built for middle-class white families," and, owing to the intense competition for housing in segregated Black communities, they were forced to pay much higher rents than were the former White occupants (Frazier, 1939/1966:342).

The number of Black families that needed to take in boarders and lodgers was considerable. According to one estimate, "at least one-third" of Black families in the urban North had lodgers or boarders during the Great Migration (Thomas, 1992:93, citing Henri, 1976). Furthermore, families often harbored several boarders or lodgers at once. A survey of northern Black families reported that "seventy-five percent of the Negro homes have so many lodgers that they are really hotels" (Haynes, 1924:69, cited in Thomas, 1992:92). An ecological study of the residential patterns of Blacks in Chicago and New York found it "significant" that Blacks were "concentrated in the zones where rooming- and lodging-houses comprise a relatively large proportion of the nonresidential structures" (Frazier, 1939/1966:238).

Thus, the practice of taking in boarders and lodgers became part of the informal family economy of Black communities in the urban North after the Great Migration. This practice was, like the migration itself, facilitated by family- and community-based networks, and women were usually at the center of such networks. They "undertook the greatest part of the burden" of helping the newcomers find interim housing, according to a study of Chicago (Grossman, 1989:133). Hence, most boarding and lodging house keepers were women, not only because cooking and cleaning—the main tasks of boarding and lodging house keepers—were "women's work," but also because women played "connective and leadership roles" in northern Black communities and because taking in boarders and lodgers helped Black women combine housework with an informal, income-producing activity (Grossman, 1989:133). In addition, boarding and lodging house keeping was often combined with other types of self-employment. Some of the Black women who kept boarders and lodgers also earned money by making artificial flowers and lamp shades at home (Frazier, 1939/1966:343).

The need to combine household chores and paid work became even more crucial during the Great Depression as the nascent Black working class in the North was decimated by wholesale layoffs of Black industrial workers. Running a boarding or lodging house was thus an attractive option to Black women who were economically distressed.[4] In contrast, domestic service—the only employment alternative for many of these women—was very difficult, if not impossible, to coordinate with family responsibilities. In addition to low pay, it demanded long hours and "provided little independence in work routines." Moreover, the domestic servant was usually on call "around the clock" and was subject to the "arbitrary power of individual employers" (Trotter, 1993:60).

Yet, boarding and lodging house keeping was also low paying, according to census data. Of all employed women in the northern states who were classified as boarding and lodging house keepers and who worked year-round in 1939 and reported earnings (49,525 of 56,854), nearly 97% made less than $1,000 that year, and almost 90% made less than $100 (U.S. Bureau of the Census, 1943a:Table 72). But these astonishingly low figures must be viewed in light of two well-known facts: (1) informal entrepreneurs tend to grossly understate their earnings in official surveys, and (2) transactions in the informal economy often involve barter rather than cash payment. Regarding the second point, it is notable that low-income residents of urban Black communities have an old tradition of informally trading goods and services through kin-based exchange networks (Stack, 1974:32–44). It is also noteworthy that the purpose of boarding and lodging house keeping was not so much to make money as it was to literally keep a roof over one's head—the essence of survivalist entrepreneurship.

---

[4]The practice of sheltering boarders and lodgers was widely denounced by social reformers, who feared that the presence of unrelated adults, and adult males, in particular, would undermine family morality (e.g., see Grossman, 1989:133; Thomas, 1992:92). Ironically, however, this practice probably enhanced the stability of families, for it permitted women "to earn money while remaining home with their children" (Grossman, 1989:133).

Hairdressing and Beauty Culture

These were important entrepreneurial pursuits for northern Blacks in the early 20th century (Boyd, 1996a:133–134). In point of fact, from 1890 to 1940, "barbers and hairdressers" were the largest segments of the Black business population, together comprising about one third of this population in 1940 (Oak, 1949:48). Blacks tended to gravitate into these occupations because White barbers, hairdressers, and beauticians were unwilling or unable to style the hair of Blacks or to provide the hair preparations and cosmetics used by them. Thus, Black barbers, hairdressers, and beauticians had a "protected consumer market" based on Whites' desires for social distance from Blacks and on the special demands of Black consumers (Drake and Cayton, 1945/1962:460–462; Kinzer and Sagarin, 1950:142, 144–145; Myrdal, 1944:310). Accordingly, these Black entrepreneurs were sheltered from outside competitors and could monopolize the trades of beauty culture and hairdressing within their own communities.

These occupations were particularly important entrepreneurial pursuits for Black women in the urban North after the Great Migration. In part, this was a result of the decisive advantage of a protected market of coethnic consumers. But another factor was that beauty culture and hairdressing were easy occupations to enter. Training was often available from a local high school or "beauty college," and a salon could be established in a vacant storefront or in one's own home (Boyd, 1996b:37, citing Drake and Cayton, 1945/1962). To those Black women who had to reconcile paid work with family responsibilities, these features made the occupation an attractive alternative to many other pursuits, such as the notoriously inflexible occupation of domestic service.

Moreover, the demand for beauticians and hairdressers in the Black communities of northern cities was high, even during the Great Depression. Despite the hard times, beauty parlors and barber shops remained the most numerous and viable Black-owned enterprises in these communities (e.g., Drake and Cayton, 1945/1962:450–451). Perhaps demand was robust because many Black women who were seeking jobs believed that one's appearance was a crucial factor in the ability to gain much-needed employment. Indeed, Black self-help organizations in northern cities, such as the Urban League and the National Council of Negro Women, stressed the importance of good grooming to the newly arrived Black women from the South, advising them to have neat hair and clean nails when searching for work. Above all, the women were told to avoid wearing "head rags" and "dust caps" in public (Drake and Cayton, 1945/1962:247, 301; Grossman, 1989:150–151). These admonitions were directed to all Black women, but they were particularly relevant to those who were looking for secretarial or white-collar jobs, for Black women needed straight hair and light skin to have any chance of obtaining such positions (Drake and Cayton, 1945/ 1962:162–163).

Beauty culture and hairdressing not only provided Black women with opportunities for survivalist entrepreneurship, these occupations also helped some Black women economically advance. Many Black hairdressers and beauticians had close business ties with beauty schools or the manufacturers of cosmetics and hair preparations, and these ties sometimes enabled Black women "to move up from home shops or salons to the ownership of several salons or a beauty school, or even to larger and highly profitable enterprises that made and sold cosmetics" (Boyd, 1996b:42, citing Drake and Cayton, 1945/1962). Indeed, it is not fortuitous that the most successful and visible Black female entrepreneurs of the early 20th century were in beauty culture and hairdressing, most notably, Madame C. J. Walker and Annie M. Turnbo-Malone (Boyd, 1996b:42, citing Harmon, 1929). Hence, many Black women in the urban North no doubt entered beauty culture and hairdressing because they saw these occupations as potential ladders of upward socioeconomic mobility.

Upward socioeconomic mobility and economic prosperity were, of course, exceptions rather than the rule. This is evidenced by census data on employed women in the northern states who were classified as barbers, beauticians, and manicurists and who worked year-round in 1939. Of those who reported earnings (124,692 of 133,926), almost 90% made less than $1,000 that year, and 42% made less than $100 (U.S. Bureau of the Census, 1943a:Table 72). Again, such low numbers must be interpreted in the context of both the understating of earnings and the bartering of goods and services that routinely occur in the informal economy.

Other Entrepreneurial Occupations

Several other occupations were also avenues of survivalist entrepreneurship for Black women in northern cities during the early twentieth century. Many of these women were self-employed as home-based laundresses, taking in the laundry of middle- and upper-class Whites. This had been a common occupation among Black women in the South and, as one might expect, it was also a common occupation among the Black women who migrated to the urban North during the Great Migration (Drake and Cayton, 1945/1962:249). Yet, mechanized, commercial laundries owned by Whites or Chinese immigrants began to replace home-based "washwomen" by the second decade of the twentieth century and thus self-employed

Black laundresses were displaced *en masse*. According to one study, the commercial laundries had taken "hundreds of thousands of job opportunities away from the Negro home laundresses," and by 1930, only 2% of such laundries were owned by Blacks (Myrdal, 1944:311). So, as the demand for home-based laundresses waned, relatively few Black women in northern cities were self-employed as laundresses by the Depression era. Nonetheless, a large number of these women worked as operatives in commercial laundries, where the specialized division of labor and fast pace of work were "comparable to a modern factory" (Grossman, 1989:192; see also Drake and Cayton, 1945/1962:250–252).

Black women entrepreneurs in the urban North also opened stores and restaurants, and such establishments proliferated during the Great Depression, as unemployed Blacks with modest savings opened small shops "as a means of securing a living" (Frazier, 1949:405). Called "depression businesses," these marginal enterprises were often classified as proprietorships, even though they tended to operate out of "houses, basements, and old buildings" (Drake and Cayton, 1945/1962:454). Food stores and eating and drinking places were the most common of these businesses, because, if they failed, their owners could still live off their stocks (Drake and Cayton, 1945/1962:454; Frazier, 1949:402).

Yet, Black entrepreneurs were much less likely to enter these retail businesses than to enter personal service occupations, such as barbering, beauty culture, and hairdressing. In part, this was because Blacks generally found it difficult to secure the financial capital, social capital, and human capital that were needed to start businesses in the retail trade, due to racial discrimination, lack of informal methods of financing (such as rotating credit associations), and difficulty organizing cooperative entrepreneurial efforts (Bates, 1973:7; Butler, 1991:75; Drake and Cayton, 1945/1962:437; Harris, 1936:22; Light, 1972:22–58, 101–126; Oak, 1949:63–65). In addition, those northern Blacks who aspired to become retailers faced stiff competition from outside merchants, most of whom were European immigrants (Myrdal, 1944:308). While these merchants often refused to provide personal services to Blacks, they were "anxious to sell food, clothing, appliances, and liquor" to them (Light, 1972:14), and owing to their greater entrepreneurial resources, they could, in most cases, offer Black consumers superior goods, lower prices, and better terms of credit than could Black merchants (Drake and Cayton, 1945/1962:445; Light, 1972:118–124). Moreover, Black retailers, unlike Black barbers, hairdressers, and beauticians, did not have a protected consumer market of coethnics, for the "tastes and buying habits" of Blacks were not markedly different from those of Whites, save for "a few cosmetic items" (Kinzer and Sagarin, 1950:145).

HYPOTHESES

Based on the foregoing literature review, I derive several hypotheses about survivalist entrepreneurship among Black women in northern cities during the Great Depression. The resource disadvantage theory of ethnic enterprise holds that the participation of Blacks in the informal economy is caused by Black disadvantage in the labor market. In the analyses that follow, the standard of labor market disadvantage will be both absolute (i.e., unemployment) and relative (i.e., the higher unemployment rate of Blacks compared to Whites). I hypothesize that the involvement of Black women in boarding and lodging house keeping—one of the most popular entrepreneurial occupations among these women—was positively associated with the disadvantage of these women in the labor market. Furthermore, because this occupation was part of the informal, home-based economy of Blacks in northern cities, I also hypothesize that this positive association was stronger than the associations between the labor market disadvantage of Black women and their involvement in the other entrepreneurial occupations discussed above.

In addition, I hypothesize that the involvement of Black women in barbering, hairdressing, and beauty culture was positively associated with the labor market disadvantage of these women. The northern Black women who tried to become survivalist entrepreneurs during the Great Depression benefited from the ease with which these occupations could be entered and from the protected coethnic consumer market created by social distance and special consumer demands. Accordingly, I hypothesize that the positive association between occupational participation and labor market disadvantage was stronger for Black women in barbering, hairdressing, and beauty culture than for Black women in retailing. Recall that Black entrepreneurs who sought to enter the retail trade found it difficult to secure the necessary capital and credit, lacked a protected market, and faced competition from outside merchants.

Finally, based on the literature review, I hypothesize that there was a positive yet weak association between the employment of Black women as laundresses and the disadvantage of these women in the labor market. According to the literature, the involvement of Black women in this occupation was traditionally heavy but began to wane in the urban North by the 1920's as commercial laundries reduced the demand for "washwomen." Nevertheless, those who faced both joblessness and resource disadvantage were no doubt motivated by their desperate circumstances to become independently employed in this pursuit. Hence, it would not be surprising to find that, while many Black women in northern cities did become laundresses in response to labor market disadvantage during the Great Depression, the decline of opportunities for self-employment in this occupation made it a less viable avenue of survivalist entrepreneurship than other pursuits, such as boarding and lodging house keeping and barbering, hairdressing, and beauty culture.

BACKGROUND

To provide a backdrop for testing the hypotheses, I will first present some descriptive data on the involvement of northern Black women in the entrepreneurial occupations discussed in the review of the literature. These data are for 1940, a year of the Great Depression when many unemployed Blacks were hard pressed to become survivalist entrepreneurs (U.S. Bureau of the Census, 1943a:Table 63). Indeed, although the wartime recovery was 2 years away, the Black unemployment rate in the 1940 census (10.9%) was higher than in any other census from 1890 to 1970 (Vedder and Gallaway, 1992:698), and as I noted earlier, the unemployment rate of Black women in the urban North was especially high.

Table I displays for the northern states of the United States (i.e., the states of the northeast and north central regions) indexes of the representation of Black women in seven occupational categories of the 1940 decennial census. While the categories include employees as well as the self-employed, they are reasonably good measures of the participation of Black women in the entrepreneurial occupations identified in the foregoing review of the literature.

The indexes of occupational representation (IOR) were computed by dividing the proportion of Black women in each occupation by the Black proportion of total employed women and then multiplying the result by 100. Index values over 100 indicate that Black women were overrepresented in the occupation; index values below 100 indicate that they were underrepresented. For comparative purposes, the index values of White women are also presented.

Table I shows that Black women in the North were greatly overrepresented among laundry operatives and laundresses and boarding and lodging house keepers. The IOR of Black women in the former occupational category (296.22) indicates that the number of these women who were laundry operatives or laundresses (13,755) was three times greater than the number "expected," based on the representation of Black women among employed women. The IOR of Black women who were boarding and lodging house keepers (251.40) indicates that the number of these women (6,796) was two-and-one-half times greater than expected. In addition, Black women were overrepresented among barbers, beauticians, and manicurists. The

Table I. Indexes of the Representation of Black and White Women in Selected Occupations in the Northern States, 1940[a]

	Black women	White women
Laundry operatives and laundresses, except private family	296.22 (13,755)	89.96 (83,176)
Boarding house and lodging house keepers	251.40 (6,796)	92.35 (49,703)
Barbers, beauticians, and manicurists	110.44 (6,677)	99.51 (119,791)
Dressmakers and seamstresses, not in factory	101.30 (3,630)	99.92 (71,290)
Proprietors, managers, and officials of eating and drinking places	63.96 (1,039)	101.78 (32,918)
Canvassers, peddlers, and news vendors	37.36 (208)	103.15 (11,434)
Proprietors, managers, and officials of retail stores	22.47 (1,087)	103.91 (100,075)
Total employed women in all occupations in the northern states	324,423	6,456,570

[a]Index values over 100 indicate overrepresentation; index values under 100 indicate underrepresentation. The number of women in each occupation is in parentheses. Occupations are ranked by the index values of Black women.

relevant IOR (110.44) indicates that the number of Black women in these occupations (6,677) was 10% greater than expected.

In contrast to these patterns, White women were slightly underrepresented in the three occupational categories, a finding that suggests that the overrepresentation of Black women in these pursuits was not simply a general pattern for women but a pattern specific to Black women.

Table I further shows that northern Black women were greatly underrepresented in entrepreneurial occupations that had to do with retailing. The IOR of Black women who were proprietors, managers, and officials of eating and drinking places (63.96) indicates that the number of these women (1,039) was 36% less than expected. Similarly, the IOR of Black women who were proprietors, managers, and officials of retail stores (22.47) indicates that the number of these women (1,087) was 77% less than expected.[5] These findings are not surprising, given the problems of Black retail entrepreneurship discussed earlier. Yet, it is remarkable that Black women were greatly underrepresented among canvassers, peddlers, and news vendors, for these pursuits represent the lowest level of retail entrepreneurship and would presumably be easy to enter, even for the disadvantaged. The IOR of Black women in this occupational category (37.36) indicates that the number of these women who were canvassers, peddlers, and news vendors (208) was 63% less than expected.

Again, these occupational patterns differ markedly from those of White women. The latter were slightly overrepresented in the three retailing occupations. Only in the case of dressmakers and seamstresses, did Black and White women have similar IORs, 101.30 and 99.92, respectively, indicating proportional representation.

In sum, the data in Table I are in line with the proposition, based on the resource constraint version of disadvantage theory, that Black women would tend to cluster into entrepreneurial pursuits with relatively low barriers to entry—namely, service occupations (specifically, laundry operative and laundress, boarding and lodging house keeper, and barber, beautician, and manicurist) rather than retail proprietorships, which require capital investment plus an inventory. The underrepresentation of Black women among canvassers, peddlers, and news vendors, however, is at odds with the proposition, for even those with few resources are capable of becoming petty entrepreneurs in these occupations.

ANALYSES

I will test the aforementioned hypotheses with city-level data from the 1940 decennial census (U.S. Bureau of the Census, 1943b:Tables 5 and 13). Cities are the units of analysis because the city accurately represents the spatial arena of local economic activity (Thompson, 1965:44–51). The dependent variables are the rates of the participation of Black women (per 1,000 employed Black women) in the seven entrepreneurial occupations examined above in Table I. I analyze the rate of occupational participation rather than the IOR because the latter is a ratio and, therefore, might be involved in a spurious relationship with one of the explanatory variables used to measure Black women's labor market disadvantage. I analyze those

---

[5]The data on women in this occupational category include wholesale as well as retail establishments. The vast majority of women in this category, however, were proprietors, managers, and officials of retail proprietorships; few women, Black or White, were in the wholesale trade, which was more capital intensive than retailing and thus more difficult to enter.

northern cities with at least 1,000 employed Black women ($N = 34$), in order to have an adequate base for calculating the dependent variables.[6]

One explanatory variable will be the percentage of Black women classified by the census as "unemployed and seeking work." This variable directly measures the disadvantage of Black women in the labor market, because it is an indicator of the "penalty" (viz., unemployment) that disadvantage inflicts (Light and Rosenstein, 1995:155–156). Unemployment is arguably the most serious form of disadvantage in the labor market (Light, 1979:35). The other explanatory variable is an alternative measure of joblessness, the employment-population ratio of Black women. This variable is a useful measure of labor market disadvantage, for unlike the rate of unemployment, it includes Black women who are not in the labor force, i.e., "discouraged workers" (Farley and Allen, 1987:212). The latter, who have abandoned the search for employment in the mainstream labor market, no doubt have a desperate need to become survivalist entrepreneurs.

Descriptive Statistics

Table II shows the mean participation rates of Black and White women in the seven entrepreneurial occupations. Not surprisingly, Black women's highest rates of participation were in the three pursuits in which these women were overrepresented (see Table I). These rates, furthermore, were significantly higher than the comparable rates of White women. As one would also expect, Black women's lowest participation rates were in the three retailing occupations, and these women had significantly lower rates of participation than did their White counterparts in retail stores and in the category, canvassers, peddlers, and news vendors.

The intragroup patterns of occupational participation differ for Black and White women. In particular, the mean participation rates of Black women in the occupations of laundry operatives and laundresses (34.05), barbers, beauticians, and manicurists (23.25), and boarding and lodging house keepers (22.32) were several times higher than the mean participation rates of these women in retail stores (3.84). In contrast, the mean participation rates of White women in the occupations of laundry operatives and laundresses (17.87) and barbers, beauticians, and manicurists (18.99) were

---

[6]These cities were: Akron, OH, Boston, MA, Buffalo, NY, Cambridge, MA, Camden, NJ, Chicago, IL, Cincinnati, OH, Cleveland, OH, Columbus, OH, Dayton, OH, Des Moines, IA, Detroit, MI, Elizabeth, NJ, Gary, IN, Hartford, CT, Indianapolis, IN, Jersey City, NJ, Kansas City, KS, Kansas City, MO, Milwaukee, WI, Newark, NJ, New Haven, CT, New York City, NY, Omaha, NE, Paterson, NJ, Philadelphia, PA, Pittsburgh, PA, Providence, RI, St. Louis, MO, Trenton, NJ, Toledo, OH, Wichita, KS, Yonkers, NY, Youngstown, OH.

Table II. Mean Participation Rates (per 1,000 workers) of Black and White Women in Selected Occupations in Thirty Four Northern Cities, 1940 (Standard Deviations in Parentheses)[a]

	Black women	White women
Laundry operatives and laundresses, except private family	34.05[b] (23.65)	17.87 (5.35)
Barbers, beauticians, and manicurists	23.25[c] (8.32)	18.99 (5.23)
Boarding house and lodging house keepers	22.32[b] (14.28)	9.80 (3.51)
Dressmakers and seamstresses, not in factory	11.02 (5.73)	12.44 (3.29)
Proprietors, managers, and officials of eating and drinking places	4.19 (3.09)	4.15 (2.18)
Proprietors, managers, and officials of retail stores	3.84[b] (4.67)	14.43 (3.50)
Canvassers, peddlers, and news vendors	.77[b] (.82)	1.98 (.76)

[a]Tests are two-tailed. Occupations are ranked by the means of Black women.
[b]Black–White difference is significant, $p < .001$.
[c]Black–White difference is significant, $p < .05$.

only slightly higher than the mean participation rate of these women in retail stores (14.43), and the latter was actually higher than the mean participation rate of these women in boarding and lodging house keeping (9.80). These mean differences were significant ($p < .001$). Thus, compared to White women, there was a marked tendency for Black women in the urban North during the Great Depression to enter service occupations (viz., laundry operative and laundress; boarding and lodging house keeper; and barber, beautician, and manicurist) rather than retail proprietorships. This disparity is consistent with the notion, derived from the resource constraint version of disadvantage theory, that groups afflicted by resource disadvantage—in this case, Black women—are particularly inclined to gravitate into those entrepreneurial occupations with low barriers to entry.

A glaring anomaly, however, is the extraordinarily low participation rate of Black women in the category, canvassers, peddlers, and news vendors. This is surprising because these occupations represent the lowest level of enterprise and are prominent in the informal economy. A possible explanation is that Black women in these pursuits, and women in general, faced stiff competition from foreign-born male entrepreneurs and hence found it difficult to gain a foothold in the petty trading sector. In northern cities during the early 20th century, this sector and other retail activities were dominated by Jewish and Italian immigrant men (Lieberson, 1980:311–313).

Regression Analyses

Table III displays the correlations (r) and slopes (b) of the bivariate regressions of the occupational participation rates of Black women on the percentage of Black women who were unemployed and seeking work. The comparable results for White women are also presented. The mean

Table III. Regression of Occupational Participation Rates on the Percentage of Women who are Unemployed and Seeking Work, Black and White Women in 34 Northern Cities, 1940 (Standard Errors of the Slopes are in Parentheses)[a]

	Black women		White women	
	r	Slope	r	Slope
Laundry operatives and laundresses, except private family	.23[b]	.89[b] (.66)	−.01	−.02 (.33)
Barbers, beauticians, and manicurists	.64[c,f]	.86[c,f] (.18)	−.45[d]	−.81[d] (.28)
Boarding house and lodging house keepers	.37[c,f]	.86[c,f] (.38)	−.14	−.16 (.21)
Proprietors, managers, and officials of retail stores	.62[c,f]	.47[c] (.11)	.26[b]	.32[b] (.21)
Proprietors, managers, and officials of eating and drinking places	.55[c,f]	.28[c,f] (.07)	−.52[d]	−.39[d] (.11)
Dressmakers and seamstresses, not in factory	.11[f]	.11[f] (.16)	−.41[d]	−.47[d] (.18)
Canvassers, peddlers, and news vendors	.15[f]	.02[f] (.02)	−.28[b]	−.07[b] (.04)

[a] Tests are one-tailed. Occupations are ranked by the slope coefficients of Black women.
[b] $p < .10$.
[c] $p < .025$.
[d] $p < .01$.
[e] $p < .001$.
[f] Black–White difference is significant, $p < .05$.

percentages of Black and White women who were unemployed and seeking work, 19.21 (SD = 6.15) and 10.60 (SD = 2.89), respectively, were significantly different (p < .001), reflecting the greater disadvantage of Black women in the labor market. To simplify the discussion of the findings, I will focus on the slopes, which are particularly relevant, because the hypotheses are about the change in occupational participation associated with the change in labor market disadvantage.

Among Black women the slopes were all positive as the disadvantage theory of entrepreneurship would predict, i.e., the greater the level of labor market disadvantage, the greater will be the level of survivalist entrepreneurship. Yet, the slope of laundry operatives and laundresses was only marginally significant (b = .89, p < .10), and the respective slopes of dressmakers and seamstresses (b = .11) and canvassers, peddlers, and news vendors (b = .02) were not significantly different from zero. These results probably reflect the dearth of entrepreneurial opportunities for women in these occupations. In this regard, recall that home-based, self-employment for Black laundresses declined precipitously during the early twentieth century and, therefore, I hypothesized that there would be a positive but relatively weak association between Black women's participation in this occupation and their disadvantage in the labor market.

My hypothesis about the slope of Black women in boarding and lodging house keeping was partly supported. This slope (b = .86, p < .025) was significantly greater than the slopes of these women in eating and drinking places (b = .28, p < .001) as well as in dressmaking and sewing and in canvassing, peddling, and news vending.[7] However, it was not significantly different than the slopes of these women in the categories of barbers, beauticians, and manicurists (b = .86, p < .001) and proprietors, managers, and officials of retail stores (b = .47, p < .001). My hypothesis about the slope of Black women in the barbering and beauty culture occupations was unequivocally supported, though. This slope was significantly greater than the slopes of these women in retail stores and in eating and drinking places as well as in dressmaking and sewing, and in canvassing, peddling, and news vending.

Overall, these results are consistent with my expectation, based on the resource-constraint version of disadvantage theory, that, in response to labor market disadvantage, Black women in the urban North during the Great Depression were more inclined to gravitate into service occupations with low barriers to entry rather than retail occupations. These findings,

---

[7]The one-tailed t-tests used in these and subsequent tests of slope differences are based on the formula, $t = (b_1 - b_2)/(SE_1^2 + SE_2^2)^{0.5}$ where b_1 and b_2 are the unstandardized slopes and SE_1 and SE_2 are their respective standard errors (Kmenta, 1971:371). The degrees of freedom of these t-tests are the pooled degrees of freedom of the two regression equations.

moreover, differ markedly from those of White women. Only in the case of retail stores ($b = .32, p < .07$) was there a positive association between the percentage of White women who were unemployed and seeking work and the occupational participation rate of these women. Indeed, in four cases—namely: barbers, beauticians, and manicurists; proprietors, managers, and officials of eating and drinking places; dressmakers and seamstresses; and canvassers, peddlers, and news vendors—the associations between unemployment and occupational participation were significantly negative, suggesting that jobless White women who were looking for work in the mainstream labor market avoided these entrepreneurial pursuits.

I now replicate these analyses using the employment-population ratio to measure labor market disadvantage. The respective means of this ratio of Black and White women, .267 ($SD = .088$) and .270 ($SD = .033$), were not significantly different. Thus, while racism did penalize Black women in the labor market, it evidently did not cause the rates of joblessness of Black and White women to significantly differ.

Table IV shows the bivariate regressions of the occupational participation rates of Black women on the employment-population ratio of these women. The comparable results for White women are also displayed. The correlations and slopes of Black women were not significantly different from zero in the cases of dressmakers and seamstresses ($b = -6.81$), canvassers, peddlers, and news vendors ($b = -1.06$), and laundry operatives and laundresses ($b = 41.34$). These findings, of course, parallel those of the previous analysis (Table III) and may reflect the dearth of entrepreneurial opportunities in these occupations. Yet, in four cases, the correlations and slopes were significantly negative, indicating inverse associations between Black women's employment-population ratio and occupational participation rates. These results are in line with disadvantage theory which predicts that the lower the employment-population ratio, the greater will be the need to find an independent means of livelihood and thus the higher will be the rate of survivalist entrepreneurship.

Consistent with my hypothesis, the slope of Black women in boarding and lodging house keeping ($b = -98.51, p < .001$) was significantly lower than the other slopes. Also in accord with my hypothesis, the slope of Black women in barbering and beauty culture ($b = -64.84, p < .001$) was significantly less than the slopes of these women in retail stores ($b = -28.24, p < .01$) and eating and drinking places ($b = -19.32, p < .001$) and in the occupations of dressmakers and seamstresses, canvassers, peddlers, and news vendors, and laundry operatives and laundresses.

So, as was the case in the analyses of Table III, the analyses of Table IV are in agreement with my prediction, derived from the resource-constraint version of disadvantage theory, that, in response to disadvantage in the

Table IV. Regression of Occupational Participation Rates on the Employment-Population Ratio, Black and White Women in 34 Northern Cities, 1940 (Standard Errors of the Slopes are in Parentheses)[a]

	Black women		White women	
	r	Slope	r	Slope
Boarding house and lodging house keepers	−.61[d,e]	−98.51[d,e] (22.72)	.37[b]	38.32[b] (17.32)
Barbers, beauticians, and manicurists	−.69[d]	−64.84[d] (12.21)	−.57[d]	−88.78[d] (22.63)
Proprietors, managers, and officials of retail stores	−.53[c]	−28.24[c,f] (7.98)	−.50[c]	−52.35[c] (16.05)
Proprietors, managers, and officials of eating and drinking places	−.55[d]	−19.32[d] (5.21)	−.41[c]	−26.68[c] (10.53)
Dressmakers and seamstresses, not in factory	−.10	−6.81 (11.52)	−.04	−4.35 (17.47)
Canvassers, peddlers, and news vendors	−.11	−1.06[e] (1.65)	−.37[b]	−8.27[b] (3.74)
Laundry operatives and laundresses, except private family	.15	41.34 (46.98)	.36[b]	57.39[b] (26.45)

[a]Tests are one-tailed. Occupations are ranked by the slope coefficients of Black women.
[b]$p < .025$.
[c]$p < .01$.
[d]$p < .001$.
[e]Black–White difference is significant, $p < .05$.
[f]Black–White difference is significant, $p < .10$.

labor market, Black women had a greater tendency to become boarding and lodging house keepers and barbers, beauticians, and manicurists than to become proprietors of retail stores and eating and drinking places. However, in contrast to the analyses of Table III, the analyses of Table IV show similarities in the intragroup patterns of Black and White women, albeit with some notable exceptions. Similar to Black women, the slopes of White women were significantly negative for barbers, beauticians, and manicurists ($b = -88.78$, $p < .001$), proprietors, managers, and officials of retail stores ($b = -52.35$, $p < .01$), and proprietors, managers, and officials of eating and drinking places ($b = -26.68$, $p < .01$). The slope of White women in barbering and beauty culture, furthermore, was significantly lower than the other slopes.

These racial similarities are interesting, because they suggest that, when "discouraged workers" are taken into account (via analysis of the employment-population ratio), Black and White women in northern cities may have had roughly common patterns of survivalist entrepreneurship during the Great Depression. Recall that the employment-population ratio, unlike the unemployment rate analyzed in Table III, includes those who have stopped searching for jobs in the mainstream labor market—i.e., those who desperately need to become survivalist entrepreneurs.

Yet, a noteworthy racial difference in Table IV was that the slope of White women in boarding and lodging house keeping was positive ($b = 38.32$, $p < .025$) rather than negative, a result that runs contrary to the disadvantage theory. In addition, the slope of White women in retail stores was lower than the comparable slope of Black women, but marginally so ($p < .10$), and the slope of White women in canvassing, peddling, and news vending was significantly negative ($b = -8.27$, $p < .025$) and lower than the comparable slope of Black women ($p < .05$). These discrepancies imply that, in the urban North during the Great Depression, (1) keeping a boarding or lodging house was a unique entrepreneurial occupation for those Black women who needed to find an independent means of livelihood and (2) survivalist entrepreneurship in retailing and in canvassing, peddling, and news vending was more common among White women than Black women.

DISCUSSION

Applying the resource constraint version of the disadvantage theory of entrepreneurship, I expected that Black women would respond to labor market disadvantage in northern cities during the Great Depression by becoming survivalist entrepreneurs. In particular, I hypothesized, these women would be most inclined to participate in entrepreneurial occupations with low barriers to entry, namely, boarding and lodging house keeping and hairdressing and beauty culture. These occupations, according to the review of historical literature, provided Black women in the urban North with their best opportunities for survivalist entrepreneurship.

The findings largely supported my hypotheses. Black women in northern cities were overrepresented in these two pursuits, and they participated in them at higher rates than did their White counterparts. The regression analyses, furthermore, showed that the participation of Black women in these occupations was, as I anticipated, positively associated with the disadvantage of these women in the labor market; and with only one exception, these associations were stronger than those between Black women's labor market disadvantage and their participation in retail stores, eating and drinking places, and the other three entrepreneurial occupations.[8]

Support for my hypotheses was particularly robust in the regression analyses of the employment-population ratio, a measure of labor market disadvantage that includes discouraged workers, many of whom had stopped looking for mainstream jobs and desperately needed to become survivalist entrepreneurs. These analyses revealed, as I predicted, that the strongest association between Black women's labor market disadvantage and rates of occupational participation would be observed for boarding and lodging house keeping. This hypothesis was based on studies that suggested that this occupation was part of the informal, family economy of northern Blacks during the early 20th century and hence was a relatively easy pursuit for Black women to enter.

The regression analyses also showed that the disadvantage of Black women in the labor market was positively associated with the involvement of these women in retail stores and in eating and drinking places. As I discussed in the literature review, Blacks encountered numerous obstacles to entrepreneurship in the retail trade and accordingly, they were greatly underrepresented in this field. Nonetheless, as the analyses demonstrated, Black women in northern cities gravitated into these retailing occupations in response to joblessness during the Great Depression. Hence, survivalist entrepreneurship among these women was not limited to pursuits in which Black female entrepreneurs had the advantage of a protected market, such as barbering and beauty culture.

Furthermore, the differences in the regression analyses of Black and White women were consistent with the disadvantage theory of entrepreneurship. The theory predicts that, the greater the penalty inflicted by labor market disadvantage, the greater will be the level of survivalist entrepreneurship. In the first regression analysis, Black women were clearly the more disadvantaged group, for the percentage of these women who were unemployed and seeking work was almost twice as high as the comparable percentage of White women. So, it is not surprising that, in this analysis, the results of Black women were in agreement with disadvantage theory, while those of White women were not, with only one exception (viz., retail stores). However, in the second regression analysis, the respective employment-population ratios of Black and White women were virtually the same, and likewise, there were roughly similar patterns of survivalist entrepreneurship among women from the two groups, albeit with some

---

[8]The lone exception was in Table III: the slope of Black women in boarding and lodging house keeping was not significantly different from the slope of these women in retail stores.

notable exceptions (viz., in boarding and lodging house keeping and in retailing occupations).

The racial differences in the indexes of occupational representation have implications, too. Black women were overrepresented in boarding and lodging house keeping and in hairdressing and beauty culture; yet White women were slightly underrepresented in these occupations. These results imply that, in northern cities during the Great Depression, boarding and lodging house keeping and hairdressing and beauty culture were "ethnic niches" for Black women.[9] An ethnic niche is an occupation in which an ethnic minority group concentrates and becomes overrepresented (not necessarily to the point where other groups are excluded) because the occupation helps its members cope with modest skills and/or employer discrimination (Model, 1993:162).

The findings of my study advance our understanding of the economic endeavors of Black women in the urban North. As I noted in the literature review, research on this topic has focused on the employment of these women in domestic service and other low-status jobs and has largely ignored the entrepreneurial responses of these women to labor market exclusion. Yet, the above results imply that the disadvantage theory of entrepreneurship is highly relevant to the experience of northern Black women during the Great Depression. So, by assuming that disadvantage in the labor market has failed to stimulate business enterprise among Blacks, many sociologists have neglected a salient aspect of the adjustment of Black women to joblessness and limited opportunity in the midst of the nation's worst employment crisis. My study, then, also supports the "economic detour" interpretation of Black entrepreneurship (Butler, 1991:71–77), which holds that, similar to other oppressed groups, Blacks have started businesses in reaction to disadvantage in the labor market. Accordingly, I recommend that future research devote more attention to how Black women have engaged in survivalist enterpreneurship as an economic adaptation strategy.

ACKNOWLEDGMENTS

I thank the reviewers of *Sociological Forum* for their many helpful comments.

[9]Black women were also overrepresented in the occupational category, laundry operatives and laundresses; but this category cannot be considered an ethnic niche because there was little evidence that Black women's participation in this category was related to their disadvantage in the labor market.

REFERENCES

Bates, Timothy
1973   Black Capitalism: A Quantitative Analysis. New York: Prager.

Bodnar, John, Michael Weber, and Roger Simon
1988   "Migration, kinship, and urban adjustment: Blacks and Poles in Pittsburgh, 1900–30." In Raymond A. Mohl (ed.), The Making of Urban America: 170–186. Wilmington, DE: Scholarly Resources, Inc.

Boyd, Robert L.
1996a   "Demographic change and entrepreneurial occupations: African Americans in northern cities." The American Journal of Economics and Sociology 55:129–143.
1996b   "The Great Migration to the North and the rise of ethnic niches for African American women in beauty culture and hairdressing." Sociological Focus 29:33–45.

Butler, John Sibley
1991   Entrepreneurship and Self-Help Among Black Americans. Albany, NY: State University of New York Press.

Drake, St. Clair, and Horace Cayton
1962   Black Metropolis. (1945) New York: Harcourt, Brace and Company (original publication date).

Du Bois, W. E. B.
1973   The Philadelphia Negro. (1899) Millwood, NY: Kraus-Thomson Organization, Ltd (original publication date).

Farley, Reynolds, and Walter R. Allen
1987   The Color Line and the Quality of Life in America. New York: Russell Sage Foundation.

Frazier, E. Franklin
1949   The Negro in the United States. New York: Macmillan.
1966   The Negro Family in the United States. (1939) Chicago: University of Chicago Press (original publication date).

Grossman, James R.
1989   Land of Hope: Chicago, Black Southerners, and the Great Migration. Chicago: University of Chicago Press.

Harmon, J. H.
1929   "The Negro as a local businessman." Journal of Negro History 10:116–155.

Harris, Abram L.
1936   The Negro as a Capitalist. Philadelphia, PA: American Academy of Political and Social Science.

Haynes, George F.
1924   "Negro migration—its effects on family and community life in the North." Proceedings of the Fifty-first Annual Session of the National Conference of Social Work. Toronto, Ontario, Canada.

Henri, Florette
1976   Black Migration: Movement North, 1900–1920. New York: Anchor Books.

Kiser, Clyde V.
1969   From Sea Island to City. New York: Athenevy.

Kinzer, Robert H., and Edward Sagarin
1950   The Negro in Business: The Conflict Between Separatism and Integration. New York: Greenberg.

Kmenta, Jan
1971   Elements of Econometrics. New York: Macmillan.

Kusmer, Kenneth L.
1976   A Ghetto Takes Shape: Black Cleveland, 1870–1930. Urbana, IL: University of Illinois Press.

Levenstein, Margaret
1995   "African American entrepreneurship: the view from the 1910 Census." Business and Economic History 24:106–122.

Lieberson, Stanley
1980   A Piece of the Pie: Blacks and White Immigrants Since 1880. Berkeley: University of California Press.

Light, Ivan
1972   Ethnic Enterprise in America. Berkeley: University of California Press.
1977   "The ethnic vice industry, 1880–1944." American Sociological Review 42:464–479.
1979   "Disadvantaged minorities in self-employment." International Journal of Comparative Sociology 20:31–45.

Light, Ivan, and Stavros Karageorgis
1994   "The ethnic economy." In Neil J. Smelser and Richard Swedberg (eds.), The Handbook of Economic Sociology: 647–671. Princeton, NJ: Princeton University Press.

Light, Ivan, and Carolyn Rosenstein
1995 Race, Ethnicity, and Entrepreneurship in Urban America. New York: Aldine de Gruyter.

Loewen, James W.
1971 The Mississippi Chinese: Between Black and White. Cambridge, MA: Harvard University Press.

Marks, Carole
1989 Farewell—We're Good and Gone: The Great Black Migration. Bloomington: Indiana University Press.

Model, Suzanne
1993 "The ethnic niche and the structure of opportunity: Immigrants and minorities in New York City." In Michael B. Katz (ed.), The "Underclass" Debate: Views From History: 161–193. Princeton, NJ: Princeton University Press.

Myrdal, Gunnar
1944 An American Dilemma. New York: Harper and Row.

Neckerman, Kathryn
1993 "The emergence of 'underclass' family patterns, 1900–1940." In Michael B. Katz (ed.), The "Underclass" Debate: Views From History: 194–219. Princeton, NJ: Princeton University Press.

Oak, Vishnu V.
1949 The Negro's Adventure in General Business. Westport, CT: Negro Universities Press.

Portes, Alejandro, and Alex Stepick
1985 "Unwelcome immigrants: The labor market experiences of 1980 (Mariel) Cuban and Haitian refugees in South Florida." American Sociological Review 50:493–514.

Smith, Shelley A., and Marta Tienda
1988 "The doubly disadvantaged: Women of color in the U.S. labor force." In Ann Helton Stromberg and Shirley Harkness (eds.), Women Working: Theories and Facts in Perspective: 61–80. Mountain View, CA: Mayfield Publishing Company.

Stack, Carol B.
1974 All Our Kin: Strategies for Survival in a Black Community. New York: Harper and Row.

Thomas, Richard W.
1992 Life for Us Is What We Make It: Building Black Community in Detroit, 1915–1945. Bloomington: Indiana University Press.

Thompson, Wilbur R.
1965 A Preface to Urban Economics. Baltimore: Johns Hopkins University Press.

Trotter, Joe W., Jr.
1985 Black Milwaukee: The Making of an Industrial Proletariat, 1915–1945. Urbana, IL: University of Illinois Press.
1993 "Blacks in the urban North: The 'underclass question' in historical perspective." In Michael B. Katz (ed.), The "Underclass" Debate: Views From History: 55–84. Princeton, NJ: Princeton University Press.

U.S. Bureau of the Census
1943a Sixteenth Census of the United States: 1940. Volume III. The Labor Force, Part 1. United States Summary. Washington, D.C.: U.S. Government Printing Office.
1943b Sixteenth Census of the United States: 1940. Volume III. The Labor Force, Parts 2–5. Washington, D.C.: U.S. Government Printing Office.

Vedder, Richard K., and Lowell Gallaway
1992 "Racial differences in unemployment in the United States, 1890–1990." Journal of Economic History 52:696–702.

Waldinger, Roger, and Howard Aldrich
1990 "Trends in ethnic business in the United States." In Roger Waldinger, Howard Aldrich, and Robin Ward (eds.), Ethnic Entrepreneurs: Immigrant Business in Industrial Society: 49–78. Newbury Park, CA: Sage Publications.

Yancy, Robert J.
1974 Federal Government Policy and Black Business Enterprise. Cambridge, MA: Ballinger.

Part III
Unemployment and Entrepreneurship

[19]

Unemployment and self-employment: a survey

The currently high level of unemployment emphasises the importance (in policy terms) of the potential contribution of a self employment alternative. Here the author examines the available UK evidence on the degree of movement from unemployment to self employment, the factors influencing this movement and the role of labour market information and training.

THIS paper examines the movement into self-employment of people who are either unemployed or likely to become so as a result of redundancy. 'Self-employment' is used here in a broad non-technical sense, and covers all situations where people have set up in business on their own account. The businesses so formed may take different organisational forms — sole proprietorships, companies or partnerships — and cover very different types of activity, from window cleaning to manufacturing. Our justification for providing a survey of the work that has been undertaken in this field is two-fold. First, we have so far been unable to trace any study that has focused specifically on this issue although, as we shall see, a number of studies have made passing reference to it. On the theoretical level the establishment of a new business by an unemployed person or indeed someone still in paid employment has not (as far as we can see) received explicit recognition as a possible option in the job search literature. Perhaps this fact in itself is not of any technical significance: self-employment may be incorporated into the models as simply

another job option. However, the absence of explicit mention does serve to emphasise the lack of interest in the transfer phenomenon that is the topic of this paper.

Second, the currently high levels of unemployment emphasise the importance of the issue from a policy viewpoint: if opportunities in *paid* employment are limited, to what extent can redundant and unemployed people create their *own* work by setting up in business? The present government is currently sponsoring training courses aimed specifically at assisting people to make this transition (see Section III) and it clearly sees the formation of entirely new enterprises by redundant workers as one means of alleviating unemployment. (The March 1981 Budget contained measures designed specifically to encourage this activity.) We shall examine the likely impact on employment of such transfers later. More generally, the government is devoting considerable effort to the encouragement of the small firm sector as a whole, in the belief that it is in this sector that the main hope for additional employment lies[1].

This paper is divided into three parts. In Section I we look briefly at the factors affecting

⊐ Peter Johnson is Senior Lecturer in Economics at Durham University

the transfer from unemployment to self-employment. Section II examines the available empirical evidence in the UK on the transfer from unemployment (or threatened unemployment) to self-employment. The final section examines the role of labour market information and training in this area.

I Factors affecting the transfer from unemployment to self-employment

In principle, the unemployed person faces several possible options in the future allocation of his time. These options may be grouped into three main categories. First, he may remain unemployed. Second, he may become an employee, i.e. enter *paid* employment. Third, he may enter *self*-employment. He may of course try to combine these categories, e.g. he may run a business 'on the side' while still remaining an employee of another company.* Within the paid and self-employment categories there may be several options open to him (e.g. he may work as an employee for x. y *or* z; he may found a business in industries a, b *or* c).

At a theoretical level, it is helpful to view the unemployed worker as comparing the anticipated returns, discounted, in each of the options open to him. These returns include non-financial elements. For example, a number of studies (e.g. Boswell, 1973, chap. 3; Cooper, 1973; Goldby and Johns, 1971; Roberts and Wainer, 1971; Scott, 1978)† have pointed to the importance of such factors as the degree of independence, job satisfaction, social status, control over others and challenge in the returns that founders obtain from their businesses. The non-financial *costs* of running a business (e.g. disruption of family life, anxiety, the possibility of bankruptcy) have to be set against these returns. Similarly, the net returns from unemployment and paid employment will also be determined in part by non-monetary factors. Some options may not of course be open to the unemployed worker: he may be unable to obtain *any* kind of paid employment even if he wanted to. Other options may not even be considered: for example, probably most unemployed manual workers do not give any thought to setting up on their own account. For our purposes, we can represent these possibilities as yielding zero or negative returns in respect of the options involved.

We are of course concerned here with the *subjective* assessment of future returns in the different options. Such assessment might be based on wildly inaccurate estimates of what the present values of those benefits are likely to be. Several writers have argued (although not usually on the basis of firm empirical evidence) that the high failure rate of small businesses (see the survey by Gudgin, 1974, and Brough, 1970) may in part be due to the tendency of people to go into well established markets which are already saturated by existing producers (for example, see Davis and Kelly, 1972, p.60, and Beesley, 1955)[4]. Such entrants may have grossly miscalculated their prospects. It is also likely that many potential founders will bias their calculations in the opposite direction, i.e. they will *underestimate* the possible returns to self-employment.‡

These returns will be subject to a constant process of adjustment. For example, the unemployed person's circumstances, his position in the labour market, his perceptions of market opportunities, social attitudes towards the different options and government policies are unlikely to remain static and all are likely to play some part in the determination of anticipated returns. The individual may also directly alter his perceptions of the returns by engaging in search activity in order to improve his knowledge about the possible options (e.g. the person considering self-employment may

---

* The formation of a co-operative represents another form of activity in which the categories mentioned in the text may be combined. The worker becomes *both* an employee — often at a wage less than the going rate — and an owner of the business, from which he receives his share of any profits. In this sense he can be regarded as being in both self-employment and paid employment. For a review of the development of co-operatives, see Wilson and Coyne[2]

† The studies by Cooper and Roberts and Wainer are limited to founders of new technologically orientated companies

‡ Some preliminary work with ex-employees of a large (private) UK company has indicated that a substantial percentage of founders may be too pessimistic about their prospects when setting up. Of a sample of 28 ex-employees who had left at various times in the past to set up in business on their own, 12 thought in retrospect that they had been *more* successful than they had anticipated when launching out originally. These answers may of course reflect some ex-post rationalisation and in any case the sample size is too small to warrant firm conclusions. However, despite these difficulties the figures serve as a useful counterbalance to the views expressed in the text

Unemployment and self-employment: a survey

undertake some market research in order to identify commercially viable activities).

The unemployed person will move into self-employment when he perceives that the discounted value of future returns from that activity exceed those from either unemployment or paid employment.* This may occur not only because anticipated returns from self-employment have *risen*, but because returns from the alternatives have *fallen*. Thus a perceived decline in employment prospects or a fall in unemployment pay will, other things being equal, generate movement into self-employment. It is not therefore surprising to see that a number of authors have argued that unemployment may stimulate new business formation[5].

II **Previous studies on unemployment and self-employment**

As we have already mentioned, we have been unable to trace any UK study that was specifically geared to examining the role of self-employment among people who had either been made redundant or who were unemployed[6]. However, there are three areas of empirical research more general in nature that might be expected to deal, in greater or lesser degree, with this particular issue. These areas are: studies of redundant workers and their subsequent experience in obtaining re-employment; studies of the unemployed and their subsequent experience; and studies of new firm formation and the backgrounds of the founders. We examine the findings of each of these in turn (we delay the main *interpretation* of these findings until the end of the section). Before we do this, however, we should note that all the studies mentioned were undertaken *before* the recent policy emphasis on small business: the results, therefore, provide a useful yardstick against which the effects of the new policy initiatives might be assessed.

(i) Redundancy studies

These are principally of two kinds.

(a) Case studies

There is now a very considerable number of studies of particular redundancies and of the subsequent job histories of the people involved. Among industries covered in the studies undertaken in the post-war period in the UK are the following: aircraft and missiles (Thomas, 1969; Wedderburn, 1964); engineering (Daniel, 1972); mining (HMSO, 1970; Bulmer, 1971); motor vehicles (Kahn, 1964; Pearson and Greenwood, 1977); railways (Wedderburn, 1965); textiles (Martin and Fryer, 1973) and shipbuilding (Sams and Simpson, 1968; Herron, 1975; Hart, 1979).†

It is difficult to summarise the findings of such a diverse collection of studies. However, it is striking that all either do not mention self-employment among redundant workers or, where they do, such employment is clearly very unimportant in quantitative terms as a source of re-employment. However, it should be noted that some of the studies were not set up in a way that would elicit a clear indication of whether someone had gone into business on his own account. Many of the classifications adopted for deciding the subsequent employment of the redundant workers could have applied equally to paid employment or self-employment. Furthermore, even where an explicit question on self-employment was included in a study, it is not always clear whether or not such employment refers only to those who *in National Insurance terms* are self-employed, or whether it also includes those who are 'self-employed' in the broad, non-technical sense of 'working for themselves' but who for National Insurance purposes, because they have set up a *company* of which they are technically 'employees', are not self-employed.‡ However, even allowing for these problems, it is quite clear that self-employment was not an important avenue for re-employment. The following table gives some indication of its importance in those case studies that give firm data. The very small

---

* Movement into any of the three states is not an irreversible decision Indeed, at any point in time an individual may envisage a future career pattern that involves all three at different stages This complication need not worry us here

† At the time of writing, a number of other redundancy studies are being undertaken or are at the report stage These include investigations into particular redundancies in the shipbuilding, jute and cash register industries
‡ Even if the studies exclude those who start their own *companies* it is unlikely that the data on self-employment would significantly understate the number of new businesses since most firms that do become incorporated start off life in a way which would make their employees self-employed in the normal National Insurance sense

7

Table 1: Redundancy and self-employment: some case studies

Industry	Company/ Companies involved	Number in sample	Nature of sample	% of sample going into self-employment	Source
Engineering	Mainly GEC	529	Males who received lump sum payment at redundancy. 67% of total sample were unskilled, semi-skilled or skilled manual workers.	3	Daniel (1972) p.97
Motor vehicles	Mainly BMC	215	Males who did not go back to original employer. Total sample of 447 males made redundant. 86% of total sample either semi-skilled or manual workers.	2	Kahn (1964) p.177
Shipbuilding	Upper Clyde Shipbuilders	264	Males who had obtained re-employment out of 300 active job seekers. Total sample of 328 useable interviews out of 400 approached. 91% of the 400 were unskilled, semi-skilled or skilled manual workers.	1	Herron (1975) p.85
Shipbuilding (Oil rig construction)	RDL	795	Total (mostly males) entering employment after redundancy. Total sample of 1030 made redundant. 85% of 795 were skilled or unskilled manual workers.	1	Hart (1979) table 55
Textiles	"Casterton Mills"	107	Males who received redundancy pay, out of total sample of 328 male leavers. 55% of 107 were manual workers.	7 mentioned starting up own business as one use to which redundancy money would be put (respondents could state two uses)	Martin and Fryer (1973) p.126

percentage of people going into business on their own account may in part be a reflection of the nature of the samples, in particular their emphasis on manual occupations. (This emphasis is also apparent in most of the redundancy studies which make no mention at all of self-employment.) Data on differences in the rate at which redundant people go into self-employment across occupations are very sparse in these case studies, but there is tentative evidence in the studies by Martin and Fryer (1973)* and more recently by Hart (1979), to suggest that *non*-manual workers are more likely to set up on their own. In an unpublished study of male 'staff' personnel who had taken voluntary severance from a large chemical company, the author found that the percentage going into business by them-

selves was about 7%, very much higher than any of the percentages reported in the first four studies in Table 1. (The 'Casterton Mills' study did not indicate how many had *actually* set up in business, it is not, therefore, directly comparable with the others). We shall return to this point later. It may also be true that the more entrepreneurially inclined of the work force in the closing plant may have left prior to the closure to set up on their own. In most cases such people would not be covered by these studies.

(b) More general studies

These include the studies by MacKay and by Parker *et al*[7], the latter being aimed at evaluating the effects of the Redundancy Payments Act. MacKay's study makes no explicit mention of self-employment, although the possibility that some of his respondents set up in business on their own account cannot be ruled out Parker *et al*[8] found in their study of

---

* This statement draws on the data Martin and Fryer provide on the use made of redundancy payments It may be of course that non-manual workers, for various reasons, received *higher* redundancy payments and were, therefore, in a better position to set up on their own

Unemployment and self-employment: a survey

Table 2: Findings of Parker, et al

Last job prior to redundancy	% in self-employment (first job after redundancy	Base figure* on which % is calculated
Senior managers	8	78
Junior managers	11	55
Professional and technical		
higher	14	42
lower	—	50
Clerical	2	157
Skilled	4	458
Semi-skilled	3	245
Unskilled	3	470

* Relates to those who *found* a post-redundancy job.

Source: Parker (1971), Table 3.38, p.100.

a random sample of just over 2000 redundant workers that at the time interviews took place about 1% were self-employed.* The percentage was the same both for workers who received no statutory payment, and for those who did receive such a payment. This suggests that redundancy payments may not be an important stimulus for people to set up by themselves. Indeed, it might be argued that redundancy payments may in part act to make unemployment relatively more attractive. In view of the comment earlier about differences across occupations, it is worth reproducing in full here their findings on different classes of redundant employees, about 80% of whom were males, who had received a statutory payment and who had subsequently gone into self-employment.

It is very striking that the percentages are substantially greater in the professional and management categories While there may be other factors which explain part of these differences, straight occupational differences are still likely to account for a substantial residual. The finding that manual and clerical workers are relatively less important sources of self-employment is confirmed in another 'general' study undertaken by Daniel (1972)

(ii) Studies of the unemployed

The fairly large scale studies conducted by Daniel (1974) and Daniel and Stilgoe (1977) make no mention, in their analyses of the jobs to which the unemployed go, of self-employment, although, as with the redundancy studies, the research was not designed to elicit

specific responses in this area. The large scale study by the Department of Employment (1977) on the characteristics of the unemployed conducted in 1976-1977 showed that 1% of males in the sample had become self-employed six months after their initial interview. (This represents nearly 2% of all those who had left the unemployment register.) Grossed up to 1976 totals this would have represented a flow of 9100 people from unemployment into self-employment. (It is not clear whether self-employment is defined in National Insurance or broader terms here.) These figures are not broken down by duration of unemployment or occupation.

Disney has shown in his study of movements between classes for a cohort of 1630 males, all of whom were born in 1933, that about 5% of all those who had experienced any period of sickness or unemployment in 1972 paid at least one month of Class 2 stamps in 1973 (although only 1% paid Class 2 stamps for the *whole* of 1973, suggesting that a significant number may have tried self-employment for a short experimental period). Again, we do not have any further breakdown of these data.

(iii) Studies of new firms

The published work on new firm formation and on the background of founders in the UK in the post-war period is relatively sparse. The studies by Boswell (1972), Gudgin (1978), Firn and Swales (1978), Little (1977), Johnson and Cathcart (1979 a and b), Gudgin et al (1979) and Storey and Robinson (1979)† probably

---

* Two per cent of those who received statutory redundancy payments claimed that the 'major use' to which they put them was to set up in business This suggests that by the time of the interview some had already moved away from running their own business

† Individual business histories do of course abound However, it would be a major task to synthesise the findings of these studies Without such a synthesis any comments would be of an anecdotal kind and would not, therefore. be particularly helpful in the present context

Table 3: Status of incubator plants of a sample of Northern Region founders

Status of incubator plant	NBEs		Founders	
	Number	%	Number	%
Closed at time of formation of new business	19.0	25.7	29.0	23.5
Closed subsequent to formation of new business	7.5	10.1	11.0	9.6
Taken over by another (existing) business at time of formation	4.0	5.4	8.0	7.0
Remaining open	34.0	45.9	56.0	48.7
Founders unemployed	1.0	1.4	2.0	1.7
Don't know	8.5	11.5	11.0	9.6
Total	74.0	100.0	115.0	100.0

constitute the bulk of the recent material[9].

None of these studies was set up to look specifically at new firms formed by redundant employees or unemployed people. However, our own study provided some background data on the previous experience and working environment of the founders. This study covered 74 entirely new *manufacturing* businesses (115 founders) founded in the Northern Region in recent years. Details of the sample can be found in Johnson and Cathcart (1979a)[10]; it is sufficient to say here that it was not, as far as we are aware, systematically biased in any way.

The finding which is of particular relevance in the context of this survey is that a substantial minority (about one-third) of founders came from incubator plants that either were actually closing at the time of the formation of the new business or were about to close. The following table provides the relevant data New Business Equivalents (NBEs)* give the number of founders weighted by their contribution to business formations.

The occupational breakdown of the founders who came from plants closing at or subsequent to formation of the new business is given in Table 4.

There were *no* unskilled manual workers in the group. Eighty-five per cent were white collar workers: and the biggest single group in this second category was management (above foreman level). The data do not of course provide information on formation *rates* across occupations since we do not know how many in total in each occupation were made redundant over the relevant period; however, it should be clear that managerial and supervisory occupations have a much higher propensity to set up in manufacturing business than manual workers, and that within the latter

* The NBE of any given founder is the reciprocal of the number of founders involved in the formation of the relevant business

Table 4: Occupational breakdown of a sample of Northern Region founders

	Founders	%
Semi-skilled manual	2	5.0
Skilled manual	4	10.0
Clerical	1	2.5
Sales representatives	5	12.5
Commercial	4	10.0
Technical	3	7.5
Supervisory (foreman or equivalent)	6	15.0
Managerial (above foreman level)	15	37.5
TOTAL	40	100.0

category, unskilled workers are less likely to set up than skilled workers. These findings are in line with the findings from the redundancy and unemployment studies (the latter are not of course limited to self-employment in *manufacturing*).

We also found from our study that 'fertility' in terms of manufacturing spin-off declines with incubator plant size, even when industry effects are accounted for. This finding is based on an analysis of the incubator size of *all* founders, whether or not they were affected by closure. However, none of the 28 founders who came from a manufacturing incubator which closed at (or subsequent to) the formation of the new firm and for whom we have data came from incubator plants or more than 500 employees Unfortunately, data on the number of employees involved in the closure of plants of different sizes are not avaialble Consequently, we do not know whether the absence of spin-off from the 500 plus plants represents a relatively lower fertility *rate*, although on the basis of the other evidence, we suspect that it does.

None of the research in the three categories mentioned above provided very detailed information on the transfer from redundancy/ unemployment to self-employment. However, the following conclusions seem reasonably

Unemployment and self-employment: a survey

clear. First, the total size of the transfer is probably very small. Consequently, even if substantial policy initiatives were taken in this area the outcome, in terms of the reduction in unemployment, would be of a low magnitude. (Such initiatives may, nevertheless, be justified in cost benefit terms, but their absolute impact on the unemployment problem would be limited.) It may of course be argued that a new business created by a person affected by unemployment may also provide employment for others and thereby *indirectly* reduce unemployment. However, the majority of new businesses are formed in the service sectors and they will often employ — even at their largest — only a few employees.* Of 43 businesses formed by ex-staff employees of the large chemical company referred to earlier, only one was employing more than five, three years after formation. (Storey, 1980, has shown that not one of the new *manufacturing* firms formed between 1965 and 1976 in Cleveland employed more than 100 people in 1976; he also shows that this finding is not unique to Cleveland.) Such firms may remain small not only because the market is limited but because the owner does not want to relinquish either internal or external control. Some businesses may of course have very high growth potential in employment terms and it is likely that the founders of such businesses will be drawn from managerial ranks rather than from manual grades.

The estimation of the *actual* numbers of people employed in the new businesses is unlikely of course to be a good guide to the overall impact of formations on unemployment since the 'new' jobs may displace workers in other businesses. Such displacement effects are difficult to estimate, although information on the nature of the employment in the new businesses may provide some guide.

Second, manual workers (and especially unskilled manual workers) seem less likely to make the transfer than managerial grades. The latter are likely to have higher anticipated earnings in self-employment than the former. Not only is their expertise more complete in terms of running a business, but they are also more aware of possible market opportunities. Skilled manual workers are likely to have more expertise to sell on a self-employment basis

than their unskilled counterparts.

Third, there are reasonable grounds for supposing that ex-employees from small plants are more likely to set up in business than those from larger plants. Employees in the smaller plants will have greater contact with individuals who have themselves set up in business. They will gain greater familiarity with the types of market that could be served by a new business which in the early years at least is almost inevitably going to be small. They are also likely to gain greater all-round experience in the running of a business. At the same time, it must be said that the evidence we have is consistent with some pre-selection by potential founders: they may deliberately seek employment in small plants before setting up in order to gain relevant experience. Nevertheless, even if this is the case, the lower fertility of large plants implies that the depressed regions of the UK are likely to be at a relative disadvantage as far as new formations are concerned.

III The role of labour market policies

Our discussion in Section II suggested two basic objectives which labour market policies might have in this area. Before we examine these below, it is worth stressing the general point that such policies cannot be considered in isolation from those relating to *paid* employment and unemployment. If, for example, labour market policies make paid employment more attractive, then (ceteris paribus) the flow into self-employment will diminish. Lowering unemployment benefit will have an opposite effect

(i) Improvement in the *accuracy* with which potential founders perceive their likely prospects in self-employment. (For one way in which these prospects can be affected, see Jackson, 1979, p.3.) Such activity may involve broadening or narrowing the potential founder's horizons. It may even generate an interest in self-employment that did not previously exist. In some cases it may lead to the abandonment of proposals for a new business, by making potential founders more realistic about (for example) their own abilities, market prospects, the availability of finance, premises, labour etc † This improvement in

---

* Even if the businesses involved employed large numbers, we would still not know what would have happened to employment in the absence of such firms

† This *reduction* in the rate of formations by such potential founders may be an indicator of success of policies in this area, if the people who would otherwise fail are deterred from setting up

accuracy of perceptions may occur *directly*, through the provision of information and advice, and/or *indirectly*, through the provision of certain types of experience which are likely to raise perceived prospects in self-employment. There can be little doubt that the overwhelming emphasis in the provision of information in redundancy situations (and, indeed, in the labour market generally) is on paid employment opportunities. As far as we can see most companies and official agencies adopt a *responsive* attitude towards self-employment, i.e. they may provide a 'sign-posting' and/or advisory service to those who express an interest, but they do not actively promote self-employment as an option. This bias stems in part from the fact that labour market information in the self-employment area must of necessity be more nebulous in character. No 'vacancy' lists exist as such. Indeed, it is in the interests of the currently self-employed to conceal as far as they can the 'vacancies' in their particular line of business. This raises the question of whether it would be possible to formulate a positive approach to information provision on self-employment opportunities which might attract people whose 'natural' perceptions of such opportunities are very limited or non-existent (for example because of their previous work experience) but for whom the probability of success in self-employment is high.

The provision of information is, in general, likely to have a cumulative impact, and our own research suggests that founders have often considered the idea of founding a business for several years before actually launching out (Johnson and Cathcart, 1979a). The impact (in terms of new formations) of information provided only immediately prior to redundancy is therefore likely to be much less than where there has been a build-up over several years. In this connection we should note the absence of such positive promotion of self-employment as a career option in the UK. A cursory examination of the official careers publications for example shows a marked absence of discussion on the opportunities for setting up (perhaps at a later date) on an 'own account' basis. It is likely that schools could take a much more active part in sowing the seeds that might bear fruit at a later stage. *Indirect* methods of altering perceptions might be achieved through (for example) employment experience in a small firm.

So far we have considered only the perceived prospects of potential *founders*. However, large *companies* making personnel redundant might also be encouraged to question whether activities that they are shutting down or rationalising might not be viable on a smaller scale, if run by some of their ex-employees as independent businesses. Such businesses often have lower unit costs than sections of a similar size which are part of a large company (often because of lower over-head costs). 'Buy-outs' of this kind appear to have become much more frequent as the result of the present recession, partly because the unit cost difference between small and large company operations becomes more marked as output falls (the overhead element becomes more significant). Companies engaged in rationalisation might also be able to assist start-ups by ex-employees by making available equipment and premises which have a low real cost in terms of alternative uses. They might also provide ex-employees with some initial orders where those employees are providing goods or services which were previously 'in house' activities of the large company. Such a policy might provide the new start-up with the breathing space in which to establish other customer contacts. The costs of such a buying policy might be small in relation to the gains in industrial terms resulting from a smoother rationalisation process.

(ii) The alteration of actual prospects through (a) changes in the economic and social environment in which formation and sub-sequent growth can occur; and/or (b) changes in potential founders' own capabilities via training both on and off the job. Under (a) there can be no doubt that the general political environment has become much sympathetic towards small firms in recent years. One effect of this has been a growth in 'local initiatives' (see Foundation for Alternatives, 1979) and of bodies which provide various forms of assist-ance to new business.* Tax and other reliefs for small firms have also been introduced; how substantially these moves have shifted the balance of advantage towards self-employment remains, however, an open question. (It must be remembered that the impact on formations of any measures which also improve the returns from paid employment — a lowering of

* The London Enterprise Agency, the Hackney Project and the St Helen's Trust, are examples of this kind of activity

Unemployment and self-employment: a survey

income tax rates is one example — will be greatly reduced; it may even be zero or negative.)

In the longer term, it may be possible to change social attitudes towards setting up in business on an own account basis through (for example) special schools programmes. Social attitudes towards business failure may also affect the formation rate. It is, for example, a commonly held view that bankruptcy has a social stigma attached to it in this country which is much less than that in the United States. (We have no definite evidence on this score.) The removal of such a stigma might thus raise perceived prospects in self-employment.

Many of the above measures cannot of course be regarded as *labour* market policies. However, it may be misconceived to focus exclusive attention on such policies since there may be far greater returns in terms of formation and growth rates of new businesses from changes in *general* economic and social policies.

Under (b), there may be scope for providing some form of formal training for self-employment The MSC has recently introduced training schemes for unemployed personnel wishing to set up in business. It is difficult, and probably too early, to assess the overall impact of these schemes. (The measurement of 'output' from the training presents formidable problems for any evaluation.) However, it should be remembered that the underlying aim of these courses is not to train an entrepreneur from scratch, but to improve the performance of someone already committed to the formation of a business The demand for such courses is therefore dependent to a large extent on the factors mentioned under (a)

It is doubtful whether there is much scope for explicit on-the-job training of would-be entrepreneurs, especially if the firm providing the training knows that the trainee will set up as a competitor. However, as we have seen, the provision of small firm experience in a more general context may lead to a greater awareness of options in self-employment on the part of people so employed.

We have discussed various ways in which policies might influence the extent and nature of transfer between unemployment and self-employment. Whether any or all of these policies would represent an efficient use of resources remains of course an open question.

Conclusions

This article has considered the movement from unemployment or redundancy to self-employment, broadly interpreted. We have suggested that an increase in unemployment or actual (or threatened) redundancy may increase the rate of new firm formation although we know very little about the elasticity of this response. Redundant workers or workers threatened by redundancy are an important source of founders for new manufacturing firms, at least in the Northern Region. Notwithstanding this finding, the formation of a new business does not appear to be an important avenue for re-employment among redundant workers. The studies of redundancy and the unemployed so far undertaken suggest that no more than about 5% of people affected by redundancies attempt to set up on their own, although the studies are biased towards manual workers and therefore towards a group that is likely to be less 'fertile' in terms of the setting up of businesses. Managerial grades have higher fertility. Nevertheless, our findings should generate caution in arguing that new business formations by unemployed/redundant workers can make a big impact on the unemployment figures. The need for caution is further emphasised when the nature of the businesses formed and the size of their subsequent labour force are analysed. This is *not* to say, however, that policies in this area would not be cost effective In the depressed regions of the UK, where unemployment is by definition higher, the problem is exacerbated by the relatively high concentrations of larger plants, since fertility appears to be inversely related to plant size.

Labour market information by training policies for self-employment (which cannot be seen in isolation from those for *paid* employment or unemployment) may be viewed as having two main aims: improvement in the *accuracy* of workers' perceptions of self-employment possibilities; and the alteration of actual self-employment prospects via changes in the economic and social environment and training. The improvement in the accuracy of perceptions may lead *inter alia* to some people who would otherwise have gone into business and then failed, deciding against self-employment. It is important to see the training/information inputs in the context of the *whole range* of economic and social variables that influence formation rates.

To date nearly all self-employment information has been provided on a responsive basis. An active approach to such information provision, though difficult to formulate, might attract successful founders who might not otherwise set up. We have also argued that the provision of information on self-employment needs to be viewed in a longer term context in shaping attitudes; there may, therefore, be a role for stimulating interest in this area at school level.

References

1 This view of the employment potential of the small firm sector received a considerable boost from Birch, D L., *The Job Generation Process*, MIT Program on Neighborhood and Regional Change, Cambridge, Mass , 1979. Birch estimated that, over the period 1969-1976, 52% of *net* employment creation came from independent businesses which had less than 20 employees in 1969 (Employment in new businesses formed *during* the period are included in this figure) There are, however, a number of problems with Birch's data and his findings have been widely misinterpreted see Storey, D J , *Job Generation and Small Firms Policy in Britain*, Policy Series 11, Centre for Environmental Studies, March, 1980 For recent estimates for employment creation by new firms in various regions of the UK, see Firn, J and Swales, J K , 'The Formation of New Manufacturing Establishments in the Central Clydeside and West Midlands Conurbations 1963-1972', *Regional Studies*, 1978, 12, pp 119-213, Gudgin, G , Brunskill, I and Fothergill, S , *New Manufacturing Firms in Regional Employment Growth*, paper given to Conference on New Firm Formation, Centre for Environmental Studies, October, 1979, Johnson, P S and Cathcart, D G , 'New Manufacturing Firms and Regional Development Some Evidence from the Northern Region', *Regional Studies*, 1979a, 13, pp 269-280, Storey, D J and Robinson, J F F , *Entrepreneurship and New Firm Formation The Case of Cleveland County*, paper given to Conference on New Firm Formation, Centre for Environmental Studies, London, October, 1979 For a comparison between the US and Britain, see Fothergill, S and Gudgin, G , *The Job Generation Process in Britain*, Centre for Environmental Studies, Research Series 32, London, 1979 None of these studies, however, answers the question of what would have happened to employment in the absence of these formations

2 Wilson, N and Coyne, J , 'Co-operatives and the Promotion of Co-operative Development in Great Britain', *Industrial Relations Journal*, Vol 12 No 2, 1981

3 Cooper, A C , 'Technical Entrepreneurship What do we know?', *R & D Management 3(2)*, 1973, pp. 59-64, Roberts, E B and Wainer, H A , 'Some Characteristics of Technical Entrepreneurs', *IEEE Transactions on Engineering Management*, EM-18(3), 1971, pp 100-109

4. See Gudgin, G , *The East Midlands in the Post-war Period*, Ph.D , Leicester University, 1974, Brough, R , 'Business Failures in England and Wales', *Business Ratios*, (Summer) 1970, pp 8-11, Davis, J. R and Kelly, M., *Small Firms in the Manufacturing Sector*, Committee of Inquiry on Small Firms, Research Report No 3, HMSO, London, 1972, p 60, and Beesley, M E., 'The Birth and Death of Industrial Establishments. Experience in the West Midlands Conurbation, *Journal of Industrial Economics*, 4(1), 1955, pp. 45-61

5 See, for example, the findings and the studies quoted in Johnson, P S and Darnell, A C , *New Firm Formation in Britain*, Department of Economics, Durham University, Working Paper No 5, 1976

6 Some limited follow-up studies of unemployed personnel who have participated in self-employment courses have been undertaken see Watkins, D , 'Practical Support for the Establishment of New Businesses', paper given to the Smaller Business Research Conference, Durham University, November, 1978 However, by their very nature these studies cover samples which have very specific characteristics

7 McKay, D I , 'After the Shake Out', *Oxford Economic Papers*, 24, 1972, pp 89-110, Parker, S R , *Effects of the Redundancy Payments Act*, HMSO, London, 1971

8 Ibid , p 97

9 Boswell, J , *The Rise and Decline of Small Firms*, Allen & Unwin, London, 1973, Gudgin, G , *Industrial Location Processes and Regional Employment*, Saxon House, 1978; Firn, J and Swales, J K , op. cit , Little, A D , *New Technology Based Firms in the UK and Germany*, Anglo-German Foundation for the Study of Industrial Society, London, 1977, Johnson, P S and Cathcart, D G , op cit., Johnson, P S and Cathcart, D G , 'The Founders of New Manufacturing Firms A Note on the Size of their 'Incubator' Plants', *Journal of Industrial Economics*, XXVIII, 2, 1979a, pp 219-224, Gudgin et al , op cit ,, Storey, D J and Robinson, J F F , op cit

10 Johnson and Cathcart, op cit , 1979a

Bibliography

Boswell, J , *The Rise and Decline of Small Firms*, Allen & Unwin, London, 1973

Brown, G , 'Characteristics of New Enterprises', *New England Business Review*, 1957

Bulmer, M I A , 'Mining Redundancy A Case Study of the working of the Redundancy Payments Act in the Durham Coalfield', *Industrial Relations Journal*, Vol 2 No 4, 1971, pp 3-21

Cooper, A D , 'Technical Entrepreneurship What do we know?', *R & D Management*, 3(2), 1973, pp 59-64

Daniel, W W , *Whatever Happened to the Workers at Woolwich?*, PEP Broadsheet No 537, 1972.

Daniel, W W , *A National Survey of the Unemployed*, PEP Broadsheet 546, PEP, London, 1974

Daniel, W W and Stilgoe, E , *Where are they now? A follow-up study of the unemployed*, PEP Broadsheet No 572, PEP, London, 1977

14

Unemployment and self-employment: a survey

Department of Employment, 'Characteristics of the Unemployed Sample Survey, June 1976, *Department of Employment Gazette*, 1977, June

Disney, R., *The Distribution of Unemployment and Sickness among the United Kingdom Population*, University of Reading, Department of Economics, Discussion paper No 87

Foundation for Alternatives, *Local Initiatives in Britain*, mimeo, Adderbury, 1979

Golby, C W. and Johns, G , *Attitudes and Motivation*, Committee of Inquiry on Small Firms, Research Report No 7, HMSO, London, 1971

Hart, D M , Internal MSC paper on redundancies at RDL (North Sea) Ltd., at Methil, Scotland, 1979

Herron, F , *Labour Market in Crisis*, Macmillan, London, 1975

HMSO, *Ryhope a pit closes a study in redevelopment* (for the Department of Employment and Productivity), HMSO, London, 1970.

Kahn, H R , *Repercussions of Redundancy a local survey*, Allen & Unwin, London, 1964

Martin, R and Fryer, R H , *Redundancy and Paternalist Capitalism a Study in the Sociology of Work*, Allen & Unwin, London, 1973

Pearson, R and Greenwood, J , *Redundancies and Displacement A Study of the Maidstone Labour Market*, Institute of Manpower Studies, Sussex University, 1977

Roberts, E B and Wainer, H A , 'Some Characteristics of Technical Entrepreneurs', *IEEE Transactions on Engineering Management*, 1971, EM-18 (3), pp 100-109

Sams, K I and Simpson, J V , 'A Case Study of a Shipbuilding Redundancy in Northern Ireland', *Scottish Journal of Political Economy*, 1968, pp 267-282.

Scott, M., 'Independence and the Flight from Large Scale Sociological Factors in the Founding Process', paper given to the Smaller Business Research Conference, Durham University Business School, November, 1978

Thomas, R (ed), *An Exercise in Redeployment*, Pergamon, Oxford, 1969

Wedderburn, D. E , *White Collar Redundancy A Case Study*, University of Cambridge, Department of Applied Economic, Occasional Paper No. 1, Cambridge U P , 1964

Wedderburn, D E., *Redundancy and the Railwaymen*, University of Cambridge, Department of Applied Economics, Occasional Paper No 4, Cambridge U P. 1965

[20]

The Birth of New Firms — Does Unemployment Matter? A Review of the Evidence*

D. J. Storey

ABSTRACT. The purpose of this paper is to review the most significant recent literature identifying the determinants of new-firm births and the role that unemployment plays. In doing so, the paper draws upon two distinct strands in the economics literature. The first strand of literature is from the field of industrial organization, where the role of entry has been examined within the structure-conduct-performance paradigm. The second strand comes from the literature on entrepreneurship. Whereas the first approach tends to focus on the industry as the unit of analysis and is concerned primarily with inter-industry comparisons, the second strand of literature is more oriented towards the firm as a unit of analysis and the impact exerted by the macro-economic environment. It is concluded that the most important development for future research is at the interface of these two approaches.

1. Introduction

The current interest in understanding the factors influencing the birth of new firms comes from two main sources. Firstly from those who relate this to the vast literature on factors influencing entry into markets (Geroski, 1990). Essentially this interest group are those conducting empirical testing of the Structure — Conduct — Performance paradigm (SCP). According to the SCP school, entry takes place in response to some combination of pre and expected post entry prices in the chosen market and in associated markets. It also depends upon the level of perceived barriers in both groups of markets. The SCP literature therefore emphasises

Final version accepted on January 17, 1991

Centre for Small and Medium Sized Enterprises
Warwick Business School
University of Warwick
Coventry CV4 7AL
U.K.

microeconomic elements rather than macro-economic considerations. Perhaps the only two significant exceptions to this statement are the studies by Highfield and Smiley (1987) and Yamawaki (1990).

It has also been recognised for many years, that no distinction is made in the SCP literature between types of entrants.[1] Acs and Audretsch (1989) quote Gorecki (1975) in saying "In published statistical studies of the determinants of entry, entrants have been treated as a homogeneous class". Yet in order to understand and predict what is happening in the market-place it *is* necessary to recognise that new small firms are likely to respond to different incentives, compared with established firms either switching or diversifying into a different industry. Theoretical and empirical support for this distinction is provided by Storey (1982), Acs and Audretsch (1989) and by Mills and Schumann (1985).

The second source of interest in the factors influencing the birth of new firms comes from those more concerned with questions of entrepreneurship. This literature is concerned to understand factors influencing the formation of new firms in aggregate and over time. It is not concerned with whether new firms enter industry i or industry j, but focuses instead upon the decision by an individual whether or not to become an entrepreneur. It takes as its historic antecedents the work of Knight (1921), who theorised that the individual would switch from employee to employer depending on the relative expected returns in these two forms of activity. The empirical work in this area tends to use time series data and is concerned to understand variations in aggregate new firm formation. In conducting this work there are a number of indices of new firm formation used — such as new company forma-tions, businesses newly registered for VAT, or the numbers of self employed workers. This literature is concerned with the nature of the macro-economic environment.

It is the purpose of the current paper to review the most significant recent empirical studies in this second stream of literature. In doing so it attempts to draw more closely together the SCP and the entrepreneurial literature.

2. Entrants, wholly new firms and self employment: Definitions and data

Before beginning such a review it is important to be clear about the terms used and their signific-ance. In this paper data will be presented on "entrants", "wholly new firms" and on "the self employed". These are not identical terms, al-though all three can be considered as overlapping sets. Hence it is important to be clear on the definitions used and the availability and coverage of data.

For the purposes of this paper we shall define an entrant as a new business unit to industry i. The entrant, in fact, comprises three sub groups, viz.:

1. Those firms which are operating in industry j and which continue to operate in j, but which now operate in i. These firms therefore cur-rently operate in both i and j, and are called diversifiers.
2. Those firms which move from j to i — and so no longer operate in j. They are called switchers.
3. Firms which have never operated in j or in any other industry. The latter are called Wholly New Firms — WNFs. The latter are therefore a subset of Entrants.

The relationship between WNFs and the self employed is even more complex. Its complexity arises from the fact that self employment combines conceptual and legal/statistical issues. It also varies from one country to another and also over time in the same country. For these reasons we will only refer to the current position in the UK. The Self Employed are broadly defined as "those who in their main employment work on their own account, whether or not they have employees". (For a discussion of the definitional problems with

Self Employment data in the UK see Johnson (1988).) The self employed include those who own firms which employ others, but are numerically dominated by individuals who work "on their own account" but do not employ others. The further complication which arises is that some individuals who are self employed may own or part own more than one firm whilst others, although they are self employed may, in practice, be little different from most employees.

We turn now to questions of data availability. In the UK, as in virtually all countries, there is no complete enumeration of the population of firms in the economy.[2] There is not even a complete enumeration of firms in the manufacturing sector. Firm coverage declines with decreasing size and coverage of new firms is less complete than coverage of longer established firms. Data prob-lems also arise in measuring the numbers of self employed workers. Partly these are due to irregu-lar surveys, partly due to questions of sampling unreliability, and partly to inconsistencies and ambiguities over definitions (Johnson, 1988).

Although, in principle, it should be a simple matter to identify the number of "entrants", new firms or newly self employed workers in either the economy as a whole, or in a given industry in a given period of time, this is not the case. The definitional issues outlined above provide only the briefest insight into the difficulties which exist in operationalising the concept. In practice, there-fore, identifying the appropriate measure of entry presents major problems.

3. Entrants and wholly new firms: A quantification

Our purpose in this section is threefold. Firstly we show that those firms defined as entrants are a mere fraction of the number of WNFs in an industry. Secondly we argue that not all entrants are WNFs, and finally it is shown that those firms defined as entrants are unrepresentative of WNFs.

To illustrate these points we draw upon Geroski (1990) who obtained a special tabulation from Business Statistics Office (BSO) of entrants in eighty six UK manufacturing sectors for the period 1975—1988. This is reproduced as Table I below.

The first row of the table shows the average number of *entrants* identified by BSO for each of

TABLE I
The five year life experience of UK entrants at a disaggregated level

	Cohort year			
	1975	1976	1977	1978
Average number of entrants per industry	106.16	99.41	69.16	77.77
Five year survival rate	68.7%	70.5%	67.5%	71.9%
Initial mean employment size: Survivors	30.7	21.91	36.8	21.3
Survivors employment growth rates	0.76%	−2.75%	−8.38%	−12.1%
Cohort employment growth rate	−39.18%	−49.78%	−43.9%	−49.29%

Source: Geroski (1990).

the 86 manufacturing sectors, so that for example there were 6,688 entrants in 1978.

Published data on businesses registered for VAT in 1978 in the Production sector does not seem to be available. However, we know that there were 10,400 newly registered firms in 1980 and 12,300 in 1981 (Ganguly, 1985). In part this discrepancy with the BSO data may be caused by the VAT definitions of "Production" being slightly more wide ranging than "Manufacturing", but this is likely to be partly offset by the exclusion of some sectors from the VAT data set because output from such firms is zero rated, or because the firms did not reach the minimum sales turnover size necessary for VAT registration.

Not all firms newly registered for VAT are wholly new firms: some, for example, will have changed ownership and will re- register for VAT. In other cases new subsidiary companies may choose to newly register for VAT, whereas others may choose to continue to be registered with their parent. The key point is that some cross entrants and diversifiers will register for VAT whereas others will not. Coverage by BSO of "entrants", as would be defined and analysed by those conducting empirical studies under the Structure-Conduct-Performance paradigm, is therefore substantially less than for new VAT registrations.

Both groups, however, combine, probably in different proportions, switchers, diversifiers and wholly new firms.

We have demonstrated that some BSO "entrants" may not be included in the new VAT registrations statistics, but that overall only around two thirds of new VAT registrations appear as "entrants". We now propose to show that those

which do appear as "entrants" in the BSO data are profoundly different from the typical WNF.

The second row of Table I shows that between 67% and 72% of "entrants" in any given year would be expected to survive for a five year period. This, however, is significantly higher than the equivalent figure for businesses registered for VAT as a whole (life-span figures are not published for Production businesses only) where about half of firms newly registered would expect to survive for 5 years (Ganguly, 1985).[3]

The third row of Table I refers to the average (arithmetic mean) employment size of entrants in their initial year. This varies from 21 to 36 employees. The VAT data base, however, does not provide information on employment, so it is necessary to look elsewhere for comparative data. The best comparison we can make is with the data in Table II below which shows *Median* employment levels, by age, for wholly new manufacturing firms in Northern England founded between 1965 and 1981.

Given the highly skewed nature of data on new firm size, the fact that Table I presents mean data and Table II presents median data does serve to magnify differences between the tables. Furthermore Table II presents data on wholly new manufacturing firms in Northern England, where small firms have traditionally prospered rather less well than in other parts of the UK. Nevertheless several points of clear difference do emerge from Tables I and II.

First the average size of firm is likely to be different in the two tables. Secondly Row 4 of Table I shows that average employment size falls with increases in age, even for surviving firms over

170   *D. J. Storey*

TABLE II
Median employment in wholly new firms, by age of firm

Age of firm	Number of employees in new firms founded 1965–1971	Number of employees in new firms founded 1971–1981
1	7.5	6.5
2	9.0	5.5
3	9.0	6.0
4	10.0	10.0
5	10.0	10.0
6	10.0	7.0
7	11.0	10.5
8	11.5	
9	11.0	
10	11.0	

Source: Storey (1985, p. 33).

a five year period. This is not the case for Northern Region firms summarised in Table II. Here surviving firms appear to grow in employment in their early years, and it is only after they have reached about five years of age that employment growth ceases.

These differences can be explained in two ways. The first is that some firms which are classified as "entrants" by BSO in a given year are not necessarily firms which have begun trading, or even entered the market in that year. Instead they may have been trading for several years, and have increased their employment size, before they become included in the BSO datafile. Once they are more than four years of age they are much more likely to have either static or declining employment, which is consistent with the characteristics of the BSO "entrants". Secondly, as was noted in the earlier section, "entrants" include not only wholly new firms, but also switchers and diversifiers. The latter are more likely to be part of a larger organisation and might, particularly in markets where minimum efficient scale (MES) considerations are present, be expected to be rather larger than wholly new firms in their early stages of life.

These comparisons therefore suggest the following. Firstly that those firms included in the BSO database, and which would be classified as "entrants" by those conducting empirical work in the SCP tradition, include switchers, diversifiers

and wholly new firms. Secondly these "entrants" are generally very much larger, have lower growth rates and higher life expectancy than wholly new firms.

4. The birth of wholly new firms

The above section has demonstrated that wholly new firms are a subset of "entrants", but with somewhat different characteristics. For this reason attempts to explain the factors influencing entry may not be wholly appropriate to an explanation of new firm formation. This section reviews a number of time series based recent econometric studies of new firm formation with a view to testing for key explanations of firm formation behaviour. The role which unemployment plays in the motivation to establish a business is our central concern.

In no sense can the review be regarded as being comprehensive, since it does not even begin to address the econometric estimation problems of such models. Its purpose is firstly to take the findings from these studies and, where appropriate, relate them to others on the same topic. Secondly it attempts to observe patterns in variables included and results obtained, and finally it makes suggestions for new directions for research. The current section begins with a discussion of the choice of dependent variables in these studies.

1. The dependent variables

Given the previously noted absence of a comprehensive data set on firms in the UK, there are three main indices of new firm formation used in time series studies, viz.:

a) New company incorporations.
b) Changes in the proportion of workers classified as self employed.
c) Businesses newly registered for VAT.

As we have shown above none of these three measures of new businesses are either comprehensive or unbiassed. New company incorporations, by definition, exclude those businesses which chose, for taxation or other purposes, to be either partnerships or sole traders. On the other hand they include new companies which are established by existing businesses — primarily those referred to earlier as diversifiers, and may or may not include switchers.

Thirdly whilst a company may be registered in a given year it need not begin trading in that year. Indeed it may be several years before trading begins. Conversely, some businesses may have been trading for many years as a sole trader or partnership before they become registered as a company. Existing companies can also be purchased 'off the shelf'. The year of incorporation is therefore an imperfect measure of the year in which the business began trading. This highlights the potential importance of both lags and leads in such models, since individuals or existing businesses may create new firms in anticipation of changes in trading conditions, whereas others may only respond once matters become more certain.

Despite their limitations, measures (a) and (b) above have been used in studies, the objective of which is to determine the factors which explain time series variations in business formations. Data on measure (c) has not been used for time series analysis in the UK since only 14 data points are currently available.

2. *The role of unemployment*

Our prime interest is to examine the evidence on the role which unemployment plays in the formation of wholly new firms. Specifically, we wish to examine whether new firm formation is positively or negatively related to unemployment. In even posing this question we distinguish ourselves from the mainstream of the SCP literature where this question is not generally addressed.

The mechanism by which unemployment can, in principle, spur new firm formation has long been recognised. Oxenfeldt (1943) articulated that individuals, faced with unemployment and little prospect of gaining work as an employee, would be more likely to work for themselves than an otherwise similar individual who is in employment. The framework articulated by Knight (1921) suggested the individual may be considered to move between three states: unemployment, self employment and employee, depending upon relative prices in the three markets.

The analytical problem facing researchers investigating the impact of unemployment on new

firm formation is that there is an *a priori* case that unemployment can either increase or decrease new firm formation. These are the so-called "push" and "pull" hypotheses.

The "pull" hypothesis is closely related to the SCP tradition. It argues that new firm formation takes place when an individual perceives an opportunity to enter a market to make at least a satisfactory level of profit. Ceteris paribus, this is more likely to happen when demand is high and when the individual is credit-worthy or has access to personal savings. In such a situation individuals are "pulled" or attracted into forming their own businesses and are more likely to have access to the assets necessary to start the business.

The converse "push" hypothesis suggests that depressed market conditions mean individuals experiencing or facing the prospect of unemployment are more likely to establish new firms. In the Knight framework, even though the expected income from self employment is low, it is higher than the expected income from unemployment or from searching for employment as an employee. Furthermore, as Binks and Jennings (1986) point out, unemployment in an economy is likely to coincide with the closure of businesses and hence lead to the increased availability and low cost of second hand equipment. In this sense a key barrier to new firm formation may, somewhat paradoxically, be lower in times of depressed than in times of buoyant demand.

A third hypothesis is explored by Hamilton (1989) who suggests that the relationship between unemployment and business formation may be non-linear. He argues that at low levels of unemployment, increases in unemployment will lead to increases in new firm formation. However, once a "critical" level of unemployment is reached, increases in unemployment lead to reductions in new firm formation. Hamilton puts forward two separate justifications for the existence of a critical or break point. The first is that at low levels of unemployment those who become unemployed recognise that market opportunities exist and are therefore "pulled" into forming their own firm. But, as unemployment continues to rise these business opportunities diminish and so new firm formation rates fall. Hamilton's second justification for a "break point" is that an economy may have a fixed supply of new firm founders which, once exhausted, will lead to a drop in formation rates.[4]

It is then an empirical question as to whether, or possibly in what situations, unemployment is related to new firm formation. Excluding the time series studies which we propose to examine in some detail shortly, there are two other types of evidence which have shed some light on this matter.

The first are Survey results of interviews with those individuals who have recently become new firm founders. The results here broadly support the hypothesis that unemployment is positively related to new firm formation. Binks and Jennings found that about 50% of new owner managers in the early 1980s in Nottingham were "forced" into starting their own business. The present author found that amongst businesses established in Cleveland during the 1970s, one quarter of founders claimed they were unemployed, or likely to become unemployed immediately prior to starting the business (Storey, 1982). These proportions are very much higher than the prevailing levels of unemployment in these localities at the time.

A second approach is to undertake cross sectional analysis, and here the results are much less clear cut. Support for the view that unemployment is positively related to new firm formation is provided by Storey and Jones (1987). They show that, in North East England, new firm formation rates are highest in those industries where job shedding is greatest, yet were not related to a range of profitability measures. Given that individuals tend to form a firm in the industry in which they were formerly employed, it suggests that "push" factors were stronger than "pull" factors.

Cross sectional analysis examining new firm formation across localities with different levels of unemployment has, however, yielded results which contradict the above findings. In the UK it has been shown that areas with the highest levels of unemployment have the lowest rates of new firm formation — Whittington (1984), Coombes and Raybould (1989).

Blanchflower and Oswald (1990a) also suggest that the likelihood of an individual choosing to become self employed is, when account is taken of other variables, greater in areas of prosperity than less prosperous areas. In reaching this conclusion the authors draw upon the National Child Devel-

opment Survey which follows a representative sample of more than 12,000 children in the UK born between 3rd and 9th March 1958. In separate work Blanchflower and Oswald (1990b) using the British Social Attitudes Survey find that whilst there has been a substantial growth in the numbers of self employed workers in the UK between 1983 and 1988 this can be 'explained' by *reductions* in unemployment.

Hamilton attempts to reconcile these findings by arguing that time series analysis needs to take account of changes in public policies which have encouraged the formation of new firms. Conversely in undertaking cross sectional analysis it is necessary to take account of differences in the entrepreneurial potential of areas (Reynolds, 1990; Moyes and Westhead, 1990). In short it is vital to ensure that specification errors are minimised in the equations through a full enumeration of relevant factors.

3. *The other independent variables*

There have been six main studies in the UK which have attempted to establish a time series relationship between unemployment and an index of new firm formation. The studies by Hudson (1987), Robson (1990) and by Binks and Jennings (1986) used data on company incorporations in England and Wales as the index, whilst Hamilton (1989) used data for Scotland. The studies by Johnson *et al.* (1988) and by Robson and Shah (1989) used data on self employment.

The independent variables used in these studies are shown in Table III, together with an indication of whether or not the variable was found to be significant. Where appropriate, the coefficient is signed.

As can be seen from the Table only the studies by Hudson, Robson, Johnson *et al.* and Robson and Shah make an attempt to fully specify the relationship between unemployment and firm formation, and it is upon these four studies which we shall primarily concentrate.

The Table shows that there are three types of public policy effects identified. The first is a simple "data effect" in which certain years or quarter years have imperfect information, for example, because of industrial disputes involving civil servants collecting the data.

A second set of policy effects is associated with

TABLE III
Independent variables

Concept	Variable used	Studies	Signif	Sign
1. Labour market	Unemployment, or U / V	Robson	Yes	+
		Hudson	Yes	+
		Binks & Jennings	Yes	+
		Hamilton	Yes	+
		Johnson *et al.*	Yes	+
		Robson & Shah	Yes	+
2. Public policy	S.E.T. &	Johnson *et al.*	Yes?	+?
		Robson	Yes?	+?
		Hudson	Yes	+
	E.A.S.	Johnson *et al.*	Yes?	+?
		Robson	No	N/A
	Data changes	Johnson *et al.*	Yes	+/−
		Robson	Yes	+/−
		Hudson	Yes	+/−
	Taxation	Robson	Yes	+/−
3. Profitability	Income from self employment	Robson	Yes	+
		Robson & Shah	Yes	+
	Share prices	Robson	Yes	+
4. Interest rates	Real interest rate	Hudson	No	N/A
		Robson & Shah	Yes	−
		Robson	No	N/A
5. Consumer expenditure	Real disposable income	Hudson	Yes	+
6. Personal savings	Sum of real savings	Hudson	No	N/A
	Real liquid assets from the personal sector	Robson	No	N/A
		Robson & Shah	Yes	+
7. Cyclical indicator	Ratio of GDP to GDP trend	Johnson *et al.*	Yes	+
8. Structural indicator	IER structural indicator	Johnson *et al.*	Yes	+/−

Key: N/A = not applicable; ? = weak significance.

specific legislative changes. For example, in the years 1966—1973 Selective Employment Tax (SET) was in operation. This tax was levied on all employed workers in businesses in much of the service sector. However, it was not levied on the self employed, and so may have encouraged businesses to opt for a partnership/sole proprietorship legal form, rather than incorporation. It also 'encouraged' firms to have their workers on a 'freelance' basis, rather than an employees.

Another potentially important public policy variable is the Enterprise Allowance Scheme (EAS), under which unemployed individuals since 1981 have received a payment of £40 per week for twelve months if they start a business. Johnson et al find some modest support for the impact of EAS, but are somewhat sceptical of this finding since the scheme has been in operation during a period in which there are a number of other policy initiatives designed to promote self employment and new business creation. Both Robson, and Robson and Shah include EAS in their original variable specification, but are unable to find an independent impact for it, upon either the self employment or the company incorporations data. However, Gray (1990) in his evaluation of EAS finds that perhaps up to 15% of the net increase in self employment in the UK in the 1982—88 period is accounted for by EAS.

The third dimension of the public policy effect

is on the choice of legal form. It is examined by Robson who assesses the impact of differential tax rates on corporate, as opposed to personal income. He argues that, as the ratio of the marginal rate of corporation tax to income tax rises, the less likely it is that individuals will choose to incorporate their business.

Item 3 in Table III shows there are two explicit profitability variables included by Robson and by Robson and Shah in their models, neither of which are examined by Hudson or by Johnson *et al*. The simple specification of income from self employment is, not surprisingly, shown to be positively associated with numbers of self employed workers and also with company incorporations. Less obviously, Robson also relates incorporations to real share prices on the grounds that these may reflect expected future profits in the corporate sector.

Three of the UK studies explicitly include an interest rate variable. Hudson argues that interest rates combine potentially conflicting factors for the new firm. The first is that a rise in interest rates reduces the net profitability of the firm. Higher rates, designed to reduce the supply of credit will also mean that it becomes more difficult for individuals to obtain credit. However he also argues that the work of Stiglitz and Weiss (1981) suggests increases in interest rates mean that high risk, high reward projects will be favoured. Since new firms are risky ventures, Hudson argues that they may, perhaps somewhat paradoxically, find it easier to obtain finance at times of high interest rates. Table III shows that in the estimation equations which Hudson presents, the interest rate variable is not shown to be significant.

The Robson, and Robson and Shah findings on the role of real interest rates are interesting. In their study of factors influencing self employment Robson and Shah find that real interest rates are significantly and negatively related to self employment. Robson does not, however, find any significant relationship with new company incorporations, except in the indirect sense that since lagged self employment levels are related to incorporations then real interest rates may be considered to have indirect impact.[5]

Hudson also includes a consumer expenditure variable and finds it positively related to formation rates. In many respects this is likely to closely follow the Johnson *et al*. measure shown in Table III as the cyclical indicator.

Much more surprising is that neither of the different indices of personal savings used by either Hudson or by Robson turn out to be significant in directly influencing new company incorporations. Robson and Shah in their study of self employment, however, do find real liquid assets to be positively associated with entry into self employment. Again Robson believes that the impact upon company incorporations is indirect, working through the lagged self employment term as with the interest rate variable discussed above.

This therefore contrasts with almost all of the interview research with new firm founders in the UK which has shown that personal savings are the prime source of funding for almost all types of new firms, ranging from "conventional" firms, primarily in the service sector (Storey, 1982) to new high technology firms (Monck *et al.*, 1988). Furthermore Blanchflower and Oswald (1990a) show that relatively modest levels of inheritance money significantly increases the likelihood of an individual becoming self employed. They present this as evidence of a binding liquid assets constraint. It is therefore somewhat surprising that the time series analyses have not been able to isolate a clearer influence for personal savings upon business formation.

5. Entrants and macroeconomic conditions

To our knowledge there are no UK studies which have attempted to relate macroeconomic conditions to industry entrants within the traditions of the SCP school. The only such studies which have been conducted world-wide are by Highfield and Smiley (1987) for the USA and Yamawaki (1990) for Japan.

The Highfield and Smiley study examined United States incorporations over the 1948 to 1984 period, and used both cross section and time series analyses. It concluded that "lower rates of GNP, lower inflation rates, and greater growth in the unemployment rate were followed by increases in the rate of new incorporations". At the cross sectional level they concluded that high entry rates were associated with high sales growth, high profits and higher R & D. No support for the existence of traditional entry barriers was provided.

The Yamawaki study of Japanese manufacturing over the 1979—84 period derived rather different conclusions. It found that net entry responded procyclically with entry being highest during cyclical upswings and lowest during downswings. At a sectoral level net entry was negatively related to capital intensity and positively related to sales growth and advertising intensity.

6. Discussion

In this section our objective is to compare the findings of the UK studies of self employment and wholly new firms in Section 4 with other econometric studies using time series analysis of new firm formation. These studies generally utilise United States data, where it has to be recalled that what we refer to in Table III as the Public Policy framework will be different. It is also likely that there will be some significant differences in other variables, reflecting cultural and historical differences such as attitudes to risk. Nevertheless our purpose in making the comparison is to point to areas where improvements to the UK studies might be made by taking account of these results.

We have been assisted in this task by the work of Hudson who, in addition to the UK study referred to extensively above, has also undertaken a broadly similar study examining births and deaths of United States companies (Hudson, 1989). Two other studies in the United States are also referred to here, viz.: Highfield and Smiley (1987); and Blau (1987). The latter is concerned with self employment and is therefore comparable to the Johnson *et al.* findings, whereas the Highfield and Smiley and the Hudson papers are more directly comparable to the UK studies by both Hudson, by Robson and by Robson and Shah.

In commenting upon the UK studies with reference to those conducted in the United States, there are the obvious Public Policy differences referred to earlier. In the UK case, the 1980s have seen a considerable effort by the government to promote the growth of "enterprise". During that decade the numbers of Self Employed have risen from 1.9m to 2.9m. No new upsurge in explicit government policy initiatives to promote enterprise has occurred in the US, although there is an upward trend in the proportion of workers who are self-employed, which began somewhat earlier in the mid 1970s.

Comparing the variables found to be significant

by Blau with those in the UK studies there are clear similarities, but also some interesting differences. The main finding of Blau — that industrial structure changes are of prime importance, parallels the Johnson *et al.* finding that growth has been high in those sectors with a high proportion of self employed workers.

It is, however, the differences between Blau and the UK studies which are of considerable interest. The first difference is that there is no testing by Blau of the role of unemployment, and the possible "push" role which this may have had in increasing self employment. The nearest which he comes to addressing this question explicitly is to include a variable which takes account of the presence of minimum wage agreements, under which jobs might be expected to be "rationed" by non-wage means. The inconsistent findings on this variable lead him to conclude that general labour market conditions do not have a clear impact upon self employment. This is somewhat surprising bearing in mind that the increasing numbers of self employed workers in the United States coincides with the slow down in growth in the world economies following the first increase in Oil prices.

In contrast the Highfield and Smiley (1987) findings on new incorporations suggest that what they describe as a sluggish macro economic climate of, low rates of GDP growth, low inflation rates and increases in unemployment are conducive to high rates of business formation. All these variables are shown to be significant in explaining quarterly changes in incorporations over the period 1948—84. Hudson (1989) also finds, from his study of United States company births 1951—84, that unemployment is positively correlated with formations, in an equation where profitability and personal consumption expenditures are also included and significant in the expected direction. The macro economic conditions influencing company births in the United States therefore broadly confirm his results for the UK.

Hudson also finds that the interest rate variable has no clearly identifiable effect. Since this finding is both confirmed by Highfield and Smiley for the United States and supports Hudsons other results for the UK, it suggests the impact of interest rates upon firm formation rates is much more complicated than has been sometimes suggested.

Somewhat disappointingly Hudson (1989) does

not appear to examine what we describe in Table III as the Public Policy framework in the United States. If, as the above studies have shown, unemployment is positively associated with firm formation then it seems reasonable to suppose that variations in the individuals income whilst unemployed will influence his or her choice of self employment or unemployment. The characteristics of the Social Security system are therefore likely to influence this choice and should be incorporated within these models.

The Blau study includes variables which are generally absent from the UK studies but which might shed considerable additional light upon the growth of "enterprise" in the UK. The key new result which Blau generates relates to the role of taxation. He finds that higher marginal tax rates for high income earners promotes self employment, but has the reverse effect for low income earners. Blau rationalises the former finding by arguing that increased tax rates will encourage high income earners to become self employed in order to increase their opportunity for under-reporting income and possible overstating expenses. He is unable to offer an explanation of why the reverse should be the case for low income groups.

This finding is, however, of potentially great importance for the UK, since the 1980s saw a major increase in all indices of new firm formation, and a general reduction in tax rates, particularly for the high income earners. There is also some evidence that the largest proportionate increase in, for example, self employment has occurred amongst former blue collar workers who have created businesses which do not employ other workers (Curran and Blackburn, 1988). Nevertheless the role of taxation has not yet been adequately incorporated into the time series models in the UK. Even the Robson study is only concerned to examine the impact which taxation has upon the choice of the legal form of a business, rather than upon the decision to start a business in the first place. It is therefore important that the role of taxation is better incorporated into a time series analysis of "enterprise".

A second variable included by Blau which, with the exception of Robson and Shah, is not incorporated into the UK studies is changes in Social Security benefits — most notably retirement

benefits. Blau argues that increases in these benefits may have encouraged employees to seek self employment status as a prelude to retirement rather earlier than has been the case in the past. Intuitively this would seem less relevant in the UK where the 1980s has seen, if anything, a general reduction in the level of State Benefits. Nevertheless for a considerable number of workers close to retirement or for those who are unemployed, the characteristics of the state benefit system is a factor which can influence their choice of employee, self employed or unemployed status. An associated issue is the growth of private pension and insurance schemes and the efforts to make them transferable between employers. Their development may also serve to encourage individuals approaching retirement age to become self employed some years before reaching formal retirement age.

In the UK context it is very relevant to consider the nature of State benefits received by the unemployed, and the potentially unemployed. Here it is necessary for the individual to consider the choice of three situations. The first is to be unemployed and to undertake no work other than job seeking. The second is to move from unemployment to self employment, but the third state is to illegally combine unemployment with self employment. The extent to which this happens would, according to the law enforcement literature initiated by Becker (1968), be expected to depend upon the probability of detection, the penalties imposed upon those convicted and rewards of combining income from both states. Only Robson and Shah address these issues in their study of self employment, and conclude that there is a short run negative effect upon self employment of the real value of unemployment benefits. To fully model the choice of employment status requires an examination of these factors.

7. Conclusions

This paper has attempted to review the overlap between two strands of literature, with a view to assessing the public policy implications and suggesting new directions for further research. Despite the difficulties of making precise comparisons, we also examine the extent to which methodologies may be applied in both the United States and the United Kingdom.

The first literature strand is the familiar Structure Conduct Performance analyses which examine firm entry rates, by industry, using cross section data. The second strand is studies which have examined the factors influencing the formation rates of firms over time. With the exception of the work by Highfield and Smiley they are generally not combined together.

Despite the tendency of some analysts to infer that the two groups are homogeneous, we demonstrate that the term "entrant" used in the SCP literature is not necessarily identical to the term "wholly new firm". Secondly that the latter is not, at least in the UK, synonymous with data on new firms registered for VAT, with company incorporations, with new self employed workers or, of course, with "entrants". We show that there are differences in the growth and expected life-span of each of these groupings of business activities. In short we support the views expressed by, for example, Acs and Audretsch, that there are likely to be differences between the reasons why these groups come to be established, and their performance once established. These differences should be clearly highlighted.

The second half of the paper probes the variables which econometric studies have used to explain variations in firm formation rates over time, in terms of data on new company incorporations and numbers of self employed workers. In particular the role which unemployment plays in influencing these data are examined in both the United Kingdom and the United States.

The broad consensus is that time series analyses point to unemployment being, ceteris paribus, positively associated with indices of new firm formation, whereas cross sectional, or pooled cross sectional studies appear to indicate the reverse. Attempts to reconcile these differences have not been wholly successful. They may reflect possible specification errors in the estimating equations, since none include all the independent variables which have been shown to be significant in the existing literature. In particular we suggest that more attention is given to the issue of taxation, savings and state benefits than has been the case in the past. This implies the need for a labour market approach to be integrated within the Structure

Conduct Performance paradigm in order to fully model the New Firm Formation/Entry Process. The need is to achieve methodological advancement at the interface of industrial and labour economics.

Notes

* I would like to thank Martin Robson, Steve Batstone, Steve Johnson and participants at the WZB conference for comments received on an earlier version of the paper. Remaining errors are my responsibility.
[1] The confusion was not apparent in the early writings of Bain (1956) who defined entry as the establishment of new productive output in an industry by a new firm. This effectively excluded cross entry and the subsequent empirical work which defined entry as the production of a good or service perfectly substitutable in the minds of the buyer which then included cross entry and takeover cases. I am grateful to Steve Batstone for pointing this out to me.
[2] The closest to an enumeration of firms comes in the efforts of Bannock (1990).
[3] Businesses may deregister for VAT for several reasons. About 60% are because the trader goes out of business, about 20% through sale, about 5% through changes in legal status and the remainder through reasons such as falling below the exemption limit or no longer being a taxable person. See British Business (1985).
[4] An alternative is to regard the relationship as a quadratic with push forces in operation at low levels of unemployment and being replaced by push factors as unemployment rises. See Batstone and Mansfield (1990).
[5] This point was made to me in a private communication from Martin Robson dated 25 July 1990.

References

Acs, Z. and D. Audretsch, 1989, 'Births and Firm Size', *Southern Economic Journal* **55**(2), 467–475.

Bannock, G. 1990, *Small Business Statistics: A Feasibility Study Prepared for Department of Employment*, London: Graham Bannock & Partners.

Batstone, S. and E. Mansfield, 1990, 'Births, Deaths and "Turbulence" in England and Wales', University of Warwick, mimeo.

Becker G. S., 1968, 'Crime and Punishment: An Economic Approach', *Journal of Political Economy* **76**, 169–217.

Binks, M. and A. Jennings, 1986, 'Small Firms as a Source of Economic Rejuvenation', in J. Curran, J. Stanworth, and D. Watkins (eds.), *The Survival of the Small Firm*, Vol. 1, Aldershot: Gower, pp. 19–37.

Blanchflower, D. G. and A. J. Oswald, 1990a, 'What Makes an Entrepreneur?', Dartmouth College, NBER Working Paper No. 3252.

Blanchflower, D. G. and A. J. Oswald, 1990b, 'Self Employment and Mrs. Thatcher's Enterprise Culture', in

R. Jowell and S. Witherspoon (eds.), *British Social Attitudes: The 1990 Report*, Aldershot: Gower Press.

Blau, D. M., 1987, 'A Time Series Analysis of Self Employment in the United States', *Journal of Political Economy* 95(3), 445—467.

British Business, 1985, 'UK Firms Grow by 11 Per Cent in Five Years', *British Business*, 23 August, 354—356.

Coombes, M. G. and S. Raybould, 1989, 'Developing a Local Enterprise Activity Potential (LEAP) Index', *Built Environment* 14(2), 107—117.

Curran J. and R. Burrows, 1988, 'Enterprise in Britain: A National Profile of Small Business Owners and the Self Employed', Small Business Research Trust, London.

Ganguly, P., 1985, *UK Small Business Statistics and International Comparisons*, London: Harper and Row.

Geroski, P. A., 1990, *Entry and Market Dynamics*, Oxford: Basil Blackwell.

Gorecki, P., 1975, 'The Determinants of Entry by New and Diversifying Enterprises in the UK Manufacturing Sector 1958—63', *Applied Economics* 7, 139—147.

Gray, C., 1990, 'Some Economic — Psychological Considerations on the Effects of the Enterprise Allowance Scheme', *Piccola Impresa* 1, 111—124.

Hamilton, R. T., 1989, 'Unemployment and Business Formation Rates: Reconciling Time Series and Cross Section Evidence', *Environment and Planning* 21, 249—255.

Highfield, R. and R. Smiley, 1987, 'New Business Starts and Economic Activity: An Empirical Investigation', *International Journal of Industrial Organisation* 5, 51—66.

Hudson, J., 1987, 'Company Births in Britain and the Institutional Environment', *International Small Business Journal* 6(1), 57—69.

Hudson, J., 1989, 'The Birth and Death of Firms', *Quarterly Review of Economics and Business* 29(2), 68—86.

Johnson, S., 1988, 'An Assessment of Industrially Disaggregated Data on Self Employment', Institute of Employment Research Project Report, University of Warwick.

Johnson, S., R. Lindley and C. Bourlakis, 1988, 'Modelling Aggregate Self Employment: A Preliminary Analysis', Institute of Employment Research Project Report, University of Warwick.

Knight, F. H., 1921, *Risk, Uncertainty and Profit*, New York: Houghton Mifflin.

Mills, D. E. and L. Schumann, 1985, 'Industrial Structure with Fluctuating Demand', *American Economic Review* 75(4), 758—767.

Monck, C. S. P., 1988, *Science Parks and the Growth of High Technology Firms*, London: Croom Helm.

Moyes A. and P. Westhead, 1990, 'Environments for New Firm Formation in Great Britain', *Regional Studies* 24(2), 123—136.

Oxenfeldt, A., 1943, *New Firms and Free Enterprise*, Washington, D.C.: American Council on Public Affairs.

Rees, H. and A. Shah, 1986, 'An Empirical Analysis of Self Employment in the UK', *Journal of Applied Econometrics* 1, 95—108.

Reynolds, P. D., 1990, 'US Regional Characteristics, New Firms and Economic Growth', Paper prepared for presentation to Cross National Workshop on the role of Small and Medium Enterprises in Regional Economic Growth, University of Warwick, 28 March.

Robson, M. T., 1990, 'Self Employment and New Firm Formation', Department of Economics, University of Newcastle upon Tyne, mimeo.

Robson, M. T. and A. Shah, 1989, 'A Capital Theoretic Approach to Self Employment in the UK', Department of Economics, University of Newcastle upon Tyne, mimeo.

Stiglitz, J. E. and A. Weiss, 1981, 'Credit Rationing in Markets with Imperfect Information', *American Economic Review* 71(3), 393—410.

Storey, D. J., 1982, *Entrepreneurship and the New Firm*, London: Croom Helm.

Storey, D. J., 1985, 'Manufacturing Employment Change in Northern England 1965—78', in D. J. Storey (ed.), *Small Firms in Regional Economic Development: Britain, Ireland and the United States*, London: Cambridge University Press.

Storey, D. J. and A. M. Jones, 1987, 'New Firm Formation — A Labour Market Approach to Industrial Entry', *Scottish Journal of Political Economy* 34, 37—51.

Whittington, R. C., 1984, 'Regional Bias in New Firm Formation in the UK', *Regional Studies* 18, 253—256.

Yamawaki, H., 1990, 'The Effects of Business Conditions on Net Entry: Evidence from Japan', in P. A. Geroski and J. Schwalbach (eds.), *Entry and Market Contestability: An International Comparison*, Oxford: Basil Blackwell.

[21]

Scottish Journal of Political Economy, Vol. 34, No. 1, February 1987
© 1987 Scottish Economic Society

NEW FIRM FORMATION—A LABOUR MARKET APPROACH TO INDUSTRIAL ENTRY*

D. J. STOREY AND A. M. JONES

University of Newcastle upon Tyne and University of York

I

INTRODUCTION

Although entrants play a central role in the structure/performance paradigm it is apparent that such firms are only indirectly included in the major empirical work on the topic. The central theme of the bulk of these studies is that variations in profitability, at an industry level, can be explained in terms of concentration, and a variety of barriers to entry (Sawyer, 1981). This barrier-orientated approach commonly features the concept of a queue of potential entrants, what Bain (1956) termed the "general condition of entry". However, due to a tendency to concentrate on the diversification of existing enterprises, the socio-economic determinants of new firm founders are invariably neglected.

There has been little attempt to directly test for a relationship between the number of entrants and perceived future profits. This is primarily a consequence of the difficulty of obtaining suitable data on entrants, whether they are wholly new firms or existing enterprises shifting or diversifying their operations.

This paper uses data for new manufacturing businesses created in Northern England between 1965 and 1978 and the East Midlands between 1968 and 1975 with a view to testing the validity of the conventional theory of entry. It is recognised that self-employment is an alternative to unemployment (or to paid employment) and an attempt is made to integrate industrial entry and labour search into a single model. This theoretical and empirical development requires that a distinction be made between entrants by transfer or diversification and wholly new firms.

II

THEORY

Much of the conventional entry theory has been built upon the concept of the limit price (Waterson 1984, Clarke 1985). This refers to industries in

* We are grateful for the many helpful suggestions made by Mike Waterson and an anonymous referee. We also thank Steve Fothergill and Graham Gudgin for allowing us access to their data on establishments in the East Midlands, but the opinions expressed are those of the authors alone.

Date of receipt of final manuscript: 21 April 1986.

38   D. J. STOREY AND A. M. JONES

which there are increasing returns to scale up to a level of output which is a significant proportion of the total market. The impact on aggregate supply of an entrant, of at least minimum efficient scale, will be to depress market price and consequently the level of profit. Post-entry profits rather than existing profit levels should therefore be the decision-making criterion for potential entrants. This fact allows existing firms to achieve actual profits at a level (above "normal") such that the level of expected post-entry profits is sufficient to discourage potential entrants.[1] The central thrust of the model is to render outcomes determinate in terms of price.[2]

As noted by Gorecki (1979), a major weakness of the limit pricing hypothesis lies in its inability to distinguish between entrants which are wholly new and existing enterprises which have diversified or transferred from other sectors. The importance of this distinction is that the two categories of firms are likely to respond to different stimuli.[3]

Total entrants into industry i (E_i) are therefore defined to be both wholly new businesses (NF_i) and existing businesses moving into i (TD_i), where wholly new businesses are independent enterprises setting up their first plant;

$$E_i = NF_i + TD_i \qquad (1)$$

An existing business, currently operating in industry j, is expected to view a move to i (whether a transfer or a diversification) primarily on the basis of expected post-entry profits in i (π_i) and expected profits in j (π_j), subject to entry barriers (X_i) and any miscellaneous factors (Z_i). An example of the latter could be the reduction in uncertainty gained by vertical integration.

$$TD_i = f(\pi_i, \pi_j, X_i^T, Z_i) \qquad (2)$$

where,

$$\frac{\partial TD_i}{\partial \pi_i} > 0 \quad \frac{\partial TD_i}{\partial \pi_j} < 0 \quad \frac{\partial TD_i}{\partial X_i^T} < 0$$

In equation (2) X is a vector representing barriers to entry, whether they are economies of scale, product differentiation or absolute cost advantages, and X_i^T refers only to those barriers which apply to this particular group of entrants. Those readers interested in a recent examination of cross entry are referred to Deutsch (1984).

---

[1] It is worth noting that the most appropriate measure of profitability in a profit maximisation model of limit pricing is the price-cost margin, equivalent to the profit-sales ratio.

[2] This simple determinancy was criticised by Caves and Porter (1977). They argued that structural barriers to entry, seen by Bain (1956) as exogenous, are in fact subject to the endogenous behaviour of incumbent firms.

[3] In developing their theory of barriers to mobility, Caves and Porter (1977) hypothesise the existence of subgroup structures within industries accompanied by group-specific entry barriers. An implication of this model is that potential entrants may also be distinguishable on the basis of the group they intend to enter. Caves and Porter define these groups primarily in terms of marketing strategies and they are therefore not strictly comparable with the distinction we propose to make between established and wholly new firms. However their approach does illustrate that much may be gained by abandoning assumptions of homogeneity.

NEW FIRM FORMATION   39

Wholly new firms are formed by individuals all of whom will have the option of obtaining employment in the formal labour market or of being unemployed.[4] Two contrasting views of this process may be offered. The first argues that individuals currently employed in industry i are faced by the alternatives of continued employment in i, possible employment in j, unemployment, or of establishing a new venture. Similarly, in the event of redundancies in industry i, the individuals involved may remain unemployed, gain employment in industry j or become self-employed.[5] Of those who exercise the latter option it is assumed that the majority will remain in industry i, primarily because their "contacts", so important in starting a new firm, will be in that industry. Individuals are more likely to be aware of market gaps, suppliers and the technology of production in the industry in which they were formerly employed.[6]

The majority of new firm founders in the ith industry begin their operations with "second-hand" equipment. The price of this equipment depends, in the short-term, primarily upon the extent to which falls in final demand result in reductions in capacity in that industry. A reduction in final demand thus increases spare capacity in the industry leading to plant and machinery being sold off by liquidators and, to a lesser extent, by existing enterprises. In recessionary conditions reductions in capacity by larger enterprises will result in a major increase in the availability of second-hand equipment, dwarfing the increased demand by entrepreneurs starting in business. These characteristics of the second-hand capital market are clearly shown by Binks and Jennings (1986). This reduces the price of second-hand equipment which is the major entry barrier that the entrepreneur faces. The effect, therefore of depressed market conditions in industry i may be both to make self-employment relatively more attractive *and* to reduce an important barrier to new firm formation in that industry.

A second view argues that whilst unemployment reduces the opportunity cost of business formation it also depletes the assets of the entrepreneur so making entry more difficult. Indeed the conventional view would be that reduced labour demand reflects poor expected profitability, so discouraging entry. It is therefore an essentially empirical question as to which of these "explanations" is more powerful.

An entry function for wholly new businesses can now be proposed. The

[4] "The labourer asks what he thinks the entrepreneur will be able to pay, and in any case will not accept less than he can get from some other entrepreneur, or by turning entrepreneur himself. In the same way the entrepreneur offers to any labourer what he thinks he must in order to secure his services and in any case will not offer more than he thinks the labour will be worth to him, keeping in mind what he can get by turning labourer himself." (Knight, 1921.)

[5] In a survey, carried out in the area which is now Cleveland county, 26 per cent of new firm founders claimed to have been unemployed prior to to starting their business (Storey, 1982). Other authors who have seen unemployment as a stimulus of new firm formation include Dahmen (1970), Wedervang (1965) and Oxenfeldt (1943).

[6] The Cleveland survey, which covered all industries except retailing, found that 60 per cent of new firm founders had remained in the same industrial order (Storey, 1982). The comparable figure produced by Johnson and Cathcart (1979) was 50 per cent.

independent variables again include expected post-entry profitabillity in industry i (π_i^1) and a specific set of barriers to entry (X_i^N). But they are now joined by an index of labour shedding (L_i), a specific indicator of employment opportunities in i. This variable plays a central role in subsequent analysis,[7] but the two hypotheses outlined above lead to conflicting signs. Two specific characteristics of L_i are possible. The first is net employment change in the ith industry i.e. gross job gains minus gross job losses, whilst the second is simply gross employment loss defined as job loss through closures and contractions. Take, now, two industries i and j, identical in size, in terms of employment and in terms of employment change over time. It is argued that if gross job losses in industry i are significantly higher than in j, then industry i will, *ceteris paribus*, have the higher rates of new firm formation since more individuals will have lost their jobs in that industry and so will be "forced" to consider the entrepreneurial option.[8]

$$NF_i = f(\pi_i^1, X_i^N, L_i) \qquad \frac{\partial NF_i}{\partial \pi_i^1} > 0 \quad \frac{\partial NF_i}{\partial X_i^N} < 0 \tag{3}$$

The net effect of an exogenous reduction in demand for products of industry i on the number of entrants in subsequent periods therefore depends on the magnitude of two conflicting influences. A fall in profitability can be expected to lead to closures and a transfer of existing enterprises out of i but at the same time redundancies may stimulate the formation of wholly new businesses, as former employees find this more attractive than either unemployment or the possibility of obtaining work in industry j. The latter will depend upon the extent to which reduced job prospects reduce their assets and the extent to which these new and small firms can be expected to fill "niches" within the existing markets.

III

THE EXISTING WORK

The main empirical study using number of entrants as the dependent variable was carried out by Mansfield on a multiplicative model of the form:

$$E_{it} = \alpha_0 \pi_{it}^{\alpha_1} X_{it}^{-\alpha_2} Z_{it} \tag{4}$$

where

$$\frac{\partial E_{it}}{\partial \pi_{it}} > 0; \quad \frac{\partial E_{it}}{\partial X_{it}} < 0$$

---

[7] In the empirical section of this paper it is assumed that NF_i is a multiplicative function, log-linear in terms, X and L.

[8] Another factor, explored by Kihlstrom and Laffont (1979) is the degree of risk aversion amongst entrepreneurs, whilst differences in wage rates in i and j could also affect the model specification.

This model was tested with data for four industries over a variety of periods, yielding 10 data points. Mansfield showed that a significant and positive relationship existed between profitability and entry rates. The latter are defined as the number of firms that entered the ith industry during the tth period (and survived until the end of the period) as a proportion of the number in the industry at the beginning of the period. This is only one of the indices of entry since it neglects those entrants which failed to survive the given period. The difference between total entrants and surviving entrants may be considerable since in most of the industries covered by Mansfield the period used is a decade. An examination of data by Dun and Bradstreet for the U.S.A. suggests that approximately half of a given year's new manufacturing firms fail to survive for a decade. Mansfield would therefore seem to be underestimating the *total* number of entrants by this amount. Since however he is attempting to explain cross-industry differences this under-enumeration may not be so important, but the absence of a reliable control sample makes even this hypothesis untestable.

The formulation of entry rates used by Mansfield differs in several respects from that used in subsequent attempts to use entries as the dependent variable in regression equations. For example the work by Orr (1974) does not use the gross surviving entry rate favoured by Mansfield, but instead uses the net entry rate. This is defined to be:

$$E_i = 1/4 \sum_{t=1964}^{1967} N_{it} - N_{i(t-1)} \tag{5}$$

where:

$E = E_i \ldots E_{71}$ industries;

N_{it} = number of reporting corporations in the ith industry in the tth year (Canada);

$N_{it} - N_{i(t-1)}$ is defined as ≥ 0.

Orr therefore selects only those industries where there are more firms in year t than in year $t-1$, consequently his data includes wholly new firms, firms transferring from other industries, and exits. Orr admits that the data may also, in some cases, include firms where the ownership has changed. Finally it has to be recognised that the data source from which Orr draws, only includes firms which have sales exceeding $500,000, at 1967 prices. This means that only firms with at least 50 workers would be included in his sample. If the size distribution of new firms in Canada during the period was the same as in the Northern region of England then only 6 per cent of all new firms would be included in Orr's data.

The study by Gorecki (1975) also uses a net entry rate, examining the increased (decreased) number of enterprises in 51 industries in the U.K. between 1958 and 1963. Gorecki attempts to distinguish between the net change in specialist and in diversifying firms. His sample includes exits, yet there are strong reasons for believing that there is an asymmetry between

42   D. J. STOREY AND A. M. JONES

factors affecting rates of entry and exit. For example, whilst gross entries are postulated to be affected by profitability and entry barriers, empirical studies of gross exits have included profitability and the number of enterprises at risk because of their size (Mansfield 1962, Marcus 1963). Furthermore the study by Henderson (1980) has shown there to be no association between an industry's profitability and the propensity of its establishments to close. More recently Van Herck (1984) has attempted to explain the interrelationships between entry and exit but his empirical work does not make clear the definitions of entry used.

It is clear that a number of formulations of entry rates are theoretically justifiable for testing the relationship between entry and profitability. However, to test for a relationship between the choices open to the individual all new businesses have to be charted, including those which have diversified from other industries. Ideally such data should include all sizes of new firms, not simply those which reach a given (usually high) minimum size, and finally it should also include all new firms rather than only those which survive until the end of the period. Such data does not exist for the U.K. economy as a whole but is available to the authors for Northern England. Valuable data is also available for the East Midlands of England, but on the slightly different basis discussed in the next Section.

Finally it seems likely that the entrepreneur's view of expected post-entry profitability and of the actual height of entry barriers may vary from one location to another. For example, some areas may specialise in the "small" specialist end of a given market whilst other areas may specialise in large scale mass production. Recently two studies have examined the locational differences in *actual* profit rates in broadly comparable firms. Bayldon, Woods and Zafiris (1984) question whether differences exist between inner city and new town locations, whilst Fothergill, Gudgin, Kitson and Monk (1984) show that such differences do exist between conurbations and other areas.

IV

SOURCES OF DATA

Data on wholly new manufacturing firms in Northern England were derived from records constructed for the County Councils of Cleveland, Durham and Tyne and Wear.[9] Coverage is virtually complete, subject to the limitations of government statistics and the data base contains nearly 5,000 manufacturing establishments which existed at any stage between 1965 and 1978. For each establishment, data on employment are available for most years. In addition further data on, for example, name, address, location, industry (MLH), ownership, date of establishment (if after 1965) and date of closure (where applicable), are available.

[9] The construction is described in detail in Storey, Keasey, Watson and Wynarczyk (1987).

The East Midlands data were kindly supplied by Graham Gudgin and Steve Fothergill. The source for this data is the Factory Inspectorate and full details are available in Fothergill and Gudgin (1982). The numbers of wholly new firms existing in 1975 which had been created since 1968 were provided. It must be emphasised that these include only new firms which survived until 1975, and in this important aspect the data differs from that available on the Northern Region.

From this population of manufacturing establishments in the two regions it is possible to identify a group which consists of new independent businesses and to identify the years in which they began operations. In principle it would also be possible to identify existing establishments which switched their industry (cross-entry). However these cases are not included in subsequent analysis because in several cases a change in MLH is a reflection of the industrial classification being initially incorrect, rather than a genuine change of activity.

Finally it would therefore be desirable to have data on profitability and entry barriers specifically for the North and for the East Midlands but unfortunately such data does not exist. It has therefore proved necessary to use national data for both of these measures.

V

THE VARIABLES

(i) *Entry rates*

Four New Firm formation rates are used in this analysis.

(a) NF_i^N; takes the total number of wholly new firms in the ith industry (locally-owned sole proprietorships, partnerships, or private limited companies) which traded for the first time between 1965 and 1978 in the counties of Durham, Cleveland or Tyne and Wear. Such firms must be legally independent enterprises, i.e. not subsidiaries of existing enterprises. To identify a formation rate, the number of such wholly new firms is divided by the number of single plant independent firms in the ith industry in Durham, Cleveland and Tyne and Wear in 1965. Hence NF_i^N represents the gross proportionate increase in the number of single plant independent firms in the three counties over the 1965–1978 period.

(b) NF_i^{NUK}; if the number of single plant independent firms in the three counties existing in industry i in 1965 were low for some temporary reason then NF_i^N would be an an inappropriate index. Instead it may be better to divide the number of wholly new firms in the ith industry by the number of enterprises in the ith industry in the U.K. since this is less likely to be affected by "exceptional" values. Data for numbers of enterprises do not exist for 1965 but the U.K. data from "Census of Production" is used for 1968 to derive NF_i^{NUK}.

44 D. J. STOREY AND A. M. JONES

(c) NF_i^{EM}; since the North of England has been shown by Fothergill and Gudgin to have a rate of new firm formation significantly below the national average, data on formation rates in the East Midlands are used to determine whether the cross section formation rates in the North are correlated with those of a region with a formation rate more typical of the U.K. as a whole. NF_i^{EM} takes the data supplied by Steve Fothergill and Graham Gudgin on wholly new firms in the East Midlands between 1968 and 1975 for each MLH. This is divided by the number of single plant independent firms in that industry in 1968. It must be emphasised, however, that the East Midlands data includes firms starting after 1968 but which *survived* until 1975. It does not include, unlike the Northern data, new firms starting after 1968 but which failed to survive until 1975.

(d) NF_i^{EMUK}; This index takes the number of wholly new firms formed in the East Midlands in the ith industry between 1968 and 1975 and divides by the number of U.K. enterprises in the ith industry in 1968 according to the Census of Production.

(ii) *Profitability index*

The concept of expected post-entry profitability is, in practice, unquantifiable and a suitable proxy is required. Empirical studies have generally used ex-post profits (See Waterson, 1984). There may also be a lag between the observed opportunity for profit and an individual forming a firm to take advantage of that opportunity. The extent of this lag is likely to vary from a matter of days to years depending partly upon the individual and partly upon the industry to be entered. It seems likely that industries where initial capital requirements are high will experience a longer period between the perception of profit and actual entry than an industry where capital requirements are small. Neither we, nor other empirical studies, are able to take this into account except through the entry barriers index. Furthermore it could be argued that is is *not* the general level of profitability in industry i which affects the willingness of the individual to form his own firm since profitability in the industry as a whole may be affected by the presence of large firms. Of more relevance is the expected return which the individual could expect to obtain by forming a new firm and this will, at least initially, be more closely related to the profitability of smaller firms in the industry. The only useable data on corporate profitability is national and taken from Census of Production, so that in the model *Regional* entry rates will be compared with *National* ex-post profitability data.

$$\pi_i = \frac{(\text{Net output} - \text{Wages and Salaries})}{\text{Net Output}}$$

From this general index a number of possible indices can be formed.

π^{68} = Gross Profits in 1968 in ith industry in U.K.
π^{70} = Gross Profits in 1970 in ith industry in U.K.
π^{73} = Gross Profits in 1973 in ith industry in U.K.
π^{76} = Gross Profits in 1976 in ith industry in U.K.

$^{99}\pi_i^{70}$ = Gross Profits in 1970 in U.K. ith industry in firms employing less than 100 workers.

$^{99}\pi_i^{73}$ = Gross Profits in 1973 in U.K. ith industry in firms employing less than 100 workers.

$^{99}\pi_i^{76}$ = Gross Profits in 1976 in U.K. ith industry in firms employing less than 100 workers.

In determining entry rates the change in the level of profit may be more important than the absolute level of profit. For example, an industry may have high entry barriers and high profits and a zero entry rate. In the event of an exogeneous increase in profitability entry could be stimulated. It could also be argued that changes in the profitability of small firms, rather than the profitability of all firms in the industry, are most likely to affect expectations.

Two types of index of change in profitability have therefore been constructed:

$\Delta\Pi_i^{t,t+1}$ = Change in U.K. profitability in ith industry between year t and year $t + 1$.

$^{99}\Delta\Pi_i^{t,t+1}$ = Change in U.K. profitability in ith industry between year t and year $t + 1$ in firms employing less than 100 workers.

(iii) *Labour market variables*

It was argued above that a factor influencing the likelihood of an individual becoming the founder of a new firm is the availability or otherwise of work locally in his/her industry.

Ceteris paribus it would be expected that those industries which were major net shedders of labour would also have the highest rates of new firm formation. However, these *net* employment changes conceal the growth in employment in some firms and the loss of employment in others. Since it is those workers in firms either *contracting* their labour forces or *closing* that are particularly "at risk", the index should express gross job losses as a proportion of total employment in industry i.

The labour market indices used are:

$L_i^{t,t+1}$ = % change in U.K. Employment in ith industry between year t and year $t + 1$, so that if $E_t > E_{t+1}$ then $L^{t,t+1} < 0$

L_i^N = Job Losses through Contractions + Closures in Northern England 1965–78 in ith industry
Total Employment in ith industry in 1965 in Northern England.

To estimate L^N, job losses through closure are defined as employment in 1965 in establishments which had closed by 1978. Job losses through contractions are defined as job losses in establishments which although trading in both 1965 and 1978 had *less* jobs in 1978 than in 1965. Gross Job Losses are defined as the summation of closures and contractions.

(iv) *Barriers to entry* (X_i^L)

Scherer (1980) reviews the variety of entry barriers used in empirical studies, but the index adopted in this paper is that formulated by Lyons

46   D. J. STOREY AND A. M. JONES

(1980). It estimates, for a variety of industries, the minimum efficient plant-size as a percentage of industry size (MEP/S) on the basis of a firm's decision to set up a second plant. Using the 1968 Standard Industrial Classification, Lyons provides estimates for 144 industries at MLH and sub-MLH level but he specifically excludes industries which have "miscellaneous" in their title. This is unfortunate in the present study since these industries frequently contain a large number of wholly new firms. Nevertheless, the advantages of having entry barrier data constructed at MLH level transcends these disadvantages.

VI

THE RESULTS

Difficulties arose in testing due to incomplete data for all industries and variables. During the period there was a major change in the Standard Industrial Classification in 1968 and a reallocation of some establishments in 1970, both of which raise problems of comparability over the time periods. Secondly, in many instances the number of wholly new firms in an MLH was less than five and so were excluded because of the risk of introducing "extreme" values. Finally, as noted above, the Lyons data does not cover all industries. Given these constraints only 31 MLH's were able to provide observations on all variables.

As noted earlier the existing empirical work has been unclear on the functional form of a relationship between entry and profitability. It is also unclear from a theoretical standpoint whether a linear or more complex functional form is appropriate. For this reason Table 1 presents a simple correlation matrix between the four endogenous variables (NF_i^N, NF_i^{NUK}, NF_i^{EM}, NF_i^{EMUK}), and the 15 exogenous variables. Table 2 identifies the correlation between endogenous variables. Table 3 presents similar data to Table 1 but with all variables subjected to a logarithmic transformation. Similarly Table 4 shows the correlation between the logarithmic transformed endogenous variables. Only after these tables are regression results presented in Tables 5 and 6.

The most striking feature of Tables 1 and 3 is the absence of any association between the absolute level of profit in a given year and entry rates, however defined, in either Northern England or the East Midlands. This statement applies to the absolute level of profit in any given year in all enterprises within that MLH and to profitability in the smaller enterprises, i.e. those with less than 100 employees.

The second group of variables shows the correlation between the two entry rates for each of the two Regions and the change in profitability for a number of time periods. A variety of different time periods was in fact tested but only three are shown here. Again there is no evidence of any association.

The third group of variables refer to labour shedding, the first three of

TABLE 1

Simple correlation matrix

	NF_i^N	NF_i^{NUK}	NF_i^{EM}	NF_i^{EMUK}
Π_i^{68}	0·0982	0·1681	0·1329	0·1405
Π_i^{70}	0·1124	0·0821	0·0753	−0·0484
Π_i^{73}	0·1049	0·1147	0·1473	0·0441
Π_i^{76}	0·0693	0·2131	0·0420	−0·0080
$^{99}\Pi_i^{70}$	−0·0091	−0·0212	−0·1003	0·0530
$^{99}\Pi_i^{73}$	0·0418	−0·0057	0·0063	0·1424
$^{99}\Pi_i^{76}$	0·1388	0·1694	0·1507	0·0071
$\Delta\Pi_i^{6876}$	0·1016	0·0391	0·0746	0·1879
$\Delta\Pi_i^{6873}$	0·0609	0·0654	−0·0145	0·1031
$^{99}\Delta\Pi_i^{7076}$	−0·1616	−0·2471	−0·2668	0·0246
L_i^{6873}	0·1101	−0·2188	0·1395	−0·0243
L_i^{6870}	0·0694	−0·2690	0·1490	−0·0717
L_i^{6876}	0·0064	−0·3429*	0·2585	0·0715
L_i^N	0·4752**	−0·1518	0·2594	−0·0803
X_i^L	−0·1158	−0·2927	−0·1542	0·2152

** Significant at 1% level.
 * Significant at 5% level.

which are based on national data taken from the Census of Production whilst the fourth identifies the gross job losses in Northern England. For the first time in Table 1 the correlation coefficient for the Northern entry rates are significant at the 5 per cent level. Thus the index of gross job losses in Northern England L_i^N is positively associated with new firm formation rates in the Region NF_i^N. On the other hand L_i^{6876} is negatively associated with NF_i^{NUK} which is the opposite to that predicted by the labour shedding theory. To determine whether these relationships are robust when subject to logarithmic transformations it can be seen from Table 3 that the significantly positive relationship between L_i^N and NF_i^N continues whereas that between NF_i^{NUK} and L_i^{6876} disappears. This suggests that labour shedding is a factor "explaining" the sectoral variations in new firm formation rates in Northern England. It is not possible to construct a similar index for the East Midlands 1968–75, but for completeness the Table shows the insignificant association between East Midlands formation rates and L^N.

TABLE 2

Correlation matrix

	NF_i^N	NF_i^{NUK}	NF_i^{EM}	NF_i^{EMUK}
NF_i^N	1·0000			
NF_i^{NUK}	0·4833	1·0000		
NF_i^{EM}	0·1671	0·1763	1·0000	
NF_i^{EMUK}	0·0846	−0·1684	−0·0555	1·0000

48   D. J. STOREY AND A. M. JONES

TABLE 3

Correlation matrix: logarithmic transformations

	NF_i^N	NF_i^{NUK}	NF_i^{EM}	NF_i^{EMUK}
Π_i^{68}	0·1580	0·1694	0·0645	0·2316
Π_i^{70}	−0·0145	0·1916	−0·0209	0·1880
Π_i^{73}	−0·0314	0·2250	0·0434	0·2186
Π_i^{76}	0·0813	0·2518	0·0814	0·1620
$^{99}\Pi_i^{70}$	−0·0819	0·0201	−0·1054	0·1880
$^{99}\Pi_i^{73}$	0·0932	0·0564	0·0424	0·2582
$^{99}\Pi_i^{76}$	0·1230	0·1660	0·0392	0·0457
$\Delta\Pi_i^{6876}$	0·1630	0·1595	0·1463	−0·0421
$\Delta\Pi_i^{6873}$	−0·1461	−0·1774	0·1041	−0·0232
$^{99}\Delta\Pi_i^{7076}$	−0·2234	−0·0600	−0·2009	0·1271
L_i^{6876}	−0·0546	0·2791	0·0460	−0·0292
L_i^{6870}	−0·0276	0·0245	0·1855	0·3148*
L_i^{6873}	−0·0513	0·0158	−0·3308*	−0·2246
L_i^N	0·4171**	−0·1950	0·0610	−0·1439
X_i^L	−0·2062	−0·3704*	−0·1149	0·1997

** Significant at 1% level.
 * Significant at 5% level.

TABLE 4

Correlation matrix: logarithmic transformations

	NF_i^N	NF_i^{NUK}	NF_i^{EM}	NF_i^{EMUK}
NF_i^N	1·0000			
NF_i^{NUK}	0·2632	1·0000		
NF_i^{EM}	0·4410	0·3044	1·0000	
NF_i^{EMUK}	−0·0169	−0·0945	0·2252	1·0000

Finally, the barriers to entry index X_i^L is shown to be significantly negatively correlated with NF_i^{NUK}, after the logarithmic transformation. This accords with the expectations from the theoretical model.

Tables 2 and 4 show the correlation between the four entry rates used in this analysis. They demonstrate the generally weak relationship between these variables, and this must be a matter of concern since it is not clear which index is the most appropriate.

Tables 5 and 6 show the "best" OLS equations, in terms of adjusted $\bar{R}^2$, using both a linear and logarithmic form. Only about 20 per cent of the variation in industry formation rates is explained by the included variables, but the values of $\bar{R}^2$ are significantly higher for NF_i^N where it is possible to identify a local index of job shedding than for other indices of formation. Of all variables included, the relationship between L_i^N and NF_i^N is the most striking. Of secondary interest is that in Table 5 there appears to be some

NEW FIRM FORMATION   49

TABLE 5

Best fit equations: linear form[1]

	NF_i^N	NF_i^{NUK}	NF_i^{EM}	NF_i^{EMUK}
C	2·853 (2·969)	0·0362 (5·434)	0·9167 (5·256)	−0·053 (1·26)
π_i^{68}				0·1123 (1·91)
$^{99}\Delta\pi^{7076}$	−4·575 (1·135)	−0·023 (1·191)	−1·1053 (1·5064)	
L_i^{6876}		−0·0295 (1·844)	0·8671 (1·458)	
L_i^N	469·52 (2·974)			
X_i^L		−0·003 (1·176)		0·0161 (1·67)
$\bar{R}^2$	0·2599	0·2202	0·1368	0·1331

Notes: 1. '*t*' values in parenthesis.

TABLE 6

"Best" fit equations: log form[1]

	NF_i^N	NF_i^{NUK}	NF_i^{EM}	NF_i^{EMUK}
C	2·025 (2·142)	−3·653 (33·788)	−0·6916 (5·452)	−3·062 (6·553)
$^{99}\pi_i^{73}$				1·1103 (1·741)
$^{99}\Delta\pi_i^{7076}$	−0·3667 (1·4628)			
L_i^{6873}			−0·1143 (1·887)	
L_i^{6870}				0·1192 (1·802)
L_i^{6876}		0·0851 (1·358)		
L_i^N	0·2583 (2·582)			
X_i^L		−0·1331 (1·5665)		
$\bar{R}^2$	0·2326	0·1522	0·1094	0·2352

Notes: 1. '*t*' values in parenthesis.

50   D. J. STOREY AND A. M. JONES

support for the view that *increases* in industrial profitability in smaller
business between 1970 and 1976 are associated with higher formation rates.
However none of the coefficients in the equations is statistically significant,
although each has a negative sign.

VII

Conclusions

This paper argues that a major local factor influencing the rate of new firm
formation is the rate at which jobs are shed in that locality. The evidence
presented shows that, at least for the Northern Region, there appears to be
no association between changes in, or absolute national levels of, profitability
in the *i*th industry and new firm formation rates in that industry. On the
other hand formation rates in the *i*th industry in the Northern Region are
positively correlated with job shedding in the region. It is not possible to
identify an identical index of job shedding in the East Midlands where new
firm formation rate data are also available, but the absence of any association
between formation rates and national profitability data is again clear.

Even with stronger statistical associations, it could be argued that such an
analysis is still compatible with conventional theory since the employment
status of those starting the businesses is not given. However work undertaken
by one of the present authors (Storey 1982) and by Binks and Jennings (1986)
shows that between 25 per cent and 50 per cent of those starting new
businesses claim to have been unemployed immediately prior to starting in
business. Furthermore since these businesses were defined as being wholly
new, i.e. not having more than 50 per cent of their share capital owned by
any other enterprise, then their founders are certainly not existing asset
holders buying up undervalued companies.

The evidence presented in this paper is not conclusive but it does suggest
that local labour market conditions are of greater importance in influencing
local rates of new firm formation than national indices of profitability.

References

BAIN, J. S. (1956). *Barriers to New Competition.* Cambridge, U.S.A.: Harvard University
   Press.
BAYLDON, R., WOODS, A. and ZAFIRIS N. (1984). Inner City versus New Towns: A
   Comparison of Manufacturing Performance. *Oxford Bulletin of Economics and
   Statistics,* Vol. 46, No. 1, pp. 21–30.
BINKS, M. and JENNINGS, A. (1986). *Small Firms as a source of Industrial Regeneration,* in
   J. CURRAN, J. STANWORTH and D. WATKINS (ed) *"The Survival of the Small Firm",*
   Aldershot, Gower.
CAVES, R. E. and PORTER, M. E. (1977). From Entry Barriers to Mobility Barriers:
   Conjectural Decisions and Contrived Deterrence to New Competition. *Quarterly
   Journal of Economics,* Vol. 91, pp. 241–261.
CLARKE, R. (1985). *Industrial Economics.* Oxford: Basil Blackwell.
DAHMEN, E. (1970). *Entrepreneurial Activity and the Development of Swedish Industry
   1919–1939.* Homewood, Illinois: Richard D. Irwin.

DEUTSCH, L. L. (1984). Entry and the extent of multiplant operations. *Journal of Industrial Economics*, Vol. 32, No. 4, June, pp. 477–487.

FOTHERGILL, S. and GUDGIN, G. (1982). *Unequal Growth*. London: Heinemann Educational Books.

FOTHERGILL, S., GUDGIN, G., KITSON, M. and MONK S. (1984). Differences in the Profitability of the U.K. Manufacturing Sector between conurbations and other Areas. *Scottish Journal of Political Economy*, Vol. 31, No. 1, February, pp. 72–91.

GORECKI, P. K. (1975). The Determinants of Entry by New and Diversifying Enterprises in the U.K. Manufacturing Sector 1958–1963: Some Tentative Results. *Applied Economics*, Vol. 7, pp. 139–147.

HENDERSON, R. A. (1980). An Analysis of Closures among Scottish Manufacturing Plants between 1966 and 1975. *Scottish Journal of Political Economy*, Vol. 27, pp. 152–174.

HYMER, S. and PASHIGAN, P. (1962). Firm Size and Rate of Growth. *Journal of Political Economy*, Vol. 70, pp. 556–569.

JOHNSON, P. S. and CATHCART, D. G. (1979). New Manufacturing Firms and Regional Development: Some Evidence from the Northern Region. *Regional Studies*, Vol. 13, pp. 269–280.

KIHLSTROM, R. E. and LAFFONT, J. (1979). A General Equilibrium Entrepreneurial Theory of Firm Formation Based on Risk Aversion. *Journal of Political Economy*, Vol. 87, pp. 719–748.

KNIGHT, F. H. (1921). *Risk, Uncertainty and profit.* New York: Houghton Mifflin.

LYONS, B. (1980). A New Measure of Minimum Efficient Plant Size in U.K. Manufacturing Industry. *Economica*, Vol. 47, pp. 19–34.

MANSFIELD, E. (1962). Entry, Gibrat's Law, Innovation and the Growth of Firms. *American Economic Review*, Vol. 52, pp. 1023–1051.

MARCUS, M. (1967). Firms' Exit Rates and their Determinants. *Journal of Industrial Economics*, Vol. 16, pp. 10–22.

ORR, D. (1974). The Determinants of Entry: a Study of the Canadian Manufacturing Industries. *The Review of Economics and Statistics*, Vol. 56, pp. 58–65.

OXENFELDT, A. R. (1943). *New Firms and Free Enterprise*. Washington, American Council on Public Affairs.

SAWYER, M. C. (1981). *The Economics of Industries and Firms*. London: Croom Helm.

SCHERER, F. M. (1980). *Industrial Market Structure and Economic Performance*. Chicago: Rand McNally.

STOREY, D. J. (1982). *Entrepreneurship and the New Firm*. London: Croom Helm.

STOREY, D. J., KEASEY, K., WATSON, R. and WYNARCZYK, P. (1987). The Performance of Small Firms. London: Croom Helm.

VAN DERCK, G. (1984). Entry, Exit and Profitability. *Managerial and Decision Economics*, Vol. 5, No. 1, pp. 25–31.

WATERSON, M. (1984). *Economic Theory of the Industry*. London: Cambridge University Press.

WEDERVANG, F. (1965). *Development of a Population of Industrial Firms*. Oslo: Scandinavian University Books.

[22]

Small Business Formation by
Unemployed and Employed Workers

David S. Evans
Linda S. Leighton*

ABSTRACT. This paper uses data from the Current Population Surveys for 1968—1987 and from the National Longitudinal Survey of Young Men to examine the relationship among unemployment and small business formation and dissolution for white men and women. We find that self-employed workers are more likely to have experienced unemployment than are wage workers because their higher entry rate into self-employment offsets their higher exit rate out of self-employment. Unemployed men and women who enter self-employment experience a larger drop in their earnings than the unemployed who return to wage work.

I. Introduction

The formation of small businesses by unemployed workers has attracted a great deal of interest in recent years. Several Western European countries have adopted programs to stimulate small-firm formation by unemployed workers.[1] These programs, which provide financial assistance to unemployed workers who start firms, were a response to chronically high rates of unemployment on the one hand and low rates of business formation on the other hand compared with the United States. In this country, several experimental programs have tried to encourage business formation by disadvantaged workers — e.g., low-income, unskilled workers, many of them on welfare — under the auspices of the The Comprehensive Employment Training Act (CETA) and the Job Training and Partnership Act (JPTA).[2] The U.S. Department of Labor is implementing experimental programs in several states to provide financial assistance and management advice to unemployed workers who start small firms.[3]

Little is known about the propensity of unemployed workers to start small businesses in the absence of governmental assistance or about the exit rate of firms started by unemployed workers relative to that of firms started by wage workers. These issues are important because they provide insights into the ability of small-business assistance programs for the unemployed to stimulate the formation of viable small businesses.

The formation of small-firms started by unemployed and employed workers are examined using data drawn from the Current Population Surveys for 1968—1987. By matching respondents who were in the CPS surveys in contiguous years, we have obtained data on over 400,000 individuals between the ages of 18 and 65. We also use data from the National Longitudinal Survey of Young Men, which tracks roughly 5,000 men over a 15 year period beginning in 1966, to examine the effect of being unemployed on business and wage earnings in 1981. These datasets are described in the second section. The third section presents summary statistics on small-business startups and exit rates by unemployed and employed workers using the CPS matched data. The fourth section estimates a model of selection into self-employment for employed and unemployed workers. In the fifth section we examine the impact of unemployment experience on self-employment participation and earnings. The last section summarizes the results and presents suggestions for further research on this topic.

Final version accepted on June 15, 1990

David S. Evans
NERA
123 Main Street
White Plains, NY 10601
U.S.A.

and

Linda S. Leighton
Department of Economics
Fordham University
Bronx, NY 10458
U.S.A.

Small Business Economics **2**: 319—330, 1990.
© 1990 *Kluwer Academic Publishers. Printed in the Netherlands.*

II. Description of the data

The March Supplements to the Current Population Surveys (CPSs), conducted by the U.S. Bureau of the Census, are based on a stratified random sample of approximately 70,000 U.S. households. Survey participants are asked a variety of questions concerning demographic characteristics, earnings, employment, and other characteristics of the household members as of the survey week as well as information about their employment and earnings in the preceding years. In theory half of all respondents are in contiguous surveys for most survey years. We have matched these respondents over the period 1968—1987 for the pairs of years where matches are possible. For each individual, we have information pertaining to the survey week for two surveys and information about the longest held job in the preceding year. See Appendix A for details.

Figure 1 summarizes the profile of an individual on the matched CPS dataset. The individual is interviewed in March of year 1 and asked what she is doing as of the survey week. This gives us information on whether she is a wage worker or self-employed and, if she is unemployed, the number of weeks she has been unemployed. She is also asked about her earnings and the longest-held job in the preceding year (Year 0). She is interviewed in March of year 2 about her activities as of the survey week in Year 2 and about her earnings and the longest-held job in the preceding year (Year 1).

The matched cross-sections are then pooled over the 1968—1987 period. We use this pooled (15 years) cross-section (2.33 years) data to calculate entry and exit rates between jobs held as of the survey week and between the longest-held jobs in the year.

We conducted separate analyses for white men and white women, because there are important labor-market differences between these groups. White men have a much higher rate of self-employment than white women and most other

INFORMATION AVAILABLE FOR MATCHED CPS OBSERVATION

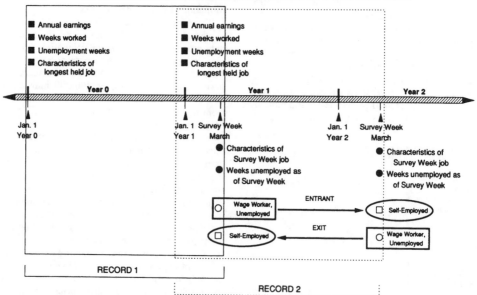

Fig. 1. Information available for matched CPS observation.

demographic groups — about twice that of white women and three times that of minorities — and comprise about 72% of all self-employed individuals in our matched samples.[4] Minorities, especially blacks, have very low rates of self-employment. Because there are relatively few minority members in our sample and because blacks (the largest minority group) are much less likely to become self-employed than are members of other races, there are very few self-employed minority members in our sample. Consequently, we do not report results for minorities. There were a total of 150,085 white men and 96,770 white women, who were in our sample during matched surveys and who were labor force participants.

We concentrate on self-employed individuals who are unincorporated — either sole proprietors or members of partnerships — because data on self-employed individuals who are incorporated were incomplete. For the job held as of the survey week, the Census Bureau includes incorporated self-employed workers among wage workers. Consequently, it is not possible to observe entry into or exit out of incorporated self-employment between survey weeks. For the job held during the previous year, the Census Bureau did not identify incorporated and unincorporated self-employed workers separately before 1976.

We have adopted the following definitions. *Entry* is defined as a switch from wage work or unemployment to unincorporated self-employment between the survey week of Year 1 and the survey week of Year 2. Exit is defined as a switch from unincorporated self-employment to wage work or unemployment between the survey week of Year 1 and the survey week of Year 2. We consider an alternative definition of entry which allows us to determine the exit rate of recent entrants into self-employment. *Entry** is defined as a switch from wage work on the longest-held job in the preceding year to self-employment as of the survey week. For most individuals the longest-held job is that job held for six months or more in the preceding year. Individuals whose longest-held job in the preceding year (Year 0) was a wage job but who were self-employed as of the March survey week (Year 1) would generally have switched into self-employment between July 1 of year 0 and the March survey week of Year 1.[5] These individuals have been self-employed for 9

months or less. We consider the exit rate of these recent entrants into self-employment below.

We describe differences in the length of time in unemployment and the reason for being unemployed on business startups.[6] Respondents in survey Week 1 (see Figure 1) who are unemployed as of the survey week are asked the number of weeks they have been unemployed and the reason they are unemployed.[7] Using this information, we estimate entry rates into self-employment in survey Week 2.

The National Longitudinal Survey is based on a national probability sample of men who were between the ages of 14 and 24 in 1966 and who were surveyed yearly between 1966 and 1971 and in 1973, 1975, 1976, 1978, 1980, and 1981. There were 3,918 white men in the initial survey of whom 2,731 were still in the survey in 1981. Using information on employment status and tenure, we calculated total experience in wage work and self-employment and total unemployment experience for each year of the sample. These data are described in detail in Evans and Leighton (1987).

III. Self-employment entry and exit by employed and unemployed wage workers

Entry and exit

Table I reports entry rates for employed and unemployed workers. An important finding is that the entry rate into self-employment is about twice as high for persons who are unemployed as for persons who are not unemployed: 4.5% vs. 2.4% for white men and 2.9% vs. 1.4% for white women.[8] The probability of switching into self-employment increases as unemployment duration becomes very long (for men, 40 or more weeks; for women, 15 or more weeks).

Table 1 also reports exit rates for employed and unemployed workers. The exit rates are for persons who entered self-employment between the longest-held job in the preceding year and the survey week.[9] We have broken down the exit rates according to the number of weeks of unemployment in the previous year. While these definitions and breakdowns are not strictly comparable to those used for the entry rate, they can give us a rough idea of whether people who have entered

322   *David S. Evans and Linda S. Leighton*

TABLE I

Entry into and exit out of rate unincorporated self-employment by weeks unemployed, 1968—1987

Employment status	Entry rate[a]	Exit rate[b]
	White males	
Employed	2.4%	37.0
Unemployed	4.5	51.5
Weeks unemployed		
1—4	4.3	46.8
5—10	3.6	42.6
11—14	5.2	53.3
15—26	4.5	56.5
27—39	4.3	54.2
40 or more	6.7	81.8
	White females	
Employed	1.4%	41.2
Unemployed	2.9	42.3
Weeks unemployed		
1—4	2.3	61.5
5—10	2.3	40.0
11—14	2.5	28.6
15—26	3.7	50.0
27—39	4.8	50.0
40 or more	3.6	33.3

[a] The entry rate is the percent of labor-force participants who were wage workers on their main current or last job as of the first survey week and who were unincorporated self-employed on their main current or last job as of the second survey week. Data were pooled for 1968—1987. The hypothesis that employed and unemployed workers have the same entry rate into self-employment can be rejected at the 0.0001 percent level using a chi-square test. Weeks of unemployment are measured as of the survey week.
[b] The exit rate is the percent of individuals who were wage workers on the longest-held job in the calendar year preceding the first survey week and unincorporated self-employed workers as of the first survey week who were wage workers as of the second survey week. Weeks of unemployment is based on total weeks of unemployment during the calendar year preceding the first survey week.

self-employment after a long spell of unemployment are more or less likely to remain self-employed. Two findings are notable. First, the exit rate is higher for white men who were unemployed in the preceding year but not for white women. Second, the figures indicate a tendency for the exit rate for white men to increase with the duration of unemployment but not for white women.

Table II reports the entry rate into self-employment for unemployed workers by reason for their unemployment. White men and white women who quit their jobs or who lost their jobs are more likely to start business than individuals who were on temporary or indefinite layoff. There is no evidence that people who have lost their jobs are more likely to start a small business than people who have become unemployed by voluntarily quitting their jobs.[10]

TABLE II

Entry into unincorporated self-employment by unemployed workers by reason for unemployment, 1968—1987[a]

Reason for unemployment	Entry rate	
	White men	White women
Lost job	5.1	2.7
Quit job	5.3	2.8
Left school	3.3	3.8
Wanted temporary work	3.1	3.0
Other	6.1	3.5
Temporary or indefinite layoff	3.5	1.8

[a] The entry rate is defined as the percent of unemployed labor-force participants who were wage workers on their last job as of the first survey week and who were unincorporated self-employed on their main current or last job as of the second survey week. Data were pooled for 1968—1987. Exit rate is not available by survey week reason.

Relative earnings changes

We have seen that white male unemployed workers are more likely to start small businesses but also more likely to return to wage work during their first year of self-employment compared with employed workers. It is interesting to compare the earnings received by self-employed workers who entered from unemployment with the earnings received by self-employed workers who entered from wage employment. Because individuals enter into self-employment from wage work or unemployment at various times during the year and because only annual earnings data are available, it is not possible to obtain an exact comparison of wages in self-employment and wage work. We approximate the average hourly earnings received in Year 0 and Year 1 by taking total earnings (wage plus self-employment) received during the calendar year and dividing by the number of hours worked during the calendar year (number of weeks worked times hours usually worked as reported by the individual). See Appendix A for a discussion of the problems and limitations of this measure.

Let us consider Table III which reports relative wage changes for entrants and nonentrants into self-employment and for entrants who entered from wage work vs. unemployment. Several findings emerge. First, individuals who have been unemployed experience a smaller increase (larger decrease) in earnings between years than individuals who have not been unemployed. This is what one would expect if poorer workers are more likely to become unemployed.[11] Second, unemployed individuals who enter self-employment experience a larger decrease in earnings than individuals who do not enter self-employment. Unemployed white men who enter self-employment suffer an earnings decline of 34.4% while unemployed white men who reenter wage work obtain an earnings increase of 3%. While part of the earnings decrease could be due to the greater

TABLE III

Average log change in real weekly earnings for workers who enter self-employment versus workers who get a wage job by unemployment status

	White males	
	Entrants	Non-entrants
Employed	−17.1	9.5
Unemployed	−34.4	3.0
Weeks unemployed		
1−4	−16.8	12.2
5−10	−50.8	−0.2
11−14	−28.1	−1.5
15−26	−50.7	1.6
27−39	−14.4	−10.6
40 or more	−38.7	−0.3

	White females[a]	
	Entrants	Non-entrants
Employed	−28.7	9.9
Unemployed	−30.2	8.0

[a] Too few observations for analysis of unemployment by weeks unemployed for white females.

opportunities self-employed workers have to underreport income, unemployed workers who enter self-employment suffer a much greater decrease in earnings than employed workers who enter self-employment (34.4% vs. 17.1%). Unemployed workers who enter self-employment do poorly compared to unemployed workers who return to wage work. Third, we examined the relationship between wage changes and weeks unemployed as of the survey week for white men. There is no evidence of a systematic relationship between changes in wages and weeks of unemployment.[12]

IV. Comparison of self-employment entry for employed and unemployed wage workers

Multivariate statistical methods are used in this section to determine whether some of the differences identified above are due to differences in the characteristics of people who become unemployed. Estimates of the probability of entering self-employment and of self-employment wages are reported separately for employed and unemployed workers.

We hypothesize that the probability of entering self-employment depends upon demographic characteristics, education, experience, the wage rate received on the current job, and the availability of liquidity for starting a business. We argue that individuals will switch from wage work to self-employment if the expected value of self-employment exceeds the expected value of wage work. The difference between these expected values depends upon the difference between expected earnings in the two occupations and upon relative tastes. Expected wage earnings depend upon current wage earnings, education and experience. Expected self-employment earnings depend upon education and experience. We conjecture that the probability of switching into self-employment will decline with current wage earnings but may increase or decrease with education and experience depending upon whether these characteristics are more important in self-employment or wage work.

Finally an individual will be more likely to switch into self-employment the greater his net worth if there are liquidity constraints as in Evans and Jovanovic (1989). Liquidity is measured by the sum of interest and dividend payments in the previous year. For unemployed workers, we expect that the probability of entry into self-employment is related positively to the number of weeks they have been unemployed. Variables are defined in Table IV.

To estimate the effect of these variables on the probability of entry, we obtained regression estimates of the "linear probability model" for which the dependent variable is 0 (for non-entrants) or 1 (entrants).[13] The model was estimated with data for 1976—1987.[14] Results are reported in Table V. While the magnitude and the significance of some of the estimated coefficients differ between unemployed and employed workers and between white men and white women, the results are generally similar. The probability of entry increases with experience, education, and liquidity and decreases with the wage rate. The probability of entry for unemployed workers does not increase significantly with the number of weeks of unemployment.

V. The long-term effects of unemployment on self-employment participation and earnings

We turn to the NLS dataset to see how unemployment experience over an extended time period affects self-employment participation and earnings for white men who were still in the NLS panel in 1981. Since the approach here and the results are described in more detail in Evans and Leighton (1987, 1989), we concentrate on the relevance of the results to the relationship between unemployment and self-employment. We calculated the amount of time individuals were unemployed and the amount of time individuals were in wage employment or self-employment from information on employment experience from 1966—1981.

Table VI reports estimates of the probability of participating in self-employment in 1981 obtained from a statistical procedure known as probit analysis. As an indicator of individuals who have had a relatively large amount of unemployment, we used weeks of unemployment experience divided by wage experience plus unemployment experience.[15] The estimated coefficient on this variable is positive and statistically significant. This result is consistent with our CPS finding that unemployed workers are about 2 times as likely to

TABLE IV
Variable definitions

Variable	Definition
Current population survey	
Urban	Dummy for resident of SMSA
Married	Dummy for married individual
High-School dropout	Dummy for individual with less than 12 years of schooling
College dropout	Dummy for individual with more than 12 and less than 16 years of schooling
College graduate	Dummy for individual with 16 years of schooling
Post-graduate	Dummy for individual with more than 16 years of schooling
Experience	Age-education-6
Previous wage	Average hourly earnings in previous year
Liquidity/1000	Dividend plus interest receipts
Weeks unemployed	Number of weeks unemployed
National longitudinal survey	
Military	Dummy for individual who served in the military
Urban	Dummy for individual who lives within an SMSA
Professional	Dummy for individual in professional occupations
Farmer	Dummy for individual in farm occupation
Married	Dummy for individual who is married
Divorced	Dummy for individual who is divorced
Handicapped	Dummy for individual who has poor health
Log earnings	Natural log of earnings in the previous year
Education	Years of education
Business experience	Years in current business
Previous business	Years in previous business
Wage experience	Years in wage experience
Military experience	Weeks of military experience
Tenure	Years in current job
Changes	Number of jobs held by indivdiual since 1966 divided by wage experience
Unemployment	Weeks of unemployment divided by wage plus unemployment experience times 100
Unemployment wks	Weeks of unemployment since 1966
Wage earnings	Wage earnings of wage workers
Self earnings	Self-employment earnings of self-employed workers who report wage but no self-employment earnings

enter self-employment and about 1.5 times as likely to leave self-employment during the first year as employed workers.

The unemployed are so much more likely to enter self-employment (2 times as likely as employed workers) that, even though they are more likely to leave self-employment (1.5 times as likely as employed workers), they are more likely than the employed to remain self-employed over time.[16]

Table VII reports earnings estimates for self-employed workers and wage workers. The important finding for our purposes is that unemployment experience — measured as the total length of

TABLE V

Linear-probability model estimates of the determinants of self-employment entry White men

Variable	Unemployed Coefficient (standard error)	Employed Coefficient (standard error)
Urban	0.0049 (0.0070)	−0.0037* (0.0011)
Married	0.0298* (0.0010)	0.0050* (0.0018)
Divorced	0.0029* (0.0141)	0.0098* (0.0028)
High-School dropout	0.0016 (0.0084)	−0.0007 (0.0017)
College dropout	0.0258* (0.0096)	0.0042* (0.0015)
College graduate	0.0269 (0.0166)	0.0112* (0.0019)
Post-graduate	0.0940* (0.0211)	0.0187* (0.0019)
Experience	0.0031* (0.0011)	0.0008* (0.0002)
Experience^2/100	−0.0071* (0.0023)	−0.0013* (0.0004)
Previous wage	−0.0006 (0.0006)	−0.0003* (0.0001)
Previous wage^2	0.0231 (0.0463)	0.0011* (0.0006)
Liquidity/1000	0.0016 (0.0027)	0.0012 (0.0002)
Weeks unemployed	0.0003 (0.0003)	—
Constant	−0.0033 (0.0113)	0.0154* (0.0020)
R^2	0.0185	0.0031
F-statistic	3.8593	12.7336
Observations	4087	81455

Table V (Continued)

Variable	Unemployed Coefficient (standard error)	Employed Coefficient (standard error)
Urban	0.0026 (0.0080)	−0.0047* (0.0010)
Married	−0.0004 (0.0114)	0.0061* (0.0016)
Number of kids	−0.0033 (0.0038)	0.0010 (0.0090)
Number of kids under 6	0.0134 (0.0080)	0.0060* (0.0012)
Divorced	0.0111 (0.0139)	0.0038* (0.0020)
High-School dropout	−0.0045 (0.0100)	−0.0009 (0.0012)
College dropout	0.0106 (0.0099)	0.0041* (0.0013)
College graduate	0.0259 (0.0150)	0.0070* (0.0018)
Post-graduate	0.0431* (0.0196)	0.0038* (0.0019)
Experience	0.0033* (0.0011)	0.0004* (0.0002)
Experience^2/100	−0.0075* (0.0026)	−0.0006 (0.0004)
Previous wage	−0.0022 (0.0013)	−0.0002* (0.0001)
Previous wage^2	0.7062* (0.3166)	0.0031 (0.0019)
Liquidity/1000	0.0013 (0.0024)	0.0006* (0.0002)
Weeks unemployed	0.0004 (0.0003)	—
Constant	0.0088 (0.0130)	0.0048* (0.0018)
R^2	0.0220	0.0023
F-statistic	2.0607	7.5238
Observations	2016	59505

* Significant at 0.05 level or less.

time spent in unemployment — carries a substantially larger penalty in self-employment than in wage work. A self-employed worker loses 0.77% of earnings per week of past unemployment while a wage worker loses 0.42% of earnings per week of past unemployment.[17]

VI. Conclusion

This report has investigated small business forma-

326   *David S. Evans and Linda S. Leighton*

TABLE VI
Estimated probability of being self-employed in 1981 (white men probit estimates)

Variable	Coefficient	Std. error	t	Prob > |t|	Mean
Self-employed					0.161165
Urban	−0.1845696	0.0788463	−2.341	0.019	0.7067961
Married	0.0705539	0.0923126	0.764	0.445	0.776699
Divorced	0.1504005	0.101406	1.483	0.138	0.1446602
Handicapped	−0.2205851	0.1354426	−1.629	0.104	0.0859223
Experience	0.0631149	0.011388	5.542	0.000	14.45653
Education	0.0468791	0.0159466	2.940	0.003	13.83447
Unemployment	0.0008846	0.0001591	5.561	0.000	138.5192
Changes	0.0129181	0.0027347	4.724	0.000	16.87336
Farmer	1.852521	0.1674885	11.061	0.000	0.038835
Professional	1.318865	0.1805655	7.304	0.000	0.0286408
Military	0.2254239	0.1098127	2.053	0.040	0.3504854
Mil. exp.	−0.0039777	0.0032259	−1.233	0.218	9.865049
Constant	−3.077114	0.3627388	−8.483	0.000	1

Number of obs = 2060.   chi2(12)   = 293.63
Log likelihood = −762.87545.   Prob > chi2 = 0.0000

tion by unemployed workers. Key findings include:

— Unemployed workers are about twice as likely to start businesses as employed workers. The entry rate into self-employment is 2.4% for employed white men vs. 4.5% for unemployed white men; and 1.4% for employed white women vs. 2.9% for unemployed white women.
— Unemployed white men who start small businesses are more likely to fail than employed white men who start small businesses. Of white men who started a small business after being unemployed, 51.5% returned to wage employment after a year. Of white men who were not unemployed before starting a business, only 37.0% returned to wage employment after a year. There is little difference for white women — 42.3% for the unemployed vs. 41.2% for the employed. Our sample of white women, however, is much smaller and the results less reliable.
— The higher entry rate into self-employment out-weighs the higher exit rate out of self-employment for unemployed workers. Conse-

quently, over time self-employed workers are more likely to have experienced previous spells of unemployment than are wage workers.
— Men and women who enter self-employment from unemployment experience a larger drop in total earnings during their first year than either individuals who enter self-employment from wage work or individuals who return to a wage job after a spell of unemployment. White men who entered self-employment from unemployment experience a decrease in their annual earnings of 34.4%. By way of comparison, white men who were employed prior to entering self-employment had an earnings drop of 17.1%; white men who got a wage job after unemployment had an earnings increase of 3.0%. The differences for white women show a similar although less dramatic pattern.
— For both unemployed and employed workers, the probability of entry into self-employment increases with experience, education and liquidity and decreases with the wage rate.
— Time spent in unemployment depresses self-employment earnings more than wage earnings. A self-employed worker loses 0.8% of

TABLE VII
Estimated log earnings equations for self-employed and wage workers, 1981 (regression estimates)

White male self-employed workers

Variable	Coefficient	Std. error	t	Prob > $|t|$	Mean
Log earnings					9.722387
Urban	0.2984078	0.0959255	3.111	0.002	0.5886525
Married	0.1426724	0.1182799	1.206	0.229	0.8262411
Handicapped	−0.7237983	0.1653379	−4.378	0.000	0.0744681
Wage exp.	0.0212041	0.0106104	1.998	0.047	8.838993
Bus. exp.	0.1127724	0.0267228	4.220	0.000	6.831969
Bus. exp.^{2}	−0.0048672	0.0012519	−3.881	0.000	78.364
Prev. Self	0.2638763	0.1084132	2.434	0.016	0.2234043
Education	0.102862	0.0187483	5.486	0.000	13.85816
Unemploy wks	−0.0076448	0.0023534	−3.248	0.001	12.71631
Changes	−0.0019309	0.0039824	−0.485	0.628	18.22286
Farmer	0.0088565	0.1262476	0.070	0.944	0.1950355
Professional	0.1607639	0.1705543	0.943	0.347	0.0957447
Military	−0.1787064	0.122895	−1.454	0.147	0.3439716
Mil. exp.	0.0065334	0.0037604	1.737	0.083	7.723404
Constant	7.547442	0.3774288	19.997	0.000	1

Number of obs = 282.
R-square = 0.3591.
Adj R-square = 0.3255.

$F(14,267) = 10.69$
Prob > F = 0.0000
Root MSE = 0.71254

White male wage workers

Variable	Coefficient	Std. error	t	Prob > $|t|$	Mean
Log earnings					9.888144
Urban	0.2116573	0.0287379	7.365	0.000	0.7239521
Married	0.2301503	0.0304746	7.552	0.000	0.7694611
Handicapped	−0.180494	0.0451322	−3.999	0.000	0.0874251
Wage exp.	0.0984876	0.0198633	4.958	0.000	13.97031
Wage exp.^{2}	−0.0024167	0.0006396	−3.778	0.000	210.6699
Self exp.	0.0447571	0.011243	3.981	0.000	0.3203938
Education	0.0706433	0.0054855	12.878	0.000	13.82814
Unemploy wks	−0.0042027	0.0005479	−7.670	0.000	16.44012
Changes	−0.0035781	0.0009934	−3.602	0.000	16.32626
Farmer	−0.4048178	0.1277192	−3.170	0.002	0.0101796
Professional	0.15914	0.1064927	1.494	0.135	0.0149701
Military	0.0213733	0.0400467	0.534	0.594	0.3556886
Mil. exp.	0.0018262	0.0010989	1.662	0.097	10.36886
Constant	7.818336	0.1790618	43.663	0.000	1

Number of obs = 1670.
R-square = 0.2813.
Adj R-square = 0.2756.

$F(13,1656) = 49.85$
Prob > F = 0.000
Root MSE = 0.51578

earnings per week of past unemployment while a wage worker loses 0.4% of earnings per week of past unemployment.

Self-employment provides an outlet for unemployed workers. While unemployed workers do not do very well at self-employment — they fail more often, earn less in the first year than entrants from wage work — the fact that many remain self-employed rather than returning to wage work suggests that they would do even more poorly at wage work. Otherwise they would not have remained self-employed.

Recommendations for further research

These results should be viewed primarily as descriptive. We must exercise considerable care in inferring a causal relationship between unemployment and small-business formation and success. People who become unemployed and choose to start a business may differ in a variety of unmeasured ways from other people. Further research will be required to address this issue.

Moreover, the fact that many self-employed workers do find temporary and sometimes permanent employment in their own businesses does not necessarily imply that the government should or should not subsidize small business startups by unemployed workers. Such programs would be desirable from the standpoint of economic efficiency only if market breakdowns currently hinder the formation of efficient businesses by unemployed workers. There are at least three possible market breakdowns. First, capital markets may provide too little capital to small firms. Recent work by Evans and Jovanovic (1989) and Fazzari, Hubbard, and Petersen (1987) finds that smaller firms are more likely to face liquidity constraints than larger firms. If these liquidity constraints are the result of a market breakdown it is possible that government assistance programs to small businesses could rectify these breakdowns. An ongoing project for the Small Business Administration is examining this issue. Second, government regulation and requirements may hinder small-business formation as a result of imposing costs that bear more heavily on smaller firms.[18] While tiering regulations so that smaller firms face lighter requirements is the preferred method for dealing with this problem, it is possible that direct subsidies to small businesses may be more cost-effective when there are large administrative costs associated with tiering. Third, it is possible that direct subsidies for small business startups reduce chronic unemployment and the welfare and other social costs associated with such unemployment. The social costs and benefits of small-business assistance programs should be considered carefully before they are adopted or expanded.[19]

Appendix A

Current population surveys, 1968—1987

The March Current Population Surveys (CPS) include a special March supplement. Responses to this supplement and to the regular survey questionnaire comprise the Annual Demographic File (ADF). From the March surveys we have constructed a dataset which contains current demographic and employment information and earnings and employment information for the previous calendar year. Our dataset includes individuals between the ages of 18 and 65 as of the March survey, who were not farm owners or workers, and who were not in institutions such as dormitories or asylums.[20] Family workers are also excluded. There were 1,781,888 responses from individuals who met this definition between 1968 and 1987, the years for which the CPS data are available on computer tape at the time of this project.

Many individuals are in two successive March surveys because of the Census Bureau's practice of "rotating" the individuals who are in the survey. Generally, households participate in the survey for two four-month periods separated by an eight-month period when they are not in the survey. In theory, 50% of the households are in contiguous March surveys. In practice, roughly 30% of the households are in contiguous surveys because some households move or dissolve or becuse household members refuse to participate in the survey. There is no overlap for the years 1985—1986, 1976—1977, 1972—1973, and 1971—1972, as a result of changes in rotation groups. The resulting data set contains roughly 2.33 years of employment information for about 400,000 individuals.

Average hourly earnings

For individuals who entered self-employment between the survey week in Year 1 and the survey week in Year 2, the average hourly earnings received in Year 0 will primarily reflect wage earnings and the average hourly earnings received in Year 1 will reflect wage earnings for the part of the year where they were still wage workers and self-employment earnings for the part of the year they were self-employed. Consider an individual who was a wage worker continuously between January 1 of Year 0 and June 30 of Year 1 and self-employed continuously between July 1 of Year 1 and the March survey week of year 2. Her hourly earnings for Year 0 will reflect her wage job and her hourly earnings for Year 1 will reflect an average of her wage job for the first half of Year 1 and her self-employment job the second half of Year 1. Some entrants into self-employment between the March survey week of Year 1 and the March survey week of Year 2, however, will have switched into self-employment between January and the March survey week of Year 2. For these individuals average hourly earnings for Year 1 will not reflect any self-employment earnings. Nevertheless, the average hourly earnings for entrants will reflect some self-employment earnings and can therefore provide at least a crude indication of how entrants overall fare relative to non-entrants.

Notes

* The authors are Vice President, National Economic Research Associates and Associate Professor, Fordham University, respectively. This research was supported by the U.S. Small Business Administration under contract no. SBA-2102-AER-87. We retain responsibility for the views expressed below.

[1] See Bendick and Egan (1987) for a summary and critique.

[2] See Balkin (1987), (1989) and Marschall (1986) for a summary.

[3] See U.S. Department of Labor (1987) for a description of the proposed project which was awarded to Abt Associates.

[4] They account for about 75% of all full-time self-employed individuals in the United States.

[5] If they worked for 12 months in the previous year and switched from a wage job to a self-employed job during the year, they would have had to have spent at least 6 months in their wage job to be classified as a wage worker.

[6] Census has reported duration of unemployment as a continuous variable since 1976 and by several categories prior to 1976. For consistency we have converted the continuous unemployment duration information to the categories used prior to 1976. The use of survey week unemployment causes well-known biases. Longer unemployment spells are more likely to be captured than shorter spells, and the truncated length of a spell is not an accurate measure of the completed spell. These limitations imply that the quantitative results should be interpreted cautiously. We do not believe the qualitative results will be affected.

[7] These unemployed are also asked to indicate which of the following factors led them to be unemployed: they were laid off, they quit their job, they left school and are now looking for a job, they wanted temporary work, they were temporarily or indefinitely laid off, or they are unemployed for some other reason. The unemployed may include people who have left a self-employed job. However, self-employed individuals generally do not experience spells of unemployment. They do not get laid off or fired. We suspect most remain at least nominally self-employed while looking for alternative employment.

[8] We reported a similar finding for the NLS men in Evans and Leighton (1987).

[9] These are people who met the entry* definition discussed in the previous section.

[10] People might not want to admit that they were fired or they may have quit their jobs in anticipation of being terminated. Thus the data may not be a reliable guide to the reason for termination.

[11] There is some evidence based on the NLS that workers with low wages and a history of instability are most likely to switch to self-employment holding assets and education constant. See Evans and Leighton (1989).

[12] Because there were few unemployed women who switched to self-employment we were unable to perform a reliable analysis for these groups.

[13] It is well known that the standard errors of this model are biased because the error term is heteroskedastic. However, the bias tends to decrease with sample size and is unlikely to be important for the extremely large sample sizes used in this study. For more on the linear-probability model, consult any elementary textbook in econometrics, e.g., Kmenta (1971).

[14] Because of resource constraints we have not retrieved all of the necessary variables from earlier years of the CPS.

[15] As mentioned earlier, self-employed individuals generally do not experience spells of unemployment. Consequently, it is not appropriate to include self-employment experience in the denominator.

[16] The exit rate for unemployed workers is 1.5 times that for employed workers for white men but just about the same for white women.

[17] The first derivative of log earnings (E) with respect to unemployment weeks (U) is $d(logE)/dU = (dE/E)/dU$ which equals the estimated coefficient on U. dE/E is the percent change in earnings due to a change in unemployment weeks.

[18] See Brock and Evans (1985, 1986, 1989) for further details.

[19] For work along these lines see Bendick and Egan (1987) and National Economic Research Associates (1988).

[20] Unpaid family workers — individuals who work without pay in a family business — were also excluded. Also, respon-

dents who were members of subfamilies were also excluded because of the difficulty of attributing a consistent family income to them due to changes in the definition of the number of persons in the family variable over the period studied. (In the earlier years, number of persons excluded subfamily members; from 1976 on, number of persons in the family included subfamily members. Government workers were included while armed forces workers were excluded.)

References

Balkin, S., 1987, *Survey of CETA Entrepreneurial Programs*, Department of Economics, Roosevelt University (June).

Balkin, S., 1989, *Self-Employment for Low Income People*, New York: Praeger Press.

Bendick, M. and M. Egan, 1987, 'Transfer Payment Diversion for Small Business Development: British and French Experience', *Industrial and Labor Relations Review* **40** (2), 132—157.

Birch, D., 1979, *The Job Generation Process*, Cambridge, Ma.: Center for the Study of Neighborhood and Regional Change, Massachusetts Institute of Technology.

Blau, D., 1987, 'A Time Series Analysis of Self-Employment', *Journal of Political Economy* **95** (2), 445—467.

Brock, W. 1988, 'The Role of Small Business in Macroeconomics and Finance', unpublished, Department of Economics, University of Wisconsin (June).

Brock, W. and D. Evans, 1985, 'The Economics of Regulatory Tiering', *Rand Journal of Economics* **16**(3), 398—409.

Brock, W. and D. Evans, 1986, *The Economics of Small Businesses: Their Role and Regulation in the U.S. Economy*, New York: Holmes and Meier.

Brock, W. and D. Evans, 1989, 'Small Business Economics', *Small Business Economics: An International Journal* **1**(1), 7—20.

Evans, David S., and Linda S. Leighton, 1987, *Self-Employment Selection and Earnings over the Life Cycle*, Washington, D.C.: Office of Advocacy, U.S. Small Business Administration (December).

Evans, David S., and Linda S. Leighton, 1989, 'Some Empirical Aspects of Entrepreneurship', *American Economic Review* **79** (3), 519—535.

Evans, David S., and B. Jovanovic, 1989, 'Estimates of Model of Entrepreneurial Choice under Liquidity Constraints', *Journal of Political Economy* **97** (August), 808—827.

Fazzari, S., R. Hubbard, and B. Peterson, 1987, 'Financing Constraints and Corporate Investment', NBER Working Paper No. 2387, Cambridge, MA.: National Bureau of Economic Research (September).

Marschall, Daniel, 1986, 'Entrepreneurship and Dislocated Workers: Lessons from Ohio's JTPA Experience', *The Entrepreneurial Economy* **4** (June), 5—6.

National Economic Research Associates, Inc., 1988, *An Evaluation of the Loan Guarantee Scheme*. Prepared for the Department of Employment, London: National Economic Research Associates, Inc. (July).

Uchitelle, L., 1988, 'Reliance on Temporary Jobs Hints at Economic Fragility', *New York Times*, March 16, p. 1.

[23]

Does Unemployment Lead to Self-Employment?*

Nigel Meager

ABSTRACT. The currently burgeoning literature on the nature of and the causes for the recent reverse in the downward trend in self-employment in many developed economies, contains a somewhat inconclusive debate on the relationship between unemployment and self-employment, and whether self-employment fluctuates pro- or counter-cyclically. This paper reviews this literature, presents some recent evidence for EC countries, and argues that the approach in the previous research of searching for relationships between unemployment and self-employment *stocks* is fundamentally inappropriate. A new approach, based on an analysis of inflows to and outflows from self-employment, is called for.

1. Introduction

In the last two decades, the long-term historical decline in self-employment as a proportion of total employment in most economically developed economies has slowed, or in some cases reversed. In some countries (such as the UK — see Meager (1991a) — and the USA), the reversal has been particularly marked. As a result, there has been a renewal of interest in self-employment among economists and other social scientists.

Even a casual observer of the applied social science literature will have noted the increasing number of studies attempting to model and

Final version accepted on July 23, 1991

Institute of Manpower Studies
University of Sussex
Brighton BN1 9RF
UK

and

Wissenschaftszentrum Berlin für Sozialforschung
Reichpietschufer 50
D W-1000 Berlin 30
Germany

explain the factors affecting self-employment. These studies can be found both at a micro level, using cross-sectional or longitudinal data to identify the factors influencing individual propensities to enter self-employment; and at a macro level, using time-series data to model the aggregate development of self-employment over time. The *micro* studies include, for example, Fuchs (1982), Rees and Shah (1986), Borjas (1986), Carroll and Mosakowski (1987), Pickles and O'Farrell (1987), Evans and Leighton (1989a), Evans and Jovanovic (1989), De Wit and Van Winden (1989), O'Farrell and Pickles (1989), Burrows (1990), and Meager (1991a); some of these studies are embedded within a (neoclassical) economic framework, others take a more sociological perspective. For examples of *macro* studies by economists, see OECD (1986), Blau (1987), Johnson *et al.* (1988), Evans and Leighton (1989b),[1] and Blanchflower and Oswald (1990); whilst Steinmetz and Wright (1989), and Bögenhold and Staber (1990) provide recent examples of aggregate time-series analyses within the sociological tradition.

The explanations put forward for the recent developments in self-employment are manifold, and the empirical evidence available on the relative importance of the various factors in explaining the self-employment experience of different countries is extremely mixed. It is not our intention to review these competing explanations here, but briefly, they include:[2]

- changing opportunities for dependent employment over the economic cycle:
- sectoral change (in particular, the decline in agriculture and manufacturing, and the expansion of the service sector);
- changing aspirations of certain sections of the workforce (with an increasing preference for "enterprise" and autonomous forms of work);

— changing strategies of employing organisations (with an increased tendency towards sub-contracting, and the use of labour only sub-contractors, and other forms of "self-employed" labour);

— government policies (in particular the widespread introduction of labour market and industrial policy instruments designed to encourage and support self-employment and the small business sector);

— demographic change (thus for example, in so far as the propensity to be self-employed tends to increase with age, the current "ageing" of the workforce in many developed economies might of itself be expected to result in an increase in the proportion of the workforce self-employed).

In the present paper we concentrate on the first of these explanatory factors, namely the cyclical sensitivity of self-employment. We should note in passing, that it is likely that some of the other factors are also themselves cyclically dependent, and thus not strictly exogenous influences on self-employment. Thus, for example, the use of sub-contractors by employing organisations might well expected to vary with the cycle (not necessarily in a straightforward manner; some models of employer behaviour generate pro-cyclical movements in sub-contracting, others imply that the variation is counter-cyclical). Similarly, in so far as government policies are labour market-driven, we might expect some counter-cyclical variation in the intensity of policies targeted at increasing self-employment.

Our emphasis here, however, on cyclical variations in self-employment, is not because we regard this as the most important factor in explaining self-employment trends, but rather because:

a) in order to establish whether there has indeed been any fundamental shift in the underlying historical trend in self-employment, and certainly before attempting to explain such a shift, we need to be able to separate out the influence of the economic cycle; and

b) the debate in the literature about the relative importance of cyclical factors has been particularly confused and inconclusive in its findings. This situation has arisen largely because,

as argued in this paper, the basic relationship being examined has been fundamentally mis-specified in most of the previous research.

The debate about the influence of labour market conditions on self-employment is paralleled in the literature on the factors influencing the birth of new firms, a small strand of which explicitly considers the role of unemployment (this latter literature is comprehensively reviewed, mainly in the UK context, by Storey (1991)). The relationship between new firms and self-employment is a complex one but it is clear that, as Storey (1991) emphasises, the two groups can at most be regarded as overlapping sets. In the present paper then, we are primarily concerned not with firm births *per se*, but with self-employment as a distinct labour market state, and with the role played by the macro-economic environment, and in particular the role played by unemployment, in influencing developments in self-employment.

2. Unemployment and self-employment: push or pull?

Underlying most of the discussion about cyclical variations in self-employment is a very simple theme. The key question addressed by the previous research is: how does the level (or rate) of self-employment vary with the level of economic activity in the economy, or with the unemployment rate? Some of the models in the literature have been cast directly in terms of economic activity (e.g., with the ratio of actual to trend GDP as the explanatory variable), others have used unemployment as the key independent variable. Given, however, the strong relationship between economic activity and unemployment (albeit a relationship which varies over time and over the trade cycle, with variable lags etc.), the substance of the arguments involved is similar between the two approaches, and in many of these models unemployment fluctuations are treated as a proxy for fluctuations in the level of economic activity (whether this treatment is the most appropriate one will be considered in more detail below).

What then are the substantive hypotheses involved here? The first, and simplest, is that high and increasing levels of unemployment constitute, in so far as they reflect a lack of employment opportunities in dependent employment, a "push" factor for people (whether they be unemployed or labour market entrants) to enter self-employment. On this model we would expect self-employment to move counter-cyclically. In the words of OECD (1986):

> ... in a slack labour market with few opportunities for paid employment, unemployed workers may seek self-employment as an alternative to joblessness, and multiple job-holders with secondary jobs in self-employment may lose their primary paid jobs, thereby becoming wholly self-employed (OECD, 1986, p. 53).

This kind of argument is at the heart of the study by Bögenhold and Staber (1990), who argue that this interpretation of self-employment growth as a response to unemployment and lack of dependent employment opportunities, is a key explanatory factor for the post-war self-employment experience of ten OECD countries.

The second key hypothesis is that the level of economic activity acts as a "pull" factor on self-employment. That is, more people will enter self-employment, and their businesses are less likely to fail, when economic activity levels are high/growing than when they are low/falling. On this model we would expect self-employment to move pro-cyclically. Again, in the words of OECD (1986):

> ... output fluctuations affect the self-employed as well as wage earners and salaried employees; for example, their businesses may fail a profit margins shrink or disappear during recessions (OECD, 1986, p. 53).

Thus we have two intuitively plausible hypotheses, working in opposite directions, and much of the interpretation of the empirical findings on the relationship between self-employment and the economic cycle (including the internationally comparative OECD study), has been cast in terms of establishing which one of these two opposing forces "dominates" the other. A series of US studies published in the Monthly Labour Review (Bregger, 1963; Ray, 1975; Becker, 1984) came to the conclusion that the unemployment "push" effect was dominant, and that self-employment fluctuated counter-cyclically. Creigh *et al.* (1986), used similar interpretations to explain their cross-sectional findings for the UK of no strong relation-

ship between regional unemployment and self-employment rates,[3] arguing:

> The net impact of unemployment on the self-employment rate is thus unclear. It depends upon the balance between the incentives which high unemployment creates for individuals to enter self-employment as an alternative to being unemployed or remaining outside the labour force altogether, and the relatively depressed business environment found in areas of high unemployment (Creigh et al., 1986, p. 188).

Of course, it might be argued (and we take up this argument in more detail below), that there are two fundamentally different types of relationship involved here, which should be modelled separately. One (which we have labelled the "pull" relationship) is a *direct* relationship between the level of economic activity and self-employment, whilst the second (the "push" relationship), is an *indirect* relationship between the level of economic activity and self-employment which operates through the mechanism of the labour market.

This distinction is recognised in some of the empirical work. Thus Johnson *et al.* (1988) in their analysis for the UK, distinguish between "cyclical" and "labour market" factors, and their estimated models include both a cyclical (GDP-based) indicator, and an unemployment variable. Interestingly, both variables record significant positive coefficients in their models, apparently confirming the existence of both the "push" and the "pull" effects. Bögenhold and Staber also include both variables in their internationally comparative study, with rather different results[4] (although, as will be argued in Section 3 below, their choice of dependent variable — the self-employment *rate* — casts some doubt on these findings).

3. Previous empirical findings

Before turning to the findings from the empirical studies which have looked at the aggregate relationship(s) between self-employment and the economic cycle and/or unemployment, which is our main concern in this paper, it is worth briefly considering whether the rather more extensive empirical research based on *micro (i.e., individual level)* data can provide any guidance to the likely existence or nature of such relationships.

Micro level studies

Most of the research on self-employment with micro-data has been cross-sectional in nature, looking at the influence of various personal, social and economic characteristics on an individual's likelihood of entering self-employment, or on his/her probability of being self-employed at a given point in time.[5] The methodological problems inherent in inferring aggregate time-series relationships from micro level cross-sectional data, are such that even if such work were to show, for example, that unemployment experience was a significant influence on individual entry into self-employment, we would not be able to conclude that aggregate unemployment fluctuations are a significant determinant of aggregate self-employment trends. Nevertheless the existence of such a relationship would provide a useful micro level corroboration of any observed aggreagate relationship, and the same ("unemployment push") theoretical explanation could clearly apply to both.

Unfortunately most of the cross-sectional micro level studies[6] do not include variables based on individual unemployment or labour market experience (this is true, for example, of the studies by Fuchs (1982), Rees and Shah (1986), Borjas (1986), Carroll and Mosakowski (1987), Evans and Jovanovic (1989), De Wit and Van Winden (1989), Burrows (1990), and Meager (1991a)). Of those that do include such variables, the findings are mixed. Thus Evans and Leighton (1989a) find, for the USA, that the effect of an individual history of unemployment on the probability of entering self-employment is inconsistent between the years for which they have data. They do, however, find a positive relationship between *current* unemployment and entry into self-employment, whilst the probability of *being* self-employed at a given time is also higher for individuals with relatively more experience of unemployment. Pickles and O'Farrell (1987), by contrast, using a data set from Ireland which includes retrospective information on individual career histories, find the opposite, and conclude that

> The baseline model offers no evidence to suggest that becoming self-employed is associated with or is a response to unemployment. . . . (Pickles and O'Farrell, 1987, p. 437).

Hakim (1989) reports the results of a nationally representative survey of inflows to and outflows from self-employment in Great Britain in 1987, and although no statistical analysis is presented, the data suggest that redundancy or unemployment constituted the main motive for entering self-employment for a minority (just over a quarter) of people who had entered self-employment during the previous four years.

At a micro level, then, the evidence is limited and mixed, but for Great Britain and the USA at least, there is some evidence of association between unemployment and entry to self-employment.

Aggregate studies

Turning to the previous research at a more aggregate level, the various studies have used different data series from different countries (in a few cases, notably OECD (1986) and Bögenhold and Staber (1990), comparative data from several countries have been used), and over different time periods. The key question to be asked, then, is whether the existing evidence enables us to conclude that there does exist a clear cyclical relationship of the type hypothesised, which persists over time and in different places, and if so, what is that relationship?

Unfortunately, despite the considerable research effort devoted to this question, the evidence to date is extremely mixed, and in places contradictory. Thus, some of the research, including many of the US studies (e.g., the Monthly Labour Review papers referred to above, as well as Steinmetz and Wright (1989)), and the internationally comparative study of Bögenhold and Staber (1990), finds evidence of a dominant "unemployment push" effect, whilst Evans and Leighton (1989b) conclude that the US self-employment rate moves (weakly) in a pro-cyclical fashion. Other studies find no clear cyclical relationship (e.g., OECD, 1986), or evidence of both effects (Johnson *et al.,* 1988). Finally, there is also some evidence, as for example in the UK study of Blanchflower and Oswald (1990), of a dominant "prosperity pull" effect, and the latter authors argue for the UK that:

> The rise in self-employment at the end of the 1980s

seems to be attributable to the fall in unemployment (Blanchflower and Oswald, 1990).

It is appropriate, therefore, to ask whether these differences in the empirical findings:

a) are due to inadequacies in the empirical methodology adopted by the various authors;

b) reflect genuine differences in the cyclical behaviour of self-employment at different times and places; or

c) imply that the underlying approach of searching for a relationship between unemployment (and/or the economic cycle), and the level (or rate) of self-employment is fundamentally flawed.

Choice of dependent variable

It is clear that much of the existing work is dogged by methodological difficulties. Perhaps the most serious, and best-documented difficulty centres on the question of whether the appropriate dependent variable should be the level or the rate of self-employment (the latter is typically calculated as a proportion of total employment). The self-employment *rate* was used by many of the earlier researchers, but their common finding of counter-cyclical fluctuations in the self-employment rate should not in this case have been used as evidence for the "unemployment push" hypothesis (although it often was), since much of the variation in the rate can be explained by changes in the denominator (total employment) rather than in the numerator (self-employment). Thus it is possible that *both* self-employment and dependent employment fall in a recession, but that the latter is more cyclically sensitive than the former (i.e. in crude terms employers respond to recession by reducing employment levels, whilst the self-employed respond by reducing hours or effort, rather than by ceasing to trade), so the self-employment rate, incorporating both variables, moves counter-cyclically. This issue is discussed in Bayliss (1990), and the problem is recognised in many of the more recent studies (e.g., OECD, 1986; Johnson *et al.* 1988), where the relevant equations are estimated both with levels, and with rates of self-employment as dependent variables.

It is now fairly widely recognised in the literature that whilst the self-employment *rate* may be the appropriate variable for certain purposes (e.g., cross sectional micro-studies of the propensity of different groups to be self-employed), if we are concerned with aggregate time-series cyclical relationships, the key relationship of interest is obscured thereby, and the use of a *level* variable is appropriate. It is particularly unfortunate that the only recent internationally comparative study of this relationship (Bögenhold and Staber, 1990) is characterised by its use only of the self-employment rate as a dependent variable, thereby throwing considerable doubt on its findings of a dominant and similar "unemployment push" effect in all ten countries over the post-war period.[7]

Level of aggregation

A further question which has often arisen in the literature, when defining the appropriate self-employment rate for inclusion in the model(s), has centred on whether or not agriculture should be included in the analysis. Most of the recent work on the topic concentrates on non-agricultural self-employment. The argument for excluding agriculture rests on the fact that the self-employment rate in agriculture is extremely high (in nearly all countries agriculture is the sector with the highest self-employment rate). Given the near universal secular trend in advanced economies for agricultural employment to decline as a proportion of total employment, it is argued that the pattern of historical development of self-employment in other sectors will be obscured if agricultural self-employment is included in the analysis. It is sometimes claimed further, that because of its "traditional" nature, and its heavy use of unpaid family labour, agricultural self-employment is in some sense, fundamentally "different" in kind from self-employment in other sectors, and should therefore be excluded.

Against this position, it can be argued, however, that in so far as agricultural self-employment accounts for a significant (it declining) proportion of total self-employment, as it still does even in some western European economies,[8] then we will miss an important component of self-employment if we exclude it from the analysis. On this view, it would be better to include agricultural self-employment, and if indeed it is subject to different influences than other types of self-employment, to try and model those influences in the analysis.

More generally, however, the discussion of agricultural and non-agricultural self-employment draws attention to an important feature of self-employment as a whole, namely its heterogeneity (see also Meager, 1991a). Much of the literature reviewed here treats self-employment as if it were (with this sole exception of the agricultural self-employed) a homogeneous group of workers subject to similar (macro-economic) influences. It is clear, however, from the micro-level sociological studies that self-employment is an extremely mixed bag. Self-employment may include, for example, everyone from highly skilled professional "own account" workers such as doctors, lawyers and accountants, to entrepreneurial small business owners (who may in turn employ others), to taxi-drivers and retailers, and many low-skilled workers in a variety of trades and occupations, Many of the self-employed (such as "labour only" sub-contract construction workers in the UK, for example), may be self-employed in name only, and their characteristics and behaviour may in most respects be similar to those of dependent employees. The key point is that all of these different groups may have little in common other than the fact of their self-employment, and *a priori* there is no reason to assume that the response of these different "segments" of self-employment to cyclical, structural or labour market policy factors will be similar. This raises the distinct possibility that the failure of the earlier studies to arrive at common coherent findings on the cyclical sensitivity of self-employment may result from the tendency in this research to treat (non-agricultural) self-employment as a single analytical category.[9]

Of course, it may be argued that the fact that the self-employed are extremely heterogeneous in this sense does not of itself imply a similar heterogeneity in the effects of unemployment on these different segments of the self-employed. Such evidence as does exist for self-employment disaggregated by industrial sector or by occupational group, however, (see Meager (1991a) for the UK, and Büchtemann and Gout (1988) for Germany) suggests that recent trends in self-employment *have* differed considerably between these groups, and there is at least a *prima facie* case for disaggre-

gation in examining the determinants of these trends. It is, moreover, relatively straightforward to construct arguments suggesting that the responsiveness to unemployment and labour market circumstances will vary between the different segments of self-employment. To take but one example, the degree of institutional and legal regulation of the various occupations in which the self-employed are found varies considerably both within and between countries. Other things being equal, *entry into self-employment* in a highly regulated occupation as a short-term response to slackness in the labour market, is likely to be dependent on a prior and longer-term choice of *entry to the occupation itself*. Thus, in most of the liberal professions (the law, medicine, architecture, etc.) entry into self-employment is legally restricted in the short-run to those who are already qualified for these occupations; in most manual occupations, by contrast, it is not (the legal and institutional regulation of manual occupations varies considerably between countries, however, and in Germany, for example, entry to self-employment in a wide range of (skilled) manual occupations is also highly regulated through the "Handwerk" system).[10] Hence we might expect to find that entry into self-employment in regulated occupations is less responsive to the economic cycle than is entry to unregulated occupations, and that there is a tendency for short-term cyclical self-employment responses to be crowded into relatively unregulated activities with low barriers to entry (the finding from some of the micro-level surveys that a high proportion of entrants to self-employment change their occupation on entry is consistent with this hypothesis — see, for example, Hakim, 1988, p. 431). As far as exit from self-employment is concerned, there seems less reason *a priori* to expect a strong variation between types of self-employment, except in so far as some economic sectors (construction, for example) tend to be more cyclically sensitive than others, but this further reinforces the key point made later in this paper, that inflows and outflows should be disaggregated in work on this question.

Choice of independent variable(s) and data period

Other technical problems can also be identified for many for the previous studies, which may in turn cast doubt on their findings. Thus, for example, we may question the use by some researchers (e.g., Johnson *et al.,* 1988; Bögenhold and Staber, 1990) of both GDP and unemployment variables in the same equation, given the strong dependence of unemployment on the level of economic activity. If the underlying structural relationship between unemployment and economic activity can be specified, then estimating the appropriate reduced form with an economic activity variable alone as a regressor may be a preferable approach.

Other findings may result from peculiarities of the particular data set or time period chosen for analysis. This seems particularly likely with regard to the distinctive findings of Blanchflower and Oswald (1990) for the UK, namely a strong negative relationship between unemployment and self-employment over 1983—89, using a pooled cross-section/time-series data set. As the authors themselves recognise, estimation on a data period covering only the upswing period of one cycle cannot be an adequate test of an underlying cyclical relationship. It seems unlikely that they would have obtained the same results had their data period also included the period 1979—83, when both unemployment and self-employment grew strongly in the UK.

We would argue, however, that further concentration on such methodological details would be fruitless, since the basic approach, common to all of the previous studies, of searching for a simple relationship between one or more "economic activity" variables (whether they be output variables, or unemployment variables) and a *stock* measure of self-employment (whether defined as a level or a rate, and whether including or excluding agriculture), is fundamentally inappropriate. Before attempting to develop an alternative approach, however (in Section 5 below), we provide a further illustration of the lack of any common or clear relationship (over time and across countries) between aggregate unemployment and self-employment stocks.

4. The unemployment/self-employment relationship in the European Community

This illustration uses data from OECD "Labour Force Statistics" and "Economic Outlooks",[11] for ten EC countries,[12] for the period 1970—88. The graphs in the Appendix below plot the movements of the level of (non-agricultural) self-employment and the unemployment rate in each of these countries (given our view of the inappropriateness of these types of model specification, we do not attempt to estimate these relationships econometrically). The clear feature emerging from the graphs (which is not surprising in the light of the earlier discussion), is the lack of any consistent pattern between the two variables, either within countries over time, or between countries.

Clearly our use of the unemployment *rate,* rather than the unemployment level in these graphs can be questioned on the same grounds that we have used to question other researchers' use of the self-employment *rate.* That is, the denominator of the unemployment rate is the total labour force, which itself includes self-employment. If all variables other than the level of self-employment remained constant, therefore, we would observe a spurious (negative) correlation between the self-employment level, and the unemployment rate. The key point in practice, however, is that the other variables are not constant, and movements of the unemployment rate are strongly dominated by movements in the unemployment level. Furthermore, although self-employment is a component of the labour force, the relationship between self-employment changes and labour force changes is rather weak, since most movements into (and out of) self-employment are movements from (to) employment/unemployment rather than movements from (to) economic inactivity (see also Section 6 below). Replacing the unemployment rate with the unemployment level, therefore, makes virtually no difference to the inter-country patterns observed in the graphs, and the only reason for using the rate rather than the level of unemployment is to deflate the data in such a way as to provide some international comparability.

It is particularly instructive to contrast these patterns with the findings of Bögenhold and Staber (1990), who also use OECD data (for a longer time period), for ten countries (five of which are also in the EC). It would seem that the positive relationship between unemployment and self-employment observed by Bögenhold and Staber, for all the countries in their study (a statistically significant relationship in all but two of the countries), probably results from their use of the self-employment *rate*, i.e., their regression is picking up the cyclical relationship between unemployment and *total employment*, rather than its effect on self-employment *per se*.

The graphs in the Appendix show that when the absolute level of self-employment is used, the only countries exhibiting a clear positive relationship between self-employment and the unemployment rate over all or most of the post-1970 period are Ireland, Italy, and arguably Spain (1975—85). In some cases the relationship is clearly in the opposite direction (i.e., increasing unemployment has occurred together with falling non-agricultural self-employment). This pattern is particularly clear in France, and to a lesser extent, in Denmark.

Most of the remaining countries show a mixed pattern. The UK graph shows clearly that the relationship observed by Blanchflower and Oswald (1990) for the post-1983 period does not hold for the period as a whole.[13] Indeed if, as the latter authors imply, the underlying relationship in the UK is a "prosperity pull" one (i.e., self-employment tends to increase as the economy grows and unemployment falls), then it would appear that this relationship has shifted over time. The pattern in the UK graph is superficially consistent with the argument that this relationship held in the UK both prior to the 1979—83 recession and subsequently, but that this recession coincided with a structural shift, such that post-1983 a given unemployment rate was associated with a much higher level of self-employment than in the pre-1979 period. More sophisticated (econometric) analysis would be required to identify whether such a structural shift had indeed occurred (and the analysis of Johnson *et al.* (1988) does suggest some form of structural break), but in the UK case at least it is relatively easy to construct hypotheses to explain such a shift. Such hypotheses might, for example, be related to the particular severity of the 1979—83 recession and labour shake-out in the UK, and the associated structural changes in employment and resulting greater friction in the labour market (a "hysteresis" argument). Alternatively, hypotheses might be constructed on the basis of attitudinal change, associated with the post-1979 Thatcher governments' attempts to promote an "enterprise culture" in Britain. Blanchflower and Oswald (1990) argue strongly against the latter type of hypothesis, on the basis of their

post-1983 analysis; but see also Meager (1991a), for further discussion of this question.

Superficially at least, the graphs for Germany and Belgium (and arguably Spain) exhibit a similar pattern to that of the UK. The pattern in the Netherlands differs from that in all the other countries, and exhibits a positive relationship pre-1981, and a negative relationship post-1981 (with some shift over 1984—86).

These patterns further support the argument against the search for simple universal relationships between aggregate self-employment and the economic cycle. Matters are clearly much more complex than this, and in so far as self-employment moves with unemployment, it does so in a different way in different times and places, and it is likely that different sub-categories of self-employment are responsive in different ways and to different extents to the economic cycle.

5. The analysis of self-employment flows

Should we, then, in the light of the preceding discussion, abandon any attempt to model the relationship between self-employment and the economic cycle? It would be unfortunate if the failures of the earlier work were to lead us to this conclusion, since it is clear that the two hypotheses underlying most of the previous research, ("unemployment push" and "prosperity pull") are not only intuitively plausible, but consistent with some of the available micro-evidence. It seems unlikely on the one hand that the tightness of the labour market and the availability of dependent employment would have no consistent influence on individuals' propensities to become self-employed, and it seems equally unlikely on the other hand that the level of economic activity would have no consistent influence on the survival chances of the self-employed and small businesses.

A more careful examination of the basic behavioural hypotheses presumed to underlie such relationships suggests, however, that the search for cyclical patterns in self-employment *stocks* is inappropriate. The level of self-employment, and changes in that level over a period, result from changes in the number of people entering self-employment during that period, and the number of people leaving self-employment over that period. The importance of such *gross* flows in explaining the behaviour of *unemployment* over time, is by now a commonplace in the theoretical and empirical economics literature (for a theoretical treatment, see Pissarides, 1990), and it is therefore surprising that this kind of approach is not generally found also in the literature on self-employment. A possible explanation for this might be that in the case of unemployment, empirically speaking, the gross flows are typically much larger relative to the stock than is the case for any other aggregate labour market variable, so the importance of flows is perhaps harder to ignore in the case of unemployment than it is for other variables. Furthermore, in purely practical terms, the widespread availability of regular (usually monthly) unemployment inflow and outflow data in most countries may well have encouraged the use of such data, and the associated attempts to develop flow-based models. Neither of these factors, however, can explain the equal dearth of *theoretical* models based on self-employment flows.

Even where the previous literature discusses the behavioural processes involved (implicitly) in terms of flows (e.g., in terms of the factors influencing "entry" to self-employment), the empirical models employed are, as we have seen, typically couched in terms of stocks or changes in stocks. Thus Storey (1991) in discussing the UK research on the factors influencing new business formation, notes that

> . . . there are three main indices of new firm formation used in time series studies, viz:
> a) new company incorporations;
> b) changes in the proportion of workers classified as self-employed;
> c) businesses newly registered for VAT (Storey, 1991).

Storey does not note, however, that whilst indices a) and c) are inflow indices, and therefore, in principle appropriate for use as dependent variables in models examining the determination of new firm formation, b) is not such an index. Rather it represents the change in a stock variable, which is itself the net outcome of gross inflows to and outflows from self-employment. Quite apart from any differences in the *coverage* of the three variables (which is what Storey's critique focuses on), it is clear that b) is a different analytical construct from the other two variables, and wholly inappropriate[14] as a measure of entry to self-

employment or new firm formation, including as it does the effects of *exit* from self-employment (or firm deaths).

If we think in terms of flows, it immediately becomes clear that the familiar "unemployment push" hypothesis is essentially based on a model positing a relationship between unemployment and *inflows* into self-employment. A strong case can also be made for the "prosperity pull" hypothesis resting on a relationship between economic activity and *outflows* from self-employment, although in this case the argument is less clear-cut, i.e., one might argue that the hypothesis is not only about *outflows* (people being more likely to leave self-employment through business failure in a recession), but also about *inflows* (people — other than those experiencing unemployment push — being less likely to enter self-employment at times of depressed economic activity). As we show below, interpreting the hypothesis this way makes the underlying model more complex, but it does not affect the core argument presented here, namely that any such model should be cast in terms of flows rather than stocks.[15]

In crude terms, then, and taking first the simplest version of the two hypotheses, there is no contradiction between them, but rather if they are both valid, then during a recession as unemployment increases, we can expect to see both an increase in the inflows to self-employment ("unemployment push"), and an increase in the outflows ("prosperity — *or in this case lack of it* — pull"). It is self-evident that the overall effect on the stock of self-employment is not predictable *a priori*, but is a *net* effect, depending on the parameters of the underlying inflow and outflow relationships.

In practice the matter may be slightly more complicated than this, since outflows from self-employment may themselves be a lagged function of earlier inflows, irrespective of the economic cycle. There is a considerable literature in the research on small firms (see the discussion on Storey and Johnson (1987), for example), which suggests that a certain amount of "churning" in the small firms sector takes place more or less independently of the overall economic climate. That is, of any cohort of new entrants to the sector, a certain proportion can be expected to fail and leave the sector within a fairly short period, largely irrespective of market conditions. This might be because the initial idea for the business was poorly thought out, or because the self-employed person possessed inadequate business management skills, or because he/she discovered that the self-employed lifestyle did not match initial expectations etc. Hence, even with no cyclical fluctuations, any surge in the inflow to self-employment can be expected to be followed by a surge in the outflow, after a lag.

Formalising the above in very simple terms, then, and assuming linear relationships (the precise functional forms involved are irrelevant to our key arguments), let:

I_t = the inflow into self-employment in period (year) t;

O_t = the outflow from self-employment in period t;

S_t = the level of self-employment at the end of period t;

U_t = unemployment at the start of period t (in line with our earlier discussion this should probably be the *level* of unemployment rather than the more usual unemployment rate, although a case could be made for the latter on the grounds that it might be a better proxy for the *perceived probability* of becoming unemployed, or of getting a job once unemployed).

The inflow equation then, is:

$$I_t = a + bU_t + ct, \qquad (1)$$

where t is a time trend variable to pick up secular trends in entry to self-employment, the effects of structural shifts in the economy etc. (in a more sophisticated approach we might attempt to model some of these effects separately). The "unemployment push" hypothesis is then simply that $b > 0$.

Similarly the outflow equation might look as follows:

$$O_t = d + eU_t + fI_{t-2} + gt. \qquad (2)$$

For simplicity in what follows, we have used unemployment in Equation 2 as a proxy for the level of economic activity. It makes no difference to the subsequent argument whether outflows are expressed as an increasing function of unemployment or as a decreasing function of economic activity — the key point is that we hypothesise outflows to move counter-cyclically.

The "prosperity pull" hypothesis is simply that $e > 0$ in Equation 2. The lagged term in I_{t-2} is to capture the automatic "churning" effect referred to above. We have assumed a two-year lag simply because an initial examination of flows data for the UK (see also Meager (1991a), and the discussion below) suggests that a surge in the inflow into self-employment in a particular category (e.g., by gender or sector), tends to be followed some one to two years later by a surge in the outflow in that category (the "second year crisis" in the development of small businesses is well documented in the case-study literature). Of course, it might be more reasonable to model this feature with some sort of distributed lag function, as it is clear that to the extent that this churning occurs it is likely to spread over a longer period than a single year. The single lag term is included here for simplicity, just to remind us of the likely existence of this phenomenon. Clearly we assume that $f > 0$.

The stock-flow accounting identity is:

$$S_t = S_{t-1} + I_t - O_t \qquad (3)$$

and substituting for I_{t-2} in Equation 2, and for I_t and O_t in Equation 3, yields:

$$S_t - S_{t-1} = f(U_t, U_{t-2}, t) \qquad (4)$$
$$\quad\quad\quad\quad\; ? \quad - \;\; ?$$

Thus, in this very simple linear formulation, the net change in the stock of self-employment over the period is a function:

a) of the current unemployment rate (of *indeterminate sign*: whether it is an increasing or decreasing function depends on the relative magnitudes of the coefficients b and e in Equations 1 and 2);

b) of lagged unemployment — in our specific formulation it is the unemployment rate two years earlier (a *negative function*); and

c) of a time trend (again this function is of *indeterminate sign* depending on the relative magnitudes of the coefficients c, g and f, and on the signs of c and g in Equations 1 and 2).

So far we have used the simplest interpretation of the "pull" hypothesis, namely that it affects outflows. As suggested above, however, a plausible hypothesis might also be that there is a pull effect on the inflows to self-employment (e.g., as unemployment increases, some groups of people experience not a "push" into self-employment, but rather are discouraged from entering self-employment because of the depressed economic climate). We argue below (in Section 6 of the paper) that this possibility is probably best handled by disaggregating the flows data to distinguish between the inflows from different sources (e.g., according to whether they come from unemployment, employment or economic inactivity). If however, data limitations preclude such disaggregation, there may still be some scope for modelling the influences on inflows in such a way as to take account of both push and pull possibilities. Thus, for example, following Hamilton (1989), who uses a similar formulation to model new business formation in Scotland, we might include a quadratic term in unemployment in the inflows Equation 1 above, which would then become:

$$I_t = a + bU_t + b'U_t^2 + ct. \tag{1a}$$

and the hypothesis would be that $b > 0$ and $b' < 0$. That is, as unemployment rises, we observe a push effect, until a point is reached beyond which the discouragement effect predominates, and

> ... the necessary 'push' towards self-employment on those made unemployed will no longer be accompanied by sufficient 'pull' of new business opportunities (Hamilton, 1989, p. 250).

Substituting Equation 1a in the above model yields a revised version of Equation 4 as follows:

$$S_t - S_{t-1} = f(U_t, U_t^2, U_{t-2}, U_{t-2}^2, t) \tag{4a}$$
$$\quad\quad\quad ? \quad - \quad - \quad + \quad ?$$

Once again it is clear that if the inflow and outflow relationships are as hypothesised here, then any estimated time-series relationship in which a *stock* measure of self-employment is treated as a function of current unemployment, is not only underspecified, but the sign on that relationship is indeterminate.

Given that most of the earlier empirical work has effectively involved an estimation of some version of the reduced form equation (4 or 4a etc.), but without any modelling of the underlying structural relationships determining the flows, and given the indeterminate sign on the relationship between self-employment and unemployment in

that equation, it is not surprising that the relationship uncovered so far has tended to be a rather unstable one. This does not imply, however, that the underlying structural relationships (such as in Equations 1 or 2 above) are themselves in any sense unstable, neither does it imply that the "unemployment push", or "prosperity pull" hypotheses are invalidated (or supported) by the evidence. It is true that many of the previous authors are apparently concerned in their analysis only with *inflows*; thus in Bögenhold and Staber (1990), it would appear that both the unemployment and the GDP growth variables are seen as "push" factors, affecting entry to self-employment. The key point, however, is that these macro variables are, as we have argued, likely to influence both inflows and outflows independently, and the use of a stock dependent variable therefore compounds both sets of influences and cannot be used to examine either the inflow or the outflow relationship. Indeed, as we have seen, there are good theoretical reasons to believe that there will be no consistent time-series relationship between the stock of self-employment and the economic cycle.

6. Conclusions

In conclusion, it would seem that future research on the behaviour of self-employment over the cycle, should not concentrate on further attempts to model the relationship between unemployment and self-employment stocks. Whilst many previous authors (including Steinmetz and Wright (1989) and Bögenhold and Staber (1990)) are clearly aware of the dynamic nature of self-employment, and their discussion of hypotheses such as "unemployment push" reflects this awareness, their tests of such hypotheses nevertheless typically rest on an examination of cyclical variation in self-employment stocks. This paper has shown that this approach is both theoretically and empirically an inappropriate means for examining the key hypotheses of interest. Rather, such work should focus on the flows into and out of self-employment, developing theoretical models to explain the cyclical behaviour of these flows, and searching for and utilising flows data to test these models.

Adequate flows data on self-employment are, unfortunately scarce (which may partly explain previous authors' reliance on stock data), but the various Labour Force Surveys now conducted on a comparable basis in EC countries, for example, enable the construction of crude flows variables, based on respondents' employment status one year prior to the survey. Given that these data do not extend back on a comparable basis before 1983, the scope for rigorous time-series modelling is extremely limited. Nevertheless, these data provide some basis for investigating in a more or less descriptive fashion, the dynamic evolution of self-employment over the recent time period in EC countries. Some countries have also, in recent years, attempted to develop consistent aggregate stock-flow accounting systems to record transitions between labour market states (a good example here is the *Arbeitskräfte-Gesamtrechnung* in Germany, the coverage of which extends back to 1970 — see Reyher and Bach (1988)), which provide, within those countries at least, the possibility for time-series analysis of self-employment flows.

As an example of the former, the aggregate self-employment flows data for Great Britain (from the UK Labour Force Survey; estimates given in Daly (1991)), are shown in Figure 1. Whilst the data period is too short for any cyclical effect to be shown up, the "churning" referred to above can be seen clearly. Thus the surges in self-employment inflows over 1983—4 and 1986—87 are followed by (smaller) surges in the outflows some two years later (at the time of writing, this pattern appears to

be further confirmed by the self-employment figures in the preliminary results from the 1990 Labour Force Survey).

Further work, therefore, should focus on examining the flows patterns for other European countries, as revealed by the European Labour Force Surveys, and on beginning to relate changes in these flows to cyclical and other factors. Furthermore, in the light of the heterogeneity in self-employment referred to above, such flows analysis should (where sample sizes allow), be undertaken at a more disaggregated level. Much more work is required to determine the most appropriate segmentation of self-employment into different categories, but key variables might include sector (and/or occupation) as well as some indicator of whether the different types of self-employed constitute a "small business", an "own account worker" or a "disguised employee",[16] if such distinctions can be operationalised from the data.

There may also be some advantage in breaking the various self-employment flows down by their sources and/or destinations, and attempting to analyse or model the behaviour of each sub-flow separately. Thus so far, we have discussed the "unemployment push" hypothesis in terms of the overall inflow into self-employment. Clearly, however, we can make an analytical and empirical distinction between the inflows from unemployment, dependent employment, and economic activity respectively, and we might expect each of these flows to respond rather differently to the economic cycle. Thus, if the "unemployment push" hypothesis holds, we would expect to observe a positive relationship between the unemployment rate and the sub-flow from unemployment to self-employment. In the case of the sub-flow from dependent employment (empirically the largest of the three sub-flows in most countries), the picture is less clear. On the one hand increased unemployment (and the associated decline in employment opportunities) might be expected to result in an increased flow into self-employment among some involuntary job-losers (choosing self-employment as a preferable alternative to unemployment). On the other hand, a certain proportion of the sub-flow from wage employment to self-employment consists of voluntary quitters, opting for self-employment rather than employment, for economic or lifestyle reasons. A deteriorating eco-

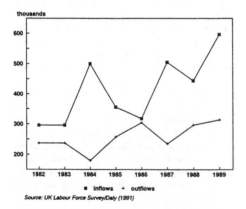

Fig. 1. Great Britian: Self-Employment Flows, 1982—89

nomic climate might, *ceteris paribus*, be expected to reduce the size of this group. Similarly, with regard to labour market (re-)entrants, an economic downswing might be expected to "push" more of these towards self-employment; but equally amongst those for whom it is an option, the downswing might also result in their postponing or abandoning the decision to enter the labour market (i.e., the traditional "discouragement" effect of increasing unemployment on labour force participation).

There is a strong case, therefore, not only for further work in this area to concentrate on self-employment flows, but for this work to attempt (in so far as the available data permit), to develop models explaining the dynamics of the different sub-components of the various gross flows. This case is reinforced by an initial examination of sub-flows data from the UK Labour Force Survey, shown in Table I (the data are taken from Meager (1991a)). These data show "inflows" to self-employment[17] over two one-year periods (1983—84) and (1986—87), broken down according to whether the entrants to self-employment were employed, unemployed or economically inactive prior to entry.

Two features stand out from Table I. Firstly, the size of the inflow to self-employment was very similar in the two periods (it increased by about 3,000, or just over half of one percent of the total inflow). Secondly, despite this similarity in the inflow between the two years, there are considerable differences in the pattern of sub-flows. Thus the inflows from employment and unemployment both increased over the period, by 13 percent and 18 percent respectively, whilst the flow from economic inactivity decreased considerably (by 28

TABLE I
Self-employment inflows: UK, 1983—84 and 1986—87

Inflow into self-employment during year	1983—84 (thousands)	1986—87 (thousands)
Total inflow	432.6	435.6
Flow from employment	204.3	231.2
Flow from unemployment	87.7	103.4
Flow from inactivity	140.7	101.0

Source: UK Labour Force Survey/Meager, 1991a.

percent). In view of the preceding discussion, it is of interest to attempt to relate these changes to changes in unemployment between 1983 and 1986. Unfortunately there is some inconsistency between the various data sources[18] as to whether the unemployment level (and rate) in the UK peaked in 1983 (as suggested by the most recent OECD internationally "standardised" data — see the UK graph in the Appendix), or in 1986 as suggested by official UK sources. There is clearly a strong general case for using internationally comparable data based on the ILO definition of unemployment, rather than internal UK data based on administrative definitions (even where these data have been adjusted to allow for discontinuities due to changes in benefit regulations etc.). It might be argued, however, that when examining hypotheses such as "unemployment push" into self-employment, it is the *perception* of the tightness of the labour market held by the relevant actors at the time which is equally or more important. It was certainly the case, for example, that the public perception of falling unemployment did not begin in the UK until 1986 at the earliest. Between 1983 and 1986, the "headline" level of unemployment continued to increase strongly (and the published unemployment rate also increased, albeit at a somewhat slower pace, due to expansion in the labour force). It is common, therefore, even in internationally comparative studies, to sue the adjusted Employment Department unemployment series for the UK, rather than the more strictly comparable OECD series.[19]

If, for the sake of argument, we interpret 1983—86 as a period during which unemployment was still increasing in the UK, the sub-flows data in Table I are consistent with the "unemployment push" hypothesis with regard to the flows from dependent employment and unemployment (i.e., they suggest an increased flow into self-employment among people losing their jobs, or who have already lost them). The large fall in the flow from economic inactivity, however, is consistent with the notion of a dominant "discouragement" effect. Clearly, an adequate exploration of these issues would require flows data for more than two years, and from more than one country,[20] and it is unfortunate that the only flows data available to the author at the time of writing are subject to these difficulties in interpreting the direction of change of unemployment. Nevertheless, the data are presented here to illustrate and support the argument that the richness of our understanding of the dynamics underlying changes in self-employment can be improved only through a detailed analysis of self-employment inflows and outflows.

Finally, it is worth noting that a more detailed examination of self-employment flows, and the factors influencing them, is likely also to be beneficial in the evaluation of labour market policies aimed at self-employment. To date, the majority of such programmes in EC countries have been targeted on increasing the inflow into self-employment (particularly the inflow from unemployment). If the churning relationship observed for the UK data in Figure 1 is typical, however, then clearly a strong case can be made for some shift of policy emphasis to reducing the *outflow* from self-employment, otherwise the long-term impact on the stock of a policy which successfully increases the inflow to self-employment, is likely to be small. Of course there may be more indirect benefits from a policy which encourages inflows (irrespective of whether they result in lasting self-employment), in that inflows may be a mechanism for introducing both product and process innovations into the economy, as well as enhancing the individual human capital of the new entrants themselves (such arguments have, for example been used by evaluators of the Enterprise Allowance Scheme in the United Kingdom — see Owens, 1989). Equally, it can be argued that a high level of outflows may also be beneficial in ridding the economy of outdated structures, [21] although to the extent that a high proportion of outflows are typically relatively recent entrants, this argument may have less force.

Nevertheless, in so far as the objective of such programmes is to increase the level of self-employment[22] in a sustainable fashion, and this is often one of the stated objectives (see Owens, 1989), then greater attention to the relationship between inflows and subsequent outflows, and the factors influencing both sets of flows can only be beneficial in improving the design and evaluation of such programmes.

Notes

* I would like to thank Steve Johnson, Günther Schmid, David Storey and an anonymous referee for helpful comments and suggestions on an earlier draft of the paper.

[1] Although this study by Evans and Leighton is included in the "macro level" category, it differs from most of the others in this category, in that it attempts to explain changes over time in the US aggregate self-employment rate with grouped micro-data ("quasi-panel" data), and includes individual characteristic variables of the type typically found in cross-sectional micro level studies, as well as the more usual aggregate variables.

[2] See Meager (1991a), and (1991b), for a more extensive account of the competing explanations.

[3] This result is questionable, however, and others have argued that the cross-sectional relationship between self-employment and unemployment rates in the UK is a negative one; see, for example, Meager (1991a). For an attempt to reconcile the apparently conflicting cross-section and time-series findings, in the context of the relationship between unemployment and new business formation, see Hamilton (1989).

[4] I.e., they find a generally positive and significant coefficient on the unemployment rate, and a negative and significant coefficient on their GDP growth variable. Hence they argue that the influence of a high level of unemployment and a depressed level of economic activity both act in the direction of increased self-employment.

[5] A key problem with research based on the relationship between various independent variables and individual *propensities* to be self-employed at a given time (e.g., as in Burrows, 1990; De Wit and Van Winden, 1989; Meager, 1991a; Rees and Shah, 1986), is that this approach confounds both *entry* and *survival* effects in self-employment. See Chesher and Lancaster (1983), for a general but rigorous account of the statistical problems involved with such an approach.

[6] We exclude here the various case-study or small sample studies (e.g., in the UK, Fevre, 1987; Johnson and Rodger, 1983; Lee, 1985), which are typically based on studies of recently redundant workers, or of particular categories of the unemployed. Whilst such studies provide useful indications of the processes and pressures which may lead such people to enter self-employment, they cannot provide any evidence on the overall existence and nature of "unemployment push".

[7] Bögenhold and Staber acknowledge, in a footnote, the possible "tautological element" introduced into their analysis by the use of the self-employment rate, but do not elaborate on its potentially serious implications for the conclusions of their research.

[8] Thus the European Labour Force Surveys for 1986, for example, showed that the proportion of self-employment accounted for by agriculture was over 50 percent in Ireland and Portugal, over 40 percent in Greece, and over 30 percent in Denmark, Spain, France, and the Netherlands.

[9] Several of the earlier authors recognise this problem, but in most cases have been precluded from separately modelling the cyclical sensitivity of different types of self-employment by lack of adequate data at a disaggregated level.

[10] For a comprehensive account of the workings of the Handwerk system, and a comparison with the UK, see Doran (1984).

[11] These are the best sources of data on these variables which have been adjusted in an attempt to ensure international comparability. The main alternative source (the EC Labour Force Survey), has fewer problems of comparability, but is not yet available in a sufficiently long time-series to allow analysis of cyclical change.

[12] Luxembourg and Portugal are excluded: the former on grounds of size, the latter on grounds of data availability.

[13] Unfortunately, the various measures of UK unemployment differ in the picture they paint for the post-1983 period. The OECD "standardised" measure used here, dates the downturn in unemployment in 1983. Data from the British Department of Employment (see Employment Department, 1990), date it as starting in 1984 (Labour Force Survey data using the ILO/OECD unemployment definition), or in 1986 (official claimant count data). These differences persist whether the data are expressed as levels or rates. Clearly, given the strong growth in self-employment throughout the 1980s, any analysis of its relationship with unemployment over this period is affected by which definition is taken. See also the discussion in Section 6.

[14] This leaves aside the problem, already discussed, that the variable is a *ratio* whose movements may be dominated by changes in the denominator (total employment), rather than by changes in the numerator (self-employment).

[15] A further complication in the case of outflows is that one element of the outflow may consist of self-employed people achieving "employed" status through the legal incorporation of their businesses. This type of outflow, then, reflects "success" rather than "failure", and is arguably likely to increase at a time of overall economic growth (I am grateful to Steve Johnson for this point).

[16] Parisotto (1991), in his examination of self-employment in Italy utilises a similar categorisation of the self-employed into "traditional", "new" and "satellite" segments.

[17] I.e., people who were self-employed at the time of the survey, and who had some other employment status one year prior to the survey. It is clear that these data are only a very imperfect approximation to true inflows, in that they fail to pick up multiple changes of status during the year (see the discussion of the various problems associated with these flows data in Daly, 1991). Nevertheless, any significant changes in the patterns of self-employment inflows and outflows over time can be expected to show up in these data.

[18] See also the discussion in Note 13 above.

[19] See, for example, Jackman *et al.* (1990), who use OECD data for all countries except the UK (for which they use the Employment Department series adjusted for definitional changes), in their comparative study of the relationship between unemployment and vacancy rates in OECD countries.

[20] The author is in the process of extending this analysis to the 1983—89 period for a range of EC countries, using secondary analysis of data from the EC Labour Force Surveys provided by EUROSTAT.

[21] I am grateful to an anonymous referee for this point.

[22] Of course, a parallel objective of such programmes is also to reduce the level of unemployment, which at least partly explains their exclusive emphasis on self-employment inflows — Meager (1991c).

References

Bayliss, F. J., 1990, *Self-Employment in Industrialised Market Economy Countries*, ILO World Employment Programme Research Working Paper No. 38, Geneva: International Labour Office.

Becker, E. H., 1984, 'Self-Employed Workers: An Update to 1983' *Monthly Labor Review* 107 (7), 14—18.

Blanchflower, D. and A. Oswald, 1990, 'Self-Employment and Mrs Thatcher's Enterprise Culture', in *British Social Attitudes: the 1990 Report*, Aldershot: Gower.

Blau, D. M., 1987, 'A Time Series Analysis of Self-Employment in the United States', *Journal of Political Economy* 95 (3), 445—467.

Bögenhold, D. and M. Staber, 1990, 'Selbständigkeit als ein Reflex aus Arbeitslosigkeit?' *Kölner Zeitschrift für Soziologie und Sozialpsychologie* 42 (2), 265—279.

Borjas, G. J., 1986, 'The Self-Employment Experience of Immigrants', *Journal of Human Resources* 21 (4), 485—506.

Bregger, J. E., 1963, 'Self-Employment in the United States, 1948—62', *Monthly Labor Review* 90 (1), 37—43.

Büchtemann, C. F. and M. Gout, 1988, *Développement et structure du travail "indépendant" en R.F.A.*, report prepared for the Commission of the European Communities and the Commissariat Général du Plan, Berlin: Wissenschaftszentrum Berlin für Sozialforschung (mimeo).

Burrows, R., 1990, 'A Socio-Economic Anatomy of the British Petty Bourgeoisie: A Multivariate Analysis', in R. Burrows (ed.), *Enterprise Culture, Entrepreneurship, Petty Capitalism and the Restructuring of Britain*, London: Routledge.

Carroll, G. R. and E. Mosakowski, 1987, 'The Career Dynamics of Self-Employment', *Administrative Science Quarterly* 32, 570—589.

Chesher, A. and T. Lancaster, 1983, 'The Estimation of Models of Labour Market Behaviour', *Review of Economic Studies* 50, 609—624.

Creigh, S. *et al.*, 1986, 'Self-Employment in Britain: Results from the Labour Force Surveys 1981—84', *Employment Gazette* 95 (6), 183—194.

Daly, M., 1991, 'The 1980s — A Decade of Growth in Enterprise: Self-Employment Data from the Labour Force Survey', *Employment Gazette* 99 (3), 109—134.

De Wit, G. and F. A. A. M. Van Winden, 1989, 'An Empirical Analysis of Self-Employment in the Netherlands', *Small Business Economics* 1 (4), 263—272.

Doran, A., 1984, *Craft Enterprises in Britain and Germany: A Sectoral Study*, London: Anglo-German Foundation for the Study of Industrial Society.

Employment Department (UK), 1990, 'Measures of Unemployment: The Claimant Count and the Labour Force Survey', *Employment Gazette* 98 (10), 506—513.

Evans, D. S. and L. S. Leighton, 1989a, 'Some Empirical Aspects of Entrepreneurship', *American Economic Review* 79 (3), 519—535.

Evans, D. S. and L. S. Leighton, 1989b, 'The Determinants of Changes in US Self-Employment, 1968—1987', *Small Business Economics* 1 (2), 111—119.

Evans, D. S. and B. Jovanovic, 1989, 'An Estimated Model of Entrepreneurial Choice Under Liquidity Constraints', *Journal of Political Economy* **97**(4), 808—827.

Fevre, R., 1987, 'Subcontracting in Steel', *Work, Employment and Society* **1**, 509—537.

Fuchs, V. B., 1982, 'Self-Employment and Labour Force Participation of Older Males', *Journal of Human Resources* **16**(3), 339—357.

Hakim, C., 1988, 'Self-Employment in Britain: A Review of Recent Trends and Current Issues', *Work, Employment and Society* **2**(4), 421—450.

Hakim, C., 1989, 'New Recruits to Self-Employment in 1980s', *Employment Gazette* **97**(6), 286—297.

Hamilton, R. T., 1989, 'Unemployment and Business Formation Rates: Reconciling Time-Series and Cross-Section Evidence', *Environment and Planning A* **21**, 249—255.

Jackman, R. *et al.*, 1990, 'Labour Market Policies and Unemployment in the OECD', *Economic Policy* **11**, 450—490.

Johnson, P. and J. Rodger, 1983, 'From Redundancy to Self-Employment', *Employment Gazette* **91**(6), 260—264.

Johnson, S. *et al.*, 1988, *Modelling Aggregate Self-Employment: A Preliminary Analysis*, University of Warwick, Institute for Employment Research.

Lee R., 1985, 'The Entry to Self-Employment of Redundant Steelworkers', *Industrial Relations Journal* **16**(2), 42—49.

Meager, N., 1991a, *Self-Employment in the United Kingdom*, IMS Report No. 205, Brighton: Institute of Manpower Studies.

Meager, N., 1991b, 'The Characteristics of the Self-Employed: Some Anglo-German Comparisons', in A. Felstead, and P. Leighton (eds.), *Making Work: Self-Employment and Small Businesses in Europe Today*, London: Kogan Page.

Meager, N., 1991c, *Self-Employment Programmes for the Unemployed in EC Countries: A Note*, Berlin: WZB, March (mimeo).

OECD, 1986, 'Self-Employment in OECD Countries', in *OECD Employment Outlook*, Paris: OECD.

O'Farrell, P. N. and A. R. Pickles, 1989, 'Entrepreneurial Behaviour Within Male work Histories: A Sector-Specific Analysis', *Environment and Planning A* **21**, 311—331.

Owens, A., 1989, *Enterprise Allowance Scheme Evaluation: Net Costs to the Exchequer, Estimates for 1987/88*, Research and Evaluation Branch, Report No. 22, Sheffield: The Employment Service.

Parisotto, A., 1991, '*The Distinctive Pattern of Non-Agricultural Self-Employment in Italy*', World Employment Programme Research, Working Paper No. 48, Geneva: International Labour Office.

Pickles, A. R. and P. N. O'Farrell, 1987, 'An Analysis of Entrepreneurial Behaviour from Male work Histories', *Regional Studies* **21**, 425—444.

Pissarides, C. A., 1990, *Equilibrium Unemployment Theory*, Oxford: Basil Blackwell.

Ray, R. N., 1975, 'A Report on Self-Employed Americans in 1973', *Monthly Labor Review* **102**(1), 49—54.

Rees, H. and A. Shah, 1986, 'An Empirical Analysis of Self-employment in the UK', *Journal of Applied Econometrics* **1**, 95—108.

Reyher, L. and H.-U. Bach, 1988, 'Arbeitskräfte-Gesamtrechnung: Bestände und Bewegung am Arbeitsmarkt', *Beiträge zur Arbeitsmarkt- und Berufsforschung* **70**, 123—143.

Steinmetz, G. and E. O. Wright, 1989, 'The Fall and Rise of the Petty Bourgeoisie: Changing Patterns of Self-Employment in the Postwar United States', *American Journal of Sociology* **94**(5), 973—1018.

Storey, D. J., 1991, 'The Birth of New Firms — Does Unemployment Matter? A Review of the Evidence', *Small Business Economics* **3**(3), 167—178.

Storey, D. J. and S. Johnson, 1987, *Job Generation and Labour Market Change*, London: Macmillan.

Appendix.   Unemployment rates and non-agricultural self-employment in EC countries (1970—1988)

Belgium

Non-agricultural self-employment (thousands)

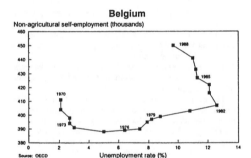

Source: OECD   Unemployment rate (%)

Denmark

Non-agricultural self-employment (thousands)

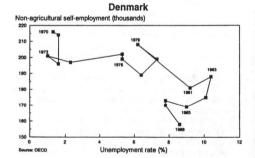

Source: OECD   Unemployment rate (%)

France

Non-agricultural self-employment (thousands)

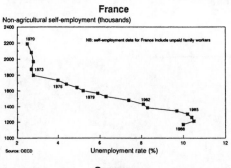

NB: self-employment data for France include unpaid family workers

Source: OECD Unemployment rate (%)

Italy

Non-agricultural self-employment (thousands)

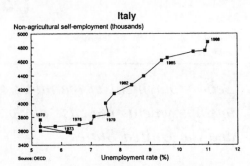

Source: OECD Unemployment rate (%)

Germany

Non-agricultural self-employment (thousands)

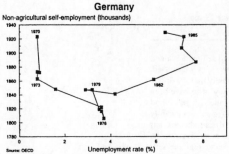

Source: OECD Unemployment rate (%)

Netherlands

Non-agricultural self-employment (thousands)

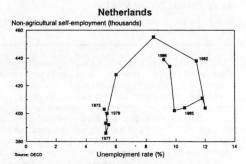

Source: OECD Unemployment rate (%)

Ireland

Non-agricultural self-employment (thousands)

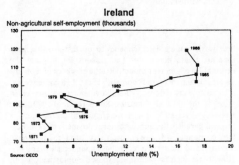

Source: OECD Unemployment rate (%)

Spain

Non-agricultural self-employment (thousands)

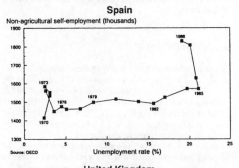

Source: OECD Unemployment rate (%)

Greece

Non-agricultural self-employment (thousands)

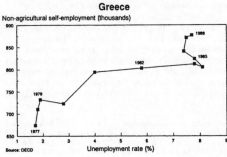

Source: OECD Unemployment rate (%)

United Kingdom

Non-agricultural self-employment (thousands)

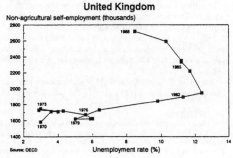

Source: OECD Unemployment rate (%)

[24]

Applied Economics, 1994, **26**, 189–204

Self-employment in the midst of unemployment: the case of Spain and the United States

ALFONSO ALBA-RAMIREZ

Universidad Carlos III de Madrid, Calle Madrid 126, 28903 Getafe, Spain

This article examines the relationship between unemployment and self-employment. The possibility that self-employment is an alternative for jobless workers is discussed. In doing so, the standard job search model is used to show informally that if workers learn about the job market in the process of looking for work, those who have been unemployed for longer are more likely to become self-employed. Indeed, it was found that for both Spain and the United States the duration of unemployment significantly increases the probability of becoming self-employed. Further analysis indicates that part-time work and the absence of social security coverage are more likely to be associated with self-employed workers. In Spain, it was also found that the self-employed without employees earn significantly less than other workers with similar characteristics.

I INTRODUCTION

Recently, economists and policy makers have become increasingly concerned with the role of small businesses in the economy. One reason for this interest is the recent growth of self-employment among some OECD countries.[1] High levels of unemployment in the late 1970s and early 1980s hint that unemployment might be a contributing factor for the observed increase in self-employment.

In general, we know little about the characteristics and circumstances associated with the workers who, sooner or later in their life, decide or are prompted to become 'entrepreneurs'. In the midst of high unemployment, establishing a business becomes a plausible alternative for the jobless.[2] Self-employment not only solves an individual's unemployment problem, but also places a potential employer in the labour market. Nonetheless, this proposition remains to be tested.

One might think that in periods of high employment and growth, there is not much incentive for self-employment

because there is a greater tendency to join fast-growing firms than to create new ones. The reasons for this are the expectation of greater productivity, the existence of economies of scale and increased competitiveness. As a consequence, a trend toward reduced self-employment was observed in most of the OECD countries. Since the mid-1970s, this tendency reversed in the non-agricultural sector. Such a reversal parallels the increased unemployment rates in western economies. Moreover, deep structural changes have occurred and the service sector has expanded substantially. How these factors contribute to self-employment is an empirical question yet to be addressed by researchers.

This article studies the relationship between unemployment and self-employment at a microeconomic level. To do that, self-employment can be linked to duration of unemployment. In order to assess if self-employment is a worthy choice for the long-term unemployed, a further attempt is made to see how well matched self-employed workers are to their jobs. Futhermore, to describe various features of self-employed workers, the demographic and

[1] See OECD (1986)
[2] Legislation aimed to help the jobless start up their own businesses has been implemented in Europe and in the United States Spain enacted a law in 1985 to provide lump-sum unemployment insurance to workers willing to become self-employed As of the autumn of 1989, jobless persons in the state of Washington (US) can apply to the Self-Employment and Enterprise Development Project (SEED), which allocates lump-sum unemployment insurance and provides training for some of those who want to create a small business This measure has been extended to other states in the US

previous job characteristics of the currently self-employed are compared to those of waged and salaried workers.[3]

The empirical work in this study focuses on Spain and the United States. Spain is a fruitful case for analysing the relationship between unemployment and self-employment. First, unemployment began to grow in the mid-1970s and reached its peak in 1985. Second, due to the predominance of small-size firms, a comparison between the United States and Spain helps in the assessment of the special features of the Spanish case. The duration of unemployment data for workers who have changed firms in Spain and for those displaced from their jobs in the United States are used.

One result of our analysis is that, after controlling for workers who did not experience unemployment in Spain or the United States, the duration of a prior unemployment spell significantly increases the probability of current self-employment status. For both countries, evidence of a higher probability of part-time work among self-employed workers is also found. This is a circumstance that is more likely to be associated with workers who suffered a longer unemployment spell before re-employment. Another result is that the wage differences between self-employed and waged and salaried workers depend on the size of firm owned by the self-employed workers. Self-employed workers without employees earn 22% less, whereas the self-employed with over five employees earn 26% more than waged and salaried workers in Spain.

II. CONCEPTUAL AND EMPIRICAL FRAMEWORK

Thus far, insufficient effort has been made to understand the generation and evolution of entrepreneurship. Some of the literature stresses that one feature distinguishing self-employment from waged and salaried work is the degree of risk-taking. Based on this fundamental aspect of self-employment, the risk involved, Knight (1921), Kanbur (1979) and Kihlstrom and Laffont (1979) have built up their models on entrepreneurship. In an aggregate context, Blau (1987) tried to model the relationships between the proportion of self-employment and variables such as relative prices, technology and tax structures.

Using a consumer discrimination framework, Borjas and Bronars (1989) generated some predictions about the distribution of income and proportions of self-employment by ethnic and racial groups Evans and Jovanovic (1989) developed a model of selection into entrepreneurship based on the existence of liquidity constraints. Lucas (1978) takes 'entrepreneurial ability' to explain the choice of self-employ-

ment. Other theories, grounded in psychology and sociology, emphasize motivation and social relations in explaining the creation of small businesses. To date, however, little attention has been paid to the relationship between unemployment and self-employment.[4]

When modelling the selection into self-employment, the typical worker is assumed to compare the expected income from waged or salaried work with the expected income from self-employment. Self-employment is chosen if greater income results (Blau, 1987; Evans and Jovanovic, 1989). A non-rationed supply of labour is implicitly assumed, i.e. there are plenty of jobs at market wages. Under high unemployment, this assumption is unrealistic. Workers who face limited opportunities for obtaining a waged or salaried job have drastically constrained income streams.

Unemployment has two main effects on workers. (1) Specific skills are lost and general human capital deteriorates. Thus, as time out of work lengthens, the probability of getting the desired job diminishes. (2) As a result of joblessness, income is lost. Furthermore, job search is costly and, in a learning environment, the reservation wage declines with job search tenure (Mortensen, 1986; Burdett and Vishwanath, 1988; McCall, 1989). Thus, duration of unemployment becomes a key variable which indicates the difficulties in finding waged or salaried work, along with the financial loss associated with pursuing it. In this context, self-employment, so long as it is endogenously determined, becomes a viable alternative for jobless workers.

Unemployed workers not only learn about the job market (job offers and wage offer distribution), but also obtain information about business opportunities. In the hardship of joblessness, the worker's underlying managerial ability (mix of creativity and boldness) flourishes or is reinforced out of necessity. For those workers who have not decided to employ themselves before experiencing unemployment, self-employment becomes more attractive or acceptable as duration of unemployment is prolonged.

The process would develop as follows. As duration of unemployment lengthens, the decline in the reservation wage reduces the expected wage or salary income. The worker will stop looking for paid work when the expected income from dependent employment falls below the expected income from self-employment. The latter is assumed to be constant over the search period. Nonetheless, it can increase if, as stated earlier, some business opportunities are realized as time passes

The above discussion suggests that, given search costs, an initial reservation wage, managerial ability, business start-up assets and other conditions, some workers become readily self-employed upon leaving or losing their jobs if

[3]Some of the factors which motivate the creation of small businesses are social environment, dissatisfaction with paid work, personality differences, family circumstances, desire for profits, availability of assets, possession of skills and technology, willingness to take risks, or simply the necessity to 'survive' Some of these factors are elusive to an economic analysis, but fortunately some of them are not
[4]See Evans and Leighton (1989) for some evidence

their expected income from self-employment is greater than their expected income from waged or salaried work.[5] Other workers must experience unemployment before they enter self-employment.

It would be expected that in an economy where self-employment is not feasible, joblessness would last for longer periods and more workers would withdraw from the labour force. In other words, economic forces driving workers into self-employment should reduce the duration of unemployment and prevent some workers from dropping out of the labour market. In this context, it can be argued that if the reason for becoming self-employed affects the likelihood that the business will improve over time, the most likely to last and grow are those businesses owned by persons who were selected into self-employment without an intervening spell of unemployment.[6]

Empirical framework

According to the previous discussion, the worker who has left or lost a waged or salaried job decides to become self-employed if the expected self-employment income is higher than the expected wage or salary from a job. When there is a spell of unemployment, expected incomes from both sources are re-evaluated throughout the search period as new information is obtained.

Assume that the expected income from self-employment is M_s and the expected income of waged or salaried work is M_w. Then the choice of self-employment is made upon the sign of the following equation:

$$P^* = M_s - M_w = Z\pi + \varepsilon$$

where P^* expresses the income differential between self-employment and waged or salaried work, Z contains all the variables which affect M_s and M_w, π indicates the reduced-form impact of the personal and economic variables on P^*, and ε is an error term. The term P^* is not observed, but the outcome of the decision process is observed, which is a dichotomous variable P. Assuming normality for ε, the probit model results:

$$P = 1 \quad \text{if } P^* > 0 (\varepsilon > -Z\pi)$$
$$P = 0 \quad \text{if } P^* \leqslant 0 (\varepsilon \leqslant -Z\pi)$$

Since expected income from waged or salaried work depends on the reservation wage, and it is assumed that the latter diminishes with duration of unemployment, the main hypothesis to be tested emerges. Given joblessness, the longer the duration of unemployment, the more likely are workers to enter self-employment. In Z, other demographic and economic characteristics are included that may affect the expected income from either waged or salaried work or self-employment, i.e. gender, marital status, age, education, tenure, reasons for job loss or quitting, and others.

A number of studies have addressed the demographic characteristics of self-employed workers in the United States and the United Kingdom.[7] Most researchers have found that the self-employed person is more likely to be male, married, older and more educated than salaried and waged workers. These four features are associated with two fundamental requirements for starting up a small business: availability of financial resources and managerial skills. However, little research has been done on the relationship between self-employment and unemployment.

III. DATA

The Spanish data used in this study are from the Working and Living Conditions Survey (hereinafter ECVT), a government-sponsored household survey carried out in Spain in the fourth quarter of 1985. Its goal, to assess the importance of the concealed sector in the labour market, together with its size of more than 60 000 interviewees, make the ECVT a nation-wide representative survey with extensive information on the Spanish labour force.

In the ECVT, all workers were asked if they had changed firms at any time in their working life. Those who responded in the affirmative were further questioned about their reason for changing firms, their previous and current job characteristics, and their duration of unemployment. The class of worker (waged or salaried, self-employed or family aid) is known for the previous and the current job.

This work concentrates on workers who have moved from a previous non-agricultural waged or salaried job. Workers who reported that they have never changed firms are excluded from the sample. In the analysis, workers are

---

[5] At times, some waged and salaried workers simultaneously hold self-employment as a secondary job Upon the threat of unemployment or actual displacement, self-employment becomes their only job. In the light of these circumstances, dual job holders tend not to report unemployment Another reason for this might be that they did some job searching while employed

[6] A successful entrepreneur is one whose firm grows. In the context of understanding entrepreneurship as a process of undertaking, innovation and profit maximization, the distinction between the self-employed with and without employees may be relevant In this work, some suggestive differences are found between the self-employed with and those without employees It is observed that the growth of self-employment in Spain corresponds to those business owners without employees Only the self-employed who hire other workers might be considered to be entrepreneurs, or 'undertakers' as expressed by Cantillon (1755). The workers who create their own jobs without hiring other workers are more likely to seek self-employment as a temporary alternative, with the underlying expectation of finding a job as waged or salaried workers at a future time. However, enterprises require lead time to develop. Those who are the sole employees of their companies are prime candidates for becoming successful employers.

[7] See Blanchflower and Meyer (1990), Blanchflower and Oswald (1990), Meyer (1990), Evans and Leighton (1989), Borjas (1986), Rees and Shah (1986), Becker (1984) and Fuchs (1982).

192   *A. Alba-Ramirez*

classified into three groups according to their reasons for moving: workers who quit or voluntarily moved, workers who were displaced from their jobs (individually fired, firm bankruptcy, cutback on work, end of contract), and workers who moved for other reasons (retirement, marriage, birth, military service, other). Workers for whom information on duration of unemployment was missing or who reported more than 120 months out of work were deleted. Also, some observations with missing values for the relevant variables were ruled out. This left 7657 individuals, of whom 20.6% were self-employed.

The US data[8] are from the Displaced Worker Survey (hereinafter DWS), a supplement to the Current Population Survey in 1984, 1986 and 1988. This data set contains ample information regarding workers' previous and current jobs, together with aspects related to the transition period, e.g. duration of unemployment and collection of unemployment insurance.[9] The reasons given for displacement are plant closing, slack work and position or shift abolished. The sample used is composed of white workers aged 20–61 years, who were displaced from non-agricultural waged or salaried full-time jobs.

Due to the impossibility of separating single and multiple spells of unemployment in the 1984 survey, only the 1986 and 1988 surveys are used. After deleting observations for which missing values in relevant variables exist, a limited

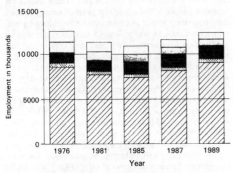

Fig. 1 *Structure and evolution of employment in Spain,* □ *waged or salaried,* ▩ *employers,* ■ *self-employed,* ▤ *self-employed in agriculture,* ▨ *others*

sample of 5282 re-employed workers is obtained. The reported class of worker allows those who hold waged or salaried jobs to be distinguished from those who are self-employed (incorporated as well as unincorporated) at the survey date.

The samples were selected with the sole condition that workers had moved from a previous non-agricultural waged or salaried job. Additional restrictions on the US sample are imposed by the data available. The reason for considering only movers is that the focus of the study is on the transition from waged or salaried work to self-employment. Thus, the results presented here do not apply to all workers. For example, workers who enter self-employment directly from the labour force are not included in this analysis. Moreover, the results on the characteristics of self-employed workers must be interpreted accordingly.

IV. SELF-EMPLOYMENT IN AN ECONOMY OF HIGH UNEMPLOYMENT: SPAIN

Using data taken from the Spanish Labour Force Survey (EPA), Fig. 1 shows the distribution of employment by class of workers for various years. The approximately 1.8 million decline in the number of jobs from 1976 to 1985 was almost recovered in the following 4 years. The evolution of the number of waged and salaried workers and the number of self-employed with employees (employers) reflects the general trend in employment. The number of employers decreased by 20% from 1976 to 1985, and grew by 24% during the following 4 years. However, the number of self-employed workers without employees grew from 1976 to 1989. The rate of increase was 5.1% from 1976 to 1981, 11.8% from 1981 to 1985, 7.5% from 1985 to 1987, and stabilized in the following 2 years. As the graph indicates, the fall in employment was much lower in the second phase of the economic recession (1981–1985). At the end of 1985, the unemployment rate reached 22% and the mass of displaced workers had little chance to escape unemployment.[10]

Table 1 reflects the proportions of self-employment by current job tenure in the ECVT sample used.[11] The table illustrates the flow of workers into self-employment, conditional on their being employed at the survey date.[12] Among previously waged or salaried workers who entered employment in 1980 or before and remained employed at the end of 1985, 21% were currently self-employed and about 16%

[8]I am grateful to Lawrence Katz for kindly providing extracts from the Displaced Worker Supplement.
[9]The absence of wage information for self-employed workers is an unfortunate feature of these data.
[10]See Alba-Ramirez and Freeman (1990) for an analysis of the duration of unemployment among displaced workers in Spain
[11]No differences were observed in the results when the sample was weighted.
[12]It should be kept in mind that, since the present sample is a cross-section of workers, those self-employed in the survey are workers who have remained so after entering self-employment

Table 1. *Current class of workers by year of entry, conditional on being employed*

Period	Frequency (row percentage) [column percentage]			
	Waged–salaried workers	Self-employment with employees	Self-employment without employees	Total
≤ 1980	3690 (79 49) [60 69]	214 (4.61) [69 03]	738 (15 90) [58.25]	4642 (100.00) [60.62]
1981–83	856 (74.43) [14.08]	51 (4.43) [16.45]	243 (21.13) [19.18]	1150 (100 00) [15.02]
1984	406 (74.77) [6.68]	14 (2.58) [4.52]	123 (22.65) [9.71]	543 (100.00) [7.09]
1985	1128 (85.33) [18 55]	31 (2.34) [10.00]	163 (12.33) [12.87]	1322 (100.00) [17.27]
Total	6080 (79 40) [100.00]	310 (4.05) [100.00]	1267 (16.55) [100.00]	7657 (100.00) [100.00]

Note· The sample is composed of workers who have moved from a previous non-agricultural waged or salaried job
Source: ECVT

were self-employed without employees. Among those who began their jobs between 1981 and 1984, the proportion of self-employed workers increased. However, Table 1 shows a substantially reduced probability of shifting to self-employment among those workers who started their new job in 1985. As previously noted, in 1985 employment began to recover in Spain. It seems that the evolution of self-employed workers without employees in Spain was counter-cyclical in the late 1970s and throughout the 1980s, whereas evolution of the Spanish self-employed with employees in the same period was pro-cyclical.

Self employment and duration of unemployment

In analysing the relationship between self-employment and unemployment in this article, some limitations with regard to the data used should be highlighted. First, when considering the transition of waged and salaried workers to self-employment, it is not possible to separate the probabilities of a worker's switch to and permanence in self-employment. Current job tenure will be used to partly control for this. Second, the data provide the last firm change of each worker. Although the numbers of times workers have changed firms are known, there is no information on whether or not those workers who have changed more than once have had

previous self-employment experience. The regressions used control for the number of firm changes. Third, during the recession period, it was a frequent practice among Spanish firms to convert waged and salaried workers into independent contractors, a form of self-employment, in order to lower costs and enhance productivity. Because it is presumed that a change in the class of a worker results from a change of firm, the likelihood of reported change in the class of a worker being due to contract conversion is reduced.[13]

In the following probit regressions on the probability of entering self-employment, the dependent variable is 1 if the previously waged or salaried worker shifted to self-employment and remained in that situation, and 0 otherwise. Table 2 shows that males, married women, older people, the less educated and workers with longer tenure in their previous job are more likely to have become self-employed. The result for older workers is well-known (Fuchs, 1982). The result for education may indicate that in an economy of high unemployment, the less educated, and hence the less competitive, workers regard self-employment as an alternative to scarce paid work.

Furthermore, it is found that, consistent with Fig. 1 and Table 1, the probability of being self-employed is higher among workers with five or fewer years of tenure in their current job. One reason for this may be that employment spells of self-employed workers are shorter than those of

[13]Note however, that some of the workers who have changed firms might have changed their worker class in the current job.

194   *A. Alba-Ramirez*

Table 2 *Probit regressions on the probability of entering self-employment among workers with a wage or salary in their previous job.*

	Coefficient		
Variable[1]	All workers	Males	Females
Constant	−2.5359 (−9.79)	−2 0391 (−6 73)	−3.4064 (−6.52)
Male	0.3224 (7.37)		
Married	0.0817 (1.87)	−0.0605 (−1.14)	0.3145 (3.86)
Age	0.0519 (4.45)	0.0468 (3.42)	−0.0774 (3.22)
Age[2]	−0 0005 (−3.55)	−0 0004 (−2.61)	−0.0007 (−2.70)
Age ≥65	0.8859 (4.76)	1.1025 (4.58)	0.8840 (2.57)
Education=6	0.0436 (0.98)	0 0137 (0.27)	0 1665 (1.63)
Education=8	−0.0483 (−0.85)	−0.0785 (−1 22)	0 1126 (0.91)
Education=12	−0 0680 (−1.17)	−0.1104 (−1.69)	0 1300 (1 01)
Education=15	−0.1546 (−1 94)	−0.2227 (−2.33)	0.0329 (0 21)
Education=17	−0.2611 (−3 15)	−0.3685 (−3 79)	0.0724 (0.44)
Tenure	0.0272 (3 97)	0.0290 (3 84)	0.0267 (1.48)
Tenure[2]	−0.0005 (−2.24)	−0 0005 (−1.95)	−0.0010 (−1.36)
Senior <1	0.1643 (−2.87)	0.1066 (1.56)	0 2596 (2.42)
Senior 1–2	0.4685 (6.82)	0.4266 (5.24)	0.5697 (4 37)
Senior 2–5	0 4124 (8.16)	0.4174 (7.06)	0 4173 (4.19)
Region ur	−0 0100 (−3.05)	−0.0104 (−2.82)	−0.0067 (−0.91)
Duration=0	0.3298 (7.10)	0.3084 (5.68)	0.3750 (3.85)
Months unemployed	0.0068 (6.09)	0 0062 (3.68)	0.0063 (3.90)
Jobchange=1	0 1818 (3.57)	0 1474 (2.49)	0.2989 (2.80)
Jobchange=2	−0.0041 (−0.09)	−0.0562 (−1.07)	0.1842 (1 78)
Jobchange=3	−0 0159 (0.33)	−0.0177 (−0.33)	0.0329 (0 28)
Quit	−0 1481 (−3.08)	−0.0447 (−0.73)	−0.2671 (−3.19)
Displaced	−0 1544 (−2.84)	−0 0545 (−0.82)	−0.3374 (−3.02)
Log Likelihood	−3664.6	−2850.2	−788.84
$\hat{P}$	0.206	0 225	0 153
N	7657	5613	2044

Note: The *t*-statistics are presented in parentheses.
Source: Spain and ECVT.
[1] For a full explanation of these terms see appendix Table A1.

waged and salaried workers.[14] An alternative explanation is that from 1981 to 1985, when unemployment soared in Spain, many workers found self-employment to be the only escape from their joblessness.

As suggested before, this hypothesis is tested by relating duration of unemployment to the probability of current self-employment among previously waged and salaried workers. Fifty-seven per cent of workers in the sample did not experience unemployment after leaving or losing their previous job. In the probit regression, one can control for this circumstance by adding a dummy variable.

Column 1 of Table 2 indicates that the dummy for workers without an intervening spell of unemployment has a mean effect of 0.22 on the probability of shifting to self-employment.[15] However, given a spell of unemployment, the longer the duration of such a spell, the more likely workers are to become self-employed; a month out of work translates to a 0.45 percentage point increase in the probability of becoming and remaining self-employed.[16] These results hold true for males and females, although the marginal probabilities are higher for the latter. Furthermore, we find that a one-point increase in unemployment rates across

[14] Using the ECVT, there are several ways to shed some light on this possible explanation First, by examining workers who have changed firms, the average duration of the previous job for workers in a prior waged or salaried job (5 5 years) is compared, with that of those previously self-employed (10.6 years) Second, the precentage of currently waged or salaried workers who have never changed firms (38.5%) is compared with that of their self-employed counterparts (40.7%). One should keep in mind that, depending on the business cycle, the probability of remaining self-employed may change over time. Moreover, the probability of both entering and remaining self-employed helps to explain workers' selection into self-employment.
[15] The mean effect on the probability of a unit change in the independent variable is calculated as the coefficient estimates of the probit regression times the mean value for the sample of the standard normal density function evaluated at $Z\pi$.
[16] For a clearer perspective on the probability of entering self-employment, only workers who have been in their current job for less than a year were considered. Both variables, dummy for absence of unemployment and duration of unemployment, resulted in positive and significant coefficients.

regions significantly lessens the probability of self-employment among males by 0.6 percentage points.[17] This result turns out to be true only for voluntary movers, as will be seen later. It indicates that a depressed local labour market offers less incentive for workers to voluntarily shift to self-employment.

The reason for moving[18] offers insight into the relationship between unemployment and self-employment, and highlights the role of other variables in explaining self-employment. According to reasons for moving from the previous waged or salaried job,[19] Table 3 presents the results of the probit regressions for the probabilities of becoming and remaining self-employed. The dummy for workers who have not experienced unemployment is always significant. However, duration of unemployment is not significant where other reasons for moving apply. The increase in the

Table 3   *Probit regressions on the probability of entering self-employment among workers with a wage or salary in their previous job.*

	Coefficient		
Variable[1]	Displaced	Voluntary movers	Other reason for moving
Constant	−3.2485 (−7.01)	−2.6597 (−7.00)	−2 9684 (−4.80)
Male	0.5203 (5.43)	0 4142 (6.53)	0.3415 (2 81)
Married	0.0266 (0.34)	0.0977 (1 55)	0.0587 (0.53)
Age	0 0704 (3.28)	0.0522 (3.06)	0.0633 (2.27)
Age²	−0.0007 (−2 97)	−0 0004 (−2 17)	−0.0006 (−2 05)
Age ⩾65	0.7298 (1.46)	1 0830 (3 98)	0.6333 (1 79)
Education = 6	0 1885 (2.22)	−0.0075 (−0.12)	−0.0257 (−0.24)
Education = 8	0 0232 (0 21)	−0.0806 (−1.01)	−0 0186 (−0.14)
Education = 12	0 2297 (2.14)	−0 1920 (−2.38)	−0.2202 (−1.50)
Education = 15	0.2146 (1.37)	−0.2037 (−1.95)	−0.4736 (−2 12)
Education = 17	−0.1670 (−0 93)	−0.3095 (−2 89)	−0.3070 (−1 45)
Tenure	−0.0029 (−0.21)	0.0399 (3.79)	0.0240 (1.49)
Tenure²	0.0002 (0 45)	−0.0008 (−2.04)	−0.0006 (−1.18)
Senior < 1	−0.0315 (−0.35)	0.3770 (3.95)	0 0710 (0.54)
Senior 1–2	0 3745 (3 48)	0 6069 (5.37)	0.2023 (1 27)
Senior 2–5	0.2499 (2.77)	0 5771 (8 06)	0.2609 (2 04)
Region ur	−0.0040 (−0.69)	−0.0170 (−3.67)	−0 0005 (−0.06)
Duration = 0	0.5111 (6.41)	0.1470 (2 14)	0.4566 (4.16)
Months unemployed	0 0099 (4.98)	0 0072 (3.75)	0.0032 (1 59)
Jobchange = 1	0 1494 (1 44)	0.2123 (3.06)	0.2332 (1 93)
Jobchange = 2	−0.0066 (−0 07)	−0 0247 (−0 39)	0.1419 (1 24)
Jobchange = 3	0.0298 (0.34)	−0 0225 (−0 34)	0 0294 (0.24)
Fired	0 0843 (0 89)		
Bankrupt	−0.0624 (−0.72)		
Cutback	0.2546 (2.09)		
Retired			0.9108 (2.95)
To marry or give birth			0 4167 (3.44)
Military			−0.1089 (−0.81)
Log Likelihood	−1033.0	−1925.4	−635 5
P̂	0.183	0.208	0 243
N̄	2330	4037	1240

Note: The *t*-statistics are presented in parentheses.
Source: Spain and ECVT
[1]For a full explanation of these terms see appendix Tables A1&2.

---

[17]Since the regional structure of unemployment has not significantly changed in Spain, the regional unemployment rate in 1985 is used
[18]The very significant negative coefficients of the dummies representing reasons for moving among females in Table 2 are due to the fact that the omitted reasons, moving because of marriage, giving birth or retirement, notably increase the probability of self-employment. See Goffe and Scase (1986) for an analysis of the married woman and self-employment
[19]The duration of the current job varies across reasons given for leaving the previous one. For example, the proportion of workers who have been in the current job for less than 5 years is 60% among displaced workers, 26% among voluntary movers, and 40% among those who responded with other reasons for moving. The reason for moving from and into a job is closely related to the business cycle. Also, the probabilities of permanency in self-employment are likely to depend upon the underlying motive for becoming so.

probability of entering self-employment after a month of unemployment is 0.77 percentage points among displaced workers and 0.51 percentage points among voluntary movers from a previous job, though the majority of voluntary movers, 75%, did not experience unemployment. A possible reason for observing unemployment among some of the workers who moved voluntarily may be that they made a mistake in assessing their work prospects.

Some other remarkable results are found. Variables for tenure in the previous job, one firm change and regional unemployment rate are significant only for voluntary movers. Those displaced workers who lost their jobs because of cutback on work are more likely to become self-employed. Among those who gave other reasons for change, it is observed that workers who left due to retirement, marriage or birth have a higher probability of self-employment.[20]

The former results indicate that, after controlling for workers who did not suffer unemployment, the duration of unemployment significantly increases the probability of becoming and remaining self-employed. This probability is enhanced when only self-employed workers without employees are considered.[21]

Although setting up a business takes time, it is unlikely that workers who decide to become self-employed soon after displacement will report the time spent setting up the business as time unemployed. In this respect, the question of the duration of unemployment was formulated in fairly clear terms: 'After leaving this job, how long did you spend (or are you) out of work and actively looking for a job?'

Three issues should be addressed at this point.

(1) *The selection bias.* Throughout this work only workers who were re-employed at the survey date were considered. Since those still unemployed are more likely to have a longer unemployment duration, this probably means that the transition rate into self-employment is understated. A way to deal with this problem, not undertaken in this work, consists of using duration models where there are three possible outcomes: unemployment, dependent employment and self-employment. The results shown in this article suggest an increasing hazard rate for self-employed workers.

(2) *Endogeneity problems are apparent.* Is duration an endogenous variable? We argued previously that according to the standard job search model, self-employment reduces the average duration of unemployment. The reason for the reduction is that some workers stop job-searching when self-employment becomes more profitable than to continue searching. That can be interpreted as meaning that the shorter duration of unemployment is determined by the decision to become self-employed. However, it is the time

out of work that makes the expected income from waged or salaried work go down and the entry into self-employment a reasonable decision. Thus, it seems plausible to use unemployment duration as an exogenous variable in explaining the decision to become self-employed.

(3) *Unobserved heterogeneity.* It is always possible that all the sources of heterogeneity were not identified in the present sample. The fact that self-employed workers are more likely to have avoided unemployment after job loss indicated that the positive relationship observed between self-employment and duration of unemployment cannot be caused solely by heterogeneity. In other words, self-employed workers are not necessarily those least able workers whose only alternative is to employ themselves. They become self-employed as a result of an efficient choice made under some exogenous conditions, e.g. scarcity of paid work.

For the sake of robust results, the next section examines the relationship between unemployment and self-employment in the United States.

V. SELF-EMPLOYMENT AMONG DISPLACED WORKERS IN THE UNITED STATES

The United States is one of the OECD countries where self-employment has grown the most in the last 15 years. On the other hand, the US proportion of self-employment is less than half the proportion of self-employment in Spain. How the duration of unemployment affects self-employment in the US as compared to the Spanish economy was tested. Differences between labour market institutions in both countries make this comparison very enlightening.

Table 4 reports the results of probit regressions for the probability of entry and permanence in self-employment among displaced workers in the United States. The sample is restricted to white workers, between 20 and 61 years of age, displaced from waged and salaried jobs during the period 1981–1987, who worked full-time in the non-agricultural sector. After deleting some observations with missing values for some variables, a sample of 5282 individuals is left, of whom 8.16% had become and remained self-employed as of the survey dates (1986 and 1988). Self-employed US workers are more likely to be males, older people, residents of the mountain or Pacific regions, non-collectors of unemployment insurance, sufferers of longer duration of unemployment, holders of fewer jobs after displacement, higher earners in the previous job, and non-participants in a group health insurance plan.

---

[20]The probit regressions were run according to occupation in the previous job. The sample was broken down into three categories of workers: skilled labourers, unskilled labourers and others. No change was observed in the results indicated earlier.
[21]We have insufficient data to answer the question of how much of the increase in self-employment is accounted for by the increase in unemployment duration in Spain.

Table 4. *Probit regressions on the probability of entering self-employment among displaced workers in the US.*

Variable[1]	Coefficient			
		Have held only one job since displacement		
	Entire Sample	All workers	Males	Females
Constant	−4 3610 (−9.32)	−4.7615 (−7.82)	−4 5734 (−6.36)	−4.8893 (−3 76)
Male	0.1654 (2 62)	0.2156 (2 65)		
Married	0.1134 (1.83)	0.0969 (1.19)	0.0287 (0.28)	0.2133 (1.39)
Age	0.0538 (2.58)	0.0640 (2.37)	0.0698 (2.18)	0.0597 (1 06)
Age^2	−0.0005 (−2 30)	−0 0007 (−2.28)	−0.0007 (−1.97)	−0.0008 (−1.19)
Education = 13	0.0075 (0.11)	0.0183 (−0.21)	0.0323 (0.31)	−0.2349 (−1 27)
Education = 14	−0.1561 (−1.57)	−0.3212 (−2.32)	−0.3748 (−2.24)	−0.2927 (−1.09)
Education = 15	−0.0550 (−0.51)	−0.0316 (−0 23)	−0.0352 (−0.22)	−0.0434 (−0 1,5)
Education = 16	0.1179 (1 17)	0.0691 (−0.55)	−0 1630 (−1 05)	0 6056 (2 51)
Education ⩾ 17	0.0519 (0.58)	−0.0027 (−0.02)	−0.0204 (−0.15)	0 0365 (0.13)
Slack	0 0566 (0.96)	0.0242 (0 31)	−0.0111 (−0.12)	0.1119 (0.65)
Abolish	0 1161 (1.53)	0.1649 (1.72)	0.0627 (0.53)	0.3261 (1 86)
Tenure	0.0079 (0.65)	0 0263 (1.72)	0.0125 (0.73)	0 1172 (2.55)
Tenure^2	−0.0005 (−1 25)	−0.0011 (−1.97)	−0 0007 (−1 23)	−0.0053 (−2 15)
Y displaced >83	−0.0522 (−0.89)	−0.0058 (−0.07)	0.1039 (1.13)	−0 3333 (−2 09)
Region 2	0.0517 (0.63)	0.1294 (1.26)	0 1259 (1 08)	0 2352 (0.98)
Region 3	0 1282 (1 64)	0.1840 (1.86)	0.1595 (1 41)	0.3446 (1.52)
Region 4	0 2196 (2 73)	0.2809 (2.71)	0.1592 (1.31)	0.6561 (2.93)
Moved	−0.0774 (−1 19)	−0.1348 (−1 46)	−0.0832 (−0.82)	−0 3542 (−1 40)
Advnotice	0.0641 (1 22)	0.0688 (1 01)	0.0772 (0 97)	0.0300 (0 21)
Collected UI	−0 1586 (−2.57)	−0.1159 (−1.46)	−0.1902 (−2.09)	0 0739 (0.41)
Duration = 0	0.0054 (0.06)	0.0737 (0 75)	−0.0107 (−0.09)	0.3120 (1.52)
Weeks unemployed	0.0029 (2.47)	0.0036 (2.34)	0.0038 (2.02)	0.0027 (0 88)
No of jobs	−0.0744 (−2 80)			
Log wage	0.2765 (4 82)	0 2787 (3.73)	0 2728 (3 18)	0.2715 (1.67)
Not covered	0.1741 (2.69)	0 2619 (3 11)	0.2742 (2 73)	0.2057 (1.26)
Log Likelihood	−1423 8	−875 7	−650.7	−206.3
$\hat{P}$	0.0816	0 0938	0.1086	0 0645
N	5282	2963	1971	992

Note: The sample is composed of white workers who were displaced from full-time non-agricultural waged and salaried jobs.
The *t*-statistics are presented in parentheses.
Source: Displaced workers survey 1986–88.
[1]For a full explanation of these terms see Appendix Table A2.

Analysis of workers who had held only one job after displacement showed no substantial change. However, some differences emerged when comparing probit regressions by gender. Women are more likely to be self-employed if they were college-educated, had longer tenure in the previous job, were displaced in 1983 or before, and lived in the mountain or Pacific regions. The variable duration of unemployment does not significantly affect displaced women's probability of becoming self-employed in the United States.

Contrary to the results for Spain, US workers who did not experience unemployment are not more likely to be self-employed after displacement. Nonetheless, according to column 2 of Table 4, 1 week out of work significantly raises the probability of becoming and remaining self-employed by 0.46 percentage points. Recall that a month of unemployment increases the probability of self-employment by 0.77

percentage points among displaced workers in Spain. However, because the data sets are not identical, it is difficult to compare the degree to which unemployment duration affects self-employment in Spain and the United States. Also, the incidence and evolution of unemployment duration and self-employment differ in both countries.

With these limitations in mind, it is nevertheless possible to sense how differently duration of unemployment affects self-employment in Spain and United States. To achieve that, displaced workers who have experienced unemployment are considered. The specifications in column 1 of Table 3 for Spain, and in column 2 of Table 4 for the United States were used. To avoid the effect of the measurement unit for unemployment duration in both countries, the logarithm of duration was taken. It was found that a 1% increase in unemployment duration raises the probability of self-

Table 5. *The job quality by class of worker in Spain*

	All workers	Waged and salaried	Self-employment with employees	Self-employment without employees
	Percentage of workers in each category			
Part-time workers	18.40	17.78	7.42	24.07
Looking for work	5.22	4.98	1 94	7.18
Holding another job	21.25	20.63	11 94	26 52
No social security	15 31	14.11	9 35	22.49
Number	7657	6080	310	1267

Source. ECVT

Table 6. *Probit regressions on job quality among Spanish self-employed males*

Dependent variable[1]	Coefficient			
	Part-time work = 1	Looking for work = 1	Holding another job = 1	No social security = 1
Constant	1 4911 (2 34)	−0 9595 (−1 10)	0.9929 (1 64)	1 3264 (2.00)
Married	−0 2249 (−1 96)	0 1808 (1 11)	0.1178 (1 04)	−0.3511 (−3.01)
Age	−0 0986 (−3 58)	−0.0100 (−0.25)	−0.0829 (−3 13)	−0.0971 (−3.40)
Age²	0.0011 (3 79)	−0.0000 (−0.00)	0.0009 (3.31)	0.0010 (3.48)
Education = 6	−0 2824 (−2.55)	−0 2565 (−1.68)	−0.0602 (−0 57)	−0 3014 (−2.40)
Education = 8	−0 3467 (−2.21)	−0 0388 (−0 20)	0.1278 (0 93)	−0 0348 (−0 22)
Education = 12	−0 5103 (−3.03)	−0 1493 (−0.73)	−0.0895 (−0 60)	−0.1291 (−0.77)
Education = 15	0 0292 (0.13)	0 1632 (0.59)	0.1824 (0 86)	−0 0221 (−0.09)
Education = 17	−0 2096 (−0 84)	−0.5883 (−1 26)	0.5089 (2.44)	0.7079 (3 34)
Tenure	−0.0366 (−2 31)	−0.0226 (−1 02)	−0.0373 (−2 54)	−0.0404 (−2.32)
Tenure²	0.0011 (2.31)	0.0006 (0.95)	0 0010 (2.28)	0.0010 (1 85)
Senior < 1	0 4005 (2.66)	0 1836 (0.97)	0.3349 (2.33)	0 3710 (2 35)
Senior 1–2	0 0538 (0 31)	0 0317 (0 14)	−0 0021 (−0.01)	0.1719 (0 96)
Senior 2–5	0 0246 (0.18)	−0 0658 (−0.38)	0 0589 (0 49)	0 0733 (0.53)
Region ur	0.0064 (0.78)	−0.0009 (−0 09)	−0.0019 (−0 24)	−0.0008 (−0.09)
Duration = 0	−0.2709 (−2.18)	−0 3040 (−1 90)	−0.1667 (−1.43)	−0.0547 (−0.41)
Months unemployed	0.0073 (2.16)	0 0069 (1.72)	0 0069 (2 07)	0 0094 (2 57)
Self with e	−0.5382 (−3 93)	−0.4866 (−2.52)	−0 4484 (−3 89)	−0 3414 (−2 52)
Displaced	0.1317 (1 28)	0.2449 (1.84)	0 2149 (2.24)	0 0752 (0 68)
Jobchange = 1	−0 1826 (−1.44)	−0 0751 (−1 10)	−0.1036 (−0.92)	−0 0154 (−0.12)
Log likelihood	−512.3	−272.1	−618.8	−442.1
$\hat{P}$	0.176	0.065	0.223	0.138
N	1264	1264	1264	1264

Note· The *t*-statistics are presented in parentheses
Source: ECVT.
[1]For a full explanation of these terms see Appendix Table A1

employment by 0.15 percentage points in the US and by 0.17 percentage points in Spain.[22] Since the probability of becoming self-employed is twice as high in Spain as it is in the US, one can conclude that unemployment duration has a relatively stronger effect on the probability of becoming

self-employed in the United States as compared with Spain.

The results shown in Table 4 merit some additional comments. It was observed that among displaced workers in the United States, previously high wage earners are more

[22]The probit coefficients (SD) and the mean of the standard normal density function were 0.104 (0.034) and 1.447, respectively, for the US and 0.186 (0.036) and 0.906, respectively, for Spain.

Self-employment in the midst of unemployment

likely to become and remain self-employed.[23] This result seems inconsistent with those obtained by Evans and Leighton (1989), and Evans and Jovanovic (1989), using the National Longitudinal Survey of Young Men (NLS). They found that workers selected into self-employment are relatively poorer wage earners. Nevertheless, their findings and the one reported here may not be incompatible if few NLS workers who shifted to self-employment did so in the aftermath of displacement. The reason is that it is unusual to find voluntary job separations among relatively higher paid workers. If the job is exogenously terminated, more specific human capital, higher reservation wage, more assets and higher managerial experience should be associated with higher paid workers.

VI. JOB QUALITY OF SELF-EMPLOYED WORKERS

The significant relationship between self-employment and unemployment suggests that the jobs which workers have created for themselves should be lower in quality than the jobs obtained by workers who remain waged or salaried. As indicators of the quality of the job obtained, the incidence of the following situations is taken: occasional or regular part-time work, search for another job, more than one job held, lack of social security coverage. Table 5 shows that in Spain, self-employed workers without employees are more likely to be in all these categories than are waged and salaried workers In the case of the US, the self-employed are more

Table 7 *Probit regressions on job quality among US males*

	Coefficient			
	Part-time work = 1		not covered by any group health insurance plan in current job = 1	
Dependent variable[1]	Self employed	Waged and salaried	Self-employed	Waged and salaried
Constant	0 6718 (0 41)	0.4692 (0 86)	1.7050 (1 16)	0 0303 (0 06)
Married	−0 3958 (−1 78)	−0.2758 (−3 78)	−0.3461 (−1 70)	−0.3245 (−5.48)
Age	0.0311 (0 43)	−0 0479 (−1.93)	0 0178 (0 27)	0.0087 (0.42)
Age²	−0.0002 (−0 27)	0 0006 (1.94)	−0 0003 (−0.42)	−0.0001 (−0.51)
Education = 13	−0.4865 (−2 09)	0.0636 (0.75)	−0 3254 (−1.60)	−0.0310 (−0.47)
Education = 14	−0.1844 (−0.52)	0 0289 (0.24)	−0.1856 (−0.63)	−0 2908 (−3 07)
Education = 15	−0.0312 (−0.09)	0.0501 (0 37)	−0 7152 (−2.24)	−0 2457 (−2 29)
Education = 16	−0.6837 (−1.90)	−0.1214 (−0 78)	−0 6106 (−2 06)	−0 2893 (−2.55)
Education ⩾ = 17	−0.4953 (−1.73)	0 1679 (1.41)	−0.3609 (−1 47)	−0 3806 (−3 78)
Slack	−0.3259 (−1.65)	0 0406 (0.56)	−0 0454 (−0 27)	0 0943 (1 66)
Abolish	0.1411 (0 54)	−0 0778 (−0.72)	−0 2920 (−1 26)	−0 1985 (−2.30)
Tenure	−0.1010 (−2 56)	−0 0211 (−1 47)	0.0605 (1.68)	−0.0112 (−0.89)
Tenure²	0.0030 (2 15)	0 0013 (2.85)	−0 0028 (−2.02)	−0.0001 (−0 31)
Y displaced > 83	0.1403 (0.71)	0.2113 (2 76)	−0 0952 (−0 56)	0.3825 (6 33)
Region 2	−0.0908 (−0 32)	0 1959 (1 91)	0.3778 (1 57)	0 2113 (2 59)
Region 3	−0 0496 (−0 18)	0.1103 (1 05)	0 9734 (4 22)	0 3583 (4 48)
Region 4	0 3618 (1 34)	0 3591 (3 42)	0 6113 (2 58)	0 4211 (5.06)
Moved	−0.4224 (−1 86)	−0.0227 (−0 29)	−0 0045 (−0 02)	0 1037 (1.72)
Advnotice	0.2244 (1 26)	−0.1113 (−1.70)	0 1268 (0 81)	−0 1399 (−2.69)
Collected UI	−0.0352 (−0 18)	−0.1356 (−1.74)	−0 2696 (−1 59)	−0.0522 (−0.84)
Duration = 0	−0.2866 (−1 06)	−0.1032 (−0.94)	−0.2132 (−0.97)	−0.0685 (−0.81)
Weeks unemployed	0.0107 (2.80)	0.0073 (5.04)	0.0083 (2.28)	0.0045 (3 67)
No of jobs	0.0356 (0.43)	0.0733 (2.53)	0.0683 (0.89)	0.1360 (5 89)
Log wage	−0.2968 (−1.57)	−0 2218 (−3 25)	−0.3277 (−2 01)	−0 2296 (−4 08)
Not covered	0.0711 (0 34)	0 2663 (3.35)	0 3190 (1 68)	0 4864 (7 77)
Log likelihood	−144 9	−910.7	−195 7	−1573 7
P̄	0.205	0.093	0 554	0.252
N	332	3209	332	3209

Note: The *t*-statistics are presented in parentheses.
Source: 1986–1988 DWS
[1] For a full explanation of these terms see Appendix Table A2.

[23] Unfortunately, the Spanish data do not contain information on earnings in the previous job.

likely to be part-timers and to lack coverage by a group insurance plan. Although this analysis is useful in assessing the quality of jobs, it is limited in that it does not take into account a number of factors which are likely to influence job satisfaction among self-employed workers, e.g. independence, flexibility and expectations of business improvement over time.

In the framework provided by our initial discussion, the positive effect of duration on self-employment implies that the longer the unemployment duration, the worse is the job match for re-employed workers.[24] Results in Tables 6 and 7 confirm our hypothesis in this regard for both Spain and

Table 8 *OLS estimates of earning equations for self-employed and waged or salaried workers. Full-time male workers (Dependent variables: log net monthly earnings)*

	All workers	Self-employed		Waged and salaried	
Head	0.1225	0.2455	0 2346	0.1002	0.0981
	(5.62)	(3.94)	(3.77)	(4.36)	(4 29)
Experience	0.0217	0.0177	0.0184	0.0207	0 0208
	(8 75)	(2 23)	(2 33)	(7 82)	(7 86)
Experience^2	−0 0003	−0 0003	−0 0003	−0 0003	−0.0003
	(−8.40)	(−3 00)	(−3 10)	(−6.88)	(−6 95)
Education = 6	0 1111	0 1506	0.1522	0 1100	0 1066
	(6 48)	(3.25)	(3.30)	(6 04)	(5.87)
Education = 8	0 2239	0 2493	0.2526	0 2260	0.2248
	(10 24)	(4 00)	(4 07)	(9 87)	(9.84)
Education = 12	0.4167	0.4239	0 4196	0 4230	0 4198
	(17.50)	(5.97)	(5.94)	(17.12)	(17.02)
Education = 15	0.7106	0.6229	0.6082	0.7304	0.7265
	(22 17)	(5.85)	(5.73)	(22.33)	(22.25)
Education = 17	0.8600	0 9889	0 9744	0.8500	0 8465
	(25.74)	(9.28)	(9 19)	(24.79)	(24.69)
Senior 1–2	0.0108	0.0088	−0.0061	0.0008	−0 0001
	(0 35)	(0.10)	(−0.07)	(0.02)	(−0.00)
Senior 2–5	0 0446	0.0467	0.0296	0 0401	0 0353
	(1 76)	(0.63)	(0.40)	(1 51)	(1 33)
Senior >5	0.0904	0 0444	−0.0023	0.1100	0.0930
	(4 01)	(0 64)	(−0.03)	(4.69)	(3.93)
Quit	0 0600	0 1465	0.1381	0.0435	0.0236
	(3 07)	(2 72)	(2 58)	(2.10)	(1 12)
Displaced	−0 0581	−0.0114	0 0217	−0 0702	−0 0616
	(−2 71)	(−0.19)	(0 35)	(−3 12)	(−2 71)
Self w/e	−0.2168				
	(−12.02)				
Self 1–5e	0.0199				
	(0.61)				
Self >5e	0.2640				
	(4.29)				
Duration = 0			0.0803		0 0442
			(1.42)		(2.48)
Months unemployed			−0.0027		−0 0016
			(−1.41)		(−2.46)
Lambda		0.0597	0 1020		
		(0 51)	(0.86)		
Constant	10 28	9 94	9.89	10.32	10.32
	(189.9)	(47.3)	(44.8)	(183 9)	(182.2)
Adjusted R^2	0.329	0.230	0.238	0.336	0.341
N	4340	823	823	3517	3517

Note: The *t*-statistics are presented in parentheses
All equations include eight dummies for sectors of the previous job
Source: Spain and ECVT

[24]Unemployment duration makes workers accept less desirable jobs. The finding that the longer unemployed are more likely to become self-employed suggests that if self-employment is not an option, less desirable working conditions would be observed among long-term unemployed workers who find a job

the United States. Other results indicate that in Spain, younger workers, self-employed workers without employees, and workers with shorter tenure in both the previous and the current job are more likely to have a poorer job match.

Self-employment and earnings in Spain

For comparable workers, earnings provide the best index of job 'quality' relative to pecuniary measures. Table 8 contains the results of estimated earnings equations for Spain. Only males in full-time jobs were considered.[25] Generally, Spanish self-employed workers earn less than their waged and salaried counterparts. When the self-employed are split according to the size of the firm, remarkable results are obtained: self-employed workers without employees earn about 22% less than waged and salaried workers. Self-employed workers with fewer than six employees do not earn significantly more than waged and salaried workers. Those who have over six employees earn 26% more than waged and salaried workers. When wage equations are estimated for self-employed and waged and salaried workers, some additional results are worthy of mention. General experience and tenure in the current job are better compensated in the wage and salary sector. This result is consistent with the Lazear and Moore (1984) finding that the self-employed have flatter age–earning profiles. The selection bias correction through the inverse Mills ratio turns out to be insignificant and has little effect on the results. When the variable duration is included in the earnings equations, its negative effect is significant among waged and salaried workers and is insignificant among self-employed workers.

VII. CONCLUSION

The objective of this work has been to analyse empirically the effects of unemployment on the selection into self-employment. In this discussion, self-employment was considered to be a plausible outcome of the job search process, suggesting that long-term unemployed workers were more likely to enter self-employment. For both Spain and the United States, it was found that duration of unemployment

significantly affects a worker's decision to become self-employed. Further inquiry into the kinds of jobs held by self-employed workers showed that those jobs have undesirable characteristics: part-time as opposed to full-time work, absence of social security coverage and other circumstances. At the same time, it was found that in Spain, most self-employed workers are the only employees of their firms, earning significantly less income than comparable waged and salaried workers.

These findings suggest several self-employment issues which call for future research. First, it is necessary to investigate whether self-employment stemming from unemployment solves or disguises joblessness. Second, the formation and evolution of small firms created by unemployed workers should be studied in order to gain a better understanding of entrepreneurship as it relates to unemployment. Unemployment can be a catalyst for talented entrepreneurs who otherwise would not have decided to take the risk associated with creating a business. Third, one needs to study earnings prior to self-employment, income obtained from self-employment and receipt of unemployment benefit, so as to shed more light on the worker's decision to become self-employed.

What policy implications can be derived from these findings? To provide clear policy recommendations, more probing analyses are necessary. The present finding that small businesses grow in economic downturns may indicate that self-employment represents a viable solution to workers' unemployment problems. More importantly, small businesses can greatly contribute to economic growth and the continuous generation of new jobs.[26] However, the relatively poorer job quality of self-employment casts doubt on the efficacy of a public policy that fosters self-employment.

It can be argued that public incentives for self-employment reduces the selection into self-employment and, therefore, increases businesses' failure rates. The opposite argument would defend public assistance in preventing business failure. A way to reconcile both positions may be to give public support only to already established businesses.[27]

While this research has provided some insight into the understanding of self-employment, it has left important questions for future investigations – should self-employment be given public support? If the answer is yes, what types of economic policy should be adopted? To respond to these questions, a better knowledge of the evolution of businesses created by self-employed workers should be pursued.

---

[25]Information on wages is reported in the ECVT as a coded variable. However, we have translated the variable into a continuous one by taking the midpoint of each interval

[26]Yet it remains to be seen how seedling firms, sown by the hardship of unemployment, grow under the impulse of subsequent economic recovery. That recovery, in turn, can be enhanced by a network of newly established enterprises.

[27]See Balkın (1989) for an analysis of self-employment for disadvantaged workers

202   *A. Alba-Ramirez*

ACKNOWLEDGEMENTS

The author gratefully acknowledges a grant from the Spanish Ministry of Education and Science in cooperation with
the Fulbright Commission during the second year of his
Post-Doctoral Fellowship at Harvard University and the
National Bureau of Economic Research. He greatly appreci-
ates suggestions made by participants in a meeting of
members of the NBERs Program in Labour Studies and by
an anonymous referee. He thanks Cynthia Costas for invalu-
able help in editing this work.

REFERENCES

Alba-Ramírez, A and Freeman, R. B. (1990) Jobfinding and wages
    when longterm unemployment is really long: the case of Spain,
    NBER Working Paper No. 3409.
Balkin, S. (1989) *Self-Employment for Low-Income People*, Praeger,
    New York.
Becker, E. H. (1984) Self-employed workers an update to 1983,
    Monthly Labor Review, 107, July, 14–18.
Blanchflower, D G. and Oswald, A. J (1990) What makes a young
    entrepreneur? *NBER Working Paper* No. 3252 (Revised June
    1990).
Blanchflower, D. G. and Meyer, B. (1990) A longitudinal analysis of
    young entrepreneurs in Australia and the United States,
    mimeo, NBER.
Blau, D. M. (1987) A time-series analysis of self-employment in the
    United States, *Journal of Political Economy*, 95, 445–67
Borjas, G. J. (1986) The self-employment experience of immigrants,
    Journal of Human Resources, 21, 485–506.
Borjas, G J. and Bronars, S. G. (1989) Consumer discrimination
    and self-employment, *Journal of Political Economy*, 97,
    581–605.

Burdett, K and Vishwanath, T. (1988) Declining reservation wages
    and learning, *Review of Economic Studies*, 55, 655–66.
Cantillon, R. (1755) in *Essai sur la Nature du Commerce en Generale*
    (Ed) H Higgs, Macmillan, London (1931).
Evans, D. S. and Leighton, L S. (1989) Some empirical aspects of
    entrepreneurship, *American Economic Review*, 79, 519–35.
Evans, D. S. and Jovanovic, B. (1989) An estimated model of
    entrepreneurial choice under liquidity constraints, *Journal of
    Political Economy*, 97, 808–27.
Fuchs, V. R. (1982) Self-employed and labor force participation of
    older males, *Journal of Human Resources*, 17, 339–57.
Goffee, R. and Scase, R. (1986) Women, business start-up and
    economic recession, in *Women in Small Business*. (Eds.)
    R Donckels and J. N. Meijer, Van Gorcum, Assen.
Kanbur, S. M. (1979) Of risk taking and the personal distribution of
    income, *Journal of Political Economy*, 87, August, 769–97.
Kihlstrom, R. E and Laffont, J. J. (1979) A general equilibrium
    entrepreneurial theory of firm formation based on risk aver-
    sion, *Journal of Political Economy*, 87, August, 719–48
Knight, F H. (1921). *Risk, Uncertainty and Profit*, Houghton
    Mifflin, New York.
Lazear, E P. and Moore, R. L. (1984) Incentives, productivity, and
    labor contracts, *Quarterly Journal of Economics*, 99, May
    275–96.
Lucas, R. E., Jr. (1978) On the size distribution of business firms,
    Bell Journal of Economics, 9, Autumn, 508–23.
McCall, B P. (1989) A theory of job search and learning behavior,
    Mimeo, University of Minnesota, Minnesota
Meyer, B. D. (1990) Why are there so few black entrepreneurs?
    NBER Working Paper No. 3537.
Mortensen, D. T (1986) Job search and labour market analysis, in
    Handbook of Labor Economics, (Ed.) O. C. Ashenfelter and R.
    Layard, North Holland, Amsterdam, pp. 849–919
OECD. (1986) *Employment Outlook*, Paris
Rees, H. and Shah, A. (1986). An empirical analysis of self-
    employment in the UK, *Journal of Applied Econometrics*, 1,
    95–108

APPENDIX

Table A1   *Variable definitions and descriptive statistics for ECVT sample.*

		Mean (SD)	
Variables and description		Waged and salaried workers	Self-employed workers
Male	=1 if male	0 7152	0.8015
Married	=1 if married	0.7116	0.8027
Head	=1 if household head	0 6809	0 7514
Age	= age	38.2268 (11.8)	42.0615 (11.7)
Age ⩾ 65	=1 if age ⩾ 65	0.0047	0.0215
Experience	= age–education–6	24.3929 (13.4)	28.9048 (13.4)
Education < 6	=1 <6 years of school	0.2769	0.3303
Education = 6	=1 if primary school	0 2824	0 3202
Education = 8	=1 if pre-secondary	0 1618	0 1369
Education = 12	=1 if secondary school	0 1544	0.1249
Education = 15	=1 if pre-university	0.0634	0.0462
Education = 17	=1 if university	0 0608	0.0412
Duration of previous and current job			
Tenure	= years of tenure in the previous job	4.6467 (5.3)	6.4309 (6 6)
Senior < 1	=1 if less than 1 year in the current job	0.1855	0.1230
Senior 1–2	=1 if ⩾1 and ⩽2 years	0.0667	0.0868
Senior 2–5	=1 if >2 and ⩽5 years	0.1407	0 1864
Senior > 5	=1 if more than 5 years	0 6069	0.6036
Region ur	= region unemployment rate	21.7357 (5.1)	21.2253 (5.2)
Duration = 0	=1 if not unemployment	0.5542	0 6442
Months unemployed	= unemployment duration in months	7.7037 (16 7)	8 9067 (20 1)
Reasons for and number of firm changes			
Quit	=1 if quit the job	0 5325	0.5383
Retired	=1 if retired	0.0013	0.0088
To marry	=1 if married	0.0358	0.0697
Birth	=1 if gave birth	0 0111	0.0095
Military	=1 if went military service	0 0277	0.0215
Displaced	=1 if displaced	0.3131	0.2701
Fired	=1 if was individually fired	0.0506	0.0500
Bankrupt	=1 if bankruptcy	0 1001	0.0849
Cutback	=1 if cut-back on work	0.0218	0 0323
Endcont	=1 if end of contract	0.1404	0.1026
Not defined	=1 if not defined	0 0661	0.0659
Not answered	=1 if no answer	0.0120	0.0158
Job change = 1	=1 if changed firms once	0 1771	0.2149
Job change = 2	=1 if changed firms twice	0.2674	0.2473
Job change = 3	=1 if changed firms three times	0.2179	0.2022
Job change > 3	=1 if changed firms four or more times	0 3365	0 3354
Self w/e	=1 if self-employed without employees		0.8034
Self 1–5e	=1 if 1–5 employees		0 1559
Self > 5e	=1 if more than 5 employees		0.0355
Log wage	= log of the monthly net earnings in current job	10.73 (0.51)	10.59 (0.57)
N		6080	1577

Table A2. *Variable definitions and descriptive statistics for 1986–1988 DWS sample*

		Mean (SD)	
Variables and description		Waged and salaried workers	Self-employed workers
Male	= 1 if male	0 6615	0.7703
Married	= 1 if married	0.6825	0 7703
Age	= age	35.6685 (10 3)	37 6496 (9 5)
Education ⩽ 12	= 1 if ⩽ 12 years of school	0.3772	0.3480
Education = 13	= 1 if 13 years of school	0.2747	0 2552
Education = 14	= 1 if 14 years of school	0.1020	0 0765
Education = 15	= 1 if 15 years of school	0.0729	0 0696
Education = 16	= 1 if 16 years of school	0.0682	0.1020
Education ⩾	= 1 if 17+ years of school	0 1047	0.1484
Reasons for job loss			
Close	= 1 if plant closing	0 5291	0.4965
Slack	= 1 if slack work	0.3318	0.3387
Abolish	= 1 if abolished position or shift	0.1374	0 1647
Tenure	= tenure in the prior job	4.6996 (6.1)	4.9489 (6 0)
Y displaced > 83	= 1 if displaced after 1983	0.6413	0.6403
Region of residence at survey date			
Region 1	= 1 if New England and Middle Atlantic	0.1978	0.1600
Region 2	= 1 if E–N Central and W–N Central	0.2661	0 2296
Region 3	= 1 if S Atlantic, E–S Central and W–S Central	0 3024	0.3062
Region 4	= 1 if Mountain and Pacific	0.2335	0 3039
Moved	= 1 if moved to other city or county	0.2234	0 2018
Advnotice	= 1 if given advanced notice	0 5256	0 5591
Collected UI	= 1 if collected unemployment insurance	0.5656	0 5127
Duration = 0	= 1 if not unemployment	0 1506	0.1740
Weeks unemployed	= unemployment duration in weeks	17 5273 (23.4)	19.0464 (25.1)
Log wage	= log of prior job weekly earnings	5.7752 (5 8)	5.9949 (6.0)
Not covered	= not covered by any group health insurance plan in previous job	0.2803	0 2830
No of jobs	= number of jobs held since displacement	1.7019 (1 1)	1 5104 (1.0)
N		4851	431

[25]

OXFORD BULLETIN OF ECONOMICS AND STATISTICS, 61, 3 (1999)
0305-9049

TRANSITIONS TO AND FROM SELF-EMPLOYMENT IN SPAIN: AN EMPIRICAL ANALYSIS*

Raquel Carrasco[†]

I. INTRODUCTION

Over recent years, self-employment has been receiving a great deal of attention, both from the point of view of labour market policy and academic research. Part of the reason for this is that self-employment has been growing in several countries since the mid-1970 after a long period of decline that dates back to at least the late 1940's. In Spain (and in many OECD countries) self-employment expanded faster than overall, non-agricultural employment during the period 1979–90: 12.7 percent of the workforce was self-employed in 1979 while this figure increased to 18.5 percent in 1990, according to the Spanish Labour Force Survey. But perhaps the most important reason for this renewed interest follows from the fact that self-employment has begun to be considered as an important source of new jobs and an alternative to paid employment. Therefore, it widens the choice facing both the potential entrants to the labour market and the unemployed. In fact, in many countries self-employment growth has been stimulated by supportive policies, including schemes to help the unemployed to set up in business and help in obtaining the financial resources and skills.[1]

The purpose of this paper is to study the factors influencing the decision of entry into self-employment and the likelihood of remaining in business, using longitudinal data from the Spanish Continuous Family Expenditure Survey (ECPF) for 1985.I–1991.IV. In particular, we are interested in estimating the effect of being unemployed on the probability of starting a business and on self-employment duration. We also analyze the effect of

---

*The work in this paper is partly based on my Master's thesis at CEMFI, a revised version of which was circulated as "El empleo por cuenta propia en España: un análisis empírico", Doc. de Trabajo 9526, CEMFI.

[†] I am indebted to Olympia Bover and Manuel Arellano for their excellent supervision. I have also benefited from the comments and suggestions of Daniel Arnal, Samuel Bentolila, Juan Carlos Berganza, Jose Ignacio García, Juan Francisco Jimeno, Rafael Repullo, Alejandro Requejo, Luis Toharia and an anonymous referee. All remaining errors are my own.

[1] According to OECD data, the largest schemes are in France, the United Kingdom and Spain. They are generally targeted to unemployed people who have already received benefits for a certain length of time, but sometimes also to people under risk of losing their jobs. They may provide either periodic payments, which may be higher than the corresponding unemployment benefits, or a lump-sum capitalization of unemployment benefits.

315

316   BULLETIN

capital and unemployment benefits on the probability of transition. More-over, we are concerned about capturing differences in the probabilities of switching into self-employment with and without employees and about distinguishing exit from self-employment into employment from exit into unemployment, controlling for personal characteristics and business cycle effects.

While recent studies have improved our empirical knowledge of the role of small business in the economy, data limitations have forced these studies to leave out dynamic aspects of entrepreneurship. Many of these studies follow Rees and Shah (1986)[2] who estimated a static model on the basis of cross-sectional data. However, as pointed out by Evans and Leighton (1989), the cross-sectional estimates confound the determinants of switching and survival. The longitudinal data used in this paper permit a closer examination of some key aspects of entrepreneurship. These data allow us to observe transitions into self-employment and to determine the length of time an individual has operated his business. This will enable us to assess whether unemployed individuals are more prone to become self-employed than paid-employed workers, how long they stay self-employed and what they do afterwards. As a result, we hope to know to what extent individuals use self-employment as a step to other forms of employment. In addition, the panel structure of our data allows us to construct durations for individuals entering self-employment, avoiding stock sample biases, and permits us to analyze a wide cycle of the Spanish economy.

From previous studies we know that the failure to find a job contributes to explain self-employment growth. There is some evidence from Evans and Leighton (1989) that men who are unemployed are more likely to enter self-employment. In this paper we also obtain similar evidence for Spain. Furthermore, we investigate the effect of unemployment benefits on the probability of entering self-employment, obtaining a strong negative effect. This reinforces the previous finding that suggests that the self-employed are poor workers and misfits for paid work. However, as regards the self-employment duration, our results show that previous unemployment experience increases the probability of leaving self-employment.[3]

The impact of liquidity constraints on the decision to become an entrepreneur has been widely discussed. Using US or UK micro data, Evans and Leighton (1989), Evans and Jovanovic (1989) and Blanchflower and Oswald (1991a) conclude that imperfect credit markets constrain entrepreneurs. Our empirical findings agree with these results, but we have found that liquidity constraints only affect significantly the probability of becoming self-employed with employees.

Another interesting issue is the role of macro-economic effects, particularly unemployment rate, on determining self-employment transitions.

---

[2] See, for example, Blanchflower and Oswald (1991a), Meyer (1990b) and Taylor (1996).
[3] Evans and Leighton (1989) obtain similar results for the US.

Evans and Leighton (1989) provide evidence supporting a positive relationship between unemployment rates and entering self-employment, while Blanchflower and Oswald (1991b) point towards the opposite effect. The inconsistency in these findings can be attributed to the differences in the populations under study. Our results suggest that labour market conditions have opposite effects on the transition probabilities of unemployed and wage-employed workers.

As far as the empirical estimation is concerned, we apply binomial and multinomial logit models to analyze the transition from employment and unemployment to self-employment. Self-employment duration is modelled by using discrete survival analysis. We use semiparametric methods to estimate by maximum likelihood single risk models with unrestricted baseline hazards, by specifying duration dependence in a flexible way. We then estimate a competing risks model to distinguish exit into employment from exit into unemployment. We use a Extreme Value formulation which is consistent with a Proportional Hazards model in continuous time.

The paper is organized as follows. Section II describes some theoretical predictions about the effects of certain variables on self-employment transitions. Section III describes the data set used. The econometric specifications and estimation methods are described in Section IV and Section V summarizes the main findings. Section VI states the conclusions and some policy implications.

II. A THEORETICAL FRAMEWORK

The dynamic aspects of self-employment are the focus of our research. Most self-employed started out as wage workers. The unemployed are a less important but still significant source. A number of questions are considered. What induces an individual to leave wage work or unemployment and become an entrepreneur? Are unemployed workers more likely to enter self-employment than are wage workers? How does the exit rate from self-employment change over the self-employment spell, and what is the effect of past unemployment on the exit rates to wage work or to unemployment?

These questions can be addressed within the comparative advantage framework (see for example Evans and Leighton (1989) and Rees and Shah (1986)). Individuals who have found a business opportunity must decide whether to follow it or not. Which they choose depends upon a comparison of the utility they expect to receive in the alternative occupations. Several (and possibly different) factors will affect their relative returns from self-employment versus wage work or unemployment. We assume that the rates of entry into and exit out of self-employment depend upon personal characteristics and cyclical trends in the economy.

The Determinants of Entry into Self-Employment

We first consider the probability of switching into self-employment from wage work. According to the comparative advantage model, this will occur if the expected value of self-employment exceeds the expected value of wage-work. We discuss some factors that affect employment status.

Years of education. Education could serve as a filter such that the more educated tend to be better informed, implying that they are more efficient at assessing self-employment opportunities. However, the skills which make "good" entrepreneurs are not necessarily those which result in the acquisition of formal qualifications and formal qualifications do not necessarily enhance the human capital of the self-employed in the same way as the paid employed. We will try to obtain some empirical evidence on this.

Assets. Entrepreneurship has a different work environment than wage work. It may be a riskier activity, so an individual must weigh the cost of risk in his calculations. Lack of capital may prevent even those individuals for whom the risk-adjusted expected returns from trying entrepreneurship is positive from starting a business. So an individual will be more likely to switch into self-employment the greater his net worth if there are liquidity constraints.[4]

Marital status and number of children. Family characteristics may also be indicators of risk aversion. On the one hand, it is possible that family support may make self-employment less demanding than it would be otherwise. On the other hand, married men will be less willing to take risks. This aspect has received much attention in the literature, so it is useful to consider the empirical evidence for it.

Unemployment benefits. Concerning the explanatory factors of the transition from unemployment to self-employment, the key variable which determines the switching is whether the unemployed worker receives unemployment benefits or not. Standard search theory predicts a disincentive effects of benefits.[5] Since benefits are the main source of income when unemployment, when they are exhausted, search intensity rises and the reservation wage falls, so that the opportunity cost of search decreases, thereby leading to an increase in the probability of leaving unemployment.

As in most European countries, unemployment benefits in Spain are of two types,[6] although our data do not distinguish between them. The unemployment insurance system (UI) pays benefits to workers who have previously contributed when employed. They must have been dismissed from a job held at least for one year. The replacement ratio is equal to 70

---

[4]For a formalization of entrepreneurial choice under liquidity constraints, see Evans and Jovanovic (1989), Holtz-Eakin et al. (1994a, 1994b) and Blanchflower and Oswald (1991a).

[5]See Bover, Arellano and Bentolila (1996) for a detailed empirical study, in the context of a duration model, of the effects of unemployment benefit duration and the business cycle on unemployment duration.

[6]See Bover, Arellano and Bentolila (1996) for a more detailed description.

percent of the previous wage during the first six months of unemployment and 60 percent afterwards. Benefit duration is equal to one-third of the last job's tenure, with a maximum of two years. The unemployment assistance system (UA) grants supplementary income to workers who have exhausted UI benefits or who do not qualify for receiving them, with dependents, and whose average family income is below 75 percent of the minimum wage. It pays that amount for up two years. Lastly, there are special UA benefits for temporary agricultural workers in the Southern regions of Spain.

Business cycle. Regarding the influence of labour market conditions on self-employment, the theory provides an ambiguous prediction. The sign of the relationship may be analyzed in terms of what has been called "pull" and "push" factors. "Pull" factors are stronger when conditions are good. The prospects for business are better and people may be drawn into self-employment, knowing that if the venture fails another job offer will not be far away. Less favourable market conditions may provide a "push" factors increasing the labour supply for self-employment. High unemployment levels result in few offers of paid employment, and hence that many prefer self-employment to spending long periods inactive and searching for work. Empirical work has not resolved this issue and there is little consensus on the role of macro-economic effects, particularly unemployment. For example, Evans and Leighton (1989) and Alba-Ramirez (1994), for the US and Spain, provide evidence supporting the unemployment push theory, while Blanchflower and Oswald (1991b) or Taylor (1996) point towards the pull argument for UK. In fact, "push" and "pull" factors may operate simultaneously on different groups of individuals depending on certain personal characteristics and on their labour market situation. For example, the unemployment rate may affect the transition from wage work and from unemployment in a different way. Assessing this becomes an empirical question.

Self-employed as "Misfits"

Recent work in sociology has sought to explain the unusually high self-employment rate of certain "ethnic minority" groups of individuals. Light (1980) argues that individuals who are disadvantaged in the labour market are more likely to start business. Discrimination may push some individuals into self-employment. In addition, language barriers, ignorance of customs, poverty and unemployment may make self-employment more desirable than available wage work. In order for this theory to make economic sense one must assume that these disadvantages reduce wage earnings relatively more than self-employment earnings. In terms of the Roy-type models analyzed in Heckman and Sedlacek (1985) the disadvantage theory says that certain characteristics have higher return in self-employment than in wage work and therefore people with these attributes will tend to sort themselves into self-employment. For example, unemployed individuals may be viewed

320   BULLETIN

unfavourably by employers and will find it progressively harder to acquire a
wage job. They may therefore find that their skills produce a relatively
higher return in self-employment than in wage work. We explore these
issues empirically analyzing whether unemployed individuals are more
likely to switch into self-employment than are wage-workers for our sample
of Spanish men below.

Self-employment Duration

Many individuals who start businesses return to wage work or to unemployment and the effect of certain variables on self-employment duration may
be different depending on the nature of exit.

Self-employment duration. Some self-employed may learn that either the
entrepreneurial opportunity they discovered is not as good as they thought it
would be or that they are not quite as good at running a business as they
expected (see Jovanovic (1982) for a model along these lines). Such
learning will take place during the early years of being an entrepreneur, so
the longer an individual has been self-employed the more likely he is to
continue. This may be due both to self-employed businesses taking some
time to become securely established and to people less suited to self-
employment giving up after relatively short time.

Previous labour market status. Workers' situation before entering self-
employment can be very informative about their probability of survival. If
the origin state is unemployment, difficulties in finding a job may induce
individuals to take self-employment as a temporary state, better than being
unemployed. Along the same line, it is possible that people that have been
employed have more chances of having success as self-employed. Consequently, the issue of whether the probability of departing from self-employment depends on previous labour market situation seems an interesting
question to analyze empirically.

III. DATA DESCRIPTION

The Data Set

The data we use come from the Spanish Continuous Family Expenditure
Survey (*Encuesta Continua de Presupuestos Familiares* (ECPF)). The
ECPF is a rotating panel based on a survey conducted by the Instituto
Nacional de Estadística (INE - Spanish National Statistics Office). The
ECPF reports interviews for about 3200 households every quarter. One
eighth of the sample is renewed quarterly and hence we can follow an
individual for a maximum of two consecutive years.

The ECPF started in 1985:I and we use the waves up to 1991:IV. This
allows us to study the influence of personal characteristics taking into
account changes in aggregate conditions during an extended period of time,

so that we can assess the relative importance of these factors. Furthermore, we can observe "*entrants*" into self-employment, which avoids stock sample biases in the duration analysis.

This survey contains an extensive set of demographic characteristics, including information about basic variables for this study such as the labour market situation, income and wealth.[7]

Our sample includes men who are household heads,[8] aged 21 to 65. A male sample was chosen because of the well-known differences in male and female labour market behaviour, and the fact that women have very low self-employment rates.[9] We select the 21–65 age band because we can find different rules of behaviour in the youngest and oldest men, and this can distort the results. We also excluded from our sample the agricultural sector, owing to the special characteristics of self-employment in agriculture and the fact that employment in general is decreasing noticeably since the 60's in this sector.

Our initial sample included 53447 observations (about 12300 individuals). After filtering the sample (see Appendix and Table A1) we obtain 25498 and 2412 observations for each transition considered. To study transitions to self-employment we select the subsample of paid-employment and unemployed respectively and we only consider transitions from employment to self-employment and from unemployment to self-employment and to employment. In the first case, out of 25498 observations, 381 enter self-employment and 25117 continue employed. In the second case the sample size is smaller. Out of 2412 observations, the number of entrants into self-employment is 68, the number of entrants into employment is 463 while the number of unemployed who continue unemployed next quarter is 1881. The dependent variable used in these estimations is equal to 1 if the individual who was a wage worker or unemployed in a survey quarter becomes self-employed in the next survey quarter observed.[10]

Concerning the duration analysis, the duration variable is the length of the spell of self-employment (completed or censored). After filtering the sample, the number of entrants into self-employment is 413, contributing 997 binary responses. Table A2 provides sample frequencies of duration of self-employment spells.

The explanatory variables used in the estimation can be classified into two groups: demographic variables relating the individual, and economic

---

[7] Another available data set for Spain is the Labour Force Survey ("*Encuesta de Población Activa*" (EPA)), which allows to observe the labour market situation of an individual for up to six quarters, rather than eight. This longer time dimension is one of the reasons for using the ECPF. Moreover, the EPA does not contain information about wealth variables.

[8] This is the group for which the survey offers the most detailed and exhaustive information.

[9] This is highlighted by our data: as out of 8368 self-employees sampled, only 8.2 percent were women, so this longitudinal data set provide too few observations on self-employment entry and exit for these group of individuals.

[10] We observe the labour force status once per quater. Thus, if there are additional changes in status within the quarter, they are missed.

322   BULLETIN

variables, relating to business cycle conditions. In the first group we include age, education, variables reflecting the family background and variables relating to the income and wealth of the individual. Most of these are grouped into categories and are treated as dummies in the estimation. In the second group, we include the National Unemployment Rate and the GDP growth to account for changes in the general economic conditions. In the Appendix we report information about the sample and the construction of the variables.

Self-employment Definition

In broad terms, self-employment can be considered to be the residual category of paid employment not remunerated by a wage. Ideally, self-employment may be defined more positively according to economic criteria such as of "risk", "control" and "responsibility". However, there are not available data based on criteria of this kind. Most current information on self-employment come from household interview surveys of the labour force. Individuals are asked to give their own assessment of their employment status. Although their reply can be supplemented by further information concerning their status for administrative purposes (for example whether considered as self-employed by social security administration), there are groups of individuals whose status may not be clear. One example is people simultaneously performing both self-employment and wage employment. In addition, whatever the details of the definition, the self-employed are a highly heterogeneous category, since it includes self-employed with and without employees, professionals and members of producers' cooperatives, which are groups whose labour market behaviour may be very different.

We found in our data a number of possible errors in the self-employment status and made several adjustments and deletions to minimize the effects of such errors. Thus, in our study we consider as self-employed a narrower group than the one defined by the ECPF. Two variables of the survey have been used: the labour market situation and the type of income the individual receives. We include in our definition those individuals who declare being self-employed (with or without employees) as their main activity and who in addition have self-employment earnings, although they may receive income from a secondary paid-work. An advantage of this criterion is that permits to capture clearly the characteristics of self-employed and to have a clean comparison of the choice between self-employment and other alternatives, since we exclude those individuals that are not "genuine" self-employed.[11]

---

[11] A tighter definition considers self-employed exclusively those individuals whose only source of income comes from self-employment yields similar results.

IV. EMPIRICAL MODELS AND ESTIMATION METHODS

Probability of Entering Self-employment

To study the effect of economic and demographic variables on the transitions into self-employment, we use discrete choice models. In terms of the random utility framework, individuals will switch from wage-work or from unemployment to self-employment if the expected utility of self-employment exceeds the expected utility of the other alternative.

Let d_i^* represent the expected difference between the utility of the alternatives, given national economic variables, Y_N, as well as other variables in the information set of individual i. We specify d_i^* as follows

$$d_i^* = X_i'\beta_0 + Y_N'\beta_1(X_i) + \varepsilon_i, \qquad i = 1, \ldots, I \qquad (1)$$

where X_i denotes a vector of individual characteristics and ε_i is a disturbance term that includes unobserved variables. In our empirical model we allow for the possibility of different effects of the macro-economic variables across subpopulations defined by personal characteristics

$$\beta_1(X_i) = \beta_{10} + \beta_{11}X_i. \qquad (2)$$

The probability that an unemployed or paid-employed person in quarter $t-1$ is observed self-employed in quarter t, can be expressed as a conditional expectation

$$P(d_{it}^* \geqslant 0 | X_{i(t-1)}, Y_N) = F(X_{i(t-1)}'\beta_0 + Y_N'\beta_1(X_{i(t-1)})), \qquad (3)$$

where we specify F as the logistic cumulative distribution function.

We have used information about the individual's characteristics a period earlier (i.e. before switching), otherwise possible consequences of transition are likely to be confused with causes of transition. With respect to the general economic variables used, we have considered that when people make their transition decision, they use prior economic indicators in assessing their choice. Therefore, we use macroeconomic variables that are averages of the values over the year ending in the quarter of the survey.

We estimate binary logit models for unemployed and paid workers separately[12] and compare the estimated impact of a set of explanatory variables on the probability of switching to self-employment for both types of workers. This will permit us to assess if the unemployed workers are more prone than wage workers to start a business.

Moreover, we have estimated multinomial logit models for each subsample. Regarding the transition from paid-employment, we consider the possibility for an individual to become self-employed without employees or self-employed hiring other people. It is important to make distinction since in principle may exist differential effects of the variables on the decision of

---

[12]In this estimates the dependent variable equals 1 if the individual becomes self-employed in t.

324   BULLETIN

entering one state or another. Respect to the transition from unemployment, we have estimated a multinomial model allowing for the possibility of switching into paid-work.[13]

Probability of Leaving Self-employment: Single and Competing Risks Models with Flexible Base-line Hazards

We examine the dependence of exit from self-employment on the length of time in business by estimating the probability that an individual will survive T periods in self-employment and the probability of leaving self-employment during the next period, given that individual has been self-employed for T periods.[14] The individuals in our dataset are asked for up eight consecutive quarters about their labour market situation. From this information we can construct complete or incomplete self-employment durations for individuals entering self-employment. This allows us to calculate quarterly empirical hazards on the basis of complete durations of entrants and the surviving non-censored samples for up to seven quarters.

In our analysis we treat self-employment duration (T) as a continuous random variable which is observed at discrete intervals. Self-employment duration is right censored when the individual is still self-employed at the time of leaving the sample. Our observational plan is such that spell lengths are unknown but the interval during which spells end are known (i.e. we never observe T_i, we only observe whether $k_i < T_i < k_i + 1$, where k_i is the integer part of T_i, or whether $T_i > C_i$, being C_i the censoring time).

Single Risk Models

We first consider a single-risk duration model. Formally, let T_i be the length of a spell of self-employment. At this stage, only one hazard exists which may cause failure: leaving self-employment, without distinguishing exit into paid-employment from exit into unemployment. The continuous time hazard for individual i at time t, $\theta_i(t)$, is parametrized using a Proportion Hazard specification:

$$\theta_i(t) = \lambda(t) \cdot \exp[x_i(t)'\beta], \qquad (4)$$

where $\lambda(t)$ is the base-line hazard at time t, $x_i(t)$ is the vector of (in some

---

[13]For the unemployed the multinomial model makes no distinction between the self-employed with employees and those without. It is hard to think than an unemployed will start an entrepreneurial activity hiring other people. Moreover, there are only two individuals in our data set making a transition of this kind.

[14]As pointed out by Evans and Leighton (1989), it is important to note that survival in self-employment is not necessarily equivalent to survival of a business since an individual may remain self-employed as he opens and closes successive business.

cases time-dependent) explanatory variables for individual i (not including a constant) and β is a vector of parameters which is unknown.

The discrete time model can be estimated semi-parametrically without restrictions on the base-line hazard (as in Meyer (1990a) and Narendranthan and Stewart (1993)). The probability of a spell being completed by time $t + 1$ given that it was still continuing at time t is given by[15]

$$h_i(t) = \Pr[T_i < t + 1 | T_i \geq t] = F(\gamma(t) + x_i(t)'\beta), \tag{5}$$

where $F(\cdot)$ is the Extreme Value cumulative distribution function and $\gamma(t)$ is an unrestricted parameter specific to each t that captures additive duration dependence.

If d_i is the observed duration of the *ith* individual (completed or censored) and c_i is an indicator variable equal to 1 if the spell is completed and 0 if it is censored, the contribution of the *ith* individual to the log-likelihood is given by

$$L_i = c_i \left(\sum_{t=1}^{d_i-1} \log[1 - h_i(t)] + \log h_i(d_i) \right) + (1 - c_i) \left(\sum_{t=1}^{d_i} \log[1 - h_i(t)] \right). \tag{6}$$

The log-likelihood of the sample, the sum of those contributions, is maximized with respect to β and a full set of γ's to provide Maximum Likelihood estimates.

An useful alternative way of thinking of this model is to regard each exit or continuation in each period as an observation (see Kiefer (1987), Narendranathan and Stewart (1993), Sueyoshi (1995) and Jenkins (1995), Bover, Arellano and Bentolila (1996)). The *ith* individual in the sample contributes d_i "observations", so this model can be considered as a sequence of binary choice equations (with cross-equation restrictions) defined on the surviving population at each duration. In the most general case where there are no parameter restrictions across the $h_i(t)$, equation (5) can be estimated by a series of binary models with an Extreme Value distribution function formulation for the exit probability in each quarter.[16]

Competing Risk Models

The previous model specifies the determinants of a single risk: that of leaving the self-employment state. But much of the interest comes in the analysis of data in which failure can arise from two (or more) sources. That

---

[15] We assume that the changes in the time varying variables occur at integer points.

[16] Within this framework, other binary models, not implied by the Proportional Hazards formulation (i.e. Probit or Logit), can be estimated as alternatives.

326 BULLETIN

is, we wish to model duration jointly with the state exited into rather than duration alone.[17]

So we consider a situation where there are competing risks. In our case, a spell of self-employment can end with either paid-employment or with unemployment. This distinction may be important, since we can find significantly different behaviour with respect to the two risks. See Lancaster (1990) for a detailed description of competing risk models.

We can formulate these models assuming the existence of 2 independent random variables, T_1 and T_2, one of each destination, and suppose that the actual destination entered is determined by the minimum of the $\{T_i\}$ ($j = 1, 2$), which is the duration we actually observe.

Assuming unique failure type, the overall hazard function is then given by

$$h_i(t) = h_{i1}(t) + h_{i2}(t). \tag{7}$$

We define indicators $c_{ij} = 1$ if i enters into state j; 0 else ($j = 1, 2$).[18] Then the log-likelihood contributions are given by

$$L_j = \sum_{i=1}^{N}\left[c_{ij}\left(\sum_{t=1}^{d_i-1}\{\log[1 - h_{ij}(t)] + \log h_{ij}(d_i)\} \right) \right.$$

$$\left. + (1 - c_{ij})\left(\sum_{t=1}^{d_i} \log[1 - h_{ij}(t)] \right) \right] \tag{8}$$

The full log-likelihood is the sum of terms like (8) over $j = 1, 2$. Thus, if distinct destinations depend upon disjoint subsets of parameters which are functionally independent, then, so far as the inference about $(\gamma_j(t), \beta_j)$ is concerned, the log-likelihood may be taken simply as L_j given by (8).

From this it can be seen that the parameters of a given cause-specific hazard can be estimated by single-risk methods by treating durations finishing for other reasons as censored at the point of completion. For example, the determinants of conditional probability of leaving self-employment by finding paid-work can be examined by treating spells which end with exit to an unemployment state as censored at the point of exit, and the same applies for the other exit.

---

[17]Competing risk models have been used by several authors to study unemployment durations jointly with the states into which the unemployed exit. Katz (1986), Ham and Rea (1987), Katz and Meyer (1988), Han and Hausman (1990) use such models to distinguish recalls to the same firm from other exits. Narendranathan and Stewart (1993) use this type of model to distinguish exit into employment from exit into other non-employment states and Gil and Serrat (1994) to distinguish exit into employment from exit into self-employment.

[18]Note that $c_i = \sum_j c_{ij}$.

Testing for the Proportionality of Baseline-hazards

Whilst the previous approach is very convenient, there is a potential disadvantage if we wish to test hypotheses involving restrictions across the cause-specific hazards. Then the joint estimation of the hazards is required. In this sense, an interesting restriction on the competing risk framework is the proportional base-line hazards model. The set of restrictions imposed by this hypothesis is the equality of the base-line hazard coefficients up to a factor of proportionality:

$$H_0 : \gamma_{i2}(t) = m \cdot \gamma_{i1}(t) \qquad \forall t. \tag{9}$$

This means that at all times the base-line hazards of the two cause-specific hazards are in the same ratio. The calculation of the likelihood-ratio test statistic of the hypothesis that the baseline cause-specific hazards are all proportional to one another is carried out by using the maximized log-likelihood values of the restricted competing risk model and the unrestricted model, which in turn is the sum of the maximized log-likelihood values of the single risk models, considering durations finishing for other reasons than the one of interest as censored at the point of completion.

V. EMPIRICAL RESULTS

In this section we estimate the influence of the business cycle and certain individual characteristics on the transition probabilities into self-employment and on the hazard of leaving self-employment. We first focus on transition for wage workers and unemployed workers separately and follow with a comparison of the predicted probabilities of transition to self-employment between both types of individuals. Given that the observations for the transition models are individuals observed in particular quarters, it is unlikely that the error terms in the logit regressions corresponding to different observations on the same individual are independent. In the absence of independence, our estimates are not maximum likelihood since the estimation criterion neglects the correlation between the errors. They remain, however, consistent and asymptotically normal pseudo ML estimates under the assumption of correct specification of the period-specific probabilities, although Hessian based standard errors are inconsistent. Therefore, we present standard errors robust to misspecification, using the Hessian and the cross-product of the first derivatives. Finally we report maximum likelihood estimates of the hazard of leaving self-employment for the single risk and competing risk models with unrestricted base-line hazards as described in Section III. The qualitative impact of the variables are discussed in terms of the sign and statistical significance of the estimated coefficients. In order to assess the economic significance of the effects we also report predicted probabilities and hazards for some individual types.

TABLE 1.
Probability of Entering Self-employment from Wage-work. Logit Estimates

	(1) Binomial Model	(2) Multinomial Model	
Variable		Without employees	With employees
Constant[2]	−6.985 (−10.98)	−7.152 (−10.22)	−9.090 (−5.90)
Age 21–35 and 45–55	−0.323 (−2.75)	−0.227 (−1.70)	−0.682 (−2.75)
Age 55–65	−0.653 (−3.29)	−0.577 (−2.54)	−0.914 (−2.71)
Univ. educ × Not prev. self	3.608 (2.25)	3.144 (1.43)	5.204 (2.07)
Rural area	0.678 (5.82)	0.684 (5.25)	0.650 (2.57)
Assets × 10^{-5}	0.185 (3.67)	0.136 (2.03)	0.257 (4.79)
Married	0.085 (0.33)	0.168 (0.52)	−0.102 (−0.18)
Children × Not prev. self	−0.812 (−5.84)	−0.743 (−4.68)	−1.070 (−3.60)
Unemployment Rate	0.175 (5.92)	0.163 (5.01)	0.226 (3.27)
Unemployment Rate × Univ. educ × Not prev. self	−0.204 (−2.49)	−0.199 (−1.77)	−0.243 (−1.91)
Number of obs.	25,498	25,498	
Log-likelihood	−1924.846	−2112.94	

Notes:
1. *t*-statistics in brackets.
2. The constant term will determine the probability of switching for individuals with the following characteristics: head of household single, without children, aged between 35 and 45, without higher education and living in an urban area.
3. There are not significant differences among individuals aged under 35 and aged 45–55.
4. In the multinomial model the alternative "remaining as wage-employed" is taken as the comparison one.
5. Switching frequency into self-employment: 1.49%; switching frequency into self-employment without employees: 1.17%; switching frequency into self-employment with employees: 0.32%.

Probability of Entering Self-employment from Wage-work

The binomial logit estimates reported in the first column of Table 1 provide first insights into a number of factors affecting entry into self-employment. Column 2 reports multinomial logit estimates in order to account for the differences in the transition probabilities into self-employment with or without employees. The specifications include variables concerning demographic characteristics (age, education[19]), family structure (dummies for marital status and children), family assets (wealth measured by return on real state, interest payments and dividends) and demand side situation (unemployment rate and interactions between unemployment and educa-

---

[19]Education can act as a proxy for the individual wage.

tion).[20] We also take into account whether the individual has had a spell as self-employed during the last 12 months. In this way we attempt to control for the fact that the factors behind self-employment decision for individuals with an "unstable" pattern of self-employment experience may respond to seasonal effects.

We begin by considering the effects of family assets. The coefficient on the wealth variable provides evidence of the importance of access to capital markets on the probability of becoming self-employed. This finding is consistent with Evans and Jovanovic (1989) and Taylor (1996) and suggests that individuals face liquidity constraints. However, it appears that this problem has a smaller effect on the probability of switching among individuals who decide become self-employed without employees.

The dummies describing the family structure indicates a negative effect of children on the probability of switching, but this effect is only significant for those individuals not self-employed during the last 12 months. It is interesting to note that marital status does not seem to significantly influence the probability of becoming self-employed.

Let us now examine the effect of Unemployment Rate. On its own, the effect of this variable suggests that employed individuals are more likely to move towards self-employment when the economic situation deteriorates. However, this effect only has a significant effect if the individual has not had prior self-employment experience and has a low or medium level of education.[21] From Table 2 we can see that the probability of switching for a person with a low level of education when unemployment is high is more than twice as high as for a person with a university degree. This implies that self-employment is a more likely choice when demand in the labour market is low, and seems to support the "push" argument explained in Section II. We also measured the aggregate effects by the rate of growth of GDP. The results are very close. We obtain a negative effect of this macroeconomic variable.[22] This effect again supports the idea that employed individuals enter self-employment when the economic situation worsens.

Finally, we consider the effect of personal characteristics. The more educated an individual, the higher his probability of entering self-employment.[23] Also it is interesting to point out that we obtain an even stronger positive effect when the individual becomes self-employed with employees.

---

[20]The chosen specification follows from the theoretical considerations presented in Section II. We started with a more general specification which included other variables, such as change in the number of children, change in the marital status, number of income earners in the household and non linear terms in the age, as well as interactions between other personal characteristics, such as family situation and age, with the national level variables. None of them were significant, and when omitted the estimated coefficients of the remaining regressors did not change.

[21]The total effect of the unemployment rate on higher educated individuals is -0.03 (t-statistic $= -0.34$).

[22]The estimated coefficient on the rate of GDP growth is -3.67 (t-statistic $= -4.85$).

[23]Rees and Shah (1986) obtain a similar result. They argue that although education has greater impact on employee earnings it, nevertheless, raises the probability of self-employment.

330   BULLETIN

TABLE 2.
Predicted Probabilities of Entering Self-employment from Wage-Work

	Low Unempl. Rate[2]	Change[3]	High Unempl. Rate	Change
Standard[1]	0.0153	–	0.0129	–
BUT				
No schooling	0.0109	−28.76%	0.0300	132.56%
Age 55–65	0.0110	−28.10%	0.0093	−27.91%

Notes:
1. Standard: head of household, single, age 21–35, without previous self-employment experience in the sample, university education, living in an urban area.
2. Low and high unemployment rates are 16% and 21.9% respectively, which are the lowest and the highest values for our sample period.
3. Percentage change related to the standard.

TABLE 3.
Probability of Entering Self-employment and Employment from Unemployment.
Logit Estimates

	(1) Binomial Model	(2) Multinomial Model	
Variable		Entry to self-empl.	Entry to empl.
Constant[2]	−1.213 (−1.57)	−0.543 (−0.63)	0.067 (0.13)
Age 21–35	0.197 (0.60)	0.178 (0.55)	0.444 (3.08)
Age 45–55	−0.406 (−1.15)	−0.520 (−1.51)	−0.550 (−3.71)
Age 55–65	−1.244 (−2.68)	−1.363 (−2.95)	−1.495 (−8.06)
No school. × Not prev. self	−0.712 (−2.15)	−0.686 (−2.09)	0.042 (0.37)
Secondary education	−0.617 (−0.93)	−0.597 (−0.92)	−0.278 (−1.06)
University education	−0.522 (−0.51)	−0.472 (−0.46)	0.089 (0.23)
Rural area	0.248 (0.83)	0.203 (0.68)	−0.029 (−0.23)
Benefits	−1.748 (−6.31)	−1.781 (−6.55)	−0.619 (−5.39)
Unem. Rate × Not prev. self	−0.126 (−3.61)	−0.158 (−3.91)	−0.068 (−2.73)
Number of obs.	1949	2412	
Log-likelihood	−251.97	−1343.18	

Notes:
1. *t*-statistics in brackets.
2. The constant term will determine the probability of switching for individuals with the following characteristics: head of household aged between 35 and 45, with secondary education and not receiving benefits.
3. In the multinomial model the alternative "remaining as unemployed" is taken as the comparison one.
4. Switching frequency into self-employment: 3.49%; switching frequency into wage-employment: 19.19%.

The effect of age is also the expected. The probability of switching is higher for middle-age people, particularly for those aged 35 to 45, and is much lower for those over 55,[24] and for those living in rural areas.

From the estimated personal characteristics and business cycle effects and their interactions with the "not self-employed in the last 12 months" dummy, we can see that the reasons that make individuals with an irregular self-employment behaviour switch into self-employment are different from the reasons that make people without prior self-employment experience doing it.

Probability of Entering Self-employment from Unemployment

Table 3 report logit estimates of the probability of switching for unemployed individuals. The most interesting result is that the receipt of any type of unemployment benefits considerably reduces the probability of entering self-employment. This is in agreement with the theoretical prediction of the model presented in Section II. Further, the coefficient on the benefit variable is the most significant estimated effect to explain the transition from unemployment to self-employment and the one that produces the greatest change in the estimated probabilities. Table 4 shows that not receiving benefits increases the probability of switching by 0.1157 -from 0.0293 to 0.1450-, when the unemployment rate is low, and by 0.0604 -from 0.0142 to 0.0746-, when the unemployment rate is high.

Given the characteristics of the data it is not possible to determine the extent to which this result is due to a disincentive effect of benefits or to their role as a proxy for the attachment of the individual to the wage labour market. The negative effect of benefits is likely to capture state dependence on past spells as self-employed.[25] Indeed, when we estimate a multinomial logit model for the transition from unemployment to self-employment and wage employment (column 2, Table 3) we can see that benefits affect negatively both transitions, but the effect is stronger on the probability of switching into self-employment. Therefore, we must be cautious when interpreting the negative effect of benefits on the probability of leaving unemployment.

Turning to the effect of the business cycle, the negative coefficient on the unemployment rate variable suggests that unemployed individuals are more likely to become self-employed when conditions are good.[26] This implies that for unemployed individuals, self-employment appears to become a

---

[24]This result is again consistent with the view that entrepreneurs face liquidity constraints. Entrepreneurship may in fact not be an option for younger workers bacause they will have had less time to obtain the capital needed to start a business.

[25]Evans and Leighton (1989) find that the probability of entry is higher for individuals who have had prior self-employment experience.

[26]We also attempted to control for business cycle conditions using the rate of GDP growth. This variable was non significant, with an estimated coefficient of 2.466 (t-statistic $= 0.91$).

332   BULLETIN

more attractive alternative when there is safety of paid employment available in case of failure.[27] This could also reflect the fact that in boom times there are more self-employment opportunities available since aggregate demand will be higher. This result adds to the evidence supporting the prosperity "pull" argument for this type of workers. Moreover, it seems again that the business cycle situation does not affect the transition decision for those individuals with an unstable self-employment conduct.

Finally, the effects of other personal characteristics influence in the expected direction, being the oldest and lowest educated individuals less likely to turn to self-employment.

Entry from Employment Versus Entry from Unemployment

The previous analysis shows some differences in the impact of various characteristics on transition probabilities among employed and unemployed workers, mainly those referred to as the business cycle. As explained in Section II, the theory does not provide a clear prediction of the effect of unemployment on the probability of becoming self-employed. Our results suggest that this effect differs depending on the transition considered: unfavourable business conditions affect positively the probability of becoming self-employed for those individuals coming from employment and having low level of education and negatively for those who come from unemployment. So we can conclude that the processes that lead unemployed and employed workers to self-employment are different.

We now turn to compare the predicted probabilities for both groups of workers. In the first column of Table 5 we kept the unemployment rate at its sample mean (19.78%). We can see that unemployed workers are more likely to enter into self-employment than employed workers, especially if not receiving benefits.

Taking into account the business cycle situation (columns 2 and 3 in Table 5), the results indicate that higher educated individuals are less likely to become self-employed if they are actually employed than if they are unemployed. When the unemployment rate is low, the probability of switching for a person unemployed receiving benefits is twice greater than for a person employed. If the unemployed worker does not receive benefits this figure rises to 9.5. This can reflect the higher opportunity cost (in terms of wages) that this group of individuals face.

We also found that for people with a low level of education, the probability of switching when the unemployment rate is low is higher again if the source state is unemployment, mainly when benefits are not received. However, when the unemployment rate is high, employed workers have a

---

[27]By interacting the benefit dummy with the unemployment rate we obtain a less negative effect of this variable on the unemployed who do not receive benefits. However, in this case the direct effect of benefits is not significant.

TABLE 4.

Predicted Probabilities of Entering Self-employment from Unemployment

	Low Unempl. Rate	Change	High Unempl. Rate	Change
Standard	0.0293	–	0.0142	–
BUT				
Without benefits	0.1450	394.88%	0.0746	425.35%
No schooling	0.0259	−11.60%	0.0125	−11.97%
Age 55–65	0.0070	−76.11%	0.0033	−76.76%

See Notes to Table 2.

TABLE 5.

Predicted Probabilities of Entering into Self-employment from Wage-employment Versus from Unemployment

	(1) Mean Unem. Rate		(2) Low Unem. Rate		(3) High Unem. Rate	
	Emp.	Unemp.	Emp.	Unemp.	Emp.	Unemp.
Standard	0.0137	0.0184	0.0153	0.0293	0.0129	0.0142
BUT						
Without benefits	0.0137	0.0952	0.0153	0.1450	0.0129	0.0746
No schooling	0.0209	0.0163	0.0109	0.0259	0.0300	0.0125
Without benefits and no schooling	0.0209	0.0848	0.0109	0.1299	0.0300	0.0603

See Notes to Table 2.

higher probability of starting a business than unemployed workers receiving benefits.

To sum up, a general conclusion from these results is that relatively poor workers -that is, unemployed not receiving benefits- are more likely to switch into self-employment, all else equal.[28] This agrees with the disadvantage theory presented earlier and with the view of some sociologists that "misfits" are pushed into entrepreneurship.[29]

Duration of Self-employment: Flexible Base-line Hazard Models

Maximum likelihood estimates for the single-risk model with unrestricted base-line hazards provides the starting point of the duration analysis. In the

---

[28] Evans and Leighton (1989) get similar results for the US.

[29] At this point we should be cautious since "misfits" coulf be pejorative for a class of individuals which includes many lawyers, physicians, accountants, musicians, etc. Nevertheless, our purpose here is to consider another types of self-employed and to point out that the disadvantage theory is consistent with some of our findings.

formulation given in the equation (5) we control for certain variables, including duration dependence and labour market situations prior to entering the self-employment spell. In particular, we include an indicator of whether the individual had been employed a quarter before the start of the spell. As in the previous section, the National Unemployment Rate is used to capture changes in the general economic conditions. Controls were also included for other individual characteristics. None of the characteristics such as education, age or marital status was statistically important. We should take into account however, that our data set has a serious limitation, in that we only observe entrants into self-employment over a short period of time (the maximum self-employment spell we can observe is 2 years).

First column of Table 6 contains parameter estimates for the single-risk Proportional Hazard model. In terms of the formulation given in equation (5), it implies that $h(\cdot)$ takes an Extreme Value distribution.[30] As pointed out before, our specification includes a flexible way to control for duration dependence by including a dummy variable for each quarterly duration. Durations of more than 3 quarters are excluded, due to their relatively small number of observations (see Table A2).

The results indicate that the hazard rate decreases with duration in self-employment - that is, the longer an individual has been self-employed, the more likely he is to continue. This may be due to the fact that a self-employed business takes some time to become securely established and it has access to more resources that when it first started.

The estimated effect of the previous labour market situation shows that those individuals who had a spell of unemployment in the 3 months before entering self-employment have a higher probability of moving out of self-employment. Therefore, one important conclusion here is that although unemployed workers are more likely to enter self-employment -as shown in the previous section-, past unemployment experience is negatively associated with staying in self-employment. This result supports the idea that these individuals enter self-employment to avoid unemployment, but at the same time they are less suited to self-employment leaving after a relatively short time. This may be due to the loss of human capital or because the lower quality of the information about their business opportunities. However, single-risk models are not very informative about the genuine effect of the variables on the probability of leaving self-employment. The reason is that the effect of some variables may be more pronounced in the unemployment hazard than in the employment hazard. This point will be considered below.

Another interesting result is shown in Table 7, which summarizes the predicted hazard for workers previously employed and unemployed, keeping unemployment rate at its sample mean. It is apparent from that table that at

---

[30]Probit and Logit models were estimated as alternative functional form specifications for $h(\cdot)$ and the fit of the models as measured by likelihood criterion is very similar.

durations of three months, the hazard for workers previously unemployed is three times greater than the hazard of those previously employed. Moreover, the decline in the probability of leaving self-employment is more pronounced among workers with a previous unemployment spell, falling from 0.40 in the first quarter to 0.26 by the second quarter in self-employment.

Finally, the National Unemployment Rate has a significant upward effect on the probability of leaving self-employment.

Single-risk Versus Competing-risk Models

The estimation of the single-risk model does not let us specify separately the effect of the variables on the self-employment duration through their effect on the probability of receiving (and accepting) a job offer and the probability of exit into unemployment. For this reason, we now consider a competing-risk model. Specifically, it will allow us to distinguish whether the previous labour market situation has a different effect on the two destination states considered.

The results for the model using the competing-risk framework are given in the second column of Table 6. As we might expect, the downward impact on the hazard of having a job in the 3 months before the start of the current self-employment spell is considerably more marked in the unemployment hazard than in the employment one: about three times the size. We can attribute this in part to those with unemployment experience in the past

TABLE 6.
Maximum Likelihood Estimates of Extreme Value Hazard Function Parameters

Variable	(1) Single-risk model Departure to empl.	(2) Competing-risks model Departure to unempl.	
Employed before	−1.119 (−3.85)	−0.870 (−2.69)	−2.623 (−3.40)
Unemployment Rate	0.112 (2.02)	0.121 (2.08)	−0.003 (−0.04)
Quarter (t)			
1	−3.031 (−2.61)	−3.495 (−2.87)	−2.516 (−1.43)
2	−3.569 (−3.04)	−4.010 (−3.25)	−3.347 (−1.64)
3	−3.647 (−3.10)	−4.221 (−3.240)	−2.083 (−1.22)
Number of obs.	821	821	821
Log-likelihood	−291.95	−280.30	−35.48

Notes:
1. t-statistics in brackets.
2. Number of individuals in the sample is 413, contributing 821 binary responses.

being more likely to exist into unemployment when they leave their self-employment period.

The results also indicate that dummy variables capturing duration dependence and the unemployment rate are significant in the single-risk model and in the competing-risk model for the exit into employment, although they are not significant for the exit into unemployment. Given the small sample size and the small fraction of sample that switches out of self-employment towards unemployment, this lack of statistical precision is not surprising.

We now turn to the test of the proportionality among the base-line hazard of the exit states. The results are contained in Table 8. The restricted log-likelihood was calculated and the test statistic, distributed as a χ^2-variate with 2 degrees of freedom is 1.336 (the 5% critical point is 5.99). The null hypothesis of proportionality is accepted.

TABLE 7.
Predicted Hazard Rates for Self-employment. Single-risk Model

	Hazard rate	
Self-employment duration in quarters	*Employed before*	*Unemployed before*
1	0.13	0.40
2	0.12	0.26
3	0.11	0.25

Notes:
1. We kept unemployment rate at its sample mean (19.78%).

TABLE 8.
Maximum Likelihood Estimates of the Restricted Competing-risks Model

Variable	*Departure to empl.*	*Departure to unempl.*
Employed before	−0.869 (−2.69)	−2.594 (−3.40)
Unemployment Rate	0.123 (2.11)	−0.055 (−0.37)
Quarter (*t*)		
1	−3.533 (−2.91)	
2	−4.064 (−3.31)	
3	−4.222 (−3.40)	
Proportionality factor	0.414 (0.52)	
Number of obs.	821	
Log-likelihood	−316.45	

Notes:
1. *t*-statistics in brackets.

TRANSITIONS TO AND FROM SELF-EMPLOYMENT IN SPAIN   337

VI. CONCLUSIONS

Our principal findings can be summarized as follows. (1) Unemployed individuals are more likely to switch into self-employment. This result is consistent with the view that the disadvantaged tend to become self-employed. (2) However, the business of those entering to self-employment from unemployment suffer more difficulties (higher failure rate) than the business set up by people who had moved to self-employment from an employee status. In addition, the negative effect of previous unemployment experience is much stronger on the probability of switching out of self-employment towards unemployment than on the probability of leaving self-employment and entering a job. (3) Receiving unemployment benefits reduces the probability of entering self-employment. (4) The probability of switching increases with assets. Liquidity constraints therefore appear to be important in determining entrepreneurial selection, mainly for those wage-workers who become self-employed with employees. (5) The probability of departing decreases with duration in self-employment. (6) Higher unemployment rates push lower educated employed individuals towards self-employment. However, self-employment appears to become a more attractive alternative for unemployed individuals when economic situation improves. (7) Better educated and middle-age workers are more likely to switch.

Our results are useful not only for the study of entrepreneurship but also for understanding the role of self-employment in the economy. The fact that self-employment provides an escape for poor workers suggests that policies which make it more expensive to start and operate a business will tend to increase unemployment. On the other hand, these policies should be focused on certain types of individuals in order to reduce business failure and improve the quality of entrepreneurship.

CEMFI, Madrid

Date of Receipt of Final Manuscript: March 1998.

REFERENCES

Alba-Ramirez, A. (1994). "Self-Employment in the Midst of Unemployment: the case of Spain and the United States", *Applied Economics*, Vol 26, pp. 189–204.

Blanchflower, D. and Oswald, A. (1991a), "What makes a young entrepreneur?", NBER Working Paper 3252.

Blanchflower, D. and Oswald, A. (1991b), "Self-Employment and Mrs. Thatcher's Enterprise Culture", CEP Working Paper 30.

Bover, O., Arellano, M. and Bentolila, S. (1996), "Unemployment Duration, Benefit Duration and the Business Cycle", Economic Studies, Series of the

338   BULLETIN

Banco de España, Research Department, n°57.
Evans, D. and Jovanovic, B. (1989), "An Estimated Model of Entrepreneurial Choice under Liquidity Constraints", *Journal of Political Economy*, Vol 97, pp. 808–27.
Evans, D. and Leighton, L. (1989), "Some Empirical Aspects of Entrepreneurship", *The American Economic Review*, Vol 79, pp. 519–35.
Gil, F.J., Martin, M.J. and Serrat, A. (1994), "Movilidad en el Mercado de Trabajo en España: Un Análisis Econométrico de Duración con Riesgos en Competencia", *Investigaciones Económicas*, Vol 3, pp. 517–37.
Ham, J.C. and Rea, S.A., Jr. (1987), "Unemployed Insurance and Male Unemployment Duration in Canada", *Journal of Labour Economics*, Vol 5, pp. 325–53.
Han, A. and Hausman, J. (1990), "Flexible Parametric Estimation of Duration and Competing Risk Models", *Journal of Applied Econometrics*, Vol 5, pp. 1–28.
Heckman, J. and Sedlacek, G. (1985), "Heterogeneity, Aggregation, and Market Wage Functions: An Empirical Model of Self-Selection in the Labor Market", *Journal of Political Economy*, Vol 93, pp, 1077–125.
Holtz-Eakin, D., Joulfaian, D. and Rosen, H. (1994a), "Entrepreneurial Decisions and Liquidity Constraints", *RAND Journal of Economics*, Vol 25, pp. 335–47.
Holtz-Eakin, D., Joulfaian, D. and Rosen, H. (1994b), "Sticking it Out: Entrepreneurial Survival and Liquidity Constraints", *Journal of Political Economy*, Vol 102, pp. 53–75.
Jenkins, S. (1995), "Easy Estimation Methods for Discrete Time Duration Models", BULLETIN, Vol 57, pp. 120–38.
Jovanovic, B. (1982), "The Selection and Evolution of Industry", *Econometrica*, Vol 50, pp. 649–670.
Katz, L.F. (1986), "Layoffs, Recall and the Duration of Unemployment", NBER Technical Report 1825.
Katz, L.F. and Meyer, B.D. (1988), "Unemployment Insurance, Recall Expectations and Unemployment Outcomes", NBER Working Paper 2594.
Kiefer, N. (1987), "Analysis of Grouped Duration Data", Cornell CAE Working Paper 87–12.
Lancaster, T. (1990), *The Econometric Analysis of Transition Data*, Cambridge University Press, Cambridge.
Light, I. (1980), "Disadvantaged Minorities in Self-employment", *International Journal of Comparative Sociology*, Vol 20, pp. 31–45.
Meyer, B.D. (1990a), "Unemployment Insurance and Unemployment Spells", *Econometrica*, Vol 58, pp. 757–82.
Meyer, B.D. (1990b), "Why Are There So Few Black Entrepreneurs?", NBER Working Paper 3537.
Narendranathan, W. and Stewart, M. (1993), "Modelling the Probability of Leaving Unemployment: Competing Risk Models with Flexible Base-line Hazards", *Applied Statistics*, Vol 42, pp. 63–83.
OECD (1992), "Employment Outlook", Paris, July.
Rees, H. and Shah, A. (1986), "An Empirical Analysis of Self-Employment in the UK", *Journal of Applied Econometrics*, Vol 1, pp. 95–108.
Sueyoshi, G. (1995), "A Class of Binary Response Models for Grouped Duration Data", *Journal of Applied Econometrics*, Vol 10, pp. 411–31.
Taylor, M.P. (1996), "Earnings, Independence or Unemployment: Why Become Self-Employed?", BULLETIN, Vol 58, pp. 253–65.

APPENDIX

Individual Data

Source. Rotating panel from the Spanish Continuous Family Expenditure ("Encuesta Continua de Presupuestos Familiares") from 1985:I to 1991:IV, provided by the National Statistical Office (Instituto Nacional de Estadística (INE)).

Sample. From a sample of men of 21 to 65 years of age we exclude those

- always self-employed during the observed period
- never in the labour force during the observed period
- observed only once
- with a missing interview in between two valid interviews

37174 observations satisfy these restrictions. Since we are interested in the transitions from employment to self-employment, we selected the subsample of individuals who are employed during a particular quarter and continue employed or switch into self-employment next quarter. Out of 37174 observations, 1466 correspond to individuals always unemployed and 10210 correspond to transitions from employment to out of the labour force, so they have been dropped from the subsample used to analyze transitions from employment. Therefore, we obtain 25498 observations, of which 25117 correspond to transitions from employment to employment and 381 from employment to self-employment. Regarding the transitions from unemployment, out of the original sample of 37174 observations, 27618 correspond to individuals always employed and 7144 to transitions from unemployment to out of the labour force, so they have been excluded to analyze this transition. Therefore, we have 2412 observations, of which the number of transitions from unemployment to unemployment is 1881, from unemployment to employment is 463 and from unemployment to self-employment is 68.

Education. We consider the following categories: Illiterate and no schooling, Primary education, Secondary education and University education.

Age. It is grouped into four categories: 21 to 35 years old, 35 to 45 years old, 45 to 55 years old and 55 to 65 years old.

Marital status. The variable takes the value 1 for married individuals and 0 otherwise.

Children. Dummy for individuals with children younger than 18.

Unemployment benefits. The variable takes the value 1 for unemployed individuals receiving benefits.

Family assets. Income received by the family, including rental income, interest and dividends.

Previous self-employment. The variable takes the value 1 if not observed a spell as self-employed in the last 12 months.

340 BULLETIN

Previous employment. Dummy equal to 1 if the individual was employed one quarter before entering self-employment and 0 if unemployed.
Rural area. Dummy for individuals who live in a rural area.

National Economic Variables

Unemployment Rate. Source: "Encuesta de Población Activa" (EPA), INE.
Gross Domestic Product. Source: "Cuentas Financieras de la Economía Española", Banco de España.
Table A3 provides the frequencies of the variables used in the analyses.

TABLE A1.
Number of Observations Per Transition

Source State		Destination State			
	SE	SE without empl.	Empl.	Unempl.	Others[1]
Empl.	381	209	25117	–	10210
Unempl.	68	–	463	1881	7144

1.– This column includes transitions from employment to unemployment and out of the labour force and from unemployment to out of the labour force.

TABLE A2.
Sample of Entrants into Self-employment

	Number	Percentage	Non-censored	Censored
Total number of spells	413	100.00	104	309
Duration of the self-empl. spell				
1 quarter	164	39.71	64	100
2 quarters	90	21.79	23	67
3 quarters	74	17.92	13	61
4 quarters	33	7.99	2	31
5 quarters	24	5.81	2	2
6 quarters	17	4.12	0	17
7 quarters	11	2.66	0	11

TABLE A3.
Frequencies of Individual Variables Sample of Entrants into Self-employment

	From wage-work		From unemployment	
	Number	*Percentage*	*Number*	*Percentage*
Age				
21 to 35 years old	7094	27.82	339	17.39
35 to 45 years old	8190	31.12	427	21.91
45 to 55 years old	6779	26.59	576	29.55
55 to 65 years old	3435	13.47	607	31.14
Education				
Illiterate and no schooling	2898	13.36	688	35.30
Primary education	15969	62.63	1143	58.64
Secondary education	3559	13.96	75	3.84
University education	3072	12.05	43	2.21
Family characteristics				
Married	24558	96.31	1827	93.74
With children	20574	80.69	1385	71.06
Benefit receipt				
Receiving benefits	–	–	1400	71.83

[26]

The Manchester School Vol LXV No. 4   September 1997
0025–2034 427–442

THE EVOLUTION OF U.K. SELF-EMPLOYMENT: A STUDY OF GOVERNMENT POLICY AND THE ROLE OF THE MACROECONOMY*

by
MARC COWLING
Centre for Small and Medium Sized Enterprises,
Warwick Business School
and
PETER MITCHELL†
ESRC Macroeconomic Modelling Bureau,
University of Warwick

This paper reports the findings of a time series analysis exploring the fundamental determinants of the substantial rise in U.K. self-employment over the period 1972–92. The key findings are that the self-employed/wage-employed income differential has a high and positive effect upon the proportion of the workforce in self-employment, supporting alternative wage theories of labour market status, as does housing wealth, supporting credit-rationing theories. Perhaps the most interesting feature concerns the relationship between unemployment and self-employment. On this we find that it is the duration structure of unemployment that matters, not simply the stock of unemployed people. This evidence may imply that self-employment is a last resort for certain individuals marginalized in the employed sector and facing lengthy spells of unemployment.

I INTRODUCTION

There was a major shift in the focus of government economic policy throughout the 1980s away from larger firms towards the small firm and the self-employed. The declared aim was to foster an "enterprise culture" by encouraging and nurturing new firm formation and increasing flows into self-employment. Policy was formulated at both the micro and macro level with the creation of a flexible, dynamic small-firms sector specifically in mind. To that end, flexibility within the labour force was a prerequisite—hence the introduction of a number of schemes designed to promote self-employment by assisting individuals at the start-up stage,

* Manuscript received 10.8.94; final version received 29.11.96.
† The authors would like to thank Clive Fraser, Ben Knight, Peter Smith, Robin Naylor and Keith Cowling at Warwick University and two anonymous referees for constructive comments and advice on various versions of the paper.

e.g. the Enterprise Allowance Scheme[1] and the Loan Guarantee Scheme[2]. This, it was hoped, would not only "free" the hitherto latent entrepreneurial talents of the U.K. workforce, but also reduce labour market rigidities characterized by the large-firm unionized sector, which many policy-makers at the time believed contributed to the poor competitiveness and hence the growth in unemployment in the early 1980s.

In the 1970s self-employment peaked at around 2 million in mid-1973 (see Fig. 1). However, the underlying trend was downward for this decade, reaching a low point between 1977 and 1979 of 1.9 million. The post-1979 period was characterized by dramatic increases in the number of self-employed which peaked at 3.3 million in mid-1990. More recently there has been a significant fall in self-employment, with a reduction of around 400,000 between mid-1990 and 1993.

If we consider growth rates of self-employment over time it is apparent that the period between 1973 and 1979 was characterized by negative growth rates (up to 10 per cent for some quarters). After a period of relative stability between 1978 and mid-1979 growth rates became positive for some 11 years thereafter. Within these 11 years, however, there were three periods of dramatic growth, between mid-1983 and mid-1984, between 1986 and 1987, and in 1989. The one period of significantly low growth rates occurred between mid-1985 and mid-1986.

One of the interesting features of our paper is that our extended time series analysis from 1972 to 1992 allows us to evaluate both of the great post-war recessions in the United Kingdom. To date little analysis has been undertaken which covers the 1990 recession, when set in the context of the previous decade in which self-employment and small business creation was actively and positively encouraged and supported. Responding to this we further question whether the 1980s will come to be seen as a positive short-run blip in what appears to be a long-term historical decline in self-employment.

The rest of the paper is set out as follows. Section II develops the theoretical framework for our analysis in a relatively informal context, by focusing on the key themes and issues that are to be investigated empirically. In identifying these fundamental areas we refer back to a number of the most prominent theoretical and empirical studies dealing with self-employment. In Section III we report empirical results and discuss our findings in the context of previous work. Section IV draws some conclusions.

---

[1]Originally set up in 1983, individuals are now paid between £40 and £100 per week for up to the whole of their first year of self-employment.
[2]Under this scheme, set up in 1981, the government acted as a guarantor for between 70 and 80 per cent of loans of up to £100,000. Loans attracted a fixed margin over base interest rates.

The Evolution of U.K. Self-employment 429

II THEORETICAL FRAMEWORK AND VARIABLE SELECTION

There have been a number of studies of self-employment over the last decade. The majority have been set up in a framework outlining the decision rules used to determine one's choice of labour market state, based on the respective utilities (often proxied by income) of being in one of three labour market states, namely self-employment, waged employment or unemployment. The standard models define (see for example Evans and Leighton, 1989; Robson, 1994) income earned in self-employment as

$$Y = R(\theta, K, \sigma) - rK \qquad (1)$$

where R denotes real business revenue, K the amount of capital invested and r the interest rate on loans, θ being a shift parameter in the revenue function which reflects the individual's entrepreneurial ability. Finally, σ is a random variable which captures fluctuations in aggregate demand around trend levels. It is assumed that income is increasing in entrepreneurial ability and capital and decreasing with interest rates. The self-employment income is then compared with the market wage in employment and the level of benefits in unemployment, the individual choosing the state that maximizes his or her income in each time period.

In the context of our paper perhaps the most interesting previous studies were undertaken by Blanchflower and Oswald (1990) and Robson (1994). The Blanchflower and Oswald study, reported in the British Social Attitudes Survey, implicitly questions whether the Conservative Government (between 1983 and 1989) actually succeeded in creating a new economic and social order within which individuals were liberated and thus able to pursue new paths of wealth creation which were previously not open to them. The Robson study is the closest to ours in terms of its use of quarterly time series data on self-employment (although Robson only considers male self-employment) and in terms of the theoretical framework used.

From the theoretical and empirical literature, we can identify a number of recurring themes that merit more detailed discussion. As indicated above, the standard theoretical models tend to discuss the self-employment decision in terms of the income differential in alternative labour market states.

However, whilst we take this essentially microeconomic foundation as our starting point, our interest also extends to much broader macroeconomic changes in the U.K. economy over the period. Furthermore we also consider socioeconomic shifts that may have occurred, for instance an increased policy focus on small businesses and a desire to increase home ownership. With this in mind we develop our discussion in three main areas, namely capital and finance, demand–supply and the business cycle, and government policy and schemes.

Further refinements to the Robson, Evans and Leighton method-ologies include the relaxation of the assumption of risk neutrality on the part of decision-makers, the introduction of uncertainty into the model, an extended focus on policy issues and an investigation of recessionary influences upon self-employment.

Capital and Finance

There is a large volume of literature dealing with the role of interest rates and collateral in the context of small-firm–bank lending contracts (see for example Besanko and Thakor, 1987; Berger and Udell, 1990; Sharpe, 1990). The majority of these studies focus on the information asymmetries implicit in the relationship and the development of contingency contracts by banks involving the posting of collateral. Empirical studies such as those of Binks *et al.* (1988) and Cowling *et al.* (1991) point to the potential for collateral requirements to constrain small-firms' borrowing. If we consider that an individual's total endowment of assets can be defined as

$$A = A^{\mathrm{NL}} + A^{\mathrm{L}} \tag{2}$$

where A^{NL} are non-liquid assets and A^{L} are liquid assets, then the total capital available to finance a start-up can be defined as $A^{\mathrm{L}} + \delta A^{\mathrm{NL}}$, where δ reflects the amount of money a bank will lend per £1 of non-liquid asset. This theme is developed by Black *et al.* (1996) who investigate the extent to which the supply of collateral affects business formation in the United Kingdom. Implicit in their analysis is the assumption that bank loans are typically secured on the value of an entrepreneur's house. They report that a 10 per cent rise in the value of owner-occupied housing stock is associated with a 5 per cent increase in new VAT registrations. One important structural change in financial markets was the deregulation that occurred in 1986 which allowed building societies, banks and other institutions to operate in key areas that were previously not within their remit. In terms of our discussion the subsequent increases in the number of potential lenders to small businesses and the self-employed is of primary importance, particularly when allied to increasing house ownership and the house price boom. To capture this effect we incorporate a housing wealth measure denoted LHW. In addition to housing variables we also consider "net financial wealth" which is intended to pick up other wealth effects, apart from housing wealth, which could affect the ability to finance the shift into self-employment either directly or by increasing an entrepreneur's ability to raise external, ostensibly bank, finance. Higher net worth in the form of financial assets is identified by Meyer (1990), Evans and Leighton (1989) and Dolton and Makepeace (1990) as having a positive effect on entry into self-employment.

The Evolution of U.K. Self-employment 431

Demand–Supply and the Business Cycle

In the short run changes in economic activity are likely to feed through to self-employment via demand-side effects. A cyclical upturn, for instance, will increase the demand for self-employed labour and also for the products and services offered by the self-employed. Yet the flexible nature of the working arrangements of the self-employed means that, *ceteris paribus*, short-run cyclical changes are partially absorbed by increases or decreases in hours worked. This means that self-employment will be less responsive to short-run changes in demand.

The supply side is characterized by contrasting views on what factors generate the supply of people seeking self-employment. Bogenhold (1985) identifies two opposing recruitment channels into self-employment—the desire for autonomy and economic necessity—whilst Stanworth and Curran (1973) argue that "Social and economic marginality may be a strong driving force motivating people to set up their own business". This concept is supported by Steinmetz and Wright (1989) who see the resurgence of self-employment as a response to declining wage-employment opportunities. There is a large volume of literature which lends support to the recession-push hypothesis, which argues that unemployment acts as a catalyst, encouraging the unemployed to start up in business for themselves. Empirical studies by Storey and Johnson (1987) in the United Kingdom and Evans and Leighton (1989) in the United States both lend support to this theory. Indeed Bogenhold and Staber (1991) using European and U.S. data between 1950 and 1987 show a strong and positive relationship between unemployment and self-employment for most countries. However, they qualify this by stating that "Blanket public assistance given to anyone wishing to start a business may simply accelerate the economic peripherali-sation of many of the self-employed". On the down side, however, is the fact that the long-term unemployed are unlikely to have either the required entrepreneurial talents or access to start-up capital. Newly unemployed individuals, LSRUN, are more likely to have access to savings and/or redundancy payments which could be used to finance business start-up. If we accept that many of the long-term unemployed, LLRUN, are marginalized anyhow and operate at the periphery of the labour market in low-paid, low-skilled employment, then the only discernible flows into self-employment, from this group, are likely to be into low-wage, low-skilled sectors. In addition, it is likely that such individuals' survival chances will be greatly reduced.

Government Policy and Schemes

Government policies can influence the levels of self-employment directly via specific schemes designed to support individuals moving into self-employment, or indirectly via fiscal policy. In Britain, an important scheme for the self-employed was the Enterprise Allowance Scheme, LEAS, set up in 1983 to offer income support to unemployed people wishing to set up in business. The allowance partially compensates the individual for the loss of unemployment benefit in the first year of self-employment. At its peak in 1987–88 in excess of 106,000 people were on the scheme. Indirect effects include changes in marginal tax rates which affect comparative returns to self-employment and employment. This issue is discussed by Blau (1987) who argues that rises in marginal tax rates in upper income brackets have had a positive effect on self-employment. Implicit in his analysis is the assumption that it is easier to "under report" income in self-employment. Johnson *et al.* (1988) also point out that "Privatisation and the enforced contracting-out of local authority and other services will create opportunities for the self-employed and small businesses". Clearly, government policy can have both demand-side and supply-side effects on self-employment.

III EMPIRICAL RESULTS

The aim of our study is to investigate, using quarterly time series data, the determinants of U.K. total self-employment as a proportion of the workforce over the period 1972–92. Our methodology is to use the two-step ordinary least squares estimator proposed by Engle and Granger (1987) to specify an error correction model.

Initially we focus on the selection of variables which determine the equilibrium or long-run behaviour of self-employment. Given the discussion above it is of interest to know whether or not this relationship has changed over time. To permit an examination of the time variation of the relative importance of each explanatory variable we also estimate their coefficients recursively using a least squares method.

Then the residuals from the first step, which are interpreted as a measure of "deviation from equilibrium", are incorporated in a dynamic model which focuses on short-run behaviour of self-employment. Essentially, if according to our steady-state description of self-employment the proportion is below its equilibrium level, then the model predicts growth in self-employment, and vice versa.

Our main interest is to investigate empirically the recession-push hypothesis, the importance of alternative wage theories, the impact of government policies and initiatives, the effect of financial market variables and in particular the role of the housing market.

The dependent variable is taken to be the natural logarithm of the ratio of the number of self-employed relative to the total workforce.

The Evolution of U.K. Self-employment   433

Long Run

The coefficient estimates of the long-run model are presented below. The model exhibits positive effects as expected from housing wealth and the self-employed/wage-employed income differential.

An interesting result is that short- and long-term unemployment (U_s and U_1 respectively) have opposite effects, with the effect on self-employment being negative for U_s but of similar magnitude. A 10 per cent increase in short-term unemployment reduces self-employment by (roughly) 1 per cent in the long run. The model residuals are stationary which is necessary for the dynamic model discussed below to be valid. The Dickey–Fuller and augmented Dickey–Fuller statistics are $-3\cdot7$ and $-3\cdot74$; hence the null of the unit root in the residuals is rejected.

$$\ln\frac{\text{SE}}{L} = -6\cdot63 + 0\cdot31\ln\text{HW} + 1\cdot85\ln\left(\frac{Y_{se}}{Y_w}\right) - 0\cdot11\ln U_s + 0\cdot08\ln U_1 \qquad (3)$$

The sample period is 1972Q2–1992Q2.

The housing wealth variable, HW, raises self-employment by increasing the individual's ability to raise finance from banks. A 10 per cent increase in housing wealth will increase the proportion of the workforce in self-employment by 3 per cent. This effect is very similar in magnitude to the result of Black *et al.* (1996) who find the elasticity of housing equity on VAT registrations to be 0·5 and supports the work of Meyer (1990) and Evans and Leighton (1989) who argue that higher "net" worth has a positive effect on entry into self-employment.

An interesting finding is revealed in the time variation of the housing wealth coefficient (see Fig. 2). The influence of housing wealth becomes more important in the mid to late 1980s in explaining the behaviour of self-employment. This period coincides with major deregulations governing the activities of financial institutions, effectively allowing owner-occupiers to unlock equity accumulated during periods of buoyant house prices. In a house price boom it is now possible to capitalize housing equity as a direct source of funds. Also since the supply of lending is proportional to housing wealth owner-occupiers are likely to face fewer borrowing constraints. Moreover the ability of housing wealth to serve as collateral becomes important in the light of ongoing changes in the banking system which require that more and more loans be collateralized (see Cowling *et al.,* 1991).

In terms of absolute size, the coefficient on the self-employed/employee income differential is the most important variable determining equilibrium self-employment. The differential increased by 6 per cent in the 1980s, implying an increase in self-employment of about 11 per cent. Figure 3 illustrates this coefficient over time and shows a dramatic increase in the importance of the income differential through the 1980s. This result compares well with other empirical studies of self-employment—see for example Fujii and Hawley (1991) who find that "by far the most powerful predictor of choice of mode of work is the predicted income differential".

Turning to the time-varying effects of unemployment the opposing signs on short-term and long-term unemployment provide an interesting contrast concerning the role of unemployment in the two recessions which fell in the middle and at the end of the sample. Within the standard error bounds of the successive coefficient estimates the effect of short-term unemployment, U_s, was consistently negative (see Fig. 4), particularly so after 1981. However, in both recessions there is upward movement in this coefficient, making it *less* negative. In other words, at the onset of a recession the short-term unemployed increase the proportion of the workforce in self-employment relative to non-recessionary periods. This effect is discussed further below in the context of the recession-push hypothesis. The positive effect on self-employment from long-term unemployment, U_l, implies that if the number of long-term unemployed goes up by 10 per cent then the proportion of the workforce in self-employment increases by approximately 1 per cent. Analysis of the recursive coefficients (see Fig. 5) shows that the role of long-term unemployment becomes even more important as we progress through the 1980s. In this context we view entry into self-employment as possibly the (only) option for long-term unemployed individuals.

Clearly in terms of the recession-push hypothesis it is the duration structure of unemployment which matters, *not* simply the stock of unemployed people. Our empirical results show that short- and long-term unemployed have (roughly) equal and opposite effects on self-employment; therefore a given percentage increase in the two categories will have little "net" effect on self-employment and therefore no recession-push effect. However, the duration structure of unemployment is of issue because it varies over the business cycle.

As the economy enters a recession there are proportionately more short-term unemployed. Whether or not this cohort eventually becomes long-term unemployed depends on the depth and severity of the recession.

Initially, the short-term unemployed can compete for waged employment and are re-employed, thus tending to lower the proportion of the workforce in self-employment. But as unemployment spells lengthen these individuals become the long-term unemployed. At the same time the likelihood of obtaining waged employment diminishes and self-employment becomes a last resort option for long-term unemployed people. However, it is quite probable that only a small proportion of the long-term unemployed actually enter self-employment since this group is characterized as having fewer financial resources, having lower levels of human capital and more likely to experience borrowing constraints. In addition, those who do enter self-employment will tend to displace existing self-employed workers owing to the types of work available to them.

Short Run

The dynamic error correction model is reported below, where the dependent variable is now the first difference of the proportion of the workforce in self-employment. In the short-run model growth in the self-employed/waged employee income differential Y_{se}/Y_w, real fixed capital formation INV, the Enterprise Allowance Scheme EAS and the Loan Guarantee Scheme LGS were all found to act positively on self-employment. Interestingly, none of the long-run determinants appeared to exert short-run effects although the growth term for the income differential did appear in the short-run equation. This may well suggest that the transitory component of the self-employed is more susceptible to self-employment when their entry is smoothed by government schemes and a low risk environment.

$$\Delta \ln\left[\frac{SE}{(L)_t}\right] = 0{\cdot}001 + \underset{(9\cdot2)}{0{\cdot}669} \, \Delta \ln\left[\frac{SE}{(L)_{t-2}}\right] + \underset{(4\cdot0)}{0{\cdot}003} \, \Delta \ln \text{EAS}_t$$

$$- \underset{(-2\cdot2)}{0{\cdot}054} \, \text{ECM}_{t-1} + \underset{(3\cdot1)}{0{\cdot}011} \, \Delta \ln \text{LGS}_{t-2} + \underset{(2\cdot2)}{0{\cdot}0102} \, \Delta \ln \text{INV}_t$$

$$+ \underset{(1\cdot9)}{0{\cdot}182} \, \Delta \ln\left[\frac{Y_{se}}{(Y_w)_t}\right] \tag{4}$$

The sample period is 1972Q2–1989Q2, $R^2 = 0{\cdot}62286$, DW $= 1{\cdot}5$, serial correlation $(4) = 8{\cdot}2415$, functional form $(1) = 0{\cdot}26215$, normality $(2) = 2{\cdot}531$, heteroscedasticity $(1) = 0{\cdot}1935\text{e}^{-3}$, residual serial correlation $(6) = 9{\cdot}1986$, forecast 1989Q3–1991Q4, predictive failure $(9) = 10{\cdot}9728$, Chow test $(7) = 10{\cdot}8031$. Figures in brackets are t ratios. Δ is the first difference operator. The size of the error correction coefficient implies that self-employment adjusts slowly towards its equilibrium level. None of the model diagnostics reported above was found to be significant at the 5 per cent level. This suggests that the model is structurally stable and an adequate model of the time variation in self-employment over the sample period.

Growth in the income differential exerted a consistently positive influence on self-employment growth, exhibiting a slight increase in importance over the last decade. This provides further support for the theory that income differentials are a powerful predictor of state in the labour market. Concerning government policy the evidence suggests that two of the most important initiatives, namely the Loan Guarantee Scheme and the Enterprise Allowance Scheme, were effective in terms of achieving their stated objectives of increasing self-employment and removing the financial barriers that the self-employed were perceived to be facing. Interestingly, both policy initiatives appear to be increasing in importance since their inception in 1981 and 1983 respectively.

The positive effect recorded on changes in real fixed capital formation, INV, is consistent with the results of Parker (1996) who uses this effect to measure risk and uncertainty. In line with his work we also assume that firms are less willing to commit themselves to new investment projects in uncertain times when the risk of not achieving the required returns on an investment is higher. To this end the positive coefficient on real investment, INV, is consistent with the view that, as risk and uncertainty are reduced, investment rises and thus entry into self-employment increases.

The model adequacy was also checked by carrying out an out-of-sample forecast test over the period 1989Q3–1991Q4. The results show that the model is stable and was able to track the decrease in self-employment that occurred in the post-1990 period.

No evidence was found to support the notion that changes in marginal and average tax rates explicitly affected the level of self-employment. We note, however, that reduced National Insurance contributions for the self-employed may act to increase the net income differential, although for waged employees holiday pay and suchlike may offset this effect.

Empirical evidence from Robson (1992) shows that real interest rates have a negative effect on the rate of new VAT registrations. However, the inclusion of interest rate measures, nominal or real, provided no improvement in the explanatory power of our model and they were therefore omitted.

IV CONCLUSION

We have estimated both long-run and short-run equations for self-employment at the aggregate level using quarterly time series data for the period between 1972 and 1993, during which there were significant changes in the importance of self-employment. Given that an important part of our analysis is to evaluate the role of the recession-push hypothesis we begin with the discussion of unemployment effects.

Our work suggests that it is *not* the stock of unemployed individuals but the duration structure of that stock which matters. In our model an equi-proportionate increase in unemployment by duration category produces no "net" change in self-employment and hence no empirical support for recession-push. We do find that when short-term unemployment increases this tends to reduce the proportion of the workforce in self-employment probably because the majority of new entrants into unemployment are successful in obtaining re-employment.

As the ratio of short-term to long-term unemployment falls, a pool of structurally unemployed workers is created. These individuals make fewer job applications and receive fewer offers—hence they are marginalized to such a degree, in terms of obtaining waged employment, that self-employment becomes a last resort option. However, there are two reasons why the long-term unemployed cannot simply become self-employed. First, this group has fewer financial resources, has lower levels of human capital and is more likely to experience borrowing constraints at the start-up stage. Second, those who do enter self-employment tend to displace the existing self-employed owing to the restricted range of activities available to them. To this end we do not view the Thatcher era as a period which released the latent entrepreneurial talents of the U.K. workforce.

We also find empirical evidence linking part of the rise in self-employment to activity in the housing market. This linkage became more important in the 1980s as financial market deregulation occurred allowing for owner-occupiers to capitalize a greater part of housing equity as a direct source of start-up funds during the housing market boom.

At the same time increased housing wealth lowers, but does not remove, entry barriers to self-employment arising from borrowing constraints for two reasons. First, the supply of lending is directly proportional to housing wealth since the latter serves as collateral; second, ongoing changes in the banking system are likely to require that more and more loans be collateralized.

Our empirical findings suggest that the most important determinant of the proportion of the workforce in self-employment is the income differential between self-employed sand employed workers.

The two key government schemes, the Enterprise Allowance Scheme and the Loan Guarantee Scheme, were both found to be important explanatory factors in the growth of self-employment in the 1980s. The Enterprise Allowance Scheme operated by effectively providing an income subsidy to the unemployed in order to encourage them to enter self-employment. We argue that this is hardly the stuff of entrepreneurs, yet it clearly induced significant numbers into self-employment. Indeed the high take-up of the Enterprise Allowance Scheme may well be attributable to its ability to reduce the income risk associated with entering self-employment. The success of the Loan Guarantee Scheme is linked to its focus on removing the collateral constraints that start-ups, and existing small businesses, were facing. It certainly appears likely that both initiatives are likely to continue for the foreseeable future.

Importantly, the evidence presented here does link increases in self-employment in the 1980s to the relaxation of capital constraints. This was possible because of a buoyant housing market and measures taken to deregulate financial markets. We are not optimistic that this combination

438   *The Manchester School*

of events will be repeated. Currently the housing market is depressed and the number of repossessions is at a historical high, while the process of financial market deregulation is more or less complete. However, entry barriers to self-employment can be reduced by expanding and extending existing government schemes, or by encouraging banks to take a more realistic long-term view of their lending policies. If the long-term unemployed are to obtain sustainable jobs in the self-employed sector they must have access to appropriate advice, training programmes and financial resources.

Changes in the nature of work organization will continue to provide opportunities for self-employment, especially where sub-contracting out of certain functions, particularly in business services and construction, is concerned. Therefore we expect self-employment to continue to be important as a form of work organization in the United Kingdom.

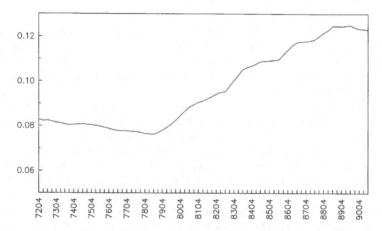

Fɪɢ. 1   Total Self-employment as a Proportion of the Workforce

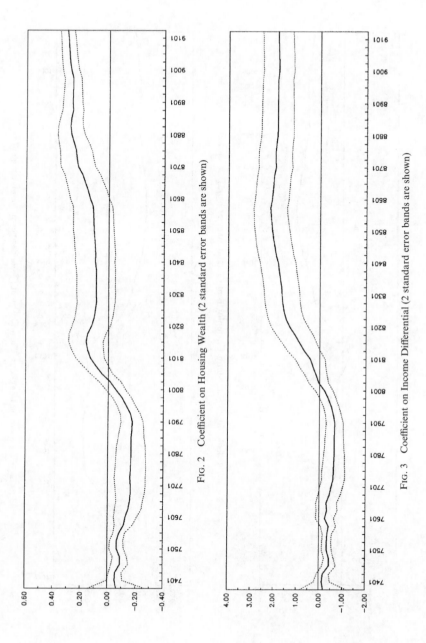

FIG. 2   Coefficient on Housing Wealth (2 standard error bands are shown)

FIG. 3   Coefficient on Income Differential (2 standard error bands are shown)

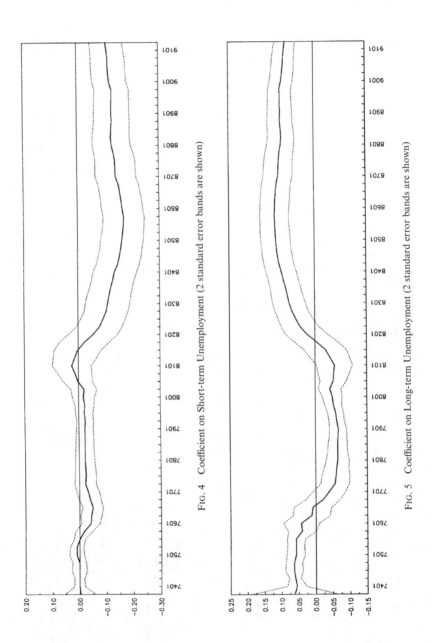

FIG. 4   Coefficient on Short-term Unemployment (2 standard error bands are shown)

FIG. 5   Coefficient on Long-term Unemployment (2 standard error bands are shown)

The Evolution of U.K. Self-employment 441

APPENDIX: LIST OF VARIABLES

$\ln(SE/L)$ The number of self-employed divided by the total workforce.
Source: LFS

$\ln(Y_{se}/Y_w)$ The ratio of self-employed income to income in waged employment.
Source: *Economic Trends*

$\ln$ HW The value of housing wealth defined as the product of the owner-occupier housing stock and the average dwelling price.
Source: Housing and Construction Statistics

$\ln U_s$ Short-term unemployment (i.e. < 52 weeks). *Source*: LFS

$\ln U_l$ Long-term unemployed (i.e. > 52 weeks). *Source*: LFS

$\ln$ LGS Number using the Loan Guarantee Scheme. *Source*: DTI

$\ln$ EAS Number using the Enterprise Allowance Scheme. *Source*: DTI

$\ln$ INV Real gross domestic fixed capital formation in transport and communications. *Source*: *Economic Trends*

REFERENCES

Berger, A. and Udell, G. (1990). "Collateral, Loan Quality and Bank Risk", *Journal of Monetary Economics*, Vol. 25, No. 1, January, pp. 21–42.

Besanko, D. and Thakor, A. (1987). "Competitive Equilibrium in the Credit Market Under Asymmetric Information", *Journal of Economic Theory*, Vol. 42, No. 1, June, pp. 167–182.

Binks, M., Ennew, C. and Reed, G. (1988). "Banks and Small Businesses: an Interbank Comparison", Report to the Forum of Private Business, Knutsford, Cheshire.

Black, J., de Meza, D. and Jeffreys, D. (1996). "House Prices, the Supply of Collateral and the Enterprise Economy", *Economic Journal*, Vol. 106, No. 434, January, pp. 60–75.

Blanchflower, D. G. and Oswald, A. J. (1990). "Self-employment and the Enterprise Culture", in R. Jowell, S. Witherspoon and R. Javell (eds), *British Social Attitudes: the 1990 Report*, Aldershot, Gower.

Blau, D. M. (1987). "A Time Series Analysis of Self-employment in the United States", *Journal of Political Economy*, Vol. 95, No.3, pp. 445–467.

Bogenhold, D. (1985). *Die Selbstandigen: Zur Soziologie dezentraler Production*, Frankfurt and New York: Campus.

Bogenhold, D. and Staber, U. (1991). "The Decline and Rise of Self Employment", *Work, Employment and Society*, Vol. 5, pp. 223–239.

Cowling, M., Samuels, J. and Sugden, R. (1991). *Small Firms and Clearing Banks: a Sterile, Uncommunicative and Unimaginative Relationship*, London, Association of British Chambers of Commerce.

Dolton, P. J. and Makepeace, G. (1990). "Self Employment Among Graduates", *Bulletin of Economic Research*, Vol. 42, pp. 35–53.

Engle, R. F. and Granger, C. W. J. (1987). "Co-integration and Error Correction: Representation, Estimation and Testing", *Econometrica*, Vol. 55, pp. 251–276.

Evans, D. and Leighton, L. (1989). "Some Empirical Aspects of Entrepreneurship", *American Economic Review*, Vol. 79, pp. 519–535.

Fujii, E. T. and Hawley, C. B. (1991). "Empirical Aspects of Self-Employment", *Economics Letters*, Vol. 36, No. 3, July, pp. 323–329.

Johnson, S., Lindley, R. and Bourlakis, C. (1988). "Modelling Aggregate Self-employment: a Preliminary Analysis", *DE Programme Project Report*, Institute for Employment Research, University of Warwick.

Meyer, B. D. (1990). "Why Are There so Few Black Entrepreneurs?", *NBER Working Paper 3537*.

Parker, S. C. (1996). "A Time Series Model of Self-employment Under Uncertainty", *Economica*, Vol. 63, No. 251, August, pp. 459–476.

Robson, M. T. (1992). "Macroeconomic Factors in the Birth and Death of UK Firms: Evidence from Quarterly V.A.T. Registrations", *Newcastle Discussion Papers in Economics*, Newcastle.

Robson, M. T. (1994). "The Determinants of Self-employment Amongst U.K. Males, 1968–90", *Newcastle Discussion Papers in Economics*, Newcastle.

Sharpe, S. (1991). "Asymmetric Information, Bank Lending and Implicit Contracts. A Stylised Model of Customer Relationships", *Journal of Finance*, Vol. 45, 4 September.

Stanworth, J. and Curran, J. (1973). *Management Motivation in the Smaller Business*, Epping, Gower.

Steinmetz, G. and Wright, E. (1989). "The Fall and Rise of the Petty Bourgeoisie: Changing Patterns of Self-employment in the United States", *American Journal of Sociology*, Vol. 94, pp. 973–1018.

Storey, D. J. and Johnson, S. (1987). *Are Small Firms the Answer to Unemployment?*, London, Employment Institute.

[27]

Alternative and Part-Time Employment Arrangements as a Response to Job Loss

Henry S. Farber, *Princeton University*

I examine the extent to which workers who lose jobs obtain work in alternative employment arrangements, including temporary work and independent contracting, and obtain voluntary or involuntary part-time work. I find that job losers are significantly more likely than nonlosers to be in both temporary jobs (including on-call work and contract work) and involuntarily part-time jobs. I also find evidence that temporary and involuntary part-time jobs are part of a transitional process subsequent to job loss leading to regular full-time employment.

I. Introduction

The purpose of this study is to examine the extent to which workers who lose jobs find work in alternative employment arrangements, including temporary work and independent contracting and in voluntary or involuntary part-time jobs rather than as conventional full-time employees. My analysis is based on data from the Displaced Worker Supplements (DWS) to the February 1994 and 1996 Current Population Surveys (CPS) that I match to the Contingent and Alternative Employment Arrangements Supplements (CAEAS) to the February CPSs in the subsequent years (1995 and 1997, respectively). These data allow me to identify job

Support for this research was provided by the Office of the Assistant Secretary of Labor for Policy, U.S. Department of Labor under Purchase Order no. B9462164, and by the Industrial Relations Section at Princeton University. Karen Conneely and Harry Krashinsky provided able research assistance. Susan Houseman and David Neumark provided useful comments on earlier drafts.

[*Journal of Labor Economics*, 1999, vol. 17, no. 4, pt. 2]

losers in the DWS, and they contain detailed information on their post-displacement employment arrangements from the CAEAS.

Interest in this subject is motivated by several factors. First, while employment in the United States has grown steadily for the last 20 years, substantial concern exists about the quality of the stock of jobs.[1] Areas of concern include increased inequality in wages, a decline in real wages at the lower end of the distribution, and reductions in important fringe benefits such as employer-provided health insurance.[2] Second, concern has developed in the last decade regarding high rates of job loss and reduced job security.[3] Finally, there has been concern about an increase in the fraction of the work force in part-time and temporary jobs.[4] The evidence also suggests that these jobs do not offer pay, fringe benefits, or opportunity for advancement comparable to those on regular jobs.[5]

The interaction between job loss and alternative work arrangements has not been examined in previous work. In my earlier work (Farber, 1997*b*) I found that workers who lose jobs are more likely to be reemployed in part-time jobs and, even when reemployed in a full-time job, they earn significantly less than they did prior to their job loss. Part of these costs associated with job loss may be related to difficulty finding conventional employment arrangements. The central goal of this study is to provide statistical evidence on the extent to which alternative employment arrangements are, in fact, a common response to job loss. I find that temporary employment and involuntary part-time employment are used disprortionately by job losers, and I also investigate in some detail

---

[1] Civilian employment was 89.9 million in January 1977 and rose to 128.6 million in January 1997, for an average annual increase of almost 2 million jobs per year. These statistics are taken from U.S. Bureau of Labor Statistics Series ID LFS11000000. This is the seasonally adjusted civilian employment level derived from the CPS for workers aged 16 and older.

[2] See Farber (1997*a*) for a brief review of and references to the literature on job quality and for an analysis of the quality of new jobs. Farber and Levy (1999) present an analysis of the decline in employer-provided health insurance that focuses on workers in new jobs and on part-time workers.

[3] The most recently available data show elevated rates of job loss in the 1993–95 period (Farber 1997*b*) and a reduction between 1993 and 1996 in the fraction of the workforce who have been in their jobs for long periods of time (Farber 1997*c*). For further analyses of job loss and its consequences see Podgursky and Swaim (1987), Kletzer (1989), Topel (1990), Farber (1993), Gardner (1995), Neal (1995), and Parent (1995).

[4] See, e.g., Howe (1986), Belous (1989), Abraham (1990), Blank (1990*b*), Golden and Applebaum (1992), Abraham and Taylor (1996), and Houseman (1997) for discussions of the incidence of and motivations for alternative employment arrangements.

[5] See, e.g., Blank (1989, 1990*a*), Tilley (1991), Montgomery and Cosgrove (1993), and Ferber and Waldfogel (1996).

whether or not these alternative employment arrangements are a transitional experience for job losers.

II. The February 1995 and February 1997 CAEAS Data

The February 1995 and 1997 CAEAS to the CPS contain information on alternative employment arrangements held at the survey date. Workers in alternative employment arrangements include independent contractors, consultants, freelance workers, other self-employed workers, temporary workers, on-call workers, and contract workers. In order to focus the analysis, I combine these into three categories. The first category, which I call independent contractors, consists of independent contractors, consultants, and freelance workers. The second category is composed of other self-employed workers (other-SE). The third category, which I call temporary workers, consists of temporary, on-call, and contract workers.[6]

In order to place workers in these categories, I use data from the basic CPS questionnaire as well as from the CAEAS. Specifically, a worker is classified as an independent contractor if he or she is employed at the survey date, is classified as self-employed in the basic CPS, and responds affirmatively in the CAEAS that he or she is "self-employed as an independent contractor, independent consultant, free-lance worker, or something else."[7] A worker is classified as other SE if he or she is employed at the survey date, is classified as self-employed in the basic CPS, and is not classified as an independent contractor as defined here.[8] A worker is classified as a temporary worker if he or she is employed at the survey date, is not classified as either type of self-employed worker, and responds affirmatively that he or she is in a temporary job, works for a temporary work agency, is an on-call worker, is a day laborer, or is a

---

[6] Another potential way to identify temporary workers is to classify those workers who report their industry of employment as personnel supply services (Census Industry Code 731). However, most workers who actually work for personnel supply firms apparently report themselves as employed in the industry to which they are assigned. Evidence for this conclusion is that the Current Employment Survey data, which are based on information collected from employers, show that 2.2% of nonfarm employment was in the personnel supply services industry (SIC 736) in 1997 (based on BLS series EEU00000001 and EEU8073601). In contrast, my tabulations of the February 1997 CPS show that 0.76% of employment was in the personnel supply services industry (CIC 731). Additionally, the personnel supply services industry includes an unknown number of workers who are not temporary workers. Thus, use of this industry classification to identify temporary workers in the CPS is not likely to be very useful here. See Segal and Sullivan (1997) for an analysis that does use this method to identify temporary workers. See also Polivka (1996).

[7] See U.S. Bureau of the Census (1995, pp. 9–21).

[8] Many of these workers are likely to be owners of small businesses.

contract employee. All other workers (including part-time) are classified as "regular" workers.

The first four columns of table 1 contain weighted breakdowns of employment arrangements for 102,318 individuals aged 20–66 who are employed at the survey date in the February 1995 and 1997 CAEASs.[9] The first row of the table contains the breakdown for the entire sample, and it shows 82.5% in "regular" employment relationships, 5.9% independent contractors, 5.4% other SE, and 6.2% temporary workers.

The last three columns of table 1 contain weighted breakdowns of full/part-time status for the same sample. The full/part-time distinction is made using data from the basic CPS information on hours of work. Part-time workers are those whose total hours on all jobs are less than 35 hours per week.[10] Those part-time workers who report a preference for working full-time and who report being part-time for economic reasons (slack work, can't find a full-time job, seasonal work) are classified as involuntary part-time. The remainder are classified as voluntary part-time. The first row of the table contains the breakdown for the entire sample, and shows 84.7% in full-time employment relationships, 10.8% voluntarily part-time, and 4.5% involuntarily part-time.

The remainder of table 1 contains breakdowns of employed workers by type of employment and full/part-time status separately by sex, education level, and age.[11] A significantly larger fraction of females than males (85.1% vs. 80.2%) are in regular employment relationships. This is due to the fact that females are significantly less likely than males (8.5% vs.

---

[9] This age range was selected to match individuals who were 20–64 in the February 1994 DWS. These percentages and other statistics presented in this study are weighted by the CPS final sampling weights. The CAEAS is distributed with special supplement weights to account for nonresponse to the supplement. These weights are based on differential response rates by demographic group, and they are highly correlated with the final sampling weights (correlation = 0.9988). Thus, while my use of the final sampling weights would understate overall population counts relative to those derived by using the special supplement weights, both weights will yield similar results with regard to computation of means and proportions.

[10] The algorithm for assigning part-time status to workers has several steps: (1) a worker is considered part-time if usual total hours are less than 35 per week; (2) where usual total hours are missing, then a worker is considered full-time if usual hours on the main job are at least 35 per week; (3) where part-time status remains unassigned, actual total hours during the reference week are used; and, finally, (4) an indicator in the basic CPS for "usually full time" is used to resolve the remaining cases.

[11] While not presented here, I also carried out multivariate probit analyses of the probability of being in employment relationships of each type. These probit models controlled for race as well as for sex, education, age, and they show the same relationships of the likelihood of alternative arrangements as the simple breakdowns in table 1.

Table 1
Fraction of Employed with Specific Alternative Employment Arrangements, February 1995 and 1997 CAEAS

Group	Workers Aged 20–66						
	Regular	Contractor	Other-SE	Temporary	Full-Time	Voluntary Part-Time	Involuntary Part-Time
All	.825	.059	.054	.062	.847	.108	.045
	(.001)	(.001)	(.001)	(.001)	(.001)	(.001)	(.001)
Male	.802	.076	.061	.061	.918	.045	.036
	(.002)	(.001)	(.001)	(.001)	(.002)	(.001)	(.001)
Female	.851	.039	.046	.064	.765	.180	.055
	(.002)	(.001)	(.001)	(.001)	(.002)	(.001)	(.001)
Education < 12 years	.823	.053	.047	.077	.818	.087	.094
	(.004)	(.002)	(.002)	(.003)	(.004)	(.003)	(.002)
Education = 12 years	.841	.054	.052	.053	.853	.097	.050
	(.002)	(.001)	(.001)	(.001)	(.002)	(.002)	(.001)
Education 13–15 years	.828	.054	.049	.069	.810	.148	.042
	(.002)	(.001)	(.001)	(.001)	(.002)	(.002)	(.001)
Education ≥ 16 years	.803	.071	.064	.062	.890	.084	.026
	(.002)	(.001)	(.001)	(.001)	(.002)	(.002)	(.001)
Aged 20–24	.851	.012	.014	.123	.705	.226	.070
	(.004)	(.002)	(.002)	(.002)	(.003)	(.003)	(.002)
Aged 25–34	.853	.042	.035	.070	.868	.088	.044
	(.002)	(.001)	(.001)	(.001)	(.002)	(.002)	(.001)
Aged 35–44	.826	.066	.057	.052	.871	.090	.039
	(.002)	(.001)	(.001)	(.001)	(.002)	(.002)	(.001)
Aged 45–54	.810	.076	.072	.043	.885	.075	.040
	(.003)	(.002)	(.002)	(.002)	(.002)	(.002)	(.001)
Aged 55–64	.767	.088	.095	.050	.812	.139	.049
	(.004)	(.002)	(.002)	(.002)	(.003)	(.003)	(.002)

NOTE.—Based on tabulations from the February 1995 and 1997 Contingent and Alternative Employment Arrangements Supplements (CAEAS) to the Current Population Surveys (CPS). See the text for definitions of the alternative employment arrangements and the full/part-time status classifications. The classifications of employment arrangements in the first four cols. are independent of full/part-time status classifications. All fractions are weighted by CPS sampling weights. The numbers in parentheses are standard errors; $N = 102,318$.

13.8%) to be self-employed (either type). There is only a small difference by sex in the rate of temporary employment. Despite being more likely to be in regular employment arrangements, females are substantially more likely than males to be employed part-time. The overall differential of 15.3 percentage points is accounted for largely by a 13.5 percentage-point differential in the rate of voluntary part-time employment that is supplemented by a 1.9 percentage-point differential in the rate of involuntary part-time employment. These differences likely reflect systematic differences in labor supply between men and women.

There is not a strictly monotonic relationship between education category and the incidence of regular employment relationships, but the most obvious pattern is that workers with at least 16 years of education have lower rates of regular employment (about two to four percentage points lower) than do workers with less education. This is accounted for by higher rates of self-employment (both types) among workers in the highest education category. With respect to part-time employment, the most striking difference is that workers in the highest education category have substantially higher full-time employment rates than do workers with less education. Workers with 12 years of education have an intermediate rate of full-time employment. The fact that the involuntary part-time rate is monotonically declining with education accounts for these findings (along with the unusually high voluntary part-time rate for workers with 13–15 years of education).

The fraction of workers in regular employment relationships declines monotonically with age. This results from an increase with age in the proportion of workers who are self-employed (both types) and a decrease with age in the fraction of workers who are in temporary jobs. The temporary job rate is particularly high for workers in the youngest age category. Full-time employment rates are lowest for workers in the youngest and oldest age categories, and this is primarily due to high voluntary part-time rates among workers in these two age categories. For the youngest workers, this may reflect part-time work while in enrolled in school. For the oldest workers this may reflect decreased labor supply of workers approaching retirement.

Note that the type of employment arrangements and full/part-time status are not independent. Table 2 contains a cross-tabulation of employment arrangements with part-time status for the 102,318 workers in the combined February 1995–February 1997 sample used in table 1.[12] Regular workers are substantially more likely to be full-time and less likely to be in either part-time category than are workers in the other

---

[12] A Pearson chi-squared text of independence in table 2 yields a test statistic of 3586.5 distributed as $\chi^2(6)$ and clearly rejects independence (p-value < .000001).

Table 2
Part-Time Status by Employment Arrangement, February 1995 and
1997 CAEAS

Group	Workers Aged 20–66 (Row Fractions)		
	Full-Time	Voluntary Part-Time	Involuntary Part-Time
Regular	.874	.092	.034
Contractor	.756	.148	.097
Other-SE	.781	.151	.069
Temporary	.638	.244	.119
All	.847	.108	.045

NOTE.—Based on tabulations from the February 1995 and 1997 Contingent and Alternative Employment Arrangements Supplements (CAEAS) to the Current Population Surveys (CPS). See the text for definitions of categories. $N = 102,318$.

employment arrangements. On the other extreme, temporary workers are least likely to be full-time and most likely to be in either part-time category. Fully 24.4% of temporary workers are voluntarily part-time and 11.9% of temporary workers are involuntarily part-time. This compares with 9.2% of regular workers in voluntary part-time jobs and 3.4% of regular workers in involuntary part-time jobs. The self-employed categories are intermediate in their full/part-time status.

III. Matching the February DWS and February CAEAS Data

The first step in matching the February 1994 and 1996 DWS with the February 1995 and 1997 CAEAS, respectively, is to define the pool of individuals eligible to be matched from the DWS. In order to be eligible to be in the CPS in both the DWS and CAEAS in the subsequent year, a household must be in one of its first 4 months in the sample in the DWS. Such a household is then eligible to be in the sample in the CAEAS in the subsequent year (in one of its 4 months back in the sample after an 8-month hiatus). But, because addresses rather than specific households or individuals are sampled and surveyed, only individuals who have not moved in the intervening year are eligible to be matched. Information contained in the CPS since 1994 is meant to allow an exact match of individuals across CPS, but, in order to reduce the likelihood of coding errors leading to inappropriate matches, I also match on a set of demographic characteristics (age, sex, and race).

I restrict my analysis to individuals aged 20–64 in the Februarys with the DWSs (1994 and 1996). There are 39,841 individuals in this age group in rotation groups 1–4 in February 1994, and there are 34,689 individuals in this age group in rotation groups 1–4 in February 1996. Thus, 74,530 individuals are eligible to be matched with individuals in the CAEAS in the subsequent year (February 1995 or February 1997). Of these, I am able to match 50,620 for a match rate of 67.9%. A problem is that the match rate depends centrally on whether or not individuals have changed residence between the survey dates. Not surprisingly, workers who lose jobs (defined precisely later in this section) are more likely to change residence. The match rate among job losers is 65.4% compared with a 69.1% match rate among nonlosers. The lower match rate among job losers is particularly unfortunate given the focus of this study, but there is no obvious solution to this problem.

It might be expected that the distribution of type of employment in the CAEAS in the subsequent year would be related to the probability of matching, with those in alternative employment relationships less likely to be matched. It turns out that there are generally small differences in the distributions of employment arrangements by whether the observation was matched. Specifically, recall that 82.5% of the overall sample from the CAEAS (including all eight rotation groups) were employed in regular jobs. Among those matched, 82.9% were employed in regular jobs. The comparisons for the other categories are fairly close: independent contractors (5.9% overall vs. 5.6% matched), other self-employed (5.4% overall vs. 6.8% matched), and temporary (6.2% overall vs. 4.7% matched). It appears that other self-employed are more likely to be matched, and this may reflect the fact that, based on the algorithm that defines this category, independent business owners are included in this category, and these businesses are not likely to be geographically mobile. In contrast, temporary workers are less likely to be matched. While there is nothing that can be done about this problem, it is important to note these differences in match rates.

Job Loss as Defined by the Displaced Worker Survey

The February 1994 and 1996 DWSs ask workers if they were displaced from a job at any time in the preceding 3-year period (1991–93 and 1994–1996, respectively). Other events, including quits and being fired for cause, are not considered displacement. Thus, the supplement is designed to focus on the loss of specific jobs that result from business decisions of firms unrelated to the performance of particular workers.

The central use of the DWS for the purposes of this study is to identify individuals who have lost a job in the relevant intervals. While job loss as measured by the DWS almost certainly does not represent all job loss about which we ought to be concerned, it does represent the best available source of data on job loss.[13] Overall, 6,637 individuals aged 20–64 reported in the February 1994 DWS having lost a job in the 1991–93 period. Similarly, 6,459 individuals aged 20–64 reported in the February

---

[13] See Farber (1997*b*) for a detailed discussion of the definition and limitations of the measure of job loss from the DWS.

1996 DWS having lost a job in the 1994–96 period.[14] Of these 13,096 job losers, 6,733 were in rotation groups 1–4, and, hence, are potentially matchable to the subsequent CPSs with the CAEAS.

The Final Match

Of the 50,620 individuals aged 20–64 in the February 1994 and 1996 CPSs who were successfully matched to the February 1995 and 1997 CPSs, 2,145 were not interviewed for the Displaced Worker Supplement, so that there is no information on job loss for these workers. These individuals are dropped from the analysis. While only the employed were eligible to be interviewed for the CAEAS, I am interested in all employment-related outcomes for displaced workers. Thus, for now I retain those who are not employed at the CAEAS date. But 3,412 employed individuals were not administered the CAEAS. When these nonrespondents are eliminated from the sample, there are 45,063 individuals including 4,102 job losers left in the matched sample, and they form the core of the analysis using the matched data. There is complete information for this sample on job loss in the 3-year period prior to the DWS and on employment arrangements in the subsequent CAEAS. Of the 45,063 individuals in the sample, 33,296 are employed at the relevant CAEAS date.

IV. Job Loss and Alternative Employment Arrangements: The Matched Data

Table 3 contains a breakdown of employment arrangements at the CAEAS date by whether the individual reported a job loss in the 3 years prior to the relevant DWS. The sample contains all individuals, whether employed at the CAEAS date or not. In particular, it shows the fraction of the sample separately for job losers and nonlosers that are in each type of employment (or nonemployment) arrangement. I also present the difference between the rates for nonlosers and the rates for losers, and I call this difference the job-loss differential.

These data include individuals who are not employed in order to highlight two issues. First, individuals who lost jobs in the 3 years prior to the DWS are more likely than nonlosers (6.2 percentage points) to report being unemployed a year after the DWS date.[15] Second, job losers are less likely than nonlosers (6.8 percentage points) to be out of the labor force (NILF) a year after the DWS date. This is because in order to have

---

[14] These represent 8.6% and 10.6% (weighted) of the total samples, respectively. However, these are not good estimates of the job-loss rates because many of those sampled had not worked and, hence, were not at risk to lose a job.

[15] Higher unemployment rates among displaced workers is well known from the literature on job displacement. See, e.g., Podgursky and Swaim (1987).

Table 3
Fraction of Individuals with Specific Alternative Employment Arrangements by Job-Loss Status (Matched DWS-CAEAS Data)

Group	Individuals Aged 20–64 in DWS					
	Regular	Contractor	Other-SE	Temporary	Unemployed	NILF
Nonlosers	.613	.047	.044	.035	.028	.234
	(.002)	(.001)	(.002)	(.001)	(.001)	(.002)
Job losers	.599	.046	.021	.078	.090	.166
	(.007)	(.003)	(.003)	(.003)	(.003)	(.006)
Difference	−.014	−.001	−.023	.043	.062	−.068
	(.008)	(.003)	(.003)	(.003)	(.003)	(.007)

NOTE.—Based on tabulations from the matched February 1994 and 1996 Displaced Worker Supplements (DWS) with the February 1995 and 1997 Contingent and Alternative Employment Arrangements Supplements (CAEAS), respectively. See the text for definitions of the job type classifications. Workers are classified as unemployed and not in the labor force (NILF) according to the standard Current Population Surveys (CPS) definitions. See the text for a description of the matching procedure. All fractions are weighted by CPS sampling weights. The numbers in parentheses are standard errors; $N = 45,063$.

lost a job, workers must have been employed at some point in the 3 years prior to the DWS. Many of the workers who were not job losers have been out of the labor force for a long period of time (or were never in the labor force).

It would be most appropriate to omit workers with no long-term attachment to the labor force from the analysis because they are not (to a first approximation) affected by job loss, but it is not possible to identify these workers. I proceed by analyzing employment status of the sample of workers who are employed at the CAEAS date. Since a substantial fraction of job losers are not employed (25.6% in table 3), this analysis errs in excluding individuals who were affected by job loss. Nonetheless, it gives the clearest picture of the distribution of employment arrangements subsequent to job loss and how this distribution is related to a history of job loss.

Table 4 is organized identically to table 3 with the difference that the breakdown in table 4 recomputes the fraction of workers in each type of employment relationship excluding those who are not employed. The results show that employed job losers have a smaller probability than nonlosers of being in a regular job. The job-loss differential for temporary work is positive, suggesting that job losers who find work are substantially more likely than nonlosers to be in temporary jobs (by 5.7 percentage points). Another difference is that job losers are less likely to be other-SE (by 3.1 percentage points), but there is not a significant job-loss differential in the probability of being an independent contractor. The analysis in table 3, which includes those not employed, yields the same qualitative results.

A word is required on the interpretation of the two self-employed

Table 4
Fraction of Employed with Specific Alternative Employment Arrangements
by Job-Loss Status (Matched DWS-CAEAS Data)

| Group | Workers Aged 20–64 at DWS Date | | | |
	Regular	Contractor	Other-SE	Temporary
Nonlosers	.830	.063	.060	.047
	(.002)	(.001)	(.001)	(.001)
Job losers	.805	.062	.029	.105
	(.007)	(.004)	(.004)	(.004)
Difference	−.025	−.001	−.031	.057
	(.007)	(.005)	(.004)	(.004)

NOTE.—Based on tabulations from the matched February 1994 and 1996 Displaced Workers Supplements (DWS) to the Current Population Surveys (CPS) with the February 1995 and 1997 Contingent and Alternative Employment Arrangements Supplements (CAEAS) to the CPS, respectively. See the text for definitions of the job type classifications. See the text for a description of the matching procedure. All fractions are weighted by CPS sampling weights. The numbers in parentheses are standard errors. All workers, $N = 33,296$.

categories. The "independent contractor" category includes self-employed workers who say that they are independent contractors, independent consultants, freelance workers, or something else. This appears to be the category that captures the sort of self-employment arrangements individuals might find themselves after leaving a company and (1) perhaps performing the same function for their old employer on a contract basis or (2) starting a "consulting" business selling their services. The "other self-employed" category is the residual and likely captures owners of small business (e.g., retail sales). As such, the "contractor" category is more likely to be used by job losers than the "other-SE." This is consistent with the tabulations in tables 3 and 4.

The next step is to carry out multivariate analyses of the probability of employment by type in order to estimate the job-loss differentials in employment probabilities controlling for demographic characteristics. Given the similarity of the relationship between job loss and type of employment found in the analysis that includes those not employed and the analysis that focuses on those employed, I continue using only the sample composed of those employed at the CAEAS survey date. I estimate simple probit models of the probability of employment of the various types as a function of job-loss status, age, education, sex, marital status, the interaction of sex and marital status, and race.[16]

[16] Note that I am not estimating a multinomial choice model of employment type, such as multinomial logit or probit. What I am interested in here is data description and summary rather than estimates of some structural choice model. The ease of interpretation of the estimates from the binomial probit models makes them a preferred method for this purpose.

Alternative and Part-Time Arrangements   S153

The key variable for the purposes of this study is the job-loss indicator. Its normalized coefficient measures the adjusted (for demographic characteristics) lost-job differential in the probability of employment of the indicated type controlling for the observable demographic characteristics.[17] The differences in the structure of employment relationships across demographic groups implicit in the probit estimates are as noted in the raw tabulations in table 1 from the February 1995 and 1997 CAEASs, and, for this reason, the estimates of the coefficients of the demographic variables are not presented here.

The first row of table 5 contains the adjusted job-loss differentials for the overall sample of 33,095 workers. The results are similar to the unadjusted differences found in table 4. Job losers are approximately 2.8 percentage points less likely than nonlosers to be in regular jobs. There is no difference by job-loss status in the probability of being an independent contractor, but job losers are significantly less likely than nonlosers to be in other-SE jobs (3.1 percentage points). Job losers are significantly more likely to be in temporary jobs (4.1 percentage points).

The job-loss differentials in the first row of table 5 control for observable differences across workers, but they constrain the job-loss differential in the employment outcomes to be the same for all types of workers. I relax this restriction by estimating separate probit models for various categories of workers. Each of these probit models contains the same set of variables as the overall model (omitting the set of variables on which the particular subsample is stratified). The remaining rows of table 5 contain the normalized probit coefficients of the job-loss dummy variable from each of these models for (1) separate models by sex and marital status, (2) separate models by educational category, and (3) separate models by age category.

The adjusted job-loss differentials estimated from separate probit models by sex and marital status are not very different. The adjusted job-loss differentials show lower probabilities of regular employment and other-SE for job losers, and these differentials are largest for unmarried workers of both sexes. This is offset largely by higher probabilities of temporary work for job losers. Single females who lose jobs also show a higher probability of being independent contractors.

---

[17] The coefficients are normalized to represent the derivative of the probability of the outcome with respect to a change in the particular explanatory variable evaluated at the means of the explanatory variables. The normalization factor is $\phi(\bar{X}\beta)$ so that the normalized coefficient is computed as $\beta\phi(\bar{X}\beta)$, where $\hat{\beta}$ is the vector of estimated parameters of the probit model, $\bar{X}$ is the vector of means of the explanatory variables, and ϕ is the standard normal probability density function. The standard errors are also normalized by $\phi(\bar{X}\beta)$, but they do not take into account the fact that the normalization itself is a random variable.

Table 5
Lost-Job Differential in Probability of Employment by Type Normalized
Probit Estimates Using Matched DWS-CAEAS Data

Group	Regular	Contractor	Other-SE	Temporary
All	−.0277	.0010	−.0313	.0414
	(.0068)	(.0042)	(.0049)	(.0033)
Single male	−.0339	−.0073	−.0242	.0514
	(.0168)	(.0107)	(.0101)	(.0096)
Married male	−.0132	−.0039	−.0548	.0416
	(.0119)	(.0085)	(.0095)	(.0046)
Single female	−.0529	.0133	.0080	.0266
	(.0126)	(.0052)	(.0055)	(.0090)
Married female	−.0259	−.0001	−.0410	.0439
	(.0132)	(.0080)	(.0106)	(.0065)
Education < 12 years	−.0105	−.0066	−.0314	.0354
	(.0252)	(.0147)	(.0174)	(.0137)
Education = 12 years	−.0196	−.0149	−.0308	.0422
	(.0116)	(.0076)	(.0084)	(.0052)
Education 13–15 years	−.0123	.0011	−.0317	.0332
	(.0118)	(.0069)	(.0079)	(.0064)
Education ≥ 16 years	−.0614	.0183	−.0311	.0514
	(.0116)	(.0076)	(.0084)	(.0052)
Aged 20–24	−.0156	.0079	−.0042	.0055
	(.0251)	(.0056)	(.0084)	(.0229)
Aged 25–34	−.0189	.0027	−.0121	.0254
	(.0122)	(.0071)	(.0071)	(.0076)
Aged 35–44	−.0378	−.0089	−.0463	.0564
	(.0118)	(.0081)	(.0092)	(.0052)
Aged 45–54	−.0346	.0161	−.0343	.0342
	(.0143)	(.0090)	(.0113)	(.0057)
Aged 55–64	.0014	−.0305	−.0632	.0569
	(.0248)	(.0166)	(.0200)	(.0100)

NOTE.—The sample includes individuals aged 20–64 at Displaced Worker Supplements (DWS) date and employed at Contingent and Alternative Employment Arrangements Supplements (CAEAS) date. The estimates are the normalized coefficients on the lost-job dummy variable from separate probit models where the dependent variable is the indicator variable for the type of employment in each column. Other variables included in the probit model include, where appropriate, a constant, three dummy variables for education category, four dummy variables for age category, and dummy variables for sex, marital status, the interaction of sex and marital status, and race. The estimates are based on the matched February 1994 and 1996 DWS with the February 1995 and 1997 CAEAS, respectively. The sample includes individuals aged 20–64 in the February 1994 and 1996 DWS who were employed at the CAEAS date. See the text for a description of the employment types and for a description of the matching procedure. See n. 16 for details of the normalization. The normalized asymptotic standard errors are in parentheses. All analyses are weighted by Current Population Surveys (CPS) sampling weights from 1994 or 1996.

The adjusted job-loss differentials estimated from separate probit models by educational category suggest that there is a contrast in the job-loss differentials between workers with less than 16 years of education and workers with 16 or more years of education. While job losers with less than 16 years of education are approximately 1 percentage point less likely than nonlosers to be employed in a regular job, job losers with at least 16 years of education are fully six percentage points less likely than nonlosers to be employed in regular jobs. This difference across education groups appears to be accounted for largely by (1) a higher adjusted job-loss differential in the probability of being an independent contractor (approximately 1.8 percentage points for highly educated workers compared with zero for less educated workers) and (2) a higher adjusted job-loss differential in the probability of being a temporary worker (approximately 5.1 percentage points for highly educated workers compared with approximately 3.5–4 percentage points for less-educated workers). Job losers in all educational categories are approximately 3 percentage points less likely than nonlosers to be other self-employed.

The remainder of table 5 contains the adjusted job-loss differentials estimated from separate probit models by age category. It appears that the largest job-loss differential in the probability of regular employment is largest for middle-aged workers (35–54 years of age). The positive job-loss differential in the rate of temporary employment is shared by workers in all age categories but the youngest. The negative relationship between job loss and the rate of other-SE is stronger among older workers.

To summarize, employed job losers are more likely to be in alternative employment arrangements, broadly defined, than are nonlosers. The largest consistent differences are that job losers are more likely than nonlosers to be in temporary jobs and job losers are less likely than nonlosers to be "other self-employed" workers. There is also some evidence that highly educated job-losers are more likely to be independent contractors relative to similarly educated nonlosers.

Is Temporary Employment Subsequent to Job Loss a Transitional Experience?

There are at least two interpretations of the finding that workers who have lost jobs are more likely to be in temporary jobs. The first finding is that temporary employment relationships are used by some workers in a transition period following job loss due to difficulty in finding regular employment. Following this transition period, displaced workers will find regular employment. The second interpretation is that the relationships between job loss and temporary employment are the result of unmeasured heterogeneity across workers, so that workers who tend to be employed in temporary jobs are also workers who are more likely to lose jobs regardless of the type of job they are holding.

While the data do not allow me to make a definitive determination of the relative importance of these two explanations, there is some evidence available that can shed some light on this issue. The first explanation (alternative employment as a transition phase) implies that the probability that a worker holds a temporary job will decline with time since displacement. The second explanation (unmeasured heterogeneity) has no such implication.

I investigate this directly using the matched sample and information

Table 6
Breakdown of Employment Arrangements by Years since Job Loss
(Matched DWS-CAEAS Data)

Years since Loss	Individuals Employed at CAEAS Date; Aged 20–64 at DWS Date			
	Regular	Contractor	Other-SE	Temporary
2 Years	.795	.055	.032	.118
	(.013)	(.008)	(.008)	(.007)
3 Years	.816	.058	.029	.097
	(.015)	(.010)	(.009)	(.009)
4 Years	.829	.074	.019	.078
	(.015)	(.010)	(.009)	(.009)
No loss	.830	.063	.060	.047
	(.002)	(.001)	(.001)	(.001)

NOTE.—Based on tabulations from the merged February 1994 and 1996 Displaced Worker Supplements (DWS) with the February 1995 and 1997 Contingent and Alternative Employment Arrangements Supplements (CAEAS), respectively. See the text for definitions of the job type classifications and for a description of the matching procedure. All fractions are weighted by Current Population Surveys (CPS) sampling weights from 1994 or 1996. The numbers in parentheses are standard errors. $N = 32,321$, including 2,056 job losers.

available in the DWS reporting the year of job loss. Unfortunately, the design of the 1994 and 1996 DWS was such that the year of job loss was asked only of individuals who reported losing a job for a subset of the allowed reasons. Specifically, individuals who reported losing a job due to (1) a plant closing, (2) slack work, or (3) position or shift abolished were asked follow-up questions including the year of job loss. Individuals who reported losing a job for other reasons were not asked the follow-up questions. Thus, information on the year of job loss is available for only 2,056 of the 3,031 workers who reported a job loss in February 1994 or 1996, who were matched to an observation in February 1995 or 1997, and who were employed at the survey date in February 1995 or 1997. I computed the number of years since job loss for these 2,056 workers. Given that job loss occurred in the 3 years prior to the DWS date, years since job loss ranged from 2 to 4 years at the CAEAS date. Of the 2,056 workers in the sample, 851 reported a loss 2 years earlier, 612 reported a loss 3 years earlier, and 593 reported a loss 4 years earlier.[18]

Table 6 contains a breakdown of employment arrangements by years since job loss, and it confirms that the likelihood of regular employment increases with time since job loss (by 3.4 percentage points from 2 to 4

[18] I have repeated the analyses of adjusted job-loss differentials using only nonlosers and this restricted sample of job losers, and the results are very similar. The declining number of job losers with time since the survey likely reflects recall bias. Such bias makes it more likely that recent events and more salient events are recalled (Topel 1990).

years, p-value $= .043$). In fact, at 4 years since job loss (3 years prior to the DWS date, 4 years prior to the CAEAS date), the fraction of losers employed in regular jobs is virtually identical to the fraction of nonlosers in regular jobs. This can be accounted for by a decline in the likelihood of temporary employment with time since job loss (by 4 percentage points from 2 to 4 years, p-value $= 0.00023$), although the likelihood of temporary employment among job losers still substantially exceeds the likelihood of temporary employment among nonlosers, even after 4 years. There are also offsetting movements with time since job loss in the likelihood of being in the two self-employment categories. However, these movements are not statistically significant at conventional levels. The movements with time since job loss in the likelihood of regular and temporary employment provide support for the view that temporary employment is used by some workers as a transition to regular employment.[19]

Brief Comments on the Results on Alternative Employment Arrangements

The advantage of using the matched DWS-CAEAS data is that detailed information on employment arrangements allows the identification of alternative employment arrangements held subsequent to job loss. But there are at least two disadvantages. First, the sample size is relatively small due to (1) the relatively small fraction of workers who report a job loss in the DWS, (2) the relatively small fraction of individuals who report being in an alternative employment arrangement in the CAEAS, and (3) the inability to match a substantial number of individuals across the two surveys. The second disadvantage is that the information on alternative work arrangements refers to a point in time substantially after the time of job loss (at least 14 months later at best and up to 4 years at worst). To the extent that alternative employment arrangements as a response to job loss are part of a transitory phase, these matched data might substantially understate the use of alternative employment arrangements as a response to job loss.[20]

---

[19] While not presented here, probit models of the probability of employment of the various types that control for age, education, sex, race, marital status, and the interaction of sex and marital status along with time since job loss do not change these findings.

[20] For example, the estimates suggest that the likelihood of temporary employment arrangements falls by about 2 percentage points with each year since job loss. Simple (weighted) tabulation of the data shows that 11.9% of those employed at the CAEAS date who had lost jobs in the year prior to the relevant DWS (2 years prior to the CAEAS) were in temporary jobs at the CAEAS date. If the point estimate is taken seriously (admittedly a stretch given the out-of-

While I cannot address these issues directly due to data limitation, I now turn to analysis of part-time employment and its relationship with job loss. I do this for three reasons. First, part-time employment, particularly involuntary part-time employment, may be experienced by job losers in a transition period. Second, information on part-time employment is available as part of the basic CPS questionnaire and is available at the DWS date (1 year more proximate to the job loss) as well as at the CAEAS date. Third, because observations on part-time status are available at two points in time in the matched data (three points in time for job losers), I can address directly the question of the transitory nature of part-time employment subsequent to job loss.

V. Job Loss and Part-Time Employment

I begin the analysis of job loss and part-time employment by carrying out an analysis of part-time employment using the matched DWS-CAEAS data that parallels the analysis presented above for alternative employment arrangements. The matched data have measures of part-time employment at two points in time: the DWS date and the CAEAS date.[21] Since the DWS date is more proximate to the date of job loss (1–3 years) than the CAEAS date (2–4 years), a comparison of the part-time rates at the two dates as well as measures of the transition rates from part-time to full-time employment can shed some light on the extent to which part-time employment is used as a transition strategy after job loss.

Table 7 provides strong evidence that involuntary part-time employment is an important transition strategy for job losers. The first three columns of the table contain the full-time, voluntary part-time, and involuntary part-time rates for nonlosers and for job losers measured at the DWS date. Also presented is the job-loss differential in these rates. The full-time employment rate is 5.6 percentage points lower for job losers than for nonlosers. This is almost entirely accounted for by a 4.9 percentage point higher involuntary part-time rate for job losers relative to nonlosers. The important contrast is with the tabulations in the last three columns of table 8, which provide the same breakdown for part-time employment status at the CAEAS date. Here there is no significant difference in the full-time rate between job-losers and nonlosers and only a 1.5 percentage point higher involuntary part-time rate for job losers relative to nonlosers.

---

sample nature of this calculation), then about 14% of those displaced in the year prior to the CAEAS would be predicted to be in temporary jobs at the CAEAS date.

[21] The DWS also has information on full/part-time status on the lost job. I use this information later in this section.

Alternative and Part-Time Arrangements   S159

Table 7
Fraction of Employed with Specific Full/Part-Time Employment Arrangements by Job-Loss Status (Matched DWS-CAEAS Data)

	Workers Aged 20–64 at DWS Date					
Group	Full Time at DWS	Voluntary Part-Time at DWS	Involuntary Part-Time at DWS	Full-Time at CAEAS	Voluntary Part-Time at CAEAS	Involuntary Part-Time at CAEAS
Nonloser	.850	.109	.041	.854	.107	.039
	(.002)	(.002)	(.001)	(.002)	(.002)	(.001)
Job loser	.794	.116	.090	.842	.104	.054
	(.007)	(.006)	(.004)	(.006)	(.005)	(.004)
Difference	−.056	.008	.049	−.011	−.003	.015
	(.007)	(.006)	(.004)	(.007)	(.006)	(.004)

NOTE.—Based on tabulations from the matched February 1994 and 1996 Displaced Worker Supplements (DWS) with the February 1995 and 1997 Contingent and Alternative Employment Arrangements Supplements (CAEAS), respectively. See the text for definitions of the job type classifications and for a description of the matching procedure. All fractions are weighted by Current Population Surveys (CPS) sampling weights from 1994 or 1996. The numbers in parentheses are standard errors. $N = 33,705$ at DWS date and $N = 33,296$ at CAEAS date.

As before, the next step is to carry out multivariate analyses of the probability of the three full/part-time categories in order to estimate the job-loss differentials in employment probabilities controlling for demographic characteristics. The first row of table 8 contains estimates of the adjusted job-loss differentials from simple probit models of the probability of employment of the various types as a function of job-loss status, age, education, sex, marital status, the interaction of sex and marital status, and race.[22] The estimates in the first three columns of table 8 use the subset of the matched sample consisting of those individuals who are employed at the DWS date, while the estimates in the last three columns use the subset of the matched sample consisting of those individuals who are employed at the CAEAS date.[23]

The first row of table 8 contains the adjusted job-loss differentials for the overall sample that are similar to the unadjusted differences found in table 7. Job losers are about 6.1 percentage points less likely than nonlosers to be in full-time jobs at the DWS date, and this difference shrinks to 2.2 percentage points by the CAEAS date. There is a small positive

[22] These differentials are the coefficients on the job-loss variable in the probit models normalized to represent the derivative of the probability of the outcome with respect to a change in job-loss status. See n. 16 for details.

[23] While the full estimates of the probit model are not presented here, the estimates based on both samples verify the common finding that married females are substantially less likely to be employed full-time, a fact that is largely accounted for by a substantially higher probability of being employed voluntarily in a part-time job. The results also support the common finding that the probability of involuntary part-time employment falls monotonically with education.

Table 8
Lost-Job Differential in Full/Part-Time Status Normalized Probit Estimates Using Matched DWS-CAEAS Data

Group	Full Time at DWS	Voluntary Part-Time at DWS	Involuntary Part-Time at DWS	Full-Time at CAEAS	Voluntary Part-Time at CAEAS	Involuntary Part-Time at CAEAS
All	−.0613	.0168	.0354	−.0219	.0075	.0130
	(.0060)	(.0049)	(.0030)	(.0059)	(.0047)	(.0032)
Single male	−.0445	.0069	.0355	−.0124	.0049	.0073
	(.0145)	(.0105)	(.0091)	(.0137)	(.0098)	(.0091)
Married male	−.0394	.0104	.0263	−.0225	.0115	.0095
	(.0053)	(.0037)	(.0036)	(.0052)	(.0032)	(.0038)
Single female	−.0744	.0164	.0480	−.0099	−.0004	.0097
	(.0164)	(.0138)	(.0089)	(.0158)	(.0128)	(.0091)
Married female	−.0920	.0413	.0410	−.0293	.0012	.0239
	(.0161)	(.0151)	(.0066)	(.0160)	(.0152)	(.0068)
Education < 12 years	−.0775	−.0056	.0667	−.0093	−.0276	.0277
	(.0243)	(.0183)	(.0162)	(.0255)	(.0176)	(.0173)
Education = 12 years	−.0666	.0279	.0334	−.0422	.0282	.0122
	(.0106)	(.0080)	(.0062)	(.0103)	(.0077)	(.0062)
Education 13–15 years	−.0666	.0279	.0334	−.0422	.0282	.0122
	(.0106)	(.0080)	(.0062)	(.0103)	(.0077)	(.0062)
Education ≥ 16 years	−.0497	.0036	.0348	.0016	−.0108	.0093
	(.0114)	(.0099)	(.0052)	(.0112)	(.0095)	(.0054)
Aged 20–24	.0276	−.0700	.0306	.0409	−.0338	−.0021
	(.0385)	(.0361)	(.0197)	(.0338)	(.0309)	(.0165)
Aged 25–34	−.0580	.0233	.0271	−.0206	.0118	.0076
	(.0108)	(.0087)	(.0056)	(.0111)	(.0086)	(.0062)
Aged 35–44	−.0582	.0095	.0371	−.0177	.0060	.0099
	(.0099)	(.0077)	(.0049)	(.0096)	(.0072)	(.0050)
Aged 45–54	−.0676	.0257	.0340	−.0209	.0015	.0173
	(.0104)	(.0080)	(.0056)	(.0106)	(.0080)	(.0060)
Aged 55–64	−.1150	.0561	.0492	−.0897	.0538	.0316
	(.0221)	(.0189)	(.0117)	(.0221)	(.0192)	(.0112)

NOTE.—The sample includes individuals aged 20–64 at Displaced Worker Supplements (DWS) date and employed at Contingent and Alternative Employment Arrangements Supplements (CAEAS) date. The estimates are the normalized coefficients on the lost-job dummy variable from separate probit models where the dependent variable is the indicator variable for the type full/part-time status in each column. Other variables included in the probit model include, where appropriate, a constant, three dummy variables for education category, four dummy variables for age category, and dummy variables for sex, marital status, the interaction of sex and marital status, and race. The estimates are based on the matched February 1994 and 1996 DWS with the February 1995 and 1997 CAEAS, respectively. The sample includes individuals aged 20–64 in the February 1994 and 1996 DWS who were employed at the CAEAS date. See the text for a description of the employment types and for a description of the matching procedure. See n. 16 for details of the normalization. Normalized asymptotic standard errors are in parentheses. All analyses are weighted by Current Population Surveys (CPS) sampling weights from 1994 or 1996.

relationship between job loss and voluntary part-time employment at the DWS date that is not apparent at the CAEAS date. Finally, job losers are 3.5 percentage points more likely to be involuntarily in part-time jobs at the DWS date, and this difference falls to 1.3 percentage points by the CAEAS date.

The estimates in table 7 and the first row of table 8 present the consistent picture that involuntary part-time employment is experienced disproportionately by job losers. However, the differential rate of involuntary part-time employment falls with time, suggesting that this is a transitional experience for many job losers.

The probit models underlying the estimates in the first row of table 8 control for observable differences across workers, but they constrain the job-loss differential in the full/part-time employment outcomes to be the same for all types of workers. As before, I relax this restriction by estimating separate probit models for various categories of workers. Each of these probit models contains the same set of variables as the overall model (omitting the set of variables on which the particular subsample is stratified). The remaining rows of table 8 contain the normalized probit coefficients of the job-loss dummy variable from each of these models for (1) separate models by sex and marital status, (2) separate models by educational category, and (3) separate models by age category.

The adjusted job-loss differentials estimated from separate probit models by sex and marital status yield results that are not very different from those derived from the overall sample. The major exception is that only married females have a significant job-loss differential in the rate of involuntary part-time employment remaining at the CAEAS date.

The adjusted job-loss differentials estimated from separate probit models by educational category imply that the job-loss differentials in full-time employment for workers in all educational categories are significantly negative at the DWS date. This is offset by significant positive job-loss differentials in involuntary part-time employment for workers in all educational categories. Moving forward one year to the CAEAS date, the job-loss differentials in full-time employment disappear for workers in the lowest and highest educational categories but remain substantial for workers in the intermediate educational categories.

With regard to age, the job-loss differential in full-time employment for the oldest workers is large and negative at the DWS date and remains so 1 year later at the CAEAS date. This is offset roughly equally by positive job-loss differentials in voluntary and involuntary part-time employment for the oldest workers.

To summarize, the estimates in tables 7 and 8 provide clear evidence that job losers are disproportionately employed involuntarily in part-time jobs. It is also clear that much of this involuntary part-time employment is part of ᴧ transition process to full-time employment.

Table 9
Fraction Employed with Specific Full/Part-Time Employment
Arrangements by Job-Loss Status and Full/Part-Time Status
on Lost Job (Matched DWS-CAEAS Data)

| | Workers Aged 20–64 at DWS Date (Row Fractions) | | | | | |
Group	Full Time at DWS	Voluntary Part-Time at DWS	Involuntary Part-Time at DWS	Full-Time at CAEAS	Voluntary Part-Time at CAEAS	Involuntary Part-Time at CAEAS
Nonloser	.850	.109	.041	.854	.107	.039
	(.002)	(.002)	(.001)	(.002)	(.002)	(.001)
Full-time job loser	.843	.078	.079	.883	.066	.051
	(.009)	(.008)	(.005)	(.008)	(.007)	(.005)
Part-time job loser	.500	.360	.140	.602	.293	.105
	(.025)	(.022)	(.014)	(.025)	(.021)	(.014)

NOTE.—Based on tabulations from the merged February 1994 and 1996 Displaced Worker Supplements (DWS) with the February 1995 and 1997 Contingent and Alternative Employment Arrangements Supplements (CAEAS), respectively. See the text for definitions of the job type classifications and for a description of the matching procedure. All fractions are weighted by Current Population Surveys (CPS) sampling weights from 1994 or 1996. The numbers in parentheses are standard errors. $N = 32,709$ at DWS date and $N = 32,246$ at CAEAS date.

The Use of Part-Time Employment by Losers of Full-Time Jobs

The 1994 and 1996 DWS provide information on the full/part-time status of the lost job for those who lose jobs due to a plant closing, slack work, or position/shift abolished. For the part-time job losers, there is no information on whether the individual was part-time voluntarily or involuntarily.[24] Analysis of post–job-loss full/part-time employment status, conditioning on the full/part-time status on the lost job, can provide more information on the extent to which part-time employment, both voluntary and involuntary, is used by job losers. Of particular interest is the postdisplacement experience of losers of full-time jobs since these workers show more commitment to full-time work than do part-time workers, many of whom are part-time voluntarily.[25]

Table 9 contains information, based on the matched data, on the postdisplacement full/part-time status of workers broken down by the full/part-time status on the lost job. The first row of table 9 reproduces

[24] Of the 2,598 job losers for whom we have information on the full/part-time status on the lost job, 10.9% (weighted) reported losing a part-time job. In contrast, 15.0% (weighted) of those workers who did not lose a job were employed part-time at the DWS survey date. Thus, the job-loss rate on full-time jobs appears to be higher than the job-loss rate on part-time jobs.

[25] Tabulations of the February 1994 and 1996 CPS data yield the result that 68.1% of part-time workers are part-time for voluntary reasons.

the first row of table 7, and it shows the postdisplacement full/part-time status of those workers who did not report losing a job. The second and third rows report the postdisplacement full/part-time employment status of full-time job losers and part-time job losers, respectively. The first three columns report the fraction in each full/part-time status at the DWS date, and the last three columns report the fraction in each full/part-time status at the CAEAS date.

Among those employed at the relevant survey date, there is a sharp contrast between the full-time job losers and the part-time job losers. By the DWS survey date, the fraction of full-time job losers who are working full-time is virtually identical to the fraction of nonlosers who are working full-time (84.3% vs. 85.0%), and, by the CAEAS date, the fraction of full-time job losers who are working full-time is significantly larger than the fraction of nonlosers who are working full-time (88.3% vs. 85.4%, p-value of difference $< .00005$). It is also the case that full-time job losers are less likely than nonlosers to be voluntarily part-time and more likely than nonlosers to be involuntarily part-time at the DWS date. By the CAEAS date, the gap in the voluntary part-time rates increases while the gap in the involuntary part-time rate decreases. This pattern is a result of the fact that the pool of nonlosers contains a core of individuals who are voluntarily part-time as a result of labor supply choices, while the full-time job losers have shown evidence of a commitment to full-time work. This interpretation of the evidence is further supported by the postdisplacement full/part-time status of the part-time job losers, who are substantially less likely than full-time job losers to be employed full-time at either the DWS date or the CAEAS date.

Transitions in Full/Part-Time Status between the DWS Date and the CAEAS Date

The analysis in the previous subsection strongly suggests that there is heterogeneity among the workforce in general and among job losers in particular in preferences for full-time work. There may also be further heterogeneity in the ability to find and hold a full-time job. Implicit in the earlier discussion is the idea that full-time workers are committed to full-time work, but it is surely the case that some full-time workers move to part-time work and vice versa, even without a job loss. This presumably reflects changes in individual constraints and in market conditions over time. In this subsection, I examine individual transitions in full/part-time status between the DWS date and the CAEAS date separately for nonlosers and for full-time and part-time job losers.

Conditioning on full/part-time status at the DWS date, I use the nonlosers as a "control group," and I measure their transition rates to full-time, voluntary part-time, and involuntary part-time employment by the CAEAS date. These are, in a sense, the "natural" rates of

Table 10
Fraction of Employed by Full/Part-Time Employment Arrangement at
CAEAS Date by Job-Loss Status and Full/Part-Time Status on Lost Job
and Job at DWS Date (Matched DWS-CAEAS Data)

	Workers Aged 20–64 at DWS Date (Row Fractions)		
Group	Full-Time at CAEAS	Voluntary Part-Time at CAEAS	Involuntary Part-Time at CAEAS
Full-time at DWS:			
Nonloser	.954	.026	.020
	(.001)	(.001)	(.001)
Full-time job loser	.961	.015	.024
	(.006)	(.004)	(.004)
Part-time job loser	.926	.027	.047
	(.023)	(.017)	(.015)
Voluntary part-time at DWS:			
Nonloser	.265	.654	.081
	(.008)	(.009)	(.005)
Full-time job loser	.481	.388	.131
	(.040)	(.043)	(.025)
Part-time job loser	.217	.711	.072
	(.056)	(.060)	(.035)
Involuntary part-time at DWS:			
Nonloser	.558	.208	.234
	(.015)	(.012)	(.013)
Full-time job loser	.676	.138	.186
	(.046)	(.037)	(.039)
Part-time job loser	.540	.170	.290
	(.101)	(.082)	(.086)

NOTE.—Based on tabulations from the merged February 1994 and 1996 Displaced Worker Supplements (DWS) with the February 1995 and 1997 Contingent and Alternative Employment Arrangements Supplements (CAEAS), respectively. Only those individuals employed at both dates are included in the analysis. See the text for definitions of the job type classifications and for a description of the matching procedure. All fractions are weighted by Current Population Surveys (CPS) sampling weights from 1994 or 1996. The numbers in parentheses are standard errors. $N = 30,383$.

transition. I then contrast these transition rates with the transition rates for full- and part-time job losers. These analyses provide further information on the incidence and persistence of part-time employment subsequent to job loss.

Table 10 contains the core of this analysis. The first panel contains the transition rates of workers who were working full-time at the DWS date. In the control group of nonlosers, 95.4% remained employed full-time a year later while 2.6% moved to voluntary part-time status and 2.0% moved to involuntary part-time status. Think of these as the natural transition rates. The picture is not far different for losers of full-time jobs who were employed full-time at the DWS date. However, part-time job losers who are employed full-time at the DWS date are less likely to remain in full-time employment (92.6%) and more likely to move to involuntary part-time status (4.7%).[26]

The second and third panels of table 10 contain the transition rates of workers who were in voluntary and involuntary part-time status, respectively, at the DWS date. The key finding is that a substantially higher fraction of full-time job losers (relative to either nonlosers or part-time jobs losers) moved from part-time jobs to full-time jobs between the DWS date and the CAEAS date. This is further evidence that full-time job losers find themselves in part-time employment as a transition to reemployment full-time.

VI. The Interaction of Alternative Employment Arrangements and Full/Part-Time Status

I have established that temporary and part-time employment, particularly involuntary part-time employment, are important transitional outcomes for displaced workers. Further, the breakdowns in table 2 clearly show that temporary workers are the least likely of all groups to be in full-time jobs. Temporary workers are more likely than other workers to be both voluntarily and involuntarily part-time. In this section, I briefly investigate how the interactions between alternative employment arrangements and full/part-time status generally and between temporary work and part-time status specifically are related to job loss.

Table 11 contains breakdowns, using the merged data, of full/part-time status by employment status at the CAEAS date separately for nonlosers and job losers. The top panel of the table uses the merged data to reproduce the breakdowns in table 2 (which used the entire 1995 and 1997 CAEASs), and the results are very similar. This verifies that the merged sample is not substantially different in these dimensions than the overall sample. The second panel of table 11 contains the same breakdowns for nonlosers. These breakdowns are very close to those for the overall sample, and this is not surprising given that only a small fraction of the sample consists of job losers. The third panel of the table contains the breakdowns for all employed job losers, and the there are some important differences here. A significantly higher fraction of temporary workers who lost jobs are employed full-time at the CAEAS date relative to nonlosers (12.0 percentage points, p-value $< .0000001$). This is entirely accounted for by an 11.8 percentage point difference in the voluntary part-time rate between nonlosers and job losers (p-value $< .0000001$).

[26] There are relatively few part-time job losers in the sample used for this analysis (173 total) and even fewer who are employed full time at the DWS date (92). As a result the standard errors on the transition rates for part-time job losers are relatively large, the differences between these transition rates and those for other groups are not generally statistically significant at conventional levels.

Table 11
Part-Time Status by Employment Arrangement at CAEAS Date

Group	Workers Aged 20–64 at DWS Date (Row Fractions)		
	Full-Time	Voluntary Part-Time	Involuntary Part-Time
All workers:			
Regular	.879	.091	.030
	(.002)	(.002)	(.001)
Contractor	.745	.153	.101
	(.008)	(.007)	(.004)
Other-SE	.784	.154	.062
	(.008)	(.007)	(.004)
Temporary	.638	.254	.107
	(.008)	(.007)	(.005)
Nonlosers:			
Regular	.880	.091	.029
	(.002)	(.002)	(.001)
Contractor	.744	.151	.105
	(.008)	(.007)	(.004)
Other-SE	.790	.150	.059
	(.008)	(.007)	(.005)
Temporary	.616	.277	.108
	(.009)	(.008)	(.005)
All job losers:			
Regular	.869	.087	.044
	(.007)	(.006)	(.005)
Contractor	.754	.179	.066
	(.026)	(.022)	(.016)
Other-SE	.651	.232	.117
	(.039)	(.032)	(.024)
Temporary	.736	.159	.105
	(.020)	(.017)	(.013)
Full-time job losers:			
Regular	.911	.052	.037
	(.008)	(.006)	(.006)
Contractor	.754	.147	.099
	(.031)	(.024)	(.021)
Other-SE	.729	.143	.128
	(.047)	(.037)	(.033)
Temporary	.768	.109	.124
	(.024)	(.019)	(.017)

NOTE.—Based on tabulations from the merged February 1994 and 1996 Displaced Worker Supplements (DWS) with the February 1995 and 1997 Contingent and Alternative Employment Arrangements Supplements (CAEAS), respectively. Only individuals employed at the CAEAS date are included in the analysis. See text for a definition of the job types and for a description of the matching procedure. All fractions are weighted by Current Population Surveys (CPS) sampling weights from 1994 or 1996. The numbers in parentheses are standard errors. $N = 33,296$.

The contrast between nonlosers and job losers is even more striking when considering only full-time job losers. The bottom panel of table 11 contains breakdowns for 1,772 full-time job losers who are employed at the CAEAS date. Full-time job losers who are employed in temporary jobs at the CAEAS date are even more likely to be in full-time jobs (76.8%) and even less likely to be in voluntary part-time jobs (10.9%).

These results imply that temporary jobs are often taken by workers who have a preference for part-time work. It may be that temporary employment arrangements are an efficient arrangement for these workers. However, it is clear that among job losers, particularly those who lost full-time jobs, temporary jobs are transitional outcomes that are more likely than the usual temporary job to be characterized by full-time hours.

VII. Final Remarks

It is clear that alternative employment arrangements are an important feature of the U.S. labor market. Tabulation of the February 1995 and 1997 CAEAS showed that 17.5% of workers were self-employed or in temporary jobs. Additionally, 15.3% of workers in these same surveys were employed part-time (10.8% voluntary, 4.5% involuntary). My analysis of the matched DWS-CAEAS data shows that job losers are more likely than nonlosers to use alternative and part-time employment arrangements. I find that job losers are significantly more likely than nonlosers to be in temporary jobs (including on-call work and contract work) and that job losers are significantly more likely than nonlosers to be employed involuntarily part-time.

I also find that the likelihood of temporary and involuntary part-time employment falls with time since job loss. Thus, it appears that these alternative employment arrangements are often part of a transitional process subsequent to job loss leading to regular full-time permanent employment. In this respect, temporary employment by job losers is of a different character than temporary employment by nonlosers. Job losers who find employment in temporary jobs are more likely to be working full-time, while nonlosers who are employed in temporary jobs are more likely to be working voluntarily part-time.

References

Abraham, Katharine G. "Restructuring the Employment Relationship: The Growth of Market-Mediated Work Arrangements." In *New Developments in the Labor Market: Toward a New Institutional Paradigm,* edited by Katharine G. Abraham and Robert B. McKersie, pp. 85–119. Cambridge, MA: MIT Press, 1990.

Abraham, Katharine G., and Taylor, Susan K. "Firms' Use of Outside Contractors: Theory and Evidence." *Journal of Labor Economics* 14 (July 1996): 394–424.

Belous, Richard S. *The Contingent Economy.* Washington, DC: National Planning Association, 1989.

Blank, Rebecca M. "The Role of Part-Time Work in Women's Labor Market Choices Over Time." *American Economic Review* 79 (May 1989): 295–99.

———. "Are Part-Time Jobs Bad Jobs?" In *A Future of Lousy Jobs?*

edited by Gary Burtless. Washington, DC: Brookings Institution, 1990. (*a*)

———. "Understanding Part-Time Work." In *Research in Labor Economics,* vol. 11, edited by Laurie J. Bassi and David L. Crawford. Greenwich, CT: JAI, 1990. (*b*)

Farber, Henry S. "The Incidence and Costs of Job Loss: 1982–1991." *Brookings Papers on Economic Activity: Microeconomics,* no. 1 (1993): 73–119.

———. "The Changing Face of Job Loss in the United States: 1981–1995." *Brookings Papers on Economic Activity: Microeconomics* (1997): 55–128. (*b*)

———. "Trends in Long-Term Employment in the United States, 1979–1996." Working Paper no. 384. Princeton, NJ: Princeton University, Industrial Relations Section, July 1997. (*c*)

———. "Job Creation in the United States: Good Jobs or Bad?" Working Paper no. 385. Princeton, NJ: Princeton University, Industrial Relations Section, July 1997. (*a*)

Farber, Henry S., and Levy, Helen. "Recent Trends in Employer-Sponsored Health Insurance: Are Bad Jobs Getting Worse?" *Journal of Health Economics* (1999), in press.

Ferber, Marianne, and Waldfogel, Jane. "'Contingent' Work: Blessing and/or Curse." Photocopied. Cambridge, MA: Radcliffe Public Policy Institute, 1996.

Gardner, Jennifer M. "Worker Displacement: A Decade of Change." *Monthly Labor Review* 118 (April 1995): 45–57.

Golden, Lonnie, and Appelbaum, Eileen. "What Was Driving the 1982–1988 Boom in Temporary Employment?" *American Journal of Economics and Sociology* 51 (October 1992): 473–93.

Houseman, Susan N. "Temporary, Part-Time and Contract Employment in the United States: New Evidence from an Employer Survey." Photocopied. Kalamazoo, MI: W. E. Upjohn Institute for Employment Research, February 1997.

Howe, Wayne J. "Temporary Help Workers: Who They Are, What Jobs They Hold." *Monthly Labor Review* 109 (November 1986): 45–47.

Kletzer, Lori G. "Returns to Seniority after Permanent Job Loss." *American Economic Review* 79 (June 1989): 536–43.

Montgomery, Mark, and Cosgrove, James. "The Effect of Employee Benefits on the Demand for Part-Time Workers." *Industrial and Labor Relations Review* 47 (October 1993): 87–98.

Neal, Derek. "Industry-Specific Capital: Evidence from Displaced Workers." *Journal of Labor Economics* 13 (October 1995): 653–77.

Parent, Daniel. "Industry-Specific Capital: Evidence from the NLSY and the PSID." Working Paper no. 350. Princeton, NJ: Princeton University, Industrial Relations Section, November 1995.

Podgursky, Michael, and Swaim, Paul. "Job Displacement Earnings Loss: Evidence from the Displaced Worker Survey." *Industrial and Labor Relations Review* 41 (October 1987): 17–29.

Polivka, Anne. "Are Temporary Help Agency Workers Substitutes for Direct Hire Temps? Searching for an Alternative Explanation for Growth in the Temporary Help Industry." Photocopied. Washington, DC: U.S. Bureau of Labor Statistics, May 1996.

Segal, Lewis M., and Sullivan, Daniel G. "The Growth of Temporary Services Work." *Journal of Economic Perspectives* 11 (Spring 1997): 117–36.

Tilly, Chris. "Reasons for the Continuing Growth of Part-Time Employment." *Monthly Labor Review* 114 (March 1991): 10–18.

Topel, Robert. "Specific Capital and Unemployment: Measuring the Costs and Consequences of Job Loss." *Carnegie Rochester Conference Series on Public Policy* 33 (1990): 181–214.

U.S. Department of Commerce. Bureau of the Census. *Current Population Survey, February 1995: Contingent Work Supplement. Technical Documentation.* Washington, DC: U.S. Department of the Census, 1995.

[28]

ELSEVIER

Available online at www.sciencedirect.com

ScienceDirect

Journal of Business Venturing 23 (2008) 673–686

JOURNAL
of BUSINESS
VENTURING

Does self-employment reduce unemployment?

A. Roy Thurik [a,b,c,*], Martin A. Carree [d], André van Stel [b,e], David B. Audretsch [c,f]

[a] Erasmus University Rotterdam, The Netherlands
[b] EIM Business and Policy Research, Zoetermeer, The Netherlands
[c] Max Planck Institute of Economics, Jena, Germany
[d] University of Maastricht, The Netherlands
[e] Cranfield School of Management, Cranfield University, UK
[f] Institute for Development Strategies, Indiana University, USA

Abstract

This paper investigates the dynamic relationship between self-employment and unemployment rates. On the one hand, high unemployment rates may lead to start-up activity of self-employed individuals (the "refugee" effect). On the other hand, higher rates of self-employment may indicate increased entrepreneurial activity reducing unemployment in subsequent periods (the "entrepreneurial" effect). This paper introduces a new two-equation vector autoregression model capable of reconciling these ambiguities and estimates it for data from 23 OECD countries between 1974 and 2002. The empirical results confirm the existence of two distinct relationships between unemployment and self-employment: the "refugee" and "entrepreneurial" effects. We also find that the "entrepreneurial" effects are considerably stronger than the "refugee" effects.
© 2008 Elsevier Inc. All rights reserved.

JEL classification: J23; J64; L26; L53; M13; O11
Keywords: Entrepreneurship; Self-employment; Unemployment

1. Executive summary

Entrepreneurship has become increasingly important to developed countries as a source of economic growth and employment creation. As public policy has turned to entrepreneurship to generate employment and economic growth, policy makers have turned to the scholarly literature for guidance about the appropriate approach and context. However, while seeking guidance about the appropriate role for entrepreneurship policy, policy makers have been befuddled with ambiguous results at best.

The relationship between entrepreneurship and unemployment has posed a complex puzzle to scholars. One view, which has been called the unemployment push, or refugee effect, suggests that the decision to become an entrepreneur is a

---

* Corresponding author. Centre for Advanced Small Business Economics, Erasmus School of Economics, Erasmus University Rotterdam, PO Box 1738, 3000 DR Rotterdam, The Netherlands. Tel.: +31 10 4082232.
E-mail address: thurik@few.eur.nl (A.R. Thurik).

0883-9026/$ - see front matter © 2008 Elsevier Inc. All rights reserved.
doi:10.1016/j.jbusvent.2008.01.007

response to either being unemployed or else the perception of dismal future employment prospects. An alternative view suggests that entrepreneurship, by virtue of creating a new venture, contributes to the reduction of unemployment. While the first view suggests a positive relationship between entrepreneurship and unemployment, the second view suggests a negative relation. Further, in each view, the causal link between entrepreneurship and employment are reversed. While the first view has high unemployment rates inducing more people to choose to become entrepreneurs, the second view suggests that the decision people make in becoming entrepreneurs will reduce unemployment at the macro-economic level.

Which of these two polar views concerning the relationship between entrepreneurship and unemployment is correct? There is both considerable theoretical and empirical support for both views and scholars have had trouble unraveling the relationship between entrepreneurship and unemployment. Unraveling it matters because understanding the true relationship can guide policy makers as they decide if, and how, to promote entrepreneurship as they strive to reduce unemployment. Using an econometric approach to disentangle the relationships, this paper attempts to reconcile the ambiguities.

A simple two-equation vector autoregression model is used to estimate both changes in unemployment and self-employment, a common measure of entrepreneurship, for a panel of 23 OECD countries over the period 1974–2002. Using lagged data to explain the current situation, we have modeled the dynamic interrelationship between self-employment and unemployment and found that the relationship between the two variables is both negative and positive. Changes in unemployment clearly have a positive impact on subsequent changes in self-employment rates. At the same time, changes in self-employment rates have a negative impact on subsequent unemployment rates. The latter effect is stronger than the former one.

The results of this study have important implications for public policy. In particular, they unequivocally suggest that public policy to generate jobs and reduce unemployment is well served by focusing on entrepreneurship but that it takes considerable time (eight years or more) for the results to become visible.

2. Introduction

Linking unemployment to self-employment dates to at least Oxenfeldt (1943), who argues that individuals confronted with unemployment and low prospects for wage-employment will turn to self-employment as a viable alternative. This is an extension of Knight's (1921) view that individuals decide between three states — unemployment, self-employment and employment. Although the actual decision is shaped by the relative prices of these three activities, implied is the prediction of a positive correlation between self-employment and unemployment. This simple theory of income choice has been the basis for a range of studies focusing on the decision of individuals to become self-employed (Parker, 2004; Grilo and Thurik, 2005; Grilo and Irigoyen, 2006). Specifically, this theory suggests that increasing unemployment leads to increasing start-up activity because the opportunity cost of starting a firm has decreased (Blau, 1987; Evans and Jovanovic, 1989; Evans and Leighton, 1990; Blanchflower and Meyer, 1994). This effect has been referred to as the *unemployment push, refugee* or *desperation* effect. There is, however, an important counterargument to this theory: The unemployed tend to possess lower endowments of the human capital and entrepreneurial talent needed to start and sustain a new firm. This, in turn, would suggest that high unemployment may be associated with a low degree of self-employment. High unemployment rates may also imply lower levels of personal wealth which also reduce the likelihood of becoming self-employed (Johansson, 2000; Hurst and Lusardi, 2004). Lastly, high unemployment rates may correlate with stagnant economic growth leading to fewer entrepreneurial opportunities (Audretsch, 1995; Audretsch et al., 2002b).

The counterarguments above suggest that entrepreneurial opportunities are not just the result of the push effect (the threat) of unemployment but also of the pull effect produced by a thriving economy as well as by past entrepreneurial activities. Indeed, while some scholars argue that unemployment influences start-up activity, others claim that the reverse holds true. Firm start-ups hire employees, resulting in subsequent decreases in unemployment (Lin et al., 1998; Pfeiffer and Reize, 2000). Furthermore, increased entrepreneurial activity may influence country-wide economic performance (van Stel et al., 2005). For example, entrepreneurs enter markets with new products or production processes (Acs and Audretsch, 2003). They also increase productivity by increasing competition (Geroski, 1989; Nickell, 1996; Nickell et al., 1997). They also improve our knowledge of what is technically viable; what consumers prefer; and of how to acquire the necessary resources by introducing variations of existing products and services in the market. The resulting learning process speeds up finding the dominant design of product–market combinations. This learning does not just come from experimenting entrepreneurs: Knowledge spillovers play also an important role

A.R. Thurik et al. / Journal of Business Venturing 23 (2008) 673–686 675

(Audretsch and Keilbach, 2004). Lastly, entrepreneurs are inclined to work longer hours and more efficiently as their income is closely related to their working effort. [See Carree and Thurik (2003) for a survey of the (positive) effects of entrepreneurship on economic growth.] A counterargument to this view points out that low survival rates combined with the limited growth of most small firms implies that the employment contribution of start-ups is very low. As Geroski (1995) has documented, the penetration rate, or employment share, of new-firm start-ups is remarkably low. In other words, the contribution of entrepreneurial activities to the reduction of unemployment is very limited at best.

The available empirical evidence, unfortunately, presents similar ambiguities and reflects these two conflicting theories. Some studies have found that unemployment is associated with increased entrepreneurial activities while others have found that entrepreneurial activity and unemployment are inversely related (Thurik, 1999). Evans and Leighton (1990), for example, found that unemployment is positively associated with the propensity to start new firms, but Garofoli (1994) as well as Audretsch and Fritsch (1994) found that unemployment is negatively related to firm start-up.[1] Carree (2002) found no statistically significant relationship between unemployment and the number of establishments. In reviewing early empirical evidence relating unemployment rates to new-firm start-up activity, Storey (1991, p. 177) concludes, "The broad consensus is that time series analyses point to unemployment being, ceteris paribus, positively associated with indices of new-firm formation, whereas cross sectional, or pooled cross sectional studies appear to indicate the reverse. Attempts to reconcile these differences have not been wholly successful." Audretsch and Thurik (2000) present empirical evidence that an increase in the number of business owners reduces the unemployment rate. They identify an "entrepreneurial" effect in terms of the positive impact on employment from new-firm entry. However, Blanchflower (2000), examining OECD countries, finds no positive impact of self-employment rates on GDP growth. Carree et al. (2002, 2007) suggest that countries with relatively low self-employment rates benefit from increased self-employment in terms of GDP growth, but that countries with relatively high self-employment rates do not.

Consequently, there are not just theoretical reasons, but also empirical evidence, albeit contested, that while unemployment causes increased self-employment, self-employment causes reduced unemployment. Unravelling the relationship between self-employment and unemployment is crucial because policy is frequently based on assumptions that do not reflect the described ambiguities. The purpose of the present paper is to try and reconcile the ambiguities found in the relationship between unemployment and start-up activity. We do this by introducing a simple two-equation vector autoregression model where changes in unemployment and self-employment are linked to subsequent changes in those variables for a panel of 23 OECD countries.

The organization of this paper is as follows. We start by providing additional background on the "entrepreneurial" effect and present an algebraic model which forms the basis for our regression exercises. In the following sections the algebraic model is extended to a two-equation vector autoregression (VAR) model, which will be used to test the "entrepreneurial" and "refugee" effects. We also present the data and methodology employed to estimate the VAR model. Finally, in the last two sections we discuss the estimation results and draw conclusions.

3. Linking self-employment to unemployment

As discussed previously, there may be both a (positive) effect of unemployment on self-employment (the "refugee" effect) and a (negative) effect of self-employment on unemployment (the "entrepreneurial" effect). And both possibilities have been studied theoretically and empirically. The "entrepreneurial effect," however, requires some further analysis.

Why an increased amount of entrepreneurial activity should have an impact on unemployment? The economics literature on Gibrat's Law provides one approach to address this question. Gibrat's Law states that firm growth is independent of firm size. Thus, Gibrat's Law implies that shifting employment from large to small enterprises should have no impact on total employment, since the expected growth rates of both types of firms are identical. And, as a result, restructuring the economy from large to small enterprises (including the self-employed) should have no impact on the overall unemployment rate.

However, there is strong and systematic empirical evidence suggesting that, in fact, Gibrat's Law does not hold across a broad spectrum of firm sizes. Sutton (1997) and Caves (1998) have produced two comprehensive and

---

[1] Other studies showing that greater unemployment serves as a catalyst for start-up activity include Reynolds et al., 1995; Reynolds et al., 1994; Hamilton, 1989; Highfield and Smiley, 1987; Yamawaki, 1990; and Evans and Leighton, 1989, 1990.

exhaustive compilations of studies relating firm size to growth and have shown that stylised fact (as Geroski (1995) puts it) that smaller firms have greater growth rates than their larger counterparts. Beginning with the pioneering studies by Evans (1987a,b) and Hall (1987), along with Dunne et al. (1988, 1989), a central finding of this literature is that firm growth is negatively related to firm size and age.[2] These findings have been confirmed in virtually every subsequent study undertaken, despite differences in country, time period, industry, and methodology used. The evidence strongly supports the claim that very young and very small firms outperform their older and larger counterparts in terms of employment creation even when corrected for their higher probabilities of exit. Some studies indicated that age and size effects disappear as firms' age and employment increase (Hart and Oulton, 1999).

The literature described above uses micro level data and shows that small firms grow faster than large firms. This suggests that, at the macro or country level, a larger presence of small firms contributes positively to economic performance as well. Self-employment rates represent a specific measure of the presence of small and very small firms in an economy. However, it is not clear that higher self-employment rates automatically lead to improved economic performance. In fact, self-employment rates in some countries may be inefficiently high (Carree et al., 2002, 2007). Too much self-employment can be characteristic of poor economies of scale in production and R&D rather than of vibrant entrepreneurial activity. Within this context, Carree et al. have introduced a model where an 'optimal' level of self-employment, E_i^*, is assumed to exist for each country i, dependent on its stage of economic development. The level E_i^* is optimal in the sense that both a level of self-employment E_i lower than E_i^* and a level of self-employment higher than E_i^* leads to a lower rate of economic growth compared to a situation where E_i equals E_i^*. In the first case, competition levels are too low, while in the second case, economies of scale and scope are not fully utilised.[3]

Similarly to their work, in the present paper we assume that the unemployment rate U_{it} in country i and period t is *positively* affected by the extent to which the self-employment rate $E_{i,t-1}$ is different from the country-specific optimal rate (in terms of employment creation), E_i^*. The unemployment rate is equal to the level U_{it}^o that would be present in case the actual self-employment rate would be equal to the optimal rate ($E_{i,t-1} = E_i^*$) plus a penalty determined by the absolute difference between $E_{i,t-1}$ and E_i^*:

$$U_{it} = U_{it}^o + \varsigma \left| E_{i,t-1} - E_i^* \right| \tag{1}$$

where $\varsigma > 0$. Taking the first difference of Eq. (1) gives

$$U_{it} - U_{i,t-1} = \varsigma \left(\left| E_{i,t-1} - E_i^* \right| - \left| E_{i,t-2} - E_i^* \right| \right) + \varepsilon_{it}, \tag{2}$$

where $\varepsilon_{it} = \Delta U_{it}^o$ stands for the effect of business cycle and other factors (with exception of the self-employment rate variable) on the rate of unemployment. The optimal self-employment rates are determined by institutional and socio-economic factors and, hence, only change very slowly over time. Therefore, there are three relevant cases for the relation between the self-employment rate and the country-specific optimal rate. First, both the self-employment rate in period $t-1$ and $t-2$ are higher than the optimal rate (case (3a)). Second, they are both less than the optimal rate (case (3b)). Third, one is higher than the optimal rate and one is lower, while both are relatively close to the optimal rate (case (3c)): $E_{i,t-1} \approx E_{i,t-2} \approx E_i^*$. Depending upon the case, Eq. (2) changes as follows:

$$E_{i,t-1} > E_i^* \quad \wedge \quad E_{i,t-2} > E_i^* : \quad \Delta U_{it} = \varsigma \, \Delta E_{i,t-1} + \varepsilon_{it} \tag{3a}$$

$$E_{i,t-1} < E_i^* \quad \wedge \quad E_{i,t-2} < E_i^* : \quad \Delta U_{it} = -\varsigma \, \Delta E_{i,t-1} + \varepsilon_{it} \tag{3b}$$

$$E_{i,t-1} > E_i^* > E_{i,t-2} \quad \vee \quad E_{i,t-1} < E_i^* < E_{i,t-2} : \quad \Delta U_{it} \approx \varepsilon_{it}^{\,4} \tag{3c}$$

Eqs. (3a) through (3c) show that the sign of the coefficient of $\Delta E_{i,t-1}$ reflects whether, on average for the countries under consideration, the self-employment rate is below, above or about equal to the optimal level. When the coefficient

---

[2] See Klomp et al (2006) for a survey of the empirical literature.
[3] Carree et al. (2002) provide empirical support for this model using a data set which is similar to the one used in the present analysis.
[4] See Audretsch et al. (2002a) for a similar approach relating economic growth to small firm presence in 17 European countries.

is positive, the self-employment rate is too high (case (3a)), while if the coefficient is negative, then the self-employment rate is too low (case (3b)). In case there is no effect of $\Delta E_{i,t-1}$ on ΔU_{it} then the self-employment rate should be close to the optimal level (case (3c)).[5] We use Eq. (4) to test for the effect:

$$U_{it} - U_{i,t-1} = \beta \left(E_{i,t-1} - E_{i,t-2} \right) + \varepsilon_{it} \tag{4}$$

The effect of self-employment rates on unemployment rates is the "entrepreneurial" effect of increased entrepreneurial activity contributing to lower unemployment rates. The coefficient β can be either positive or negative, while the coefficient ς introduced in Eq. (1) must be positive. The *expected* sign of β is negative though. That is, we expect that, for the majority of countries in our data base, self-employment levels are below optimum (case (3b)) so that an increase of self-employment results in a subsequent decrease in unemployment. We supplement our main Eq. (4) with the complementary equation relating the change of the unemployment rate to the subsequent change in the self-employment rate:

$$E_{it} - E_{i,t-1} = \lambda \left(U_{i,t-1} - U_{i,t-2} \right) + \eta_{it} \tag{5}$$

The effect of unemployment rates on self-employment rates is the push ("refugee") effect of recently unemployed workers starting their own venture to escape unemployment. Coefficient λ is expected to be positive.

The ambiguity in the relationship between self-employment and unemployment is reflected by the opposite (expected) signs of the parameters in Eqs. (4) and (5). We expect β to be negative but λ to be positive. Hence, although there is both a positive and a negative association between self-employment and unemployment, the model formed by Eqs. (4) and (5) enables us to unravel the complex relationship. In the model and method section Eqs. (4) and (5) will be extended to a simple VAR model, which will be estimated using a data base of 23 OECD countries over the period 1974–2002.[6] Also, although the period length is left undefined in the mathematical version of the model, in our empirical application, one period is defined as four years.

4. Measurement issues

Following Storey (1991), we operationalize entrepreneurial activity in terms of the number of self-employed. More precisely, we use the change in the number of non-agricultural self-employed (unincorporated as well as incorporated) as a fraction of the labour force. This measure has two significant advantages: First, while not being a direct measure of entrepreneurship, it is a useful and well-established proxy for entrepreneurial activity (Storey, 1991). Second, it is available for a large number of countries and, after applying appropriate harmonizations (van Stel, 2005), it can be compared across countries and over time. Of course, some important qualifications should be emphasized when using and interpreting this variable. First, the variable combines heterogeneous activities across a broad spectrum of sectors and contexts into one single measure. This measure treats all businesses as the same, both high- and low-tech. Second, the data are not weighted for magnitude or impact: all self-employed businesses are identically measured, even though some clearly have a greater impact than others. Third, this variable measures the relative change in the stock of self-employed businesses and not new start-ups.[7]

The panel data set of unemployment and self-employment rates for the 23 OECD countries for the 1974–2002 period is constructed as follows: For the unemployment data, U, we use the standardized unemployment rate of the OECD Main Economic Indicators. The data for self-employment, E, are from the Compendia 2002.1 data set of EIM in

---

[5] The intuition is that in case the actual self-employment rate changes from just below the optimal level to just above, or the other way around, this change has no net positive or negative effect on economic performance, here the rate of unemployment.

[6] Note that Eqs. (4) and (5) are in first differences, so that country-specific effects are differenced out. It is obvious that the rate of new venture formation is country-specific since for example entrepreneurial traits may be culture-dependent (Mueller and Thomas, 2000, and Shane et al., 1991).

[7] Basically, our measure of change in self-employment rate is a measure of net entry of entrepreneurs (i.e. the number of entrepreneurs starting a new business in a given period minus the number of entrepreneurs closing their business). Indeed, our measure of net changes in self-employment may or may not correlate with (gross) measures of entrepreneurial activity available from other sources. For instance, the correlation between the change in the self-employment rate over the period 2002–2004 and the Total-early-stage Entrepreneurial Activity (TEA) Index 2004 of the *Global Entrepreneurship Monitor* is 0.374 (*p*-value 0.105; correlation based on 20 countries). See Acs et al., (2005). Note that correlations may not be high as our measure is a net measure of entrepreneurial activity and not a gross measure. For example, in the US economy both entry and exit levels are relatively high. However, the net change in the self-employment rate has been relatively low in the last decades.

Table 1
Ranking of countries with respect to change in self-employment rate (in % points) for periods 1978–86 and 1986–94

Country	Year (t)	$E_t - E_{t-8}$	$U_{t+8} - U_t$
Portugal	1994	4.5	−2.0
Ireland	1994	2.6	−10.3
Iceland	1994	2.6	−1.4
United Kingdom	1994	2.2	−4.5
Italy	1986	2.1	0.5
Canada	1994	2.1	−2.6
Portugal	1986	−0.9	−1.5
Austria	1986	−1.1	0.5
Luxembourg	1994	−1.1	0.2
Luxembourg	1986	−1.4	1.1
Denmark	1986	−1.6	2.6
Japan	1994	−2.0	2.5

Source: Compendia 2002.1.
E_t and U_t are the self-employment and unemployment rates in period t.

Zoetermeer, The Netherlands. The Compendia data set uses data from the OECD Labour Force Statistics and other (country-specific) sources to make the self-employment data as comparable as possible across countries and over time.[8] The data in Compendia are available on a bi-annual (even years only) basis. Because our focus in the current paper is the effect of self-employment on unemployment, in Table 1 we show some data of the six country/period combinations (out of 46) with the highest and lowest values of the change in the self-employment rate from 1978 to 1986 and from 1986 to 1994. Out of six countries with the strongest *increase* in self-employment five show a subsequent *decrease* in unemployment. Italy is the exception.[9] Out of six countries with the strongest *decrease* in self-employment five show a subsequent *increase* in unemployment. Portugal, with a substantial net inflow of EU funds ('Cohesion Funds') which probably exerts a downward pressure on unemployment rates, is the exception.

5. Model and method

The previous sections explain why the dynamic interrelationship between changes in self-employment and unemployment is complex, and, in particular, why the direction of causality between the two variables is not clear a priori. The previous sections suggest two testable hypotheses — that increases in self-employment rates lead to a decrease in subsequent unemployment, and that increases in unemployment rates lead to an increase in subsequent self-employment. In order to evaluate the causal linkages involved in the relationship, the most natural way of testing these two hypotheses is to estimate a vector autoregression (VAR) model (for example, see Sims, 1980). This means that a vector of dependent variables is explained by one or more lags of the vector of dependent variables, i.e. each dependent variable is explained by one or more lags of itself and of the other dependent variables.[10]

In our application, we have a two-equation VAR model with the change in unemployment and the change in self-employment as dependent variables. Eqs. (4) and (5) are extended in three respects in order to obtain a testable

---

[8] In Compendia, self-employment rates are defined as the number of non-agricultural self-employed (unincorporated as well as incorporated), as a fraction of total labor force. The harmonizations mainly concern corrections for the number of incorporated self-employed (harmonization across countries) and corrections for trend breaks (harmonization over time). The 23 countries included in Compendia are the (old) EU-15 as well as Iceland, Norway, Switzerland, USA, Japan, Canada, Australia and New Zealand. See van Stel (2005) for details about the Compendia data base.

[9] Italy has a very high self-employment rate, approaching 20% in the first decade of the 21st Century. Further increases in this rate may be counter-productive (Carree et al., 2002). On the other hand, the strong decrease in unemployment in Ireland between 1994 and 2002 cannot entirely be attributed to the increase in self-employment between 1986 and 1994. The strong economic performance of Ireland can also be attributed to factors like foreign direct investments and European Union subsidies. The Netherlands is an example of a country with decreasing self-employment rates (-0.5% point between 1978 and 1986) and subsequently decreasing unemployment rates (-3.6% point between 1986 and 1994). The appraised Dutch 'Poldermodel', which was launched by the 1982 Wassenaar Treaty between employers' organizations and unions, is an important reason for the huge decrease in unemployment during the late 1980s and the 1990s in The Netherlands (Thurik, 1999). Therefore, entrepreneurial activity is not the only route to achieving low unemployment rates.

[10] Note that, because the same list of independent variables appears in both equations, OLS and SUR estimation are identical: it is not necessary to take into account possible correlation between the two error terms.

A.R. Thurik et al. / Journal of Business Venturing 23 (2008) 673–686   679

empirical model. First, we include lagged dependent variables on the right hand side in the VAR model to test for the direction of causality. We will report Granger-causality test statistics when discussing our results.[11] Second, we allow for multiple time lags as the "entrepreneurial" and "refugee" effects may come with a lag and we do not know a priori how long this lag may be. Third, we use time dummies as additional explanatory variables. These dummies correct for business cycle effects over the sample period for the countries covered by our dataset. The model reads as follows:

$$ U_{it} - U_{i,t-L} = \alpha + \sum_{j=1}^{J} \beta_j \left(E_{i,t-jL} - E_{i,t-(j+1)L} \right) + \sum_{j=1}^{J} \gamma_j \left(U_{i,t-jL} - U_{i,t-(j+1)L} \right) + \sum_{t=1}^{T} \delta_t D_t + \varepsilon_{1it} \tag{6} $$

$$ E_{it} - E_{i,t-L} = \kappa + \sum_{j=1}^{J} \lambda_j \left(U_{i,t-jL} - U_{i,t-(j+1)L} \right) + \sum_{j=1}^{J} \mu_j \left(E_{i,t-jL} - E_{i,t-(j+1)L} \right) + \sum_{t=1}^{T} \nu_t D_t + \varepsilon_{2it} \tag{7} $$

where i is a country-index, L is the time span in number of years, J is the number of time lags included, D_t are time dummies and ε_{1it} and ε_{2it} are possibly correlated error terms. The expected sign of the joint impact of the β coefficients is negative and the expected sign of the joint impact of the λ coefficients is positive.

Using the panel data set consisting of 23 OECD countries between 1974 and 2002, Eqs. (6) and (7) are estimated using weighted least squares. We consider changes in self-employment and unemployment over periods of four years, i.e. L equals 4.[12] Furthermore, we test for the number of time lags, in order to gain insight into the lag structure between unemployment and self-employment. Inclusion of more lags seems relevant because the employment impact of entrepreneurial ventures is not instantaneous: it requires a number of years for the firm to grow. In this respect Geroski (1995, p. 148) notes that "Even successful entrants may take more than a decade to achieve a size comparable to the average incumbent." Beesley and Hamilton (1984) point at the seedbed role of new and small firms challenging incumbent firms. The essentially innovative seedbed activities, with the inevitable trial and error (birth and death) mechanism, may take a long time to cause the 'creative destruction' of incumbent enterprise, the emergence of new enterprise and subsequent growth. Audretsch (1995) shows that the share of total employment accounted for by a cohort of new-firm start-ups in U.S. manufacturing more than doubles as the firms age from two to six years.

Rather than imposing a lag structure for the impact of the lagged variables in Eqs. (6) and (7), we test for the statistically most adequate lag structure by using likelihood ratio tests. We start by including only one lag, and then, one lag at a time, we include further lags until the likelihood ratio test rejects inclusion of further lags. In terms of Eqs. (6) and (7), this procedure determines the value of J. We avoid using data for overlapping periods as this may cause a downward bias in the estimated standard errors of the coefficients. In other words, given that we chose L equal to 4, this implies that we use data for 2002, 1998, 1994, ..., 1974.

6. Empirical results

Estimation results for the two-equation VAR model consisting of Eqs. (6) and (7) are reported in Table 2.[13]

---

[11] Eqs. (6) and (7) can be used for testing Granger-causality. The Granger (1969) approach to the question of whether x causes y is to establish how much of the current y can be explained by past values of y and then to establish whether adding lagged values of x can improve the explanation. y is said to be Granger-caused by x if x helps in the prediction of y, or equivalently if the coefficients on the lagged xs are statistically significant. This can be tested using a simple F-test on the lagged x's.

[12] Given that our data are available on a bi-annual basis, the minimum lag length is two years. However, if we measure the variables over two-year periods, chances are that two consecutive periods fall within the same business cycle. An important disadvantage then is that the lagged dependent variable dominates the regression outcomes. Regressions using $L=2$ are available upon request. With the exception of Model Ia, these produced R^2-values considerably lower than the values reported in the upper half of Table 2.

[13] Before starting our regression analysis we tested whether the dependent variables in our model are stationary. In particular, we tested for unit roots using the Dickey–Fuller method (Dickey and Fuller, 1979) and found no evidence for a unit root. More specifically we applied a t-test for ρ in the augmented Dickey–Fuller regression $\Delta_4 y_t = \alpha + \beta t + \rho y_{t-4} + \lambda_1 \Delta_4 y_{t-4} + ... + \lambda_{p-1} \Delta_4 y_{t-4(p-1)} + \varepsilon_t$ where y_t is the four-year change in unemployment or self-employment, t is a time trend, and p is the order of the autoregressive (AR) process. For each dependent variable we ran nine variants, assuming AR processes of order one, two or three, and assuming that the AR process has no constant and no trend (i.e. $\alpha = \beta = 0$), a constant but no trend ($\beta = 0$) or both a constant and a trend. The t-values for ρ varied from -6.6 to -14.3 for the change in unemployment series, and from -4.2 to 8.2 for the change in self-employment series. As these values are well below the (negative) critical values, the null hypothesis of a unit root was rejected. Note that this is in line with expectations given that our dependent variables are in first differences.

Table 2
Estimation results VAR model for 1, 2 and 3 four-year period time lags

		Model Ia	Model Ib	Model IIa	Model IIb	Model III
		1 lag	1 lag	2 lags	2 lags	3 lags
Eq. (6): dependent variable $U_t - U_{t-4}$						
Constant	α	0.030 **	0.005	0.007	−0.008	−0.009
		(7.3)	(1.1)	(1.4)	(1.8)	(1.8)
$E_{t-4} - E_{t-8}$	β_1	−0.587 *	−0.462	0.091	0.309	0.279
		(2.5)	(1.8)	(0.3)	(1.0)	(0.9)
$E_{t-8} - E_{t-12}$	β_2			−1.13 **	−1.06 **	−0.793 *
				(3.8)	(3.4)	(2.4)
$E_{t-12} - E_{t-16}$	β_3					−0.630
						(1.8)
$U_{t-4} - U_{t-8}$	γ_1	−0.143	−0.175	−0.246 **	−0.234 *	−0.334 **
		(1.6)	(1.9)	(2.7)	(2.3)	(3.1)
$U_{t-8} - U_{t-12}$	γ_2			−0.027	−0.112	−0.157
				(0.3)	(1.1)	(1.5)
$U_{t-12} - U_{t-16}$	γ_3					0.093
						(0.8)
R-squared		0.439	0.319	0.403	0.444	0.474
P-value		0.015	0.076	0.000	0.003	0.002
Granger-causality test						
Eq. (7): dependent variable $E_t - E_{t-4}$						
Constant	κ	0.004 **	−0.001	−0.002	−0.000	−0.001
		(2.7)	(0.3)	(1.5)	(0.3)	(0.7)
$U_{t-4} - U_{t-8}$	λ_1	0.031	0.042	0.067 *	0.057	0.046
		(1.1)	(1.4)	(2.2)	(1.5)	(1.1)
$U_{t-8} - U_{t-12}$	λ_2			0.090 **	0.088 *	0.093 *
				(2.8)	(2.4)	(2.4)
$U_{t-12} - U_{t-16}$	λ_3					0.056
						(1.3)
$E_{t-4} - E_{t-8}$	μ_1	0.416 **	0.422 **	0.329 **	0.289 *	0.246 *
		(5.4)	(5.0)	(3.5)	(2.5)	(2.0)
$E_{t-8} - E_{t-12}$	μ_2			0.167	0.213	0.220
				(1.7)	(1.8)	(1.7)
$E_{t-12} - E_{t-16}$	μ_3					0.016
						(0.1)
R-squared		0.340	0.333	0.385	0.366	0.379
P-value		0.284	0.176	0.006	0.044	0.074
Granger-causality test						
N		138	115	115	92	92
Loglikelihood		−563.9	−469.0	−457.0	−368.6	−364.7

Absolute *t*-values are between brackets. The results are from a weighted vector autoregression (VAR) with population as weighting variable. Coefficients for year dummies are not reported.
 * Significant at 0.05 level.
** Significant at 0.01 level.

As explained above, initially we include only one lag of the dependent variables (Model Ia). We compute the coefficients using the largest possible sample, given the lag structure. As the oldest year in the data set is 1974 and using one lag implies going back eight years, we can use data for 1982, 1986, up to 2002. For each year we have 23 countries, which gives us 138 observations in Model Ia. From the results for Eq. (6) we find that changes in self-employment have a significantly negative impact on unemployment in the subsequent period. Indeed, the Granger-causality test indicates that self-employment causes unemployment to decrease (p-value below 0.05). From the results for Eq. (7), we see that in Model Ia, unemployment does not Granger-cause self-employment to increase.

However, results using Model Ia may be biased because our lag structure is too restrictive. As previously noted, considerable lags may be involved in the relationship. To test this we include a second lag, representing changes in unemployment or self-employment between $t-12$ and $t-8$ (basically an eight year lag). Using the extra lag implies that

A.R. Thurik et al. / Journal of Business Venturing 23 (2008) 673–686 681

Table 3
Impulse response functions for unit changes in self-employment and unemployment

Lag (years)	Effect of unit change in self-employment on unemployment [Eq. (6)]		Effect of unit change in unemployment on self-employment [Eq. (7)]	
	Direct effect	Cumulative effect	Direct effect	Cumulative effect
4	0.09	0.09	0.067	0.067
8	−1.12	−1.03	0.095	0.163
12	−0.07	−1.10	0.023	0.186
16	−0.26	−1.36	0.022	0.208
Asymptot		−1.29		0.190

Effects are based on model IIa.

we lose a year in our sample, hence the model is estimated for 115 observations (Model IIa). We apply a likelihood ratio test to see whether including the extra lag improves the statistical fit of the model. For this purpose we re-compute the one lag model using the 115 observations sample (Model Ib). Testing Model IIa against Model Ib gives a likelihood ratio test statistic of 24.0. As the critical value at 5% level is 9.5 (four restrictions), it implies that a model using two lags is to be preferred over a model using one lag. Analogously, testing Model III against Model IIb we conclude that adding a third lag to the model does not improve the statistical fit. Hence, we conclude that model variants using two lags are statistically superior. Focusing on the results of Models IIa and IIb, we find that self-employment Granger-causes unemployment to decrease, and also that unemployment Granger-causes self-employment (p-values below 0.05 in all four cases) to increase.

From the signs of the coefficients and t-values in Models IIa and IIb it appears that entrepreneurial activity, as hypothesized, reduces unemployment but that the impact appears after an eight year lag. The positive effect of unemployment on self-employment seems to capitalize somewhat faster. However, given the interrelationship between the two variables in the model, a more insightful way to capture the impact is to use impulse response functions. These functions capture and compute the impact over time of an exogenous shock in either of the dependent variables, taking into account the interrelationships reflected by the estimated system of equations. In Table 3 we present the impulse response function for a unit shock to entrepreneurial activity (impact on unemployment) and for a unit shock to unemployment (impact on entrepreneurial activity) for Model IIa. Focusing on Eq. (6) we see that the direct effect is greatest for the second period of four years. For instance, a 1% point increase in the self-employment rate brings down the unemployment by 1.12% point eight years later. The time pattern of the effect of self-employment on unemployment is illustrated in Fig. 1, which pictures the impulse response function for Model IIa. The *cumulative* effect converges to −1.29 (note that Fig. 1 relates to the *direct* effect).

Table 3 shows that the initial impact of more entrepreneurial activity on unemployment is positive. Perhaps, initially, the increased competition by new entrants leads to higher labour productivity at the industry level, while industry output remains constant (Fritsch and Mueller, 2004). This implies a negative effect on employment. After some time, the new entrants may grow and actually contribute to economic growth.[14] One must be careful with this type of conclusions as t-values for the one lag self-employment variables are low, as shown in Table 2.

The finding that countries with a greater increase in entrepreneurial activity also experience systematically higher employment growth rates may be linked to a Schumpeterian process of new and small firms generating new products and production processes with the consequence that older products and production processes are replaced. This Schumpeterian process is driven by a sequence of independent and isolated opportunities (Sutton, 1997, p. 48). In the Kirznerian perspective (Kirzner, 1973), entrepreneurship is the response to these previously undiscovered profit opportunities.[15] This may lead to increased consumer satisfaction at a lower cost, hence to economic growth and lower unemployment. Profit opportunities might not only spur entrepreneurial activity but may also be generated by

---

[14] In their study of new business formation and regional development over time Fritsch and Mueller (2004) find that the peak of the positive impact of new businesses is reached about eight years after entry. This is similar to the time lag in our study. Fritsch and Mueller, however, apply the Almon lag model and discriminate between indirect effects of new business formation (crowding out of competitors, improvement of supply conditions and improved competitiveness) and a direct effect (the jobs created in the new businesses). See also Carree and Thurik (2008) and van Stel and Suddle (2008).

[15] See Yu (1998) for an examination of the role of adaptive entrepreneurship and its role in the dynamics of Hong Kong's economy.

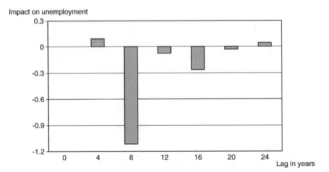

Fig. 1. Impulse response function for unit change in self-employment, model IIa.

entrepreneurs starting new firms. This idea dates to Schumpeter (1934) and Hayek (1945): modern decentralized economies allow individuals to act on their entrepreneurial views and allow them to be rewarded.

Table 3 shows that changes in unemployment have a positive impact on subsequent self-employment. This is in line with earlier findings as documented in the introduction. This is the "refugee" effect of unemployment: it stimulates start-up and self-employment rates. Our results indicate that the impact of a 1% point increase in unemployment leads to a 0.16% point increase in self-employment after eight years. Note that the "refugee" effect is considerably smaller than the "entrepreneurial" effect, i.e. the magnitude of the impacts in the right part of Table 3 is much smaller compared to the effects reported in the left part of the table.

6.1. Testing for coefficient heterogeneity

The set-up of our model assumes that the relationships are identical across the countries in our estimation sample. In this subsection we test for coefficient heterogeneity across countries for the intercept terms and the coefficients reflecting the "entrepreneurial" and "refugee" effects, i.e. coefficients α, β, κ and λ in Eqs. (6) and (7). For the intercept terms α and κ we apply likelihood ratio (LR) tests to investigate whether inclusion of country dummies improves the model fit. Regarding coefficients β and λ we multiply the corresponding self-employment and unemployment variables with per capita income and include these cross-terms as additional variables in the model.[16] This way we test whether the "entrepreneurial" and "refugee" effects vary with the development level of a country. For example, van Stel, Carree and Thurik (2005) find that the effect of entrepreneurial activity (TEA) on economic growth is higher for highly developed countries than for less developed countries. We may find a similar dependence on per capita income in the current analysis. All tests are conducted relative to Model IIa, the statistically preferred model in Table 2.

Regarding Eq. (6) where the change in unemployment is to be explained, we find no evidence for country-specificity of the intercept term α. The LR test statistic equals 23.1 while the critical value at the 5% significance level equals 33.9. Interestingly, when adding the multiplicative variable $(E_{t-8} - E_{t-12}) \times YCAP_{t-8}$ to model specification IIa, this cross-term is significant at the 5% level and an LR test supports inclusion of this variable.[17] The coefficients imply that the effect of the variable $E_{t-8} - E_{t-12}$ can be written as $1.468 - 0.173 YCAP_{t-8}$. Hence, the (negative) impact of entrepreneurial activity on unemployment increases with per capita income. To give an impression of the variation across countries, per capita income values for 1994 imply an effect of 0.18 for Greece and an effect of -2.50 for the United States. In conformity with van Stel, Carree and Thurik (2005) we see that the "entrepreneurial" effect is greater for higher developed countries.

---

[16] We use real per capita income levels in thousands of US dollars, harmonized across countries using purchasing power parities.

[17] We also estimated specifications including the multiplicative term corresponding to one lag (i.e. $(E_{t-4} - E_{t-8}) \times YCAP_{t-4}$), both added separately and simultaneously with the two lag cross-term. In addition, we estimated specifications including the per capita income variable. All these alternative specifications turned out to be statistically inferior to the one solely adding the two lag cross-term to Model IIa.

A.R. Thurik et al. / Journal of Business Venturing 23 (2008) 673–686 683

Regarding Eq. (7) where the change in self-employment is to be explained, we find evidence that coefficient κ varies by country. Inclusion of country dummies significantly improves the model fit. The LR test statistic equals 40.9 for a critical value of 33.9. Closer inspection of the dummy coefficients reveals that France and Japan have the two highest coefficients, in the absolute sense. The two countries are exceptional: the self-employment rate in these countries has been continuously declining since the 1970s. When we include country dummies for France and Japan only, R^2 equals 0.489 (compared with 0.385 in Table 2). Coefficients and t-values of the unemployment variables are similar to Model IIa in Table 2 though: 0.067 (t-value 2.3) for the one lag variable and 0.083 for the two lag variable (t-value 2.7). Hence the magnitude of the "refugee" effect is robust: the inclusion of country dummies makes no difference. Finally, no evidence is found for heterogeneity of the λ coefficients in that they depend upon per capita income levels.

7. Conclusions

The small business sector, and hence self-employment, has become increasingly important to modern OECD economies as they attempt to generate economic growth and employment. New and small firms have emerged as a major vehicle for entrepreneurship to thrive (Audretsch and Thurik, 2001). The present paper shows the important role that changes in self-employment can play in reducing unemployment.

As public policy turned to entrepreneurship to generate employment and economic growth, policy makers have turned to the academic literature seeking guidance. The advice they have found is ambiguous at best, conflicting and contradicting at worst. While some studies find a positive link between unemployment and start-up or self-employment rates, as a result of what we refer to in this paper as the "refugee" effect, other studies find evidence supporting a negative link between unemployment and start-up or self-employment rates, as a result of what we call the "entrepreneurial" effect. These two findings suggest radically different policy approaches. On the one hand, the literature focusing on the decision to become an entrepreneur suggests that public policy can reduce unemployment by providing instruments to promote entrepreneurship but does not necessarily stimulate economic growth. This literature implies policies encouraging the unemployed to become entrepreneurs. On the other hand, literature suggesting that by generating economic growth, entrepreneurship will mitigate unemployment results in policy focusing on instruments inducing high-growth entrepreneurship. The disparate recommendations resulting from these literatures have resulted in ambiguous implications for public policy concerning entrepreneurship.

Even further ambiguities emerging from the literature concerning the link between self-employment and unemployment involve the business cycle. Studies reveal a positive impact of economic downturns, which encourages unemployed workers to become self-employed, but also a positive impact of economic upturns, where growth opportunities induce an increase in entrepreneurial activity. The unemployed do not enjoy the benefits of a paid job and will tend to search for one, "pushing" people into self-employment. However, low unemployment is likely to coincide with a lively market demand for products and services "pulling" the (un)-employed towards self-employment (Parker, 2004). Thus, there is both a "recession-push" and a "prosperity-pull" aspect of the relation between unemployment and self-employment.

Overall, the relationships between self-employment and unemployment are fraught with complexity resulting in confusion and ambiguity for both scholars and policy makers. This paper attempts to unravel these complex relationships. Explicitly modelling self-employment and unemployment within the context of a simultaneous relationship, this paper uses a rich data set of OECD countries for a recent period to identify that the relationship between unemployment and self-employment is, in fact, both negative and positive. Changes in unemployment clearly have a positive impact on subsequent changes in self-employment rates. At the same time, changes in self-employment rates have a negative impact on subsequent unemployment rates. The latter is even stronger than the former. Because these are dynamic inter-temporal relationships, previous studies estimating contemporaneous relationships have confounded what are, in fact, two relationships each working in opposite directions and with different time lags. Our model shows that it is crucial to allow for different and variable time lags. It shows that both the effect of self-employment on unemployment and that of unemployment on self-employment are rather long. This is one of the reasons why policy makers – favouring quick responses and results – have been slow to discover the prominent role of entrepreneurship in the economy.

An additional finding of our analyses is that the impact of entrepreneurial activity on macro-economic performance increases with per capita income. This is also found in van Stel, Carree and Thurik (2005) where an entirely different data set is used. Hence, the many policy initiatives of the highly developed European countries to stimulate entrepreneurship seem justified.

One limitation of our research, which is inherent to working with country data, is that we cannot directly trace the factors that influence the probability of moving from unemployment to self-employment at the micro level. For instance, heterogeneity across individuals (concerning education, former experience, etc.) is of great importance when we want to explain the success rate of exiting unemployment. Likewise, concerning the "entrepreneurial" effect, we know that heterogeneity across individuals plays a role as well. For instance, research at the micro level shows that education levels of entrepreneurs positively influence the probability of achieving firm growth (Congregado et al., 2005). In our study this heterogeneity is aggregated away into self-employment and unemployment statistics at the country level. This shortcoming can only in a limited way be addressed by incorporating possible additional variables determining self-employment and unemployment rates, thereby extending the VAR model to a VARX-model.

Notwithstanding the above limitation, the results of this study are of significant policy importance because policy often aims at achieving desirable effects at the economy-wide level. For this purpose it is important to understand the relations at the macro-economic level, as studied in the present paper. For instance, Germany, a country with high unemployment, recently adopted policies designed to encourage unemployed individuals to exit unemployment by self-employment (Audretsch et al., 2007). However, as the current paper shows that the "refugee" effect is relatively small, one might wonder if such policies are worthwhile. Based on the larger "entrepreneurial" effect we suggest that it might be more effective to encourage entrepreneurship in general as higher levels of entrepreneurial activity significantly lower subsequent unemployment levels. In other words, unemployed individuals may have a bigger chance to escape unemployment by way of being hired by (new) entrepreneurs than by way of trying to start and maintain a new firm. This, in turn, may be related to the – on average – relatively low human capital levels of unemployed individuals making them less competent to run a firm (van Stel and Storey, 2004). Thus, the results of this paper unequivocally suggest that public policy to generate jobs and reduce unemployment would be best served by focusing more on innovative and high-growth entrepreneurship than on inducing the unemployed into entering into self-employment.

Acknowledgement

This paper is the result of a series of visits by David Audretsch as a Visiting Research Fellow at the Tinbergen Institute; by Roy Thurik and Martin Carree as Ameritech Research Scholars at the Institute for Development Strategies, Indiana University; and by André van Stel and Roy Thurik to the Max Planck Institute of Economics in Jena, Germany. Martin Carree is grateful to the Royal Netherlands Academy of Arts and Sciences (KNAW) for the financial support. The authors acknowledge the comments of Adam Lederer, Maria Minniti and Lorraine Uhlaner. Starting with the descriptive Thurik (1999), this paper has evolved through many iterations while early versions have been presented at many workshops and conferences. Two anonymous referees provided valuable comments. The usual disclaimer applies.

References

Acs, Zoltan J., Audretsch, David B., 2003. Innovation and technological change. In: Acs, Z.J., Audretsch, D.B. (Eds.), Handbook of Entrepreneurship Research. Kluwer Academic Publishers, Boston/Dordrecht, pp. 55–79.
Acs, Zoltan J., Arenius, Pia, Hay, Michael, Minniti, Maria, 2005. Global Entrepreneurship Monitor, 2004 Executive Report. London Business School and Babson College, Wellesley, MA and London, UK.
Audretsch, David B., 1995. Innovation and Industry Evolution. MIT Press, Cambridge, MA.
Audretsch, David B., Fritsch, Michael, 1994. The geography of firm births in Germany. Regional Studies, 28 (4), 359–365.
Audretsch, David B., Thurik, A. Roy, 2000. Capitalism and democracy in the 21st century: from the managed to the entrepreneurial economy. Journal of Evolutionary Economics 10, 17–34.
Audretsch, David B., Thurik, A. Roy, 2001. What is new about the new economy: sources of growth in the managed and entrepreneurial economies. Industrial and Corporate Change 10 (1), 267–315.
Audretsch, David B., Keilbach, Max, 2004. Entrepreneurship capital and economic performance. Regional Studies 38, 949–959.
Audretsch, David B., Carree, Martin A., van Stel, Adriaan J., Thurik, A. Roy, 2002a. Impeded industrial restructuring: the growth penalty. Kyklos 55, 81–97.
Audretsch, David B., Thurik, A. Roy, Verheul, Ingrid, Wennekers, Sander, 2002b. Entrepreneurship: Determinants and Policy in a European-US Comparison. Kluwer Academic Publishers, Boston/Dordrecht.
Audretsch, David B., Grilo, Isabel, Thurik, A. Roy, 2007. Handbook of Research in Entrepreneurship Policy. Edward Elgar Publishing Ltd, Cheltenham, UK.

Beesley, M.E., Hamilton, M.T., 1984. Small firms' seedbed role and the concept of turbulence. Journal of Industrial Economics 33, 217–231.

Blanchflower, D.G., 2000. Self-employment in OECD countries. Labour Economics 7, 471–505.

Blanchflower, Danny, Meyer, Bruce, 1994. A longitudinal analysis of young entrepreneurs in Australia and the United States. Small Business Economics 6 (1), 1–20.

Blau, David M., 1987. A time series analysis of self employment in the United States. Journal of Political Economy 95 (3), 445–467.

Carree, Martin, 2002. Does unemployment affect the number of establishments? A regional analysis for U.S. states. Regional Studies 36, 389–398.

Carree, Martin A., Thurik, A. Roy, 2003. The impact of entrepreneurship on economic growth. In: Acs, Z.J., Audretsch, D.B. (Eds.), Handbook of Entrepreneurship Research. Kluwer Academic Publishers, Boston/Dordrecht, pp. 437–471.

Carree, Martin A., Thurik, A. Roy, 2008. The lag structure of the impact of business ownership on economic growth in OECD countries. Small Business Economics 30 (1), 101–110.

Carree, Martin, van Stel, André, Thurik, Roy, Wennekers, Sander, 2002. Economic development and business ownership: an analysis using data of 23 OECD countries in the period 1976–1996. Small Business Economics 19 (3), 271–290.

Carree, Martin, van Stel, André, Thurik, Roy, Wennekers, Sander, 2007. The relationship between economic development and business ownership revisited. Entrepreneurship and Regional Development 19 (3), 281–291.

Caves, R.E., 1998. Industrial organization and new findings on the turnover and mobility of firms. Journal of Economic Literature 36, 1947–1982.

Congregado, E., Golpe, A., Millán, J.M., 2005. Determinantes de la Oferta de Empresarios. In: García, J., Pérez, J. (Eds.), Cuestiones Clave de la Economía Española, Perspectivas actuales 2004, Ed. Comares, pp. 165–187.

Dickey, D.A., Fuller, W.A., 1979. Distribution of the estimators for autoregressive time series with a unit root. Journal of the American Statistical Association 74, 427–431.

Dunne, Timothy, Roberts, Mark J., Samuelson, Larry, 1988. Patterns of firm entry and exit in U.S. manufacturing industries. RAND Journal of Economics 19, 495–515.

Dunne, Timothy, Roberts, Mark J., Samuelson, Larry, 1989. The growth and failure of US manufacturing plants. Quarterly Journal of Economics 104, 671–698.

Evans, David S., 1987a. The relationship between firm growth, size and age: estimates for 100 manufacturing industries. Journal of Industrial Economics 35 (2), 567–581.

Evans, David S., 1987b. Tests of alternative theories of firm growth. Journal of Political Economy 95 (4), 657–674.

Evans, David S., Boyan, Jovanovic, 1989. Estimates of a model of entrepreneurial choice under liquidity constraints. Journal of Political Economy 97 (3), 657–674.

Evans, David S., Leighton, Linda S., 1989. The determinants of changes in U.S. self-employment. 1968–1987, Small Business Economics 1 (2), 111–120.

Evans, David S., Leighton, Linda, 1990. Small business formation by unemployed and employed workers. Small Business Economics 2 (4), 319–330.

Fritsch, Michael, Mueller, Pamela, 2004. The effects of new business formation on regional development over time. Regional Studies 38, 961–975.

Garofoli, Gioacchino, 1994. New firm formation and regional development: the Italian case. Regional Studies 28 (4), 381–394.

Geroski, Paul A., 1989. Entry. Innovation, and Productivity Growth, Review of Economics and Statistics 71, 572–578.

Geroski, Paul A., 1995. What do we know about entry? International Journal of Industrial Organization 13, 421–440.

Granger, C.W.J., 1969. Investigating causal relations by econometric models and cross-spectral methods. Econometrica 37, 424–438.

Grilo, Isabel, Thurik, Roy, 2005. Entrepreneurial engagement levels in the European Union. International Journal of Entrepreneurship Education 3 (2), 143–168.

Grilo, Isabel, Irigoyen, Jésus-Maria, 2006. Entrepreneurship in the EU: to wish and not to be. Small Business Economics 26 (4), 305–318.

Hall, Bronwyn H., 1987. The relationship between firm size and firm growth in the U.S. manufacturing sector. Journal of Industrial Economics 35, 583–605 June.

Hamilton, Robert T., 1989. Unemployment and business formation rates: reconciling time series and cross section evidence. Environment and Planning 21, 249–255.

Hart, P.E., Oulton, N., 1999. Gibrat, Galton and job generation. International Journal of the Economics of Business 6, 149–164.

Hayek, F.A., 1945. The use of knowledge in society. American Economic Review 35, 519–530.

Highfield, R., Smiley, Robert, 1987. New business starts and economic activity: an empirical investigation. International Journal of Industrial Organization 5, 51–66.

Hurst, E., Lusardi, A., 2004. Liquidity constraints, household wealth and entrepreneurship. Journal of Political Economy 112 (2), 319–347.

Johansson, E., 2000. Self-employment and liquidity constraints: evidence from Finland. Scandinavian Journal of Economics 102, 123–134.

Kirzner, Israel M., 1973. Competition and Entrepreneurship. University of Chicago Press, Chicago.

Klomp, Luuk, Santarelli, Enrico, Thurik, Roy, 2006. Gibrat's Law: an overview of the empirical literature. In: Santarelli, E. (Ed.), Entrepreneurship, Growth, and Innovation: The Dynamics of Firms and Industries: International Studies in Entrepreneurship. Springer Science, Berlin, pp. 41–73.

Knight, Frank H., 1921. Risk, Uncertainty and Profit. Houghton Mifflin, New York.

Lin, Zhengxi, Manser, Marilyn E., Picot, Garnett, 1998. The Role of Self-Employment in Job Creation in Canada and the U.S. OECD-CERF-CILN International Conference on Self-Employment, Burlington.

Mueller, Stephen L., Thomas, Anisya S., 2000. Culture and entrepreneurial potential: a nine country study of locus of control and innovativeness. Journal of Business Venturing 16, 51–75.

Nickell, S.J., 1996. Competition and corporate performance. Journal of Political Economy 104, 724–746.

Nickell, S., Nicolitsas, P., Dryden, N., 1997. What makes firms perform well? European Economic Review 41, 783–796.

Oxenfeldt, A., 1943. New Firms and Free Enterprise. American Council on Public Affairs, Washington, D.C.

Parker, Simon C., 2004. The Economics of Self-Employment and Entrepreneurship. Cambridge University Press, Cambridge, UK.

Pfeiffer, F., Reize, F., 2000. Business start-ups by the unemployed — an econometric analysis based on firm data. Labour Economics 7 (5), 629–663.

Reynolds, Paul, Storey, David J., Westhead, Paul, 1994. Cross-national comparisons of the variation in new firm formation rates. Regional Studies 28 (4), 443–456.

Reynolds, P., Miller, B., Maki, W.R., 1995. Explaining regional variation in business births and deaths: U.S. 1976–1988. Small Business Economics 7 (5), 389–707.

Schumpeter, Joseph A., 1934. The Theory of Economic Development. Harvard University Press, Cambridge, MA.

Shane, S., Kolvereid, L., Westhead, P., 1991. An exploratory examination of the reasons leading to new firm formation across country and gender. Journal of Business Venturing 6, 431–446.

Sims, Christopher A., 1980. Macroeconomics and reality. Econometrica 48, 1–48.

Storey, David J., 1991. The birth of new firms — does unemployment matter? A review of the evidence. Small Business Economics 3 (3), 167–178.

Sutton, John, 1997. Gibrat's legacy. Journal of Economic Literature 35, 40–59.

Thurik, Roy, 1999. The Dutch Polder Model: Shifting from the Managed Economy to the Entrepreneurial Economy. Annual Meeting of the American Economic Association New York, NY. January 3–5, 1999.

van Stel, André, 2005. COMPENDIA: harmonizing business ownership data across countries and over time. International Entrepreneurship and Management Journal 1 (1), 105–123.

van Stel, Adriaan J., Storey, David J., 2004. The link between firm births and job creation: is there a Upas Tree effect? Regional Studies 38 (8), 893–909.

van Stel, André, Kashifa, Suddle, 2008. The impact of new firm formation on regional development in the Netherlands. Small Business Economics 30 (1), 31–47.

van Stel, André, Carree, Martin, Thurik, Roy, 2005. The effect of entrepreneurial activity on national economic growth. Small Business Economics 24 (3), 311–321.

Yamawaki, Hideki, 1990. The effects of business conditions on net entry: evidence from Japan. In: Geroski, P.A., Schwalbach, J. (Eds.), Entry and Market Contestability: An International Comparison. Basil Blackwell, Oxford, pp. 168–186.

Yu, Tony Fu-Lai, 1998. Adaptive entrepreneurship and the economic development of Hong Kong. World Development 26 (5), 897–911.